1000 WOMEN in HORROR 1895-2018

1000 WOMEN in HORROR 1895-2018

By Alexandra Heller-Nicholas

BearManor Media

2020

1000 Women In Horror, 1895-2018

© 2020 Alexandra Heller-Nicholas

All rights reserved.

Published in the United States of America by:

BearManor Media
4700 Millenia Blvd.
Suite 175 PMB 90497
Orlando, FL 32839

bearmanormedia.com

Printed in the United States.

Typesetting and layout by John Teehan
Cover design by Darren Cotzabuyucas

Paperback ISBN 978-1-62933-386-1
Hardback ISBN 978-1-62933-387-8

This book is dedicated to the many women who at one stage or another changed my life for the better, including Robbie Adkins, Lisa Busuttil, Di Cooper, Fiona Drury, Anna Dzenis, Marie Gator, Jade Henshaw, Hanna Hoyne, Cerise Howard, Tracey Kent, Susannah Lim, Anne Marsh, Angela Ndalianis, Di Sneddon, Jan Tonkin, Emma Westwood, Rowdy Wisbey and Pam Wright.

And most of all, to my number one girl-team;
Lorraine and Elizabeth Heller-Nicholas.

ACKNOWLEDGEMENTS

THIS BOOK IS THE RESULT of the kindness of Lee Gambin, whose support of his friends and colleagues is equalled only to his own astonishing output as a film critic, author and programmer. Many of the women I interviewed for the book I met through Lee, and his enthusiasm is matched only by his unrelenting encouragement. Special thanks also to Darren Cotzabuyucas for the beautiful cover artwork, and to Ben Ohmart at Bear-Manor Media. Actual hero Josh Nelson deserves a major shout-out, too: he went above and beyond the call of duty, and this book would not be here without him.

While I fear I haven't remembered everyone, I am also grateful to the following who've helped with this project in both direct and indirect ways: Bill Ackerman, Cesar Albarran-Torres, Rutanya Alda, Tara Anaïse, Craig Anderson, Rodney Ascher, John Atkinson, Tonjia Atomic, Prano Bailey-Bond, Conor Bateman and *4:3 Film*, Bret Berg and the American Genre Film Archive team, Anna Biller, Anton Bitel, Ashlee Blackwell, Kansas Bowling, Dean Brandum, Sophia Cacciola, Thomas Caldwell, Max Calzini, Michelle Carey, Axelle Carolyn, Abraham Castillo Flores, Sally Christie, Cinemaniacs, Aislinn Clarke, BJ Colangelo, Jarod Collard, Martyn Conterio, L.C. Cruell, Jordan Crucchiola, Sarah Daly, Derek Davidson, Samm Deighan, Winston Wheeler Dixon, Mattie Do, Heidi Lee Douglas, Julia Ducournau, John Edmond, Giles Edwards, Kat Ellinger, Brad Michael Elmore, Faith Everard, Fantastic Fest (especially Evrim Ersoy and of course Brother James Shapiro), Final Girls Berlin Film Festival (Elinor Lewy, Sara Neidorf and Lara Mandelbrot), Final Girls UK (Anna Bogutskaya and Olivia Howe), Gwendolyn Audrey Foster, Mark Freeman, Hannah 'Neurotica' Forman, Tamae Garateguy, Jill Gevargizian, James Gracey, Jordan Hall, Catherine Hardwicke, Heidi Honeycutt, Ian Gouldstone, Kier-La Janisse, Dave K. (The Fiend!), Katherine Kean, Briony Kidd, Caitlin Koller, Karen Lam, Izzy Lee, Melanie Light, Stacy Livitsanis, Barbara Magnolfi, Nicole Maines, Iain Marcks, Craig Martin, Marsha Mason, Donna McRae, Jennifer Merin (film critic and President of the Alliance of Women Film Journalists), Maude Michaud, Patrushkha Mierzwa, Shaun Miller, the Miskatonic Institute of Horror Studies, Alfonso Monroy, Monster Pictures (Neil Foley, Grant Hardie, Jarret Gahan and Ben Hellwig), Tony Nagle and Elise O'Dea, Jan Napiorkowski, Amy Nicholson, Tim O'Farrell, Alexandra Paul, Isabel Peppard, Cassandra Peterson, Lisabona Rahman, Christina Raia, Amanda Reyes, Debbie Rochon, Mia'Kate Russell, Gigi Saul Guerrero and Luchagore Productions, Elizabeth E. Schuch, Kate Shenton, Elizabeth Shepard, Amy Simmons, Fran Simeoni and the Arrow Video team, Devi Snively, Jillian Sorkin, Brinke Stevens, David Surman, Rebecca Thomson, Andrew Tong, Nacho Vigalondo, Emma Westwood, Mike White, Barbie Wilde, Peter Zablud and Silvana Zancolò.

And special thanks—always and forever—to Richard, Christian and Casper.

Jamie Lee Curtis and Michael Myers costumed guest at the sCare Foundation Benefit at Conga Room - LA Live on 30 October 2011 in Los Angeles, California. Credit: Kathy Hutchins / Shutterstock.com

INTRODUCTION

FROM THAT FOUNDATIONAL MOMENT in 1818 when Mary Shelley's classic gothic horror novel *Frankenstein* dared to make an outsider the centre of its story, horror has at its best been about giving a voice to those who otherwise struggle to be heard. Horror often tells stories about things we'd rather not hear about; it forces us to face our darkest fears, admit our basest desires and acknowledge the reality of our inescapable mortality. From splatter films to ghost stories, horror reminds us we are all ultimately little more than cognizant meat sacks, and that our place in the world of the living hangs by often the thinnest of membranes. Horror is, at its core, fundamentally democratic: at the end of the day, we're all just big old fleshy bags of bones who can bleed, suffer and experience physical pain.

I grew up in 1980s suburban Australia, where—like so many places around the world—it was all but assumed horror was for deviant young men. All those topless blondes, the blood-and-guts and chainsaws were *surely* intended only for the most toilet-brained, dead-headed hormone-dizzy adolescent boys, right? Only here's the thing: if that's the case, why did so many of my girlfriends and I get such an intense kick out of them, watching them as we so often did on the sly when our parents weren't looking during the endless stream of sleep-overs that formed the basis of my entire teenage nerd-girl social life? Maybe part of it was simply that we got a thrill out of watching films that we were culturally told weren't appropriate for blossoming young ladies. But as I've discovered in the years since, there was more going on than mere transgression.

For myself and for so many of my women friends—those when I was a kid, and those today—horror spoke to us on what was often a primal level about living in a world where physical threat is a constant presence, where danger quite possibly *is* hiding just around the corner. In this context, pretending the world is all sunshine and rainbows just doesn't cut it. Any woman who has walked home alone in the dark at night and even once looked behind her or quickened her step or crossed the road away from that stranger behind us just to be sure has first-hand experience of the fears and anxieties that horror often speaks to, whether they personally enjoy horror movies or not.

And of course, it's not just women. It's anyone who has ever felt different or had their identity defined through negations: of being not-white, not-male, not-straight, not-middle-class, or the hundreds of other points of difference that human beings at our worst use as excuses to discriminate against each other. Collectively, these "nots" are often horror's most memorable Others. While it would be useless to deny that in so many horror films these Others are often configured as monstrous, to consider this alone as an ideological baseline denies horror's perverse pleasures of allegiance—a far more useful concept than mere 'identification'. I don't need to personally identify with a character to be on their team.

The reasons for this are crystal clear: no matter how bad they are, no matter what their body count, the Other in horror is in so many famous cases *strong*. Horror is a space where Otherness is not an instant shorthand for 'victim' like it is so often in the real world. Rather, it's a fantasy space where outsiders *might* just be a force to be reckoned with. This provides a subversive thrill, especially for those of us who are so often rendered invisible in the testosterone-drunk, dog-eat-dog world of alpha masculinity.

There are, of course, more than a handful of famous horror villains who don't fall into this category, but even then, there's frequently an aspect of playful insubordination against the dominant norms at play. Think, for example, of *Halloween*'s Michael Myers, a walking parody of white masculinity with his flat blank mask and almost ludicrous, parodic physical strength. Or Leatherface from *The Texas Chain Saw Massacre*, who curiously wears for much (although, importantly, not all) of that film a suit and tie, the supposed symbol of acceptable white-collar masculine success.

That Leatherface wears a femininzed mask in that film's iconic dinner table scene is worthy of note, too: from Norman Bates in Alfred Hitchcock's *Psycho* to Bela Lugosi in Tod Browning's *Dracula*, there has often been an aspect of the effeminate—if not the outright feminine—to many of horror's most famous monsters. Horror has long provided a space for queering gender norms long before we even had a language to describe what that was; as monstrous as they may be, as noted above, even if just for a brief flickering flash, *they still had power*. While I can't speak for the pleasures (or lack thereof) that others might find in the genre, for myself at least the thrill of horror is that these feminized characters have—for once—any kind of power at all. They might be punished for it, they might be social outcasts because of it, but often—for even just one glimmering, shining, transgressive moment—they have real power.

My love for horror stems on a fundamental level from the fact that for once, a woman or feminized character walking home alone at night in the dark might not be the one scared half to death, but the one doing the scaring. It's a revenge fantasy, perhaps, but with the presence of male violence against women today at the level of a global epidemic, I will frankly take whatever pressure release I can get.

And I'm not alone. In 2003, Lorenza Munoz at the *Los Angeles Times* noted that women were "half, if not a majority, of the audience for such successful spine-tinglers as *The Ring, Scream, Jeepers Creepers 2, Final Destination*, and *Identity*". Likewise, in 2016 Phoebe Reilly at *Rolling Stone* noted "female horror fans are hardly unicorns. Quite the opposite—we go to the movies to get scared, often in greater numbers than men." But if women horror audiences have been broadly ignored in the continuing gendering of the genre's fandom being a boy's club, it's even more dire for women in the film industry who have been involved in making horror films.

It is, in short, these women who this book is about. While there's doubtlessly a widespread assumption that the only role of women in horror is to be the lambs to the slaughter, the starlets in the gauzy nightgowns who get their throats pierced by cloaked Eastern European vampires, and the bare-chested cannon fodder for a seemingly never-ending parade of slasher film killers, this book shows there's much more going beyond these dominant clichés.

That being said, there are many important women actors who have worked in horror who have often played exactly these roles. But as I argue throughout this book, their work is diverse and—more importantly—"work" is very much the key term here. This is *labor*. It's vital to not dismiss those women in their gauzy nightgowns or the unfortunate girls of the slasher film; these characters are played by real women who turned up to work to earn a living, build a career, and establish themselves in a heavily male-dominated industry. Rethinking these performances as the result of real, actual labor might not be sexy, but it's a cold, hard and important reality.

Acting—like directing, writing, camera operating, editing, art designing, producing, composing and the thousand other tasks it takes to make a film—is a job. Some of the women in this book have been paid millions of dollars for their work, and some have received almost nothing. Others choose to work on horror films for no money at all, instead fulfiling a desire to create. But in all these cases, *it's still work*.

The 1000 women in this book are people who—from my perspective at least—collectively provide a snapshot of a huge labor demographic in the horror industry that has long more-often-than-not been overlooked, underrated, or taken for granted. But these women are just the tip of the iceberg: there are 1000s and 1000s more who could be added, with 1000s and 1000s more to come. Together, they demonstrate the scope, impact and endurance of women's labor across horror film history, from 1895 through to today, in a range of different cultural, geographical and production contexts.

As Jennifer Kent told Michael O'Sullivan at The Washington Post in December 2014, "A lot of people, when I spoke to them, as a woman, and said, 'Oh, I'm directing a horror film,' it was like I was directing a snuff film or porno or something terrible". This was absurd for Kent, whose mainstream success with *The Babadook* helped recently shone a light on women filmmakers across the genre; "Women do love watching scary films. It's been proven, and they've done all the tests. The demographics are half men, half women. And we know fear".

This reflects broader comments made by women in the industry more generally about the gender biases working against women. There are legitimately hundreds of quotes to choose from, but one I think about often is this: in 2014, at a press conference for the 67th Cannes Film Festival, jury head (and the only woman winner of the prestigious *Palme d'Or*) Jane Campion said, "Time and time again, we don't get our share of representation". For Campion, ignoring a filmmakers' work because of their gender results in cinema becoming an echo chamber: "It's not that I resent the male film making, but there is something that women are doing that we don't get to know enough about."

It's perhaps no surprise, but these challenges women have faced in the film industry have strong precedent in the visual arts more broadly. In 1971, American art historian Linda Nochlin wrote a famous essay called "Why Have There Been No Great Women

The dark minds of forgotten women artists: Annibale Carracci (Italian, Bologna 1560–1609 Rome), *Two Children Teasing a Cat*, oil on canvas. Purchase, Gwynne Andrews Fund, and Bequests of Collis P. Huntington and Ogden Mills, by exchange, 1994. Open Access via The Metropolitan Museum of Art www.metmuseum.org

Artists?". The conclusion she provokes is that the question is rigged from the outset, because art history—like film history—is told from a perspective that *automatically* privileges men.

It's not that women don't have a long history of making art (cinema included), but that the system has long hindered not just their canonization, but even just acknowledging that they *exist at all*. In terms of the artworld, there's an almost never-ending list of statistics that reveal that this institutional blindness has endured. By one count, 83% of the artists in London's Tate Modern gallery in 2010 were men, and feminist artist/activist group Guerrilla Girls have worked tirelessly since 1985 to place the international ubiquity of precisely these kinds of imbalances in the art world under the spotlight.

Riffing on Nochlin's essay, the questions we need to think about become clearer. It's not "Why Have There Been No Great Women Artists?" or "Why Have There Been No Great Women Horror Filmmakers?", but rather how do we break free from the dominant assumptions about cultural history that have so often privileged white men over everyone else? How do we get a clearer picture of *who* has been making art, be it sculpture, painting or horror movies?

In a fascinating article called "Horror Grrrls" at the online film journal *Offscreen*, filmmaker Maude Michaud drew a direct parallel to the ethos of the DIY '90s Riot Grrrl punk-feminist movement and the contemporary Women in Horror movement. In the United States, Michaud identifies its origins somewhere in the late aughts, where feminist horror film events like the Los Angeles-based Viscera Film Festival established in 2007 by Heidi Honeycutt and Shannon Lark intersected with the tireless work of Hannah Neurotica (aka Hannah Forman), who gave birth to the Women in Horror Recognition Month in February 2010 by dropping the mother of all diversity manifestos on the blog for her legendary zine, *Ax Wound*.

Of Women in Horror Recognition Month, Michaud said, "The goal of the celebration was to urge people around the world to seek out the work of women writers, filmmakers, photographers or journalists working within the horror genre, and invite them to create sister events that would showcase the work of these women. The idea went viral [and] … as a result, an entire community of female horror media makers was discovered through the different WIHM events."

The Women in Horror movement and WIHM have significantly also prompted vital debates. Questions of tokenism, ghettoization, and essentialism are important to acknowledge here. These debates amongst women in the genre themselves demonstrate a simple truth: there's still a long way to go. Yet WIHM continues to grow; even in Australia we have Tasmania's Stranger with My Face International Film Festival, founded by filmmakers and artists Briony Kidd and Rebecca Thomson in 2012.

This is not just happening in English-speaking countries, either. Founded in late 2016 by co-directors Elinor Lewy, Sara Neidorf and Lara Mandelbrot, Germany's Final Girls Berlin Film Festival is another vibrant indicator of the desire for the focus on women in horror to be amplified. For Lewy, "As a lifelong horror fan, I was getting bored of horror festivals screening films that were predominantly made by the 'norm,' meaning white, straight, able-bodied, middle-class cis men. These 'horror norm' films only reflect a specific viewpoint; they aren't the be-all and end-all of the genre. We want to showcase different perspectives, namely those of women making horror. There weren't many platforms for us, so we created one for ourselves." Neidorf adds, "I love horror's ability to dissect social ills and scratch away at the surface to expose the darker, less palatable recesses of our minds. Horror is fun, yes, *and* it's so much more than that. Final Girls Berlin is about digging into both aspects: the sociopolitical potentiality of the genre *and* rejoicing in the gnarly, gruesome, and grotesque, but with a different bend, a different eye." Neidorf continues, "There's a tremendous wealth of untold horror stories, unseen visions, and we wanted to play a part in bringing those to more viewers, and creating a space of dialogue around those stories, a place for women and non-binary people in horror to come together, share, spectate, and collaborate."

Just like Nochlin's "Why Have There Been No Great Women Artists?" essay, the title of this book too is more a provocation than a statement of fact: there are *obviously* more than 1000 Women in Horror. But for some, even this in itself is a relatively radical statement, and it really shouldn't be: if we think only of those gauzy-nightgowned women or the screaming teenage girls of the slasher films of the '70s and '80s, there are doubtlessly some people (perhaps, depressingly, many) who might be stuck to make it even make to 100. But as I illustrate throughout this book, those women—and plenty of others—are there, and they have been since the earliest days of the cinema, all around the world.

Even a cursory glance at the films and filmmakers in this book make it readily apparent that not only have different women made different kinds of horror movies, but they have done so across an impressive range of cultural and historical contexts within a variety of budgets and local industry frameworks; just think, for instance, of early silent era pioneers like Alice Guy, Lois Weber, Luise Fleck and Germaine Dulac, Czech New Wave director Věra Chytilová's *Wolf's Hole* (1987), Hong Kong New Wave filmmaker Ann Hui's *Visible Secret* (2001), American grindhouse director and pornographer Roberta Findlay's *The Oracle* (1985) and acclaimed Indigenous Australian visual artist Tracey Moffatt's *beDevil* (1993). But just as important are the emerging filmmakers, actors, and other women who work on making horror movies whose names we might not be as familiar with, those who don't get to the red carpets. These lesser-known figures are just as much a part of this book as the big names.

Like all histories, horror film history is consciously written. By choosing what and who to privilege, decisions have also been made—no matter how inadvertently—about who gets left out. Historically, across the arts in general, the latter has typically been anyone who's not a straight white man. God bless them, many of these men have made some incredible horror movies, and this book is absolutely not intended to undermine their achievements: it doesn't have to be an either/or scenario.

In this book, I also inescapaby face the same challenge of selection (and, by default, omission), because by choosing these particular 1000 women there are consequently a vast number of women I therefore could *not* include. The issues are bluntly practical; a book called *Every Single Woman, Who Ever Worked in Horror, Ever* would not just be a hard sell to a publisher but would also land me in an early grave due to the impossibility of its scope.

In this light, this book hopes to play a small part in helping to set the record straight. It's about leveling the playing field in even just a tiny way in regard to how we think about horror film, not only in terms of gender, but also considering how that intersects with other factors like race, sexual identity, class, and other ubiquitous markers of social and cultural difference that have kept so many important women hidden from view. It is in this spirit that the greatest indicator of this book's success would be the criticism; "What, *only* 1000?".

THE RULES OF ENGAGEMENT

I once met a very nice young man at a horror film festival who told me he had a spreadsheet of his favorite horror movies that he organized according to the specific codes and conventions of the genre, in terms of subgenres, iconography and recognizable 'authorized' directors whose involvement in a project automatically bestowed it with the magical label "horror". Throughout this project, I have often thought of this spreadsheet and how flagrantly I have disregarded the logic that this young man held so sacred.

But for me, horror is more about the adverbs and adjectives than the nouns. I'm less interested in defining the genre through object-centric words like "skeleton", "thunderstorm", and "zombie", as I am through more descriptive, even poetic language. Horror for me is about the "disturbing", the "unsettling", the "bleak", the "disorienting".

While this approach allows me to drill down in a more satisfying manner to the core of what makes horror tick, in terms of constructing an entire book about the genre I confess I have at times envied that spreadsheet, as oppositional in nature as it may be to how I conceive what lies at the dark heart of horror. But as Briony Kidd recently told me when I spoke to her for this book, even this question of definition has a gendered aspect. "One of the things I've noticed with running a women's horror festival is that genre definitions themselves can be quite gendered and political," she said. "For example, a lot of work made by women tends to sit outside of the most conventional notion of what 'horror' entails. If that's the case their work is likely to be strongly criticised on that basis, whereas a male director's work that's similarly challenging will be granted the label more easily and he will be considered an innovator. In other words, the male filmmaker has earned the right to define the genre himself, the female filmmaker is still seen as 'other', and maybe 'getting it wrong' in a sense."

From this perspective, it may be worth stating from the outset how I have approached what kinds of films to include in this book. I consider "horror" in a far more fluid, flexible, and elastic way than any spreadsheet like that discussed above would allow, focusing more on mood and tone at times than explicit, text-book iconography. I also take the origins of horror in gothic literature seriously: not just in terms of writers like Mary Shelley, but the influence of earlier 18th century gothic romance novelists like Ann Radcliffe and Clara Reeve. I flatly reject the dude-bro assumption that so-called 'chick flicks' and horror don't mix—the kind of argument that became almost suffocating from some hostile corners when Catherine Hardwicke's *Twilight* was released in 2008, for example—largely because the very origins of the genre itself prove this emphatically wrong.

And then there's the question of feminism itself. We'll all have different takes on this, but for myself I do not for one second believe that "women filmmakers" must necessarily make "feminist films", whatever that may be. "Feminism" is one of those terms thrown around with such force—by those both passionately for it and venomously against—in online discourse especially that only on very rare occasions does anyone on either side stop to really carefully and clearly clarify *precisely* what they mean by the term. The word "feminist" can, does, and has for a long time meant different things to different people, and that meaning has changed and evolved dramatically over time: if you've been paying attention, feminism is less a point of passive agreement than a site of furious debate. Which is how it should be: that's how you work shit out.

So a definition, however loose, may be useful to inform how I at least conceive feminism. In 2012, art theorist Peggy Phelan bravely attempted a broad definition that might be valuable when thinking through women in horror. For Phelan, "feminism is the conviction that gender has been, and continues to be, a fundamental category for the organization of culture. Moreover the pattern of that organization usually favors men over women." As hesitant as it might sound, I'd argue that any definition of feminism necessarily has to be so in order to provide space for *all* the different—and often conflicting—perspectives and points of view that the term can apply to.

While I argue for the place of the women in this book in horror history, I would never attempt—and nor do I believe I have the right—to christen each and all of them collectively as 'feminists'. Rather, my feeling is that it's up to them to make that call. In her "Horror Grrrls" essay cited above, Michaud makes an important observation: "even if a lot of femme-made films include a feminist message, the films directed by women do not automatically produce feminist content." This is important; maybe ideology is in the eye of the beholder. Maybe horror films—like all art—isn't perhaps so easily slotted into clear distinctions of 'feminist' and 'not feminist'. Maybe the real site of interest in in the gaps and contradictions and tensions and anxieties that make horror so interesting, dangerous, and important. Maybe we need to be paying closer attention rather than trying to reduce everything to reductive ideological categories like 'problematic' or 'progressive'.

For the purposes of this book at least, we may be served better again by stepping away from that spreadsheet mentality of splitting things up into clear binaries, seeking solid, definite categories of 'feminist' or 'not feminist', 'horror' or 'not horror' when talking about particular films and/or filmmakers. There are women in this book who embrace the label feminism, and there are others who are on the record for rejecting it explicitly, even though I would personally argue that their films can engage sometimes directly with what I would broadly conceive as 'feminist' issues. And vice versa: there are women who publicly identify as feminists whose films I struggle to wholly embrace in terms of their gender politics. Either way, I propose that rather than decrying them, we should leave the door wide, wide open so we can talk more about this stuff rather than the futile project of trying to lock feminism down.

Many women over many, many years have taken up precisely this challenge of talking about horror. Even in academia alone, important, urgent work on rethinking horror has been published by a number of key women in the field for decades, from Carol J. Clover's *Men, Women, and Chain Saws: Gender in the Modern Horror Film* (1992) and Barbara Creed's *The Monstrous-Feminine: Film, Feminism, Psychoanalysis* (1993) to Isabel Cristina Pinedo's *Recreational Terror: Women and the Pleasures of Horror Film Viewing* (1997) and Robin R. Means Coleman's *Horror Noire: Blacks in American Horror Films from the 1890s to Present* (2011), the latter recently the inspiration for the 2019 Shudder documentary *Horror Noire: A History of Black Horror.*

It's not just academics who are interested in talking about horror film. Amanda Reyes is a writer and film historian who edited the exhaustive collection *Are You in the House Alone? A TV Movie Compendium: 1964-1999* (2017), runs the blog *Made for TV Mayhem,* and is a loud and proud slasher fan. "Despite the criticism that labels slasher films as misogynistic, I've always felt that the genre works as a tool to illustrate the importance of female friendship in ways that other films can't", she says. "While we all attempt to put on a 'face' for the world to see, horror allows us to explore our true human nature because it's one of the only filmic venues where characters drop the façade and deal with the basest of emotions." Reyes continues, "Bonding often occurs, and women draw strength, or learn lessons from each other. For example, *The House on Sorority Row* (1983) looks at the toxicity of groupthink, the supporting friends in *He Knows You're Alone* (1980) help the protagonist recognize that she has agency, and despite the dark end for the trio of gal pals in *Killer Party* (1986), their presentation as authentic buddies is so good, it gives female viewers a wonderful sense of representation, and it makes us care about their outcome." Reyes is passionate in her defence and unambiguous about the ideological potential of these films. "Throwaway cinema to some, I suppose, but don't dismiss the power of women who work together, and the female spectators who grow from seeing these images."

Likewise, for film critic, broadcaster, and author Emma Westwood—whose books include *Monster Movies* (2008) and a book on David Cronenberg's *The Fly* (2018)—women are not just central to the genre, but also offer women themselves a valuable framework for rethinking ourselves. "Horror is such an important and bountiful creative wellspring for women because it allows them to be more than just the yin to male yang. As a film genre, it facilitates unfettered deep-dives into the 360-degree vortex of female consciousness—the light, the shade and everything in-between—where darkness in a woman is not seen as 'problematic' but, instead, as an essential part of her human expression," she says. "For some, horror may be 'unladylike' but, on the contrary, horror enables honesty in the representation of women, and honesty of voice for female filmmakers. And it is far more effective than therapy." Westwood continues, "women are inherently creators and horror—being one of, if not the, most creative of film genres—gives women an alternate channel for creation, rather than through their bodies. The opportunities horror affords are interminable; it works by filtering everyday issues and neuroses, and then distorting them through a magical lens. Everything gets magnified; disruption becomes cataclysmic, normal becomes paranormal and women get to create something that is bigger than them alone, that gets them heard." As Westwood argues, horror offers women a safe, even liberating space for release; "For a woman to go nuts with a horror movie is a cathartic experience. You can't afford to throw caution to the wind with your children; horror is the next best option."

As writers of the calibre of Reyes, Westwood, and literally hundreds of other women critics suggests, an entire volume dedicated only to 1000 Women Horror Critics would itself not be such an impossible project. So while women horror film critics do not feature in the book that follows, it must be emphasized that they too play an important part in horror's workforce of women. Recalling Phelan's observation above that "the pattern of … [cultural] organization usually favors men over women" applies just as much to women horror film critics as it does women elsewhere in the industry, and as such should permeate *any* consideration of women in horror film history more broadly. The very act of a woman working *in any way* in what has for so long been assumed to be the terrain of men is certainly—on some level, and in some way, no matter how small—an attempt to challenge a patriarchal status quo. It might be for money and it might result in films that would be virtually impossible to champion as particularly "feminist" in terms of their content, but heck, credit where credit's due.

This question of "credit" itself is another can of worms. With the broader privileging of men and male artists across visual culture more broadly that Nochlin spoke about in her 1971 essay discussed above, it is therefore little surprise that actual historical and archival records regarding the work of women in horror are far from complete. The internet has—surprise, surprise—only complicated this further.

There are a number of examples I can give to demonstrate this fact, but one of the more interesting examples concerns a woman called Rosemary Horvath. Although now the credit has been deleted, at the time of researching this book, she was listed on IMDb.com as an "uncredited" co-director with William Castle on his cult 1959 Vincent Price-fronted horror film, *House on Haunted Hill*. Assuming IMDb is the 'ground zero' of that information, it has since first appearing been replicated numerous times across the internet; she still is listed as a co-director on the film on high-profile websites like Amazon and Barnes & Noble, and a 2018 article in *Morbidly Beautiful* magazine notes "although she is uncredited in the film, Rosemary Horvath co-directed *House on Haunted Hill* with famed horror movie producer and director William Castle. This is the one and only credit in her filmography."

Digging deeper, however, I found no other traces of Hovarth's involvement in the film. Instead, I discovered a CV for a San Diego-based graphic designer of the same name that, next to the film's title, provides the description "Creative Director, Color Design, DVD Cover Design", relating to the 2008 DVD release by Legend Films, Inc. Now I might be wrong; it may be coincidence and there was in fact a shadowy co-director who worked with Castle on the original film who just coincidentally had the same name.

But here's what I thnk: Rosemary Hovarth worked on a kick-ass DVD release of the film and a database glitch saw her entered into the "director" field at IMDb. Even though that has now been removed, it got picked up and dispersed elsewhere online, and has now become part of the film's unfolding history. In one instance, her name was even listed as co-director by a hugely popular film criticism account on Twitter with over 14,000 followers. Needless to say, as impressive as her work as a designer is, Hovarth is therefore not included in this book.

There are even trickier cases. Indonesian actor Sofia Waldy (often called Sofia W.D.) worked for almost four decades on screen as an actor, with credits including H. Tjut Djalil's 1981 horror film, *Mystics in Bali*. Across the internet, on websites including IMDb.com and Wikipedia, her single feature film directorial effort *Badai-Selatan* (1962) is labeled as a horror film that played at the Berlin International Film Festival. Yet almost Indonesian cinema expert I reached out to—academics, archivists, and others with vast knowledge of the film history of that country—could not verify this. In fact, more than one pointed out that the first 'real' Indonesian horror film is broadly considered to be M. Sharieffudin A.'s *Lisa* (1971), starring Lenny Marlina.

And then, through some kind souls on Twitter, I met the extraordinary Lisabona Rahman, the Indonesian Film Online catalogue editor and an independent consultant for moving image preservation and restoration. Explaining to her my research problem, she too reiterated what I had been told elsewhere. But Rahman went a step further; while in Berlin, she dug up the Berlin International Film Festival program for the year Waldy's film played. Here's what it said about the film:

> In order to expiate, a young man comes to the loneliness of a poor village. There he is is killed after many troubles. Just the moment when the man, to whom he felt guilty, is ready to forgive.

While obviously the translation in the original program here is a little wobbly, in relation to my question about its generic specificity it ultimately raises more questions than it answers; does the phrase "there he is killed after many troubles" indicate this is a horror film, or something entirely different? Without seeing the film, I guess it depends on the nature of the "many troubles".

This does not mean that *Badai-Selatan* might not have aspects that might align it with the horror genre in some way, but at the time of writing I could not verify this either way. While I have no doubt that there is someone somewhere who knows the story be-hind this film, I myself have yet to talk to anyone—even Indonesian film specialists—who have actually seen it, let alone who can verify its generic status.

I raise these research challenges because it is far too easy to assume in the current day that old cliché that 'everything is online': firstly, it's not, and secondly, what is there is often incorrect. When dealing with films from other cultures, too, questions of access and other issues come to the fore. There are also broad cultural issues of the gendering of names; the 2012 Indian horror film *?: A Question Mark* directed by Allyson Patel and Yash Dave is, despite Patel being a man, often listed by western critics as being co-directed by a woman, 'Allyson' assumed to be a woman-specific variation of the westernized 'Allyson'.

Accordingly, I have worked with the research I have had available to me, both online and off, and have verified what I can, where I can. But if there are gaps, omissions or—god forbid—errors, I plead an unambiguous *mea culpa*. In these (what I hope are rare) in-stances, the archive let me down, because history has for a long, long, long time let women and their place in history down more generally. We need to do more work remembering, and this book hopes to play a small part in helping us do that when it comes to horror cinema.

LOOKING BACK, LOOKING FORWARD

The best part of writing this book is how much *I* learned. When I began, I had a fair idea of who to include, but as I dug deeper I realized that if gender has been a historical cloak-ing device that has excluded women from the mainstream pop cultural memory about horror film history, that has only been compounded for women of color. I had never heard of Eloyce Gist, for example, until I started reading work specifically dedicated to highlighting the work of Black women in horror such as Ashlee Blackwell's essential blog *Graveyard Shift Sisters*, as well as broader work on the subjectsuch as Robin R. Means Coleman aforementioned book *Horror Noire* and the influential work of Tananarive Due amongst many others.

Blackwell (who also co-wrote, co-produced and appeared in the *Horror Noire* docu-mentary) in particular has established her website as an urgent, timely, and hugely ac-cessible archive about Black women in horror. "The more work I do that is focused on writing about Black women in front and behind the camera in horror cinema, the more I both understand their lack of representation as a part of a bigger system of silencing, and the absurdity of this." Says Blackwell. "If horror as always stood separate, in a sense, from the mainstream, the respectable, the rewarded, then it should mirror its steadfast ethos allowing the marginalized to shine in some of the wildest most and imaginative waves. Those who love horror inherently understand its ability to be sharply intelligent and pro-duce a way to confront our fears in the healthiest and communal manner." She continues, "Yet the presence of Black women has remained sparse at best. Our beings written and directed by mostly white men who often refuse the range and forget the extraordinary obstacles Black women have endured for the sake of survival, especially within the wealth

America accumulated on free and forced labor upon Black bodies, and the terror inflicted in order to do so successfully. As an untapped figure of fragility, strength, perseverance, and the struggle for mental and physical well-being, Black women are arguably some of the best horror storytellers that the world has yet to acknowledge." With her website only increasing in visibility and popularity, there is a clear hunger to hear what Blackwell has to say, and I can vouch for that first hand in terms of what I have learned from Graveyard Shift Sisters. "What five years of research has taught me is that Black women filmmakers, and women of color in general who use horror to examine society and entertain are on the cusp of truly giving the horror genre its rightful stamp as the place where the revolution in artistic expression will continue to thrive", she says.

For filmmaker L.C. Cruell, questions of visibility are also key. She has spoken passionately and intelligently about her work as a Black woman filmmaker, noting "Every day we hear about the lack of diversity in Hollywood. Where are the minority filmmakers? Where are the diverse writers? Where are the women behind the camera? We would hire Black writers but we can't find any! In genre circles, it is even worse. And for writer/directors who happen to be both Female and Black, many people genuinely seem to believe we do not exist at all. The thing is we do. But they say 'Perception is reality' and that is truer in Hollywood than anywhere." Currently working on an all-woman, all-Black filmmaker anthology, of this project Cruell has stated "*7 Magpies* is our way of saying, 'We are here! We are here! We are here! And, we are GOOD!' It is not a question of not existing, it is a question of not being seen, thus not believed in, thus not backed, funded, represented or hired. Which, ironically, is why we are having difficulty raising funding for it. But I for one, won't give up, not on any of my work."

The work of incredible women like Blackwell and Cruell was a revelation and discovering the stories they told about women in the genre whose work I was previously unaware of was like having a blindfold removed. Frankly, that experience becomes addictive; for every person who was new to me, there were 10, 20, 50, 100 more out there that I was yet to hear about. If this book accomplishes anything, it is to do much more than simply provide a list of names you already know.

As I've argued above, while there have been a range of long-institutionalized structures in place throughout history that have worked against women artists getting the same recognition as their male counterparts, for women of color this often becomes doubly the case as it's the brutal double whammy of sexism *and* racism working against them. I have therefore attempted to include as many Black women and other women of color in this book who have done important work in the genre that I could find, even if—in the case of actors, at least—those roles have been small. As I argue, they are regardless hugely important.

And then, of course, is the question of sexuality and gender identity. As I was working through this book, when it came to filmmakers at least I admit I was surprised just how many women who made horror films publicly self-identified as lesbians or otherwise queer. Not all, not most, but significant enough a number that I took note of it. These women—like all women—aren't tied down to making specific 'types' of horror films, and if anything struck me about woman-made horror films across the board in this book it is their very diversity and unrelenting rejection of any kind of singular vision of a 'female

Poster for Brad Michael Elmore's *BIT* starring Nicole Maines. Artwork by Tula Lotay. (Used with permission, thanks to Brad Michael Elmore).

gaze' or an essentialist 'kind' of movie that women make. But that gaze is simultaneously united by the fact that it is, at its core, not-a-male-gaze. To play devil's advocate, however, it is curious that horror is an area that has clearly been of interest to so many queer women filmmakers: could it be that horror in fact has the potential to provide a space for women to talk about a whole range of things relevant to their different experiences and interests? Of course it is—just ask any woman who loves horror.

And then there's our transgender sisters, without whom this book would not be complete. Think, for example, of the legendary composer of Stanley Kubick's *The Shining* (1980) Wendy Carlos, fellow musician Angela Morley who performed the unforgettable drum solo in Michael Powell's notorious *Peeping Tom* (1960), Eva Robbins' iconic femme fatale played with *those* red stiletto heels in Dario Argento's *Tenebrea* (1983), Candis Cayne from Jane Clarke's *Crazy Bitches* (2014), Dee McLachlan's *Out of the Shadows* (2017), *Maskhead* (2009) writer and co-director Rebecca Swan, Zoey Luna from the forthcoming remake of *The Craft*, or Nicole Maine's in her breathtaking feature film debut, starring in Brad Michael Elmore's queer feminist terrorist vampire teen film *Bit* (and let's not forget the genre-loving Lana and Lilly Wachowski who wrote horror comics earlier in their career). There are doubtless many other trans women who have worked in this film genre; despite my efforts to identify as many as I could, the difficulty I experienced when trying to find more names is perhaps further evidence of the substantial challanges these women face in the industry more broadly when it comes to getting work and being recognized for it. For those of you I missed, I'm sorry I didn't find you: I tried, and the onus is on me to keep trying harder. I promise I am still looking for you.

It is in this spirit that I sign off on this introduction with this statement: the work I have started in this book is not a beginning, not an end, but part of a continuum. It's part of a long line of projects that have sought to acknowledge women's work in horror, and to change how we widely think about the genre more broadly, both in terms of its history right down to who we as audiences want to be making the films that we want to see.

Now it's your turn. Read this book, then add names I missed or names to come in the space below. Maybe you've made a horror film and add your own:

AALIYAH◊

The screen adaptation of Anne Rice's 1988 novel *Queen of the Damned* was released almost 6 months to the day after its star, Aaliyah, died in a plane crash on 25 August 2001. The film's promotional materials thus heavily featured the late R&B singer's image, even dedicating the film to her. Born in 1979 in Brooklyn, she died at only 22 years of age, her tragic death perversely feeding into the transcendent, other-worldly aspects of her on-screen character Akasha. As the original mother of the vampires, Akasha was central to Rice's beloved *Vampire Chronicles*, published between 1976 and 2016. Largely filmed in director Michael Rymer's home town of Melbourne, Australia, his vision of Rice's vampire universe failed to ignite the box office like Neil Jordan's dazzling 1994 Rice adaptation *Interview with a Vampire*. But like the character that she played in *Queen of the Damned*, the legend of Aaliyah endures well beyond death.

Aaliyah: Studio Publicity Still of from *The Queen of the Damned* © 2002 Warner Brothers / Village Roadshow. Credit: PictureLux / The Hollywood Archive / Alamy Stock Photo

AARONS, BONNIE

American character actor Bonnie Aarons has a long and illustrious relationship to horror and the macabre. One of her first roles as an ominous hobo loitering outside a diner in David Lynch's 2001 film *Mulholland Drive* is enough in itself to warrant her an enduring cult reputation, but Aarons' work on the dark side was only beginning. Despite being discouraged from perusing an acting career because she was supposedly not considered 'attractive' enough, Aarons has played some of the most unforgettable horror characters in recent years in movies including *I Know Who Killed Me* (Chris Sivertson, 2007), *In-Alienable* (Walter Koenig, 2008), *Drag Me to Hell* (Sam Raimi, 2009), *Dahmer Vs. Gacy* (Ford Austin, 2010), *The Conjuring 2* (James Wan, 2016), *Annabelle: Creation* (David F. Sandberg, 2017), and in the title role of the 2018 Corin Hardy film, *The Nun*.

ABRAHAM, VALERIE

British screenwriter Valerie Abraham was born in England in the early 1930s. Co-writing with Edward Abraham the short story that Donovan Winter adapted to the screen in his 1961 mystery thriller, *The Trunk*, they would work together on a number of similarly dark screen adaptations, such as *Serena* (Peter Maxwell, 1962) and, later in their careers, *Murder Elite* (Claude Whatham, 1985). But it is because of two horror films that their donation to the genre is most readily visible, Michael Anderson's 1970 ghost film *Dominique* (starring Cliff Robertson, Jean Simmons, and Jenny Agutter) and Roy Ward Baker's *The Monster Club* (1981), featuring horror icons John Carradine, Donald Pleasence, and Vincent Price.

ACQUANETTA

Despite the ideologically dubious exoticization of her screen image, the woman known simply as Acquanetta is broadly believed to have been born in Philadelphia in 1921 as Mildred Davenport. While appearing uncredited in her 1942 film debut, John Rawlins's *Arabian Nights*, it was in horror films like *Captive Wild Woman* (Edward Dmytryk, 1943) and Reginald Le Borg's sequel *Jungle Woman* (1944) where she earned her cult reputation, playing ape-turned-human femme fatale Paula Dupree. While her film career continued into the early 1950s, her last major screen appearance was her biggest film, *Tarzan and the Leopard Woman* in 1946.

ADAMS, JANE 'PONI'

Jane Adams was born Betty Jane Bierce in 1921, but throughout her career was known as 'Poni' due to her love of horses. Growing up in California, her early talents led her towards a career as a musician, but she rejected a scholarship at Julliard in New York City to pursue acting. Dabbling in radio and modeling, she played often-uncredited roles in adventure films, westerns, comedies, and film noir like *Lost City of the Jungle* (1946), *He Walked by Night* (1948) and *Tarzan's Magic Fountain* (1949). Adams is most immediately linked to her memorable role as Nina in Erle C. Kenton's *House of Dracula* (1945) alongside John Carradine, Lon Chaney Jr., and Lionel Atwill. She returned to the genre the following year in *The Brute Man* (Jean Yarbrough, 1946) as a blind piano player.

ADAMS, JANE

Jane Adams was born in Washington D.C. in 1965 and began her career on stage, later establishing an impressive career in film. Working across both film and theater, Adams won a Tony Award for her work on Broadway, and numerous prizes for her acting on screen. Across her lengthy filmography, Adams appeared in horror movies including *Silver Bullets* (Joe Swanberg, 2011), *Poltergeist* (Gil Kenan, 2015), *Always Shine* (Sophia Takal, 2016), and the gothic children's blockbuster *Lemony Snicket's A Series of Unfortunate Events* (Brad Silberling, 2004). Her many television credits also include the horror series *Night Visions*, *Tales from the Dark Side*, and the third series of Mark Frost and David Lynch's *Twin Peaks* in 2017.

ADAMS, JULIE

Julie Adams took to acting from an early age and made her screen debut in 1949 on the television series *Your Show Time*. Born in Iowa in 1926, Adams was linked closely to westerns and was awarded a "Golden Boot" by the Motion Picture & Television Fund in 1999 for her services to that genre. In terms of horror, she appeared in TV series including *Kolchak: The Night Stalker*, *The Night Gallery*, and 3 episodes of *Alfred Hitchcock Presents* in the late 1950s and early '60s, as well John Korty's cult teen drugsploitation movie *Go Ask Alice* in 1973. Adams also appeared in the horror films *Psychic Killer* (Raymond Danton, 1975), *The Fifth Floor* (Howard Avedis, 1978), *Black Roses* (John Fasano, 1988) and Burt Kennedy's *The Killer Inside Me* (1976). But it is in Jack Arnold's 1954 classic *Creature from the Black Lagoon* that Adams is most instantly recognizable.

ADDAMS, DAWN

Born in 1930, Dawn Addams starred alongside everyone from Peter Lawford to Charles Chaplin to Spencer Tracy in films by directors including Otto Preminger and Fritz Lang. Working in a diverse range of films, it was in the final years of her acting career she turned to horror in films including Hammer's *The Two Faces of Dr. Jekyll* (Terence Fisher, 1960) and *The Vampire Lovers* (1970), and the 1973 Amicus anthology *The Vault of Horror* (the latter two both directed by Roy Ward Baker).

ADELIYI, OLUNIKÉ

Born in Canada in 1977, actor and singer Oluniké Adeliyi studied at the American Academy of Dramatic Arts in New York before returning north to establish her career. Beginning her career on stage, for horror fans at least her first major credit was as Sidney in

Kevin Greutert's *Saw 3D* (2010). Her other horror credits include *DoUlike2watch.com* (Josh Levy, 2003) and the 2015 horror anthology *A Christmas Horror Story*. She also appeared in the horror/supernatural television series *Being Human* and *Lost Girl*.

ADJANI, ISABELLE

One of the most accomplished French actors of the late 20th century, Isabelle Adjani is an icon of European cinema. While the diversity of her filmography make her difficult to claim for horror alone, it is a genre in which she has a close relationship. Born in Paris in 1955, Adjani made her debut in Bernard Toublanc-Michel's *Le Petit bougnat* (1970), testing the waters in television before winning the first of her many awards for Claude Pinoteau's *La Gifle* in 1974. Adjani's career exploded in 1975 when she starred in the title role of François Truffaut's *The Story of Adèle H.*, leading the following year to her performance as Stella in Roman Polanski's horror film *The Tenant* (1976). In 1979, she starred in Werner Herzog's *Nosferatu the Vampyre*, and in 1981 her dual performances as Anna and Helen in Andrzej Żuławski's *Possession* won her Best Actress Awards at the French Césars and the Cannes Film Festival. Adjani also appeared in many films with distinctly dark and gothic themes, such as in Claude Miller's 1983 serial killer film *Deadly Circuit* and Patrice Chéreau's *Queen Margot* (1994). Similarly, her flair for gothic theatricality was brought to the fore in her performance in Jeremiah S. Chechik's otherwise regrettable 1996 remake of Henri-Georges Clouzot's *Les Diaboliques* (1955).

Isabelle Adjani attends the *Mammuth* Premiere during of the 60th Berlin International Film Festival at the Berlinale Palast on February 19, 2010 in Berlin, Germany. Credit: Denis Makarenko / Shutterstock.com

ADRIAN, CAROLINE

Caroline Adrian is a French producer with Delante Productions. Amongst her many credits, she was a key figure behind-the-scenes in two of the country's strongest recent entries into the horror genre, both co-helmed by women filmmakers: Caroline and Éric du Potet's co-directed *In Their Sleep* (2010), and the wartime set *Stranded* (2010), co-directed by Hugues and Sandra Martin.

ALAOUI, MORJANA

Growing up in Casablanca, Morjana Alaoui moved to France in her late teens where she met Moroccan filmmaker Laïla Marrakchi, who cast her in her celebrated debut feature *Marock* in 2005. Marrakchi's husband Alexandre Aja—like Alaoui herself—would become a key figure in the so-called New French Extremity movement, he as the director of *Haute Tension* (2003), and Alaoui in front of the camera in Pascal Laugier's unflinching *Martyrs* (2008). While she has acted in a range of different movies, Alaoui's connection to horror is not limited to *Martyrs* alone: she also appeared in *The Hybrid* (Billy O'Brien, 2014) and *Broken* (Shaun Robert Smith, 2016).

ALDA, RUTANYA—INTERVIEW (MAY 2018)

With credits spanning back half a century and having collaborated with filmmakers including Robert Altman, Sam Peckinpah and Michael Cimino, Rutanya Alda is one of cinema's most enduring and memorable screen performers. While certainly not limited the horror genre, it is here that she has garnered a particularly loyal fan following, appearing in films including *The Fury* (Brian De Palma, 1978), *When a Stranger Calls* (Fred Walton, 1979), *Amityville II: The Possession* (Damiano Damiani, 1982), *Girls Nite Out* (Robert Deubel, 1982), *The Stuff* (Larry Cohen, 1985), *The Dark Half* (George A. Romero, 1993) and *Late Phases* (Adrián García Bogliano, 2014).

As outlined with intelligence and deep emotional insight in her 2015 book *The Mommie Dearest Diary: Carol Ann Tells All*, Alda is far more than the sum of her filmography. Born in Latvia as Rutanya Skrastiņa, she spent much of her early childhood in a German displaced persons camp during World War II before arriving in America as a child refugee. Through her determination, talent and force of will, she established a impressive career as an actor, despite enduring a number of professional horror stories of her own.

It is no understatement that yours is one of the most impressive of filmographies, Rutanya, and looking at a list of filmmakers you have worked with across your career it feels almost sacrilegious to narrow our interview only down to horror! But is there anything about this genre in particular that is

close to your heart, both personally and as a performer? What can you do in your craft in horror that is difficult to find room for elsewhere?

I don't think of horror as a genre when I am acting in a horror film. I think of it from the actor's point of view of speaking for the character truthfully. I'm part of telling a story and if that story winds up in a genre that's fine with me. But as an actor I don't think that way. I don't think—oh I'm doing a horror film—I think how can I most truthfully express what this character is feeling. I take the point of view of the character and always in support of the character. I don't label the person as good or bad—I think of her as a human being exposed to certain circumstances in her life. It's about adversity and crisis and how my character deals with it in the story.

It's hard to pick one of your best horror performances, but *Girls Nite Out* was certainly the most fun! As an actor, was that kind of extreme character hidden in clear sight for much of the film fun to play? What was the experience of making that movie like?

Girls Nite Out we filmed in a weekend, and tried to rest as best we could between all the chaos that was going on. I basically had one take—that was all there was time for. Again, I spoke for my character—who thinks she is doing what she needs to do. The fact that I did not get paid for my performance and the $5000 they promised makes me not happy with the people involved in this film. I consider it theft of my services and I think this happens more often than is known. Stealing from actors is easy for the unprincipled people out there. We are the most vulnerable, and I think it's disgraceful. So I don't look back on this project with a good heart. Still, I think it's a good trashy fun film.

There's so much strength in your performance as Dolores in *Amityville II: The Possession*, she is such a grounded character and I think the audience right from the outset turn to her as a stabilizing force as things increasingly get out of hand. What was your experience of making that film more generally, and how did you approach the role considering the huge success of the original *Amityville* film?

I never saw the original film of *Amityville*, so that made it easier for me to just create my own person. This is a bonus for an actor. I think they should not see anything that they are doing a sequel to if possible. Don't let other actors affect your own original thoughts. I felt our film was terrific due to the wonderful director, Damiano Damiani. When you have a great director, the work rises in scope. It elevates the film. I think Damiano did this, he took it on as a film about the disintegration of a family that was already in crisis, and moving into the house just made the family relationships more dangerous. How Damiano shows it, I think, makes this film a classic.

Rutanya Alda (as Dolores Montelli) in *Amityville II: The Possession* (Daimano Damaini, 1982).
Credit: Orion Pictures/Photofest © Orion Pictures

It's not just a cheap knock off—it's original in its scope and size. Our film was not well received at the time because it was so real and so disturbing, but through time it has stood up and people that have seen the series think *Amityville II* is the best of them. It has an authenticity that the other films lack. I spoke for Delores as a woman who tries her best for her family and ultimately, she has no control over what happens. I broke it down into sections so that her life disintegrates at each level. Through the years, I feel that our film has stood up while the others have not.

I know it technically doesn't fall under what is classically understood as "horror", but for me personally *Mommie Dearest* is absolutely terrifying—one of the most shocking and upsetting stories about monstrous motherhood ever put to film or paper. I ve recently read your brilliant book *The Mommie Dearest Diary: Carol Ann Tells All,* and while a fascinating account of your career more generally, it so powerfully brought to life the fact that the reality you endured on set was no less a horror story in its own right. Your tone is so measured and sensible, but the way that Faye Dunaway used the method approach as an excuse to be so sadistic for me at least was just shocking: I found it even as a reader and a film watcher quite liberating to read you getting it off your chest,

and was impressed by how level-headed your tone was throughout. Was the process of writing the book cathartic? I can't imagine it was particularly pleasant to revisit emotionally.

Mommie Dearest indeed has horror to it. The horror of childhood and abuse…I don't think anything is more horrible and frightening. I wrote my diary about the day to day experience of *Mommie Dearest* while filming so I could keep focus on my work in the film. I found myself (and so did everyone working on the set, crew and all) … [terrorized by] a star who had the power to get people fired. At the time, I had to deal with that fear and also to do my best in speaking for Carol Ann, my character. By journaling the daily experience, I felt I could better deal with the daily goings-on.

I tried to be objective as best as I could and also included the 'other characters' on the film set, the wonderful hair, makeup, and other people on the set, and their feelings about what was going on. I never intended to publish the diary, but years later when the film became the biggest cult film of all, there was tremendous interest in what happened behind the scenes.

In my personal appearance with host Hedda Lettuce at the Zigfield Theater in New York City and a crowd of 1800 people, I got the message that 'people want to know'. I think the book reveals to readers outside the business what film making is about day to day, and all the stress, personality challenges, and reality of what it takes to make a film. I think it's good that people read the book and kind of have an awakening—that is not all glamour and roses. It's as complicated, and even more so.

Your own childhood was far outside the terrain of what many people reading this interview would have experienced, and your success is an extraordinary story of strength and perseverance. What was your vision of the United States before you arrived? How do you think the things you experienced when you were young impacted your journey to professional success?

I was a starved, sick refugee child in the aftermath of World War II, and this of course it something that will always be in my life. While in a sick camp for children, I saw my first film—a western with Gary Cooper and Paulette Goddard (I only learned their names later when as an adult I happened to see the film and remembered a scene from it). The film changed my life because it told a story that was very different from the life I was living. It was magical. it had cowboys and Indians and a life so different than anything I had ever seen. At that moment, right then and there, I knew I wanted to be a story teller. I wanted to be an actress and tell stories. That never changed. I must have been about 6 years old at the time.

When I arrived in America, I thought it would be full of Indians and cowboys—of course it was much more than that. But westerns were a big part of my growing up in America as I went to the double features every Saturday and they were mostly westerns. Joy oh joy! I think every actor brings his life journey to his or her work, while at the same time putting the needs of their character first.

Adrián García Bogliano is one of my favorite contemporary horror directors, and I did not know that you were in his glorious werewolf film *Late Phases* until I started watching it—what a wonderful film it is, and what a delightful surprise you were! Could you tell me a little about the experience of working on that movie and your character Gloria? It's an unusual werewolf film in many ways, even though it adheres to the sub-genre so clearly; I'd love to hear your thoughts on it.

I adored Adrián García Bogliano. I was not aware of who he was when I started working on the film and he asked me to autograph a still and a poster. I was stunned. Later, I was to discover his background. He is a wonderful director and well-known in his own right. There were challenges with filming a low budget film—weather, etc. I think his brother who was the DP did a remarkable job in a very short and tight schedule, and I would love to work with them again anytime. He has a vision for his work and I admire him for it.

I'm curious to hear if you have noticed any trends across cinema—horror particularly, but more generally also—in terms of the representation of women characters? I think we very arrogantly always assume that things are getting more progressive on this front, but watching older horror movies especially I am not convinced this is always the case. I'd like to hear your thoughts on this, and if you could give advice to women wishing to enter the realm of horror filmmaking in particular, what would you tell them?

I don't watch horror films. They scare me and I don't want to be scared. Life is scary enough. This may come as a surprise to people considering I have been in several, including working with George Romero in *The Dark Half*. In my scene where I get brutally murdered by Timothy Hutton, George edited the scene down and down. I asked him why—he said because it scares me so much, I have to be less scared. I loved working with George, he was very sensitive with actors.

So I can't speak to how women are represented in horror films. I can say that I think women in films are labeled and not explored. Looking back at film noir and the '30s and '40s, there were mothers, grandmothers, aunts, and storekeepers, etc. There was variety. I feel now these women are missing. To me it's the woman 'cookie-cutter', the women as written all feel the same, and they are usually 25 years old. They don't grow. I'm sure there are always exceptions, but many young writers have not experienced life and there is a lot of shallow writing about women. The European films do a much better job with women characters—much deeper and more interesting.

I don't know what to tell a woman about getting into the realm of horror making, this was never a goal of mine. I thought they were good parts when I took them on. Maybe women should write their own horror films—that would be most interesting.

ALDEN, PRISCILLA

Born in 1939 in San Francisco, American actor Priscilla Alden made her debut in Nick Millard's schlock classic *Criminally Insane* (1975) and its 1987 sequel as Ethel Janowski, an escaped psychiatric patient who murders those who seek to curb her passion for food. Across the 3 decades she worked on both stage and screen, Alden scored bit parts in more highbrow fare like Alan Parker's *Birdy* (1984) and Chris Columbus's *Nine Months* (1995), but it was her horror roles—not just the *Criminally Insane* movies, but her last appearance in Millard's adaptation of Henry James's classic novella *The Turn of the Screw* in 2003— that make her an important but often overlooked horror figure.

ALLAN, ELIZABETH

Making her film debut in 1931, Elizabeth Allan took her first steps towards the dark side in Leslie S. Hiscott's *Alibi;* an adaptation of Michael Morton's 1928 play of the same name, itself based on Agatha Christie's 1926 proto-slasher novel *The Murder of Roger Ackroyd.* Born in 1910 in Britain, Allan made over 65 films in a career spanning almost 4 decades. Her horror work includes the 1932 Maurice Elvey version of *The Lodger* (adapted more famously by Alfred Hitchcock in 1927), Edgar Selwyn's pre-code serial killer film *The Mystery of Mr X* (1934), Ken Hughes's *The Brain Machine* (1956), and Robert Day's *The Haunted Strangler* in 1958 with Boris Karloff, before she shifted solely to television. Allan is most renowned for starring alongside Lionel Barrymore, Béla Lugosi,and Carroll Borland in horror king Tod Browning's *Mark of the Vampire* in 1935, where she played the desired prey of Lugosi's thinly-disguised Dracula figure, Count Mora.

ALLBRITTON, LOUISE

Born in Oklahoma in 1920, an early start in the theater led Louise Allbritton to Universal Studios in the early 1940s. Initially starring in a number of westerns, comedies, spy films, thrillers, musicals, dramas, and war films, her stand-out performance was in Robert Siodmak's *Son of Dracula* (1943) alongside Lon Chaney Jr. and Evelyn Ankers. As Katherine, Allbritton puts in one of the great she-vamp performances of Universal's underrated 1940s horror output, and she later turned to roles in episodes of spooky television series like *The Invisible Man* and *Alfred Hitchcock Presents*.

ALLEN, NANCY ●

Early dance lessons gave the young Nancy Allen a taste for performance that would see her study at the famous High School of Performing Arts that inspired Alan Parker's 1980 film *Fame*. Born in New York City in 1950, her film debut was in Hal Ashby's *The Last Detail* (1973), later appearing in Jim Sotos' *Forced Entry* (1975), a less-extreme remake of the nasty 1973 porn/horror film of the same name. Allen shot to widespread public attention through her role as Chris in Brian De Palma's *Carrie* (1976). Marrying De Palma in 1979, their future collaborations would include *Dressed to Kill* (1980) and *Blow Out* (1981), until they divorced in 1984. Allen continued to be a familiar face in horror in films like *Strange Invaders* (Michael Laughlin, 1983) and *Poltergeist III* (Gary Sherman, 1988), her fame peaking in Paul Verhoeven's scifi classic *RoboCop* (1987) and its sequels. Her connection to horror continued, however, with appearances in an episode of *The Outer Limits* and starring in Kari Skogland's horror film *Children of the Corn 666: Isaac's Return* (1999).

AMARAL ALMEIDA, GABRIELA

Brazilian filmmaker Gabriela Amaral Almeida began her screenwriting career in 2004, writing initially for television and documentary shorts. In 2010 she directed her first short *Náufragos* (2010), directing a further 5 shorts including the horror film *Estátua!* in 2014. Collaborating with esteemed Argentine cinematographer Bárbara Álvarez on her 2017 film *O Animal Cordial* (*Friendly Beast*), Amaral Almeida's feature film was followed in 2019 by *A sombra do pai* (*The Father's Shadow*) which began as a short film she developed in the 2014 Sundance's Director's Lab program.

AMES, RAMSAY

Model and B-grade movie regular Ramsay Ames was born Phillps Ames in New York in 1919 and is most readily associated with her dual roles as Amina Mansori and Princess Ananka in Reginald Le Borg's 1944 sequel to *The Mummy's Tomb*, *The Mummy's Ghost*. That same year, Ames would play a small part in Edward F. Cline's horror-comedy *Ghost Catchers*, and for film noir fans has an uncredited blink-and-you'll-miss-her role as a party guest in Michael Curtiz's classic Joan Crawford-fronted *Mildred Pierce* in 1945.

AMICK, MÄDCHEN

Nevada-born Amick moved to Los Angeles in 1987 at the age of 16 where, after a few small television parts, she was cast as Shelly Johnson in David Lynch and Mark Frost's cult television series *Twin Peaks*. She reprised the role in the feature film *Twin Peaks: Fire Walk with Me* (1992), and the much-anticipated third series in 2017. In 1990, she starred alongside Anthony Perkins in Tobe Hooper's underrated made-for-TV movie *I'm Dangerous Tonight*, Amick latter appearing in Mick Garris's *Sleepwalkers* in 1995 (written by

Stephen King). Amick's other horror credits include John Lafia's television horror movie *The Rats* in 2002, noteworthy for its original (and understandably postponed) release date of 11 September 2001. A more star-studded affair was Scott Stewart's 2011 adaptation of Hyung Min-woo's eponymous Korean dystopian horror comic *Priest*, starring Paul Bettany, Maggi Q, Lily Collins, and Brad Dourif. Most recently, she returned to the small screen in the Lifetime series *Witches of West End* (2013-2014), and *American Horror Story: Hotel* (2015-2016).

AMIRPOUR, ANA LILY

Iranian-American director, producer and writer Ana Lily Amirpour was born in Britain in 1976, moving to the United States as a child and studying at San Francisco State University and UCLA. Demonstrating a passion for filmmaking from her early teens, she wrote and directed a number of shorts, and co-wrote and starred in Evan Cholfin's horror film *The Garlock Incident* (2012). In 2014, she expanded her earlier 2011 award-winning short *A Girl Walks Home Alone at Night* into the Persian-language horror-western feature of the same name starring Sheila Vand in the title role, bringing its director international acclaim. Premiering at Sundance Film Festival and garnering Amirpour the "Someone to Watch" label at the Independent Spirit Awards, she followed the success of her feature debut with the dystopian cannibal film *The Bad Batch* in 2016.

Director Ana Lily Amirpour poses with the Special Jury Prize for *The Bad Batch* during the 73th Venice Film Festival on 10 September 2016 in Venice, Italy. Credit: Matteo Chinellato / Shutterstock.com

ANAÏSE, TARA—INTERVIEW (JULY 2018)

Tara Anaïse's debut as writer, director, and producer was *Dark Mountain* (2013), a rare exception in the bewildering dearth of women filmmakers working in the found footage horror subgenre. Set in an Arizona desert, *Dark Mountain* follows director Kate (Sage Howard from Pearry Reginald Teo's 2011 horror film *The Evil Inside*) and two male companions as they search for the mysterious Lost Dutchman gold mine. Based on a local legend, Anaïse shrewdly weaves actual local folklore into a script that she discovered through her co-writer and co-producer Tamara Blaich, whom she met while completing her MFA in film production from USC's School of Cinematic Arts. Since *Dark Mountain*, Anaïse co-produced Jennifer Harrington's thriller *Housekeeping* (2015) and has worked in television. She is currently developing a project called *Bombay Blood*, and she kindly took time to speak to me about this, *Dark Mountain,* and her filmmaking craft more generally.

www.taraanaise.com

In 2015, I wrote an entire book on found footage horror film, and I'm always amazed at how few women filmmakers have made them. What lead you to decide this was the best format to tell the story you wanted to with *Dark Mountain*? The story about the Lost Dutchman gold mine at the heart of *Dark Mountain* is really something else …

My producing partner, Tamara Blaich, is from Arizona and grew up with the legend of Jacob Waltz and the Lost Dutchman Mine. She told me about the legend when we were in grad school together at USC, and we both thought the story would make a great film, but we couldn't quite get a handle on what approach to take. We kicked around some ideas in completely different genres—kid's movie, scifi along the lines of *The X Files*—but when we landed on found footage horror, it seemed like the perfect fit. Found footage works best when it makes the audience wonder if any part of the film could actually be real, and the truth behind the legend and the air of mystery surrounding the Superstition Mountains let me blur the line between fiction and documentary in a way that did just that.

I drew on the existing legend and expanded a bit, but most of the theories about the curse that are in the film are theories that people actually have. The Superstition Mountains do feature prominently in the myths of the Apache and Pima tribes. There are stories about people disappearing into vortexes or portals to another dimension, and of people seeing beings emerge from them. People do see strange lights in the sky all over that part of Arizona. And of course, people have died of exposure and been murdered out there ever since Jacob Waltz first wandered into Phoenix with a gold nugget back in the 1860s.

To add even more authenticity to the film, I knew from the beginning that I wanted to interview real townspeople about the Lost Dutchman legend instead of writing and casting those parts. So, Tamara and I went out to the Superstitions to do research a few months before we shot. We met George at the Historical Society (he really is a docent there), and Whiplash at the bar in Goldfield Ghost town (he drives the Goldfield train). Whiplash put me in touch with Ron Eagle, who is a wealth of information. He's been looking for the mine for decades and has his own theories about what the Dutchman's gold really is. I met Adam during production and got him to do an interview on the spot because I loved his look. Each of these guys had such great insight into the legend and totally looked the part—there's no way I could've written anything or cast anyone better. There's actually so much interview footage that didn't make it into *Dark Mountain* that we tossed around the idea of putting together a real doc on the Dutchman Mine.

In found footage more generally, so much of the film's strength comes from the interpersonal dynamics between the film crew and this is especially true with *Dark Mountain*. How much of your own experience of making films came to this interplay between characters, or is it entirely fictional?

I think as a filmmaker, or any kind of artist, one always draws on one's own life to some extent. The dynamic between Ross and Kate is one you see a lot in film school. Ross is the guy who wants to make an art house doc, and Kate wants to make something more commercial. In the characters' backstory, they went to film school together. Ross is a dilettante who comes from money, so he can afford to be as arty as he wants. Kate can't do that. She had to get a job as a reality TV producer out of grad school, and brings this perspective to the doc they're making.

The cast of *Dark Mountain* is so strong—I believe Sage Howard already had some horror experience with her role in Pearry Reginald Teo's 2011 *The Evil Inside*, but how did the cast come together?

Our producer, Megan Peterson, had directed Andy Simpson, who played Paul, in her own feature, *Heathens and Thieves*. Andy and Sage are a couple in real life (now married, they were engaged when we shot), and I loved the idea of casting a couple to play a couple in a found footage film—it's very meta, and also adds to the authenticity. We brought them in to read together, and they were both great. I'd originally cast Shelby as one of the voices on the tape that Kate, Paul, and Ross find at the 1970s campsite and we had another actor cast as Ross. But as it happens sometimes, we lost our original Ross about two weeks before we were scheduled to shoot. I loved Shelby's energy, and when I asked him to read for Ross, he and Andy and Sage played off one another really well, so it was settled!

I'm fascinated to hear from a formal learning perspective what you gained from your studies that was the most helpful for you on a project like this, and what nothing—not even a great degree!—could prepare you for, that you could only learn when out there doing it?

Tara Anaïse. Photo credit: Jillian Sorkin (used with permission).

This isn't technical, but for this project, the most helpful thing I learned from USC was use your connections. Almost every crew member on *Dark Mountain* was a USC grad or student. Our budget was really low, so we called in all favors from friends and former classmates. We couldn't have made the movie without their willingness to work for deferred pay or very little money.

We shot the film in 7 days in really rough conditions, and I learned that I never want to do something like that again! We were working long days out in Angeles National Forest in late May/early June, so during the day it was scorching hot, but as soon as the sun went down it was freezing. We had to get hand warmers for people on set because the nights were so cold! We had to shoot so much in a day I was really limited to the number of takes I could do. My DP, AD, and I went through before shooting and timed out each shot as best as we could so I would know how many takes I could afford to do and still make our day. The most we shot in a day was 15 pages. We did have a good time, and we made it all work, but it was really intense. On the next one I need a bigger budget and more time.

I believe you were involved with Jennifer Harrington's film *Housekeeping* – can you tell me a little about that project, what lead you to that role, and what different challenges you found producing the work of another director as opposed to directing your own film?

I actually didn't come on board *Housekeeping* until it was in post-production. I knew Jen from USC and she'd produced and edited *Dark Mountain*, so when she asked me to help out with securing distribution and putting together deliverables for her feature I said "yes" immediately. We'd been going through the same process for *Dark Mountain* so I knew what to expect. It was basically a lot of phone calls and emails to sales agents and potential distributors. Once we accepted the offer from Lionsgate, Jen and I worked together to get all of the elements in place to hand over to them—video and audio files, contracts, release forms, publicity stills, etc.

Aside from *Dark Mountain*, you have an impressive diversity of experience in different kinds of filmmaking. *Bombay Blood* sounds fascinating—can you tell us a little about that project and your experience at the Sundance Screenwriters Intensive?

Thank you! *Bombay Blood* is a tale of forbidden love, familial bonds, and cultural identity, unfolding across two timelines (the present and the summer of 1968), that explores the relationships between Raj, an older Indian man who emigrated to the States in his late twenties; his daughter Caroline, a first-generation half-Indian American music journalist; and his old friend Devi, a former singer in a band in India's all but forgotten late '60s rock scene. When Caroline accompanies Raj to Mumbai to attend a funeral, she uncovers her father's secret history—a history that has the potential to either tear their relationship apart or bring them closer together.

It's a story that's loosely inspired by my own family's history. My father grew up in Bombay, and when he was in his twenties, he moved to New York, where he met my mom. She was born in Brazil and came to the States when she was 5. When writing the script, I drew on my own experiences as a first generation American, and used the story to kind of understand where I came from, in a way. A lot of it is ficitionalized, but the themes and emotions are rooted in reality. I'm also a fan of psychedelic rock, so when I found out that there had been a tiny psych rock scene in India in the late 60s/early 70s, I knew I needed to incorporate it into the story.

The Sundance Screenwriters Intensive was a short but powerful workshop that took place over two days in Los Angeles. We had a full day of writing exercises led by the amazing Joan Tewkesbury, in which we used different techniques to flesh out our characters and explore their motivations. One of my favorites was writing a character's dream. The next day we were paired with two mentors and discussed the script with both. Sundance fosters an incredibly supportive environment for its filmmakers, and all of the staff and mentors are insightful and committed to helping their filmmakers solidify her or his own unique perspective in telling their stories. It was a fantastic experience.

There's so much energy in *Dark Mountain* and it really feels like a project that had a strong driving ambition behind it. What advice would you give to other women horror filmmakers who want to make their own movie but are hesitating about taking the plunge?

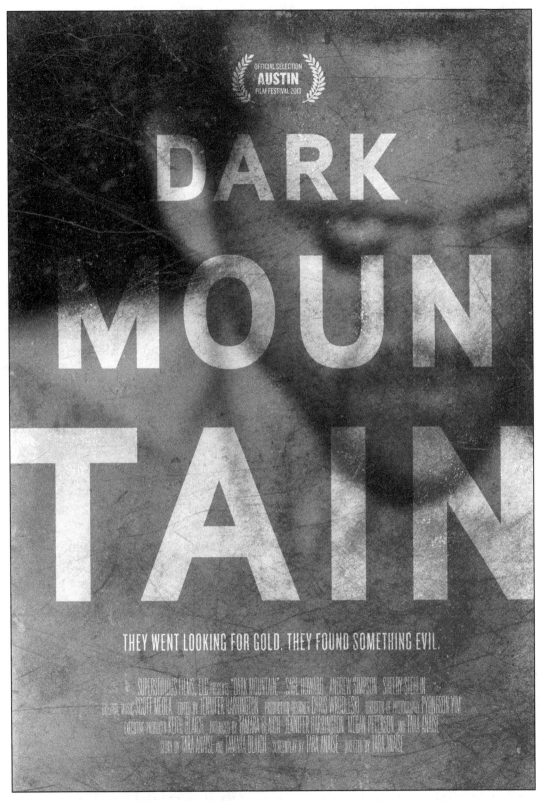

Dark Mountain (Tara Anaïse, 2013)—promotional poster (used with permission)

Set a start date for production and tell everyone you know you're making a movie. Do it even if you don't know where the money's going to come from or how you're going to pull it off. Do it *especially* if you don't know those things. And say it like you mean it. Making a movie is like moving a mountain, and it's so easy to push things off into the future until you're ready and everything is perfect. But then next week becomes next month becomes next year…and you still haven't shot. Once you start acting like it's real and happening imminently, things will somehow start falling into place.

The *Dark Mountain* crew was about 80% female—all of the key positions with the exception of our production designer were filled by women. That's really rare on film sets in general, and practically unheard of in the genre world. Although it appears we are in the midst of a cultural shift demanding gender parity in the entertainment industry, the reality is we're nowhere close. According to the Center for the Study of Women in Television and Film, only 8% of the 100 top-grossing films of 2017 had a female director, and only 2% had a female cinematographer. Television statistics are even more abysmal. The best way to change these stats is for women in positions of power to support and hire other talented women. I'm a member of a few organizations for female directors that are working towards this goal—the Film Fatales, the Alliance of Women Directors, and the USC alumnae group Women of Cinematic Arts.

ANDERS, LUANA

Actor Luana Anders was born in 1938 in New York and began her 45-long career in the mid-1950s. Working across film and television, her early career was marked by her work with Roger Corman's American International Pictures, where she made the majority of her work in the horror genre. Her credits include *The Pit and the Pendulum* (Roger Corman, 1961), *Dementia 13* (Francis Ford Coppola, 1963), *The Manipulator* (Yabo Yablonsky, 1971) and *The Killing Kind* (Curtis Harrington, 1973).

ANDERSON, JUDITH

Born in in Adelaide, Australia in 1897, Frances Margaret Anderson would become one of Britain's most celebrated actors. As Judith Anderson, she played Mrs Danvers in Alfred Hitchcock's *Rebecca* (1940), one of the most unholy feminine forces ever unleashed in gothic cinema. Starting her career on the Sydney stage, she achieved great success in both New York and London, making her first feature film appearance in Rowland Brown's film noir *Blood Money* in 1933. It was in *Rebecca*, however, that Anderson played one of her most famous roles as the sadistic housekeeper. Nominated for an Academy Award for Best Supporting Actress, she would, across her hugely successful screen and stage career, return to dark-themed and gothic terrain in films including Otto Preminger's *Laura*

(1944), René Clair's adaptation of Agatha Christie's *And Then There Were None* (1945), Joseph Stefano and Robert Stevens's TV movie *The Ghost of Sierra de Cobre* (1964), and Terry Bourke's *Inn of the Damned* (1975), the latter seeing Anderson returning to Australia.

ANDERSON, MELISSA SUE

Considering her squeaky-clean origins as Mary Ingalls on the long-running television series *Little House on the Prairie*, that Melissa Sue Anderson later became an unexpected horror darling is a perverse coup for the genre. But she always had spooky leanings: one of her first screen appearance was as an unnamed young girl in the *Bewitched* episode "Tabitha's First Day of School" in 1972. But it was her film debut as Ginny in J. Lee Thompson's classic Canadian slasher *Happy Birthday to Me* in 1981 that revealed Anderson's true flare for horror. That same year she also starred as Vivian Sotherland in Rod Holcomb's TV horror movie *Midnight Offerings*, and Anderson was part of the ensemble cast for the Aaron Spelling-produced *Dark Mansions* in 1986, a television movie revival of the gothic soap opera *Dark Shadows*. She would appear in two episodes of *The New Alfred Hitchcock Presents* and starred alongside Elliot Gould in Malcom Marmorstein's 1990 horror-comedy *Dead Men Don't Die*.

ANKERS, EVELYN

Born in Chile in 1918, Evelyn Ankers' educational background at a string of impressive British schools—culminating in a stint at the Royal Academy of Dramatic Art—may have added to the distinctly 'posh' quality that made her the go-to performer whenever a classic-era Hollywood horror film needed a 'classy dame'. After a string of uncredited roles in the mid-to-late 1930s, she joined Universal in the early 1940s and would star in a number of horror films including Arthur Lubin's Bud Abbott and Lou Costello horror-comedy vehicle *Hold That Ghost* (1941), *The Wolf Man* (George Waggner, 1941), *The Ghost of Frankenstein* (Erle C. Kenton, 1942), *Captive Wild Woman* (Edward Dmytryk, 1943), *Son of Dracula* (Robert Siodmak, 1943), *The Mad Ghoul* (James Hogan, 1943), *Weird Woman* (Reginald Le Borg, 1944), *Jungle Woman* (Reginald Le Borg, 1944), *The Invisible Man's Revenge* (1944), and *The Frozen Ghost* (Harold Young, 1945).

ANSLEY, MELANIE

Author and filmmaker Melanie Ansley was born in Canada and raised in China, now working between Los Angeles and Beijing. Focusing her talents across novel-writing, film production and screenplays, she runs the production company Peking Pictures and her horror credits include directing the features *Walking the Dead* (2010) and *Watch Me* (2006), the latter which she also co-wrote.

ARGENTO, ASIA ‹

While frequent collabora-
tors with her parents—Italian horror royalty Daria
Nicolodi and Dario Argen-
to—Asia Argento's accom-
plishments both behind
and in front of the camera
have seen her stray well beyond the generic bounda-
ries for which her family
name is broadly aligned.
An action film star on the
back of *XXX* (Rob Cohen,
2002), Argento is no stranger to independent and art
cinema with films like *New
Rose Hote*l (Abel Ferrara,
1998), *Last Days* (Gus Van
Sant, 2005), *Marie Antoinette* (Sofia Coppola, 2006),
Boarding Gate (Olivier Assayas, 2007), and *The Last
Mistress* (Catherine Breillat, 2007). As a director, she
herself made *Scarlet Diva*
(2000), *The Heart Is Deceit-
ful Above All Things* (2004),
and *Incompresa* (2014). But
it is horror where Argento
took her first formative
steps into directing, with
the segment "Prospettive"

Asia Argento, Milan, Italy, 4 April 2018.
Credit: Andrea Delbo / Shutterstock.com

in the 1994 Italian anthology film *DeGenerazione* (in which she also acted). Making her
screen debut in the Italian mini-series *Sogni e bisogni* in 1985, it was as Ingrid in Lamberto Bava's *Demons 2* (1986) that saw her first appear in a horror context, followed by
roles in *The Church* (Michele Soavi, 1989), *Love Bites (*Antoine de Caunes, 2001), and
Land of the Dead (George A. Romero, 2005). With her father Dario in the director's
chair, she also starred in *Trauma* (1993), *The Stendhal Syndrome* (1996), *The Phantom of
the Opera* (1998), *The Mother of Tears* (2007) and *Dracula 3D* (2012).

ARTERTON, GEMMA:

Born in England in 1986, actor Gemma Arterton studied at London's Royal Academy of the Dramatic Art, graduating in 2008. Beginning with an acclaimed stage career and soon moving to film, she worked across a variety of genres and contexts—from comedy to Bond girl—and appeared in a number of major blockbuster films including *Clash of the Titans* (Louis Leterrier, 2010). Arterton has starred in a number of horror films including Neil Jordan's *Byzantium* (2012), as Gretel in *Hansel & Gretel Witch Hunters* (Tommy Wirkola, 2013), and in Marjane Satrapi's *The Voices* (2014). In 2016, she offered what is arguably the best performance of her career in Colm McCarthy's powerful zombie film *The Girl with All the Gifts*.

Gemma Arterton at the *Hansel & Gretel Witch Hunters* Los Angeles Premiere, Chinese Theater, Hollywood, California, 24 January 2013. Credit: s_bukley / Shutterstock.com

ARNERIĆ, NEDA

One of the region's most prolific and revered actors, Neda Arnerić was born in what was then known as the Socialist Federal Republic of Yugoslavia in 1953. Recognizable to international audiences for her role in the Blaxploitation film *Shaft in Africa* (John Guillermin, 1973), she made her screen debut in Mladomir 'Purisa' Djordjevic's 1966 war film *Drömmen*. But in terms of horror, she appeared in the 1971 British film *Venom* (aka *The Legend of Spider Forest*), directed by Peter Sykes. Arnerić also appeared in the Austrian/Yugoslavian co-production *Dark Echoes* in 1977 about a zombie sea captain with a taste for revenge. Still acting up until 2015, Arnerić was also active in politics in the early 2000s.

ARNOLD, DOROTHY

Born in Minnesota in 1917 and making her screen debut in 1937 in two short films—William Watson's *Freshies* and Al Christie's *Going, Going, Gone!*—Dorothy Arnold had a string of small and uncredited roles in her early career until earning her two most recognized credits in 1939 with Joe May's *The House of Fear* and Ford Beebe's serial *The Phantom Creeps*. Her ex-husband, American baseballer Joe DiMaggio, would famously elope with Marilyn Monroe in 1944, and Arnold returned to the screen only tentatively after 1940.

ARNOLD, JANA K.

Jana K. Arnold is a frequent collaborator of director David DeCoteau, having penned screenplays for *The Sisterhood* (2004), *Witches of the Caribbean* (2005), and *Stem Cell* (2009). *The Sisterhood* is a lesbian vampire film starring Barbara Crampton. *Witches of the Caribbean* is about a teenage girl haunted by nightmares of being burned alive in the 16th century which she investigates while in the eponymous tropical locale. *Stem Cell* is a mad scientist film featuring another horror icon, Dee Wallace. Arnold is the co-founder of Dallas-based production company Madman Pictures.

ARQUETTE, PATRICIA '

A strong advocate for gender equality in her industry, Patricia Arquette's presence behind the scenes is as significant as it is in front of the camera. One of 5 children of actor, writer, and producer Lewis Arquette, she made her screen debut as Kristen Parker in Chuck Russell's *A Nightmare on Elm Street 3: Dream Warriors* (1987). She returned to horror in 1990 in an episode of *Tales from the Crypt*, and in 1994 she starred in Tim Burton's *Ed Wood* playing Kathy O'Hara's, the cult director *of Plan 9 from Outer Space*'s famously woke girlfriend who accepted his transvestism without question. In the dual roles of Renee Madison and Alice Wakefield, Arquette also pulled off the good girl/bad girl dichotomy in David Lynch's *Lost Highway* (1997) and starred in Ole Bornedal's *Nightwatch* that same year. She also starred in Rupert Wainright's 1999 theological horror movie *Stigmata* and made a small off-camera cameo in M. Blash's 2013 film *The Wait* as the voice of a psychic, a neat reference to her 6-year stint starring in the television series *Medium* (of which she also directed a number of episodes).

ARRIGHI, NIKE

Born in France and growing up in Australia, Nike Arrighi lived in Paris and London as a young adult, studying at the Royal Academy of Dramatic Art in the latter. She made her screen debut in 1966 in the British horror television series *Out of the Unknown* and appeared in a number of television shows including *The Prisoner*. Returning to horror in Hammer's *The Devil Rides Out* in 1968—based on Dennis Wheatley's novel, adapted to the screen by Richard Matheson and directed by Terence Fisher—she appeared in another Hammer film in 1971, Peter Sasdy's *Countess Dracula* with Ingrid Pitt and Lesley-Anne Down. But arguably it is her appearance as the blind psychic Orchidea in Francesco Barilli's 1974 *giallo The Perfume of the Lady in Black* that gave us Arrighi's most unforgettable performance.

ARTHUR, KAREN

Karen Arthur's screen career began as an actor, making a brief uncredited appearance in the Gene Kelly-directed *A Guide for the Married Man* in 1967, followed by a string of bit-parts in TV series. The following year she made her directorial debut with the fierce feminist drama *Legacy* (starring and written by Joan Hotchkis), and while juggling TV work to pay the bills, she directed her magnum opus, the independently-produced horror film *The Mafu Cage* (1978) starring Carol Kane and Lee Grant. Picking up in part where *Legacy* left off, *The Mafu Cage* amplifies in both outrageousness and intensity Arthur's previous exploration of women struggling with mental health issues. After struggling to attain artistic autonomy in the studio system, her last feature film was the thriller *Lady Beware* in 1987, and she then commited herself wholly to television where she excelled as an award-winning director.

ASAKURA, KAYOKO

Japanese director, writer, producer, and editor Kayoko Asakura was born in Japan in 1977 and studied at Tokyo Zokei University. A fan of films like Tobe Hooper's *The Texas Chainsaw Massacre*, in 2010 she made the short films *Off Season* and *Don't Peep*, and an episode of the horror television series *Tales of Terror from Tokyo and All Over Japan* titled "Empty House". In 2013, she released her breakout horror film *It's a Beautiful Day* and the short *Hide and Seek*, followed by *Girls, Dance with the Dead* (2015), and *Dokumushi* (2016).

ASATO, MARI

Born in Japan in 1976, Mari Asato began as an assistant photographer on Kiyoshi Kurosawa's *Barren Illusions* (1999). Asato was assistant director of Hiroshi Takahashi's *Sodom the Killer* in 2004 (in which she also received her only acting credit), and in 2004, she directed the action film *Samurai Chicks* and an episode *of Hideshi Hino's Theater of Horror* "The Boy from Hell". This was followed in 2008 by the quirky coulrophobic horror film *Twilight Syndrome: Dead Go Round*. In 2009, Asato made her debut as writer with the screenplay for *Ju-On: Black Ghost* which she also directed, continuing the internationally popular *Grudge* series. This was followed by the horror films *Cellular Girlfriend* and *Gomennasai* in 2011, and the 3rd, 4th, and 5th instalments of *The Chasing World* horror franchise. In 2013, Asato adapted Haruka Hôjô's supernatural mystery novel *Bilocation* to the screen in a film of the same name, with the sequel *Bilocation Ura* the following year. Her most intriguing film, however, remains her 2014 film adaptation of the videogame *Fatal Frame*.

ASELTON, KATIE

Katie Aselton was born in Maine in 1978 and made her acting debut in the television series *Undressed* in 2001, later acting in movies like Gus Van Sant's *The Sea of Trees* (2015) and the *X-Men* series *Legion*. The first film she directed was the feature-length comedy *The Freebie* in 2010. Aselton both directed and starred in her second directorial effort, the horror movie *Black Rock* with Lake Bell and Kate Bosworth, collaborating with her husband Mark Duplass who wrote the screenplay. In 2015, Aselton appeared in Joel Edgerton's horror film *The Gift* and made a brief audio cameo in the 2014 found footage horror movie *Creep*, directed by her brother-in-law Patrick Duplass and starring, co-written and co-produced by Mark. In 2019, she appeared in Justin Benson and Aaron Moorhead's film *Synchronic*.

Katie Aselton at the *Game of Thrones* Season 7 Premiere Screening at the Walt Disney Concert Hall on July 12, 2017 in Los Angeles, CA. Credit: Kathy Hutchins / Shutterstock.com

ASENSIO, ANA

New York-based writer, actor, and director Ana Asensio was born in Madrid in 1978, making her first appearance as an actor on Spanish television in the late 1990s. Asensio attained widespread attention for her starring role in the series *Nada Es Para Siempre* in the early 2000's, and as well as a string of short films she continued her work in television well into the century's second decade. She made the move to acting in feature films with movies including *The Afterlight* (Alexei Kaleina and Craig Macneill, 2009), *The Archive* (Ethan Spigland, 2015), and the horror-themed *Fresh Flesh* (Tirso Calero, 2011), *The Kovak Box* (Daniel Monzón, 2006) and *Zenith* (Vladan Nikolic, 2010). Asensio's critically acclaimed directorial film debut *Most Beautiful Island* has strong horror elements with its shrewd reimagining of the genre's iconography in its tale about the lengths an illegal immigrant will go to survive and was included in Vulture's 2018 list "100 Scares That Shaped Horror".

ASHIZAWA, AKIKO

Beginning her film career as an assistant camera operator on Banmei Takahashi's *Tattoo Ari* in 1982, Akiko Ashizawa's filmography as cinematographer includes Hideyuki Hirayama's 1994 horror short *Yoi ko to asobô* and the horror features *Naked Blood: Megyaku* (Hisayasu Satô, 1996), *Yabu no naka* (Hisayasu Satô, 1996), *Loft* (Kiyoshi Kurosawa, 2005), *Screaming Class* (Tetsuya Sato, 2013), and *Hana-Dama: The Origins* (Hisayasu Satô, 2014). Having worked with Kurosawa on numerous other films—not just *Loft* but *Journey to the Shore* (2015) and *Tokyo Sonata* (2008)—it is arguably his 2006 film *Sakebi* where Ashizawa's skills as a horror cinematographer come to the fore. A winner of the Ministry of Education Award for Artistic Excellence (*Geijutsu Sensho Monbudaijinsho*), she is one of the most highly regarded cinematographers in Japan.

ASPINALL, JENNIFER

New York-based make-up artist Jennifer Aspinall's lengthy résumé reveals her that across her vast experience in television, theater, commercials, and film, is a passion for horror. Credited for special makeup effects on *The Toxic Avenger* (Michael Herz and Lloyd Kaufman, 1984), *Spookies* (Genie Joseph, Thomas Doran and Brendan Faulkner, 1986) and *Street Trash* (Jim Munro, 1987) she did both hair and makeup in Larry Cohen's *The Ambulance* (1990). Aspinall also worked on special effects make up and props for *Psychos in Love* (Gorman Bechard, 1987) and *Toxic Tutu* (Joe Nardelli, 2017).

ATOMIC, TONJIA—INTERVIEW (JUNE 2018)

A broad skill set marks Washington-based Tonjia Atomic's filmography, both in front of the camera as an actor and behind it. In regard to the latter, she has credits for not just directing, producing, writing, composing and editing, but in makeup/SFX, costuming, art and camera departments also. To date, Atomic has directed five shorts alone, including the horror films *Awesome Ouija Board* (2009, co-directed with Forrest Baum), *Companion* (2011), *Closing In* (2014), *Reborn* (2015), the Tristan Risk-fronted *Just a Prick* (2018, co-directed with Michelle Nessk), as well as a segment in the anthology *Hobo with a Trash Can* (2015). Her feature films as director include *Walking to Linas* (2012), *Plain Devil* (2014), and the horror films *Claudia Qui* (2012) and her upcoming sequel to *Manos: The Hands of Fate* (Harold P. Warren, 1965) called *Manos Returns* (2018). Atomic is also a writer, musician and jewellery maker. At the time of our interview, Atomic was working on a new slasher film starring Bill Oberst Jr.

When did you realise that horror was going to play such a key role in your life?

I was a big fan of horror as a kid. My father loved horror films and B movies. I wasn't allowed to watch some of them at a young age and I used to sneak out of bed and watch whatever my Dad was watching on TV from the hallway. I had an interest in vampires and dark fairy tales from a very young age. I had no idea that I would be making horror films as an adult but it seems to make sense. I feel like this is a comfortable place for me to be.

It's no understatement to suggest that you're quite the polymath, Tonjia—an all-round renaissance woman! Directing, producing, writing, composing, editing, acting, as well as working in art, makeup and camera departments. Serious question: is there anything you can't do?!

Tonjia Atomic, photo by Joseph P. Traina
(used with permission)

A lot of the jobs that I've had to do are out of necessity. As an indie filmmaker that often works with little to no budget I've had to do many things myself. There are a few things that I'm not as comfortable with, although I've had training in every aspect of filmmaking. The different departments in filmmaking are so specialized and often require technical skill. It's best to find out what interests you and specialize in it. For me, writing, directing, editing, music, and acting are what I'm best at.

As director, you've clearly a real flair for horror material, although this is not your exclusive terrain. What does the genre allow you space to do that make it so useful to your art practice?

I am drawn to the psychological aspects of horror. Within horror I am able to explore sensitive and dark topics in a way that is fantasy-based. It is a safe place to explore the darker themes of life.

You've directed a few films in a co-directorial capacity which I find fascinating. How does this collaborative process differ from when you are the sole driver behind the wheel, so to speak?

I've co-directed with both Michelle Nessk and Rachel Jackson. Both experiences have been great. One of the reasons that each project went so well was because I get along so well with each of the directors. It's been a joy working with both of them. They each bring different things to the table than I would by myself while being nice to work with at the same time. I love what we've been able to produce.

You are quite prolific in terms of making both shorts and features—do you have a preference for one over the other, or do each have strengths and weaknesses?

I actually prefer feature films. I like being able to flesh out the stories and the characters. I like being able to sit with the stories and characters too. I'm better at letting themes unfold in a larger time frame than I am telling a complete story in a short amount of time. I've made my share of shorts and enjoyed doing so, but I always struggle with how to end them without feeling like I'm ending them with a gimmicky punchline.

***Claudia Qui* is your most overt horror feature, can you tell us a little about the inspiration behind that film and the circumstances around its creation?**

I was inspired by the idea of someone being possessed in their sleep and their talking in their sleep reflecting that. I also fell in love with the music of Luminol. Luminol is Barbara Burgio and Don Ayers. I decided to make the film as a love letter to their music. The film is completely improvised and edited together with full versions of their songs. We made it for no money. I wouldn't do another movie that same way as there were certain things that I wish could have been different that I had little control over at the time. I think it suffers a bit due to the limitations that we had but it was good experience for me.

Your other feature films again reveal a creative vision that is quite broad— ***Plain Devil*** **and** ***Walking to Linas*** **in particular. Can you talk us through each of these films, and what is it that you think unites them the most strongly?**

Plain Devil and *Walking to Linas* are both comedy features of mine. *Plain Devil* is a campy send up of juvenile delinquent films of the '50s set in modern times. It's a silly comedy with themes of social inclusion. *Walking to Linas* also happens to be a silly comedy. The scenes and dialogue are all improvised. It's about a pair of aspiring artists on the search for a director that they hope will help them hit the big time.

I'm fascinated by the sound of your project ***Manos Returns***, **the sequel to** ***Manos the Hands of Fate***. **Can you tell us a bit about this?**

We recently finished *Manos Returns*. It is the sequel to *Manos the Hands of Fate* and includes Jackey Neyman Jones, Tom Neyman, and Diane Mahree Rystad from the original film. Our sheriff is played by Bryan Jennings who is the son of William Jennings, the sheriff in the original. The story slightly parallels the original film in that travellers get lost and find themselves drawn into Manos' lair.

It's 50 years after the original story and Debbie is all grown up and twisted from her years in the lodge. Other characters are back and have also been changed by living in the evil lodge for so many years. Jackey Neyman Jones is one of the producers along with me, Rachel Jackson (*Manos: The Hands of Felt*), and Joe Sherlock (*Beyond the Wall of Fear*). We worked hard to make the film enjoyable and well made within a small budget that we'd raised via Kickstarter. From the responses so far, I think we succeeded.

You've had work featured in quite a few horror anthologies and shorts compilations—what are your thoughts on these kind of feature-length compendiums as an outlet to showcase the work of an array of filmmakers?

I love anthology films. I think it's really a way to provide a home for short films. I think it's so much fun to collaborate with others and also to work with a set of rules to follow. *Hobo with a Trash Can* is my most well-known anthology so far. We each made a short film using $1 as our budget. It's a fun film especially for low- and no-budget fans.

Outside filmmaking, I understand you make jewellery and are a musician. As an artist, what do these different creative outlets allow you to satisfy that you would struggle to achieve if you focused solely on one artistic field?

Manos Returns promotional image created by Joe Sherlock (used with permission)

Music and filmmaking definitely take up most of my creative energies. If I had to focus only on those I could. However, they are both so time consuming and intense that I usually take breaks after I'm done with a project and spend time relaxing in whatever way I can. When not working on a film or music project I still need a creative outlet. That's where jewellery making, soap making, and other smaller creative projects come in. I've always felt the need to create since I was very young. As a child, I had a strong imagination and made up stories and my own toys to go along with those stories.

AUBERT, LENORE

Born in Slovenia and raised in Vienna, Eleanore Maria Leisner used the more Hollywood-friendly name Lenore Aubert throughout her screen career. She turned to acting after working as a model in New York City, initially on stage and then shifting to film with her new moniker. Her first film appearance was an uncredited role in Ernst Lubitsch's 1938 film *Bluebeard's Eighth Wife* with Claudette Colbert and Gary Cooper, and she worked steadily in film and television until the early 1950s. She had key roles in Lesley Selander's horror film *The Catman of Paris* (1946) and the film noir *The Return of the Whistler* (D. Ross Lederman, 1948). But her fame stems primarily from her appearances in Charles T. Barton's horror-comedies *Abbott and Costello Meet Frankenstein* (1948) and *Abbott and Costello Meet the Killer, Boris Karloff* (1949).

AUGER, CLAUDINE

Claudine Oger (later Auger) was born in Paris in 1941, and in 1958 she was crowned Miss France. The fame that accompanied this title garnered her the role as Domino in the James Bond film *Thunderball* (Terence Young, 1965), but her horror credentials are even more memorable if only for her performance as Renata in Mario Bava's *Twitch of the Death Nerve* (1971). Earlier in her career, she appeared uncredited in iconic French filmmaker Jean Cocteau's 1969 film *Testament of Orpheus*, having made her screen debut in Pierre Gaspard-Huit's *Christine* two years earlier, marrying the director when she was 18 years old. She returned to horror in 1978 in René Cardona Jr.'s *The Bermuda Triangle* with John Huston, but her strongest performance in the genre next to *Twitch of the Death Nerve* was in Paolo Cavara's *giallo Black Belly of the Tarantula* in 1971.

AUMONT, TINA

Tina Aumont is the daughter of revered French actor Jean-Pierre Aumont and Dominican actor Maria Montez. Born in the United States, her reputation largely remains based on her starring role in *Casanova* (Federico Fellini, 1976) and her collaborations with

Tinto Brass, *The Howl* (1968) and *Salon Kitty* (1975). Aumont also appeared in a number of horror films, including the experimental Italian-British horror co-production *Necropolis* (1970), Giulio Questi's *Arcana* (1972), Sergio Martino's *giallo Torso* (1973), and N.G. Mount's *Dinosaur of the Deep* (1993), which co-starred Jean Rollin. Aumont would later appear in Rollin's *Two Orphan Vampires* in 1997.

AVELLÁN, ELIZABETH

Elizabeth Avellán is a film producer born in Venezuela and is known primarily for her work on many films directed by Robert Rodriguez, to whom she was married to from 1990 to 2006. These include horror films *From Dusk till Dawn* (1996), *The Faculty* (1998), and the two films that made up the 2007 *Grindhouse* release, Quentin Tarantino's *Death Proof* and Rodriguez's *Planet Terror*. She continued producing Rodriguez's work after their separation, including the 2010 film *Machete* which he co-directed with Ethan Maniquis. Avellán's other horror credits include *From Dusk till Dawn 2: Texas Blood Money* (Scott Spiegel, 1999), *From Dusk till Dawn 3: The Hangman's Daughter* (P. J. Pesce, 2000), and *Predators* (Nimród Antal, 2010). She is the Vice President of the production company Troublemaker Studios, co-founded with Rodriguez in 2000.

AXELROD, NINA

A casting director by trade, New York-born Nina Axelrod also appeared in front of the camera in many horror films. Coming from a showbiz family, her father was writer, producer and director George Axelrod, himself the son of silent era actor Betty Carpenter. Nina Axelrod was the casting director for almost 20 films including the horror movies *Nightflyers* (T.C. Blake, 1987*)*, *Fright Night Part 2* (Tommy Lee Wallace, 1988), *Critters 3* (Kristine Peterson, 1991), *Critters 4* (Rupert Harvey, 1992), *Netherbeast Incorporated* (Dean Ronalds, 2007) and *The Graves* (Brian Pulido, 2009). Famously auditioning for the role of Rachael in Ridley Scott's *Blade Runner* (1982) that ultimately went to Sean Young, as an actor Axelrod is most recognizable for her role as Betty in *Critters 3* and Terry in *Motel Hell* (Kevin Connor, 1980).

AYKAÇ, EBRY

Turkish actor Ebru Aykaç was born in the Aegean Region in 1975 and studied at Celal Bayar University before focusing on a screen career. In 2006 she starred as Hande in Hasan Karacadag's internationally acclaimed cult horror film *D@bbe*.

B

BABBIT, JAMIE

Hailing from Ohio, Jamie Babbit's filmmaking career began as an intern on Martin Scorsese's *The Age of Innocence* (1993), and later worked as a script supervisor on David Fincher's *The Game* (1997). As a short film director, her movie *Stuck* (2001) won a jury prize at the Sundance Film Festival, and she directed episodes of popular television series including *Girls* and *Looking*, and more recently episodes of dark-themed series including *Santa Clarita Diet* and *Ghosted*. As a feature film director, her most recognizable movie might be *The Itty Bitty Titty Committee* (2007), but her 2005 gothic incest feature *The Quiet* with Edie Falco and Martin Donovan exemplifies her skills with darker, brooding subject matter.

BACH, BARBARA

Barbara Bach was a tremendous horror actor in her own right, despite her broader fame stemming from a number of other factors: the one-time Mrs Ringo Starr, the former Countess Gregorini di Savignano di Romagna, and a Bond girl in *The Spy Who Loved Me* (1977). Born in New York City, she was a highly successful model during the 1960s before turning towards acting. Her credits include the *gialli Black Belly of the Tarantula* (Paolo Cavara, 1971) and *Short Night of Glass Dolls* (Aldo Lado, 1971), as well as Sergio Martino's eco-horror *The Great Alligator River* (1979) and Danny Steinmann's *The Unseen* (1980).

BACKLINIE, SUSAN

The iconic image of Susan Backlinie being attacked by a shark in Steven Spielberg's legendary 1975 film *Jaws* is not just one of the most famous scenes in 1970s US cinema, but one of the most instantly recognizable horror movie images of all time. Born in California in 1946, the actor, stuntwoman, and animal trainer played the first character in the movie we see killed by the shark. Backlinie wore a harness while making the famous scene that tethered her to the ocean floor; Spielberg caught her legendary look of surprise by not telling her exactly when she would be grabbed by a diver underneath the water. Backlinie collaborated again with Spielberg in a parody of the scene in his 1979 film *1941*, and she also appeared in the 1977 eco-horror movie, *Day of the Animals*.

BACLANOVA, OLGA

Olga Vladimirovna Baklanova left Russia to professionally conquer the United States in a career that spanned stage, screen and radio as an actor, singer and dancer. While Baklanova worked across a number of genres, it her two most famous roles were in the horror genre; Paul Leni's *The Man Who Laughs* (1928) alongside Mary Philbin and Conrad Veidt, and as the doomed, conniving trapeze artist Cleopatra in Tod Browning's *Freaks* (1932).

BAILEY-BOND, PRANO

Born and raised in Wales within a creative family of actors and artists, Prano Bailey-Bond's short films have played around the world at prestigious festivals including the London Film Festival, Tampere Film Festival, Slamdance, and Sitges Film Festival. Her short *Nasty* (2015) played at more than 100 film festivals and received several accolades. Other shorts such as *Shortcut* (2016)—which was made for Film4's Fright Bites series— *The Trip* (2013), *Man Vs. Sand* (2012), *Short Lease* (co-directed with Jennifer Eiss in 2010), and her first film *The House of Virgins* (2007) have similarly received widespread recognition. She cites her influences as Cindy Sherman, Douglas Sirk and David Lynch, saying that she "grew up on a diet of *Twin Peaks* in a strange Welsh community". Prano has participated in talent development schemes including the Berlinale Talent Campus and BFI Network@LFF. In 2018 she was selected as a Screen Daily 'Star of Tomorrow' and is currently gearing up to shoot her feature film debut, the psychological horror film *Censor*. It is supported by the BFI, Film4, Ffilm Cymru Wales, and Creative England, and was shortlisted for the Sundance Writers Lab.

BAKER, BETSY

As Ash Williams' luckless girlfriend Linda in Sam Raimi's *The Evil Dead* (1981), Iowa-born Betsy Baker carved her way into cult film history despite only committing fully to an acting career in later years. Working predominantly in television, her credits include *True Blood* and *American Horror Story*, and on horror movies such as the horror-comedy mockumentary *Brutal Massacre: A Comedy* (Stevan Mena, 2007), *2084* (George Blumentti and Maurice Kelly, 2009), and *Lake Eerie* (Chris Majors, 2016). She also appeared in the horror shorts *The Premonition* (James Ersted, 2018) and the fan film *Ash vs. Evil Dead: Aunt Linda's Bake Off* (Michael Kallio, 2017).

BAKER, CARROLL

Carroll Baker shot to international stardom with her starring role in Elia Kazan's Tennessee Williams adaptation *Baby Doll* (1956), and she would continue to appear in a number of impressive films such as *Giant* (George Stevens, 1956) with James Dean. Her first turn towards low-brow exploitation fare was in Jack Garfein's *Something Wild* (1961) and, after a poorly received starring role as Jean Harlow in a 1965 biopic and a much-publicized contract dispute, she moved to Italy and starred in a number of *gialli* and horror films including *The Sweet Body of Deborah* (Romolo Guerrieri, 1968), *Orgasmo* (Umbert Lenzi, 1969), *So Sweet…So Perverse* (Umberto Lenzi, 1969), *A Quiet Place to Kill* (Umberto Lenzi, 1970), *The Devil with Seven Faces* (Osvaldo Civirani, 1971), *Knife of Ice* (Umberto Lenzi, 1972), *Baba Yaga* (Corrado Farina, 1973) and *The Flower with the Petals of Steel* (Gianfranco Piccioli, 1973). Baker would return to the United States to work in more mainstream fare later in her career, with a key role in John Hough's beloved *The Watcher in the Woods* (1980).

BALASKI, BELINDA

California-born Belinda Balaski's career as an entertainer began when she was only 5 years old. While her filmography is long and impressive in both television and film, for horror fans, she is most immediately renowned for her collaborations with filmmaker Joe Dante including *Pirahna* (1978), *The Howling* (1981), *Gremlins* (1984), and *Gremlins II: The New Batch* (1990). She also starred in Bert I. Gordon's cult horror film *The Food of the Gods* (1976) and John Moffitt's *The Werewolf of Woodstock* (1975).

BALDIN, REBECCA

Born in Arkansas in 1955, actor Rebecca Balding worked for 30 years from the mid-1970s onwards, appearing mostly on television. In 1979 she starred alongside Barbara Steele and Yvonne De Carlo in the classic horror film *The Silent Scream*, returning to a lead role in the genre in her soon-to-be husband James L. Conway's 1981 horror movie *The Boogens*.

BALK, FAIRUZA

A child actor, Fairuza Balk was catapulted to fame as Dorothy Gale in Walter Murch's *Return to Oz* in 1985. Through Andrew Fleming's *The Craft* (1996), Balk became synonymous with her bad goth girl character as she and her friends dabbled in schoolgirl sorcery. That same year, she would star in the ill-fated screen adaptation of H. G. Wells' *The*

Island of Doctor Moreau (1896), initially helmed by cult filmmaker Richard Stanley and later taken over by John Frankenheimer (Balk is one of the interview subjects in David Gregory's 2014 documentary about the production fiasco, *Lost Soul: The Doomed Journey of Richard Stanley's Island of Dr. Moreau*). In 2006, she starred in Larry Cohen's donation to the *Masters of Horror* television series, "Pick Me Up", and in 2018 appeared in Orson Oblowitz's brutal home invasion film *Hell is Where the Home Is*.

BANG, CAROLINA

Spanish actor Carolina Bang was born in the Canary Islands in 1985 and is renowned for her frequent collaborations as both actor and producer with her husband Álex de la Iglesia. Together Band and de la Iglesia have been responsible for some of the most original and euphoric genre films to emerge from Europe over the last decade, most of which have horror, gothic, supernatural or otherwise dark themes. With de la Iglesia directing, Bang acted in *The Last Circus* (2010) and *Witching & Bitching* (2013), and produced *The Bar* (2017). Bang has also appeared in the horror film *Shrew's Nest* (Juan Fernando Andrés and Esteban Roel, 2014) and produced the *The Devil and the Blacksmith* (Paul Urkijo, 2017).

BANKHEAD, TALLULAH

Self-defined "ambisextrous" Hollywood superstar Tallulah Bankhead never minced words, whether acting or in person. Her quick wit, sharp tongue and open bisexuality rendered her a stand-out figure amongst Hollywood's stereotypical image of idealized womanhood. While her skills were primarily associated with the theater, two roles in particular—Alfred Hitchcock's brutal proto survival horror film *Lifeboat* (1944) and Hammer's glorious *Die! Die! My Darling* (Silvio Narizzano, 1965), the latter of which she chose over the part in *Whatever Happened to Baby Jane?* (Robert Aldrich, 1962) that eventually went to Bette Davis—solidify her place as a key figure in horror history.

BANNER, JILL

As the title character in Jack Hill's legendary *Spider Baby* (1964), Jill Banner's Laura raised the bar for excessive, over-the-top girl-child horror villains. Although the film was tangled in legal issues that delayed its release, it has demonstrated impressive longevity with cult audiences in large part due to the electricity between Banner and her co-stars, Sid Haig and Elizabeth Washburn. Despite other appearances in films including the horror movie *Weekend of Fear* (Joe Danford, 1966), it is *Spider Baby* upon which Banner's cult reputation largely rests. Passing away at the age of 35 in a car accident, it is tempting to speculate what the future could have held for the young actor had she survived.

BARA, THEDA

The original vamp, silent era superstar Theda Bara was one of cinema's first sex symbols, pushing a star persona heavily reliant upon a femme fatale-like combination of dark sexuality and perverse power. Despite little of her work surviving, Bada was a prolific actor, and while not horror *per se* even the titles and synopses of many of her films underscore how Bara's image was linked to a dark, dangerous eroticism tinged with the transgressive and exotic: *The Devil's Daughter* (Frank Powell, 1915), *The Serpent* (Raoul Walsh, 1916), *The Tiger Woman* (J. Gordon Edwards, 1917), *The Rose of Blood* (J. Gordon Edwards, 1917), *Salomé* (William Fox, 1918), *The She-Devil* (J. Gordon Edwards, 1918), *When a Woman Sins* (J. Gordon Edwards, 1918, and *The Unchastened Woman* (James Young, 1925). *A Fool there Was* (Frank Powell, 1915) is one of her most famous surviving films, which more concretely established her association with the vamp archetype.

Theda Bara, circa 1915. Credit: PictureLux / The Hollywood Archive / Alamy Stock Photo (32557 217THA)

BARBEAU, ADRIENNE *

Born in California in 1945, American actor and writer Adrienne Barbeau began her career in musicals in the early 1960s and soon relocating to New York to perform on Broadway. A Tony Award winner, she later made the switch to television and film. Barbeau has well over 400 screen credits, and for cult film fans her work in horror is of great significance, particularly her many collaborations with one-time husband, director John Carpenter. Her credits in the genre include *Someone's Watching Me!* (John Carpenter, 1978), *The Fog* (John Carpenter, 1982), *Swamp Thing* (Wes Craven, 1982), *Creepshow* (George A. Romero, 1982), *Bridge Across Time* (E. W. Swackhamer, 1985), *Open House* (Jag Mundhra, 1987), the segment "The Facts in the Case of M. Valdemar" in *Two Evil Eyes* (George A. Romero, 1990), *Burial of the Rats* (Dan Golden, 1995), *Ring of Darkness* (David DeCoteau, 2004), *Unholy* (Daryl Goldberg, 2007), *War Wolves* (Michael Worth, 2009), and in a lovely homage to her role in *The Fog*, she plays a DJ who delivers the wraparound narrative in the 2015 horror anthology *Tales of Halloween*.

BARRETT, ADRIENNE

John Parker's 1955 film *Dementia*—aka *Daughter of Horror*—is a classic of art horror, a surreal low-budget film that follows the psychological decline of its unnamed woman protagonist, played to perfection by Adrienne Barrett. Although little remains known of Barrett, her performance is powerful and provocative, doubly impressive because the film's conscious decision to rejet spoken dialogue and rely solely on physical performance and the avant-garde soundtrack by composer and Hedy Lamarr's co-inventor, George Antheil.

BARRETT, EDITH

Taking to the stage in her teens and later joining Orson Welles's Mercury Theater, Edith Barrett met Vincent Price when appearing in the group's production of Thomas Dekker's *The Shoemaker's Holiday* and they married soon after. Although her screen credits dwindled after their divorce in 1948, she made a few notable appearances in *Alfred Hitchcock Presents* in the 1950s. Her major credits, however, are two Val Lewton-produced horror films for RKO Pictures: in Jacques Tourneur's *I Walked with a Zombie* (1943), and in Mark Robson's *The Ghost Ship* (1943).

BARRYMORE, DREW [1]

One of the most famous child actors of the 1980s, the rise-and-fall-and-rise-again of Drew Barrymore's career is Hollywood legend. Coming to public attention in *E.T. the Extra-Terrestrial* (Steven Spielberg, 1982), she made her debut in Ken Russell's horror-scifi hybrid *Altered States* in 1980 and would consistently return to horror throughout her career. As a child, she was cast in Mark L. Lester's screen adaptation of Stephen King's 1980 novel *Firestarter*, tackling another King adaptation in 1985 in Lewis Teague's *Cat's Eye*. Later horror films included *Poison Ivy* (Katt Shea, 1992), a cameo in *Waxwork II: Lost in Time* (Anthony Hickox, 1992), reviving her career in Wes Craven's postmodern horror blockbuster hit *Scream* in 1996. In 2017, Barrymore announced she would be producing a woman-focused horror television series called *Black Rose Anthology*.

Drew Barrymore at the Natural Resources Defense Council's Oceans Initiative, 6 June 2011 in Mailbu, California. Credit: DFree / Shutterstock.com

BASKOVA, SVETLANA

Russian diretor Svetlana Baskova is a graduate of the renowned Moscow Architectural Institute but has built her reputation on a series of films, many of which feature extreme violence and engage with horror in a range of ways, frequently as a critique of patriarchy. Of these, her 1999 film *The Green Elephant* is perhaps the most well-known, a brutal horror film about prisoners in a Russian gulag. While English language translations of her work are not easy to find, her debut film *Cocki, the Running Doctor* was released the year before *The Green Elephant*. Baskova's other horror films include *Five Bottles of Vodka* (2001), and she has also made a number of dramas, including *Mozart* (2006), *The Head* (2004), and *For Marx...* (2012).

BASSETT, ANGELA

American actor and political activist Angela Bassett was born in 1958 in New York. She has appeared in a range of highly acclaimed films and television shows since she launched her career in the mid-1980s, most recently as Ramonda in Ryan Coogler's 2018 super-hero blockbuster *Black Panther*. She worked in theater before moving to television, with breakthrough roles in films such as John Singleton's *Boyz n the Hood* (1991) and Spike Lee's *Malcolm X* (1992). Her horror credits include John Landis's *Innocent Blood* (1992), *Critters 4* (Don Keith Opper, 1992), *Vampire in Brooklyn* (Wes Craven, 1995), and David C. Wilson's horror-scifi hybrid *Supernova* (2000). She also appeared in the television series *Nightmare Cafe*, *American Horror Story: Hotel* and *American Horror Story: Roanoke*.

BASTEDO, ALEXANDRA

British actor Alexandra Bastedo was born in the United Kingdom in 1946 and was a popular sex symbol during the 1970s. Famous for her appearance in the British scifi series *The Champions*, her cinema debut was in William Castle's 1963 horror film *13 Frightened Girls*, later starring in Vincente Aranda's cult Spanish adaptation of Joseph Sheridan Le Fanu's novella *Carmilla* (1872), *The Blood Spattered Bride* (1972). She later starred alongside Peter Cushing and John Hurt in Freddie Francis's 1975 horror movie *The Ghoul*.

BASU, BIPASHA

New Delhi-born Bipasha Basu is one of the most famous faces in Indian horror cinema. With a background in modeling, her starring role in the smash hit horror film *Raaz* (Vikram Bhatt, 2002) linked her closely to the genre, a relationship she would continue in later horror movies including *Aetbaar* (Vikram Bhatt, 2004), *Rakht* (Mahesh V. Manjrekar, 2004), *Rudraksh* (Mani Shankar, 2004), *Darna Zaroori Hai* (Chekravarthy, 2006), *Aatma* (Suparn Verma, 2013), *Creature 3D* (Vikram Bhatt, 2014), and *Alone* (Bhushan Patel, 2015). Basu is a vocal feminist activist who also champions animal rights.

BATES, JEANNE

Born in California in 1918, Jeanne Bates's career spanned almost 60 years on radio, television and film, but it is her performance as Mrs. X in David Lynch's horror film *Eraserhead* (1977) that largely established her cult reputation. She would appear in the genre frequently throughout her career, however, including in films such as *The Soul of a Monster* (Will Jason, 1944), *Back from the Dead* (Charles Marquis Warren, 1957), *The Strangler* (Burt Topper, 1964), *Silent Night, Deadly Night 4: Initiation* (Brian Yuzna, 1990), *Mom*

(Patrick Rand, 1991), as well as episodes of television series including *The Twilight Zone*. Her last film appearance was as Irene in David Lynch's *Mulholland Drive* (2001).

BATES, KATHY

Kathy Bates was born in 1948 in Memphis and is an award-winning stage and screen actor who has worked with filmmakers including Miloš Forman, Robert Altman, James Cameron and Mike Nichols. It is in the role of Annie Wilkes in Rob Reiner's 1990 screen adaptation of Stephen King's 1987 novel *Misery*, however, that Bates's name is most immediately associated, winning her an Academy Award for Best Actress. While her repertoire is broad, Bates's other horror work includes *My Best Friend is a Vampire* (Jimmy Huston, 1987), *Diabolique* (Jerimiah Chechik, 1996), and two other Stephen King adaptations: *Dolores Claiborne* (Taylor Hackford, 1995), and an uncredited appearance in the television mini-series *The Stand* (Mick Garris, 1994). Bates has also appeared in *Six Feet Under* and *American Horror Story*.

BAUER, MICHELLE

American B-grade horror star Michelle Bauer began her career in adult magazines and films, including the horror-themed adult movie *Nightdreams* (Francis Della, 1981). Impressing exploitation producer and director Fred Olen Ray in an audition, she was cast in his 1986 film *The Tomb* alongside Cameron Mitchell, John Carradine and Sybil Danning. Bauer would collaborate on numerous horror movies with Ray including *Hollywood Chainsaw Hookers* (1988), *Evil Toons* (1992), *Beverly Hills Vamp* (1989), Scream *Queen Hot Tub Party* (1991), *Witch Academy* (1995), *Tomb of the Werewolf* (2004) and *Voodoo Dollz* (2008). Other regular directors she worked with include David DeCoteau on *Nightmare Sisters* (1988), *Sorority Babes in the Slimeball Bowl-O-Rama* (1988), *Puppet Master III: Toulon's Revenge* (1991) and *3 Scream Queens* (2014); as well as legendary Spanish director Jess Franco on 1998's *Lust for Frankenstein* and *Mari-Cookie and the Killer Tarantula*, both in 1998. Bauer's other horror credits include *Terror Night* (Nick Marino, 1987), *Demonwarp* (Emmett Alston, 1988), *Death Row Diner* (B. Dennis Wood, 1988), *Camp Fear* (Thom Edward Keith, 1991), *Demented* (Richard Martin, 1994), *Vampire Vixens from Venus* (Ted A. Bohus, 1995), *Gingerdead Man 2: Passion of the Crust* (Silvia St. Croix, 2008) and *Megaconda* (Christopher Olen Ray, 2010).

BEACHAM, STEPHANIE

British actor Stephanie Beacham is a familiar face in soap operas including *The Colby's*, *Dynasty*, and *Coronation Street*, but it is through her horror roles that she has earned a cult audience. Studying mime in France before concentrating on acting at London's

Royal Academy of Dramatic Art, Beacham's performance skills come to the fore in many of her horror roles, including *The Devil's Widow* (Roddy McDowell, 1970), Hammer's *Dracula A.D. 1972* (Alan Gibson, 1972), Amicus's *And Now the Screaming Starts!* (Roy Ward Baker, 1973), and two films by Pete Walker, *Schizo* (1976) and *House of Mortal Sin* (1976). Beacham would star with Marlon Brando as Miss Jessell in *The Nightcomers* (Michael Winner, 1971), the prequel to Henry James's famous gothic novella *The Turn of the Screw* (1898). Her later horror films include *Inseminoid* (Norman J. Warren, 1981) and *The Witches Hammer* (James Eaves, 2006).

BEALS, JENNIFER,

Following her breakout performance in the international blockbuster *Flashdance* (Adrian Lynne, 1983), Chicago-born Jennifer Beals starred in the title role of Franc Roddam's *The Bride*, a reimagining of Mary Shelley's novel *Frankenstein* alongside pop star Sting. Having studied literature at Yale, Beals' screen credits include many horror, gothic and dark-themed roles including Robert Bierman's cult black comedy *Vampire's Kiss* in 1989 with Nicolas Cage, and the following year in French New Wave filmmaker Claude Chabrol's *Dr M*, a reimagining of Fritz Lang's *Dr Mabuse the Gambler* (1922). In 1998, she appeared in Greg Spence's *The Prophecy II* alongside Christopher Walken, and in 2006 Beals acted in Takashi Shimizu's *The Grudge 2*, the second film in the American remake series of the popular J-horror *Ju-On* series. While working steadily across film and television, Beals would continue to work in horror in series including *The Outer Limits* and *The Hunger*.

BEAUMONT, GABRIELLE

Little about British director Gabrielle Beaumont would suggest that she would be responsible for one of the darkest evil child films of the 1980s. Beyond *The Godsend* (1980), Beaumont's filmography shows the output of a dedicated workhorse, with credits including episodes of *M*A*S*H, Miami Vice, Hill Street Blues, Doogie Howser, M.D.*, and *Star Trek: The Next Generation*. Earlier in her career, Beaumont had received producer credits for Viktors Ritelis's *The Corpse* (1971)—a remake of Henri-Georges Clouzot's 1955 French classic *Les Diaboliques*—and she later directed an episode of the television series *Nightmare Classics*.

BECERRIL, SANDRA

Bestselling author of nine novels and filmmaker supreme Sandra Becerril was born in Mexico City in 1980 and studied extensively before turning her attentions to creative work that often intersects with the horror genre. As a director, her notable credits are

El Escondite (2011), *Están Aquí* (2014), *Sustefest 2018* (2018) and the short *La Venganza* (2015), all of which she wrote with additional screenwriting credits including the anthology *Nightmare Cinema* (2018) and Alexis Pérez Montero's horror feature *Desde tu infierno* (2018). Becerril has also worked as an editor and producer on many of these projects.

BECKINSALE, KATE '

Born in London in 1973, English actor Kate Beckinsale has a long association with horror through her recurring starring role in the *Underworld* series. With a background in theater, she studied at Oxford's New College and soon turned her attention to film and television. Her first horror film credit was Lewis Gilbert's *Haunted* (1995), with later work in the genre including Stephen Sommers' *Van Helsing* (2004), Nimród Antal's *Vacancy* (2007) and Brad Anderson's *Stonehearst Asylum* (2014). But it is in *Underworld* that her connection to the genre is strongest, starring in *Underworld* (Len Wiseman, 2003), *Underworld: Evolution* (Len Wiseman, 2006), *Underworld: Rise of the Lycans* (Patrick Tatopoulos, 2009), *Underworld: Awakening* (Måns Mårlind, 2012) and Anna Foerster's *Underworld: Blood Wars* (2016).

Kate Beckinsale at the presentation of *Underworld Awakening* at the Villamagna hotel on 25 January 2012 in Madrid, Spain. Credit: Shelly Wall / Shutterstock.com

BELL, ASHLEY

Concentrating on her acting career after graduating with a degree in Fine Arts from New York University, American actor Ashley Bell played one of the more interesting women protagonists in a found footage horror film as Nell in Daniel Stamm's 2010 film *The Last Exorcism* and its non-found footage horror sequel, *The Last Exorcism Part II* (Ed Gass-Donnelly, 2013). Aside from her role in Douglas Aarniokoski's post-apocalyptic horror film *The Day* (2011), Bell would collaborate with horror filmmaker Mickey Keating on both *Carnage Park* (2016) and his 2017 film, *Psychopaths*.

BELL, KRISTA

Canadian stunt woman Krista Bell initially trained as a wrestler for the WWE before getting her big break in stunts when The Rock noticed her while making Kevin Bray's 2004 action film *Walking Tall*. She has worked on a number of blockbusters, ranging from the *Planet of the Apes* to *Pirates of the Caribbean* franchises, and has signficant experience with stunt work in horror films such as *Scary Movie 4* (David Zucker, 2006), *Hollow Man II* (Claudio Faeh, 2006), *Black Christmas* (Glen Morgan, 2006), *Resident Evil: Extinction* (Russell Mulcahy, 2007), *Devil's Diary* (Farhad Mann, 2007), *Lost Boys: The Tribe* (P.J. Pesce, 2008), *Possession* (Joel Bergvall and Simon Sandquist, 2008), *The Seamstress* (Jesse James Miller, 2009), *Jennifer's Body* (Karyn Kusama, 2009), *The Twilight Saga: Eclipse* (David Slade, 2010), *The Tortured* (Robert Liberman, 2010), *30 Days of Night: Dark Days* (Ben Ketai, 2010), *Saw 3D: The Final Chapter* (Kevin Gruetert, 2010), *Red Riding Hood* (Catherine Hardwicke, 2011), *Dream House* (Jim Sheridan, 2011), *The Twilight Saga: Breaking Dawn—Part 1* (Bill Condon, 2011), *The Cabin in the Woods* (Drew Goddard, 2012), *House at the End of the Street* (Mark Tonderai, 2012), *The Twilight Saga: Breaking Dawn—Part 2* (Bill Condon, 2012), *Shut In* (Farren Blackburn, 2016), and television series including *The Dead Zone*, *Masters of Horror* and *iZombie*.

BELLUCCI, MONICA

European cinema icon Monica Bellucci was born in Italy in 1964. While her cult reputation began in earnest with an unforgettable performance in Gaspar Noé's shocking *Irréversible* (2002), her earliest horror performance was as a Bride of Dracula in *Bram Stoker's Dracula* (Francis Ford Coppola, 1992). Bellucci began her career as a model in her early teens where she was hugely successful and attained global recognition and success. Across her lengthy acting career, her other horror credits include *Brotherhood of the Wolf* (Christophe Gans, 2001), *Don't Look Back* (Marina De Van, 2009), a small cameo in *Sheitan* (Kim Chapiron, 2006), and the Australian horror film *Nekrotronic* (Kiah Roache-Turner, 2018).

Monica Bellucci in *Brotherhood of the Wolf* (aka Le Pacte des Loups, 2001) © Universal/ courtesy Everett Collection. Credit: Everett Collection Inc / Alamy Stock Photo

BENJAMIN, ROXANNE

Raised in Pennsylvania and beginning her career as a writer, Roxanne Benjamin developed her passion for film when she worked at a cinema while she was at college in Nashville. Renowned as an actor, director, writer and producer, after moving to Los Angeles to develop her career she began largely in executive capacities and proved to be a key behind-the-scenes player on several indie horror films. In recent years, she has moved to more creative roles. As a producer, her credits include the anthology series *V/H/S* (2012), *V/H/S 2* (2012), and *V/H/S Viral* (2014) as well as the horror anthology *Southbound* (2015) and *XX* (2017). In *Southbound* she co-wrote and directed the segment "Siren", while in the latter she wrote and directed the segment "Don't Fall". Benjamin also wrote the screenplay for Annie Clark's (aka St. Vincent) *XX* entry, "The Birthday Party". She was a producer on Sean Byrne's 2015 horror film *The Devil's Candy*, and in 2018 she directed the short film *Final Stop*. In 2019, she released her feature film debut, the survival horror movie *Body at Brighton Rock*.

BENNETT, JILL

British actor Jill Bennett's career is broadly overshadowed by her tragic death, yet her career was extraordinary: on stage, she played everyone from Ophelia to Hedda Gabler, and in film she worked with directors including John Huston, Vincente Minnelli, Joseph Losey, Tony Richardson, Lindsay Anderson and Bernardo Bertolucci. Her work in horror cinema was significant, including two classic British horror films from 1965: Freddie Francis's *The Skull* with Peter Cushing and Christopher Lee, and Seth Holt's *The Nanny* with Bette Davis. In 1977, she would appear alongside Mia Farrow in Richard Loncraine's chilling *The Haunting of Julia*.

BENNETT, JOAN

Coming from a show business family, American actor Joan Bennet had long worked on stage before moving to cinema, beginning in the silent era through the 1920s to the early 1980s. With co-stars including Spencer Tracy, John Barrymore, Katharine Hepburn and Gregory Peck, Bennett was famously shortlisted for the role of Scarlett O'Hara in *Gone with the Wind* (Victor Fleming, 1939). But her most celebrated role from the early part of her career is the femme fatale in Fritz Lang's *Scarlet Street* in which she co-starred with Edward G. Robinson, a role that arguably established the early roots of her flair for darker characters. In later years, Bennett would continue this trajectory with a key role in the long-running gothic soap opera *Dark Shadows* (1966-1971), revisiting the role for the film based on the series, *House of Dark Shadows* (Dan Curtis, 1970). Bennett was later cast as the legendary coven leader Madame Blanc in Dario Argento's Eurohorror classic *Suspiria* in 1977, a role today broadly considered her most memorable achievement.

BERNAL, JOYCE E.

Prolific Filipino filmmaker Joyce E. Bernal began her career as an editor and then moved to directing film and television. While working predominantly in romance and comedy terrain, Bernal has frequently dabbled in horror territory including *Segunda Mano* (2011), *D'Anothers* (2005), *Kimmy Dora and the Temple of Kiyeme* (2012) and *Da Possessed* (2014), the latter a remake of Raghava Lawrence's Tamil film *Muni 2: Kanchana* (2011).

BEST, AMY LYNN

Hailing from Pittsburgh and with a background as a dancer and actor, Amy Lynn Best's first foray into horror was in a production capacity for *The Resurrection Game* (Mike Watt, 2001), in which she also stars. Her directorial debut was 2003's *Severe Injuries* (produced by Happy Cloud Pictures, which she co-founded), followed by the documentary *Spicy Sister Slumber Party* (2004), the feature *Splatter Movie: The Director's Cut* (2008) and a number of shorts. As an actor, her credits include *Dr. Horror's Erotic House of Idiots* (Paul Scrabo, 2004), *Church of the Eyes* (Andrew Copp, 2013), *Demon Divas and the Lanes of Damnation* (Mike Watt, 2009) and *A Feast of Flesh* (Mike Watt, 2007).

BESWICK, MARTINE

With British, Portuguese and Jamaican heritage, British actor and model Martine Beswick was a two-time Bond girl and made a significant impact on horror cinema. Beginning her relationship with Hammer with the Raquel Welch-fronted *One Million Years B.C.* (1966), Beswick would feature in Hammer's *Prehistoric Women* (Michael Carreas, 1967) before moving on to more explicit horror territory in the Peter Collinson's hugely underrated home invasion film *The Penthouse* (1967), Hammer's *Dr Jekyll and Sister Hyde* (Roy Ward Baker, 1971), *Queen of Evil* (Oliver Stone, 1974), *Devil Dog: The Hound of Hell* (Curtis Harrington, 1978), *From a Whisper to a Scream* (Jeff Burr, 1987), *Critters 4* (Rupert Harvey, 1992), and *Night of the Scarecrow* (Jeff Burr, 1995).

BETTI, LAURA

Italian actor Laura Betti was born in Italy in 1927 and would become one of the country's great screen presences. She worked with filmmakers including Federico Fellini and Pier Paolo Pasolini, appearing in the latter's notorious *Salò, or the 120 Days of Sodom* (1975). For horror fans, Betti is most immediately recongizable as Anna, the psychic in Mario Bava's *Twitch of the Death Nerve* (1971), and as Mildred in Bava's earlier film *Hatchett for the Honeymoon* (1970). In 1987, she appeared in long-time Dario Argento collaborator Franco Ferrini's *giallo Sweets from a Stranger* (1987).

BETTIS, ANGELA

Born in Austin in 1973, Angela Bettis is an actor, producer and director with a close association with the horror genre. While she attracted mainstream attention with her role in James Mangold's *Girl, Interrupted* (1993), it was as the title character in Lucky McKee's *May* (2002) that garnered Bettis several awards and solidified her role in horror. McKee and

Bettis would become frequent collaborators; she appeared in his films *The Woods* (2006), *The Woman* (2011), and his 2006 donation to the *Masters of Horror* series "Sick Girl", and she directed McGee's script for *Roman* (2006), in which he also starred. Bettis would also appear in horror films including *Bless the Child* (Chuck Russell, 2000), *Toolbox Murders* (Tobe Hooper, 2004), *Scar* (Jeb Weintrob, 2007), and was cast in the lead role of Bryan Fuller's 2002 television movie adaptation of Stephen King's classic horror novel *Carrie* (1974). Aside from directing *Roman*, in 2012, Bettis was one of only two women directors involved in the first *The ABCs of Death* anthology with her short "E is or Exterminate".

BEY, MARKI

Marqueeta 'Marki' Bay was born in Philadelphia in 1947, and while her filmography is not extensive, her starring role in the Blaxploitation horror movie *Sugar Hill* (Paul Maslansky, 1974) offers one of the most memorable performances by a Black woman in horror of that decade. In the previous year, she appeared in the serial killer film *The Roommates* (Arthur Marks, 1973).

BIGELOW, DEEDEE

Washington-born actor DeeDee Bigelow made her first horror appearance in Jeff Bühler's *Insanitarium* (2008), with later horror credits include *Dead Air* (Corbin Bernsen, 2009), *Horrorween* (Joe Estevez, 2011), *Legend of the Reaper* (Tara Cardinal, 2013), *Scarlet Samurai: Incarnation* (Tara Cardinal and David R. Williams, 2013) and *Pain is Beautiful* (Chris Staviski, 2015).

BIGELOW, KATHRYN

Winner of the 2009 Academy Award for Best Director and Best Picture for her war film *The Hurt Locker*, California-born Kathryn Bigelow has worked across genres since her feature debut, the biker movie *The Loveless* (1982). Bigelow followed this with her cult vamprie film *Near Dark* (1987), one of the greatest hillbilly horror films of all time. In her 1990 thriller *Blue Steel*, Bigelow consciously reworks questions about violence and womens' autonomy later linked to the critical concept of the Final Girl, casting Jamie Lee Curtis from *Halloween* to make a clear reference to this character type despite the film straying from strictly horror terrain. Amongst other achievements, Bigelow would also experiment

Kathryn Bigelow at the Los Angeles premiere of *Zero Dark Thirty* held at the Dolby Theatre in Hollywood on 10 December 2012. Credit: Tinseltown / Shutterstock.com

dark-themed scifi territory in both *Strange Days* (1995) and an episode of the 1993 mini-series *Wild Palms*.

BILLER, ANNA—INTERVIEW (JULY 2016)

The following interview was published in 2016 at 4:3 Film and is republished with permission. The original article can be found online here https://fourthreefilm.com/2016/07/the-love-witch-an-interview-with-anna-biller/

In her second feature film *The Love Witch*, multi-skilled filmmaker and all-round renaissance woman Anna Biller—writer, director, producer, editor, production and costumer designer—proves on the back of 2007's *Viva* that she is very much an artist with a driving, defining vision. That this vision is both smart and fun makes the experience of watching her films not merely insightful but unambiguously delightful. *The Love Witch* is a film that is, in many ways, a lot smarter than its deliberately glossy, hyper-stylised surfaces might initially suggest, and this is an extraordinarily refreshing feeling when the opposite is sadly far more common. *The Love Witch* is the antidote to all those films with pompous, intellectual airs that collapse under the weight of their own smugness when scrutinised.

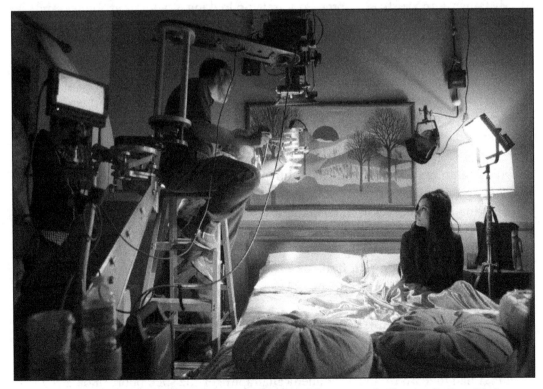

M. David Mullen and Samantha Robinson on the set of *The Love Witch*. Photo credit: Steve Dietl.
Courtesy Anna Biller Productions.

Growing up among what she has called the "ghosts" of Hollywood filmmaking in Los Angeles, the very materiality of cinema itself—the meat of it, the flesh of it—are central to Biller's filmmaking practice. Both *The Love Witch* and *Viva* were shot on 35mm, and her earlier shorts—*A Visit from the Incubus* (2001), *The Hypnotist* (2001) and her first film, *Three Examples of Myself as Queen* (1994)—were all shot on 16mm. This tangibility and tactility of film also manifests through the lush textures and colors: *The Love Witch* is a feast for the senses as much as the mind.

It is also very funny. Following the story of Elaine (Samantha Robinson), a 1960s-era witch who employs her craft to make herself irresistible to the opposite sex, the sweetness and sincerity of Robinson's performance render *The Love Witch* thoughtful, hilarious and, at times, tragic. A love letter to Technicolor and the vibrant aesthetics of the 1950s and '60s, *The Love Witch* is the most charming feminist film manifesto of 2016.

http://www.lifeofastar.com/

As a starting point to those new to your work, *The Love Witch* is clearly the product of someone with a strong background in visual design. In terms of filmmaking, you are quite the Renaissance woman and have a lot of skills in your toolbox, so I'm fascinated to hear how they all coalesced in your practice. Can you tell me briefly what your background is?

My father is an artist—a painter. So I grew up looking at a lot of art books, and going to a lot of art galleries and museums. And my mother is a fashion designer, so I was always around beautiful fabrics and clothes. I also watched a lot of classic movies growing up, and was fascinated with production design and costumes. In school I did my studies in studio art, and only later in graduate school did I switch to film. I was making experimental art videos and small, handmade Super 8mm films where I'd build little sets and make costumes, and this naturally segued into making "film-films" for me.

Wearing so many (beautiful) hats during the production process with both *Viva* and *The Love Witch*, I would assume that the process would be less a traditional collaboration in terms of the major components (writing, directing, production design, editing, etc). When there's different people in all these roles, there are necessarily times that horns clash and opinions differ, but when it's just you, do you find the process challenging in other ways (aside from the sheer workload, of course)?

Working on my own during pre-production, sometimes it's hard to keep the motivation up when the actual physical work becomes too tedious or too demanding. And I'm constantly having new learning curves thrown in, as when, for this film, I had to learn to do left-handed calligraphy for the spell book, hook a rug, and compose for a period wind ensemble. Sewing in particular can get really

Poster for *The Love Witch*. Artwork by Michael Koelsch, poster design by Fred Davis.
Courtesy Oscilloscope Laboratories (thanks to Anna Biller Productions).

exhausting. I wish I had an assistant to do hems and things, but my space is not large enough to accommodate two people and I only have one sewing machine.

Sometimes it feels inappropriate how labor-intensive the process is and I feel like Rapunzel sitting sadly in front of a pile of straw that I need to spin into gold, but then again all of this labor gives me time to keep reworking the themes and ideas in the film, which only makes it richer over time. I also would love to have assistants help me pick things I need, but that hasn't worked so far. Much of the time if I can't find a kind of fabric or furniture that was in my sketch, I come up with something totally different, but that still works with the fantasy themes I have in my head, which are quite specific. I have no way to explain any of that to an assistant.

I'd like to talk to you a little about your influences: we very much crossed paths due to a shared love of European directors with a distinct visual style and thematic drive (Fassbinder, Borowczyk, Franco, Fulci, etc). I think we also share a real love of Classical Hollywood and the spaces filmmakers found to be subversive when working under the Hays code, when there was so much pressure to steer clear of controversy. How do you find in practice these influences— and others, of course—manifest in your own work? Are there any filmmakers or artists that have influenced you in other ways that do not necessarily seem as apparent in the kinds of films you make?

This is an interesting question. In terms of influences, a lot of people think I am pulling mostly from the '60s and '70s, when most of the time (except for Fassbinder and work from a few other key filmmakers) I am pulling from much earlier films. I love working within the limitations of codes and other strictures. I set my own limits on what I will or will not film. I never use profanity for instance, and I try never to make anything ugly, as if working within a studio system that would require such things. Yet unlike earlier filmmakers, I'm not doing it because I have to, but because I think it makes for better art. I think that when the censorship codes lifted in the late '60s everyone started to think that the more ugly, violent, or pornographic something was, the more cutting-edge it was, and we're still suffering somewhat under that mentality. I'm interested in culture much more than I am interested in the annihilation of culture, so in that sense I am out of time. The filmmakers that have influenced me the most that may not be apparent are Jacques Démy and Joseph Von Sternberg.

The word 'erotica' is an eternally fascinating one for me, as it is so culturally loaded—I think, with a lot of these Eurosleaze directors we're drawn to (Borowczyk, Franco, honorary Eurosleaze director Radley Metzger), there is something proudly 'pornographic' about them, but this word seems to actively deny the overwhelming artistry that drives their work. Sexuality is—to put it mildly—a centrepiece of your work that I'd like to talk to you about a little. What do you think is the difference between erotica and pornography? What marks the kind

of sexually explicit (be it hard or softcore) work that you are drawn to as a spectator, and how does that influence the way you depict sexuality?

Well, the word pornography is pejorative in the sense that it refers to erotic content with no cultural value. Radley Metzger made hardcore films, but he was trying tell great literary stories and to make sex movies for couples, which was a social and human project, and he had a special interest in giving full agency and dimension to female characters. So I don't think you could say his films are pornographic even though they are hardcore. Catherine Breillat also makes hardcore films that are not pornographic, because they are academic—they are teaching the audience about female sexuality. In my view, if a film has no thematic, social, political, or cultural value, then it is pornographic. And this applies to both erotic and non-erotic films.

My project is aligned with Catherine Breillat's in that I am trying to teach about female sexuality, even in areas where it's uncomfortable or seems regressive—or, especially in those areas, because there are so many misunderstandings and stereotypes about women and sex. We know so much about male sexuality and so little about female sexuality. Sexuality after all is an extension of identity, so we need to see more films where women's sexuality isn't just an extension of male fantasy. People think my filmmaking is so bizarre in its ideas, and yet these ideas about female desire and fantasy have been well-known and studied by psychologists for decades—stuff about women being in love with their own image rather than wanting to look at a man, about getting turned on by the level of a man's desire or by the thought of being passively taken by a man, that kind of thing.

Elaine is a fantastically complex character. From a post-feminist position, she's so easy at first to dismiss as a comic foil, a kind of Stepford Wife run amok and very much a part of the historical universe that your film is set in. But when considered more closely, I'm struck by how thoroughly likeable and sweet she is, and that she's not rendered villainous or objectionable because she drank the Stepford Wife Kool-Aid. I'm curious how you went about constructing Elaine in terms of her politics?

Part of the likeability of Elaine is due to Samantha Robinson's performance. She has a natural sweetness that comes through, and I encouraged her to be true to herself when playing the role. But the script is also sympathetic towards her. Elaine is coping with a history of abuse the best way she knows how. Everything and everyone in society has conspired to make her what she is, so she can't really be blamed for making the choices she makes. But she is also sociopathic, either from birth or through life experience or both. She is a psychologically realistic, dimensional character, who has been driven crazy just trying to negotiate her place as a woman in the world. I based her character on women I've known who have constructed a false self, a mask of beauty and subservience to men that they can't sustain, so the mask cracks after a while.

Elaine has internalized all of the male animus characters that have blocked her, judged her, and acted upon her in her life, from her father to her husband to the men we see in the film. So although Griff for instance is a romantic, handsome guy, he is also a judge, he refuses to love her, and he represents the law. I think women watching the film are going to viscerally respond to these judges and have sympathy for her struggle, because it's a struggle we all have with men in our lives.

In terms of the politics of creating a character: although I'm always thinking about politics when I construct a script as a whole, thinking about politics when constructing a character is deadly. It's why we have so many unrealistic female characters. Characters are people, and people are good and bad, and they don't neatly represent the ideals that screenwriters may wish to embody.

Publicity still for *Viva*. Photo credit: Steve Dietl. Courtesy Anna Biller Productions

What remains unrelentingly fascinating about Elaine is despite her actions, she never becomes monstrous. Partially of course this is due to the light-hearted comic tone of the film, but it feels more than that to me: a kind of sympathy to her position, a vague sense memory that I had the same kind of training, and that it remains dormant somewhere in my brain. I had the experience watching the film that this was the case with Trish as well, that as grounded and as comparatively 'normal' as she is, there's a kind of buried level of cult programming that makes Elaine as irresistible conceptually to her as she is sexually to other men.

I do have sympathy for Elaine's position, because her beauty has taught her hard life lessons which never have to be learned by a man, and has made her the object of abuse by various men in her life. And of course all women are trained to be subservient, to value our looks and the ability to offer sex above anything else, and to not pursue our goals, if not directly than indirectly through the brutality of the culture. So in some twisted way Elaine can be admired because she has succeeded so well in playing the game, in a way that most women are unable to. She has made herself into everything a man could possibly want. But even Elaine can't do it in the end. Her dilemma—and the dilemma of many women—is that in order to get love from a man, she has to allow herself to be swallowed up in him, and to lose her reflection in the mirror. Men can't see who she is, even when they've drunk her potion. All they can see is their own desire, their own lust, their own suffering. So love makes them not more attached to her, but more self-centered.

As for Trish, she is fascinated with Elaine's image, and then becomes fascinated with her own image in the mirror. Trish sees the intactness of Elaine's "beautiful" image as a sort of bravery in standing out and being different that she's never been able to muster, and she feels empowered when she tries to emulate it. Because you know, that's another sort of trap women can fall into—the fear of looking sexy because of being disrespected or of making oneself too different from a man. Elaine establishes herself as utterly feminine and distinct from a man and finds strength in that. So there is a double meaning to her mask of beauty: on the one hand it's a sign of submission to male desire, and on the other hand it's a costume that establishes her fabulousness as a woman. I tend to think of it more as the latter, especially when she wears costumes that are so strongly the stuff of female fantasy, like her Victorian outfits, which most men would find over-the-top and maybe even a little creepy.

How would you describe the relationship between *Viva* and *The Love Witch*, both in terms of the material they address, and in regards to your own artistic practice and what you've learned now being on the festival circuit the second time around?

The character Barbi that I play in *Viva* is a love-starved housewife, and the character of Elaine in *The Love Witch* is a love-starved witch. They both hit a wall when trying to go out in the world and find what they desire, because men don't understand them and can't or won't give them what they want. Barbi, who is passive, depressed, and has mostly given up on her dreams, is mainly looking for sexual fulfillment, but this fulfillment comes at the price of her safety, her reputation, and her home. Elaine is more aggressive and tactical in her search for love, but is unable to find what she wants because men ultimately are unequal to the task of submitting to her demands.

The Love Witch is more explicit in its themes than *Viva*, because what I learned on the festival circuit with *Viva* is that people are very literal-minded and don't look much at metaphor and symbolism—at least not with my work. I feel I was usually not given the benefit of the doubt when it came to conscious choices I was making. Reviews often spoke of inadvertent meaning, unconscious meaning—or even no meaning—when I worked so meticulously to put all of those ideas there. People also objectified me because I was playing the lead role and there was partial nudity. So I thought, next time I'm not going to act in it, and I'm going to have to put my ideas even more explicitly in the text.

From an industrial perspective how much do you find you get reduced to essentialist ideas about the kinds of films 'women' make? I'm consistently struck by the diversity of women's filmmaking practice (both today and historically), yet this to me feels like it works in opposition to critical and industry tendencies to reduce 'women's filmmaking' almost to its own genre. I'd love to hear your insight and experience on this.

I've never been lumped in with other female directors. If anything, I've been compared way too much to male filmmakers whom I have little to nothing in common with except visual style. It's true that women's filmmaking is incredibly diverse, but I am personally interested in how female consciousness might shape artwork differently, especially in the way female characters are constructed. So I actually would encourage people to try to group women's films together to see if there are any threads that connect them, and to try to create a sort of canon of women's films that critics can talk about as women's films.

One reason I want to be thought of as a female filmmaker is that my work can only be understood in that context. So many critics want to see my work as a pastiche of films that men have created. When they do that, they deny the fact that I am creating my own world, something completely original. Women are so often thought of as being unable to make meaning. So they are allowed to copy what men make—to make a "pastiche" out of what men have created—but not to create original work. My work comes from a place of being female, and rewrites film genres from that place. So it's essential for me to be placed into a history of female/feminist artmaking practice, otherwise it's taking the work completely out of context.

I wrote an article earlier this year about Robert Eggers' *The Witch* where I argued quite strongly for it as an urgent and timely re-articulation of the

figure of the witch as an important symbol for feminine power that has culturally been defanged over recent years; an identity women can adopt and
embrace themselves to kind of 'get in' before men can try to configure them
as monstrous. Elaine in *The Love Witch* relates to this premise in some pretty
complex, fascinating ways: I'm intrigued to hear how you see Elaine in the
long history of cinematic witches, from *Wizard of Oz* to *Suspiria* to Eggers'
film?

There are two types of cinema witches: the old, ugly hag which is the type featured
in most movies and literature, and the young, beautiful siren embodied by Circe and
Medea, who appeared in films mostly starting in the '60s and was a continuation of
the noir femme-fatale siren. I think of all of Bergman's female characters as witches
also, in the siren sense. Elaine is obviously also a siren. But unlike most cinematic
witches, who embody male fear of female desirability or ugliness or power, I'm trying
to tell her story mostly from the inside. She's split into two images: the one the world
has of her as dangerous and evil, and the one she has of herself, which is resourceful
and loving. To the world, her beauty is a source of pain, torture, and bondage; to herself, it's about trying to construct an identity and create loving bonds. Historically all
witches have been interested in and experts on love, so Elaine in that sense is a classic
witch.

One last question: I was lucky enough to see Prince earlier this year, and he played
his 1996 song 'The Love We Make' which includes the line "wicked is the witch
that stands for nothing". Not delving too far into semantics, what to you does
Elaine "stand for"?

Elaine stands for the witch as a metaphor for all women—for the split we have as
women between our own self-image, and the various images and expectations
imposed on us by history, culture and desire.

BIRD, ANTONIA

Late British director and producer Antonia Bird only worked in horror once, but her
efforts produced a classic of the genre. Her 1990 cannibal film *Ravenous* starred Guy
Pearce and Robert Carlylse and featured a memorable score by celebrated composer Michael Nyman and Blur's Damon Albarn. Initially slated to be directed by Macedonian
filmmaker Milcho Manchevski, Bird was recommended by Carlylse after Manchevski quit
the production after less than a month into the project after citing difficulties with producers. While Bird shared similar complaints and noted later that the released version
had been recut without her approval, the film still stands as one of the finest and most
intelligent cannibal films ever made.

BISSET, JACQUELINE

British-born actor Jacqueline Bisset would work across her lengthy career with filmmakers such as François Truffaut, Sidney Lumet, John Huston, Claude Chabrol and Stanley Donen, and alongside actors including Frank Sinatra, Audrey Hepburn, Steve McQueen, Dennis Hopper and Jean-Paul Belmondo. Bissett's work in horror includes Peter Collinson's 1975 remake of Robert Siodmak's 1945 film *The Spiral Staircase*, Luigi Comencini's *The Sunday Woman* (1975), Peter Yates's 1977 *Jaws*-inspired *The Deep*, and most interestingly she led the body swap satanic cult film *The Mephiso Waltz* (Paul Wendkos, 1971) with *M*A*S*H*'s Alan Alda as a distinctly against-type demonic goth composer.

BLACK, KAREN

One of the unchallenged queens of horror, Karen Black was born in Chicago in 1939 and starred in some of the most important films of New Hollywood including *You're a Big Boy Now* (Francis Ford Coppola, 1966), *Easy Rider* (Dennis Hopper, 1969), *Five Easy Pieces* (Bob Rafelson, 1970) and Robert Altman's *Nashville* (1975) and *Come Back to the Five and Dime, Jimmy Dean, Jimmy Dean* (1982). But it was in horror that Black flourished, beginning with Dan Curtis's television horror anthology *Trilogy of Terror* (1975) and *Burnt Offerings* with Bette Davis and Oliver Reed the following year, *Invaders from Mars* (Tobe Hooper, 1986), *Family Plot* (Alfred Hitchcock, 1976), *It's Alive III: Island of the Alive* (Larry Cohen, 1987), *Out of the Dark* (Michael Schroeder, 1989), *Mirror, Mirror* (Marina Sargenti, 1990), *Haunting*

Karen Black at the World Premiere of *The Nightmare Before Christmas*, El Capitan Theater, Hollywood, California. 16 October 2006.
Credit: s_bukley / Shutterstock.com

Fear (Fred Olen Ray, 1990), *Evil Spirits* (Gary Graver, 1990), *Children of the Night* (Tony Randel, 1991), *Children of the Corn IV: The Gathering* (Greg Spence, 1996), *Curse of the Forty-Niner* (John Carl Buechler, 2002), *House of 1000 Corpses* (Rob Zombie, 2003), *Some Guy Who Kills People* (Jack Perez, 2012) and *Ooga Booga* (Charles Band, 2013).

BLACK, CATHERINE

Canadian painter, actor and filmmaker Catherine Black began her performing career on the stage and appeared in both *American Psycho* (Mary Harron, 2000) and with Crispin Glover in The *Donner Party* (Terrence Martin, 2009). Additional horror credits also include Douglas Rath's *Shock Value* (2014) and *Mary Loss of Soul* (Jennifer B. White, 2014). Black is also a director, and her 2018 comedy-horror short *Girl Trip* won a number of awards.

BLACKTHORNE, MELANTHA

With a performance background beginning with ballet lessons as a young child, Melantha Blackthorne—aka Countess Bathoria—has been a force behind many horror projects, be it in an acting, production, directing, stunts or writing capacities. Blackthorne's directorial credits include *Sinners and Saints* (2004), and she acted in many directed by Sv Bell such as *Purple Glow* (2005), She-*Demons of the Black Sun* (2006) and *Rise of the Ghosts* (2007). Other horror credits include *Prison of the Psychotic Damned: Terminal Remix* (D.W. Kann, 2006), *Fable: Teeth of* Beasts (Sean-Michael Argo, 2010), *Sineaters* (Sean-Michael Argo, 2012), *Bloody Slumber* Party (Larry Rosen, 2014), *Gilgamesh* (Richard Chandler, 2014), *Bleeding Hearts* (Dylan Bank, 2015) and *Krampus: The Devil Returns* (Jason Hull, 2016).

BLAIR, LINDA*

As one of the most famous faces of 1970s horror, as Regan O'Neill in *The Exorcist* (William Friedkin, 1973), Linda Blair lifted the bar for child actors in horror like few before or since. Born in Missouri in 1959, Blair would star in her teen years in the film's sequel *Exorcist II: The Heretic* (John Boorman, 1977), which while not achieving the same critical or commercial success as the original, has grown in its cult reputation over recent years in large part due to Blair's performance. Her later horror credits would include *Summer of Fear* (Wes Craven, 1978), *Hell Night* (1981), *Grotesque* (Joe Tornatore, 1988), *Witchery* (Fabrizio Laurenti, 1988), *The Chilling* (Deland Nuse and Jack A. Sunseri, 1989), the horror-comedy *Repossessed* (Bob Logan, 1990), *Dead Sleep* (Alec Mills, 1992), *Sorceress* (Jim Wynorski, 1995), *Cousin Sarah* (Jenni Gold, 2011), *The Green Fairy* (Dan Frank, 2015) and a cameo in Wes Craven's *Scream* (1996).

Linda Blair in *The Exorcist* (1973), directed by William Friedkin.
Credit: Warner Bros. Pictures/Photofest © Warner Bros. Photographer: Josh Weiner.

BLAISDELL, JACKIE

Jackie Blaisdell was born Jacqueline Mary Boyle and grew up in Massachussetts. She moved to California in the 1950s with her husband Paul Blaisdell, a renowned American visual FX artist famous for his work in horror and scifi during this era. Jackie and Paul met while students at The New England School of Art & Design and she was his often-unsung collaborator, and together they worked on costumes, props and special effects for films including *The Day the World Ended* (Roger Corman, 1955), *The She-Creature* (Edward L. Cahn, 1956) and *Invasion of the Saucer Men* (Edward L. Cahn, 1957). Despite this, Blaisdell herself only ever received two official film credits; as a special designer on Bert I. Gordon's *Attack of the Puppet People* (1958) and *The Spider* (1958).

BLANC, ERIKA

Erika Blanc was born in Northern Italy in 1942 and would star in a number of cult horror films and *gialli* including *Lady Morgan's Vengeance* (Massimo Pupillo, 1965), *The Third Eye* (Mino Guerrini, 1966), *Kill, Baby...Kill!* (Mario Bava, 1966), *So Sweet...So Perverse* (Umberto Lenzi, 1969), *The Night Evelyn Came Out of the Grave* (Emilio P. Miraglia, 1971), *The Devil's Nightmare* (Jean Brismée, 1971), *The Red Headed Corpse* (Renzo Russo, 1972), *Mark of the Devil Part II* (Adrian Hoven, 1973), *A Dragonfly for Each Corpse* (León Klimovsky, 1975) and *Erotic Games of a Respectable Family* (Francesco Degli Espinosa, 1975).

BLANC-BIEHN, JENNIFER

Jennifer Blanc (also credited Jennifer Blanc-Biehn) was born in New York City in 1974 and began acting as a child, appearing in sitcoms such as *Married...With Children* and *Saved by the Bell*. In 2013 she directed the horror/scifi hybrid *The Night Visitor*, and in 2016 she directed *The Girl*, receiving a co-writing credit to the sequel to *The Night Visitor*, *The Night Visitor 2: Heather's Story* (Brianne Davis, 2016), and Kate Rees Davies' 2017 dystopian scifi film *Altered Perception*. Blanc-Biehn has an extensive list of producer credits to her name, and on screen, her acting credits include horror films such as *The Crow* (Alex Proyas, 1994), the all-woman directed horror anthology *Prank* (2008), *The Absent* (Sage Bannick, 2011), *The Divide* (Xavier Gens, 2011), *Among Friends* (Danielle Harris, 2012), *Havenhurst* (Andrew C. Erin, 2016), *Deadly Signal* (Brianne Davis, 2016) *She Rises* (Larry Wade Carrell, 2016), *The Night Visitor 2: Heather's Story* (Brianne Davis, 2016), *Deadly Retreat* (Jon Artigo, 2016) and *Fetish Factory* (Staci Layne Wilson, 2017).

BLANCHARD, FRANÇOISE

Renowned mostly for her work with French filmmaker Jean Rollin, Françoise Blanchard was born in 1954 in Paris. She began her career as a hand model and making movies with filmmakers including Bruno Mattei and Pierre Chevalier, before starring as Catherine Valmont in Rollin's *The Living Dead Girl* in 1982. Blanchard would again work with Rollin on *The Sidewalks of Bangkok* (1984), *Chasing Barbara* (1991) and *The Night of the Clocks* (2007), as well as making numerous films with Jess Franco including his 1983 film *Revenge in the House of Usher*.

BLOCH, JULIA

Film editor Julie Bloch studied literature at Columbia University in New York before studying film at Denmark's European Film College. She began her career as an assistant editor at Lars Von Trier's film studio Zentropa, before moving back to the United States and working with acclaimed director Terrence Malick on his 2011 film *Tree of Life* as an editorial assistant. It is her collaborations with filmmaker Jeremy Saulnier however that have firmly established her reputation—the revenge film *Blue Ruin* (2013), 2015's terrifying neo-Nazi horror film *Green Room* and the 2018 thriller *Hold the Dark*. In 2017, she also edited Kate and Laura Mulleavy's psychological horror film *Woodshock*, starring Kirsten Dunst.

BLOOM, CLAIRE

With a 60-year career on stage and screen, British actor Claire Bloom was discovered by Charlie Chaplin and appeared in his 1952 film *Limelight*. While her filmography is extensive, her performance as Theodora ("Theo") in Robert Wise's 1963 film *The Haunting*—adapted from Shirley Jackson's 1959 novel *The Haunting of Hill House*—is significant beyond the high standard of her acting. Unlike the book, Theo's lesbianism is made more explicit in the film, and importantly it is not presented as monstrous or perverse: Bloom's casual, naturalistic performance is crucial to making this important moment of queer screen representation a tasteful and respectful one.

BLOUNT, LISA

Lisa Blount is famous for her work as an actor but is also an Oscar-winning producer for her husband Ray McKinnon's 2001 short comedy, *The Accountant*. Born in Arkansas in 1957, she studied at San Francisco State University before beginning her career on stage. Working across film and television, in 1987 she starred in John Carpenter's horror film *Prince of Darkness*, and her other horror credits include *Dead & Buried* (Gary Sherman, 1981), *Nightflyers* (Robert Collector, 1987) and *Needful Things* (Fraser C. Heston, 1993).

BLYTHE, JANUS

While Janus Blythe is of course most immediately known for her spectacular performance as Ruby in Wes Craven's 1977 film *The Hills Have Eyes*, her other horror credits are just as impressive, including early small roles in *The Centerfold Girls* (John Peyser, 1974), *The Phantom of the Paradise* (Brian De Palma, 1974), *Eaten Alive* (Tobe Hooper, 1976) *Drive In Massacre* (Stu Segall, 1976), *The Incredible Melting Man* (William Sachs, 1977) and *Spine* (John Howard and Justin Simmonds, 1986), notably returning to work again with Craven on *The Hills Have Eyes 2* in 1984.

BOGART, ANDREA

Andrea Bogart is a familiar face with recurring roles on television series such as *General Hospital* and, more recently, *Ray Donovan*, but she has substantial horror form as an actor also. Born in Missouri in the late 1970s, apart from her lengthy list of television credits include the horror movies *Dark Wolf* (Richard Friedman, 2003), *Greed* (Ron Wolotzky, 2006), *Dark Ride* (Craig Singer, 2006), *Something's Wrong in Kansas* (Louis Paul Tocchet, 2008), and *Nite Tales: The Movie* (Deon Taylor, 2008)

BOLKAN, FLORINDA

One of the shining lights of Italian cinema, the Brazilian model-turned-actor Florinda Soares Bulcão—who used the stage name Florinda Bolkan—learned Italian during her career as a flight attendant. She was discovered by revered Italian filmmaker Luchino Visconti, and would later apper in his 1969 film *The Damned* alongside Dirk Bogarde and Ingrid Thulin. Amongst her filmography, she appeared in a number of *gialli* and horror films including *A Complicated Girl* (Damiano Damiani, 1968), *A Lizard in a Woman's Skin* (Lucio Fulci, 1971), *Don't Torture a Duckling* (Lucio Fulci, 1972), *Footprints on the Moon* (Luigi Bazzoni, 1975), *The Last House on the Beach* (Franco Prosperi, 1978), and the nunsploitation film *Flavia the Heretic* (Gianfranco Mingozzi, 1974). Bolkan won 3 David di Donatello Awards (the Italian equivalnt of the Oscars) during her career for her acting work.

BONHAM CARTER, HELENA:

Helena Bonham Carter arriving for the European Premiere of *Dark Shadows* at Empire Leicester Square, London, 5 September 2012. Credit: Alexandra Glen / Featureflash Photo Agency / Shutterstock.com

Boasting an impressive screen career that began in earnest with James Ivory's *A Room with a View* (1985) and the title role of the gothic melodrama *Lady Jane* (Trevor Nunn, 1983), celebrated British actor Helena Bonham Carter was born in London in 1966 and has won several awards across her career. While initially aligned with period pieces, Bonham Carter rapidly broke out of this typecasting with movies like *Fight Club* (David Fincer, 1996) and *Novacaine* (David Atkins, 2001). While her association with horror span back as early as the 1994 Kenneth Branagh-directed *Mary Shelley's Frankenstein*, this aspect of her craft was emphasized by her long collaboration with filmmaker Tim Burton—with whom she also had a personal relationship—beginning with their work together on *Planet of the Apes* in 2001. Burton and Bonham Carter's gothic-themed collaborations would include *Corpse Bride* (2005), *Sweeney Todd: The Demon Barber of Fleet Street* (2007) and *Dark Shadows* (2012). She would play Death Eater Bellatrix Lestrange in a number of the *Harry Potter* films, and Bonham Carter also made a small cameo appearance in Brad Silberling's 2004 gothic children's film *Lemony Snicket's A Series of Unfortunate Events*.

BONNOT, FRANÇOISE

Learning the craft of editing through her mother, the celebrated French film editor Monique Bonnot, across almost 50 years Françoise Bonnot worked with many big-name directors including Costa-Gavras, Michael Cimono, Ridley Scott, and in the final years of her career, on numerous occassions with filmmaker Julie Taymore. Bonnot made two significant donations to the horror genre through her work as editor; firstly on Dario Argento's sophmore *gialli Four Flies on Grey Velvet* in 1971, and in 1976 on Roman Polanski's psychological horror film *The Tenant*.

BOONYASAK, LALIA

Born in Bangkok in 1982, model and actor Laila Boonyasak is a familiar face in Thai horror for her recurring role as Buppah Rahtree in the *Buppah Rahtree* series—*Buppah Rahtree* (Krit Sriphoomset, 2003), *Buppha Reborn* (Mario Maurer, 2009) and *Rahtree's Revenge* (Mario Maurer, 2009). She also acted in Parkpoom Wongpoon's segment "Flight 244" in the cult 2008 horror anthology *4bia*, and Andrew Lau's 2003 Hong Kong horror film *The Park*.

BOORAEM, DOROTHY

Dorothy Booraem began making films as a child, teaching herself a range of micro-budget filmmaking skills with her first short *Good Wise Mischief* (1993) including writing, directing, cinematography and editing. Having made a number of short films, her first feature was *Wake the Witch* (2008), followed by the horror films *Blood Rites* (2010) and *Corruptor* (2016).

BOREL, ANNIK

French-born Annik Borel's cult reputation stems almost solely from her remarkable performance in Rino Di Silvestro's *Werewolf Woman* (1976), where she starred alongside fellow horror icon Dagmar Lassander. While this was her primary claim to fame, she is said to appear in a small uncredited part in Ted V. Mikels *Blood Orgy of the She-Devils* (1973).

BORLAND, CARROLL

Carroll Borland was born in San Francisco in 1914 and would become a cult horror icon for her performance as Luna, the daughter of Béla Lugosi's Count Mora in Tod Browning's *Mark of the Vampire* (1935). She studied acting at the University of California, and while only have a small number of film credits, in her later years she returned to acting, featuring in Fred Olen Ray's horror films *Scalps* (1983) and *Biohazard* (1985).

BOWER, ANTOINETTE

British-American actor Antoinette Bower was born in the south of Germany in 1932 and worked on stage and screen for almost 40 years. Across her many films are the horror movies *Superbeast* (George Schenck, 1972), *Prom Night* (Paul Lynch, 1980), *Blood Song* (Alan J. Levi, 1982) and *Time Walker* (Tom Kennedy, 1982). She also worked on television series including *The Twilight Zone*, *Thriller* and *Alfred Hitchcock Presents*.

BOUCHET, BARBARA

Although born in Germany, the bulk of actor Barbara Bouchet's film work has been in Italy. Beginning her career as a dancer and model, while she appeared as Miss Moneypenny in *Casino Royale* (Ken Hughes, 1967), she was unhappy with the lack of interesting roles she was being offered and she moved to Italy where she acted in a number of *gialli*. These include *The Man with Icy Eyes* (Alberto De Martino, 1971), *Black Belly of the Tarantula* (Paolo Cavara, 1971), *Amuck!* (Silvio Amadio, 1972), *The Red Queen Kills Seven Times* (Emilio P. Miraglia, 1972), *The French Sex Murders* (Ferdinando Merighi, 1972) and *Don't Torture a Duckling* (Lucio Fulci, 1972). Bouchet's later horror films include *Darkside Witches* (Gerard Diefenthal, 2015).

BOWLING, KANSAS

Kansas Bowling began writing her first script in high school and was 17 when she made her first feature film, the feminist slasher movie *B.C Butcher* (2016) for Troma Entertainment. She has made over 25 music videos—one recently with Iggy Pop—and is currently directing a feature film starring Caroline Williams.

BOWMAN, LAURA

Born in 1881 and raised in Ohio, Laura Bowman was a frequent collaborator of pioneering Black filmmaker Oscar Micheaux. Of the films they made togther, Micheaux's *Murder in Harlem* (1921) combines elements of the murder mystery with racial politics, and aside from her other roles she also acted in the 1934 voodoo film *Drums O'Voodoo*, directed by Arthur Hoerl (famous today as the writer of the 1936 film *Reefer Madness*).

BOYNTON, LUCY

Actor Lucy Boynton is closely linked to the horror films of Osgood Perkins (son of *Psycho*'s Anthony Perkins) who together have collaborated on two of the more interesting horror films of recent years: *The Blackcoat's Daughter* (2015, also released as *February*), and *I Am the Pretty Thing That Lives in the House* (2016). Boynton's other horror credits include Caradog W. James's 2016 British re-imagining of the Baba Yaga legend *Don't Knock Twice* and Gareth Evans' *Apostle* (2018).

BRAIER, NATASHA

Argentine cinematographer Natasha Braier has won many awards around the world for her work in advertising and film. She graduated from Argentina's *Instituto Vocational De Arte* in 1996, going on to study photography at *Escuela de Fotografia Creativa* and completing a Masters degree in Cinematography at the British National Film and TV School in 2001. While she has worked on documentaries, art installations, music videos and both short and feature films, it is her work as Director of Photography on Nicolas Winding Refn's 2016 horror movie *The Neon Demon* that saw Braier win awards for Best Cinematography at both the Danish Academy Awards and the Boston Online Critics Association.

BRANDT, CAROLYN

Appearing on screen under a range of aliases including Eva Gaulant, Nora Alexis and Caroly Flynn, Carolyn Brandt acted solely in the films of her husband, legendary exploitation director Ray Dennis Steckler, including *The Thrill Killers* (1964), *The Incredibly Strange Creatures Who Stopped Living and Became Mixed-Up Zombies* (1964), *The Mad Love Life of a Hot Vampire* (1971), *Blood Shack* (1971), *The Sexorcist* (1974), *Perverted Passion* (1974) and *The Hollywood Strangler Meets the Skid Row Slasher* (1979). Less a muse than an active collaborator with Steckler, in the context of B-grade genre film Brandt's repertoire was impressive. In 1994, Steckler released a documentary about her work, *Carolyn Brandt: Queen of Cult*.

BREIEN, ANJA

Despite being entered in competition in the 1981 Venice Film Festival, little is known of Anja Breien's 1981 Norwegian film *The Witch Hunt*. As an important figure in Norwegian film history, Breien has championed womens issues across her work in both feature films and documentaries. Breien was born in Oslo in 1944 and studied French at university, moving to France to study filmmaking in 1964. Her first commercial success was the 1975 film *Wives,* a feminist reply to John Cassavetes's *Husbands* (1972). With *The Witch Hunt*, the filmmaker used the story of the persecution of accused witches in Norway in the 17th century as a metaphor through which to explore gender politics.

BRESSE, BOBBIE

Model turned actor Bobbie Breese began her screen career on television in the late 1970s and early '80s before turning to horror. Her first horror role was as Susan Walker Farrell in Michael Dugan's *Mausoleum* (1983), followed by *Ghoulies* (Luca Bercovici, 1984),

Evil Spawn (Kenneth J. Hall and Ted Newsom 1987) and *My Lovely Monster* (Michael Bergmann, 1991). Much of her cult reputation has been solidified by her appearances in documentaries including *Drive-In Madness* (Tim Ferrante, 1987) and *Famous Monster: Forrest J Ackerman* (Michael MacDonald, 2007).

BRIGANTI, ELISA

Screenwriter Elisa Livia Briganti was a frequent collaborator with her husband Dardano Sacchetti. Together they wrote a number of cult films, amongst them many beloved Italian *gialli* and horror movies including Lucio Fulci's *Zombi 2* (1979), *The House by the Cemetery* (1981), and *Manhattan Baby* (1982), and Lamberto Bava's *A Blade in the Dark* (1983) and *Until Death* (1987).

BROCK, DEBORAH

Deborah Brock made her directorial debut with *Slumber Party Massacre II* (1987), the sequel to Amy Holden Jones's iconic 1982 *The Slumber Party Massacre*. Made on a low budget but pulling over $3,500,000 at the box office, despite Brock's success she would not return to horror but instead went on to co-produce films including Randal Kleiser's *Honey I Blew Up the Kid* (1992) and the Vincent Gallo-directed *Buffalo '66* (1998). In 2012, Brock directed the black comedy *The Misadventures of the Dunderheads*.

BROWN, BLAIR

Blair Brown is an American actor who has worked across stage and screen since the early 1970s. She studied at the National Theater School of Canada and made her feature film debut in James Bridge's *The Paper Chase* (1973). In 1980 she played Emily Jessup in Ken Russell's cult horror-scifi film *Altered States*, and her other credits in the genre include Paul Wendkos's 1985 made-for-television movie adaptation of *The Bad Seed*.

BROWN, ERIN

Erin Brown—known also to her fans as Misty Mundae and Sadie Lane—was born in St Louis in 1979 and has developed a cult reputation based on her work in horror and adult movies. Beginning in softcore, she moved to hardcore and horror-themed material with director and her then-partner William Hellfire with the 1999 movie *Vampire Strangler*. Brown's career would continue with adult/horror hybrids or more straightforward horror material across films including *Duck! The Carbine High Massacre* (William Hellfire and

Joey Smack, 1999), *Witchbabe: The Erotic Witch Project 3* (Terry M. West, 2001), *Mummy Raider* (Brian Paulin, 2002), An *Erotic Vampire in Paris* (Donald Farmer, 2002), *My Vampire Lover* (George Freeway, 2002), *Lust in the Mummy's Tomb* (William Hellfire, 2002), *Satan's School for Lust* (Terry M. West, 2002), *Dr. Jekyll & Mistress Hyde* (Tony Marsiglia, 2003), *An Erotic Werewolf in London* (William Hellfire, 2006), *Shadow: Dead Riot* (Derek Wan, 2006), *The Rage* (Robert Kurtzman, 2007), *Holocaust Cannibal* (Bill Zebub, 2014), *The New York Butcher* (Sean Weathers, 2016) and *Woodsman: Forest of Pain* (Victor Bonacore and Louis C. Justin, 2016). Brown has also received directing credits on a number of shorts, including *Lustful Addiction* (2003), *Confessions of a Natural Beauty* (2003) and *Voodoun Blues* (2004).

BROWN, RAINE

Horror actor Raine Brown studied at New York's American Academy of Dramatic Arts and was a member of the Hudson Shakespeare Company. Despite appearing on television shows including *Sex In the City* and *Strangers With Candy*, Brown's filmography is largely linked to horror and her credits include *Nightmare in Shallow Point* (Alan Miller, 2000), *Horror* (Dante Tomaselli, 2003), *Woods of Evil* (Director: Conrad Glover, 2005), *Satan's Playground* (Dante Tomaselli, 2006), *Plasterhead* (Kevin Higgins, 2006), *Under Surveillance* (Dave Campfield, 2006), *Vindication* (Bart Mastronardi, 2006), *Barricade* (Timo Rose, 2007), *Pink Eye* (James Tucker, 2008), *Darkness Surrounds Roberta* (Giovanni Pianigiani, 2008), *Angel's Blade* (Robert Stock, 2008), *Beast* (Timo Rose, 2009), *Experiment 7* (Joe Davison, 2009), *Game Over* (Timo Rose, 2009), *Psycho Holocaust* (Krist Rufty, 2009), *As Night Falls* (Joe Davison, 2010), *Braincell* (Alex Birrell, 2010), *The Reunion* (Jeff Stewart, 2011), *The Ascension* (Robert Stock, 2011), *Deer Crossing* (Christian Jude Grillo, 2012), *Torture Chamber* (Dante Tomaselli, 2013) and *Sickness* (Brandon E. Brooks, 2017).

BROWN, RITA MAE

Famed American novelist and lesbian activist Rita Mae Brown is also somewhat of a feminist horror icon for having penned the screenplay for Amy Holden Jones's *The Slumber Party Massacre*, titled *Sleepless Nights* in Brown' original script. Brown wrote the screenplay as a parody of the slasher subgenre, but she felt the film's producers instead chose to undermine those elements and present the material less ironically. Despite Brown's disappointment that her original intentions were not fully represented in the final film, the movie—perhaps due to its then-unusual woman's authorship in terms of both director and screenwriter—makes *The Slumber Party Massacre* an enduring and important film in the history of women in horror.

BROWNING, EMILY ↵

Australian actor Emily Browning was born in Melbourne in 1988 and began her career on Australian television. Her breakthrough role was as Violet Baudelaire in Brad Silberling's 2004 gothic comedy *Lemony Snicket's A Series of Unfortunate Events*. Her horror credits include *Ghost Ship* (Steve Beck, 2002), *Darkness Falls* (Jonathan Liebesman, 2003), *The Uninvited* (Charles and Thomas Guard, 2009), and Catherine Hardwicke's 2013 erotic thriller/stalker film/goth rock musical *Plush*.

BRUCKNER, AGNES

Agnes Bruckner is a Hollywood-born actor who worked intensively since the 1990s with a particular flair for horror. Shifting from modeling to acting, she worked in soap operas and television movies and in 2005 starred in Jim Gillespie's horror film *Venom*, followed other movies in the genre including *The Woods* (Lucky McKee, 2006), *Blood & Chocolate* (Katja Von Garnier, 2007), *Vacancy 2: The First Cut* (Eric Bross, 2008), *Kill Theory* (Chris Moore, 2009) and *The Pact* (Nicholas McCarthy, 2012). Bruckner continues to work across film and television, maintaining her close relationship to horror.

BUITENHUIS, PENELOPE

Award-winning Canadian filmmaker Penelope Buitenhuis has made a wide range of films but has primarily been drawn to dark-themed thrillers and mystery films and television movies. In 2010, she directed the horror film *Hard Ride to Hell* starring cult horror star Katherine Isabelle. Buitenhuis's other work thematically reminiscent of horror also includes *Killer Bees* (2002), *Time and Again* (2007) and *The Secret of Pine Cover* (2008).

BURING, MYANNA

MyAnna Buring was born in Sweden in 1979 and started her horror career as Sam in Neil Marshall's cult 2005 British horror film *The Descent*, revisiting the part in the Jon Harris's 2009 sequel. After a very small part in John Moore's 2006 remake of Richard Donner's 1976 horror blockbuster *The Omen* and Edgar Wright's faux trailer "Don't" in Quentin Tarantino and Robert Rodriguez's *Grindhouse* (2007), Buring's horror credits continued with *Lesbian Vampire Killers* (Phil Claydon, 2009), *Devil's Playground* (Mark McQueen, 2010) and *Kill List* (Ben Wheatley, 2011). Bringing Buring to a much wider audience was her appearance as Tanya in the gothic vampire blockbuster franchise *The Twilight Saga*, acting in both *Breaking Dawn Parts 1* and *2* in 2011 and 2012 respectively.

BURKE, KATHLEEN

Kathleen Burke was working for a dentist in Chicago when she won a talent competition held by Paramount Studios that received approximately 60,000 entries. The prize was a $200 a week contract for 5 weeks to play the panther woman Lota in Erle C. Kenton's 1932 pre-code screen adaptation of H.G. Wells's 1896 novel, *The Island of Dr. Moreau* (retitled for the film version to *Island of Lost Souls*). After this, her film debut, she worked in many movies over the following 6 years, most notably the horror film *Murders in the Zoo* (A. Edward Sutherland, 1933). She retired from the industry at 25 years old.

BURKE, KRISTIN M.

The work of costume designer Kristin M. Burke has featured in a range of horror movies, the genre offering her creative opportunities to develop her craft. Mentored by celebrated theatrical costume designer Virgil C. Johnson, Burke studied at Evanston's Northwestern University. Her horror credits include *Carnosaur* (Adam Simon and Darren Moloney, 1993), Within the Rock (Gary J. Tunnicliffe, 1996), *Casper: A Spirited Beginning* (Sean McNamara, 1997), *Terror Tract* (Lance W. Dreesen and Clint Hutchison, 2000), *The Grudge 2* (Takashi Shimizu, 2006), *Insidious* (James Wan, 2010), *Paranormal Activity 2* (Tod Williams, 2010*), The Conjuring* (James Wan, 2013), *Insidious: Chapter 2* (James Wan, 2013), *The Conjuring* 2 (James Wan, 2016) and *Lights Out* (David F. Sandberg, 2016). Burke has written two books about her work in the film industry—*Going Hollywood: How to Get Started, Keep Going, and Not Turn into a Sleaze* (2004) and *Costuming for Film: The Art and the Craft* (2005)—and is also a visual artist, specializing in collage.

BURNS, LOUISE AND LISA

Their film credits may be a short list, but as the so-called '*Shining* twins', English sisters Lisa and Louise Burns are two of the most famous faces of 20th century horror. Playing the terrifying Grady sisters in Stanley Kubrick's famous 1980 horror film, the girls' answered an open casting call, and despite the characters not being twins in neither the book nor film, the director found their appearance striking. With their blue dresses and side-parted hair, the Burns twins are undoubtedly horror icons.

BURNS, MARILYN '

As Sally Hardesty in Tobe Hooper's genre-defining *The Texas Chain Saw Massacre* (1974), Marilyn Burns is one of the most revered horror actors of her generation. Born in Pennsylvania in 1949, she made early film appearances in movies by screen luminaries such as Robert Altman and Sidney Lumet, but it is as Sally that her close association with horror was established. Burns would later act in Kim Henkel's rebooted *Texas Chainsaw Massacre: The Next Generation* (1994), and she would reunite with Hooper in his 1977 film *Eaten Alive.* In 1976. she played Linda Kasabian in Tom Gries's famous television movie *Helter Skelter* about the Manson murders, and she would continue to work in horror in movies including *Kiss Daddy Goodbye* (Patrick Regan, 1981), *Future-Kill* (Ronald W. Moore, 1985) and *Sacrament* (Shawn Ewert, 2014),

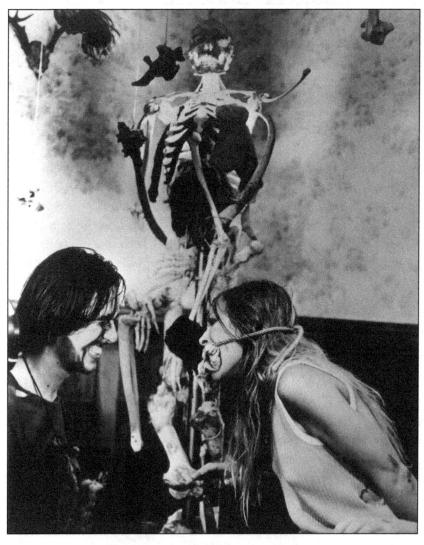

Edwin Neal and Marilyn Burns in *The Texas Chainsaw Massacre* (Tobe Hooper, 1974).
Credit: Moviestore collection Ltd / Alamy Stock Photo (TCSM 002P) (Tobe Hooper, 1974)

BURRELL, SHEILA

Born in 1922 in London, Sheila Burrell came from an acting family; her famous cousin was celebrated actor Laurence Olivier. Burrell herself established an impressive career on the stage, working in theater for over 50 years. While her lengthy film credits saw her in a range of film and television programs, it was in Freddie Francis's 1963 Hammer film *Paranoiac* alongside Oliver Reed where she excelled as Aunt Harriet. She later appeared in Mark Peploe's horror movie *Afraid of the Dark* in 1991 and a number of horror television shows such as *Spooky* and an episode of *Tales of the Unexpected*.

BURROUGHS, JACKIE

Canadian actor Jackie Burroughs was born in England in the late 1930s and moved to Canada in her teens. She is a highly acclaimed actor who began her career on stage in Ontario and soon moved to film and television. Burroughs' horror credits include *The Dead Zone* (David Cronenberg, 1983), *Food of the Gods II* (Damian Lee, 1989), *Bleeders* (Peter Svatek, 1997), *Rhinoceros Eyes* (Aaron Woodley, 2003) and *Willard* (Glen Morgan, 2003).

BURSTYN, ELLEN

One of the most famous faces of American horror of the 1970s, Ellen Burstyn was born in 1932 in Detroit. Beginning her career on television, her early film roles saw her acting alongside Donald Sutherland, Jeff Bridges, Jack Nicholson and Bruce Dern, and working with directors including Martin Scorsese and Peter Bogdonovich. She received an Oscar nomination for her role as Chris MacNeil, the mother of Linda Blair's possessed Regan in William Friedkin's classic horror film *The Exorcist* (1973). Burstyn has maintained an impressive career until the present day with films like Darren Aronofsky's nightmarish *Requiem for a Dream* (2000), a rare glitch in quality being Neil LaBute's 2006 remake of Robin Hardy's 1973 film *The Wicker Man* as the bewilderingly gender-swapped Sister Summerisle.

Ellen Burstyn at the Los Angeles premiere, in Hollywood, of *Requiem for A Dream*, 16 October 2000. Credit: Paul Smith / Featureflash Photo Agency / Shutterstock.com

BUTLER, SARAH

Reviving Camille Keaton's prototypical rape avenger in Steven R. Monroe's 2010 remake of Meir Zarchi's 1978 film *I Spit on Your Grave*, Sarah Butler would bring the rape-revenge trope to an entire new generation. Born in Washington in 1985, she studied theater at the University of Southern California while working at Disneyland. After a number of small television roles, she scored the lead role in the exploitation remake, revisiting the role again in R.D. Braunstein's *I Spit on Your Grave III: Vengeance is Mine* in 2015. Butler's other horror film credits include *The Demented* (Christopher Roosevelt, 2013), *Nightmare Nurse* (Craig Moss, 2016), *All Light Will End* (Chris Blake, 2018) and an episode of the horror television series *Twisted Tales*.

BYRNE, ROSE

The filmography of Australian actor Rose Byrne is diverse, and throughout her career she has played a number of siginficant roles in the horror genre. Born in New South Wales in 1979, she studied at The University of Sydney and began acting in film and television in her teens. In 2007, she played Scarlet in Juan Carlos Fresnadillo's *28 Weeks Later*, returning to the horror genre with force with starring roles in James Wan's hugely popular *Insidious* and *Insidious: Chapter 2* (2013).

BYRON, KATHLEEN

While most immediately associated with her central performance as Sister Ruth in Michael Powell and Emeric Pressburger's proto-nunsploitation film *Black Narcissus* (1947), British actor Kathleen Byron had a career on stage and screen that spanned more than 60 years. During this period, she appeared in a number of horror films, including *Night of the Eagle* (Sidney Hayers, 1962), Hammer's *Twins of Evil* (John Hough, 1971), *Craze* (Freddie Francis, 1974) and *Nothing but the Night* (Peter Sasdy, 1973).

C

CACCIOLA, SOPHIA

Los Angeles-based feminist artist and filmmaker Sophia Cacciola has co-directed two feature horror films with her partner Michael J. Epstein; the all-woman surrealist murder mystery *Ten* (2014) and the lesbian vampire film *Blood of the Tribades* (2016). Her most recent horror feature is the social satire *Clickbait* (2018), and apart from a number of short and anthology films, Cacciola and Epstein also co-directed the science fiction feature film *Magnetic* (2015). She also works as a cinematographer and plays drums and sings in a no-wave post-punk band called Do Not Forsake Me Oh My Darling.

Sophia Cacciola, Filmmaker http://sophiacacciola.com (image used with permission).

CALAMAI, CLARA

As one of the *grande dames* of the Italian cinema, Clara Calamai rounded off her legendary screen career with an homage to her earlier stardom in her macabre performance as Marta in Dario Argento's *Deep Red* (1975). Born in 1909 and rising to the peak of her success in the 1930s and '40s, it was as the desperate femme fatale Giovanna in *Ossessione*—Luchino Visconti's 1943 adaptation of James M. Cain's 1934 novel *The Postman Always Rings Twice*— that Calamai offered one of her strongest and most memorable performances. A proto-*giallo* of sorts, *Ossessione* bookends neatly with *Deep Red* as it consolidates Calamai's strong abilities playing complex, violent women. A crowning achievement to the end of an impressive career, it is as *Deep Red*'s Marta that Calamai became a horror star.

CAMERON, JESSICA

Canadian filmmaker Jessica Cameron initially studied fashion before moving to the United States where she caught the movie bug when taking acting lessons. As an actor, her horror credits include *The Sleeper* (Justin Russell, 2012), *Silent Night* (Steven C. Miller, 2012), *To Jennifer* (James Cullen Bressack, 2013), *A Grim Becoming* (Adam R. Steigert, 2014) and *All Through the House* (Todd Nunes, 2015). With over 70 on-screen credits, in 2013, she turned her attention to directing with her feature debut *Truth or Dare*, which she also co-wrote. Playing at film festivals internationally, it would make Cameron a familiar name on the horror festival circuit. In 2015, she directed the feature horror film *Mania* starring Tristan Risk through her production company, Small Town Girl Productions.

CAMP, COLLEEN.

In a career that has straddled exploitation film, mainstream movies, television, and indie cinema, Colleen Camp's filmography includes films as diverse as *Police Academy 2: Their First Assignment* (Jerry Paris, 1985), *The Swinging Cheerleaders* (Jack Hill, 1974) and *American Hustle* (David O. Russell, 2013). Born in 1953 in San Francisco, Camp studied singing and acting and gained early roles on television. One of her most impressive horror credits is alongside Sondra Locke in Peter S. Traynor's *Death Game* (1977), with Camp and Locke both acting as co-producers (it was recently remade by Eli Roth in 2015 under the title *Knock Knock*). In 2018, she appeared in Roth's much-anticipated Cate Blanchett fronted dark fantasy film, *The House with a Clock in Its Walls*. Camp also acted in horror films such as Larry Cohen's *Wicked Stepmother* (1989) alongside Bette Davis, Chris Wales' *The Vagrant* (1992), George Huang's *How to Make a Monster* (2001), Patrick Dinhut's *Dead and Deader* (2006) and Andrew Shortell's *Psych 9* (2010), also producing a number of these and other films.

Colleen Camp at the 2016 LACMA Art + Film Gala at Los Angeles County Museum of Art on October 29, 2016 in Los Angeles, CA. Credit: Kathy Hutchins / Shutterstock.com

CAMPBELL, NEVE

In 1996, Neve Campbell starred in two of the biggest horror films of the 1990s—Wes Craven's *Scream* franchise and Andrew Fleming's *The Craft*. Born in Canada in 1973, she studied dance and, in the early 1990s, began working in television commercials and several popular television series, culminating in a key role in *Party of Five* in 1994. Although she had made a small earlier appearance in Craig Pryce's horror film *The Dark* (1993), it was the box office success of *The Craft* and the *Scream* franchise that made Campbell a star, returning to the role of Sidney Prescott in Craven's sequels *Scream 2* (1997), *Scream 3* (2000) and *Scream 4* (2011).

Actor Neve Campbell at the premiere of the movie *Scream 4* at Grauman's Chinese Theatre, 11 April 2011, Hollywood, California. Credit: RoidRanger / Shutterstock.com

CARDINAL, TARA

Despite a troubled early life, Tara Cardinal was always driven by an inherent desire to perform. As a director, she has helmed both *Legend of the Red Reaper* (2013) and *Scarlet Samurai: Incarnation* (2013), while her acting credits include *Bloodstruck* (Joe Hollow, 2010), *Bite Nite* (Ernest E. Brown and Scott Kunkle, 2011) and *Zombie Massacre* (Luca Boni and Marco Ristori, 2013). With the latter produced by Uwe Boll, Cardinal also acted in the segment he directed for the 2013 horror anthology, *The Profane Exhibit*, called "Basement".

CARDIN, MARGARET

Negative cutting and matching might not be the most glamourous job in the film industry, but according to Byron Kennedy—producer of George Miller's *Mad Max* (1979)—Margaret Cardin is largely responsible for saving that film. With over 50 credits in a range of editorial capacities, Cardin worked with some of Australia's greatest filmmakers including Miller, Peter Weir and Fred Schepisi. But it is in her work on a range of Australian genre films that Cardin's talents shone the brightest, including gothic and horror films such as *Picnic at Hanging Rock* (Peter Weir, 1975), *Inn of the Damned* (Terry Bourke, 1975), *Patrick* (Richard Franklin, 1978), *Thirst* (Rod Hardy, 1979), *The Survivor* (David Hemmings, 1981), *Strange Behavior* (Michael Laughlin, 1981) and Brian Trenchard-Smith's notorious exploitation film *Turkey Shoot* (1982).

CASTEL, MARIE-PIERRE AND CATHERINE

Born in suburban Paris in 1950, twin sisters Marie-Pierre and Catherine starred in a number of films made by cult French filmmaker Jean Rollin including the horror films *The Nude Vampire* (1969), *Lips of Blood* (1975), and *Phantasmes* (1975). Marie-Pierre also appeared in *The Shiver of the Vampires* (1970) and *Requiem for a Vampire* (1971) and retired in the late 1970. Catherine returned to make another film with Rollin in 2002, *Dracula's Fiance*.

CARLOS, WENDY

Famed electronic musician and film composer Wendy Carlos is renowned for her breathtaking soundtrack work, most famously used by Stanley Kubrick to chilling effect on his 1980 film *The Shining* after having collaborated with the filmmaker on his 1971 film *A Clockwork Orange* in 1971. Long having experienced gender dysphoria, Carlos is a transgender horror icon who began hormone treatment in 1969; *The Shining* was released a year after Carlos had gone public about her transition. Carlos also wrote the soundtrack for *Tron* in 1982.

CARRILLO, SOFIA

With her wrap-around sequence providing the glue for the much-hyped 2017 all-women-directed horror anthology *XX*, Mexican stop-motion animator Sofia Carrillo was clearly an impressive and unique talent with a strong grasp of the beautiful and disturbing. Carrillo would win a number of awards including an Ariel (the Mexican equivalent of an Oscar) for her 2012 film *Prita Noire*. Currently working on a feature film project, Carrillo's other shorts include *Vertigo* (2005), *Out of Control* (2008), *Adaptación* (2012), *La Casa Triste* (2013), *El corazón del sastre* (2014) and *Cerulia* (2017).

CAROLYN, AXELLE—INTERVIEW (JUNE 2018)

Born in Brussels, Los Angeles-based Axelle Carolyn is a filmmaker with a background in acting and journalism. Writing on film for publications including cult genre magazine *Fangoria*, Carolyn published her award-winning first book *It Lives Again! Horror Movies in the New Millennium* in 2008 and is also a fiction writer. Turning to filmmaking in 2011, she wrote and directed a few shorts that achieved widespread acclaim, leading to her debut feature film, the haunting, tragic ghost story *Soulmate*.

Despite surprising edits by British censors, the film premiered at the prestigious Sitges International Fantastic Film Festival in 2013 and brought Carolyn's directorial work to a broader audience. This continued with her driving the horror anthology *Tales of Halloween* in 2015 (in which she directed the segment "Grim Grinning Ghost"), both it and *Soulmate* also introducing her long-time collaborator, Anubis the dog. Carolyn recently worked as a writer on the popular Netflix series *The Chilling Adventures of Sabrina*, a reboot of the iconic comic of the same name, and in 2018 released her latest book, *The Frightfest Guide to Ghost Movies*.

Axelle Carolyn. Photographer: Jan-Michael Losada. Used with permission.

I understand that you were born and raised in Belgium, so I'd love to ask you about the origins of your affinity with horror: did it come to you through an early experience with film and television, or can you trace it back even earlier than that to something else?

I've been attracted to horror for as long as I can remember. I didn't have much exposure to horror movies, but I would focus on whatever I could get my hands on—images of skeletons, pictures of scary films in the TV program, dark Disney movies like the *Black Cauldron*—and obsess over them. My horror education mostly came through books though; I didn't really get access to movies until my mid-teens. I also remember I would always write little stories about haunted houses and ghosts…

Oh, and here's a weird fact. My family found out a few years ago that the house I grew up in, in Brussels, used to host the workshop of a Jewish painter called Felix Nussbaum, who fled the Nazis and lived in hiding in Brussels. He was eventually arrested in his workshop in 1944 and sent to die in Auschwitz. His paintings are incredibly dark, pessimistic, haunted. Look up *The Triumph of Death*; it's a masterpiece—and it's the kind of imagery, with skeletons and depictions of Death, I've been obsessed with my whole life. I like to think that a little bit of his spirit remained in his workshop and somehow influenced me growing up.

Belgian horror is so distinct a form of national cinema, although not exactly millions of them I'm continually impressed by the quality of generic output from the country. Is there something in the Belgian national sensibility that you think aligns it with such a striking and unique kind of dark, gothic sensibility?

I have to admit that having spent my entire adult life and career between the UK and the US, I'm not overly familiar with the Belgian genre scene, although there are directors like Fabrice du Welz and Jonas Govaerts I'm a huge fan of. I also love Belgian painters, from Rene Magritte, Paul Delvaux and Felicien Rops, to Bruegel, Bosch and Van Eyck, who all delved in dark, surreal material.

One of my main gateways into horror was Belgian author Jean Ray, who wrote several volumes of short ghost stories. I read them all when I was about 10 or 11, along with *Frankenstein* and *Dracula* (then I discovered Stephen King, and life was never the same again!) And then there's a great horror festival in Brussels, the Brussels Fantastic Film Festival (BIFFF for short), which I've been attending since I was 16. That event was the highlight of each year for me as a teenager, and really nurtured my love of the genre. It allowed me to meet filmmakers from all over the world, and to get a first insight into the business and craft of filmmaking.

What brought around your move to the United States?

I fell in love with L.A. the first time I visited, while I was still living in London. I was instantly welcomed into an awesome, tight-knit group of horror nerds and filmmakers, and they're still my best friends to this day. It took a few years for the stars to align and the move to actually happen, but it just felt right.

I read *It Lives Again*! at such an important moment—as a beautiful big glossy book, it really felt like the first tangible, concrete evidence I'd seen that contemporary horror at the time was really flourishing, which was something that so urgently needed to be said. It feels like that book was really hit on something so urgent about the direction the genre was taking after the 90s. Can you tell me a little about how that project came to fruition?

Thank you! I started my career as a horror reporter, first for *Fangoria*, then also for *IGN*, *SFX*, and some French magazines…But I've always considered journalism an entry point, my goal being to write and direct. The book was meant as a swan song to non-fiction writing when I started being more active behind the camera.

At the time, it seemed like there was such a great revival in the genre, and yet mainstream opinion dismissed it as nothing but remakes and torture, so I thought I'd offer a different POV and point out hidden gems, and try to figure out why certain trends were so popular. One of the most influential books for me was *The Monster Show* by David Skal, and that's the spirit I attempted to recreate.

I actually have another book coming out this summer, about ghost movies! As you can probably tell from my movies, I'm have a bit of a ghost obsession. In this one I basically reviewed the 200 best ghost movies from around the world, since the birth of cinema. It was incredibly fun to do.

Soulmate is such a quiet, creeping film, and so beautifully and carefully directed. So much of that film's energy feels like it stems not just from the screenplay but from the cast, the location, and the cinematography with the emphasis on light and shadow. I'd love to hear how these elements in particular came together for you, what inspired the project, and what your experience of the nuts-and-bolts production side of making your debut feature was like.

I had the idea for *Soulmate* while on a road trip in the British countryside. I drove through this creepy, beautiful little village, and it made me think that it had been a while since I'd seen a classical British ghost story—it was before *Woman in Black* came out. I wrote it with the idea of making it on a super tight budget (I saw that Imdb says estimated budget is $600k; I wish I'd had a third of that!) so the story is basically two people in a house, only one of them is dead.

We filmed it in a holiday cottage in Wales, which is incredibly beautiful. My cinematographer, Sara Deane, is incredibly talented; it was such a joy to work with her and capture these beautiful landscapes. I also lucked out with the cast; I'd worked with Anna Walton briefly on my short film *The Halloween Kid*, so she was attached very early on and we had time to discuss the script scene by scene, get her feedback, discuss the part extensively…I miss that process, and it was great to have so much freedom!

It's almost absurd to recall the incomprehensible treatment Soulmate received at the hands of British censors. At the time, I remember much social media outrage, but looking back it seems even more random and nonsensical. Can you tell me how that aspect played out at the time, and now—5 years later— how you have retrospectively come to understand it?

I haven't. It's still puzzling to me. I can sort of understand that they have a strict rule for depictions of suicide—although they've made exceptions, and I found a couple of movies which showed the same amount we did, and didn't get cut—but then once we'd cut the whole scene (because the 16 seconds of mandatory cuts not only mangled the scene, but more tragically, in my opinion made suicide seem appealing by making it look painless!), they gave us a 15 certificate for "strong violence and gore". Um, what? Where did they see that…?

From *Soulmate* (Axelle Carolyn, 2013). Used with permission.

Tales of Halloween is so much fun, and it's such a great cast and group of film-makers that came together for the project. What inspired the project, how did you get everyone together, and what are your feelings about anthology films more generally?

Tales of Halloween was such a great experience. I'd just moved to L.A. and hanging with my friends, I thought it'd be great to work on something all together, since we all work in horror. Since so many of us were filmmakers, an anthology was the most appropriate format. I mentioned it to a couple of friends, and they loved the idea, so I started approaching a few more.

Once we had a rough line-up, Mike Mendez offered to pitch it to Epic Pictures, who had just produced his movie *Big Ass Spider!*, and they came on board right away. We wrote the scripts over the summer, and shot it between Halloween and Christmas. Each short would have two to three days to shoot—it was a bit of a logistical nightmare—and towards the end, we had to avoid framing people's Christmas decorations whenever we filmed on the street…Mike and I were also producing so we got to help all our friends and see what their style is like on set, which was interesting and fun and really, really challenging.

Your segment "Grim Grinning Ghost" is for me the perfectly weighted anthology segment—I think far too often in other portmanteau films there's a tendency for directors to try and squeeze an entire feature into a -20minute segment, but "Grim Grinning Ghost" felt like it was just the right size to really create a strong mood piece. The casting of Alex Essoe and Lin Shaye was also perfect, too—I loved this bringing together of a new horror star with a more established one. Can you tell me about the making of this segment in particular?

The way we developed the stories was that in the beginning, everyone would meet in my backyard and we'd pitch each other ideas. It was a great process, because

On the set of "Grim Grinning Ghost"—directed by Axelle Carolyn—from the 2015 anthology *Tales of Halloween*. Used with permission.

you could immediately see what bombed and what got everyone excited. Then we'd all start writing, and I'd collect the scripts and make sure they weren't too similar, etc. And right away I could tell that a lot of the filmmakers had chosen to go for at least some degree of comedy, so I thought I should make something quick, spooky, to give the audience a jolt.

I also hadn't done much of that in *Soulmate*, which is more atmospheric than scary, so I thought it was a great opportunity to just focus on a technical exercise: how to craft a jump scare in just a few minutes. It's more complex than it seems! Not just the technical aspect of it, but you also have very little time to make the audience care about the characters.

Thankfully I was lucky enough to have Alex Essoe as my lead, and she's instantly likable and so much fun to watch. I'd just seen her at the L.A. premiere of *Starry Eyes*, and we hit it off; a couple of days later I thought I'd write the part for her.

I also liked the idea that since the other segments focused on kids and teenagers, I'd show where the grown-ups spend the evening, so I got to cast a few friends in cameo roles: Mick Garris, Stuart Gordon, Lisa Marie, Barbara Crampton, and Lin. When we started screening it in festivals, I got to see the audience jump and yelp, it was awesome.

The question on everyone's lips: will we be seeing more of your canine star and muse, Anubis?

I certainly hope so! I give her a part, or at least a guest appearance, in everything I write. She's also appeared in a couple of small ad campaigns; I'd love for her to act more! She's so talented. And she gets lots of attention and treats, so she loves it.

CARTER, ANN

Child star Ann Carter was born in New York in 1936, and during her brief career her co-stars included screen luminaries such as Barbara Stanwyck, Katharine Hepburn and Humphrey Bogart. With a childhood frequently disrupted by poor health and her family moving from state to state, her career proved a central focus and one of her earliest roles was as Veronica Lake's daughter in René Clair's supernatural comedy *I Married a Witch* (1942). Her most famous role, however, was in Robert Wise's Val Lewton-produced *The Curse of the Cat People* (1944).

CARTER, LAUREN ASHLEY

Demonstrating her passion for horror, scifi and dark fantasy material from the outset, Ohio-born Lauren Ashley Carter delivered a stand-out performance as Peggy in Lucky McKee's 2011 film *The Woman*. Carter's later horror films include starring roles in *Jug Face* (Chad Crawford Kinkle, 2013) and *The Mind's Eye* (Joe Begos, 2015), collaborating twice in 2015 with cult director Mickey Keating on *Pod* and her career stand-out performance in the title role of his film *Darling*. In 2017, she played dual roles in Natasha Kermani's dark scifi film, *Imitation Girl*.

CARPENTER, CHARISMA˙

Earning an enduring cult reputation based on her long-running role as Cordelia Chase in both *Buffy the Vampire Slayer* and *Angel*, Vegas-born Charisma Carpenter was discovered while working as a waitress. Carpenter's later film credits maintained her association with supernatural and horror-themed movies, including *Voodoo Moon* (Kevin VanHook, 2006), *House of Bones* (Jeffery Scott Lando, 2010), *Psychosis* (Reg Traviss, 2010), *Haunted High* (Jeffery Scott Lando, 2012), *Girl in Woods* (Jeremy Benson, 2016), and appearances in horror-themed television series such as *Supernatural* and *Scream Queens*.

CARPENTER, JENNIFER

In the title role of *The Exorcism of Emily Rose* (Scott Derrickson, 2005), Jennifer Carpenter revealed she was an actor with few inhibitions, making her well-suited to the genre's demands. Born in 1979 in Kentucky, she studied theater at New York's Julliard School before moving to the stage. *Emily Rose* was considered her breakthrough performance, and her other credits would include the slasher film *Lethal Eviction* (Michael Feifer, 2005), *Quarantine* (John Erick Dowdle, 2008)—the American remake *of [REC]* (Jaume Balagueró and Paco Plaza, 2007)—and Christian E. Christiansen's *The Devil's Hands* (2014). Carpenter also had an ongoing role in the serial killer series *Dexter*.

CARTWRIGHT, VERONICA

British-born US émigré Veronica Cartwright built an impressive career as a child star, with early career highlights revealing a flair for the dark side with films like Alfred Hitchcock's horror movie *The Birds* (1963) and the gothic lesbian melodrama *The Children's Hour* (William Wyler, 1961). While her filmography numbers well into the hundreds, some of her most memorable roles are in horror/scifi hybrids including *Invasion of the Body Snatchers* (Philip Kaufman, 1978) and the 2007 Oliver Hirschbiegel remake *The Invasion*, *Alien* (Ridley Scott, 1979), and television series like *The X-Files*. Cartwright has also acted in more straightforward horror films such as *Nightmares* (Joseph Sargeant, 1983), *Mirror, Mirror 2* (Jimmy Lifton, 1994), *The Town That Dreaded Sundown* (Alfonso Gomez-Rejon, 2014), and *The Dark Below* (Douglas Schulze, 2015). If there is one scene that encapsulates Cartwright's flair for the grotesque and disturbing, however, it is surely the famous cherry-puking scene in George Miller's 1987 film, *The Witches of Eastwick*.

CASABÉ, LAURA

Argentine director, cinematographer and editor Laura Casabé wowed audiences with her 2016 film *Benavidez's Case*. While Casabé has been hesitant to define the film purely as horror, it is a genre that clearly influenced her adaptation of fellow Argentine author Samanta Schweblin's short story for the screen with its tale about an artist exploited by his psychiatrist. Making her directorial debut with the scifi film *El hada buena—Una fábula peronista* (2010) and followed that same year with the horror short *La vuelta del malón*, Casabé had also appeared on screen in the feature *Plaga Zombie: Zona Mutante: Revolución Tóxica* (2011).

CASCONE, ANNETTE AND GINA

Sisters Annette and Gina Cascone are credited with co-writing the script for cult horror film *Mirror, Mirror* (1990), and also received writing credits for *Grave Secrets* (David Hillenbrand, 2013). Together they wrote the popular children's horror book series *Deadtime Stories* under the alias A.C. Cascone from 1997 to 2013, which—like the similarly themed *Goosebumps* series—also spawned a popular children's television series. They also wrote two autobiographical books, *Pagan Babies and Other Catholic Memories* (1982) and *Life al Dente: Laughter and Love in an Italian American Family* (2003).

CASH, ROSALIND ⸰

Rosalind Cash was born in 1938 in New Jersey and was one of the first members of New York City's Negro Ensemble Company, a theater group formed in 1967 by playwright Douglas Turner Ward. Across a screen and stage career that spanned more than 30 years, Cash worked on film and television including a number of horror movies such as the Blaxploitation horror film *Dr. Black, Mr. Hyde* (William Crain, 1976), *From a Whisper to a Scream* (Jeff Burr, 1987), *Death Spa* (Michael Fischa, 1989), and her final role was the cult horror anthology *Tales from the Hood* (Rusty Cundieff, 1995).

CASSAVETES, XAN

Xan (Alexandra) Cassavetes comes from strong cinema stock: her mother is actor Gena Rowlands, father director-actor John Cassavetes, and her brother and sister Nick and Zoe are both actors and directors themselves. As the eldest of the three Cassavetes children, Xan was cast in small roles in a number of her father's films, many starring her mother, including 1974's *A Woman Under the Influence* and 1984's *Love Streams*. As a director, Xan established herself as a figure with a close relationship to cult film with the 2004 documentary *Z Channel: A Magnificent Obsession*, later aligning herself with horror specifically with her 2012 vampire film *Kiss of the Damned* which won her Octopus d'Or at the Strasbourg European Fantastic Film Festival.

CASSIDY, KATIE

Moving from television to film, Katherine Evelyn Anita Cassidy—credited as Katie for short—established her big-screen reputation with a number of horror films including a many remakes such as *When a Stranger Calls* (Simon West, 2006), *Black Christmas* (2006) and *A Nightmare on Elm Street* (Samuel Bayer, 2010). Cassidy also featured in the slasher film *The Lost* (Chris Siverston, 2006), the Mansonploitation horror movie *Wolves at the Door* (John R. Leonetti, 2016) and the gothic noir *The Scribbler* (2014), as well as appearing in the popular television series *Supernatural*.

CASTO, SHANNON

Frequently working with co-director Michelle Henderson, Casto and Henderson together ran Little Oak Film Group in Texas, together producing a number of independent horror movies. Beginning her film career as an extra and moving to cinematography, their first feature collaboration as directors was *Sinner* (2008) and other horror credits as co-director and co-writer with Henderson include *The Caretaker* (2008), Protege (2009), *His Will Be Done* (2009), *Dark Spaces* (2009), and *House Call* (2013), the latter also joined by Parrish Randall on directing duties and co-written by Ty Schwamberger instead of Henderson. Casto was cinematographer on all these films except *Protege* and *Dark Spaces*, but her credits in the area also include Parrish Randall's *Slaughterhouse* (2008) and the Henderson solo-directed horror feature *Gut Instincts* (which Casto also co-wrote).

CATALDI-TASSONI, CORALINA

Born in America but raised in Italy, Cataldi-Tassoni is renowned for her collaborations with Dario Argento on films including *Opera* (1987), *Phantom of the Opera* (1998) and *Mother of Tears* (2007). Her other horror credits include *Demons 2* (Lamberto Bava, 1986), *Evil Clutch* (Andreas Marfori, 1988), *The Childhood Friend* (Pupi Avati, 1994), *The Room Next Door* (Pupi Avati, 1994) and *Ghost Son* (Lamberto Bava, 2007). In 2017, she played Lady Macbeth in Mariano Baino's short film *Lady M 5.1*, and beyond her film career, Cataldi-Tassoni is also a writer, musician and artist.

CATTET, HÉLÈNE

With her professional collaborator and husband Bruno Forzani, Hélène Cattet's filmography of shorts and features are experimental and often explicit homages to Italian genre cinema, particularly *giallo*, that seek to provoke intense physical sensations from their audiences. Born in Paris in 1976 and, with Forzani, now based in Belgium, Cattet's films as co-director include the shorts *Catharsis* (2001), *Chambre jaune* (2002), *La Fin de notre amour* (2003), *L'Étrange Portrait de la dame en jaune* (2004), *Santos Palace* (2006) and their segment for the 2012 horror anthology *The ABCs of Death* called "O is for Orgasm". Their feature films *Amer* (2009) and *The Strange Color of Your Body's Tears* (2013) engage heavily with *giallo* tropes and conventions, while their most recent film *Let the Corpses Tan* (2017) holds spaghetti westerns and *poliziottescho* as its core subject of fascination.

CAYNE, CANDIS

Candis Cayne was born in Hawaii in 1971 and is a renowned transgender performer who has appeared in television shows including *CSI: NY, Dirty Sexy Money, Transparent,* and *Grey's Anatomy*. Beginning her career in drag in the early 1990s and transitioning later that decade, she worked in many films from 1995 onwards. Of these, her memorable role as Vivianna in Jane Clark's horror-comedy feature film *Crazy Bitches* (2014) is a standout performance.

CHANDLER, HELEN

Born in 1906 in South Carolina, despite her hesitancy to play the role of Mina in Tod Browning's *Dracula* (1931) alongside Béla Lugosi, it is without doubt that role which rendered her a key figure in the history of women in horror. Beginning her career on the stage, she would play a number of famous roles including Ophelia in a 1925 stage adaptation of *Hamlet* with British actor Basil Sydney. The success of *Dracula* was not again repeated for Chandler, whose emotional deterioration and decline into alcohol abuse from the end of the 1930s onwards have been heavily documented, resulting in a serious fire that caused irreversible damage to her appearance. She never returned to acting.

CHANEY, REBEKAH

Rebekah Chaney wrote and directed the slasher film *Slumber Party Slaughter* in 2012, in which she also appeared in front of the camera in the role of Casey Reitz. Her feature debut followed on from her previous short *Waste Land* (2007) about a woman who seeks the help of a psychiatrist after being attacked by a demon.

CHANG, PEARL

As both an actor and director, Ling Chang—more commonly credited as Pearl Chang—both starred and directed in the 1982 Taiwanese horror film *Wolf Devil Woman* and apparently its sequel *Wolf Devil Woman 2* that same year under the alias Ma Peng Sze. While the sequel was written by cult Hong Kong genre filmmaker Godfrey Ho, Chang also had writing duties on the first film in the series which follows her title character who seeks revenge on the ominous Red Devil, leaving her as an orphan who was raised by wolves.

Helen Chandler and Bela Lugosi in *Dracula* (Tod Browning, 1931). Credit: Moviestore collection Ltd / Alamy Stock Photo (DRCA 007P)

CHASE, DAVEIGH

Born in Las Vegas in 1990, Daveigh Chase hit the child actor horror film payload with a double whammy early in her career with two roles; first as the title character's younger sister Samantha in Richard Kelly's cult 2001 film *Donnie Darko* (reviving the role in Chris Fisher's 2009 sequel *S. Darko*). The following year she would play Samara Morgan, the supernatural force out to cause havoc via a haunted videotape in *The Ring* (Gore Verbinski, 2002), the American remake of the J-horror blockbuster *Ringu* (Hideo Nakata, 1998). Chase would later appear in the horror films *Killer Crush* (Anthony Lefresne, 2015) and *Jack Goes Home* (Thomas Dekker, 2016), and has numerous credits as a voice actor.

CHASTAIN, JESSICA ᐧ

Despite her impressively diverse filmography, celebrated American actor and producer Jessica Chastain has spoken highly of the potential of horror for ideological commentary, and has featured in a number of horror films. Born in California in 1977, she studied at Julliard in New York before making her screen debut in the 2004 pilot for a remake of the gothic soap opera *Dark Shadows*. In 2013, she starred in Andy Muschietti's horror film *Mama*, and in 2015 had a leading role in Guillermo del Toro's *Crimson Peak*. In 2019 she reunited with Muschietti for *It: Chapter Two*.

CHICA, PATRICIA

Canadian-Latina filmmaker Patricia Chica has a diverse and lengthy filmography, with horror-related shorts including *Serpent's Lullaby* (2014), *A Tricky Treat* (2015), *Crimson Dance* (2016), and *Las Cholas* (2017). Her films have been selected for over 300 official selections at a range of international film festivals, and her 2017 coming-of-age short film *Morning After* saw her awarded the Best Director Award at Oaxaca Film Fest and the Ambassador's Grand Prize at the Rhode Island International Film Festival. In 2018, her project *Montreal Girls* was selected for the Toronto International Film Festival's Filmmaker Lab, which she had developed through her participation at the SODEC_LAB Immersion Cannes.

CHONG, RAE DAWN ᐧ

Rae Dawn Chong is a Canadian actor and filmmaker who early in her career was noted for her relationship to her famous father, comedian Tommy Chong of Cheech and Chong fame. But she swiftly proved herself on her own merits in films like *The Color Purple* (Steven Spielberg, 1985), and developed a fascinating career in the horror genre in particular. Her credits as an actor in the genre include *Tales from the Darkside: The Movie* (John Harrison, 1990), *The Borrower* (John McNaughton, 1991), *Hideaway* (Brett Leonard, 1995) and *Cyrus: Mind of a Serial Killer* (Mark Vadik, 2010). In 2000, she also wrote and directed the horror-comedy short film *Cursed: Part III*, which remains her only directorial credit.

CHRISTIE, JULIE '

One of the most iconic faces of British film and television, despite working with directors including David Lean, François Truffaut, Robert Altman and Hal Ashby, it is in horror where two-time Oscar nominee Julie Christie has revealed the range and power of her acting talent most forcibly. Studying at London's Royal Central School of Speech & Drama, in 1973 Christie co-starred with Donald Sutherland in Nicolas Roeg's Venice-set *Don't Look Now*, adapted from a 1971 short story by British writer Daphne du Maurier. In 1977, she starred in another dark genre film, Donald Cammell's horror/scifi hybrid *Demon Seed*, where Christie's character Susan Harris is forcibly impregnated by a computer with god delusions. In 2001, she acted alongside Sophie Marceau in Jean-Paul Salomé's Belphegor's *Phantom of the Louvre*, followed in 2011 by her appearance as the grandmother in Catherine Hardwicke's gothic reimagining of the fairy-tale *Red Riding Hood*.

CHRISTINE, VIRGINIA

Born in Iowa in 1920, Virginia Christine Ricketts dropped her surname for her acting career and would go on to a career on stage and screen that would span almost 40 years. Linked closely to the horror genre, her many credits include Princess Ananka in *The Mummy's Curse* (Leslie Goodwins, 1944), *House of Horrors* (Jean Yarbrough, 1946), *Invasion of the Body Snatchers* (Don Siegel, 1956) and *Billy the Kid Versus Dracula* (William Beaudine, 1966), and she would also appear in episodes of *Alfred Hitchcock Presents*, *The Twilight Zone* and *Thriller*.

CHURCHILL, MARGUERITE

Although most famous for starring alongside John Wayne in Raoul Walsh's western *The Big Trail* (1930), Marguerite Churchill acted in a number of classic horror films that make her a key figure in the genre. Born in Kansas in 1910 and studying acting in New York City, in 1936 she played in both Michael Curtiz's *The Walking Dead* alongside Boris Karloff, and the lesbian vampire classic *Dracula's Daughter* with Gloria Holden, directed by Lambert Hillyer.

CHYTILOVÁ, VĚRA

A key figure in the influential Czech New Wave, avant-garde filmmaker Věra Chytilová made some of the most original and dazzling films of 20th century European cinema, including her peerless feminist masterpiece *Daisies* (1966), which was banned by the Czech government. Amongst her many impressive movies is her 1987 film *Wolf's Hole* which entered the 37th Berlin International Film Festival: while ostensibly a slasher film with a scifi twist, the film—in typical Chytilováian style—can also be read as a less-than-subtle allegory for the country's recent political history and the pressures to submit to oppressive, authoritive regimes. While hardly exclusively a genre filmmaker, Chytilová often returned to experiment with the codes and conventions of popular cinema tropes, such as in her later rape-revenge film *Traps* (1998).

CIARDI, FRANCESCA

Francesca Ciardi is an Italian actor who was born in 1954. Her notoriety stems largely from her performance as one of the unfortunate victims in Ruggero Deodato's controversial video nasty *Cannibal Holocaust* (1980). So realistic was Ciardi's character's death in the film that police investigated it as an actual murder, matters further complicated by the fact that she had a contractual obligation to hide from the press in order to promote this sense of authenticity. Ciardi has recently returned to acting in Spencer Hawkins' 2016 horror film *Death Walks*.

CIPRIANI, ANGELA

While very little is known of editor Angela Cipriani, she is a notably rare exception to the otherwise heavily masculine world of Italian horror and *giallo* production. Thus, while her credits are limited to *Frankenstein all'italiana* (Armando Crispino, 1975) and the *giallo The House of the Yellow Carpet* (Carlo Lizzani, 1983), Cipriani's name is an important one in the history of women in Italian horror cinema in particular.

CLARK, ANNIE

Known more readily by her moniker St Vincent, Annie Erin Clark was born in Oklahoma in 1982 and would go on to become one of the most celebrated art-rock singer and musicians of her generation. In 2017, Clark directed a segment of the all-woman horror anthology *XX*, adapting "The Birthday Party" to the screen from a script by Roxanne Benjamin. Clark has recently announced that she will be directing an adaptation of Oscar Wilde's 1890 novel *The Picture of Dorian Gray* for her feature film directorial debut.

CLARK, JANE

Filmmaker Jane Clark is the founder of FilmMcQueen Productions, through which she has made many of her horror projects. Beginning her career in front of the camera as an actor, she moved to directing to have more control over the storytelling process. After making a number of shorts she directed her feature debut, the 2013 drama *Meth Head*, following it up in 2014 with the queer feminist horror-comedy *Crazy Bitches* which was nominated for Best Film at Portugal's Fantasporto Film Festival.

CLARK, KATHIE

Inspired heavily by the music video aesthetics of the 1980s in her most famous films, Kathie Clark was an influential costume designer during that decade. Working broadly in cult and low-budget indie genre films, her horror credits include *The Dungeonmaster* (Dave Allen, Charles Band, John Carl Buechler, Steven Ford, Peter Manoogian, Ted Nicolaou, and Rosemarie Turko, 1984), *Ghoulies* (Luca Bercovici, 1984) and *TerrorVision* (Ted Nicolaou, 1986), and she worked on a range of films in the genre in other capacities including *Evil Speak* (Eric Weston, 1981), *Cat People* (Paul Schrader, 1982), *Deadly Eyes* (Robert Clouse, 1982), *Cujo* (Lewis Teague, 1983) and *Rumpelstiltskin* (Mark Jones, 1995).

CLARK, MARLENE

As Ganja Meda in Bill Gunn's iconic horror film *Ganja & Hess* (1973), model and actor Marlene Clark became an important part of horror film history in a genre that all too rarely gives women of color starring roles. Born in 1949, Clark was raised in Harlem and her film career was marked by early uncredited roles in *Midnight Cowboy* (John Schlesinger, 1969) and *Putney Swope* (Robert Downey Sr., 1969). She later appeared in Hal Ashby's *The Landlord* (1970), based on a script written by *Ganja & Hess* director Gunn. Clark would also work in other horror films including *Night of the Cobra Woman* (Andrew Meyer, 1972), *Black Mamba* (George Rowe, 1974), *Lord Shango* (Ray Marsh, 1975) and Jack Hill's girl gang exploitation classic *Switchblade Sisters* (1975). But it is the legacy of *Ganja & Hess* that remains the strongest, remade in 2014 by Spike Lee as *Da Sweet Blood of Jesus*, Clark's role revived by British actor Zaraah Abrahams.

Marlene Clark in Ganja & Hess (Bill Gunn & Fima Noveck, 1972). Credit: Kelly/Jordan Ent. Photofest ©Kelly/Jordan Enterprises

Aislinn Clarke, image by Ivan Ewart. Used with permission from Aislinn Clark.

CLARKE, AISLINN —INTERVIEW (DECEMBER 2018)

The following interview with Aislinn Clarke was originally published in December 2018 by AWFJ.org, the official website and online magazine of the Alliance of Women Film Journalists (AWFJ), an international non-profit professional association of prominent female film critics, reporters and commentators. The original publication of the interview may be accessed at https://awfj.org/blog/2018/12/19/aislinn-clarke-on-found-footage-belfast-and-the-devils-doorway-alexandra-heller-nicholas-interviews-exclusive/ The interview may not be republished or quoted in whole or in part without written permission from the Alliance of Women Film Journalists.

Released in the United States through IFC Films in mid-2018, Aislinn Clarke's feature film debut *The Devil's Doorway* is an remarkable accomplishment for a number of reasons. The first feature-length horror movie directed by a woman in Northern Ireland, it is also one of the very rare feature-length found footage horror films directed by a woman. A lecturer at the Seamus Heaney Centre at Queen's University in Belfast, Clarke's prowess as an academic researcher granted her unique insight into how to most effectively unite the thrills and pleasures of the horror genre with what lies at the heart of the project: a passionate and intelligent interrogation of a very real and profoundly dark element of her country's history and its mistreatment of women.

Set in 1960, *The Devil's Doorway* tells the story of two priests who take their analogue audio-visual equipment to a Magdalene Laundry in Ireland to investigate a possible miracle. What they discover is far more profane, setting the scene for a genre film that shrewdly intersects the very real horrors of these real-life asylums where the Catholic church housed young women deemed to be morally dubious in character, particularly in regard to their sexuality (hence the reference to Mary Magdalene). Prostitutes, unmarried pregnant women and women suffering mental health issues were all institutionalized in these homes, first established in Dublin in 1765.

Played by Lalor Roddy and Ciaran Flynn, as genre codes and conventions often dictate these priests discover far more than they bargained for when their investigation begins to reveal the shocking secrets that lay hidden in the Laundry they are investigating, both worldly and—as they ultimately discover—of a far more supernatural nature.

Aislinn kindly took the time to talk to me at length about her impressive film, it's history and development, and the role of women in horror filmmaking more broadly.

I'd like to start by asking about how the Magdalene laundries 'fit' in your experience of growing up as a woman in Ireland. I confess for me in in Australia *The Devil's Doorway* was really the first I'd heard of them—although I certainly had heard of other variations—but I'm fascinated to hear about your research process and how that intersected with their wider notoriety or what was perhaps common knowledge?

I think it is difficult to say to what extent the laundries were part of common knowledge. They have a much higher profile now because of recent revelations at Mother and Baby Homes, because of campaign groups seeking justice over unnecessary medical procedures performed in these places, for lives wasted. However, before that, when they were in operation, they were neither secret nor overt—they just were. My da was a breadman and he delivered bread to a number of local convents, one of which was a laundry—he used to describe the awful heat of the place, the rooms that weeped water, the damp floors, the miles of white sheets stretched across the rafters, and the red-faced girls working there. That intimate knowledge of the inner workings probably wasn't common, but everyone knew there was somewhere that bad girls went. You may not have been able to point out the building, but it was an unarguable truth—they were somewhere. A childhood friend of my mother was snatched from the street and taken away, although, if you were to speak to her now, as an adult, she would say that she was well-treated.

Not everyone was. Not ever convent was that sort of place. My husband's aunt spent her formative years in a children's home that is now notorious for the mistreatment of its boarders, but she too would tell you she was well-treated. That seems to be the way, there was a system of retaining church power that rested on the exploitation and mistreatment of the weakest in its care, but it wasn't all clergy, it wasn't every church building. Like an abusive relationship, it is the threat, as well as the execution, that maintains the power balance. There was the threat that bad girls went somewhere, even if most people couldn't say where the place was, even if they didn't have a name for it—the abstraction was part of its power. It loomed there.

My colleague at Queen's University, the playwright Michael West, said of the film that the power of its premise was identifying the Magdalene Laundry as "Ireland's haunted house" and that's a good analogy for what Ireland knew of the laundries at the time: the house on the hill that you know to keep out of, nothing else needed to be known. It was part of the national landscape—like our other institutions: the reformatory, the borstal, the mother and baby homes, the special needs homes—these were places that people were put so not to be seen and, thus, the places themselves were visible and invisible.

My husband remembers a boys home beside his school in the early nineties; it had a high, wrought iron gate and a long lane that ran to a distant building up a hill. He never saw anybody come in or go out, even though it was in operation. That was where bad boys went. The building a sort of bogeyman—it didn't come to you, you went to it. Of course, it wasn't the priests he was scared of, as a child, but the bad boys or being a bad boy himself. All the institutions were the same.

That's the context of the laundries when I grew up. It's hard to say how present they were. They were even in the background. The last one closed in 1996, which was the year before I had my son—I was 17 and, in a not too distant world, I could have been one of those girls. Any of us could have been, of course. We were all sinners and all a hair's breadth from being sent somewhere for correction—and we would have been thankful for it too, apparently.

My real research began when I started looking into making a documentary in 2005. I spoke to lots of survivors. I spoke to lots of people who had been born in these places. The stories were harrowing and there were lots of them. It doesn't take you to go far to find some connection to any of these places, but the all-powerful Irish shame meant that no one talked about it for a long time, for fear of being the only ones talking. Everyone was touched in some way, but everyone felt as though they experienced it in isolation.

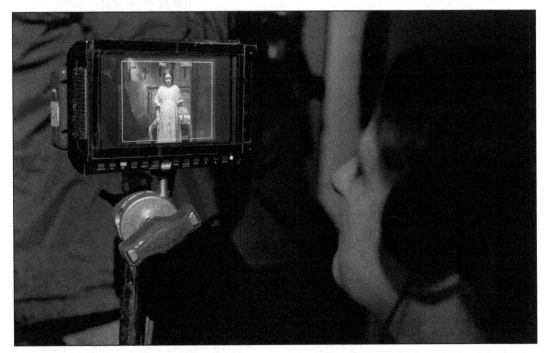

On the set of *The Devil's Doorway*. Image by Joanne Mullin, used with permission from Aislinn Clark.

I'm intrigued by the choice to use this real-life horror story as the foundations for a found footage horror film in particular; of all the ways to present this material, this is a really fascinating choice in regards to the tensions between factuality and fantasy. I'd really love to hear what made you focus on this sub-genre in particular format-wise; did you always intend it to be a found footage horror film?

The found-footage came first. The producers wanted to make a found-footage film first and foremost—as many low-budget film-makesr do. Then they had the idea to incorporate Magdalene Laundries. When they came to me, looking for a director, they had a one-pager on a contemporary found-footage film, captured on go-pro, in an abandoned building. I thought there was much more in the idea than that. If I was going to do a Magdalene Laundry story, it had to be in their heyday—the 1960s. And if I was going to do a found-footage film, it would have to add to the story and the aesthetic. It was my first feature and it was a lot to risk, but I told them I would only do it if it was a period piece, shot on film. The girls couldn't be the villains. The possession had to be ambiguous. Thankfully, they went for it.

Really, the found-footage approach was perfect for the story. I wanted to create a Gothic piece and so many of the great Gothic novels are written as episolatory novels or diaries. They are presented as documents of things you won't believe. In one sense, they are documentaries—documents that present one perspective on the story. The Gothic is also about uncovering hidden things, the heroines—it's always heroines!—pry, that's their main activity and it generally doesn't go well. Found-footage seemed like a continuation of something like *The Awful Disclosures of Maria Monk* (1836), or, *The Hidden Secrets of a Nun's Life in a Convent Exposed* (1836). If I could combine that with the aesthetic of the Maysles Brothers film, then I would have something that presented heightened truth—something that begs you to believe in it. The something that is revealed is almost too much to be true. That's why our cameraman is called Fr. John, he is John the Revelator.

I think found-footage and religion are a very definite fit. As you say, they both have at their heart and investment in the truth, in the believability of what is experience. They believe in an objective reality that is observable and, in the case of found-footage, it is recordable. Where narrative film has the sense of being curated, found-footage purports to be raw, like the footage of an objective, omniscient observer. That's why I wanted scenes like the birth scene, for example, where there is no one behind the camera: it is no longer John's point of view, but an eye that watches without acting in the world—the eye of God maybe or just the objective reality that can be looked in on.

John's last words—although they're not completely audible—are "You've got to hope someone is watching." He's probably talking about God, but he's talking about the audience too. Those who believe in God and those who survive to the end of a found-footage film share this in common: their experience is not in vain because—indeed, it is motivated by the fact that—it is validated by an external observer. They are not alone.

There's an stunning moment very early in the film where Helena Bereen's Mother Superior strips back almost from the outset the line between text and subtext; *The Devil's Doorway* **thoroughly won me over when she tells Lalor Roddy's Father Thomas that far from being the enemy or an oppressor, the role of her and her colleagues was to cover up the results of the male clergy's sexual abuse of young women, and she goes as far I believe to even use the phrase "dirty laundry". I'd love to hear from you how you balance the political power of horror for social and cultural critique in** *The Devil's Doorway*, **and how you weave that through the more overt 'horror' codes and conventions?**

I think it's important to start with the drama, to be conscious of what the characters' experience is within the world of the story, even before the supernatural elements appear. For me, the supernatural elements wouldn't have the same potency if the audience didn't connect with the characters—they must have complex relationships outside their shared horror experience. Therefore, it is impossible to write an effective horror story—that is, one that horrifies, rather than just scares—without it having some socially recognisable component—we have to recognize something in it. Monsters, ghosts, and all the things we're afraid have mean something, we are scared of them for a reason, because of what they mean, what they represent, what they say about us or people we know. Therefore, their place in a story becomes almost natural, self-explanatory—our myths are metaphors for our real fears; in a story, they are extensions, manifestations of the horrific truth. In a place like a Magdalene Laundry, where female innocence and sexuality were contained, where the duality of the Catholic view of woman—as innocents and temptresses, as powerless and powerful—is institutionalized, a possession was a completely natural extension—those places existed because Ireland and the Catholic church viewed women like that, as vessels of an evil sexuality that must be restrained.

In terms of that speech, it was suggested, once I'd delivered the script, that the Mother Superior should hold her tongue a while and curtail her treatment of the girls in the home. The note thought it would be stronger if the barbarism of the institution was revealed over time and that the nun should initially play deferential or coy. No Irish person—indeed, no Catholic –would believe that for a second. In presenting her that way—with that degree of candour and unselfconsciousness—I wasn't levelling anything at nuns in particular. The revelation was not that these places were awful—everyone knows that now. The revelation is the Church-State system that supported these places—and the other institutions and the other practices—in Ireland was self-sustaining, that these people were part of it, and they knew their part and they didn't know how—or if—to break out of it.

The setting of the film in a past historical moment is a really interesting choice, and I love how the use of analogue media that is so present in every scene is aligned so tightly with this designation of a previous time. But that being said, the film feels so urgent and contemporary in what it has to say. Can you talk

me through this relationship between the past and the present in *The Devil's Doorway*, both in terms of the technology that defines its diegetic 'documentary' and this broader question of how the past more thematically feeds into the present in a political/ideological sense?

I've always been inspired by techniques and tropes of the past. I had shot on film before; I've staged radio plays; I've made silent films. I'm interested in all these forms and how different media and times offer different textures and different opportunities. In *The Devil's Doorway*, for example, I was interested in how the characters would mostly record image and sound on separate devices and the opportunities there were to disassociate the two in order to see and hear things differently. In silent film, there is a different relationship between visual, sound, and audience experience. I am interested in how the audience will experience what they see and hear and placing a piece in the past or using techniques from the past bring that to the forefront as a film-maker—there are moments when the audience feel very intimate with the characters and moments when they feel very estranged from them.

That said, as a storyteller, I care about human stories, emotional stories, and these, I think, are timeless. The emotional arcs for characters are recognisable, no matter when the story is set. However, I will bring modern sensibilities to my stories and the temptation to compare the past and present or underline similarities and differences between then and now. Horror, especially, with its licence to tweak reality, allows us to make have that commentary, in a way that a straight historical drama might not be able to.

The film had its world premiere on the day that the Republic of Ireland voted to repeal the 8th Amendment, which constitutionally criminalized abortion in the country. Given the long-lingering mark of the Church-State's power in Ireland, it would be impossible to make a film about the recent past that didn't also have contemporary relevance. Indeed, even know, abortion is illegal in Northern Ireland—where I live—and proposed legislation drafted in the Republic after the referendum now looks like it will not bring about any realistic change. We are still very tied to and by the past here.

There's clearly a lot of love for *The Exorcist* here, and while a distinct reference point, it's more of a love letter than fan service. I'd be very keen to hear your thoughts on how *The Exorcist* 'fits' into your broader vision of *The Devil's Doorway* on this front?

I saw *The Exorcist* when I was 7. I watched it with my da, who let us watch all the horror films, but nothing with sex in it. I was terrified, but, then, I was a little Catholic girl in Ireland—all that stuff was very real and possible to me.

That said, *The Exorcist* wasn't a prime reference for me in making the film. Of course, it came up in conversation, but my mind was elsewhere. In terms of the challenges to faith, I was influenced by the questions raised in Charles Beaumont's *The Howling Man*—the power of ambiguity to undermine faith. Of course, the elements of possession are codified by the Catholic church, but I wanted to avoid the tropes of possession films as much as possible—no demon voice; using physical violence sparingly. I wanted the possession to be a side note. That's not what the film is about. The possession underlines the horror of the place—the girl may or may not warrant the treatment that she's given and, certainly, that's how the church saw women: partly possessed, partly in need of protection.

The Exorcist does show an optimistic view. Living in Ireland, I invariably end up making small-talk with a lot of priests at a lot of weddings. They love horror films and they love *The Exorcist*. It validates their worldview. However, I think *The Devil's Doorway* does to some extent too. In *The Exorcist*, Fr. Karras' faith is restored by his actions—the possession is reversed! In *The Devil's Doorway*, neither the possession nor priest wins out—the system that governs them both wins. That might seem pessimistic, but I think that, while no one's faith in God is restored in the film, they are still emboldened morally. Even without faith, in fact, in their darkest despair and hardest test, the priests make the courage leap. They fight for the right thing, even when everything within their faith system directs them to act otherwise. The kernel of their faith in a good God wins out over their "faith" as directed by the church. I think there is optimism too in the fact that it's a period piece—it may address contemporary issues, but the specifics are relegated to the past. Things can change, but it takes courage rather than faith.

There seems to be a real tension in the film that I really liked that was torn between this reverence to the iconography and iconology of Roman Catholicism and the ugly 'truth' that lies underneath. Was this a conscious strategy, and how does one approach the question of style and form in the context of the supposed 'realism' that found footage horror maintains as its central aesthetic and narrative conceit?

I reckon that Catholicism's longevity is down to its strong visual branding. The iconography is so strong and transmits it mixed messages so easily that it is readable and alluring, even for those without faith. If you based a research study on horror films alone, it would be easy to believe that Catholicism was the same cultural force it was 500 years ago and that all other beliefs are fringe cults. This is because it looks so good on film and everyone recognizes a Catholic priest, they recognize a Catholic nun, and they recognize the Blessed Virgin. They may not know the specifics of any part of the mass or of the sacraments, but they recognize that—within a horror film, at least—these are the good guys.

Certainly, as a girl growing up Catholic in Ireland, the aesthetic kept me devout much longer than the theology. I don't think there is any Catholic girl who doesn't dream of being a nun, who doesn't look longingly at the images of the BVM with an aspiration to be her. Given how poorly women are treated within Catholicism, the Virgin's power must be strong to keep so many women on side. It's like being in an abusive relationship: I know they treat other women badly,

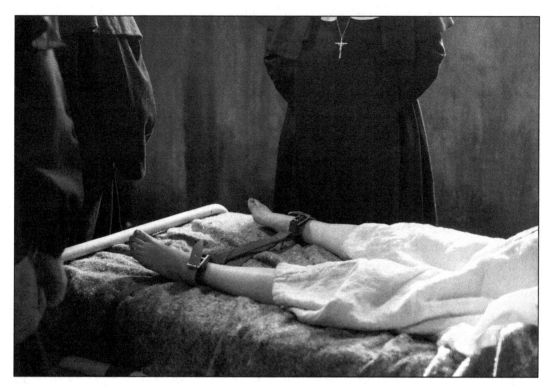

From *The Devil's Doorway*. Image by Joanne Mullin, used with permission from Aislinn Clark.

but, if they just treated me like they treated her, it would be worth it. Or to be a nun, a bride of Christ, to marry a man who really loves and will treat you well. When Kathleen, the possessed girl, says she "really love(s) the statues," she is serious—the statues are real, they're powerful, aspiration, they represent everything we want to, but cannot be, they are are conduit to the divine.

Thus, there isn't any real distinction between style and substance in Catholicism. The Catholic mindset is one of duality, both things are true at once—it is bread and body; he is fully god and man; she is both virgin and mother. A thing can be simultaneously surface and substance. Indeed, the surface counts, even while the observer is debased. Catholicism comes from the experienced, rather than the understood, and it is experienced through repetition and objects standing in place of abstracts.

John's long lingering shots of religious artefacts feels completely natural to me. That's what a Catholic film-maker would focus on. He focuses on the statue, hoping it will bleed, but he films all the other paraphernalia as well, hoping for the same thing. The Catholic search for truth is funneled through these objects, so the substance in the film he is making is found in the style of Catholic iconography.

A lot of the press the film has received really emphasises its status as the first feature-length horror film written and directed by a woman in Ireland, and I am curious about your thoughts on this. I'm also doubly interested in this as found footage horror is an area where I've found a surprising absence of

women filmmakers—there's Tara Anaïse's *Dark Mountain*, Amanda Gusack's *In Memorium* and a few others, but I've long been surprised how few women filmmakers have experimented with the form. I'm very curious to hear your thoughts on this labelling of "woman filmmaker" as opposed to just "filmmaker", particularly considering the intense focus on gender politics in *The Devil's Doorway*?

As a woman—and an Irishwoman at that—gender issues are hard for me to ignore, when emotional honesty is such an important part of why I do what I do. I am conscious of being perceived as a "woman filmmaker" and I am happy to be visible as a woman making films. As long as it is visible and not obstructive, I can see the value of that. It is certainly easy to feel ghettoised within the genre of "female stories." I am also an "Irish filmmaker," however I don't feel the adjective Irish prevents my work being judged objectively against the work of my peers, whereas I think the adjective female does—it seems to delineate who is allowed to be my peer.

As for the found-footage question, I don't think I have anything that I would say publicly, but I would be interested in carrying on that conversation, if it is something you've thought about. Anecdotally, my experience of other female directors is that many of them tend to be very diligent, realizing that they have to hold themselves to a higher standard to be taken seriously. They are on top of everything, have every detailed work out, and won't go until everything is in place. It is too big a risk to be otherwise—they're not granted the luxury of doing work that is roughly-hewn. By the same experiential measure, many male directors I meet feel much more entitled to attention, to respect, and are confident that their talent will be seen through whatever limitations they have. As found-footage is something that film-makers do at the beginning of their career, I imagine many female directors simply wouldn't risk their few opportunities on a form that has so many built-in imperfections and that is already a magnet for heavy-handed amateur critique. They'll take their chance on the script they've perfectly honed, with the shot list they've worked through carefully. Even then they'll be held to a ridiculous standard. Even in my case, the producers came to me wanting to make a found-footage film. It's not something I would planned to make myself, but the opportunity arose, I had a vision for it was interesting, and I had a moral obligation to make sure that a horror film about the laundries was intelligent and compassionate and not exploitative.

The film is unusual in the genre, I think, in being fully scripted—most are not. And my producers and co-writers didn't want a script at all, but there is no way that we could have created that world and those characters—almost 60 years ago—through improvisation alone. There was too much specific knowledge, too much priestly jargon. But the (male) producers would have been happy to hoof it, because they wouldn't have been under the scrutiny as I would have been as a female director.

CLARKE, MAE

Actor Mae Clarke was born Violet Mary Klotz in Philadelphia in 1910. She began her stage career in vaudeville as a child, and as a professional dancer she moved to New York. Moving to California, she appeared in a number of films for Universal Studios during the 1930s, famous in particular for her role as Dr Frankenstein's bride Elizabeth Lavenza in James Whale's classic 1931 horror film *Frankenstein*. The iconic image of Karloff's monster chasing her remains one of the most famous images from that decade's prolific horror output.

CLEMENS, ADELAIDE

Australian actor Adelaide Clemens was born in Brisbane in 1989 and began working on television in her teens. Making her debut performance in a small role as a carnival girl in *X-Men Origins: Wolverine* (Gavin Hood, 2009), her first major film role was in Ben C. Lucas's Australian rape-revenge film *Wasted on the Young* (2011). While career highlights would include a role as Catherine in Baz Luhrmann's 2013 screen adaptation of *The Great Gatsby*, Clemens' horror film credits include *Vampire* (Shunji Iwai, 2011), *No One Lives* (Ryuhei Kitamura, 2012), *Silent Hill: Revelation* (Michael J. Bassett, 2012) and *Rabbit* (Luke Shanahan, 2017).

CLOSE, GLENN·

With her Oscar-nominated performance as scorned lover Alex Forrest in Adrian Lyne's 1987 blockbuster *Fatal Attraction*, American actor Glenn Close redefined monstrous femininity for an entire generation, influencing contemporary cinema in a profound way. Born in Conneticut in 1947, she has worked on screen and stage and is a 6-time Oscar nominee. Amongst her many credits include the Jekyll and Hyde film *Mary Reilly* (Stephen Frears, 1996), *The Stepford Wives* (Frank Oz, 2004), and most recently she appeared in the zombie movie *The Girl with All the Gifts* (Colm McCarthy, 2016).

CLOVER, CAROL J.

Californian Professor Carol J. Clover may be an expert in Scandavian mythology and languages, but it is as one of the most famous feminist film theorists of the late 20th century that her legacy lies due to her coining the term "Final Girl" and her broader work on gender and horror cinema. Inspired by slasher films when her teenage son started bringing horror videos home, Clover's 1992 book *Men, Women, and Chainsaws: Gender in the Modern Horror Film* is one of the very few feminist academic film texts to find a broad mainstream audience, and her notion of the Final Girl has since become part of common pop cultural parlance. As used by Clover, the term refers to a woman protagonist who fights and survives, thus demonstrating the fluidity of gender identification in whom Clover assumes to be horror's predominantly male audience. While an interview subject in documentaries including *The American Nightmare* (Adam Simon, 2000) and *Science of Horror* (Katharina Klewinghaus, 2008), it is in J.T. Petty's 2006 mockumentary *S&Man* that Clover makes her most curious cameo, combining actual interview, documentary-style footage with fictional material framed within the movie's narrative as a snuff film.

CODY, DIABLO

Author, screenwriter and producer Brook Busey-Maurio—aka Diablo Cody—was born in Illinois in 1978. After her breakthrough memoir *Candy Girl: A Year in the Life of an Unlikely Stripper* (2005), she would write the Oscar award-winning script for the celebrated *Juno* (Jason Reitman, 2007). She wrote the screenplay for the much-hyped Karyn Kusama directed 2009 horror movie *Jennifer's Body* with Megan Fox and Amanda Seyfried, which—despite initial lackluster responses—has become a beloved cult feminist horror classic. Cody is also widely reported to have provided uncredited script doctoring work on Rodo Sayagues and Fede Álvarez's screenplay for Álvarez's 2013 *Evil Dead* remake.

Diablo Cody at The Orange British Academy Film Awards 2008 held at the Royal Opera House on 10 February 2008 in London, England. Credit: Entertainment Press / Shutterstock.com

COHEN, EMMA

Born in Barcelona in 1946, Spanish actor, writer and director Emma Cohen is said to have made an uncredited early appearance in the Christopher Lee and Klaus Kinski fronted Jess Franco horror film *Count Dracula* (1970), followed by roles in films including *The Cannibal Man* (Eloy de la Iglesia, 1972), *Horror Rises from the Tomb* (Carlos Aured, 1973), *Inside a Dark Mirror* (Jess Franco, 1973), *The Lady with Red Boots* (Juan Luis Buñuel,

1974), *Cross the Devil* (John Gilling, 1975), *Night of the Walking Dead* (León Klimovsky, 1975), and—later in her career—in Antonio Hernández's supernatural drama *The Hidden* (2005).

COLANGELO, BJ—INTERVIEW (AUGUST 2018)

Cleveland-based Brittney Jade Colangelo is a force of nature, both as a filmmaker, performer and film critic. In the latter capacity, she has written for *Birth.Movies.Death*, *Playboy*, *Blumhouse*, *Dread Central*, and her feminist horror blog, *Day of the Woman*. Although also working in comedy, Colangelo wrote, produced and directed the 2016 horror short *Margaret*.

She has produced and acted in a range of other horror films including *Benny and Steve Almost Die* (Dustin Mills, 2017), *Halloween Spookies* (Dustin Mills and Dave Parker, 2016) and the horror shorts *Snuffet* (Dustin Mills, 2014) and *Seven Minutes* (R. Zachary Shildwachter, 2015), the latter which she also co-wrote. At the time of our interview, Colangelo had completed her first feature film *Powerbomb*, again co-written and co-directed with Shildwachter.

https://www.patreon.com/dayofthewoman

There's an almost unspoken law in the universe that critics and filmmakers are two separate beasts, and outside a few very famous cases, never the twain shall meet. I love that you have single-handedly proven this wrong, excelling in both fields. Can you tell me a little about your experiences and background in both fields—performance and critical writing? Which came first?

I've been performing since I was a little girl. Whether it be on stage in a musical, delivering a public speech in a pageant, or as a competitive baton twirler, I've never not been performing. Performance was always an extension of self, and it wasn't until college that I started really diving into *why* there was such a personal impact from performing or watching the performances of others. Performing is my way of expression, but writing has always been my therapeutic medium. Sometime in my late teens, after I was armed with the confidence of every college freshman after taking Creative Writing 101, academic analysis of film and other styles of performance art became a passion of mine. Hyper-analyzing film and television helped me gain a better understanding of the world around me, and why artists choose to put on screen what they do.

Filmmaking was always something I was interested in, but something I had always believed was a 'man's field.' That makes me sound like a 'bad feminist,' but enlightenment and education is a huge part of growth. It honestly wasn't until I was about 18 or so that I realized how many films I adored were directed by women, and how little respect they were given. Realizing the existence of that

BJ Colangelo. Photo Credit: Yoshi Andrego. Used with permission.

disproportion bothered me on an incredibly visceral level, and it then became a challenge I wanted to dominate.

My critical writing background heavily influences the scripts that I write and the way that I plan to shoot a film, and my background in performance largely dictates my style as a director.

Do you think being a filmmaker and actor yourself makes you a stronger critic or provides you with insight other critics may not have?

All of our personal experiences dictate how a film will affect us, and I like to think that my background in film and musical theater offers a different perspective. When critiquing another actor's performance, I like to put myself in their shoes. What would it be like to handle this material? What would it be like to act opposite of the other players? Analyzing the performance from an actor's standpoint potentially offers a better understanding of the process.

In the same way, my experience as a filmmaker directly influences how I critique film as a whole, particularly independent films with lower budgets. A great example of this was watching Jeremy Gardener's *The Battery*. The film was shot for 6,000$, less than what some big budget films would spend on craft services. There›s an appreciation of the brilliance of that film that is difficult to capture unless you have also tried to make a film on a shoe-string budget. Sure, plenty of critics love that movie (because it›s truly exceptional), but there›s another level of inspiration that the film offers to someone that has endured that struggle.

You do so much: acting, directing, producing, writing. How do you juggle these identities on a film project? Are they separate, or do they more organically bleed into each other?

I like to think that I'm good at compartmentalizing, but the truth is that I'm an adult-goth Tracy Flick from *Election*. I'm an obsessive over-achiever, a multi-tasker, and borderline anal retentive when it comes to organizing film projects. I'm always wearing every hat at once, but I hope that I'm good at realizing when the time and place is for one hat to be on the front line. If anything, the acting aspect is usually at the forefront because directing and producing require me to 'act' a certain way in a given circumstance. Writing is personal, and it's the one time I'm not acting.

I first became aware of you and your work at a time when you were recovering from serious illness and I was so rocked by how openly and frankly you spoke about it on social media. Later, I discovered in your critical writing that you were similarly honest and unflinching about other experiences in your life and how that related to your understanding of and engagement with cinema—I think your piece on surviving sexual assault and Abel Ferrara's *Ms. 45* is one of my all-time favourite pieces of film writing. How do you conceive of this

relationship between private and public in both your critical writing and as an artist more generally?

I started writing publicly when I was only 18 years old, so my development as a writer and analyst is public record for the world to see. My writing career also began as Facebook began to gain popularity, so I'm from a generation of selfie-takers and oversharers. Because of this, it's difficult to remember a time when I wasn't a 'public figure.' I've had people recognize me at conventions and talk to me about my work, because unlike many writers during that time, I wasn't writing under a pseudonym and my 'author's picture' was the same as my Facebook profile picture.

Being in the public eye at such a crucial time of my development from teenager to adult was really difficult. I was hit with trolls and online harassment every day, and I sought therapy to help deal with it. There were plenty of times when I wanted to give up and quit, but I didn't want terrible people to feel any sense of victory by quitting. After a few years, my therapist and I discussed being more open about my experiences. We agreed that I was in a great place on my path to healing from previous traumas and felt that it might be therapeutic to be honest about my life. If I was going to write about what made a film 'tick,' it was only logical to offer background as to where my perspectives and insights were formed.

There are obviously things that I do not share (I've never publicly named my rapist, for example), but for the most part, I will talk openly about pretty much everything. My sexuality, my personal relationships, my traumas, the deaths of people close to me, my geographical changes, my changes in appearance, my kinks, my political opinions, and my core values are all available for public consumption.

Most of my life was already part of the public eye, and when you offer your opinions and criticisms publicly, you as a person are also putting yourself out there for scrutiny.

I'd rather be the one in control of telling my story or framing the narrative about who I am and what I stand for.

While your filmmaking work—like your criticism—obviously privileges horror, but there's also a strong flair for the comedy in there, too. How do you conceive the relationship between these two genres both creatively and critically?

Comedy and horror are similarly linked in that enjoyment and fear are universal emotions, but what makes us laugh and what scares us are not universal. These emotions are elicited by different elements, and it's fascinating to try and figure out what combination of those elements works the best. Like horror, comedy is a genre that has never died in its popularity, and part of my obsession with comedy comes from it existing on the other side of the horror pendulum. I want to know what scares people, but I also want to know what makes people laugh. It's like determining aftercare in a BDSM relationship

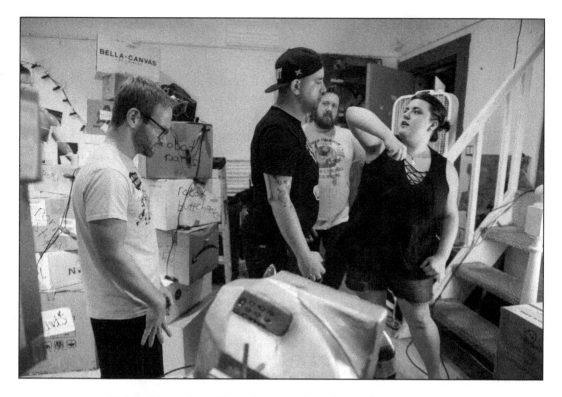

BJ Colangelo on the set. Photo Credit: Andy Dudik. Used with permission.

I know that I don't need to tell you that horror has for far too long been an assumed boys club , when so many women know even just as fans this is far from the truth. What's your story with the genre, and why do you think it holds a particular appeal to women creatives, critics and audiences?

Horror was always the bonding tissue between my mother and I. She loves horror but my father (though he'll never admit it) gets really scared when watching the films. As a child, she realized quickly that I could hang with even the scariest of the spookies, so I have a very sentimental attachment to the genre. As far as why women are interested in horror, I think it's because it offers us a safe outlet for the negative emotions that surround us 24/7.

As an assault survivor, I can speak from firsthand experience that being a woman is scary as hell. I don't know if I can trust someone I'm walking past on the street. I don't know if I'm going to be killed for rejecting a stranger's advances. There's a lot of fear directly related to simply existing while a woman. Horror allows us to process those fears and experience a cathartic release from those fears without actually being in any imminent danger.

I'd argue that it's similar to why women are so fascinated with true crime. We're often the victims of these serial killer stories, and our obsession allows an ease in our anxiety from the real world.

Pop quiz!

> **o Best film directed by a woman?**

Lizzie Borden's *Working Girls* (1986)

> **o Best performance by a woman in a horror film?**

Toni Collette in *Hereditary* changed my damn life. I'm going to be David Lynch and Laura Dern levels of obsessed with her until the day I die.

> **o Best horror film for collapsing assumed heteronormative gender binaries?**

The Hunger. Give me David Bowie and androgynous bisexual Susan Sarandon or give me death.

> **o If there was a remake on the cards, what horror film would be on your ultimate wish list as an actor, writer and/or director?**

I want to do a retelling of *Carrie* from the perspective of Margaret White more than I've ever wanted anything else in the world.

One last question: if you could issue one demand to horror filmmakers around the world, what cliché or bad habit would you beg them to avoid?

Please stop insulting your characters' intelligences by acting as if horror movies don't already exist. The teens who use smartphones know what a zombie is. The girl shopping at the mall knows a vampire doesn't have a reflection. The babysitter being chased by a masked killer is not going to run up the stairs. Let your characters use their brains.

COLLETTE, TONI

Born in Sydney in 1972 and studying at Australia's National Institute of Dramatic Art, Toni Collette showed an ability to flex performative muscle with darker themes in movies like the cult 1998 Australian film *The Boys* (1998), based on the brutal real-life murder of Australian nurse Anita Cobby. In her Oscar-nominated international breakthrough role as Lynn in M. Night Shyamalan's horror movie *The Sixth Sense* (1999), Collette forged the formal beginnings of her relationship with the genre, consolidated in later years with films including *Like Minds* (Gregory J. Read, 2006), *Fright Night* (Craig Gillespie, 2011) and *Krampus* (Michael Dougherty, 2015). Most recently Collette's strengths as a horror actor excelled in Ari Aster's blockbuster 2018 film *Hereditary*, whose impact relies heavily upon Collette's convincing portrayal of her deeply traumatized character, Annie. In 2019, Collette starred alongside Jake Gyllenhaal and Rene Russo in Dan Gilroy's artworld horror film *Velvet Buzzsaw*.

COLLINS, JOAN ∙

Even at her peak of excessive monstrous femininity in the epoch-defining '80s soap opera *Dynasty* as Alexis Colby, British actor Dame Joan Collins rarely disguised her passion to play outrageous, over-the-top women. Born in 1933 in London, she studied at the Royal Academy of Dramatic Art and while her career began in earnest in the early 1950s, it was during the 1970s in particular that she flourished as a horror actor. Films from this era include *Revenge* (Sidney Hayers, 1971), *Fear in the Night* (Jimmy Sangster, 1972), *Dark Places* (Don Sharp, 1973), *I Don't Want to Be Born* (Peter Sasdy, 1975), and two Freddie Francis horror anthologies, *Tales from the Crypt* (1972) and *Tales that Witness Madness* (1973). More recently, Collins has joined the cast of the television series *American Horror Story*.

Toni Collette at the Los Angeles premiere of her movie *Krampus* at the Arclight Theatre, Hollywood, Los Angeles, California, 30 November 2015. Credit: Featureflash Photo Agency / Shutterstock.com

Joan Collins walks the runway for Stephane Rolland at the Heart Truth's Red Dress Collection for Fall 2010 during Mercedes-Benz Fashion Week on 11 February 2010 in New York. Credit: lev radin / Shutterstock.com

The Collinson twins in *Twins of Evil* (John Hough, 1971). Credit: © Universal Pictures/ Photofest

COLLINSON, MADELINE AND MARY

Famous for being the first identical twin Playboy Playmates of the Month in 1970, Madeline and Mary Collinson were born in Malta in 1952. They may have had a limited film career, but it peaked spectacularly with their performance as the title sisters in Hammer's classic *Twins of Evil* (John Hough, 1971)—the third in Hammer's Karnstein Trilogy—in which they appeared alongside Peter Cushing.

COLUCCI, FLORENCIA

Uruguayan actor and filmmaker Florencia Colucci was born in Montevideo in 1986 and won a number of national film awards for her debut role as Laura, the lead character in Gustavo Hernández's shocking horror film *The Silent House* (2010). She has continued to work as an actor in Uruguayan film and television.

COMER, ANJANETTE

Texan actor Anjanette Comer worked primarily on television from the early 1960s, first showing her flair for gothic-themed material in the funeral home black comedy *The Loved One* (Tony Richardson, 1965) as Aimee Thanatogenous. In the 1970s, she was cast in a number of cult horror films, including René Cardona Jr.'s *Night of a Thousand Cats* (1972) and *The Baby* (Ted Post, 1973), and Dan Curtis's television horror anthology *Dead of Night* in 1977. In 1992, she also appeared in David Schmoeller's demonic cult horror movie *Netherworld*.

COMMENGE, ÈVE

Belgian-based French ex-pat Ève Commenge is a producer who has worked extensively with experimental genre filmmakers Hélène Cattet and Bruno Forzani, renowned for their many feature films and shorts that explore the experimental potential of Italian *giallo* cinema such as *Amer* (2009) and *The Strange Color of Your Body's Tears* (2013). Commenge studied at Université Paul Valéry in Montpellier, meeting Cattet and Forzani in 2005 and beginning their lengthy collaboration. Her work with the pair also includes the shorts *Santos Palace* (2006), and their most recent feature, *Let the Corpses Tan* (2017).

CONNELLY, JENNIFER ·

Beginning her career modeling and a brief star turn as a child pop star in Japan, New York-born Jennifer Connelly studied at both Yale and Stanford Universities while establishing her career as a major contemporary film star. Making her screen debut in Sergio Leone's *Once Upon a Time in America* (1984), her second screen credit saw her again collaborating with a master of Italian cinema in Dario Argento's *Phenomena* (1985), starring as an American student at a Swiss private school who possesses a supernatural connection with insects. With her status as a movie star set into motion with her appearance in Jim Henson's *Labyrinth* (1986) alongside David Bowie, it was in the dark fantasy *Etoile* (Peter Del Monte, 1989) that Connelley's role as an American ballet student at an elite European dance academy recalled the premise of Argento's *Suspiria* (1977), while concretely foreshadowing Darren Aronofsky's *Black Swan* (2010). Her blossoming career continued to feature dark-themed films such as *Dark City* (Alex Proyas, 1998) and *Requiem for a Dream* (Darren Aronofsky, 2000), with Connelly moving back to more overt horror territory with her starring role in Walter Salles' 2005 film *Dark Water*, a remake of Hideo Nakata's 2002 J-horror of the same name.

COOK, PENNY

Actor Penny Cook became a household name in Australia during the 1980s for her role as Vicki the vet in the popular soap opera *A Country Practice*. Graduating from the National Institute of Dramatic Arts, she developed a strong career on stage and screen as an actor and later as a host for the popular magazine travel series, *The Great Outdoors*. Less known, however, is Cook's brief career as one of the country's more interesting horror actors appearing in Craig Lahiff's slasher film *Coda* (1987) and, the following year, in Mario Andreacchio's haunting and politically-charged colonialist critique horror film *The Dreaming*.

COOKE, OLIVIA

Born in Manchester in 1993, British actor Olivia Cooke began her acting career on UK television before becoming familiar to international viewers as one of the primary cast members in the A&E cable series *Bates Motel*, a teen-centred prequel to Alfred Hitchcock's 1960 film *Psycho*. On the back of her association with the genre, in 2014 Cooke starred in two horror films; as the possessed Jane Harper in John Pogue's *The Quiet Ones*, and as Laine Morris, the main character in Stiles White's board-game inspired *Ouija*. In 2016, Cooke starred in Juan Carlos Medina's gothic horror film *The Limehouse Golem*, scripted by Jane Goldman and based on Peter Ackroyd's 1994 novel *Dan Leno and the Limehouse Golem*. In 2017, she co-starred with Anya Taylor-Joy in Cory Finley's teenage psychopath film *Thoroughbreds*.

COOTE, SUZANNE

Filmmaker Suzanne Coote is an American writer, director and producer who in 2018 released the taut home invasion horror film *The Open House* which she co-directed with actor Matt Angel. Driven by a passion for filmmaking since she was a child, she cites Austrian auteur Michael Haneke as a major influence on her work.

CORBETT, GRETCHEN

Gretchen Corbett is an American actor who has worked across film and television since the late 1960s. Born in Oregon in 1945, she studied at Carnegie Tech in Pittsburgh and her fame rests largely on her 4-year role playing Beth Davenport on the popular 1970s television series *The Rockford Files*. Corbett can also claim cult film fame for her performance in John Hancock's 1971 classic *Let's Scare Jessica to Death*, and in 1981 she also starred in Bob Claver's horror film *Jaws of Satan*.

CORMAN, JULIE

Wife of legendary producer and director Roger Corman, Julie Corman is a formidable film producer in her own right and has worked closely with Corman since their marriage in 1970, beginning with Martin Scorsese's *Boxcar Bertha* in 1972. Forming New Horizons with Roger in 1983 after they sold New World Productions in 1982, Julie additionally formed Trinity films in 1984 to produce family movies. Her horror credits alone include *Saturday the 14th* (Howard R. Cohen, 1981), *Chopping Mall* (Jim Wynorski, 1986), *The Nest* (Terence H. Winkless, 1988), *Saturday the 14th Strikes Back* (Howard R. Cohen, 1988), *Brain Dead* (Adam Simon, 1990), *Sorority House Massacre II* (Jim Wynorski, 1990), *Dinoshark* (Kevin O'Neill, 2010), *Sharktopus* (Declan O'Brien, 2010), *Sharktopus vs. Pteracuda* (Kevin O'Neill, 2014) and *Sharktopus vs. Whalewolf* (Kevin O'Neill, 2015). Julie Corman won the Producer of the Year award from the Academy of Film and Television in 1996 and has been a visiting professor at a number of universities including Penn, Yale, UCLA and Duke.

CORRI, ADRIENNE

Putting in an unforgettable performance in the notorious rape scene in Stanley Kubrick's *A Clockwork Orange* (1971), Scottish-Italian actor Adrienne Corri was born Adrienne Riccoboni in 1930 in Glasgow. worked with an impressive range of directors on less controversial films including Jean Renoir, David Lean and Otto Preminger, and her horror work includes Ernest Morris's *Corridors of Blood* (Robert Day, 1958), *The Tell-Tale Heart* (1960), *The Anatomist* (Dennis Vance, 1961) and *Vampire Circus* (Robert Young, 1971), with another career highlight in Jim Clark's 1974 film *Madhouse* with Vincent Price and Peter Cushing.

CORSAUT, ANETA

Aneta Corsaut was born in Kansas in 1933 and studied at Northwestern University before moving to California and continuing her studies at UCLA. Famed for her work across film and television, she began her acting career in the mid-1950s, working for 40 years until her death in the mid-90s. Corsaut had a number of horror credits including *The Blob* (Irvin Yeaworth, 1958), *Bad Ronald* (Buzz Kulik, 1974), and *The Toolbox Murders* (Dennis Donnelly, 1978).

COURT, HAZEL

British actor Hazel Court was a familiar face in mid-20th century horror, learning the trade at J. Arthur Rank's The Company of Youth acting school (the media moguls attempt to build a stable of young talent to equal that of Hollywood). Court's many horror credits include *Ghost Ship* (Vernon Sewell, 1952), *The Curse of Frankenstein* (Terence Fischer, 1957), *The Man Who Could Cheat Death* (Terence Fisher, 1959), *Doctor Blood's Coffin* (Sidney J. Furie, 1961) and a number of the Roger Corman-directed Poe Cycle films including *The Premature Burial* (1962), *The Raven* (1963) and *The Masque of the Red Death* (1964). In 1981 she made her final horror film appearance in Graham Baker's *Omen III: The Final Conflict*. Court also acted in episodes of a number of popular horror television series such as *Alfred Hitchcock Presents*, *The Invisible Man* and *Thriller*.

COX, COURTENEY ⸰

With her fame resting primarily on her long-running association with sitcoms including *Family Ties* and *Friends*, Courteney Cox was one of the central actors of Wes Craven's hugely successful *Scream* franchise and appeared in all 4 films: *Scream* (1996), *Scream 2* (1997), *Scream 3* (2000) and *Scream 4* (2011). In 2006, she also produced the slasher film *The Tripper*, directed by then-husband David Arquette

CRAIG, SARAH

Make-up artist Sarah Craig is based in Toronto and has worked in film and television for almost 15 years. Her horror film credits include *Dawn of the Dead* (Zack Snyder, 2004), *Silent Hill* (Christophe Gans, 2006) and Andy Muschietti's 2017 remake of Stephen King's 1986 novel *It*. In the latter she revamped Tim Curry's iconic evil clown make-up from Tommy Lee Wallace's 1990 television miniseries of the same name for Pennywise actor Bill Skarsgård, introducing the character to whole new generation.

CRAMPTON, BARBARA

One of the shining lights of North American horror since the 1980s, American actor Barbara Crampton was born in New York in 1958. After beginning her career in soap operas, she arrived with a splash with the cult film double whammy of Brian De Palma's *Body Double* (1984) and Stuart Gordon's *Re-Animator* (1985). Crampton's many credits include films such as *Chopping Mall* (Jim Wynorski, 1986), *From Beyond* (Stuart Gordon, 1987), *Puppet Master* (David Schmoeller, 1989), *Castle Freak* (Stuart Gordon, 1995), *The Sisterhood* (David DeCoteau, 2004), *You're Next* (Adam Wingard, 2011), *The Lords of Salem* (Rob Zombie, 2012), *We Are Still Here* (Ted Geoghegan, 2015), *Beyond the Gates* (Jackson Stewart, 2016), *Death House* (Gunnar Hansen, 2017), *Puppet Master: The Littlest Reich* (Sonny Laguna and Tommy Wiklund, 2018), *Culture Shock* (Gigi Saul Guerrero, 2019) and and the gothic black comedy *Little Sister* (Zach Clark, 2016). Amongst many other roles, in 2015 she also featured in Axelle Carolyn's segment "Grim Grinning Ghosts" in the horror anthology *Tales of Halloween*.

CRAWFORD, JOAN ⟨

Born in Texas as Lucille Fay LeSueur in the mid 1900s (the exact date is a subject of debate), Joan Crawford is one of the most famous faces of Classical Hollywood cinema. With a career spanning almost half a century, she worked in silent cinema through the pre-code period to the peak of the golden age through to television. She starred alongside Lon Chaney in Tod Browning's 1927 silent horror movie *The Unknown*, and while working in film noir and other dark-themed movies during the peak of her career, it was with her later-career renaissance with *What Ever Happened to Baby Jane?* (Robert Aldrich, 1962) that she returned to horror with force in her final years on screen. This saw her play memora-

The Unknown (Tod Browning, 1927), with Joan Crawford. Credit: Everett Collection Inc / Alamy Stock Photo)

ble central roles in movies such as *Strait-Jacket* (William Castle, 1964), *I Saw What You Did* (William Castle, 1965), *Berserk!* (Jim O'Connolly, 1967), and *Trog* (Freddie Francis, 1970). Crawford's broader notoriety as an abusive, sadistic mother stems from the 1978 memoir *Mommie Dearest* (written by her adopted daughter Christina), and in 2017 the television series *Feud* focused on her complex relationship with *Baby Jane* co-star Bette Davis, with Jessica Lange and Susan Sarandon in their respective roles.

CRAVEN, VERONICA

Veronica Craven is a graphic artist, writer, director, editor, producer and SFX make-up artist who has worked on music videos, television, short films, and features. Amongst her many credits, she produced and wrote her sole feature length credit as director, the horror movie *Pocahauntus* (2006), starring Eliza Swenson and Stephanie Basco.

CRONENBERG, DENISE

Canadian costume designer Denise Cronenberg is the sister of cult filmmaker David Cronenberg and mother of director Aaron Woodley. She has collaborated with her brother on numerous films including *The Fly* (1986), *Dead Ringers* (1988), *Naked Lunch* (1991), *Crash* (1996), *eXistenZ* (1999), *Spider* (2002) and *A History of Violence* (2005), and horror movies such as *The Guardian* (William Friedkin, 1990), *Bless the Child* (Chuck Russell, 2000), *Dracula 2000* (Patrick Lussier, 2000), *Dawn of the Dead* (Zack Snyder, 2004), and *Resident Evil: Afterlife* (Paul W. S. Anderson, 2010). Cronenberg also designed the costumes for the 2008 opera version of *The Fly*, based on her brother's 1986 film of the same name, composed by Howard Shore who wrote the score for the original movie.

CROSBY, DENISE

While linked most famously to scifi for her role on *Star Trek: The Next Generation*, Hollywood-born Denise Crosby has starred in an impressive number of horror films. Granddaughter of Classical Hollywood screen idol Bing Crosby, she began her career modeling for *Playboy* magazine and acting in soap operas and other television shows. In 1989, she appeared in Mary Lambert's *Pet Sematary* (based on Stephen King's 1986 novel of the same name) and starred in Maria Lease's 1991 cult horror film *Dolly Dearest*. Her other horror credits include *Relative Fear* in 1994 by *My Bloody Valentine* (1981) director George Mihalka, *Mutant Species* (David A. Prior, 1994), *Mortuary* (Tobe Hooper, 2005), *Born* (Richard Friedman, 2007) and *The Watcher* (Ryan Rothmaier, 2016).

CROWLEY, SUZAN

Suzan Crowley is a British-born actor who worked in film and television since the late 1970s. Amongst her credits are the horror films *Born of Fire* (Jamil Dehlavi, 1987), *The Devil Inside* (William Brent Bell, 2012), *The Den* (Zachary Donohue, 2013) and Elizabeth E. Schuch's extraordinary *The Book of Birdie* (2017). Crowley also appered in the horror television series *Escape the Night*.

CRUELL, L.C.

American screenwriter, director and author Lucy Cruell is a prolific creator with an affinity for the scifi/horror genre. Cruell graduated with honors from both Duke University and Harvard Law School, and aside from working as an attorney, freelance writer/editor, film critic and entrepreneur, she has also published over 20 short stories. Her screenplays, pilots, and films have won over 3 dozen awards for competitions, festivals, and fellowships, including a National Endowment of the Arts Selection, a NATPE fellowship, and one of the first AMC/Shudder Labs Fellowships. Cruell's films include shorts like *I Need You* (2016) and *Flesh* (2017), features such as the anthology *Cemetery Tales: Tales from Morningview Cemetery* (2017), and web series such as the critically acclaimed *31*. Current feature projects include *Crimson*, *Last Call for Angels*, and *7 Magpies*, the first all African-American woman written and directed anthology.

CULPEPPER, HANELLE

Hanelle Culpepper has had a hugely impressive career as a director and writer, working primarily in television and running her production company Hillview 798 Productions. Hailing from Alabama, amongst her many achievements she is the first Black woman to ever direct an episode of *Star Trek*, and has received a nomination for a directing award from the National Association for the Advancement of Colored People (NAACP). In 2009 she directed the supernatural horror feature *Within*, and she has also directed episodes of the horror-themed television series *Sleepy Hollow* and *American Gothic*.

CUMMINGS, AUDREY

Canadian filmmaker Audrey Cummings is a graduate of the Canadian Film Centre's Directors' Lab and has won a number of awards including the WIT Kodak New Vision Fellowship Award for Best Emerging Canadian Female Director and the Barry Avrich Award at the Toronto Film Festival. She has directed a number of scifi, fantasy, and horror shorts, and the feature-length horror films *Tormented* (2014), *Berkshire County* (2014) and *Darken* (2017).

CUNTAPAY, LILIA

Making her debut acting performance in the third film of the popular Filipino horror franchise *Shake Rattle and Roll* in 1991, Lilia Cuntapay's dedication to the genre has earned the reputation as the oft-cited "Queen of Philippine Horror Movies". Cuntapay was born in 1935 and moved from an early career as a school teacher to a number of jobs, eventually starting her film career as an actor. Often typecast as the folkloric Aswang figure (an evil, shape-shifting Filipino spirit), she appeared in the title role of Peque Gallaga and Lore Reyes's 1992 film of the same name, as well as *Shake Rattle & Roll IV* (1992), *Shake Rattle & Roll V* (1994), and other horror movies such as *Anak ng dilim* (Nick Lizaso, 1997), *Dugo ng birhen: El kapitan* (Rico Maria Ilarde, 1999) , *Demons* (Mario O'Hara, 2000), *Bahay ni Lola 2* (Joven Tan, 2005), *Island of the Living Dead* (Vincent Dawn, 2007), *Scaregivers* (Uro Q. dela Cruz, 2008), *Segunda mano* (Joyce Bernal, 2011) and *Kamandag ni Venus* (Dyzal M. Damun, 2014). Cuntapay's career is explored in Antoinette Jadaone's essential, award-winning 2011 mockumentary *Six Degrees of Separation from Lilia Cuntapay.*

CURTIS, JAMIE LEE *

Jamie Lee Curtis is horror royalty, and with her mother Janet Leigh's starring role in Alfred Hitchcock's proto-slasher *Psycho* (1960), it may be in her blood. Born in 1958, her first film is one of the most important horror films ever made; John Carpenter's *Halloween* (1978), leading to her being cast in a number of sequels including *Halloween II* (Rick Rosenthal, 1981), a small voice cameo in *Halloween III: Season of the Witch* (Tommy Lee Wallace, 1982), *Halloween H20: 20 Years Later* (Steve Miner, 1998), and *Halloween: Resurrection* (Rick Rosenthal, 2002). Curtis's other horror credits are equally impressive, including *The Fog* (John Carpenter, 1980), *Prom Night* (Paul Lynch, 1980), *Terror Train* (Roger Spottieswood, 1980), *Roadgames* (Richard Franklin, 1981) and *Virus* (John Bruno, 1999). Curtis played Cathy Munsch in the television series *Scream Queens,* and in 2018 reprised her role as Laurie Stroud for David Gordon Green's *Halloween* reboot.

Jamie Lee Curtis and Michael Myers costumed guest at the sCare Foundation Benefit at Conga Room— LA Live on 30 October 2011 in Los Angeles, California. Credit: Kathy Hutchins / Shutterstock.com

CUTHBERT, ELISHA ҙ

Elisha Cuthbert was born in Canada in 1982 and began her career on the kids horror television series *Are You Afraid of the Dark?* in the late 1990s. Moving to Los Angeles in her late teens to further her career, across her many successful film and television roles are a number of horror film credits such as *Believe* (Robert Tinnell, 1999), *House of Wax* (Jaume Collet-Serra, 2005) and *Captivity* (Roland Joffé, 2007).

CUTLER, MIRIAM

While today working almost solely on documentary films, Emmy-nominated composer Miriam Cutler worked on many horror films earlier in her career. These primarily involved the *Witchcraft* series, with Cutler's music appearing on *Witchcraft II: The Temptress* (Mark Woods, 1989), *Witchcraft III: The Kiss of Death* (Rachel Feldman, 1991), *Witchcraft IV: The Virgin Heart* (James Merendino, 1992), *Witchcraft V: Dance with the Devil* (Talun Hsu, 1993), *Witchcraft VI: The Devil's Mistress* (Julie Davis, 1994), *Witchcraft 7: Judgement Hour* (Michael Paul Girard, 1995) and *Witchcraft 8: Salem's Ghost* (Joseph John Barmettler, 1996). Her other horror credits include *Silent Scream* (James Chean, 1999) and *Body Parts* (Michael Paul Girard, 1992). Cutler was a co-founder of the Alliance of Women Film Composers.

CYRAN, CATHERINE

Harvard graduate Catherine Cyran moved to London after her studies to be a management consultant at the Royal Shakespeare Company, before relocating to Los Angeles and dedicating her life to making movies. Beginning her film career by producing and writing for Roger Corman, she later turned to directing. In 1995, she directed the medical horror film *Sawbones*, and she wrote and produced *Slumber Party Massacre III* (Sally Mattison, 1990).

D'ATRI, ELENA

Italian filmmaker Elena D'Atri began experimenting with filmmaking as a teen and spent time in her youth also working in theater and with painting. As a writer, director, editor, and actor, after the 2006 short film *Tatuaggio Reale* she made her feature debut, the horror movie *Il Mistero di Villa De Mahl*. Her later films include the gothic-themed *08:27* (2008), *Mortis Scelerum: The Reaper's Sin* (2009), *Interferenza* (2009), *Il Quadro: The Painting* (2012) and *Parole Nel Buio* (2014).

DABROWSKY, URSULA

Canadian filmmaker Ursula Dabrowsky has been living in the Australian city of Adelaide since the 1990s and has released two impressive feature-length horror films that she both wrote and directed, *Family Demons* (2009) and its follow-up, *Inner Demon* (2014). *Family Demons* was a self-funded project receiving international festival acclaim and consequent distribution. Funded by the South Australian Film Corporation's FilmLab project, *Inner Demon* likewise found an international audience on the genre festival circuit, with its rendering of the Final Girl trope in a uniquely Australian context appealing to audiences internationally.

DADE, FRANCES

Born in 1910 in Philadelphia, American actor Frances Dade was handpicked by powerful film executive Samuel Goldwyn for a contract, her career peaking in 1931 when she starred in Tod Browning's *Dracula* as Lucy alongside Béla Lugosi. Appearing on stage as well as screen, *Dracula* was her most famous role, and she retired from film acting a few years later after struggling to convert that performance into a more enduring career.

DAGOVER, LIL

Marie Antonia Siegelinde Martha Seubert—known simply as Lil Dagover—was born in Indonesia's Java (then the Dutch East Indies) and would become one of the great superstars of the German screen in a career that spanned almost 70 years. She flourished during the Weimar Republic—a period of great experimentation for artists, in particular—and Dagover would star during this period in one of the most famous European horror films ever made, Robert Wiene's masterpiece of German Expressionism *The Cabinet of Dr. Caligari* (1920). Working well into the 1970s, Dagover would often return to gothic and dark-themed material, such as *Madame Bluebeard* (Conrad Weine, 1931) and the mad doctor film, *Chased by the Devil* (Viktor Tourjasky, 1950).

DALE, HOLLY

Over more than 40 years, Canadian filmmaker Holly Dale has produced an astonishing body of work as a director, spanning feature films, television series, commercials, and documentaries. Across her prolific filmography are episodes of *The X-Files, The Dead Zone, Dexter* and *Mary Kills People*. In 1995, she directed the feature film *Blood and Donuts*, a vampire comedy that includes a cameo by fellow Canadian filmmaker David Cronenberg.

DALLE, BÉATRICE

French actor Béatrice Dalle was one of the most famous cult film stars of the 1980s due to her debut film role as the title character in Jean-Jacques Beineix's *Betty Blue* (1986). Across her career, she has worked with directors such as Jim Jarmusch, Abel Ferrara, Olivier Assayas and Michael Haneke. Her horror credits include Marco Bellocchio's *The Witches' Sabbath* (1988), *The Dark Woods* (Jacques Deray, 1989), *To the Limit* (Eduardo Campoy, 1997) and *You and the Night* (Yann Gonzalez, 2013), and she has collaborated on numerous horror films with Julien Maury and Alexandre Bustillo including *Inside* (2007), *Livid* (2011), *Among the Living* (2014) and their segment 'X is for Xylophone' from the 2014 horror anthology *ABCs of Death* 2. In 2001, however—in the second of her three collaborations with director Claire Denis—Dalle starred as feral cannibal Coré in

French actress Beatrice Dalle attends the screening of the film The Ladykillers at the Palais during the 57th Cannes Festival May 18, 2004 in Cannes, France. Credit: Denis Makarenko / Shutterstock.com

Trouble Every Day in one of contemporary horror's most unrestrained and unforgettable performances.

DALY, JOANN

Joann Daly was an artist famed for her cult horror film posters of the 1980s and '90s. Her many credits include *Creepshow* (George A. Romero, 1982), *Scanners* (David Cronenberg, 1981), *The Initiation* (Larry Stewart, 1984), *Killer Party* (William Fruet, 1986), *Prison* (Renny Harlin, 1987) and *The Video Dead* (Robert Scott, 1987). Daly also illustrated book covers, record covers and trading cards.

DALY, SARAH

The co-founder of Scottish horror outfit Hex Studios, Irish screenwriter Sarah Daly has collaborated with director Lawrie Brewster on some of the most original horror films seen in recent years such as *Lord of Tears* (2013), *The Unkindness of Ravens* (2016), *The Black Gloves* (2017) and 2019's *Automata* (also released as *The Devil's Machine*). With influences including M.R. James, Daphne Du Maurier and C.S. Lewis, Daly studied Media Arts at Dublin Institute of Technology which revealed her passion for scriptwriting. She moved to Scotland in 2010, where she established boutique horror production company Hex Media (later Hex Studios) with Brewster. Her other horror feature film credits include *Insatiable* (Jessie Kirby, 2008) and *Kids vs Monsters* (Sultan Saeed Al Darmaki, 2015).

DANNING, SYBIL ʼ

Austrian-born actor, model and producer Sybil Danning was a major figure in 1980s cult film, beginning her screen career in Europe with films like Emilio P. Miraglia's 1972 *giallo The Red Queen Kills Seven Times*. Moving to the United States in the late 1970s, later horror credits include *Nightkill* (Ted Post, 1980), *Julie Darling* (Paul Nicholas, 1983), *Howling II: Your Sister Is a Werewolf* (Philippe Mora, 1985), *The Tomb* (Fred Olen Ray, 1986), *Halloween* (Rob Zombie, 2007) and *Virus X* (Ryan Stevens Harris, 2010).

DAVIES, DONNA

Donna Davies is a Canadian director, writer, and producer who has worked across fictional and documentary filmmaking. She studied journalism at Nova Scotia's King's College, and amongst her documentary work is the 2005 television series *Shadow Hunter*, a 13-part series about the paranormal and popular culture that she wrote, directed and co-produced. She has continued her interest in these darker themes with the documentaries *Zombiemania* (2008) and *Pretty Bloody: The Women of Horror* (2009), which focused on woman-made horror and was nominated for an award at the Yorkton Film Festival. In 2011, she also wrote, produced and directed the documentary *Nightmare Factory* about special effects. She is the president of the production company Ruby Tree Films Inc.

DAVIS, BETTE ◈

A major star of Hollywood's Golden Age, Bette Davis was born in Massachusetts in 1908 and worked through to her death in 1989. Winning the Best Actress Oscars in both 1935 and 1938, she was nominated or the same award another 8 times, including her starring role alongside long-time rival Joan Crawford for Robert Aldrich's *What Ever Happened to Baby Jane?* (1962). Renowned for her sharp wit, fearless performances, and refusal to hold back, she was a pioneer who fought aggressively for the ability to continue acting on screen well beyond what Hollywood typically saw as a 'use by' date for women actors. Whether simply because it was where she could get work or a genuine affection for the roles available for women in horror, it is a terrain where she has many credits including *Hush... Hush, Sweet Charlotte* (Robert Aldrich, 1964), *The Nanny* (Seth Holt, 1965), *Scream, Pretty Peggy* (Gordon Hessler, 1973), *Burnt Offerings* (Dan Curtis, 1976), *The Watcher in the Woods* (John Hough, 1980) and her final film credit, Larry Cohen's 1989 film *Wicked Stepmother*. In 2017, Davis was played by Susan Sarandon in the television series *Feud* based on her ongoing professional and personal tensions with Joan Crawford.

DAVIS, BRIANNE

Actor, producer and director Brianne Davis is familiar for on-screen roles in horror films such as the 2008 remake of *Prom Night* and television series like *True Blood*, but she also has significant experience as both an actor and director of indie horror films. Davis was discovered by a modelling agency when she was 12 years old and began her career working in commercials, later turning to work behind the camera with her feature film directorial efforts *The Night Visitor 2: Heather's Story* and *Deadly Signal*, both in 2016. Her acting credits in horror features include *House of Grimm* (Desmond Gumbs, 2005), *The Haunting of Marsten Manor* (Dave Sapp, 2007), *Something's Wrong in Kansas* (Louis Paul Tocchet, 2008), *The Victim* (Michael Biehn, 2011), *Chromeskull: Laid to Rest 2* (Robert Hall, 2011), *Among Friends* (Danielle Harris, 2012), *The Night Visitor* (Jennifer Blanc-Biehn, 2013), 2013) and *Magi* (Hasan Karacadag, 2016).

DAVIS, ESSIE

A familiar face in Australian film and television, Essie Davis's starring role as Amelia in Jennifer Kent's breakthrough horror film *The Babadook* (2014) brought the actor international attention. She was born in Hobart in 1970 and studied at Sydney's National Institute of Dramatic Arts. Beginning her career in theater, she was a member of the acclaimed Bell Shakespeare Company and later moved to screen work in films including the Wachowski's back-to-back 2003 sequels *The Matrix Reloaded* and *The Matrix Revolutions*. Davis had previously starred in the Irish horror film *Isolation* (Billy O'Brien, 2005).

DAVIS, GEENA

Putting her money where her mouth is by launching the Geena Davis Institute on Gender in Media which researches representations of women, Geena Davis is an important woman in screen history for reasons that far transcend her role as writer, producer and Oscar-winning actor. Born in Massachusetts in 1956, Virginia Davis studied drama at Boston University. Early screen roles included Mace Neufeld's 1985 horror film *Transylvania 6-5000* and David Cronenberg's *The Fly* in 1986 (both co-starring ex-husband Jeff Goldblum), but she is forever linked to the genre for her starring role in Tim Burton's horror-comedy *Beetlejuice* (1988) with Winona Ryder and Michael Keaton. In 2017, she appeared in the first season of *The Exorcist*, a television spin-off series inspired by William Friedkin's 1973 film of the same name.

Geena Davis at the 2006 Writers Guild Awards at the Hollywood Palladium February 4, 2006 Los Angeles, CA 2006. Credit: Paul Smith / Featureflash Photo Agency / Shutterstock.com

DAVIS, JULIE

American filmmaker, writer and actor Julie Davis was featured alongside Atom Agoyan, Nick Cassavettes and Kevin Smith in *Vanity Fair*'s 1998 Hollywood issue in a section on New Wave Directors: curiously, she also is shown in this photograph alongside both Katja von Garnier and Mary Harron, two other women filmmakers who have made feature-length horror films. A one-time editor at the Playboy Channel, Davis is known primarily for her breakthrough indie film *I Love You, Don't Touch Me!* (1997) that premiered at

Sundance, amongst her many credits she was the director and co-writer of the 1994 horror film *Witchcraft VI: The Devil's Mistress*.

DE CARLO, YVONNE •

Born in 1922, Margaret Yvonne Middleton—known professionally by her middle name and her mother's maiden name—had a lengthy career across a range of genres. But it is as Lily Munster that her enduring legacy is most closely linked. While her Classical Hollywood career was marked by her role as Sephora in Cecil B. DeMille's *The Ten Commandments* (1956), it was her many horror films—both with *The Munsters* and after—that made her a genre icon. De Carlo reprised the role of Lily in two *Munsters* television movies, *Munster, Go Home!* (1966) and the later *The Munsters' Revenge* (1981). Her other horror credits include *Satan's Cheerleaders* (Greydon Clark, 1977), *Nocturna: Granddaughter of Dracula* (Harry Hurwitz, 1977), *The Silent Scream* (Denny Harris, 1979), *Play Dead* (Peter Wittman, 1981), *American Gothic* (John Hough, 1988), *Cellar Dweller* (Bob Wynn, 1988) and the feminist horror classic, *Mirror, Mirror* (Marina Sargenti, 1990).

DE CAROLIS, CINZIA

At only 10 years old, Italian ator Cinzia De Carolis co-starred with Carl Malden as Lori in Dario Argento's *The Cat o' Nine Tails* in 1971, filmed in Berlin, Turin and Rome. The following year she acted in Giorgio Ferroni's horror film adaptation of Tolstoy's 1884 gothic novella, *The Family of the Vourdalak*, called *The Night of the Devils*. De Carolis returned again to the genre as a young woman in Antonio Margheriti's *Cannibal Apocalypse* (1980) with John Saxon and Giovanni Lombardo Radice.

DE HAVILLAND, OLIVIA

Born in Tokyo in 1916, Dame Olivia de Havilland—like her sister Joan Fontaine—are synonymous with Classical Hollywood cinema. Winner of an Academy Award for Best Actress and nominated for 4 others, she starred alongside Errol Flynn in Michael Curtiz's *The Adventures of Robin Hood* (1938) and played Melanie in Victor Fleming's epic *Gone with the Wind* (1939). A later-in-life turn to horror saw de Havilland star in a number of gothic-themed films including *The Screaming Woman* (Jack Smight, 1972), *Hush... Hush, Sweet Charlotte* (Robert Aldrich, 1964), the killer bees film *The Swarm* (Irwin Allen, 1978) and in the home invasion film *Lady in a Cage* (Walter Grauman, 1964). Earlier films such as *The Dark Mirror* (Robert Siodmak, 1946) and *The Snake Pit* (Anatole Litvak, 1948) can also retrospectively be understood as being psychological thrillers with horror themes.

DE MARE, VICTORIA

Self-identifying "Scream Queen", actor, dancer, musician, writer and DJ Victoria De Mare is an agile, prolific creative proudly linked to horror. Linked most readily to the character Batty Boop in the *Killjoy* series, her other horror credits include *Slaughter Studios* (Brian Katkin, 2002), *Shadows* (Dan Donley, 2005), *Cutting Room* (Ian Truitner, 2006), *Werewolf in a Womens Prison* (Jeff Leroy, 2006), *Azira: Blood from the Sand* (Vinnie Bilancio and Scott Evangelista, 2006), *George's Intervention* (J.T. Seaton, 2009), *Deadly Beloved* (Gregori Holderbach, 2009), *Bio Slime* (John Lechago, 2010), *The Awakening* (Vince Rotonda, 2010), *Horrorween* (Joe Estevez, 2011), *Stripped* (Mark LaFleur and J.M.R. Luna, 2013), *Feast of Fear* (John Lechago, 2016), *The Black Room* (Rolfe Kanefsky, 2017), *Two Faced* (John Kearns Jr., 2017), *Dracula in a Women's Prison* (Jeff Leroy, 2017), *Grizzled!* (Rycke Foreman, 2018), *Hell's Kitty* (Nicholas Tana, 2018), *Monster Party* (Chris von Hoffmann, 2018) and *State of Desolation* (Jim Towns, 2018).

DE VAN, MARINA

Born in 1971, French director, writer and actor Marina de Van is a significant contemporary woman horror director from France. Her directorial debut was the shocking, intimate and highly intelligent self-mutilation film *In My Skin* (2002) which de Van wrote, directed and starred as the main character, Esther. In 2009, she wrote and directed the psychological horror movie *Don't Look Back* with Sophie Marceau and Monica Bellucci. In 2011, she directed an adaptation of Charles Perrault's fairy tale *Hop-o' My-Thumb*, de Van's horror-fantasy folktale adaptation produced by Sylvette Frydman and Jean-François Lepetit who also produced Catherine Breillat's dark fairytales, *Bluebeard* (2009) and *Sleeping Beauty* (2010). In 2013, de Van wrote and directed the disturbing Irish-set evil child film *Dark Touch*, her first English language feature.

Marina De Van (left) and Sophie Marceau at the photocall for their movie *Don't Look Back*, 16 May 2009, Cannes, France. Credit: Jaguar PS / Shutterstock.com

DECKER, JOSEPHINE

Josephine Decker is a highly acclaimed American actor, filmmaker and artist. Born in 1981, she has worked across documentaries, feature films and shorts as both actor, director, and writer. In 2013, her feature film debut *Butter on the Latch* was a deeply poetic psychological horror film starring Isolde Chae-Lawrence that received widespread acclaim, followed by the equally dark feature *Thou Wast Mild and Lovely* in 2014. As an actor, Decker has appeared in the horror films *Sisters of the Plague* (Jorge Torres-Torres, 2015) and *Saturday Morning Mystery* (Spencer Parsons, 2012). In 2016, her segment "First Day Out" featured in the horror anthology *Collective: Unconscious*. In 2018 Decker received widespread international praise for her dark drama *Madeline's Madeline*.

DEE, FRANCIS

Born in 1909 in Los Angeles, Frances Dee starred in one of the most beloved horror films of the 1940s, Jacques Tourneur's *I Walked with a Zombie* (1943). Produced by Val Lewton, Dee stars as Canadian nurse Betsy, sent to care for the seemingly comatose Jessica Holland (Christine Gordon), the wife of a plantation owner on a fictional Caribbean island called Saint Sebastian. Told from Betsy's perspective, Dee is central to the unfolding narrative that reveals her patient's true malady.

DELPY, JULIE 🏳

The multi-talented Julie Delpy has a lengthy filmography as actor, and—having studied filmmaking at New York's Tisch School of the Arts—has successfully turned her hand to both screenwriting and directing. Discovered by French New Wave figure Jean-Luc Godard for his 1985 film *Détective*, she has starred in films by directors including Agnieszka Holland, Krzysztof Kieślowski, Richard Linklater and Jim Jarmusch. In 1997, she starred in Anthony Waller's *An American Werewolf in Paris*, the sequel to John Landis's *An American Werewolf in London* (1981), and in 2009 she wrote, directed, produced, starred and composed the score for her gothic biopic *The Countess* in which she played the notorious title character, the real-life Hungarian serial killer Elizabeth Báthory.

Julie Delpy at the 2014 *Vanity Fair* Oscar Party at the Sunset Boulevard on 2 March2014 in West Hollywood, Los Angeles, California. Credit: Kathy Hutchins / Shutterstock.com

DEMES, MONICA

Brazilian filmmaker Monica Demes initially studied law and then turned her attention to filmmaking, studying in Madrid and New York City. Working across documentary, commercials, animations and live-action films, with Carmelo Calvo she collaborated on the short animation *Halloween* which prompted David Lynch to invite her to study in his Master Film program at Maharishi University. In 2016, she made her feature film debut as director, writer, editor and producer on the vampire film *Lilith's Awakening* set in Iowa.

DENIS, CLAIRE

Born in Paris in 1946, filmmaker Claire Denis is one of the most important contemporary French filmmakers working today. Beginning with her debut feature *Chocolat* (1988), Denis's films have been driven by her own distinct visual and formal style, often considered a unique language in its own right. Her 1994 film *I Can't Sleep* starring Yekaterina Golubeva was based inspired by the 1980s French serial killer Thierry Paulin (aka the so-called "Monster of Montmartre"), and in 2000 she directed the brutal horror film *Trouble Every Day* with Vincent Gallo and Béatrice Dalle which has attained a strong cult following.

Claire Denis attends the *Les Salauds* Photocall during the 66th Annual Cannes Film Festival on 22 May 2013 in Cannes, France. Credit: Denis Makarenko / Shutterstock.com

DENNIS, SANDY

Famed for playing nervous ingénue types, Sandy Dennis won an Oscar for her supporting role in Mike Nichols's screen adaptation of *Who's Afraid of Virginia Woolf?* (1966), co-starring Elizabeth Taylor and Richard Burton. Born in Nebraska in 1937, Dennis would also star in the lead role in Robert Altman's powerful deconstruction of the psycho-biddy category, *That Cold Day in the Park* (1969), in a haunting and subtle performance. In later years, she also starred in many overt horror films, including Bob Balaban's 1989 cannibal comedy *Parents*, Larry Cohen's *God Told Me To* (1976), *976-EVIL* (1988) directed by Freddie Krueger actor Robert Englund, and the Steven Spielberg-directed horror TV movie *Something Evil* in 1972.

DENEUVE, CATHERINE ·

From musicals to dramas to horror movies, Catherine Deneuve is a French cinema icon. Her impressive filmography spans from 1957 to the current day, having worked with directors including Agnès Varda, Luis Buñuel and François Truffaut. In 1965 she starred as Carole, the housebound protagonist in *Repulsion*, the first of Roman Polanski's so-called 'apartment trilogy' with *Rosemary's Baby* (1968) and *The Tenant* (1976). Just as loved by horror audiences is her role as bisexual vampire queen Miriam Blaylock in Tony Scott's exquisite 1983 horror film *The Hunger*, in which she starred with Susan Sarandon and David Bowie.

Catherine Deneuve attends *The Midwife (Sage Femme)* press conference during the 67th Film Festival Berlin at Hyatt Hotel on February 14, 2017 in Berlin, Germany. Credit: Denis Makarenko / Shutterstock.com

DEREN, MAYA

Ukrainian-born American artist Maya Deren was nothing less than a polymath, her acclaimed talents stretching across writing, filmmaking, photography and dance. As one of the most significant figures in American experimental and avant-garde filmmaking history, her most famous film *Meshes in the Afternoon* (1943) demonstrates her ongoing fascinations with the poetics of the ritualistic and otherwordly, often represented through abstracted supernatural figures. These fascinations continue through the title and imagery of her later 1943 film, the unfinished short *The Witch's Cradle*.

DEVONSHIRE, PAULA

Film producer Paula Devonshire began her career in television and short films, and her horror credits are impressive—aside from producing both *Ginger Snaps 2: Unleashed* (Brett Sullivan, 2004) and *Ginger Snaps Back: The Beginning* (Grant Harvey, 2004), she also collaborated with horror great George A. Romero as producer on his 2007 film *Diary of the Dead* and 2009's *Survival of the Dead*. Her other horror credits include Chris Trebilcock's *The Dark Stranger* (2015).

DIETZ, EILEEN

Albeit uncredited, with the flicker of a high-contrast black and white shot of her face, Eileen Dietz's terrifying, near-subliminal cameo as the demon Pazuzu in William Friedkin's *The Exorcist* (1973) is one of the most iconic images of 1970s horror. Born in New York in 1944, Dietz began acting as a child on stage and screen and through her career would appear in soap operas and sitcoms. But it is in horror that her fame primarily rests, with her many credits in that genre including films such as *The Clonus Horror* (Robert S. Fiveson, 1979), *The Freeway Maniac* (Paul Winters, 1989), *Exorcism* (William A. Baker, 2003), *Constantine* (Francis Lawrence, 2005), *Neighborhood Watch* (Graeme Whifler, 2005), *Creepshow 3* (Ana Clavell and James Dudelson, 2006), *Halloween II* (Rob Zombie, 2009), *The Queen of Screams* (Margo Romero, 2009), *Sibling Rivalry* (Margo Romero, 2009), *Butterfly* (Edward E. Romero, 2010), *Snow White: A Deadly Summer* (David DeCoteau, 2012), *Little Big Boy* (Kim Sønderholm, 2012), The Devil *Knows His Own* (Jason Hawkins, 2013), *Demon Legacy* (Rand Vossler, 2014), *Abaddon* (Michael J. Sarna, 2014), *Lake Alice* (Ben Milliken, 2017) and *Estella's Revenge* (Carlos Dunn and Steve Olander, 2018).

DIPRIMO, EMILY

Emily DiPrimo received much media attention when she directed her first feature film—the slasher film *Carver* (2014)—when only 14 years old. Soon after she came second in a Crypt TV competition to make a 6-second scare short for her film "The Director", leading her to collaborate with Crypt TV on the supernatural revenge series *Violet*. In 2015, she was one of 7 directors involved in the horror anthology *Bye Felicia* with her short "Night Shift".

DO, MATTIE—INTERVIEW (JULY 2018)

Filmmaker Mattie Do's very name signifies a series of impressive firsts: Lao's first woman director and helmer of the first Lao movies to play at international film festivals, and her most recent 2016 *Dearest Sister* (*Nong hak*) became the first from the country to be submitted to The Oscars' Best Foreign Language category. Of the 17 feature films made in Laos, Do has directed two of them: aside from *Dearest Sister* (also the country's first international co-production), her debut *Chanthaly* (2012) was the ninth feature film ever produced there, as well as being Lao's first horror movie.

Dearest Sister was developed in part through the Cannes Film Festival's La Fabrique des Cinemas du Monde emerging filmmaker development program, and although a familiar face on the international genre film festival circuit, Do's astonishing achievements are very much due wider recognition. Although she spent much of her early life in the United States and worked for a time in Europe, Do returned to live in Laos in 2010 to look after her father following the death of her mother, an event that inspired her debut feature *Chanthaly*. Like *Dearest Sister*, both films focus explicitly on the tensions within families that are brought to the fore by supernatural elements.

Do kindly took time out from working on her third feature *The Long Walk* (2019) to speak to me about her career.

You have such a remarkable story in terms of how you got into filmmaking— can you fill us in on how it all came together for you?

I would have to say that the whole film thing all came together for me by luck... followed up by a ton of hard work! Haha! Seriously, I never intended or dreamt of being a filmmaker, but when the opportunity presented itself, and I found myself thrown into the director's chair (onto the hard, cold floor in this case), I seized the moment and did my best. It was the result of actually making and completing a film that turned me into a filmmaker and made me realize I wanted to continue being one. It's a very rare and special occupation, surrounded by a lot of mystique and exclusiveness... so when I blundered into it, I figured it was really lucky and fortunate as well as fun, so I stuck with it!

Of course, I always tell the funny story of how I accidentally became a filmmaker. I came to Laos to make sure my dad wasn't being taken advantage of by a potentially suspect woman (they both were fine), ended up meeting the producers of Lao Art Media because my husband was interested in Lao films and there was no available info since in 2010, internet hadn't proliferated through most of the country yet, and when they offered him a writing job, he accepted! Of course, they then offered him a directing job because they were eager to keep Lao films afloat, since there weren't many at the time, and he rejected the chance to direct. He admitted to them he couldn't speak the language, plus he didn't really like to interface with actors... which is pretty important when directing. So he casually suggested I should do it since I had the language skills and experience in performing arts.

Director Mattie Do and friend. Used with permission.

The President and Vice President of Lao Art Media were too busy celebrating that they had a new director, one that would be the first woman in their history to direct a feature narrative, to realize that my experience in performing arts was as a ballet teacher... for 7 year olds. In any case, my husband had me read a thick book called "Directing", study the films I liked and analyze what about them I liked, and eventually I made a film. In general, he had told me that my ability to get 7 year olds to perform for five minutes straight, uncut on a stage, was already quite an impressive feat that was possibly more difficult than even film. At least in film, an adult actor is pretty easy to communicate a complicated emotion to, has a more established memory, and if we mess up, we can just call cut and try another take. Imagine what it's like to explain to a 7 year old what flirtation means when we learn certain old, established excerpts in ballet.

"Lao's first woman filmmaker" is a phrase used in relation to you almost as much as your actual name! Does this place pressure on you, and in your experience, are you finding other women filmmakers—not just in Laos but also around the world—are taking inspiration from your success?

Being Lao's first female filmmaker is kind of fun in that it almost feels like a title now! Many of my friends in South East Asia joke about how it has that weight. However, there is an immense pressure on me, and I quite frankly feel like I have a lot to prove. It's a little difficult to explain, because logically, if you're a man making film here amongst a bunch of other men, you'd think you'd strive even harder to try to stand out from the white noise of your fellow colleagues, right? I don't get that sense so much. However, for me, I feel like I can't make just any kind of film, I have to do something daring, something that improves vastly every time, and something completely bold to be able to stay afloat in film at all. I don't even mean local films. It's like having this title draped on my shoulders means that people are expecting me to be deserving and worthy of it, and if I make a subpar film, there'll be a ton of people who just kind of roll their eyes and think, "See? She's not talented at all. She only gets notice because she's the first female of Lao film."

I've been told as much. I was even told, "People notice your work because you're a girl making ghost films about other girls."

Wow. Like what the fuck? I'd like to believe that whether I had a penis or not, people would still notice my films. I'd like to believe that I can make a film about anything, girls and ghosts, or dogs and hamsters, or even men and chickens and still be noticed because the quality of my work is worthy of it. That sort of statement is kind of bullshit, and I can't help but feel that if I were a guy making ghosts films about girls, or any film for that matter, that they wouldn't utter that. It's moments like that that make me feel both burdened and extremely motivated to put something out into the world that garners attention. However, it also makes me feel like my job is harder simply because I'm a woman... especially the first.

As for being inspirational, I'm not sure. I hope I am. I hear from a lot of youth that they're inspired by me, and I try to talk to them and motivate them, but I can never tell if my words are just trickling off of them like water off of a duck's back, or if they're being absorbed. I'm very open and willing to build new filmmakers, but at the same time, I cannot waste time in my short life to put a stop to my own career, so the young people who reach out to me learn quickly that to work with me and be taught by me is like baptism by fire. So far, there only seems to be a handful that were able to stick around, and they've transitioned into different roles in filmmaking rather than directing. I have one young man that remains diligent and interested, though he prefers lighthearted films versus my very dark, bleak, and genre style. Haha! I'm also getting to know another group of young filmmakers to see if they take the dive like I did.

I think what a lot of people forget is after my stroke of luck, how much work and learning hours I put into maintaining and improving my skills as a filmmaker. It wasn't like I luckily got the opportunity to make my first film and then it was smooth sailing from there. We estimated that for my first film, I probably clocked in about 4000 hours of work between just the efforts that my husband and I put into that film. I don't even want to think about the amount of time I put into *Dearest Sister* and now my new film. I literally watch every single English speaking film that comes out in our cinema, even if I know I'll hate it, because I consider it part of my job. I probably watch one film every day or two now too, just to understand how people are approaching films. My cinema knowledge is still filled with huge gaps and spaces, however, and at the moment I'm mostly only watching new works to stay updated with what's happening now. Besides *Vertigo, The Thing, and Psycho* (two of which I only saw this year), I hadn't ever seen any classic films before.

With your debut film *Chanthaly*, the learning curve must have been very steep. What things took you the most by surprise, and what skills did you find you had a natural affinity for?

Haha, every film is a steep learning curve. In some ways, every film has some new surprise to throw at us. Honestly, I miss the laid back and carefree days of *Chanthaly* when I didn't feel like I had anyone to possibly disappoint. I think what took me by surprise was how widespread the film world was, but how connected it also was, so when one person took notice of my film then it was also noticed by a bunch of other people in the film festival world too. Whether that was sometimes positive or not, heh, well it was a learning experience!

I'm still not sure what I have a natural affinity for yet in film. It's just become something that I do. I treat film like it's a do or die part of my life. There's rarely a moment I'm not thinking about my film projects, the film I'm working on now, and what films I'm going to try to embark on next, or other people's films. Sometimes, when I'm just sitting around having a snack with my dog, then maybe I'm not thinking about anything but how cute my dog is, but generally I'm always thinking about film in one capacity or another. I figure that life is short, and I have

Poster for *Dearest Sister* (Mattie Do, 2016). Used with permission.

to make as many as I can before I die. I think I'll probably die pretty young like my mother did, so that's a large motivating factor in my life.

As your second feature, was *Dearest Sister an* easier project or did it present its own, new challenges?

Dearest Sister was more difficult in that we could not be as easy going as we were with *Chanthaly*. With *Chanthaly*, it was filmed with no definite time limit, the schedule was tailored around whenever everyone or anyone was free, and it was really leisurely in that we didn't know what the hell we were doing so if something didn't work out, we were like, "Whatever. We'll figure out a different way to do it somehow tomorrow or something."

Dearest Sister had a definite timeline because I had foreign crew coming from Estonia and France, and they had planes to catch going home at certain dates, so we couldn't just mess around and experiment. It was very challenging also to work with such professional and talented technicians in an environment that was as unstable, unpredictable, and also lacking any professional equipment or stand-ard as Laos. Culturally, we had to find a balance for working with each other, as well as through language and surviving the strange new food and weather. It was very challenging, but very rewarding as well.

The technicians I worked with were undeniably talented and amazing, and they were also very willing to find that balance of working in a foreign environment and country after a while. In some ways, it was a lot easier than I expected because they were so skilled and could get me exactly what I wanted and needed. Once we got over the adjustment period, it was pretty awesome, but of course, there's always that difficult moment where we haven't figured out our flow yet.

The hardest part about *Dearest Sister* and any film after, is all the official business stuff like financing the film, and what happens to the film after we finish with it. We didn't have to worry about any of that stuff with the first film, and now suddenly it's like... ok, how do we get this film distributed, played at festivals, on what platforms? Just the deliverables list of the formats a film must be completed in is dizzying already! These were all technical things in our industry that I had to learn about and learn quick!

Laos has such a rich cultural history whose folkloric threads you bring together with such haunting beauty in your films, with a particular emphasis on the experience (and isolation) of young women. How do you balance the broader demands of making 'spooky' movies with speaking to the very real pressures faced by these characters and women like them?

I don't know if I think at all about what the demands are for a film outside of technical quality and standard. My whole purpose of making a film is to be un-like any other existing films, and to have stories charged with emotion, power, and authenticity according to my perspective and experience. I want my films to resonate with my local audience, but also with anyone who might pick it up and watch it. Hopefully after watching one of my films, it leaves an impression and gives them something to think about. I get really annoyed and disappointed with films when I walk out of the cinema and can't even recall what they were about because they were so generic.

I impose demands on myself to not make films that cater to what occidentals expect of Laos and South East Asia for that matter. I hate how cliché so many films have become, glorifying poverty porn or mystic Asians that have some sort of indiscernible Zen quality simply because they're Asian. Apparently, a film where people do nothing for hours except stare into space and languidly drift from place to place, stiffly interacting with each other is what occidentals consider authentic. That is so far from my experience of this place, so by all means, I guess that I'm a bit ok with dashing the usual demands from the broader market and just setting it all on fire and doing what I want… which is a film that is both truthful, outstanding, entertaining, and not pretentious. Because fuck that shit.

Why horror in particular? What was it about the genre that you felt was the best way to tell the stories you wanted to share, and what was your background with the genre?

Horror, or genre in general, is seriously in my opinion the most associative kind of film. Whenever I watch a romance, I can hardly stay awake. I don't get twitter-pated or feel that warm and fuzzy feeling in my heart ever, because that's not how I fall in love, and rarely are the qualities of the people I see in those romance films attractive to me. I don't give a shit about how handsome, rich, and successful the hero is in those films, and how sad that he's dating a gorgeous woman who is kind of a selfish bitch and he doesn't realize just yet that the goofy, clumsy, manic pixie dream girl orbiting their lives is the one for him. Often when I see that manic pixie dream girl heroine character, I often think, "Honey needs a healthy dose of reality or maybe has a touch of Asperger's."

They always seem so high maintenance and out of touch. Don't even get me started with foreign romance films. I've found myself thinking the protagonist of Indian films was a creepy chauvinist, who basically almost date rapes his way into romance, or that the hopelessly oblivious Thai hero in their romances and dramas should be texted a memo for, "Hello! She's into you! Are you clueless?" Plus why are they always so homogenous? I'd like to see a romance that involved a Black hero and a white woman, or a Korean man and an Indian woman or something. Wouldn't that be something?

So yeah, people don't fall in love the same way. A lot of drama isn't drama for other cultures and countries. I watch some dramas and I think, "Yawn. First world problems." Which may be a bit derisive, but having spent almost a decade living in a country where I can't drink the tap water and where I live on a dirt road, it's hard for me to sympathize with someone who has to put up with being so beautiful, living in cute little homes with drinkable tap water and hot running water, bemoaning their sad romantic state of affairs. When did stories get so formulaic and non-memorable? However, it's undeniable that horror taps into something much more deep, and that tension, nervousness, and fear is pretty universal no matter what country it comes from. Everyone understands what it's like to be creeped out or afraid of the dark.

In fact, when I think about my genre audiences, they're much more willing to watch a film with subtitles, in another language, from another culture or country, and of varying levels of quality and standard… just because they love horror and genre. You don't find that so much with other types of film audiences. I think the genre audience is very accepting and open, and always appreciate when something new is brought to the screen.

I grew up watching inappropriate genre. I was terrified of it, and to be honest, I still am! It's a feeling I enjoy, even though I watch the majority of a movie from behind my hands and fingers, but that's how much it's affecting me! When I was little, my dad would take us to the rental video store every weekend, and he'd let us pick out a film as well. The shelves back then were lined with the empty cardboard boxes displaying the covers and the short summaries of the film in the back, with small still images from the film. The horror films were always the best boxes and covers. I'd pick those out, and even though they were horribly not appropriate for children, I guess maybe my immigrant father didn't understand the ratings system or care for that matter. In fact, he'd watch them with us and dismiss them, but would chide us if we couldn't handle it because he'd spent his hard earned money renting them for us. He'd sometimes fast forward through the really scary scenes, and so I'd still see a murder or something taking place… just really really fast. Maybe it's because of these experiences from my youth that horror really stuck with me.

I am still struck by how generous and powerful a gesture it was that you shared all the bits and pieces of _Chanthaly_ online for free so other emerging filmmakers could see the 'raw' materials of what it takes to pull a film together. What inspired you to do this, and what feedback have you got since?

I did that because after speaking to a lot of people who felt content has been owned and controlled by not the creator but the middleman, I could understand their frustration. It's probably pretty frustrating for creators too, and it's not like _Chanthaly_ was going to be distributed in any commercial way at all. There was also a huge gap for me when I became a filmmaker.

Part of the problem for people aspiring to be filmmakers is that they really don't know what they don't know. I kind of circumnavigated that by just blunt-force trauma-ing my way into making my first film. Of course, because I didn't know what I was doing, I had a lot of difficulties and made a lot of mistakes, and that's when I realized that you simply don't know what you don't know. Do aspiring young filmmakers even know what the pieces of an edited film looks like? How is it assembled? What are the building blocks of film?

It always seems like film students and film lovers always talk about it as a finished piece in its entirety, or they talk about the romance of making the pieces in production on set, but no one talks about what they do with it after it's shot and before it's completed. It's sort of a shame, because that is a crucial part of filmmaking... the actual making it into a film part. I didn't know any of that shit, so I was super happy to share it with other people who might not know.

I got some fun re-edits of parts of my film back. It was awesome. One person even re-edited the film so there was no ghost in it, but just *Chanthaly* and her dog (my dog!). It was a very still and beautiful arthouse kind of film, with almost no dialogue because I'm almost certain that whoever did it could not speak Laos. It felt like a very still life portrait of the life of a lonely hermit girl and her dog. It was cool.

A familiar face on the international film circuit, what have you gained most from visiting other countries in a professional capacity?

Besides gaining a huge network of likeminded individuals who are also professionals, I think what I've gained most is knowledge. There is so much to learn when visiting other countries and other festivals, but mainly what you get to witness is the business of film and how it's conducted, as well as experience the different kinds of films that exist from every country that are completely different from anything you've ever seen before. That influenced my take on film a lot... making a film that can't be compared to any other existing film. I love that, and you find those kinds of films at festivals. You also find a bunch of serious people who are passionate about making new cinema, finding new voices and new perspectives. It's very important and refreshing.

There's a big difference though, from going to a festival to party and rub elbows with important people in film industry, versus actually doing work. It's like being a part of the conversation... you're either in the conversation and getting something sincerely accomplished, or you're out of the conversation and hearing all the white noise around you, but aren't able to formulate or transform that into anything useful. In that case, you've just paid a ton of money to say you hung out with so and so big name in film, watched a lot of movies, probably bought a new wardrobe to look cool at aforementioned parties, and got nothing done. They got to hang out with cool people, sure, and maybe ate a bunch of canapes and drank a bunch of free wine... but does it get them any closer to making a film? Maybe not. There's a seriousness to the way we casually conduct business in film, but because that line is so thin, it's very easy to not be doing anything at all. Of course, thankfully I discovered this by visiting festivals and other film events in various places.

What do emerging filmmakers tend to ask you the most, and what's your advice for any women wanting to make their own horror movies?

They usually ask me what I did to end up making a film, or what the first steps are... but when I try to explain it, there seems to be a lot of nodding and tuning out. There also seems to be a sort of misdirected voraciousness towards making a film that skips all the priorities, and that worries me. The first time I learned about a deck or one of these visual reference books was when an aspiring film-maker sent me one to look over. I kind of thought, "Huh. Ok cool..." but offended them when I said they were kind of jumping the gun. I guess my advice is pretty boring, so it goes unheeded. I can list it for you if you want, it's exactly what I do for every film project.

First, have a good idea. That may sound numbskulled, but believe it or not, that's important. Next, if you don't write yourself (which I absolutely do not and would not), get that idea turned into a logline, synopsis, and short treatment. Be ready to pitch it at any given point, but DO NOT BE ANNOYING. Read your audience. You can always tell if they're interested or not, or you ought to be able to tell. Don't just pitch at anyone or word vomit on their shoes, it's rude and an-noying. You should be able to clearly pitch your idea within a minute, or 5 min-utes, and if you have to do it on stage at a competition or a table pitch, within 10 minutes.

Know your budget and keep your expectations tempered. People get inter-ested in an idea right away, but they lose interest when it seems like you have no idea how it's going to be executed, how you plan on making it a reality, and if you seem generally oblivious to the business of film and sales and recoupment at all. This is just the world of independent film, we aren't privileged celebrity children who have a pre-built network and a safety net to fall back on, so we have to be logical about the fact that film is a risk, and anyone interested in your idea or joining your team is also taking a risk. It's no longer about you, but about every-one involved. Director or not, we can be the ones who are acknowledged as the creative artist behind an idea, but it takes an entire team to execute that idea and to develop it and complete it. The image of the god like Director that I think film school instills in some people is just plain selfish, I personally feel it sets people up for failure.

Next, find a way to make that film come hell or high water, in a cost-efficient way. Don't just wait for all the conditions to be perfect, or you'll be waiting for-ever. Rarely are all the conditions perfect. Rarely do you have the budget you want, the equipment you desire, or the perfect locations... RARELY, but if you keep waiting, you probably never make the first film.

My last bit of advice is also very simple—your job as a director is to commu-nicate with the actors and to be able to identify a good performance and get said performance onto the screen. All the other stuff is someone else's job with your guidance... don't stress so much over the other stuff that you lose track of your main job, which is getting a good performance. The minute you let a bad perfor-mance onto the screen, it shows you don't have a propensity for directing, and god knows how bad the other takes were that THAT was the instance/take you decided to put on screen. I hear hopeful filmmakers talking about camera work, sound, music, color, all of that. It's great, it's fine, it's good... and it's all very fun, but if you can't even get the actors to actually perform, god knows no one gives a damn how awesome the rest of your film was if your directing sucks.

We are all replaceable, so if your picture is bad, but you are a talented director, some producer will hire you a better DoP. If your edit was subpar, but you are a good director, they'll replace your editor with someone more suited to your pacing. However, you as a director are also replaceable, so if all the other pieces of the film were amazing, but your actors performances were lacking and the overall flow of the performances were shakey, then they'll probably replace you as a director. Never forget, we women don't typically get as many second chances at this directing thing as often as most men do, so know your job, do your job and do it well.

DOMERGUE, FAITH

Faith Domergue was a staple in horror/scifi hybrids of the 1950s, despite her career spanning from the early 1940s to mid-'70s. Born in New Orleans in the mid-'20s, she was discovered by Howard Hughes (with whom she was also personally involved) and joined RKO in a 3-picture deal. Domergue's most famous genre work includes *Cult of the Cobra* (Francis D. Lyon, 1955), *This Island Earth* (Joseph M. Newman and Jack Arnold, 1955), *It Came from Beneath the Sea* (Robert Gordon, 1955), and *Timeslip* (Ken Hughes, 1955). Later in her career she worked in Italian *gialli*, including Lucio Fulci's *Perversion Story* (1969) and *The Man with the Icy Eyes* (Alberto De Martino, 1971), as well as the American horror films *Will to Die* (Carl Monson, 1971) and *So Evil, My Sister* (Reginald Le Borg, 1974).

DOILLON, LOU

Daughter of Jane Birkin and half-sister of Charlotte Gainsbourg, French actor, model, artist and musician Lou Doillon was born in 1982. She made her film debut at 5 years old in Agnès Varda's *Kung Fu Master* (1988) in which her mother co-wrote and starred, and in 2004 she put in a remarkable performance in the debut feature film of Pascal Laugier, *House of Voices* (2004). In 2006, she played the eponymous twins Angelique and Annabel in Douglas Buck's remake of Brian De Palma's 1973 horror film *Sisters*.

Lou Doillon attends the 60th International Cannes Film Festival on 21 May 2007 in Cannes, France. Credit: Denis Makarenko / Shutterstock.com

DOLLAR, PHOEBE

As the title character in Brad Sykes 2003 horror film *Goth*, Phoebe Dollar is also a writer and producer. She was born in North Carolina in 1984, and as an actor her horror credits include *Hell's Highway* (Jeff Leroy, 2002), *The Hazing* (Joe Castro, 2003), *Blood Sisters* (Joe Castro, 2003), *Creepies* (Jeff Leroy, 2004), *Werewolf in a Womens Prison* (Jeff Leroy, 2006), *Orgy of the Damned* (Creep Creepersin, 2010) and *Rat Scratch Fever* (Jeff Leroy, 2011). In 2018, she wrote, co-directed, co-produced and acted in the horror feature *Sunset Society*, starring Ron Jeremy.

DONAHUE, HEATHER

In 1999 and early 2000, Heather Donahue was one of the most famous horror actors on the planet for her role in the surprise blockbuster hit *The Blair Witch Project* (Daniel Myrick and Eduardo Sánchez, 1999). Largely responsible for kickstarting the mainstream popularity of the found footage horror subgenre, the film was heavily improvised by Donahue and her co-stars Joshua Leonard and Michael C. Williams. Despite this, later roles did not propel her career in the manner that the sheer scale of her breakthrough would have suggested: outside the television movies *Manticore* (John Wenrer, 2005) and the straight-to-DVD film *The Morgue* (Halder Gomes and Gerson Sanginitto, 2008), Donahue's screen credits were limited. Quitting acting in 2008, she began a new career growing medical marijuana, releasing a book about her change in life in 2011 called *Growgirl*.

DONALDSON, LESLEH

Born in Toronto in 1964, Lesleh Donaldson was a familiar face in Canadian horror in the 1980s, appearing in some of the country's most well-known cult horror films of the period. Studying music and beginning her career acting in television commercials, Donaldson's primary horror credits include *Funeral Home* (William Fruet, 1980), *Happy Birthday to Me* (J. Lee Thompson, 1981), *Deadly Eyes* (Robert Clouse, 1982) and *Curtains* (Richard Ciupka, 1983). In 1987, she featured in an episode of *Friday the 13th: The Series* for television, and in the horror anthology *Tales of Poe* (2014) alongside fellow horror legends Debbie Rochon, Amy Steel and Adrienne King.

DORIA, DANIELA

One of Lucio Fulci's favourite actors, Daniela Dora features in a number of his most notorious horror films such as *The Black Cat* (1980), *City of the Living Dead* (1980), *The House by the Cemetery* (1981) and *The New York Ripper* (1982). Born in Milan in 1957, she began her film career in 1976 and although working with directors including Joe D'Amato and Flavio Mogherini, it is her collaborations with Fulci that garnered her a cult reputation. In *City of the Living Dead*, she allegedly swallowed and regurgitated actual sheep entrails for optimum realism, and her charcters met equally grizzly deaths in his other films.

DOUGLAS, HEIDI LEE

Heidi Lee Douglas is an award-winning Australian horror filmmaker and documentarian. Douglas was born in the Australian city of Newcastle and studied Video Production and Film Studies at the University of Newcastle. In 2008 she formed her production company Dark Lake Productions, to develop and produce her many diverse projects and champion those of other filmmakers, with an emphasis on diversity and inclusivity. As writer, co-producer, director and editor, Douglas's 2014 horror short *Little Lamb* premiered at Austin's Fantastic Fest and played at film festivals around the world, and was included in the 2017 anthology of women genre filmmakers *7 From Etheria*. Her 2018 horror short *Devil Woman* premiered at Fantasia International Film Festival in Montreal and FrightFest, London. Amongst her many roles as an active participant to nurture

Director of Photography Meg White and Director Heidi Lee Douglas, on set for *Devil Woman* (2018). Photo by Eryca Green, used with permission.

other creatives she is the co-chair of Film Fatales in Sydney, who work within an international network of women filmmakers to formally mentor and support each other's work.

DOWN, LESLEY-ANNE

Born in London in 1954, Lesley-Anne Down started modeling and entering beauty competitions at 10 years old, soon beginning to work on television. In 1971, she starred as Countess Ilona in Hammer's *Countess Dracula*, with later horror credits including the Amicus anthology *From Beyond the Grave* (Kevin Connor, 1974), the punk anthropology ghost story *Nomads* (John McTiernan, 1986), *Night Trap* (David A. Prior, 1993), *13th Child* (Thomas Ashley and Steven Stockage, 2002), *Rosewood Lane* (Victor Salva, 2011) and *Dark House* (Victor Salva, 2014).

DOWNE, ALLISON LOUISE

Often acting under the stage name Vicki Miles and credited across her filmography as A. Louise Downe, Louise Downe and Allison Louise Downe, she was an established team member in the filmmaking team of David Friedman and Herschell Gordon Lewis. Married to Lewis for close to a decade, she was largely responsible for the core ideas that formed the screenplay of the latter's cult horror film *Blood Feast* (1963). According to Lewis, they tag-teamed writing the script at the typewriter, each taking over from the other when tiredness would strike. Downe also received assistant director credits on Lewis's horror films *A Taste of Blood* (1967), *The Wizard of Gore* (1970) and *The Gore Gore Girls* (1972), and both for assistant director and screenwriter of *The Gruesome Twosome* (1967).

DRAKE, FRANCES

Although most famous for playing Eponine in the 1935 Richard Boleslawski screen adaptation of *Les Misérables*, New York-born Frances Drake became a horror legend for her role as the doomed *Grand Guignol*-styled stage actor that is the source of Peter Lorre's monstrous obsession in Karl Freund's 1935 gothic horror film *Mad Love*. She also starred with Boris Karloff and Béla Lugosi in Lambert Hillyer's 1936 horror/scifi hybrid *The Invisible Ray*.

DREW, ELLEN

Ellen Drew worked for 30 years in American film from the early 1930s, discovered while working in an ice cream shop in Hollywood. Co-stars across her career included Bing Crosby and William Holden, and in 1941 she starred in her first horror film, Stuart Heiser's *The Monster and the Girl*. But it is as Thea in Mark Robson's *Isle of the Dead* (1945)—produced by iconic horror producer Val Lewton—for which she is primarily remembered.

DU POTET, CAROLINE

In 2010, Caroline du Potet co-directed the horror film *In Their Sleep* with her brother Éric du Potet. The siblings studied filmmaking in Paris, and before their feature debut they collaborated on a number of short films together in both directorial and scriptwriting capacities. Starring Anne Parillaud from *La Femme Nikita* (Luc Besson, 1990), *In Their Sleep* is a twist on the traditional home invasion narrative.

DUBLIN, JESSICA

Although born in New York in 1918, Jessica Dublin made her name in a range of internationally-produced horror films. In Italy, she appeared in the *giallo So Sweet, So Dead* (Roberto Bianchi Montero, 1972) with Farley Granger, and *Sex of the Witch* (Elo Pannacciò, 1973). Dublin starred in the cult Greek horror film *Devils in Mykonos* (Nico Mastorakis, 1976), and a smaller role in Kostas Karagiannis's *Land of the Minotaur* (1976). In North America, she acted in Brian Thomas Jones's 1988 film *Rejuvenatrix* (a loose reimagining of Roger Corman's classic 1959 film *The Wasp Woman*), *Voodoo Dolls* (Andrée Pelletier, 1991), and Lloyd Kaufman's 1989 splatter classics *The Toxic Avenger Part II* (co-directed with Michael Herz) and *The Toxic Avenger Part III: The Last Temptation of Toxie* (1989).

DUCOURNAU, JULIA—INTERVIEW (NOVEMBER 2016)

The following is a transcribed excerpt of an interview that took place at the 2016 Monsterfest in Melbourne, Australia, and excerpts appeared on the Monster Pictures home entertainment release of Raw. *Many thanks to Neil Foley, Grant Hardie, Jarret Gahan and Ben Hellwig, and that year's festival director Kier-La Janisse who organized the interview. Thanks also to Faith Everard for her assistance with transcription.*

http://cultofmonster.com.au

In 2016, French director and screenwriter shocked audiences around the world with her cannibal film *Raw*. Premiering at the Cannes Film Festival that year after being developed through the 2013 TorinoFilmLab, it would garner Ducournau international attention and win her awards at the London FIlm Festival, Austin's Fantastic Fest, the Sitges Film Festival, and the FIPRESCI Prize at Cannes.

Starring Garance Marillier as a young vegan vegetarian student who travels away from home to study, the film follows the unusual backstory about her eating habits that culminate with spectacular results. Ducournau was born in Paris in 1983 and studied screenwriting at the film and television school *La Fémis*. She won the *Petit Rail d'Or* at Cannes in 2011 for her debut short *Junior* in 2011, and in 2012 wrote and directed a television movie called *Mange*.

> **This is a film about ritual; what I found so fascinating was how shrewdly *Raw* collapses binary distinctions between what is considered acceptable ritual— socially familiar ritual—and outright transgression; I love that every moment in the film that something familiar happens, you take it to an extreme, a contrast that blurs them together which made me question the things I take for granted, the rituals in my own world.**

The first thing with rituals is that they are always come from tradition, so you

Julia Ducournau in Melbourne, Australia, 2016 for Monsterfest. Author's photograph.

never really know why you have to do some stuff because it's so archaic. It's something transmitted from generation to generation, which is the case with hazing, by the way—generally when you have a history of hazing it comes from generation to generation…

…And you reference that in the film

Absolutely, with the parents. It's pretty much for me a synonym with determinism, and my movie is about escaping determinism in many ways. The movie in itself actually; I tried to make it outside of every box, I really do not like boxes and I tried to deviate from what was expected from such a character and such a genre because for me at one point, this thing with the hazing is something that I knew instantly that the audience would rebel against because we feel trapped by many determinisms…you know, almost every day when we hear about politicians getting away [with not paying] taxes, going to the Bahamas to hide money, this is something incredibly violent and we cannot do anything about it. It's just like that, and we love to accept it gently without asking why, because there is a history behind it this we cannot handle.

And so I knew that this hazing would stand for that for many people because it's part of an establishment, it's cruel… and it's against the individual. I knew that the empathy of the audience would be with my character and it was very important that she would commit the ultimate act of transgression afterwards and that at this moment I really want my audience to fully understand her. For that matter, I think cannibalism in Justine's journey kind of stands for an act of rebellion against this establishment that is embodied by her own sister, because her own sister is a very good soldier, isn't she? She chants, she does the rituals, she eats her little steaks and stuff…

She obeys orders.

Absolutely, she obeys orders. So firstly, for me it was a…gesture, this act of cannibalism, more than anything, and then it becomes many other things in the relationship between the two sisters…It stands for many things, but this act against ritual was very important to me…It means complete freedom for me, but the freedom has a cost. Freedom only exists with responsibility, the responsibility you have to others, and at this point she's really not responsible yet, but she will become responsible.

I think that notion of responsibility in a lot of the scenes where these moments where she finds a kind of ethical or moral grey area—I'm thinking specifically of the moment when she is having sex and she chooses to bite her own arm. I think that's the first time in the film we see her taste for flesh turn to her *own* body, which is quite a dramatic shift in the film…

Absolutely.

… It's her finding an ethical space for *herself* through her own body.

I really do not like sex scenes generally in movies because most of the time it's just two people fucking…we know what it is to fuck, we all do it, it's not very interesting per se. However, I thought if she's going to get deflowered it has to mean something, to link to her journey…and at this moment she really is on the verge of not coming back. We are always on the verge of losing her in this scene, and more and more we see that she might actually hurt that guy that she loves very much.

I really wanted to play with this stretch between us and her where we're like "Oh no no no! We're not going to be with her anymore" and then at the end, at the last minute, there's this glimpse, it's a spark of humanity in her that allows her to turn it against herself. And then there's a relief in the scene.

It's interesting, I think it's only in retrospect that I realise the significance of that moment. There was an intellectual delay that I experienced quite a few times in *Raw* that I really love...One of my favourite scenes is the waxing scene, and I love the proximity of that is for me personally a very familiar horror. We do these weird things to our body that hurt like hell and having that in such close proximity to something that is so out of my experience, it's almost like I carried the intense emotion from that sensory familiarity into the next moment.

When I got the idea of waxing of course I got it at the beauty parlor and I thought 'you know this is funny, I've never seen this on screen and I thought this is really unfair because I'm really suffering right now and a lot of women at this exact moment in the world are probably suffering as well and like me they probably [are asking] why really they are doing this but they are doing this against determinism and the idea that we have to be hairless and stuff like that, to which we abide by as well'. And I thought 'this is not fair, because you see a lot of the trivialities of men's bodies—like it's OK to show men's bodies in their most organic states and we still accept it and we don't find it gross'. But women's bodies have to be glamorized, and I don't get it...it exists, and it exists for a lot of people so how come we've never seen it on screen?

So this is where I got the idea for my scene. And then, afterwards, it's different when you want to shoot it because you ask yourself different questions: how am I going to show that? What kind of feeling do I want to convey with this?

And this is what I love about body horror: in a way it makes us all equal in the room, because we all have bodies, and we do know what it means to ache, and we do know what it feels like somebody's skin... and we can relate to any body, actually. I thought it's interesting to put a very so-called feminine situation (because mostly it is linked to women—waxing and being waxed) and to try to aim for universality through it.

This is where your energy of where to place the camera comes into the camera: where am I going to put the camera for everyone to feel the same pain of this moment? And this is where ideas about close ups and stuff like that really show for what it is for *everyone*, and to never say it concerns only one part of the room, it concerns everyone...

I think the magic of that moment is that the things that happen after the waxing really expose and defamiliarize exactly what's wrong with this attitude—we need to think about the things we take for granted...I really found the moments that shocked me are because of their proximity to these more overtly taboo moments. The use of mobile phone cameras was very shrewd: screens are quite absent—laptops and phones—in the earlier part of the film, but then they have really interesting roles later on.

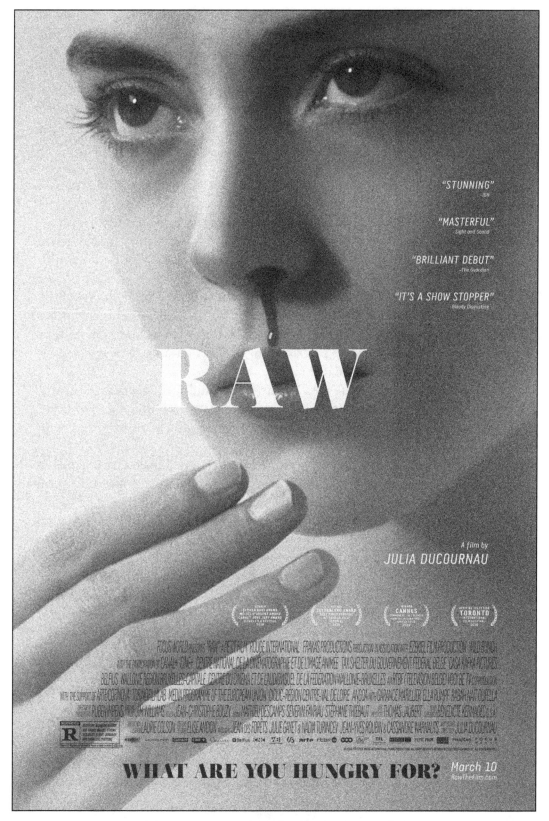

Raw (Julia Ducournau, 2016). Credit: Album / Alamy Stock Photo.

I really resist technology…it's not in my imagination, I don't care about it. However, the thing with the phone and the relationship with each other's image and the kind of is snowballing all the time. This is driving me crazy, I think it is a big disease of our time. I was thinking about a story I read about a girl who had been shot with an iPhone having sex or something like that and afterwards it was found in the high school and of course the poor girl went into a depression…how cruel that is and how unfair that is…

…It's a violation…

Yeah, I think this is unfortunately now almost has become very mundane. I play with images, this is my job, so the fact that somehow everyone thinks that it doesn't come with *any* sense of responsibility *is so wrong*. You cannot take anyone's image like that, it is not OK.

So that's why I made that scene… it's also with a kind of dynamic of 'oh you think you're better than me, I'm going to show you're just like me' between the two sisters, which is also violent. But the whole thing between them at the end when they are on the big terrace and they are on the ground and everyone is filming them when they're like dogs…

…I found that *shocking*…

This is shocking to me as well.…

… and that earlier scene in the morgue, the question of *what* was being filmed, the subject matter was less shocking to me than the act of filming, the casual way that those phones were used to film.

When we see them we are shocked because we're not behind the phones, but you can see the face of the extras when I directed them, they are bland: it's going to be over in five seconds after I put it on Facebook… it's the distance that makes them cold.

And then again in my questioning of what's human and what's inhuman, for me it's always about putting thing in perspectives. They are like dogs, but they are there for each other and they help each other because they are sisters, but in that scene they are completely empty people.

So who's the monster?

Always the question…My movie is clearly very dark, however I really wanted at the end to understand that there is a solution, and that the solution is in her. We see her growing as a moral identity. She can now know what's human and what is inhuman, for her, for herself, for the people she loves, and for people around her in her own world. She has grown into being moral, which is not the case for her sister…

I really needed for people to hear that when you've been through that and when you've been able to open your eyes to who you really are and what your humanity is and do the vacuuming of the carpet as usual, then there is a solution and that solution is in you…

DUDGEON, ELSPETH

Born in the late 19th century, Elspeth Dudgeon played mostly uncredited roles in a range of films, including Alfred Hitchcock's *Foreign Correspondent* (1940) and *The Paradine Case* (1947), and James Whale's *Bride of Frankenstein* (1935). Her most interesting role, however, is in James Whale's classic 1932 horror film *The Old Dark House* where—acting against biological gender type—she was cast as the elderly Sir Roderick Femm, resident of the spooky abode of the film's title. As such, she is credited in the film as "John Dudgeon", not Elspeth.

DUFF, DENISE

Denise Duff is an actor and filmmaker who was born in New York in 1965. She appeared in many popular television series and soap operas as an actor during the 1990s and 2000s in particular, and as an actor her horror credits include a number with filmmaker Ted Nicolaou such as *Bloodstone: Subspecies II* (1993), *Bloodlust: Subspecies III* (Ted Nicolaou, 1994), *Subspecies: The Awakening* (1998). Her other horror credits include *The Monster Man* (Jose Prendes, 2001), *Dr. Rage* (Jeff Broadstreet, 2005), and *Night of the Living Dead 3D: Re-Animation* (Jeff Broadstreet, 2012). Duff also co-directed *I, Vampire* in 2000 and directed *Song of the Vampire* in 2001, starring in both.

DUKE, PATTY °

Patty Duke's status as an all-American girl is challanged by a fascinating and diverse career that included extensive work in horror. Winning an Oscar for her starring role as Helen Keller in *The Miracle Worker* (Arthur Penn, 1962) when she was only 16 years old, she worked in film, stage and television for a remarkable 65 years. In 1972 she starred in Lamont Johnson's horror films *You'll Like My Mother* and *She Waits*, followed in 1977 in Dan Curtis's *Curse of the Black Widow* (another made-for-TV horror movie). In 1976, she starred as Rosemary in Sam O'Steen's *Look What's Happened to Rosemary's Baby* (the sequel to the 1968 blockbuster starring Mia Farrow). In 1978, she was part of the all-star cast of Irwin Allen's killer bee film *The Swarm*, and in 1989 had a central role in Sandor Stern's *Amityville 4: The Evil Escapes*.

DULAC, GERMAINE

French feminist filmmaker and writer Germaine Dulac is often credited with making the first Surrealist film. Written by fellow key French avant gardist Antonin Artaud (famous for his concept of 'the theater of cruelty'), Dulac's *The Seashell and the Clergyman* (1928) delves deep into dark, gothic imagery with a focus on death, murder and sexual repression. Despite the experimentation and poetry of her early work, after the introduction of sound Dulac primarily worked on newsreels. The influence of her early work on European art cinema is significant, and the legacy of *The Seashell and the Clergyman* can be felt in everything from David Lynch's films to Herk Harvey's *Carnival of Souls* (1962).

DUNST, KIRSTEN ⸙

American actor Kirsten Dunst was born in New Jersey in 1982, a child model who made her mainstream breakthrough in 1994 as Claudia in Neil Jordan's *Interview with a Vampire*. Beginning a career that would see her work in mainstream films like Sam Raimi's *Spider-Man* (2002), Dunst is largely considered an indie darling and works with filmmakers including Sofia Coppola and Lars Von Trier. Aside from *Interview with a Vampire*, Dunst's other horror credits include *Tower of Terror* (D.J. MacHale, 1997), *The Crow: Salvation* (Bharat Nalluri, 2000), and Kate and Laura Mulleavy's psychological horror film *Woodshock* (2017). Dunst was also an executive producer on that project, and she is currently attached to direct a feature length screen adaptation of Sylvia Plath's cult 1963 novel *The Bell Jar*.

DUPREE, MONIQUE

Monique Dupree was born in New Jersey in 1974 and is often branded as "first Black scream queen". An actor, model, musician and producer, she began acting in her midteens and her horror career began when she met Troma's Lloyd Kaufman at a Scream Queen competition for *Fangoria*. She has appeared in well over 50 movies, and her horror credits include *Pot Zombies* (Justin Powers, 2005), *Bachelor Party in the Bungalow of the Damned* (Brian Thomson, 2008), *Skeleton Key 2: 667 Neighbor of the Beast* (John Johnson, 2008), *Satan Hates You* (James Felix McKenney, 2010), *Skeleton Key 3: The Organ Trail* (John Johnson, 2011), *Bloodbath in Creightonville* (Matt Cloude, 2012), *Sheriff Tom Vs. The Zombies* (Ryan Scott Weber, 2013) and *Dead Woman's Hollow* (Libby McDermott, 2013). In 2015, Dupree also directed, produced and starred in *Shadowhunters: Devilspeak* (2015).

DUSHKU, ELIZA ˙

Closely associated with her ongoing role as Faith on the cult television series *Buffy the Vampire Slayer* and its spin-off *Angel*, American actor Eliza Dushhku was born in Massachusetts in 1980 and began acting as a child. Her horror film credits include *Soul Survivors* (Stephen Carpenter, 2001), *Wrong Turn* (Rob Schmidt, 2003), *The Alphabet Killer* (Rob Schmidt, 2008), *Open Graves* (Álvaro de Armiñán, 2009), *The Scribbler* (John Suits, 2014) and *Eloise* (Robert Legato, 2017). She also starred in the title role of the supernatural television series *Tru Calling*.

DUVALL, CLEA

Actor, writer and director Clea DuVall was born in Los Angeles in 1977. She studied at the Los Angeles County High School for the Arts and made her film debut in Jane Simpson's horror film *Little Witches* in 1996. She has worked primarily in film and television, including the horror movies *The Faculty* (Robert Rodriguez, 1998), John Carpenter's *Ghosts of Mars* (2001), *How to Make a Monster* (George Huang, 2001), *Identity* (James Mangold, 2003), *The Grudge* (Takashi Shimizu's 2004 US remake of his 2002 J-horror film *Ju-on*), the art history serial killer film *Anamorph* (Henry S. Miller, 2007) and *The Watch* (2008). She has also acted in horror television series such *as Buffy the Vampire Slayer*, *The Lizzie Borden Chronicles* and *American Horror Story*.

DUVALL, SHELLEY˙

In her iconic performance as Wendy Torrance in Stanley Kubrick's 1980 horror film *The Shining*, Shelley Duvall initially presents the character as gaunt and anxious, letting it slowly build to a crescendo of unexpected strength, courage and endurance. A regular actor in many of Robert Altman's most celebrated films, Houston-born Duvall worked across musicals, comedies, dramas, and family films, winning acting awards at both the Cannes Film Festival and a BAFTA. Her other horror credits include *Shadow Zone: My Teacher Ate My Homework* (Stephen Williams, 1997), Mike Elliott's *Casper Meets Wendy* (1998) and Tim Burton's famous short Disney film *Frankenweenie* (1984) about a dog called Sparky brought back to life by his child owner, Victor Frankenstein. In 1998, she featured in Australian director Russell Mulchay's *Tale of the Mummy* which starred Christopher Lee.

DZIUBINSKA, ANULKA

Credited simply by her first name, Anulka Dziubinska was a *Playboy* model-turned actor who found cult horror stardom in her role as Miriam in José Ramón Larraz's classic 1974 lesbian vampire film *Vampyres*, co-starring Marianne Morris. Afterwards she made small appearances primarily in television before giving up acting altogether.

E

ECHEVARRÍA, ARANTXA

Spanish filmmaker Arantxa Echevarría has worked extensively across film and television, and is renowned for her 2018 feature film, *Carmen and Lola*, which screened in the 2018 Directors' Fortnight program of the Cannes Film Festival. Born in Bilbao in 1968, Echevarría has been widely recognized in the Spanish industry for her work, including a nomination for a Goya Award for her 2012 short horror film, *De noche y de pronto*. In 2016, she also made the horror short *The Last Bus* and her work was included in the all-woman directed genre anthology, *7 from Etheria* (2017).

EGGAR, SAMANTHA

Beginning her career in theater, Victoria Louise Samantha Marie Elizabeth Therese Eggar—known simply as Samantha Eggar—studied fashion and drama, focusing on Shakespeare before her breakout film role in William Wyler's abduction thriller, *The Collector* (1965). Her international horror credits include the *giallo The Etruscan Kills Again* (Armando Crispino, 1972), *A Name for Evil* (Bernard Girard, 1973), the British horror anthology *The Uncanny* (Claude Héroux, 1977), *Demonoid* (Alfredo Zacarías, 1981) and Richard Ciupka's cult slasher film, *Curtains* (1983). In a career highlight, she starred as one of horror's greatest monstrous mothers of all time in David Cronenberg's 1979 film, *The Brood*.

EJOGO, CARMEN

Born in 1973 in London and now based in New York, actor and musician Carmen Ejogo began her career in her adolescence hosting a Disney television morning program in the early '90s, later turning to films. Flourishing in the horror genre, while she has appeared in many other highly regarded types of movies her work in *The Purge: Anarchy* (James DeMonaco, 2014), *Alien: Covenant* (Ridley Scott, 2017) and *It Comes at Night* (Trey Edward Shults, 2017) are career highlights.

EKLAND, BRITT

One of the most famous faces of the 1960s and '70s as a so-called 'sex symbol', Britt Ekland was a hard-working performer who has rarely received the professional credit she deserves for a career that has endured for almost 60 years. Ekland was born in Stockholm in 1942 and began her career as a teen with a travelling theater company, beginning her film career in London. Eckland has worked in many horror films and her credits include *What the Peeper Saw* (Andrea Bianchi and James Kelley, 1972), *Asylum* (Roy Ward Baker, 1972), *Endless Night* (Sidney Gilliat, 1972), *The Wicker Man* (Robin Hardy, 1973), *The Monster Club* (Roy Ward Baker, 1973), *Satan's Mistress* (James Polakof, 1982), *Moon in Scorpio* (Gary Graver, 1987) and *Beverley Hills Vamp* (Fred Olen Ray, 1988).

ELMI, NICOLETTA

Name a great Italian horror director and, chances are, they worked with impish child star Nicoletta Elmi. Born in 1964, while her early performances including Luchino Visconti's *Death in Venice* (1971), horror is where the celebrated red-head made her most famous appearances in films including Mario Bava's *Twitch of the Death Nerve* (1971) and *Baron Blood* (1972), *Who Saw Her Die?* (Aldo Lado's 1972), *Flesh for Frankenstein* (Paul Morrissey, 1973), *Footprints on the Moon* (Lugio Bazzoni, 1975), *The Night Child* (Massimo Dallamano, 1975) and Dario Argento's *Deep Red* (1975). As a teenager, she also played an usher in the cursed cinema at the heart of Lamberto Bava's *Demons* (1985).

ESSOE, ALEXANDRA

Daughter of a stage actor mother, Alexandra Essoe was born in Saudi Arabia in 2014. She starred in Kevin Kölsch and Dennis Widmyer's horror film *Starry Eyes*, followed by roles in horror and dark-themed movie dramas including *The Neighbour* (Marcus Dunstan, 2016), *Fashionista* (Simon Rumley, 2016), *The Blessed Ones* (Patrick O'Bell, 2016), *Midnighters* (Julius Ramsay, 2017), *The Super* (Stephan Rick, 2017), *Red Island* (Lux, 2018), *The Drone* (Jordan Rubin, 2019), *Homewrecker* (Zach Gayne, 2019) and Axelle Carolyn's segment "Grim Grinning Ghost" in the 2015 anthology, *Tales of Halloween*.

ESTELLE, JULIE

Although having voiced a lack of interest in pursuing horror roles, Indonesian actor Julie Estelle has built an impressive list of credits in the genre. Born in Jakarta in 1989, she stud-

Alexandra Essoe in "Grim Grinning Ghost"—directed by Axelle Carolyn—in the anthology *Tales of Halloween* (2015). Used with permission (thanks to Axelle Carolyn).

ied at the city's French international school, Lycée Français Louis-Charles Damais. Starring in Rizal Mantovani's horror movie *The Chanting* (2006) and its two sequels in 2007 and 2008, she later appeared in the Mo Brothers' *Macabre* (2009). In 2016, she worked again with Mantovani in his later horror film, *Firegate*. She also starred as the memorable 'Hammer Girl' in Gareth Evans' cult *pencak silat* action film *The Raid 2* in 2014.

EVANS, AMANDA

After a number of shorts and commercials, South African filmmaker Amanda Evans made her feature film debut with the stylish 2017 Cape Town-shot, snake-in-a-tent horror film, *Serpent*. Also a producer and writer, her script for the film was selected for the 2012 Berlinale Co-Production Market.

EVIGAN, BRIANA

Actor Briana Evigan was born in California in 1986 and, aside from her famous role in the *Step Up* films, she has worked extensively in the horror genre. Studying at Los Angeles Valley College, her horror credits include *Spectre* (Scott P. Levy, 1996), *S. Darko* (Chris Fisher, 2009), *Sorority Row* (Stewart Hendler, 2009), *Burning Bright* (Carlos Brooks, 2010), *Alleluia! The Devil's Carnival* (Darren Lynn Bousman, 2014) and *Paranormal Island* (Marty Murray, 2014). She also appeared in horror television series such as *Fear Itself* and *From Dusk till Dawn: The Series*.

F

FALK, ROSSELLA

Most recognizable for her performance in Federico Fellini's Oscar-winning *8½* (1963), Rome-born Rossella Falk worked in film and television for over 50 years with directors including Franco Zeffirelli, Joseph Losey and Robert Aldrich. She acted in a number of *gialli* including *Black Belly of the Tarantula* (Paolo Cavara, 1971), *The Fifth Cord* (Luigi Bazzoni, 1971), *Seven Blood-Stained Orchids* (Umberto Lenzi, 1972), *The Killer Is on the Phone* (Alberto De Martino, 1972) and Dario Argento's *Sleepless* (2001).

FANNING, ELLE

Elle Fanning began her career as a child, starting with mainstream blockbusters and increasingly moving into more daring, independent productions. She was born in Georgia in 1998, the younger sister of fellow actor Dakota Fanning. Her first association with the genre was the blockbuster horror-scifi hybrid *Super 8* (J. J. Abrams, 2011) and the gothic Disney film *Maleficent* (Robert Stromberg, 2014). It was, however, her starring role in Nicolas Winding Refn's 2016 horror film *The Neon Demon* that marked her most famous connection to the genre, later also playing literary feminist horror icon *Mary Shelley* in Haifaa al-Mansour's self titled 2017 biopic.

FARGEAT, CORALIE

Writing the screenplay for *The Telegram* (2003), and writing and directing *Reality+* (2014), French filmmaker Coralie Fargeat gained broad international recognition with her debut feature film, the gory, glossy rape-revenge film *Revenge* (2018). She studied at The Paris Institute of Political Studies and also worked as an assistant director on a number of American films made in France.

FARIS, ANNA

Although renowned primarily for her work in comedy, American actor Anna Faris also has a long relationship with horror. Born in Baltimore in 1976, she joined a theater group in Seattle after her interest in acting was piqued. Her horror film credits include *Lovers Lane* (Jon Steven Ward, 1999) and *May* (Lucky McKee, 2002), but most famously she starred in the first 4 *Scary Movie* horror parody films, beginning with Keenen Ivory Wayans's original in 2000 and making her final appearance in the franchise in *Scary Movie 4* (David Zucker, 2006).

FARMIGA, VERA ⸰

Vera Farmiga is a hugely successful actor who has worked with some of the biggest names in contemporary cinema. In recent years, her starring role in *The Conjuring* franchise has seen her closely associated with horror. The Oscar-nominated Farmiga was born in New Jersey in 1973, and after making her breakthrough in indie cinema, she would attain higher profile roles throughout her career, peaking with her multiple acting nominations for Jason Reitman's 2009 film *Up in the Air* with George Clooney. Her horror credits include *Joshua* (George Ratliff, 2007*)*, *Orphan* (Jaume Collet-Serra, 2009), and James Wan's *The Conjuring* (2013) and *The Conjuring 2* (2016) where she played Lorraine Warren. Farmiga also starred in the television series *Bates Motel*. Farmiga's sister Taissa is also an actor renowned for her work on American Horror Story, and recently starred in horror features including *The Nun* (Corin Hardy, 2018) and Stacie Passon's 2018 adaptation of Shirley Jackson's gothic thriller *We Have Always Lived in the Castle*.

FARMER, MIMSY

With her name inspired by Lewis Carroll's poem "Jabberwocky" from Lewis Carroll's *Through the Looking-Glass, and What Alice Found There* (1871), this Chicago-born American actor and artist had a close connection to the dark fantastic from birth. Although working broadly across film and television, she earned a cult reputation based on her starring roles in Italian horror, including the *gialli Four Flies on Grey Velvet* (1971), *The Perfume of the Lady in Black* (Francesco Barilli, 1974) and *Autopsy* (Armando Crispin, 1975), as well as Lucio Fulci's *The Black Cat* (1981) and Ruggero Deodato's *Body Count* (1985).

FARROW, MIA ⸰

Few screen actors have been able to use their supposed *ingénue* status to such dark and powerful effect as María de Lourdes Villiers Farrow, or Mia for short. Daughter of Hol-

Mia Farrow from *Secret Ceremony* (Joseph Losey, 1968). Credit: Everett Collection Inc / Alamy Stock Photo

lywood royalty Maureen O'Sullivan and John Farrow, despite a broad career in television and on the stage, it is her film work that has remained the most enduring. She became synonymous with the genre with her starring role in Roman Polanski's *Rosemary's Baby* (1968). Her flair for dark, gothic material was further illustrated in her starring role in Joseph Losey's *Secret Ceremony* (1968) with Elizabeth Taylor. Her horror credits continued in 1971 with Richard Fleischer's *See No Evil*, followed in 1977 with her performance in the title role of Richard Loncraine's *The Haunting of Julia*. In 2006, she reprised Billie Whitelaw's role of Mrs Blaylock in John Moore's remake of Richard Donner's *The Omen* (1976).

FARROW, TISA

Like her older sister Mia, Theresa Magdalena Farrow—credited as Tisa—also shared a flair for horror cinema, although working in distinctly different subgeneric territory to her more famous sister. Born in 1951 in Los Angeles, Tia's first horror film was Robert

Day's American made-for-television movie *The Initiation of Sarah* (1978), in which she appeared with Kay Lenz and Shelley Winters. It was Italy, however, where Tisa provided her most significant donation to the genre, starring the notorious British Video Nasties *Zombi 2* (Lucio Fulci, 1979) and *Antropophagus* (Joe D'Amato, 1980).

FEATHERSTON, KATIE

When Katie Featherston starred in a low-budget found footage horror film called *Paranormal Activity* in 2007 directed by Oren Peli, little could either of them have known the international blockbuster the film would become after its widespread cinema release in 2009. Despite claiming she was only paid $500 for the original film, she would go on to appear in the majority of the film's numerous sequels including *Paranormal Activity 2* (Tod Williams, 2010), *Paranormal Activity 3* (Henry Joost and Ariel Schulman, 2011), *Paranormal Activity 4* (Henry Joost and Ariel Schulman, 2012), *Paranormal Activity: The Marked Ones* (Christopher B. Landon, 2014) and a cameo in the Japanese spin-off *Paranormal Activity 2: Tokyo Night* (Toshikazu Nagae, 2010). In 2010, she was cast in Mel House's horror film *Psychic Experiment* and featured in several episodes of Peli's found footage horror/scifi hybrid television series *The River*.

FELDMAN, RACHEL

New York-born filmmaker Rachel Feldman began as a stage actor as a child, then moved to working as a director on television as an adult on a number of sitcoms and dramas. She received a Master of Fine Arts at New York University, and amongst her early credits as director is *Witchcraft III: The Kiss of Death* (1991) under the name R. L. Tillmans. Feldman is an awarded screenwriter, and a vocal activist for gender equality for women filmmakers.

FELISHA, RATU

Indonesian actor Ratu Felisha was born in Jakarta in 1982 and began her career as a model and soap opera actor, her horror credits include *The Chanting* (Rizal Mantovani, 2006), *The Virgin Ghost of Jeruk Purut* (Nayato Fio Nuala, 2008),) *Kain kafan perawan* (Nayato Fio Nuala, 2010), *Nakalnya anak muda* (Nayato Fio Nuala, 2010), *Badoet* (Awi Suryadi, 2015), and *Midnight Show* (Ginanti Rona Tembang Sari, 2016).

FENN, SHERILYN ⚜

Born in Detroit in 1965, American actor Sherilyn Fenn is closely associated with her enduring role as Audrey Horne in David Lynch and Mark Frost's darkly surreal television series *Twin Peaks*. Fenn left high school in her junior year to pursue acting and studied at the Lee Strasberg Theater Institute in New York before beginning her career in a number of low-budget genre films. While *Twin Peaks* and her work with Lynch in *Wild at Heart* (1990) made Fenn a cult star, her other work in the horror genre includes *Zombie High* (Ron Link, 1987), *Boxing Helena* (Jennifer Lynch, 1993), *Raze* (Josh C. Waller, 2013), *The Secrets of Emily Blair* (Joseph Genier, 2016) and *Wish Upon* (John R. Leonetti, 2017).

Sherilyn Fenn at the world premiere, in Hollywood, of *Sleepy Hollow* which stars Johnny Depp and Christina Ricci, 17 November 1999. Credit: Paul Smith / Featureflash Photo Agency / Shutterstock.com

FERDIN, PAMELYN

Animal rights activist Pamelyn Ferdin began her career as a child star on film and television, moving into horror territory during her late teens as she neared the end of her career, although she would return sporadically from 1999 onwards. In 1969 she co-starred with Gene Tierney and Ray Milland in Walter Grauman's made-for-television horror film *Daughter of the Mind*, followed in 1971 with a smaller role in Paul Wendkos's *The Mephisto Waltz*. But it was in Dennis Donnelly's *The Toolbox Murders* (1978) that Ferdin's cult reputation as a horror star largely stems, playing abducted teenager Laurie Ballard.

FERRANTI, SHARON

Filmmaker, editor and playwright Sharon Ferranti received a Masters of Fine Arts from the California Institute of the Arts. Her 2002 feature film debut *Make a Wish* was a lesbian slasher film that won the Best in Fest award at the Paris Women's Film Festival that year. Released in the United Kingdom with the less subtle title *Lesbian Psycho*, the film received widespread international distribution.

FIES, BRENDA AND ELISABETH

Director, writer and actor Elisabeth Fies and her sister, producer Brenda Fies, have worked together on numerous projects together, the least of which beyond filmmaking itself includes being the team behind Bleedfest, the Californian monthly film festival that showcased cutting-edge genre films made by women that ran until 2011. Making number of horror and thriller shorts together, they also collaborated on the 2009 horror feature *The Commune*.

FENECH, EDWIGE

Born in 1948 in what was then colonial French Algeria, despite acting in a number of sex comedies Edwige Fenech's cult status is resultant largely of her iconic work in Italian *giallo* cinema. Of these, she frequently starred in a number of movies directed by her brother-in-law Sergio Martino, including *The Strange Vice of Mrs Wardh* (1971), *Your Vice Is a Locked Room and Only I Have the Key* (1972) and *All the Colors of the Dark* (1972). Her other *giallo* credits including *Five Dolls for an August Moon* (Mario Bava, 1970), *The Case of the Bloody Iris* (Giuliano Carnimeo, 1972), *Strip Nude for Your Killer* (Andrea Bianchi, 1975) and *Phantom of Death* (Ruggero Deodato, 1988). In 2007, she featured in a small cameo as an art teacher in Eli Roth's *Hostel: Part II*, and in 1991 a perfume called *Edwige Fenech Donna* was released as tribute to the famous actor.

FIELD, SHIRLEY ANNE

British actor Shirley Anne Field appeared on both film and television since her first un-credited film role in 1955. Born in 1936, she lived in children's homes from the age of 6, outlining her remarkable life in her 1991 autobiography *A Time for Love*. Her horror credits include *Horror in the Black Museum* (Arthur Crabtree, 1959), *Peeping Tom* (Michael Powell, 1960), *These are the Damned* (Joseph Losey, 1962) and *House of the Living Dead* (Ray Austin, 1974).

FIELDER, PAT

Often considered one of the first women scriptwriters to specialize in the macabre, Pat Fielder was born in Pasadena. She was working as a secretary for the producer of *The Monster that Changed the World* (Arnold Laven, 1957) and asked if she could have an attempt at rewriting the screenplay when the original version was unable to be filmed in its initial Japanese location. Celebrated for her focus on autonomous and independent women characters, although she predominantly wrote for television later in her career, her genre credits include *The Vampire* (Paul Landres, 1957) and its sequel *The Return of Dracula* (Paul Landres 1958), and co-writing Landres' 1958 scifi film, *The Flame Barrier.*

FERRARE, CRISTINA

With a career in modeling and acting, Cleveland-born Cristina Ferrare stems from Italian descent, and moved to Los Angeles in her teens to further her career. Turning towards talk shows and writing later in her career, her sole horror credit is in the title role of Juan López Moctezuma's cult vampire classic, *Mary, Mary, Bloody* Mary in 1975 in which she co-starred with John Carradine.

FHIONA-LOUISE

Very little is known about the mysterious director of the bleak, unrelenting 1989 film adaptation of the story of notorious British serial killer Dennis Nilsen, *Cold Light of Day*. While there is little solid information available, rumors are in circulation that she either vanished or died by suicide at the age of 21. What is known, however, is that the film was produced by Richard Driscoll. Based on this, there is speculation that the mysterious disappearance of Fhiona-Louise was simply a PR stunt and that she never existed at all. What remains undeniable, however, is that despite its low budget, *Cold Light of Day* is a brutal, raw and undeniably memorable serial killer film.

FIELDS, VERNA

Oscar-award winning film editor Verna Fields was born in St Louis in 1918 and is in large part credited with providing the kinetic energy to Steven Spielberg's killer shark blockbuster *Jaws* in 1975. Before *Jaws*, Fields other editing credits included Peter Bogdonavich's *Targets* in 1971—Boris Karloff's final film where he plays a notably semi-autobiographical character. Beginning her career as a sound editor and working with filmmakers such as Fritz Lang, in 1960 she turned her attention to film editing and worked extensively across film and television. Fields also taught editing at the University of Southern California, and while her most famous student might be George Lucas, of note here is her other ex-students Willard Huyck and Gloria Katz who would go on to co-direct the cult 1973 horror film *Messiah of Evil*. After *Jaws*, Fields moved largely into executive roles at Universal and became the studios Vice President; she has thus been largely credited as an important ground-breaker for future women film executives in major studios. Aside from winning the Oscar for editing *Jaws*, she also won a Best Editing award with the American Cinema Editors and a 1981 Women in Film Crystal Award for her work in cinema.

FINDLAY, ROBERTA

Beginning her career in partnership with her then-husband Michael Findlay, Findlay is a cult figure in exploitation film history. Taking on many tasks both in front and behind the camera, the couple's *Her Flesh* trilogy—*The Touch of Her Flesh* (1968) *The Kiss of Her Flesh* (1968), and *The Curse of Her Flesh* (1968)—were so-called 'roughies' that established them on the grindhouse circuit. While Roberta herself is hazy about what actual jobs she did on what films, at different stages she wrote, edited, acted, filmed and directed many of movies with Michael, the most notorious of which was undeniably 1971's *The Slaughter* that would be re-released in 1976 by the film's distributor with a tacked-on supposedly 'real' murder scene and released under the name *Snuff*. While working largely in pornography, Michael and Roberta would also make the Yeti film *Shriek of the Mutilated* together in 1974, before Roberta would leave Michael and branch out independently to focus solely on adult filmmaking. Later in her career she would shift from pornography back to horror feature filmmaking with the movies *The Oracle* (1985), *Tenement* (1985), *Blood Sisters* (1987), *Lurkers* (1988) and *Prime Evil* (1988).

FLANAGAN, FIONNULA

Fionnula Flanagan was born in Dublin in 1941 and would earn a reputation in her homeland as much for her acting work as a political activist. Moving to the United States in the late 1960s to further her acting career, across her lengthy filmography include a number of horror film credits such as *Mad at the Moon* (Martin Donovan, 1992), *The Others* (Alejandro Amenábar, 2001), *Blessed* (Simon Fellows, 2004), *Havenhurst* (Andrew C. Erin, 2016) and the horror-comedy *Trash Fire* (Richard Bates Jr., 2016).

FLECK, LUISE

Broadly considered the second woman feature film director after French filmmaker Alice Guy, Luise Fleck was born in 1873 in Vienna. In 1910, she established *Erste österreichische Kinofilms-Industrie*, Austria's first major movie production company, with her brother and husband. She worked prolifically, moving to Berlin in the 1920s and eventually fleeing to China in 1940 after her husband was released from Dachau Concentration Camp. Of her many impressive credits, in 1911, Fleck and her brother adapted Jacques Offenbach's dark fantasy *The Tales of Hoffman* in a short film, and amongst their many credits as feature film co-directors were the 1919 ghost story *Die Ahnfrau* and the 1920 movie *Anita* about a woman menaced by an evil hypnotist.

FLEMING, LONE

Spanish horror superstar Lone Fleming was born in Denmark in 1945 and appeared in a number of classic horror films by Amando de Ossorio, including *Tombs of the Blind Dead* (1972), *Attack of the Blind Dead* (1973) and *The Possessed* (1975). As well as the Spanish *giallo Sexy* Cat (Julio Pérez Tabernero, 1973), she also acted in *Evil Eye* (Mario Siciliano, 1975) and later horror features such as Víctor Matellano's *Wax* (2014), *Vampyres* (2015), *Nasciturus: El que va a nacer* (Miguel Barreto, Sofía Guillén, and Alberto Luengo, 2015) and *Escaping the Dead* (Martin Sonntag, 2017). In 2017, she was kickstarting funds to support her directorial debut, *The Barefoot Virgin*.

FLETCHER, LOUISE

Winning the triple whammy of an Oscar, BAFTA and Golden Globe award for her chilling performance as Nurse Ratched in Miloš Forman's *One Flew Over the Cuckoo's Nest* (1975), Louise Fletcher might have put in one of the great monster performances in a film that was in no other way ostensibly a horror film. Born in Alabama in 1934 and working with filmmakers including Robert Altman and Sergio Leone, Fletcher would have a long connection to horror in many films, including *Exorcist II: The Heretic* (John Boorman, 1977), *Mama Dracula* (Boris Szulzinger, 1980), *Strange Behavior* (Michael Laughlin, 1980), *Strange Invaders* (Michael Laughlin, 1983), the unfinished *Grizzly II: The Predator* (André Szöts, 1983), *Firestarter* (Mark L. Lester, 1984), *Invaders from Mars* (Tobe Hooper, 1986), *Flowers in the Attic* (Jeffrey Bloom, 1987), *Shadowzone* (J.S. Cardone, 1990), *Nightmare on the 13th Floor* (Walter Grauman, 1990), *The Stepford Husbands* (Fred Walton, 1996), *Frankenstein and Me* (Robert Tinnell, 1996) and episodes of horror and scifi television series including *Tales from the Crypt* and *The Twilight Zone*.

FOCH, NINA

Born in the Netherlands in 1926, Nina Foch moved to New York City as a child where her mother encouraged her interest in drama and music, and she studied method acting with Lee Strasberg. Although appearing in films by directors including Stanley Kubrick, Vincente Minnelli and Robert Wise (winning a Best Supporting Actress Oscar nomination for the latter's 1954 film *Executive Suite*), early in Foch's lengthy career she worked predominantly in film noir and horror. In 1944, she starred in both Henry Levin's *Cry of the Werewolf* and Lew Landers's *The Return of the Vampire*, followed the next year with the central role in Budd Boetticher's supernatural film noir *Escape in the Fog*. Later in her career she featured in Brice Mack's *Jennifer* (1978) and had a small role in John McTiernan's underrated 1986 horror film *Nomads* with Lesley-Anne Downe and Pierce Brosnan.

Nina Foch from *Cry of the Werewolf* (Henry Levin, 1944). Credit: Everett Collection Inc / Alamy Stock Photo

FOLDES, JOAN

Working with her British-Hungarian husband Peter, Joan Foldes wrote, produced, and co-directed (despite not receiving a credit for the latter) one of the most controversial animated films of the 1950s, the British short film *A Short Vision* (1956). Shown on the popular *Ed Sullivan Show* on 27 May 1956, their short anti-nuclear horror film *A Short Vision* caused shockwaves with its gory flesh-melting detail of the effects of the atomic bomb.

FOERSTER, ANNA

Born in Germany, before becoming a director herself American filmmaker Anna Foerster worked as a cinematographer on films including *Alien Resurrection* (Jean-Pierre Jeunet, 1997) and *Godzilla* (Roland Emmerich, 1998). In 2016, she direccted the feature film *Underworld: Blood Wars* starring Kate Beckinsale, the fifth in the popular vampire/werewolf franchise. She has also worked extensively in scifi on film and television.

FONTAINE, JOAN

Oscar-winning actor Joan Fontaine was nominated 3 times for the Best Actress award, winning for her starring role in Alfred Hitchcock's 1941 psychological thriller *Suspicion*. In 1940, however, she was nominated for her lead performance in Hitchcock's brooding gothic adaptation of Daphne Du Maurier's 1938 novel *Rebecca* as a character simply known as The Second Mrs. de Winter. Fontaine was the younger sister of another Classical Hollywood star, Olivia de Haviland, and was born in Tokyo in 1917 before moving to California. Collaborating with Max Ophüls, Orson Welles and Fritz Lang, before moving solely to television her last feature film role was in Cyril Frankel's 1966 Hammer horror film *The Witches*, based on screenplay by Nigel Kneale. In 1986, she appeared in the pilot television movie for Jerry London's *Dark Mansions*—an attempt by Aaron Spelling to revamp the *Dark Shadows* gothic soap opera template for the '80s.

FORD, ANITRA

Anitra Ford may have made her fame being a model on the popular game show *The Price is Right*, but as Laura she also starred in one of the most original American cult horror films of the 1970s; Willard Huyck and Gloria Katz's 1973 movie *Messiah of Evil*. Ford worked on film and television throughout the 1970s with another notable credit being Dr Susan Harris in Denis Sanders' horror film *Invasion of the Bee Girls* (1973).

FORD, MARIA

Little is known of prolific B-grade horror actor Maria Ford who made her reputation primarily throughout the 1990s in horror films. Amongst her many credits in the genre are *Slumber Party Massacre III* (Sally Mattison, 1990), *The Unnamable II: The Statement of Randolph Carter* (Jean-Paul Ouellette, 1993), the 1993 anthology film *H.P. Lovecraft's: Necronomicon*, *The Wasp Woman* (Jim Wynorski, 1995), *Night Hunter* (Rick Jacobson, 1996) and *Bram Stoker's Burial of the Rats* (Dan Golden, 1995).

FOREMAN, DEBORAH

American actor Deborah Foreman was born in California in 1962. Modeling in her teens after encouragement from her parents, after arriving in Hollywood she quickly turned to acting and worked in commercials and television. In the dual roles of Muffy and Buffy in *April Fool's Day* (Fred Walton, 1986) she appeared in a number of other horror films including the unfinished *Grizzly II: The Predator* (André Szöts, 1983), *Destroyer* (Robert

Kirk, 1988) *Waxwork* (Anthony Hickox, 1988), *Lobster Man from Mars* (Stanley Sheff, 1989), and *Sundown: The Vampire in Retreat* (Anthony Hickox, 1989).

FORREST, CHRISTINE

Actor and producer Christine Forrest met filmmaker George A. Romero on the set of his 1973 film *Season of the Witch*, and they were married from 1980 to 2010. She appeared in a range of often uncredited parts in many of his films during this period and was a producer on Romero's *The Dark Half* (1993), the horror anthologies *Deadtime Stories: Volume 1* (2009) and *Deadtime Stories: Volume 2* (2011), and Tom Savini's 1990 remake of Romero's 1968 zombie classic *Night of the Living Dead*. She also received an Assistant Director credit on Romero's *Dawn of the Dead* (1978).

FOSTER, JODIE ι

Jodie Foster's Best Actress Academy Award for her performance as Clarice Starling in Jonathan Demme's *The Silence of the Lambs* was her second Oscar after previously winning one for her performance in Jonathan Kaplan's 1988 rape drama *The Accused*. Well-known as a successful child actor, Alicia Christian Foster was born in 1962 in Los Angeles and throughout her career, she would work across genres and later turn to directing and producing. It was earlier in her career, however, that Foster made her other significant donation to the genre in Nicolas Gessner's *The Little Girl Who Lives Down the Lane* where she plays a fiercely independent 13-year-old who reveals her strength in the face of ominous threats.

FOSTER, MEG ♪

Born in Pennsylvania in 1948, Meg Foster was raised in Connecticut and began her career on stage in New York City. She has worked extensively across both film and television and has an impressive list of horror credits including *Welcome to Arrow Beach* (Laurence Harvey, 1974), *The Legend of Sleepy Hollow* (Henning Schellerup, 1980), *They Live* (John Carpenter, 1988), *Leviathan* (George P. Cosmatos, 1989), *Stepfather II* (Jeff Burr, 1989), *Go Straight to Hell* (Edward G. Norris, 2011), *Lords of Salem* (Rob Zombie, 2012), *31* (Rob Zombie, 2016) and *Jeepers Creepers 3* (Victor Salva, 2017).

FOX, MEGAN *

Much hype surrounded American actor and model Megan Fox's foray into horror, starring in the title role of Karyn Kusama's *Jennifer's Body* in 2009. Despite an initially disappointing critical and box office response, the film has been increasingly celebrated as a feminist cult movie well ahead of its time. Fox also starred in Jimmy Hayward's 2010 horror-western *Jonah Hex*, and in 2018 was attached to star in the Travel Channels series *Mysteries and Myths with Megan Fox*, which she also co-created.

FOX, SIDNEY

Born in 1911 in New York City, Sidney Leiffer—who would act professionally as Sidney Fox—worked hard when her parents were negatively affected by the 1929 stock market crash, turning to modeling through necessity and a stage career followed from there. She first appeared in film in 1931, acting the following year with Béla Lugosi in *Murders in the Rue Morgue*, directed by Robert Florey. Despite her success being a pet project of Carl Laemmle Jr., her potential was cut unexpectedly short when she died of an accidental drug overdose at 30 years old.

FRANK, CAROL

Little is known about Carol Frank who worked as an assistant to Amy Holden Jones on *The Slumber Party Massacre* (1982) and Lina Shanklin's *Summerspell* (1983). Produced by Roger Corman's Concorde Pictures—which had previously produced *The Slumber Party Massacre*—Frank is credited for both writing and directing the 1986 slasher film *Sorority House Massacre*.

FRANKLIN, DIANE

A familiar face in 1980s teen films, Diane Franklin was born in New York in 1962. Aside from teen comedies such as *The Last American Virgin* (Boaz Davidson, 1982), *Better Off Dead* (Savage Steve Holland, 1985), and *Bill & Ted's Excellent Adventure* (Stephen Herek, 1989), she worked in two cult horror films; *Amityville II: The Possession* (Damiano Damiani, 1982) and Ted Nicolaou's *TerrorVision* (1986). She also appeared in the made-for-television horror movie *Deadly Lessons* in 1983, and her more recent horror credits include *The Final Interview* (Fred Vogel, 2017).

FRANKLIN, PAMELA

British actor Pamela Franklin was born in 1950 and would study ballet in Britain when she settled there when she was 8. Her first film role was as Flora in Jack Clayton's 1961 film *The Innocents*, adapted from Henry James's famous ghost story, the novella *The Turn of the Screw* (1898). Across her career on film and television she would return to horror, starring in films including *The Nanny* (Seth Holt, 1965), *And Soon the Darkness* (Robert Fuest, 1970), *Necromancy* (Bert I. Gordon, 1972), *The Legend of Hell House* (John Hough, 1973), the made-for-TV horror film *Satan's School for Girls* (David Lowell Rich, 1973) and her final role in Bert I. Gordon's *The Food of the Gods* in 1976 with Ralph Meeker and Ida Lupino.

FRANZ, VERONIKA

Austrian filmmaker Veronika Franz met her regular collaborator Severin Fiala when he babysat her children while he was at film school. Initially a journalist, Franz's turn towards filmmaking extended from her friendship with Fiala. Together they would watch movies that would later influence their work together as co-directors. Initially making a documentary together, their award-winning 2014 horror film *Goodnight Mommy* was their narrative feature debut, co-writing the script while Franz nursed a broken leg after wearing heels at the Cannes Film Festival. In 2018, they co-directed a segment of the horror anthology *The Field Guide to Evil* with their dark medieval queer fantasy "Die Trud", and their English-language debut—the horror film *The Lodge*—premiered at the 2019 Sundance Film Festival.

FUENTES, AMALIA

Filipino actor Amalia Fuentes was born in 1940 and was one of the country's greatest film stars. Beginning her career initially in romantic films alongside Juancho Gutierrez after winning a competition, she was nominated for many FAMAS (Filipino Academy of Movie Arts and Sciences) awards for her acting. Across her more-than-60 year career, she starred in two cult Filipino horror movies, Gerardo de Leon's 1964 film *The Blood Drinkers* and his 1966 movie, *Blood of the Vampires*.

FUJI, TAKAKO

Japanese actor Takako Fuji is renowned for her ongoing role as Kayako Saeki in Takashi Shimizu's *The Grudge/Ju-On* franchise. Born in Tokyo in 1972, she appeared in the role in *Ju-on: The Curse* (2000), *Ju-On: The Curse 2* (2000), *Ju-on: The Grudge* (2002), *Ju-*

on: The Grudge 2 (2003), and Shimizu's American remakes *The Grudge* (2004) and *The Grudge 2* (2006). Fuji's other horror credits include Shimizu's earlier short *Katasumi and 4444444444* (1998) and his 2005 film *Reincarnation*.

FUJIWARA, KEI

Kei Fujiwara began her film career as an actor in the American scifi film *The Neptune Factor* (Daniel Petrie, 1973), but would become a cult film figure with her role as the protagonist's girlfriend in Shin'ya Tsukamoto's iconic 1989 splatterpunk film *Tetsuo, the Iron Man*. In 1996 she would act, write and direct in her feature horror filmmaking debut *Organ*, a gore film about body part harvesting, followed by 2005's experimental horror film *Id*.

Kei Fujiwara (as Woman) and Tomorowo Taguchi (as Man) in *Tetsuo* aka *Tetsuo: The Iron Man* aka *The Ironman*, directed by Shinya Tsukamoto (1988). Credit: Original Cinema/Photofest © Original Cinema.

FUHRMAN, ISABELLE

Born in Washington D.C. in 1997, despite her youth American actor Isabelle Fuhrman already has established an impressive career with a close relationship to the horror genre. She is immediately recognizable for her lead role as Esther in Jaume Collet-Serra's 2009 horror film *Orphan*, and she was later cast in Tod Williams's *Cell*, adapted from the 2006 Stephen King novel of the same name. Fuhrman provided voices for Donald P. Borchers's 2009 television movie remake of *Children of the Corn*. She also appeared in the supernatural television series *Ghost Whisperer*.

G

GABRIEL, BETTY

Betty Gabriel became a horror icon for her breathtaking performance as Georgina in Jordan Peele's Oscar-winning 2017 horror film, *Get Out*, but her relationship with horror spans well beyond that single role. Born in Washington D.C. and studying drama at Julliard in New York, with a background in theater, Gabriel's other horror roles include *The Purge: Election Year* (James DeMonaco, 2016), *Unfriended: Dark Web* (Stephen Susco, 2018) and *Upgrade* (Leigh Whannell, 2018). She also appeared in *12 Deadly Days*, a horror-comedy web series anthology from 2016.

Betty Gabriel arrives for the 2018 Movies for Grownups Awards on 5 February 2018 in Beverly Hills, Los Angeles, California. Credit: DFree / Shutterstock.com

GALBÓ, CRISTINA

Eurohorror regular Cristina Galbó is a familiar face to fans of the category. She was born in Madrid in 1950, began acting as a child, and would work in almost 40 films across her

30-year screen career. Her credits include *The House That Screamed* (Narciso Ibáñez Serrador, 1970), *Satan's Five Warnings* (José Luis Merino, 1970), *What Have You Done to Solange?* (Massimo Dallamano, 1972), *The Living Dead at Manchester Morgue* (Jorge Grau, 1974) and *The Killer Must Kill Again* (Luigi Cozzi, 1975).

GALLEANI, ELY

Although her name may not be as immediately recognizable as some of Italian horror's other women, Ely Galleani is instantly familiar to anyone who knows the genre well. Born in Northern Italy in 1953 as Federica Elisabetta De Galleani, she worked on-screen under a variety of names including Justine Gall, Elisabetta De Galleani, and Edy Gall. Making her debut in Luchino Visconti's *The Damned* (1969), her horror and *giallo* credits include *Five Dolls for an August Moon* (Mario Bava, 1970), *A Lizard in a Woman's Skin* (Lucio Fulci, 1971), *Baba Yaga* (Corrado Farina, 1973), *Naked Massacre* (Denis Héroux, 1976) and *Damned in Venice* (Ugo Liberatore, 1978).

GALLI, IDA

Horror fans might know her as Evelyn Stewart but Italian *giallo* regular Ida Galli was also credited as Isli Oberon (or simply sometimes Arianna) across her 30-year film career. In her early years, she had a small role in Federico Fellini's iconic *La Dolce Vita* (1960) and, she acted in *gialli* and horror films such as *The Whip and the Body* (Mario Bava, 1963), *The Sweet Body of Deborah* (Romolo Guerrieri, 1968), *Queens of Evil* (Tonino Cervi, 1970), *The Weekend Murders* (Michele Lupo, 1970), *The Bloodstained Butterfly* (Duccio Tessari, 1971), *The Case of the Scorpion's Tail* (Sergio Martino, 1971), *Spirits of Death* (Romano Scavolini, 1972), *Manic Mansion* (Francisco Lara Polop, 1972), *Knife of Ice* (Umberto Lenzi, 1972), *Footprints on the Moon* (Luigi Bazzoni, 1975), *The Night Child* (Massimo Dallamano, 1975) and Lucio Fulci's underrated Poe-inspired masterpiece, *The Psychic* (Lucio Fulci, 1977).

GANCE, MARGUERITE

While her screen credits are hardly extensive, Marguerite Gance starred in one of the most beautiful and most important silent horror films ever made, Jean Epstein's 1928 adaptation of Edgar Allan Poe's *The Fall of the House of Usher* (1839). As Madeleine Usher, she starred alongside Jean Debucourt as Sir Roderick Usher, and her only other screen credit was as Charlotte Corday in her husband Abel Gance's famous historical epic, *Napoleon* (1927).

GARATEGUY, TAMAE

Tamae Garateguy discovered her taste for blood and sex with *Pompeya*, her violent solo debut, which won Best Argentinean Film at Argentina's International Festival of Mar del Plata in 2010 and the Free Spirit Award at the Warsaw International Film Festival in 2011. *Pompeya* also screened in festivals such as the Toronto International Film Festival in 2011, South Korea's Puchon International Fantastic Film Festival in 2012, and SXSW in Austin, Texas in 2012. In 2013, her latest project exploring sex and death, *Shewolf*, was in the International Competition (Vanguard and Genre) at the Buenos Aires International Festival of Independent Cinema, and also played México's Mórbido Film Festival, Cuba's Festival Internacional de Nuevo Cine Latinoamericano de La Habana, and Fantastic Fest. It later played in 2014 at highly-regarded international festivals including Brazil's Fantaspoa International Fantastic Film Festival and the Puchon International

Tamae Garateguy (Photo credit: Pablo Tesoriere). Used with permission.

Fantastic Film Festival. She prides herself on being the most popular mother amongst all her children's friends because of her Reagan tattoo from Fantastic Fest.

GARCIA-MOLINA, CATHY

Filipino director Cathy Garcia-Molina has worked steadily across film and television since beginning her work in the industry in 1990. Born in Quezon City in the Philippines in 1971, she is primarily known for her box-office-topping romantic comedies but made her horror debut in the supernatural anthology *Cinco* (2010) with the zombie segment "Puso".

GARCIADIEGO, PAZ ALICIA

Renowned for her frequent collaborations with acclaimed Mexican filmmaker Arturo Ripstein (who is also her husband), Paz Alicia Garciadiego is a screenwriter and academic. Amongst their many projects together, Garciadiego wrote the screenplay for Ripstein's award winning 1996 film *Deep Crimson*, based on the story of real-life serial killers

Raymond Fernandez and Martha Beck, who also provided the inspiration for cult films including *The Honeymoon Killers* (Leonard Kastle, 1970) and Fabrice Du Welz's 2014 Belgian horror film *Alleluia*.

GARLAND, BEVERLEY

Known primarily for her appearance on the whitebread 1960s American sitcom *My Three Sons*, Santa Cruz-born actor Beverly Garland had strong form in low-budget genre films. Born in 1926, she studied drama as a young woman and, in the 1950s, played in several horror/scifi hybrids directed by B-grade king Roger Corman—*Swamp Woman* (1956), *It Conquered the Earth* (1956) and *Not of this Earth* (1957). Her other horror credits are *The Neanderthal Man* (E. A. Dupont, 1953), *The Alligator People* (Roy Del Ruth, 1959), *Twice-Told Tales* (Sidney Salkow, 1963) and *The Mad Room* (Bernard Giraud, 1969).

GARRY, JACQUELINE

There is something rather disappointing that *The Curse* (2001), a microbudget feminist werewolf comedy shot in New York City for US$37,000, is Jacqueline Garry's only current film credit. Although superficially recalling *Ginger Snaps* (John Fawcett, 2000), Garry's film was allegedly shot earlier in late 1998. For any distributors reading this, surely there's room in the world for more than one late '90s werewolf-as-menstruation-metaphor film? Garry's work is ripe for rediscovery.

GASTINI, MARTA

Born near Turin in 1989, Italian actor Marta Gastini was only 20 when she co-starred with Anthony Hopkins in the exorcism film *The Rite* (Mikael Håfström, 2010), and in 2012 played Mina in Dario Argento's *Dracula 3D*. She also appeared in the horror films *Evil Things* (Simone Gandolfo, 2012) and *Compulsion* (Craig Goodwill, 2016), and played Giulia Farnese in the television series *Borgia*.

GEBBE, KATRIN

Filmmaker, writer and teacher Katrin Gebbe was born in Germany in 1983 and studied at the Academy of Visual Arts and Design in The Netherlands, Boston's School of the Museum of Fine Arts and the Hamburg Media School. Her final student film *Sores & Sirin* (2009) saw her awarded the European Union's European Young CIVIS Media Prize.

Gebbe's debut feature film was the 2013 movie *Nothing Bad Can Happen*, a brutal horror-drama film that screened at the 2013 Cannes Film Festival in the *Un Certain Regard* program. In 2018, her segment "A Nocturnal Breath" was included on the horror anthology *The Field Guide to Evil*, followed by her 2019 feature *Pelican Blood*.

GEESON, JUDY

Working on film, stage and television for well over 60 years, Sussex-born actor Judy Geeson worked in Britain early in her career but later became famous for roles in popular American television series such as *Gilmore Girls* and *Mad About You*. One of her earliest film roles was in *Berserk!* (Jim O'Connolly, 1967) with Joan Crawford, and she later appeared in a range of horror movies like *Goodbye Gemini* (Alan Gibson, 1970), *10 Rillington Place* (Richard Fleischer, 1971), *Fear in the Night* (Jimmy Sangster, 1972), *Doomwatch* (Peter Sasdy, 1972), *It Happened at Nightmare Inn* (Eugenio Martín, 1973), *Dominique* (Michael Anderson, 1979), *Inseminoid* (Norman J. Warren, 1981) and the Rob Zombie-directed *The Lords of Salem* (2012) and *31* (2016).

GELLER, SARAH MICHELLE ꙮ

In the title role of the popular television series *Buffy the Vampire Slayer*, Sarah Michelle Geller was one of the biggest cult TV stars of the late 1990s and early 2000s. Born in New York in 1977, the series sparked what would be her long association with the horror genre, starring in mainstream genre blockbusters *I Know What You Did Last Summer* (Jim Gillespie, 1997), *I Still Know What You Did Last Summer* (Danny Cannon, 1998), and *Scream 2* (Wes Craven, 1997), as well as the US remakes of the popular J-horror *Ju-on* franchise, *The Grudge* (Takashi Shimizu, 2004) and *The Grudge 2* (Takashi Shimizu, 2006). In 2009, she starred in Joel Bergvall and Simon Sandquist's *Possession*, the American remake of Park Young-hoon's 2002 South Korean film *Addicted*.

GEMSER, LAURA

Born in Indonesia in 1950, cult actor Laura Gemser was raised in the Netherlands and studied fashion at Artibus Art School. While renowned primarily for her work in many of the *Emmanuelle* films, her work on-screen often spilled into horror territory particularly with filmmakers Joe D'Amato and Bruno Mattei with whom she regularly worked. Of these, notable credits include *Emanuelle in America* (Joe D'Amato, 1977), *Emanuelle and the Last Cannibals* (Joe D'Amato, 1977) and *Erotic Nights of the Living Dead* (Joe D'Amato, 1980). Later in her career she would return to fashion to design costumes for horror films including *Metamorphosis* (George Eastman, 1990), *Beyond Darkness* (Claudio Fragasso,

1990), *Troll 2* (Claudio Fragasso, 1990), *Frankenstein 2000* (Joe D'Amato, 1991), *Door Into Silence* (Lucio Fulci, 1991) and *The Crawlers* (Fabrizio Laurenti, 1993), the latter also released under the title *Troll 3*.

GENÉE, HEIDI

German filmmaker Heidi Genée was born in Berlin in 1938 and across her career worked as a director, editor and screenwriter. Amongst the credits that span her 25-year career she notably edited Fritz Böttger's classic 1960 West German horror film *Horrors of Spider Island*, known to international audiences primarily for its inclusion on the television series *Mystery Science Theater 3000*.

GEORGE, SUSAN

Beginning her career in 1962, Susan George would become synonymous with unflinching cinema of the 1970s through her starring role in Sam Peckinpah's brutal rape-revenge film *Straw Dogs* (1971). Born in London in 1950, George had a long association with the horror genre and appeared in films including *The Sorcerers* (Michael Reeves, 1967), *Sudden Terror* (John Hugh, 1970), *Die Screaming Marianne* (Pete Walker, 1971), *Fright* (Peter Collinson, 1971), *Tintorera: Killer Shark* (René Cardona Jr., 1977), *Venom* (Piers Haggard, 1981) and *The House Where Evil Dwells* (Kevin Connor, 1982). She also acted in television movies *Dracula* (Patrick Dromgoole, 1968) and *Dr. Jekyll and Mr. Hyde* (David Winters, 1973), and episodes of horror series such as *Tales of Unease, Tales of the Unexpected* and *Tales of Mystery and Imagination*.

GERETTA GERETTA

Geretta Giancarlo aka Geretta Geretta made an early appearance in Susan Seidelman's feminist masterpiece *Smithereens* in 1982 and has worked in films made around the world. She is most famous for her work in Italian horror cinema including *Murder-Rock: Dancing Death* (Lucio Fulci, 1984), *Rats: Night of Terror* (Bruno Mattei and Claudio Fragasso., 1984), *Demons* (Lamberto Bava, 1985), *Shocking Dark* (Bruno Mattei, 1989), *The Becoming* (Geovanni Molina and Marty Marrero, 2012), *Bloody Christmas* (Michael Shershenovich, 2012) and *Domination of The Becoming* (Geovanni Molina and Marty Marrero, 2018). She is a prolific writer and studied a Masters of Fine Arts in screenwriting at the American Film Institute. She has also directed two drama feature-length drama films, *Whitepaddy* (2006) and *Sweets and Teats* (2008).

GERMAN, LAURA

Born in California in 1978, Laura German has appeared in many horror movies including the slasher film *Dead Above Ground* (Chuck Bowman, 2002), Marcus Nispel's 2003 remake of Tobe Hooper's classic *The Texas Chain Saw Massacre* (subtly renamed *The Texas Chainsaw Massacre*) and Xavier Gens' nuclear survival horror movie *The Divide* (2011). In 2007, however, she attained her most impressive role as Beth in Eli Roth's superior sequel to his 2005 so-called 'torture porn' film *Hostel*, *Hostel: Part II*.

GEVARGIZIAN, JILL

Hailing from Missouri, Jill Gevargizian—aka Jill Sixx—is a director, screenwriter and producer who began her career as a hairstylist, a career that inspired her 2016 festival favourite horror short, *The Stylist*. In 2014 she founded Sixx Tape Productions with her directorial debut *Call Girl*, that short is also included in the 2017 anthology *Dark Web*.

Jill Gevargizian (Photo credit: Brian Paulette). Used with permission. www.sixxtape.com

As writer and director, her other horror shorts include *Police Brutality* (2015), *Grammy* (2015), *The Luhrmanns* (2016) and *42 Counts* (2018). She produced the shorts *Pity* (2014) and *BFF Girls* (2018) and was Assistant Director on the 35mm feature film *Frankenstein Created Bikers* (2016) and the Second Unit Director on Jen and Sylvia Soska's "T is for Torture Porn" segment in the 2012 anthology *The ABCs of Death 2*. She founded Missouri's Slaughter Movie House in 2012, a regular movie screening event that runs on the first Monday of each month and hosts indie horror, exploitation and scifi films. It is through these screenings that Gevargaizian herself was first inspired to make her own movies.

GISH, LILLIAN

Possibly the greatest American film star of the silent era, Lillian Gish was born in 1893 in Ohio, and worked in film for three-quarters of a century. Early in her career she worked regularly with filmmaker D.W. Griffith, including in her debut film with her sister Dorothy, the 1912 home invasion short *An Unseen Enemy*. In 1928, she would star in one of her greatest roles as Hettie in Victor Sjostrom's haunting gothic tale of women and insanity, *The Wind*. Later in her career, she returned to the gothic once more in Charles Laughton's chilling *The Night of the Hunter* (1955) in which she starred alongside Robert Mitchum and Shelley Winters.

GIST, ELOYCE

Pionnering African American filmmaker Eloyce Gist was born in Texas in 1892. She grew up in Washington D.C. and studied at Howard University. Her husband James was an evangelist, and together they felt that cinema held enormous potential in spreading their message of religious faith and redemption. Dated roughly in the early 1930s, James and Eloyce made one of their two films together, the extraordinary *Hell Bound Train*, and it is understood that she wrote most of the screenplay and directed many scenes. The film shows a dancing man in a devil costume picking up a range of sinners on the eponymous train, each who are depicted in a variety of stand-alone scenarios as representing different kinds of afronts to God. The Gists would take their positively-received films to Black churches where Eloyce would play piano to provide the music which accompanied their movies.

GLOVER, KATE

Australian director, writer and producer Kate Glover gained a taste for horror at adolescent slumber parties with films like *Friday the 13th* (Sean S. Cunningham, 1980) and *Candyman* (Bernard Rose, 1992), and was heavily influenced by fellow Australian filmmaker Peter Weir's Australian gothic classic *Picnic at Hanging Rock* (1975). Glover relocated to the United Kingdom from Australia while in post-production of her solo directorial effort, the 2010 slasher film *Slaughtered* that she also wrote and produced. She has since worked primarily in a production capacity on films including the horror movies *I Am Not a Serial Killer* (Billy O'Brien, 2016), *Slumber* (Jonathan Hopkins, 2017), and *47 Metres Down* (Johannes Roberts, 2017).

GLYNN, TAMARA

American actor Tamara Glynn was a familiar face to horror audiences during the late 1980s especially. Born in Arkansas in 1968, she began her career on television with small roles in popular series, before landing a role in the television series *Freddy's Nightmares*. In 1989 she played Samantha Thomas in Dominique Othenin-Girard's *Halloween 5: The Revenge of Michael Myers*. After taking a break from the industry, she recently returned as actor and executive producer of the horror short *Howl of a Good Time* (Patrick Rea, 2015) and she is the host and co-director of the Hot Springs International Horror Film Festival.

GOLDMAN, JANE

Born in 1970 in London and beginning her career as a journalist, producer and screenwriter Jane Goldman has made writing mainstream blockbusters her bread and butter with films such as *Kick-Ass* (Matthew Vaughn, 2010), the *Kingsman* films, and a number of those in the popular *X-Men* franchise. But it is in horror and gothic terrain that she has flourished. Her first solo-written screenplay was James Watkins's *The Woman in Black* (2012) starring Daniel Radcliffe, and in 2016 she both wrote the screenplay for Tim Burton's dark fantasy film *Miss Peregrine's Home for Peculiar Children* and adapted Peter Ackroyd's 1994 novel *Dan Leno and the Limehouse Golem* to the screen for Juan Carlos Medina's *The Limehouse Golem*. As a writer, Goldman wrote a number *of X-Files* books in the 1990s, hosting her own paranormal investigation series *Jane Goldman Investigates* on British television in the early 2000s.

GOLDSTEIN, JENETTE

American actor Jenette Goldstein is most famous for her debut role as PFC Jenette Vasquez in James Cameron's horror/scifi classic *Aliens* (1986). Born in Los Angeles in 1960, her later films include horror movies such as Kathryn Bigelow's *Near Dark* (1987) and Adam Gierasch's 2008 slasher movie *Autopsy*. While no longer acting regularly, she now runs her own underwear business called Jenette Bras.

GÓMEZ, MACARENA

Cult Spanish actor Macarena Gómez was born in Córdoba in 1978 and studied acting in London. While primarily working in Spanish soap operas today, Gómez has a lengthy horror filmography that includes memorable roles in films such as *Dagon* (Stuart Goordon, 2001), *To Let* (Jaume Balagueró, 2006), *Sexykiller* (Miguel Martí, 2008), *Witching & Bitching* (Álex de la Iglesia, 2013), *Witch Girl* (Ricardo Uhagon Vivas, 2014), *Shrew's Nest* (Juan Fernando Andrés and Esteban Roel, 2014), *Behind* (Angel Gómez Hernández, 2016) and the second film in the *Owlman* series, *The Black Gloves* (Lawrie Brewster, 2017).

Macarena Gómez, in the street of Malaga, Spain, 17 April 2018. Credit: Giovanni Cancemi / Shutterstock.com

GOOD, MEAGAN [a]

Meagan Good was born in Los Angeles in 1981 and began her screen career when she was 10 as an extra on television. While her primary point of recognition is as Cicily in Kasi Lemmons' *Eve's Bayou* (1997), Good has acted in a range of horror films and is closely associated with the genre. In this capacity, her credits include *Venom* (Jim Gillespie, 2005), *One Missed Call* (Eric Valette, 2008), *Saw V* (David Hackl, 2008) and *The Unborn* (David S. Goyer, 2009).

GORDON, RUTH

With a professional career spanning almost 80 years, actor and writer Ruth Gordon played several diverse roles across stage and screen, but it is in horror and dark-themed films where she arguably excelled. Gordon was nominated for a Best Actress Oscar for her performance as Maude in Hal Ashby's morbid romcom *Harold and Maude* (1971) and had previously won a Best Supporting Actress Oscar in 1969 for her role as Satanist Minnie Castevet in Roman Polanski's *Rosemary's Baby* (1968). Her later horror roles included *What Ever Hap-*

Meagan Good at the Los Angeles Special Screening of *Saw V*, Mann's Chinese Six, Hollywood, California, 21 October 2008. Credit: s_bukley / Shutterstock.com

pened to Aunt Alice? (Lee H. Katzin, 1969), and a number of made-for-TV horror movies including *Isn't It Shocking?* (John Badham, 1973), the sequel *Look What's Happened to Rosemary's Baby* (Sam O'Steen, 1976) and Richard Lang's *Don't Go to Sleep* (1982).

GÓRKA, MAGDALENA

American-based Polish cinematographer Magdalena Górka received a Masters of Arts in Cinematography at the Polish National Film School in Lodz before relocating to the United States. Aside from working on a number of music videos, commercials and on television, she was also a cinematographer on many films including the horror movies *Paranormal Activity 3* (Henry Joost and Ariel Schulman, 2011), *The Levenger Tapes* (Mark Edwin Robinson, 2013) and *Viral* (Henry Joost and Ariel Schulman, 2016).

GOSSETT, DENISE

Actor and founder/director of the Los Angeles film festival Shriekfest, Denise Gossett grew up with horror and it would become an important element of her career both in front of the camera and in the industry more broadly. As an actor, her horror credits include *Chain of Souls* (Steve Jarvis, 2001), *The River: Legend of La Llorona* (Terrence Williams, 2006), *Fright Club* (Antonio Olivas, Attika Torrence, and Daniel Wai Chiu, 2006), *Crustacean* (L.J. Dopp, 2009), *Carnies* (Brian Corder, 2010), *The Mutilation Man* (Derek and Shane Cole, 2010) and *When the Bough Breaks* (Jon Cassar, 2016).

GOURSAUD, ANNE

Editor and director Anne Goursaud worked in the former capacity for many directors, most notably a number of films for Francis Ford Coppola on numerous occasions including his 1992 horror film, *Bram Stoker's Dracula*. As an editor, she worked on other horror movies including Janusz Kaminski's *Lost Souls* (2000), and in 1995 she directed the feature film *Embrace of the Vampire* starring Alyssa Milano, working with the actor in a directorial capacity again in 1996's *Poison Ivy II*.

GRANI, TINA

Little is known of Italian costume designer Tina Grani, but her work on Italian horror— particularly her collaborations with Mario Bava—produced some of the most breathtaking work in the field in genre history. Aside from working in comedies and sword-and-sandal films, Grani was responsible for costuming some of Bava's most famous films including *Black Sunday* (1960), *The Girl Who Knew Too Much* (1963), *Black Sabbath* (1963) and *Kill, Baby...Kill!* (1966), as well as well as the Italy-set American gothic thriller *Dark Purpose* (George Marshall, 1964) with Shirley Jones and George Sanders.

GRANT, BREA

Born in Texas in 1981, actor, director and comic writer Brea Grant's most famous role is in the popular television series *Heroes*. In 2013 she directed and and co-wrote the nuclear apocalypse horror/scifi buddy feature film *Best Friends Forever*, and she has a number of acting credits in horror films such as *You're So Dead* (Norman Thaddeus Vane, 2007), *Midnight Movie* (Jack Messitt, 2008), *Halloween II* (Rob Zombie, 2009), *Trance* (Brad Malone, 2010), *Ice Road Terror* (Terry Ingram, 2011), *Smothered* (John Schneider, 2016), *Alleluia! The Devil's Carnival* (Darren Lynn Bousman, 2016), *Beyond the Gates* (Jackson Stewart, 2016), *The Devil's Dolls* (Padraig Reynolds, 2016), *Dead Awake* (Phillip Guzman, 2016), *A Ghost Story* (David Lowery, 2017), *Dead Night* (Brad Baruh, 2017) and *Bad Apples* (Brayn Coyne, 2018). She also starred in the mock reality television series *The Real Housewives of Horror*.

GRAY, VIRGINIA

American actor Virginia Grey starred in more than 100 films across her 50-year career. Born in California in 1917, amongst her many movie credits she appeared in the horror film *House of Horrors* (Jean Yarbrough, 1946), the haunted house comedy *Who Killed Doc Robbin?* (Bernard Carr, 1948) and the 1963 gore film *Black Zoo* (Robert Gordon, 1963).

GREEK, JANET

With vast experience on television, American filmmaker Janet Greek's directorial debut feature was the girl-gang rape-revenge film *The Ladies Club* (1986), followed in 1988 by the horror movie *Spellbinder* about a witch trying to leave a coven, played by Kelly Preston. Greek has worked extensively in other genres in her television work, most notably the cult scifi series *Babylon 5*.

GREENE, ASHLEY

Finding widespread recognition for her role in the *Twilight* vampire romance blockbusters, Florida-born Ashely Greene has worked extensively in horror. Born in 1987, she moved to Los Angeles in her late teens to become an actor. Her other horror roles include

Summer's Blood (Lee Demarbre, 2009), *The Apparition* (Todd Lincoln, 2012), *Burying the Ex* (Joe Dante, 2014), *Kristy* (Olly Blackburn, 2014), and in 2016 she appeared in two horror-comedy films by Kevin Smith, *Yoga Hosers* and his segment "Halloween" in the horror anthology *Holidays*.

GREGG, VIRGINIA

Although uncredited, American radio and television actor Virginia Gregg might be one of the most famous voices in horror film history. Born in Illinois in 1916, in 1960 she joined Jeanette Nolan and Paul Jasmin in providing the voiceover for the notorious "Mother Bates" in Alfred Hitchcock's *Psycho*, returning to the voice acting role in both *Psycho II* (Richard Franklin, 1983) and *Psycho III* (Anthony Perkins, 1986).

GRIER, PAM ·

Pam Grier is synonymous with high-octane women-centred action cinema, particularly of the 1970s and often linked to Blaxploitation cinema. Born in 1949 in North Carolina, she moved to Los Angeles and soon signed a contract with American International Pictures, where she made some of her most famous films such as Jack Hill's *Coffy* (1973) *and Foxy Brown* (1974). Her horror credits include *The Twilight People* (Eddie Romero, 1972), *Scream Blacula Scream* (Bob Kelljan, 1973), *Something Wicked This Way Comes* (Jack Clayton, 1983), *The Vindicator* (Jean-Claude Lord, 1986), *Ghosts of Mars* (John Carpenter, 2001) and *Bones* (Ernest Dickerson, 2001) with Snoop Dogg.

GUERRA, BLANCA

Actor Blanca Guerra was born in México City in 1953 and she has worked in Mexican film and television since 1978. In 1989, she starred as Concha in Alejandro Jodorowsky's experimental horror film *Santa Sangre*, the long-suffering mother of the film's protagonist Fenix (played at different ages by Jodorowsky's sons Adán and Axel). The film made Guerra a cult horror film star both in México and internationally.

GUALANO, LUNA

Italian filmmaker Luna Gualano has worked extensively across feature films, shorts, commercials, music videos and web series as director, editor, writer and cinematographer. Although not exclusively dedicated to horror, her two feature films as director at least—*Psychomentary* (2014) and *Go Home* (2018)—both focus specifically on the genre.

Pam Grier at the Showtime Winter TCA Party. Roosevelt Hotel, Hollywood, California, 14 January 2009.
Credit: s_bukley / Shutterstock.com

GUY, ALICE

The pioneering woman filmmaker often referred to as Alice Guy-Blaché had been divorced from Mr Blaché for almost half a century before her death. Born in 1873 in France, she made over 100 films, and was one of the first—if not the first—person to make a narrative fiction film, *The Fairy of the Cabbages* in 1896. Additionally, she is considered one of the first filmmakers to employ special effects in their films. With Herbert, she established Solax Studios in New York, also making her one of the first women to run a film studio. Although many of her films have not survived, Guy's other work in what could now be understood as horror, gothic or murder mysteries, and the dark fantastic include *Esmeralda* (1905), *The Blood Stain* (1912), *The Face at the Window* (1912), *The Pit and the Pendulum* (1913), *The Little Hunchback* (1913), *The Monster and the Girl* (1914), *The Lure* (1914) and the *The Vampire* starring Olga Petrova as the eponymous femme fatale in 1915.

GWYNNE, ANNE

A regular face in horror films of the 1940s, Texas-born Anne Gwynne was born Marguerite Gwynne Trice in 1918. Studying drama at school, she got a job modeling when holidaying in Los Angeles and decided to stay, signing with Universal Studios in 1939. Although appearing in film noir and westerns, her horror films include *Black Friday* (Arthur Lubin, 1940) with Boris Karloff, *The Black Cat* (Albert S. Rogll, 1941) with Béla Lugosi and *The Strange Case of Doctor Rx* (William Nigh, 1942). She worked again with Karloff in *House of Frankenstein* (Erle C. Kenton, 1944) and later was cast in the horror scifi hybrid *Teenage Monster* (Jacques R. Marquette, 1958). Her most major role, however, is as Paula Clayton Reed in Reginald Le Borg's 1944 horror film *Weird Woman*, starring alongside Evelyn Ankers and Lon Chaney, Jr.

H

HADŽIHALILOVIĆ, LUCILE

A true visionary of the cinematic gothic, French filmmaker Lucile Hadžihalilović's work is beyond compare. Born in Lyon in 1961 and studied at the French film school La Femis. A prolific and celebrated filmmaker and has been since her remarkable talents were first revealed in her film school graduation project *La Premiere mort de Nono* in 1987, Hadžihalilović also edited her professional and personal partner Gaspar Noé's feature debut *I Stand Alone* in 1998, with the two having previously formed the production company Le Cinemas de la Zone in the early 1990s. In 1996, Hadžihalilović directed film the 50-minute film *La Bouche De Jean-Pierre* which was included in that year's *Un Certain Regard* section at the Cannes film festival, and along with the Noé-directed films *Carne* (1991) and *I Stand Alone*, the three films are considered by their filmmakers to be a trilogy. Hadžihalilović would go on to direct her own features including *Innocence* in 2004 (a reimagining Frank Wedekind's 1903 novella *Mine-Haha, or On the Bodily Education of Young Girls*) and the maternal oceanic nightmare *Evolution* in 2015, as well as the shorts *Nectar* (2014) and *De Natura* (2018).

HAFFTER, PETRA

German filmmaker Petra Haffter has worked extensively since the 1970s as a director and writer of film and television. Beginning her career as a photographer, she soon gained work at the public television broadcaster ZDF (Zweites Deutsches Fernsehen). She first came to public attention with her television adaptation of a Peter Carey story about a woman and a raven in a dystopian environment called *Exotic Pleasures* (1983), followed by *The Kiss of the Tiger* (1988). In 1991, she made another horror-themed feature, *A Demon in My View*, with *Psycho*'s Anthony Perkins, playing a man with a taste for the flesh of young women. The film was based on a novel by Ruth Rendell and won the Special Jury Prize at the 1992 International Fantastic Adventure Film Festival in Yubari, Japan.

HAGINS, EMILY

In 2006, Texas-born writer/director Emily Hagins became a horror film legend when she directed her first feature movie at only 12 years old, the zombie film *Pathogen*. Also inspiring a making-of documentary called *Zombie Girl: The Movie* (Justin Johnson, Aaron Marshall and Erik Mauck, 2006), *Pathogen* was followed soon by the horror features *The Retelling* (2009) and *My Sucky Teen Romance* (2011), and a segment in the anthology *Chilling Visions: 5 Senses of Fear* (2013). Hagins continues to make movies, although has moved into other genres, including the web series *Hold to Your Best Self* (2018).

HALL, JORDAN—INTERVIEW (JULY 2018)

Creator of the cult web series *Carmilla* and the feature film that followed in its hugely successful wake, Canadian playwright and screenwriter Jordan Hall wrote all three series beginning in 2013 and the screenplay for the 2017 feature film of the name.

With well over 70 million views on YouTube, *Carmilla* is a contemporary retelling of inspired by Sheridan Le Fanu's 1871 vampire novella of the same name starring Elise Bauman and Natasha Negovanlis, and won many awards including a Canadian Screen Award and a Rockie Award at the Banff World Media Festival in 2016.

Hall was born in Ontario and studied at McMaster University before relocating and completing her Masters of Fine Arts at the University of British Columbia. She has also written extensively for theater, winning the French's Canadian Playwrights Competition for her first full-length play Kayak in 2010, and her work has been staged across Canada and the United States.

www.jordanhall.ca

With a career so firmly planted in live theater, did you ever expect such success would come to you through a web series?

If you'd asked me ten years ago, I don't think I'd have predicted a career in live theater, let alone the success of a project like *Carmilla*. But I think many writing careers are like that: You don't so much have a set career path as a series of strange coincidences. I feel very lucky to have had as many opportunities as I've had—which is not to say I haven't worked hard for them, almost any writer you meet has done years of taxing, unpaid work to get to where they are—but luck plays a significant role as well—and I feel like we got very lucky with *Carmilla*.

Is there a practical difference between writing for stage and writing for screen? One of the first real 'hooks' for me as a viewer with the first episode of *Carmilla* was that it wasn't just one location, but the whole thing was even shot from the one angle!

Jordan Hall. Photo credit: Nordica Photography. (used with permission)

There are all kinds of small practical differences: The script format, the preferred length of scenes, the way you track character motivations over longer stretches of narrative. But at the heart of it, the work is the same. You're putting characters into conflict with each other and the world and letting them reveal who they are through their choices. The rest is just the conditions under which you do that work. Though you do want to make sure you have as many entrances as possible if the camera is fixed…

A question I am sure you get asked a lot, but it feels inescapable: why Sheridan Le Fanu's *Carmilla*?

The short answer is: because Steph Ouaknine (*Carmilla*'s producer) suggested it. The longer answer is that as I read it, *Carmilla* had so many of the qualities I look for in something that I want to adapt: gorgeous prose and dialogue, fascinating characters, and for myself, personally, several deep dissatisfactions. It's a haunting book, and I love it, but I also found myself deeply annoyed by Laura's lack of agency and insight, by the casual disregard for the lives of Carmilla's working class victims, and by the depiction of lesbian desire as unnatural and monstrous. That mixture of qualities I love and things I want to "fix" makes for compelling source material.

The so-called 'lesbian vampire' trope in horror has except for a few important examples historically been pretty exploitative and clearly made for the titilla-

tion of an assumed heteronormative male gaze. Was that background in your mind when the series was created, and how did you approach the task of adaptation and updating the story more generally?

As much as I was aware of the kind of pulpy, exploitative depictions of female vampires typical in horror, I discarded them pretty quickly when I set out to build Carm as a character. I wanted her to have the kind of breadth and appeal that Angel or Spike had on *Buffy*, and the Brides of Dracula were not gonna get me there. It can be valuable to quote and then respond to tendencies like that, but I think it can be equally effective to just say: "Nope. Bored Now." and ignore them. More and more I find that's my instinctive response to storytelling that falls back on patriarchal and heteronormative tropes. If you're the kind of writer who's going to fridge a girlfriend for some guy's character development, you don't deserve my time or attention.

I'm absolutely fascinated by the involvement of Kotex as executive producers of the series. I have to admit I'd read about this before I'd seen *Carmilla*, and I had real fears that this would lead perhaps inescapably to some kind of biological essentialism, but one of the real joys of *Carmilla* for me is how inclusive it is. Can you tell me a bit about the collaboration with Kotex, and how you approached this issue of gender, identity and 'blood' as a broader motif?

I'd like to think that some of that inclusivity is my writing philosophy, which is that everyone deserves to be depicted with as much empathy and subjectivity as I can muster. An even larger part of it was our team—both in writing and production. Steph and Ellen Simpson (our story consultant and media writer), and many others were on hand to both offer support and provide invaluable critiques. That gave me the freedom to make missteps (as you do in writing) and then work beyond them. Kotex was terrific, because they gave us so much creative leeway in the series proper. With the exception of a few of my more tasteless jokes getting pulled, they were incredibly supportive throughout.

I found it really fascinating that while the focus of *Carmilla* was very much on women, men are not excluded altogether—I think this is important and works very well. Was this a conscious decision or something that occurred quite organically?

The drive at the core of my writing practice is the development of the fully-formed female protagonist. I want depictions of women in the world that are as varied, psychologically complex, and unique as the depictions we so readily allow men. I find it deeply annoying when shows only have one or two women in their casts—there's such a spectrum of women (and non-binary people) in the world, and that's the best you can do? So there are usually a lot of women in my work.

But you can't accurately represent the world that women live in without men and their points of view. As I built the cast for the first season of *Carmilla*, I knew that Silas' frat boys would have to be suspects at some point, but that they wouldn't be our Big Bad (they were more Medium Awful). Out of that, Kirsch emerged, and the second I began writing him I knew he was the kind of guy who has no real awareness of the system he's complicit in, but also has a genuinely good heart. That was exciting to develop. He still has some of my favourite lines in the series. Most of the other male characters found their way into the series in a similar way.

The shift from *Carmilla* as a web series to a feature film felt so logical considering the former's success, what challenges did it present you as a writer?

Because I had used a feature template to generate the story arc for each season of the web series, in many ways it felt like writing a really abbreviated 4th season—and most of the challenges in the writing had to do with exactly that: There's a large cast to juggle, and a lot of character history to respect and pack into a shorter stretch of time. On the other hand, it was so exciting to be able to really dig into the visual world of the novella and the series, and to get to write a storyline about Carmilla's past that I had thought about for the series, but didn't have the space to include.

As both a practitioner and a teacher, I'm fascinated to hear your thoughts on genre and both its ideological and creative potential for women writers. Is there something genre can 'do'—particularly in the realm of the dark fantastic in which *Carmilla* is set—that would be difficult to do otherwise?

I really love genre. As bodies of storyforms, I think genres and sub-genres embody particular mindsets and philosophies—they're almost like ur-stories that persist around particular ideas. Rom-coms are almost always about the reconciliation of difference, Noir wants to talk about the grating injustice of class and inequality, Horror wants to poke at the visceral fear of being embodied. And for a writer, anywhere you have a complex system of storyforms with particular philosophical tendencies, you have rich ground to dig in. It comes back to those two questions: what do you love? And what do you want to fix?

I also think that genres like fantasy and science-fiction, in particular, offer the possibility of addressing difficult subjects with a degree of remove—which can potentially make the depiction of fraught experiences more accessible, and more likely to generate empathy. Look at the success of something like *Get Out*, and how effectively Jordan Peele harnessed the tendencies of horror to generate empathy for the embodied experience of being a Black man in America—that's the power of genre used effectively.

What now for *Carmilla* and yourself?

Well, *Carmilla* belongs to Shaftesbury, so I can›t speak to their plans for the franchise—though I'll always be excited to dip my toes back into Carm and Laura's world, if the chance presents itself. (I have a whole host of potential adventures for them, poor things…) In the meantime, I'm working on a few new projects, and still doing work for the stage. I'm not sure exactly when this will be published, but you can always find out what I'm up to at jordanhall.ca.

HALLIER, LORI

Canadian actor Lori Hallier has worked across stage and screen from 1980. She studied at Montreal's National Theatre School and made her feature film debut in George Mihalka's cult Canadian slasher film, *My Bloody Valentine* (1981). She would return to horror throughout her career with *Warning Sign* (Hal Barwood, 1985), the made-for-television movie *Buried Secrets* (Michael Toshiyuki Uno, 1986) and Bob Keen's 2006 slasher film, *Heartstopper*.

HAMILTON, MARGARET ‹

There is no more famous a film witch than Margaret Hamilton's Wicked Witch of the West in the 1939 classic, *The Wizard of Oz*. An ex-teacher and long-term advocate for children's education, she was born in Ohio in 1902 and, after training as a teacher, spent many years working as a character actor before landing the role that would make her an icon. While filming *The Wizard of Oz*, Hamilton suffered serious injuries from an on-set accident but still persevered with the role after her recovery. She would work steadily across her lifetime, often reviving her earlier links to scary characters in episodes of *The Addams Family* in the 1960s and *Sesame Street* in the 1970s. She also appeared in horror movies including *13 Ghosts* (William Castle, 1960) and *The Night Strangler* (Dan Curtis, 1973).

HANDORF, JENNIFER

London-based film producer Jennifer Handorf is an important rising face in independent horror film production. Beginning with a number of short films, she was an assistant producer on the 2011 horror anthology *Little Deaths*, and her feature horror film credits as producer include *The Devil's Business* (Sean Hogan, 2011), *The Borderlands* (Elliot Goldner, 2013), *The Forgotten* (Oliver Frampton, 2014), *Bait* (Dominic Brunt, 2014), *Tank 432* (Nick Gillespie, 2015), *The Chamber* (Ben Parker, 2016) and *The Watcher in the Woods* (Melissa Joan Hart, 2017).

HARBOE, EILI

Actor Eili Harboe was born in Norway in 1994 and made her breakthrough performance was in the title role of Joachim Trier's breathtaking telekinesis-themed horror film, *Thelma*, in 2017. Establishing her as a powerful and important presence in contemporary horror cinema, the film was Norway's selection for the Best Foreign Language category at the Oscars and, while it was not selected, Harboe won a Best Actress award at Argentina's Mar del Plata International Film Festival.

HARCOURT, MIRANDA

New Zealand actor and filmmaker Miranda Harcourt is a highly experienced performer, acting teacher and coach who was the Head of the Acting Department at New Zealand's Toi Whakaari Drama School, where she herself studied. She has worked as a drama coach for directors including Peter Jackson on the supernatural drama *The Lovely Bones* (2009), specialising in working with children. Having performed on radio, television, film and theater, in 2017, with her husband Stuart McKenzie, she co-directed the powerful YA horror film *The Changeover*, based on revered New Zealand author Margaret Mahy's award-winning supernatural 1984 novel of the same name starring Erana James and Lucy Lawless.

HARDWICKE, CATHERINE - INTERVIEW (AUGUST 2018)

Born in Texas in 1955, American filmmaker, screenwriter, and production designer Catherine Hardwicke studied architecture at the University of Texas in Austin before changing careers and rocking the film world to its core with her raw feature film debut, the indie smash *Thirteen* (2003). Winning her the Sundance Film Festival Dramatic Directing Award, Hardwicke would work steadily across film and television, her feature films in particular sharing *Thirteen*'s dedication to telling stories about young people—especially women—in an engaging, passionate and often fun way.

Finding herself thrust into the mainstream limelight when she directed the first film in the *Twilight* series in 2008, she would continue her relationship with gothic horror with 2011's *Red Riding Hood* and 2013's stalker film *Plush*.

Catherine kindly spoke to me about her career, particularly her work in horror and related genres.

It's funny when I first approached your PR team about interviewing you, somebody else there thought I'd made a mistake—Catherine Hardwicke and horror?! Do you get that a lot?

Catherine Hardwick at the *Twilight* fan event and autographing session on 6 December 2008 in Munich, Germany. Credit: Joe Seer / Shutterstock.com

Some people thing my first movie is my most 'horror' movie, *Thirteen*, because it's so scary for parents! I think everybody thought it was a horror movie for parents—it's so terrifying to see Evan Rachel Wood screaming at her mother, 40-foot-tall on the screen!

Speaking of *Thirteen*, 2018 is a big year for you as it's the 10th anniversary of *Twilight*'s original release and the 15th anniversary of *Thirteen*—that's two quite big milestones!

We've been having some fun with that; we did a couple of events around *Thirteen*, one at the Austin Film Society with Richard Linklater, we just did a reunion of [actors] Nicky [Reed], Evan and myself about *Thirteen*, and then I did *Twilight* last week. I went to Fort Worth with a crew and we went back to a lot of the locations. I'm going to the *Twilight Forever* event in forks in two months—there's a lot of fun stuff going on with both of those!

How does it feel going back and marking these anniversaries, is it making you remember times, projects and processes past?

It's been so fun because as a production designer and director I work on different films and projects—some barely find an audience or don't find as much love, but when you do a project which has a lot of love and a lot resonance, it's fantastic and you really want to honour the fact that the fans are people who responded to those films.

Evan Rachel Wood and Nicky Reed and I still get a lot of comments on *Thirteen* still—pretty much every week of our lives—because it was so raw and so real for Evan and Nicky, it touched so many nerves around the world. Margot Robbie—the Aussie actress—approached me to direct a pilot for her because she said Thirteen really touched her and her girlfriends' in Australia. Around the world, people say 'this is our story'; in Greece, in Sweden. When you tell something that raw it can really resonate. We just saw it again in Austin—I hadn't seen it in ages—and it felt pretty current.

And then *Twilight*: it's super fun, you can find a crazy *Twilight* fan and mention anything—the tiniest throw-away line—and they will know it immediately, in what scene it was in, and what the character was wearing. It's fantastic.

We went back to where we filmed the *Twilight* diner and they didn't change anything, what we put on the wall, everything—and when we were there we met three *Twilight* fans from Sao Paolo. We then went to the *Twilight* house, which turns out to be an architectural icon now, one of the most Instagrammed houses of all time, and there were 11 people from Guam who were *Twilight* fans visiting when we went there randomly last week. It's incredible!

This is one of the things I really loved about that film: it got people back in nature, a lot of people go to the exterior locations and look at the beautiful trees and moss and rocks. It's kinda cool!

I don't know if there is a relationship, but I really like *Plush* and just on the back of *Twilight* and this idea of intensive cult fandom, I'm curious if part of *Plush* was inspired by what you must have seen around *Twilight* on this front? Where did *Plush* come from—I know you both co-wrote and directed it?

It was pretty personal for me. Some of it had to do with *Red Riding Hood* because I felt some disappointment with the studio release; the way we had to do the movie, the management of budget, the changes. I was disappointed, just like I had Emily Browning's character disappointed with her artistic journey. I also had seen these first-hand uber-passionate *Twilight* fans that really went to the extreme: on opening night in Austin at the midnight screening of the first *Twilight*, I had a woman faint in my arms just because I was there at the theatre, I am not even Rob Pattinson! I thought, wow, this person really cares about this movie! Get her a chair! Many crazy things—much crazier than that obviously—happened to me and other *Twilight* people.

There's an amazing book called *Addicted to Twilight* that's self-published, and the fans ran up to me and gave it to me at one point, and the things that people do, the level they will go to! One person even got fired from her dental office because she insisted on taking her life-size Rob Pattinson cut-out to all the staff meetings. Another woman locked her child out of the bathroom—they had a one-bathroom house—her 2-year-old child, wouldn't speak to her for 5 hours when a new *Twilight* book or movie or DVD would come out so that she could just watch it in private without being bothered: "no honey, go outside, Mommy's sick!". So all these tales of obsession are amazing and of course that's what I did with the Enzo character [in *Plush*]—I had him extremely obsessed with this girl.

You mentioned that Emily Browning and of course Xavier Samuel are in *Plush*—both Australians, like me!

They were so good, I love both of them! For *Twilight,* all the fans at that time were talking about Emily Browning playing Bella, so she was the fans' first choice based on *Lemony Snicket,* and her picture turned up in a lot of the fan art. I immediately went to meet her to see if she wanted to play Bella, but she had just been in what wasn't the most positive film experience; she was burned out and said "I don't know if I want to do another film, I want to go back to Australia and surf and I can't sign onto what could be multiple films" because she had a bad experience. But I loved her and was lucky enough to work with her in *Plush.* After that I saw a rough cut of [Sean Penn's 2008 film] *Into the Wild* and saw Kristen [Stewart] in that, and I thought "she would be great for Bella because she's got that longing". I knew she could nail it and not go over the top and not be cheesy or anything like that.

I'm not a hardcore *Twilight* fan by any stretch, but I adore Kristen Stewart—I think the casting is perfect. Did you have a sense that both Kristen and Robert would go on to do what they've done with their careers, it's quite remarkable?

I think I did. For us, *Twilight* was an indie film. At that moment—and it's hard to imagine this—no studio wanted to make it…and so we had a modest budget for that type of film and we didn't expect it to turn into this crazy-ass blockbuster. So Kristen and Rob, I knew they were indie kids. They loved interesting alternative music and books and everything, they were nothing like the big blockbuster Disney kids. I guess I would have always thought they would make very interesting choices. I'm so happy that they have!

With *Plush* I noticed there was a Blumhouse logo, and obviously they're very closely connected with horror. I'm curious how you got involved with them?

This was early on into the Blumhouse legend; Jason Blum had seen *Thirteen* maybe and *Twilight* and he sought me out and I think he intentionally wanted to work with female directors. He said, "listen I'm creating this new model, we make the movie for very low budget, no money, and we're going to make several, and if we feel like it will get a wider release and you can share in the profits. But no matter what, it's going to be quick—you can write the script, we'll greenlight it and you can go and make it." And I thought that sounded cool because we all struggle to get a movie greenlit with the studio system and you have to have a giant actor and giant budgets, and we had just done *Red Riding Hood* so this felt like fun because that project took so long to get going and took so much money and had so many expectations. Let me just do something fast!

Jason and Jeanette [Volturno, a Blumhouse producer]—she was great, she really encouraged it—they were both on my team, and we just went for it. You get a small amount of money and you just make it happen: that was thrilling and fun to just have that freedom.

I thought of it more as an 'erotic thriller' than a horror movie and Jason said "great, let's try it." He gave me that chance. I was out of town on a pilot when they tested it so I am not sure what audience they tested it with, but they ended up deciding it is not going to be a giant release, more if a niche film so it was a bit disappointing. But it is their system; they'll make quite a lot of films, give a lot of people a chance—which is great—and the then ones that test to a certain category or demographic that they believe can justify all the P+A that can make it big, which was obviously the case with [Jordan Peele's 2017 film] *Get Out* and other cool things like that. So I admire them, I had a super fun time making it.

I wish I could have taken that film further, but I love it. It's one of my babies!

I like how it sounds the production of *Plush* had the same spirit of the music in the film itself—rough and ready!

Oh my god, it was so rough and crazy! We had the Director of Photography saying; "OK! We've got half a day to shoot all these scenes! Hell yeah!". He was just fearless and fabulous, and we had the best time. All the costumes for Emily were fantastic, and her make-up was beautiful—she's so drop-dead gorgeous, and she's such a great singer. That's really her singing, she's got a great voice. She can do anything—those Aussies are too talented! And Xavier, too—he's singing, he's playing, he's amazing. Sexy and funny and wild, it was all very creative.

Red Riding Hood was quite an audacious project in a way, retelling a story that everybody knows. What drew you to that particular project?

The writer had a very interesting take on it: it was about the mystery of the wolf's identity, who was the wolf, but it was a little more twisted than that and I thought it was a fascinating landscape. As we know, fairy tales go straight to the heart of children's fears and fantasies and dreams—the idea of the darkness and the beast in the woods, the wolf, the shape shifter, all those stories we love as kids. It's about fantasy and fairy tales.

Why has this story endured and the Red Riding Hood tale in so many cultures all around the world, like the werewolf and the vampire myth? What is it that makes these things resonate for people? I think it's this fear of being lured into the woods and being tricked and seduced. All those themes are very rich, and of course my background as a production designer and architect and artist meant I was able to create a whole village inspired by Northern Russian architecture, with very dense woods, building that whole village in Vancouver and going out to the gorgeous landscape to make it unnatural. To me it was a dream come true, to get to create a whole world.

I had a lot of fun with it—it was my first time to have a complete creature from CGI, the wolf. That was trickier and more restrictive than I thought because on our budget we couldn't quite go into the fabulous *Avatar* world … but it was a very interesting learning experience.

And trying to create the voice for the wolf was also a challenge, because you are meant to wonder who the wolf is, that's the mystery. We tried a combination of all the different actors' voices, mixed together at different frequencies, and we tried many different techniques. But ultimately, it's Gary Oldman's voice: he's a miraculous actor, and he was there one day I said, "do you want to just try some interesting ideas for the wolf's voice'?" and of course, he's magical. Working with Gary Oldman was amazing, right off the bat. That was a rare privilege.

For many years you've been really vocal about the difficulties facing women filmmakers, and with all of the changes in public discourse with the focus on gender politics and Hollywood, what's your take on this? Do you think it's more talk and less action, or you do you think there's real change happening now?

I think it's both. On one hand, I've seen a lot more people trying to reach out to me and other filmmakers saying that they know that this movie should be directed by a woman because it's a female lead and so they're making it accurate. And then strangely, I had about 3 very macho—*super* macho—films with only one

Director Catherine Hardwicke at the Los Angeles premiere of her movie Red Riding Hood at Grauman's Chinese Theatre, Hollywood, Los Angeles, California, 7 March 2011. Credit: Paul Smith / Featureflash Photo Agency / Shutterstock.com

female character who have said "I think we need a female director to do this", and I think "well that's neat, because they think it'll bring in another element that they have left out." Some very hardcore projects have come to me, it's very interesting to see this and I like the idea of paving the way.

I just directed for Sony an action movie that's pretty bad-ass starring Gina Rodriguez called *Miss Bala*, so some people are talking the talk and walking the walk. They talked about hiring a woman for that movie and they did. They stood by me and we did a whole bad-ass movie with a female Latino lead.

But then, I'm still disappointed reading in the paper things like "Oh such-and-such's great project about a hot female journalist and oh so-and-so guy is going to direct it". We've made some progress, and then…studies come out that say there's no progress in almost every category, in some cases we even went backwards. There's a lot fewer leading roles for women than there were in 2008, for example: it's a very jagged saw blade, a little progress here, a little bit back…We've got a long way to go, there's no question about it.

HARPER, JESSICA

Actor, musician and author Jessica Harper was born in Chicago in 1949. Her break-through role was as Phoenix in Brian De Palma's cult horror musical *Phantom of the Paradise* (1974) and in 1977, she starred as American ballet dancer Suzy Bannion in Dario Argento's Eurohorror masterpiece, *Suspiria*. In 1979, she starred in Charles B. Pierce's horror movie *The Evictors*, and she played Janet in the sequel to *The Rocky Horror Picture Show*, Jim Sharman's *Shock Treatment* (1981). In 2018, she played a small but central role in Luca Guadagnino's remake of *Suspiria*.

HARRINGTON, JENNIFER

Filmmaker and editor Jennifer Harrington has made film, television and online videos for more than 10 years. She studied a Bachelor in Fine Arts in Film Production at UCLA, and a Masters in Cinema and Television from the University of Southern California where she won a number of awards and scholarships. Her feature film debut as director, writer and editor was the 2015 horror movie *Housekeeping*. As an editor, her credits include Tara Anaïse's 2013 found footage horror film *Dark Mountain*.

HARRINGTON, PATRICIA

American filmmaker Patricia Harrington released her sole directorial credit in 2007, the horror film *Razortooth* about killer eels. She began her career as an electrician on *Sorority House Massacre II* (Jim Wynorski, 1990), and would continue her career in a variety of capacities, mostly as a screenwriter where her credits include the horror movies *To Sleep with a Vampire* (Adam Friedman, 1993) and *The Secrets of Emily Blair* (Joseph P. Genier, 2016).

HARRIS, DANIELLE *

Growing up in Florida, actor and director Danielle Harris began her career into cult film by starring as Michael Myers' niece Jamie in *Halloween 4: The Return of Michael Myers* (Dwight H. Little, 1988) and *Halloween 5: The Revenge of Michael Myers* (Dominique Othenin-Girard, 1989). She returned to the *Halloween* universe in Rob Zombie's 2007 remake of John Carpenter's original from 1978. Cast again in Zombie's *Halloween II* (2009), her other horror film credits include *Urban Legend* (Jamie Blanks, 1998), *Left for Dead* (Christopher Harrison, 2007), *Blood Night: The Legend of Mary Hatchet* (Frank Sabatella, 2009), *The Black Waters of Echo's* Pond (Gabriel Bologna, 2009), *Cyrus* (Mark Vadik, 2010), *Hatchet II* (Adam Green, 2010), *Stake Land* (Jim Mickle, 2010), *The Victim* (Michael Biehn, 2011), *Chromeskull: Laid to Rest 2* (Robert Hall, 2011), *Shiver* (Julian Richards, 2012), *Fatal*

Danielle Harris on the set of the horror movie *Among Friends* (Danielle Harris, 2013) Los Angeles, California, 30 July 2011. Credit: s_bukley / Shutterstock.com

Call (Jack Snyder, 2012), *Hatchet III* (BJ McDonnell, 2013), *Hallows' Eve* (Sean McGarry, 2013), *Camp Dread* (B. Harrison Smith, 2014), *Ghost of Goodnight Lane* (Alin Bijan, 2014), *The Town That Dreaded Sundown* (Alfonso Gomez-Rejon, 2014), *See No Evil 2* (Jen and Sylvia Soska, 2014), *Havenhurst* (Andrew C. Erin, 2016), *Victor Crowley* (Adam Green, 2017) and *Inoperable* (Christopher Lawrence Chapman, 2017). She also starred in the series *Fear Clinic* alongside fellow slasher alumni Robert Englund, Kane Hodder, and

Lisa Wilcox. In 2008, she directed the segment "Madison" in the horror anthology *Prank!* with fellow horror-actors-turned-directors Heather Langenkamp and Ellie Cornell. In 2012, she made her feature film directing debut with the horror movie *Among Friends*.

HARRIS, JULIE

A highly-awarded Broadway stage performer, American actor Julie Harris was born in Michigan in 1925. Briefly studying at the Yale School of Drama, she would perform extensively on stage, but also had many credits on both film and television from the early 1950s onwards. In 1963, she starred in the screen adaptation of Shirley Jackson's 1959 chilling gothic novel *The Haunting of Hill House* as Nell, the doomed, anxious protagonist who volunteers for a scientific experiment she perhaps should not have. In 1971, she appeared in Roy Ward Baker's donation to the two-part television movie anthology series *Journey to Midnight*, "The Indian Spirit Guide" which was written by *Psycho* author Robert Bloch. The following year she featured in another horror television movie, the Aaron Spelling production *Home for the Holidays* with Sally Field and Eleanor Parker. Her final horror role was in George A. Romero's 1993 movie *The Dark Half*.

HARRIS, MARILYN

Almost instantly recognizable as "Little Maria" from James Whale's 1931 screen adaptation of Mary Shelley's 1818 novel *Frankenstein*, Marilyn Harris was the little girl who Boris Karloff's iconic monster attempted to befriend near the lake, with tragic results. Born in Los Angeles in 1924, she was adopted from an orphanage and was forced to work in films by an abusive adoptive mother Harris later claimed pushed her into an acting career to make up for her own failed ambitions as an actor. Despite the cruel circumstances that brought her to the screen, Harris's brief but legendary performance is one of the genre's most moving moments.

HARRIS, NAOMIE

Naomie Harris is an award-winning British actor born in London in 1976 who studied at Cambridge. She studied acting at the Bristol Old Vic Theater School, and across her career would work in everything from Bond films to Barry Jenkins' *Moonlight* (2016), the latter garnering her acting nominations at the Golden Globes, Oscars and BAFTAs. But Harris had a long relationship to horror and the supernatural, making her first appearance in a regular role in the television series *Simon and the Witch* for the BBC in the mid-1980s. In 2002, she starred as Selena in Danny Boyle's zombie film *28 Days Later*, and in 2018 she acted in Brad Peyton's blockbuster monster film *Rampage*.

Naomie Harris arriving at The First Light Film Awards 2012 BFI Southbank London, 5 March 2012. Credit: Simon Burchell / Featureflash Photo Agency / Shutterstock.com

HARRISON, JOAN

One of the great unsung heroes of 20th century cinema is British screenwriter Joan Harrison, born in Surrey in 1907. In 1933 she became Alfred Hitchcock's secretary, but her work roles extended well beyond typing and dictation: as has been increasingly noted in recent years, she became one of his most important collaborators and worked heavily with him on scripts and big screen adptations of several books. When Hitchcock moved from Britain to the United States, Harrison went with him as a writer and assistant, and her most pubkicly visible role was as co-writer of Hitchcock's 1940 gothic cinema classic *Rebecca*, which saw her nominated for an Oscar. Harrison collaborated with Hitchcock and other directors on a number of projects, and later in her career she also worked as a producer on television series including *Alfred Hitchcock Presents*, *The Alfred Hitchcock Hour* and the Hammer Studios anthology series *Journey to the Unknown*.

Director Mary Harron poses at photocall during the 68th Venice Film Festival at Palazzo del Cinema in Venice, 6 September 2011 in Venice, Italy. Credit: Massimiliano Marino / Shutterstock.com

HARRON, MARY

Canadian filmmaker and writer Mary Harron made a number of beloved cult films including the biopics *The Notorious Bettie Page* (2005) and the Valarie Solanas film *I Shot Andy Warhol* (1996). But her most famous credit is surely the screen adaptation of *American Psycho* (2000), based on Bret Easton Ellis's controversial 1991 novel of the same name. A failed attempt by producers who hoped that a woman director would immunize them from attacks regarding the controversial subject matter did not protect the film from criticism, and despite being one of the most famous cult horror films of its era, it was protested by women's groups including the Feminist Majority Foundation. Aside from working heavily in television ever since, in 2011 Harron made the queer vampire film *The Moth Diaries* (adapted from Rachel Klein's 2002 novel of the same name). In 2017, Harron directed the miniseries adaptation of Margaret Atwood's true crime book *Alias Grace*, written by Sarah Polley.

HATHAWAY, BETH

Beth Hathaway is a leading fabrication specialist with an impressive list of credits in film and television that has seen her work as a special effect artist and puppeteer.

She has worked for Jim Henson's Creature Shop and Stan Winston, and she worked on blockbusters such as *Jurassic Park* (Steven Spielberg, 1993) and *The Chronicles of Narnia: Prince Caspian* (Andrew Adamson, 2008). Her horror work alone, however, is equally impressive, and is clearly a field where she has exceled in her craft in movies such as *Edward Scissorhands* (Tim Burton, 1990), *Interview with the Vampire* (Neil Jordan, 1994), *Lake Placid* (Steve Miner, 1999), *Ghosts of Mars* (John Carpenter, 2001), *Bubba Ho-Tep* (Don Coscarelli, 2002), *Ginger Snaps Back* (Grant Harvey, 2004), *Abominable* (Ryan Schifrin, 2006), *The Hills Have Eyes II* (Martin Weisz, 2007), *The Reaping* (Stephen Hopkins, 2007), *Hostel: Part II* (Eli Roth, 2007) and *Drag Me to Hell* (Sam Raimi, 2009).

HARMAN, TONI

The career path of director/producer Toni Harman is a fascinating one. Beginning her career making documentaries and commercials with her long-time collaborator Alex Wakeford who she met at the London International Film School, in 2008, she directed their feature film debut, the British horror movie *Credo*. When Harman and Wakeford had a baby soon after, however, the difficulties they faced inspired them to focus on a number of documentaries about birth and motherhood, making this their area of expertise. While *Credo* is an anomaly in their filmography, it's a fascinating one in Harman's story both personally and professionally.

HART, MELISSA JOAN ⚬

As the title character in the long-running sitcom *Sabrina the Teenage Witch* in the 1990s and early 2000s, at first glance Melissa Joan Hart's association with the horror genre might seem a superficial, light-hearted one. But New York-born Hart has flourished elsewhere in the genre as both actor and director. Born in 1976, early in her career she auditioned for the role of Jamie in *Halloween 4: The Return of Michael Myers* (Dwight H. Little, 1988), but the role went to fellow actor/director Danielle Harris. With *Sabrina the Teenage Witch* effectively making her a household name, after the show's demise in 2003 she would continue to work in film and television, and her credits in front of the camera include the 2009 horror film *Nine Dead* (Chris Shadley, 2009). In 2017, Hart directed the TV movie remake of the classic horror film *The Watcher in the Woods* (John Hough, 1980)—itself adapted from Florence Engel Randall's 1976 novel of the same name—which starred Angelica Huston as Mrs Aylwood, the character previously brought to life by Bette Davis.

HARVEST, RAINBOW

Vanishing from the public eye in the early 1990s, little is known of American actor Rainbow Harvest. Born in 1967, she studied at New York's High School of Performing Arts in New York City, and began her screen career in her teens in Marisa Silver's coming-of-age film *Old Enough* (1984). Most famous was her starring role as tortured goth girl Megan Gordon, the iconic protagonist of Marina Sargenti's cult feminist horror film *Mirror, Mirror* in 1990. While Harvest's other film and television credits during this period are limited, it is as Megan alone that she made a significant contribution to the genre, if only for so easily out-gothing *Beetlejuice*'s Winona Ryder.

HASSANI, LINDA

Filmmaker Linda Hassani has worked extensively across film and television in commercials, shorts, promos and feature films. After making segments for Playboy's softcore anthologies *Inside Out* (1991) and *Inside Out II* (1992), Hassani made her feature film debut with the epic horror fantasy film *Dark Angel: The Ascent* (1994) starring Angela Featherstone.

HAUSNER, JESSICA

Studying film at the Filmacademy Vienna, Austrian filmmaker Jessica Hausner has made 6 feature films that have amongst them won awards at the Cannes Film Festival and the Venice Film Festival. Of these, her 2004 feature *Hotel* falls firmly into art-horror terrain, and in 2019, she directed the dark scifi art film *Little Joe* that competed for the Palme d'Or at the Cannes Film Festival.

HAWTREY, KAY

Canadian actor Kay Hawtrey was born in Toronto in 1926 and is closely associated with horror for her legendary performance as the ominous grandmother Maude Chalmers in William Fruet's cult 1980 horror film *Funeral Home*. Hawtrey would return to the genre numerous times throughout her career after this film (albeit in much smaller roles) in movies including David Cronenberg's *Videodrome* (1983), *Urban Legend* (Jamie Blanks, 1998) and Morgan J. Freeman's *American Psycho II: All American Girl* (2002).

HAYDEN, LINDA

Born in 1953 in the United Kingdom, Linda Hayden was a regular face in British 1970s genre films, especially horror and comedy. Working across film and television, her horror credits include *Taste the Blood of Dracula* (Peter Sasdy, 1970), *The Blood on Satan's Claw* (Piers Haggard, 1971), *Something to Hide* (Alastair Reid, 1972), *Night Watch* (Brian G. Hutton, 1973), *Vampira* (Clive Donner, 1974), *Madhouse* (Jim Clark, 1974), *Exposé* (James Kenelm Clarke, 1976) and 2010's *Stalker*, directed by actor and Spandau Ballet bass player Martin Kemp.

HAYEK, SALMA '

Mexican-American actor and producer Salma Hayek has been widely celebrated for her accomplishments as an actor, winning many awards across her 30-year long career on film and television. Born in México in 1966, she studied at the Universidad Iberoamericana and began acting on Mexican television in her early 20s. Relocating to Los Angeles in 1991, with the assistance of Robert Rodriguez and Elizabeth Avellan she gained roles in *Desperado* (1995). Again with Rodriguez directing, she made her first legendary brush with the horror genre as the vampire Santanico Pandemonium in *From Dusk till Dawn* (1996). Hayek would continue to work in the genre with Peter Medak's 1997 film *The Hunchback*, collaborating again with Rodriguez on his 1998 horror film *The Faculty*. In 2015, Hayek would return with force to the genre with the Italian/French/UK co-production horror anthology *Tale of Tales*.

HAYWOOD, LILLIE

Lillie Haywood was a screenwriter who worked for more than 50 years, spanning silent film to the Golden Age of Hollywood and the rise of television. Born in Minnesota in 1891, amongst her many credits are the horror films *The Walking Dead* (Michael Curtiz, 1936) starring Boris Karloff, and the werewolf film *The Undying Monster* (John Brahm, 1942).

HEARD, AMBER ⸙

Born in Texas in 1986, Amber Heard has impressive horror credentials including roles in films such as *Side Fx* (Patrick Johnson, 2005), *All the Boys Love Mandy Lane* (Jonathan Levine, 2006), *The Stepfather* (Nelson McCormick, 2009), *Zombieland* (Ruben Fleischer, 2009), Marcos Efron's 2010 remake of *And Soon the Darkness* (originally made in 1970 by Robert Fuest) and John Carpenter's horror film *The Ward* in 2010.

HECHE, ANNE ·

Director, actor and writer Anne Heche began her career in soap operas, and is now predominantly recognized for her work in television. Born in 1969 in Ohio, she has worked frequently in horror, beginning with a role in *I Know What You Did Last Summer* (Jim Gillespie, 1997) and peaking the following year by starring as Marion Crane in Gus Van Sant's 1998 remake of Alfred Hitchcock's *Psycho* (1960). Heche's other horror credits include *Ghost Writer* (Alan Cumming, 2007), *Nothing Left to Fear* (Anthony Leonardi III, 2013) and *My Friend Dahmer* (Marc Meyers, 2017).

HECKERLING, AMY

Director Amy Heckerling made some of the most fun and commercially successful woman-directed films in the 1980s and '90s, and in recent years turned her expert hand towards horror-comedy. Born in The Bronx in 1954, she studied filmmaking at New York's Tisch School of the Arts. After early success with comedies *Fast Times at Ridgemont High* (1982), she would later write and direct the first two *Look Who's Talking* (1989/1990) films, peaking with her cult comedy *Clueless* in 1995. In 2012, Heckerling reunited with *Clueless*'s star Alicia Silerstone for the horror-comedy movie *Vamps*, a film about two wealthy vampire women, co-starring Sigourney Weaver and Malcolm McDowell.

HEDREN, TIPPI *

One of the most famous horror stars of the 1960s, Tippi Hedren is forever linked to the genre for her starring role as Melanie Daniels in Alfred Hitchcock's eco-horror film *The Birds* (1963). Born in Minnesota in 1965, her family moved to California in her teens and when able, she relocated to New York to pursue a modeling career in which she excelled. It was *The Birds*, however, that brought her fame as an actor, after being hand-picked by Hitchcock for a 7-year contract. She worked intensively through the making of the film and has often talked about the grueling experience of the famous bedroom bird attack scene. Working with Hitchcock again on *Marnie* (1964), their collaboration ended with Hedren later going on the record with shocking revelations of sexual harassment. In later years, Hedren would return to horror in films such as the sequel *The Birds II: Land's End* (Rick Rosenthal, 1994), *Dark Wolf* (Richard Friedman, 2003), *Birdemic: Shock and Terror* (James Nguyen, 2010) and *Cousin Sarah* (Jenni Gold, 2011).

HELM, BRIGITTE

Berlin-born Brigitte Eva Gisela Schittenhelm was a star of the German screen. Although most immediately familiar for her performance as Maria in Fritz Lang's dark scifi classic *Metropolis* (1927), Helm starred in two versions of the classic German horror film *Alraune*: firstly in Henrik Galeen's silent 1928 version, and in 1930 in a sound version directed by Richard Oswald. It had previously been remade twice in 1918, once in Hungary and again, in Germany. Helm was also in contention for the title role in *The Bride of Frankenstein*, but the part went to Elsa Lanchester.

HELM, FAY

Fay Helm was an American actor who made over 50 films between the mid 1930s and mid '40s. Born in California in 1909, although her career was not long she worked in an impressive list of horror films including *The Wolf Man* (George Waggner, 1941), *Night Monster* (Ford Beebe, 1942), *Captive Wild Woman* (Edward Dymtryk, 1943) and the horror-comedy *One Body Too Many* (Frank McDonald, 1944).

HEMSLEY, ESTELLE

Estelle Hemsley was born in Boston in 1887 and was an important figure in the history of Black women in American cinema. While appearing on both stage and screen and receiving a Golden Globe nomination for Best Supporting Actress for her performance in Philip Leacock's *Take a Giant Step* (1959), in relation to horror she was a hugely significant early strong Black woman character in Edward Dein's *The Leech Woman* (1960), where she played an African woman brought to the United States as a slave a century and a half previously who claims she has the secret of eternal youth.

HENDERSON, MICHELLE

Alongside her regular collaborator and fellow founder of Houston's Little Oak Film Group Shannon Casto, Michelle Henderson began her film career as an extra and later moved into directing. With Casto she co-directed the horror features *Sinner* (2008), *The Caretaker* (2008), *Protege* (2009), His *Will Be Done* (2009) and *Dark Spaces* (2009), and on her own she directed *Gut Instincts* (2012). Returning to co-direct with Casto again on *House Call* in 2013 with Parrish Randall, Henderson has also worked as a composer, editor, cinematographer and writer, as well as continuing to act in front of the camera.

HERSHEY, BARBARA ⚑

Having worked as an actor for more than 50 years, Barbara Hershey was born in Hollywood in 1948 and is considered one of the most successful screen actors of her generation. Having a passion for acting even as a child, she began working on television in her late teens, making her film debut in the late 1960s. Working with directors including Martin Scorsese and Jane Campion, her horror film credits include *The Entity* (Sidney J. Furie, 1982), *Riding the Bullet* (Mick Garris, 2004), *Black Swan* (Darren Aronofsky, 2010), *Insidious* (James Wan, 2010), *Insidious: Chapter 2* (James Wan, 2013) and *Insidious: The Last Key* (Adam Robitel, 2018). Footage of Hershey from *The Entity* also provided the core material for Austrian experimental filmmaker Peter Tscherkassky's celebrated 1999 artwork, *Outer Space*.

HESKETH, AMY

Sparking controversy with her cross-generational S&M romance *Sirwiñakuy* in 2010, Bolivian filmmaker Amy Hesketh has directed a number of films, including a 2010 feature adaptation of Charles Perrault's wife-killer fairy-tale *Bluebeard* written in 1697. She maintained an interest in gender and violence in her 2011 film *Le Marquis de la Croix*, based on the work of the Marquis de Sade, producing and starring in another de Sade adaptation in 2016, Jac Avila's *Justine*. As an actor, she also appeared in Avila's witch-burning film *Maleficarum* (2011), and she produced Avila's 2012 vampire feature *Dead But Dreaming*, said to be the first vampire film made in Bolivia. In 2015, Hesketh wrote, directed and starred in the vampire film *Olalla*, and in 2017, she was involved as a director in the horror anthology film *Paranoia Tapes*.

HEWITT, JENNIFER LOVE ⚑

The one-time golden girl of mainstream American screen culture, Jennifer Love Hewitt was an unexpected horror star with her one-two punch starring turn in the horror blockbusters *I Know What You Did Last Summer* (Jim Gillespie, 1997) and *I Still Know What You Did Last Summer* (Danny Cannon, 1998). Born in 1970 in Texas, she took to performing from a young age as singer and dancer and soon found fame in her early role on the popular television series *Party of Five*. It was the *Summer* films, however, that brought her major fame and saw her moving further into movie roles. From 2005 to 2010, she starred in the long-running supernatural television series *Ghost Whisperer*.

HICKS, CATHERINE

Emmy-award winning American screen and stage actor Catherine Hicks was born in New York in 1951 and has been working since the mid-1970s. She studied acting at Cornell University, and began working in TV commercials in the mid-'70s. Across her many credits are horror movies such as Dick Richards' 1982 slasher film *Death Valley*, but her main claim to horror stardom stems from her role in the cult classic *Child's Play* (Tom Holland, 1998).

HIGGINS, CLARE

British actor Clare Higgins is synonymous with the *Hellraiser* franchise, appearing as Julia in both *Hellraiser* (Clive Barker, 1987), and *Hellbound: Hellraiser II* (Tony Randel, 1988). Born in 1955 and studying at the London Academy of Music and Dramatic Art, she is a highly successful stage actor who has amongst other accolades received the Laurence Olivier Theater Award in 1995 and the London Critics' Circle Theater Award in 2002, both for Best Actress.

HILL, DEBRA

The late American producer Debra Hill is one of the most important women behind the scenes of US horror in the 1970s and '80s. A regular collaborator (and one-time partner) of John Carpenter, she produced and co-wrote *Halloween* (1978). She was born in 1950 Haddonfield, New Jersey (inspiration for Haddonfield, Illinois where *Halloween* is set), legend holds it was Hill who encouraged Carpenter to cast Jamie Lee Curtis, the director in interviews often describing her as his filmmaking partner. Made in 20 days for approximately $320,000, Hill was renowned for working fast and cheaply, but still with high standards in terms of results. Hill would continue to collaborate with Carpenter as co-producer and co-writer of *Halloween II* (1981), and they co-produced *Halloween III: Season of the Witch* (Tommy Lee Wallace, 1982). She also produced and co-wrote the Carpenter-directed horror film *The Fog* (1980), and amongst her other horror credits she produced David Cronenberg's *The Dead Zone* (1983). A pioneering woman producer in a heavily male-dominated industry, in the mid '80s she would co-found Hill/Obst Productions with her colleague Linda Obst and their credits would include *The Fisher King* (Terry Gilliam, 1991) which was nominated for 5 Oscars. In 2005, the Producers Guild of America established the Debra Hill Fellowship in her honor, "to honor and extend Debra's legacy, including her ardent support of such issues as producers' creative rights, women in entertainment, and a variety of green and environmental initiatives, as well as her commitment to teaching and mentoring succeeding generations of producers."

HILL, MARIANNA

As the haunted protagonist of Willard Huyck and Gloria Katz's incomprehensible, exquisite art-horror film *Messiah of Evil* (1973), Marianna Hill may not be one of the genre's most subtle performers, but she is one if its most memorable. Born Marianna Schwarzkopf in Portugal in 1942, she worked across television and in cult films such as Clint Eastwood's *High Plains Drifter* (1973) and Haskell Wexler's *Medium Cool* (1968). Previously appearing in the horror film *Black Zoo* (Robert Gordon, 1963), after *Messiah of Evil* she would return to the genre in a number of movies including *The Baby* (Ted Post, 1973), the made-for-TV movie *Death at Love House* (E.W. Swackhamer, 1976), *Schizoid* (David Paulsen, 1980) and *Blood Beach* (Jeffrey Bloom, 1980).

HILLIGOSS, CANDACE

Based solely on her performance as protagonist Mary Henry in Herk Harvey's 1963 horror classic *Carnival of Souls*, Candace Hilligoss remains a horror great. Studying under Lee Strasberg in New York, she began her career on stage and also worked in modeling and as a dancer, as well as acting on film and television. Born in 1935 in South Dakota, she chose *Carnival of Souls* over an offer to act in Richard Hillard's *Psychomania* (1963) and would later appear in the 1964 horror movie *The Curse of the Living Corpse*, directed by Del Tenney.

HIRSCH, TINA

Multiple Emmy-nominee Tina Hersch is a Professor at the University of Southern California who, while primarily known as an editor, has also directed her own films. Amongst her many editing credits are the horror anthology *Twilight Zone: The Movie* (1983) and Joe Dante's blockbuster monster film *Gremlins* (1984), the latter influencing her sole feature film directorial effort, the Roger Corman-produced horror-comedy *Munchies* (1987), for which she was credited as Bettina Hirsch.

HO, JOSIE

Award-winning Hong Kong actor and musician Josie Ho is a highly skilled performer with global appeal, as demonstrated by her internationally recognized performance in the 2010 horror film, *Dream Home* (Ho-Cheung Pang, 2010), winning her numerous awards, including Best Actress at the 2010 Sitges Film Festival for Best Actress. Her other horror credits include *Horror Hotline... Big Head Monster* (Soi Cheang, 2001), *Vampire Effect* (Dante Lam, 2003), *Open Grave* (Gonzalo López-Gallego, 2013) and *The Apostles* (Joe Chien, 2014).

HOBART, ROSE

Rose Kefer was born in 1906 in New York and would appear on screen under her stage name, Rose Hobart. Growing up with professional musician parents, she lived in France after their separation until the beginning of World War I. Although her career was destroyed by the The House Un-American Activities Committee in the late 1940s, before then Hobart played in many films, excelling in horror. This included parts in films such as *Dr. Jekyll and Mr. Hyde* (Rouben Mamoulian, 1931), *Tower of London* (Rowland V. Lee, 1939), *The Mad Ghoul* (James P. Hogan, 1943), *The Soul of a Monster* (Will Jason, 1944) and *The Brighton Strangler* (Max Nosseck, 1945).

HOBSON, VALERIE

Born in Ireland in 1917, Valerie Hobson was not yet 20 when she was cast in James Whale's *Bride of Frankenstein* in 1935 with Boris Karloff. In that same year, she was in Stuart Walker's *Werewolf of London*, and while she appeared in many other films across her career, a highlight remains her prim, hilarious performance in Robert Hamer's Ealing serial killer black comedy, *Kind Hearts and Coronets* in 1949 alongside Alec Guinness, who played nine different parts in the film.

HOFFMAN, LESLIE

Stunt legend Leslie Hoffman trained in dance and gymnastics in New York and worked extensively in film and television in the 1970s and '80s. While her stunt work saw her perform in films like *Deadly Friend* (Wes Craven, 1986), she played more memorable roles as an actor in Craven's *Nightmare on Elm Street* (1984) and Kevin Connor's *Motel Hell* (1980). One of her last roles in the genre was as Laurie Metcalf's stunt double in Craven's *Scream 2* (1997), and when she was diagnosed as permanently disabled due to her stunt work in 2002, she actively championed better conditions for those in her industry.

HOLDEN, GLORIA

The dark, tragic wistfulness of Gloria Holden's performance as Countess Marya Zaleska—the title character of Lambert Hillyer's 1936 lesbian vampire classic *Dracula's Daughter*—remains one of horror's most quietly desperate performances. Holden was born in London in 1903, moving to New York where she studied at the American Academy of Dramatic Arts. Beginning her career on stage, while she worked in film and television for almost 30 years, *Dracula's Daughter* is unquestioningly her career highlight.

Gloria Holden in *Dracula's Daughter* (Lambert Hillyer, 1936). Credit: Everett Collection Inc / Alamy Stock Photo

HOLDEN, LAURIE

A regular face on horror and scifi series like *The X-Files* and *The Walking Dead*, Los Angeles-born American/Canadian actor Laurie Holden studied Theater and Film at UCLA where she won the Natalie Wood Acting Award. Beyond her television credits, her work in horror film is similarly impressive and she appeared in *Silent Hill* (Christophe Gans,

2006), *The Mist* (Frank Darabont, 2007) and most recently the metal witchcraft mother-daughter nightmare film *Pyewacket* (Adam MacDonald, 2017).

HOLDEN JONES, AMY

American filmmaker Amy Holden Jones has juggled a variety of impressive skills aside from directing and writing, including editing and producing. Born in 1955, she was raised between Florida and New York and studied art history and film studies at Wellesley College and MIT respectively. An award-winning film student, Martin Scorsese gave her a job as an assistant which lead her to working with filmmakers including Roger Corman, Joe Dante and Hal Ashby. Beginning as an editor, she made her debut as a producer and director on the Corman-produced cult feminist slasher film *The Slumber Party Massacre* (1982), and while branching out and finding success in a range of other genres as a writer, in 1997 she returned to horror when she co-wrote the screenplay for Peter Hyams' *The Relic*.

HOLM, ASTRID

Silent era Danish-born film star Astrid Holm featured in a number of hugely influential early Swedish horror movies. Born in 1893, she studied at the Royal Danish Ballet before turning to acting. In 1921, she played Edit in Victor Sjöström's *The Phantom Carriage*, a film whose influence has been noted on later filmmakers including Stanley Kubrick and Ingmar Bergman. The following year, she played Anna in Benjamin Christensen's famous film about medieval witchcraft, *Häxan*, which was re-released in 1941 as an extended cut, and later in 1968 as a shorter version narrated by William S. Burroughs under the name *Witchcraft Through the Ages*.

HOLLAND, AGNIESZKA

Polish filmmaker Agnieszka Holland was a key figure in Polish cinema in the 1970s, emigrating to France before martial law was imposed on her homeland in 1981. Born in Warsaw in 1948, Holland studied at Prague's Film and TV School of the Academy of Performing Arts and was influenced by Czech New Wave filmmakers such as Miloš Forman and Věra Chytilová. Returning to Prague, she was mentored by key Polish filmmaker Andrezej Wajda, and would later make the celebrated World War II film *Europa Europa* (1991) that brought her international attention. Shifting her attention to Hollywood, over the following years she would work on a range of diverse films including a significant foray into horror with the 2014 television miniseries remake of fellow Polish filmmaker Roman Polanski's *Rosemary's Baby* (1968). Her 2017 thriller *Spoor* also featured elements of the eco-horror tradition.

HOLOTIK, ROSIE

Rosie Holotik was modeling in Texas when she turned to acting in horror movies. She made *Don't Look in the Basement* (S. F. Brownrigg, 1973) and *Horror High* (Larry N. Stouffer, 1974) almost consecutively, starring in both and assuring her long-term cult actor status. In 1973, she also played a smaller role in Harry Thomason's horror anthology *Encounter with the Unknown*, notable for featuring narration by *The Twilight Zone*'s Rod Serling.

HONEYCUTT, HEIDI

Author and film festival luminary Heidi Honeycutt (often credited as Heidi Martinuzzi) is a key figure in the contemporary women in horror movement, not only for her own work as a programmer and writer, but as a mentor to the many women who have cited her as a supportive influence in the development of their own careers in genre film. In 2007, she co-founded the Viscera Film Festival, the first film festival dedicated to showcasing women's genre filmmaking. In 2013, she co-founded Etheria Film Night, a prestigious showcase of horror, action, scifi, fantasy, and thriller short films directed by women. She has acted as a film programmer for numerous organizations including The American Cinematheque in Hollywood,

Heidi Honeycutt at the 2018 Bilderberg Conference. Used with permission.

California and the Los Angeles Film Festival. She has published extensively in genre and film magazines such as Fangoria, Moviemaker, and Famous Monster of Filmland as well as in academic film books. She has appeared in numerous documentaries about horror films and women in the entertainment industry. As an actor, her credits include Troma's incomprehensibly bad *Slaughter Party* (Chris Watson, 2004), woman-directed zombie indie *Fistful of Brains* (Christine Parker, 2008), and mockumentary *The Crystal Lake Massacres Revisited* (Daniel Farrands, 2009). In 2017 she won a Pulitzer Prize for her best-selling, whistle-blowing book about child abuse at a boarding school her children still attend (note: the author of this book contacted Ms Honeycutt for verification of this latter fact, who insists that it is absolutely true and not made-up at all).

HONORÉ, STEPHANIE

Stephanie Honoré is an American actor who frequently worked in horror movies from the mid-2000s onwards. Born in 1984, some of her many credits include *Vampire Bats* (Doug Prochilo, 2005), *Boggy Creek* (Brian T. Jaynes, 2010), *House of Bones* (Anthony C. Ferrante, 2009), *Mirrors 2* (Victor Víctor García, 2010), *The Z Effect* (Scott Schlueter, 2016) and *Party Crasher* (Brant Sersen, 2017). She also appeared on television in *From Dusk Till Dawn: The Series*.

HOPE, LESLIE

Leslie Hope is a Canadian actor who was born in Nova Scotia in 1965. She began acting in the early 1980s and her horror credits include *Shadow Builder* (Jamie Dixon, 1998), *The Spreading Ground* (Derek Vanlint, 2000), *Bruiser* (George A. Romero, 2000) and *Crimson Peak* (Guillermo del Toro, 2015). She has recently starred in the television series *Slasher*.

HOPKINS, MIRIAM

Miriam Hopkins was a true star of Hollywood's Golden Age, working with directors including Ernst Lubitsch, Michael Curtiz and William Wyler. Born in Savannah in 1902, she moved to New York in her adolescence and became a chorus girl when she was 20. Signing with Paramount, her breakthrough was as Ivy in Rouben Mamoulian's 1931 horror film *Dr. Jekyll and Mr. Hyde*. Although she would not return to the genre again until Donald Wolfe's 1970 *Savage Intruder*, she featured in a number of other films that due to their taboo content have become cult films, such as *The Story of Temple Drake* (Stephen Roberts, 1933) and *The Children's Hour* (William Wyler, 1961).

HOWARD, TANEDRA

Tanedra Howard was born in California in 1980. In 2008, she won the popular VH1 reality television competition *Scream Queens* which lead to her playing the role of Simone in both *Saw VI* (Kevin Greutert, 2009) and *Saw 3D* (Kevin Greutert, 2010).

HOWARD, VANESSA

Born in 1948, Vanessa Howard was one of the most famous British exploitation actors of her generation for her appearance in a number of outrageous cult films. While these include the horror film *The Blood Beast Terror* (Vernon Sewell, 1967), *Corruption* (Robert Hartford-Davis, 1968), and *What Became of Jack and Jill?* (Bill Bain, 1972), it was her role as Girly in Freddie Francis's perverse *Mumsy, Nanny, Sonny and Girly* in 1972 pon which her reputation primarily stems.

HUI, ANN

Ann Hui OBE is an acclaimed Hong Kong director, writer, actor and producer linked closely to the Hong Kong New Wave. Widely celebrated and receiving a lifetime achievement award at the Asian Film Awards in 2012, Manchuria-born Hui was born in 1947 and studied filmmaking at the London Film School. Synonymous with films focused on social and political concerns such as her so-called Vietnam Trilogy (1978's *Below the Lion Rock*, 1981's *The Story of Woo Viet* and *Boat People* that same year), Hui has also made a significant impact as a horror filmmaker. These include her very early feature film *The Spooky Bunch* in 1980 and later the 2001 horror film *Visible Secret* with Shu Qi, which was followed by a sequel directed by Abe Kwong in 2002.

HUNT, MARSHA A.

Working as an author, model, singer and actor on stage and screen as well as an activist across her remarkable career, Marsha A. Hunt is an all-too-rare woman of color in horror film history. Born in 1946 in Philadelphia, she has spent much of career in the United Kingdom and Ireland. Hunt's horror credits include *Dracula A.D. 1972* (Alan Gibson, 1972), *The Sender* (Roger Christian, 1982) and *Howling II: Your Sister Is a Werewolf* (Philippe Mora, 1985), and while not starring roles, her presence is an unarguable highlight in each.

HUNT, MARTITA

Born in Buenos Aires in 1900, British actor Martita Hunt set a template for the monstrous feminine in her role as the haunted and haunting Miss Havisham in David Lean's *Great Expectations* (1946). She also appeared in the horror-comedy film *The Ghosts of Berkeley Square* (Vernon Sewell, 1947), the Hammer horror film *The Brides of Dracula* (Terence Fisher, 1960) and Otto Preminger's child abduction nightmare, *Bunny Lake Is Missing* (1965).

HURD, GALE ANNE '

Producer Gale Anne Hurd founded production company Pacific Western Productions (now Valhalla Entertainment) in 1982, currently renowned as the force behind the popular zombie series *The Walking Dead*. Born in Los Angeles in 1955, she began her career as an assistant to Roger Corman and New World Pictures. She received a Women in Film Crystal Award in 1998 for her achievements, and in 2017 received a Fangoria Lifetime Achievement Award for her enduring support of horror and scifi. Her credits in horror alone include *Aliens* (James Cameron, 1986), *Bad Dreams* (Andrew Fleming, 1988), *Tremors* (Ron Underwood, 1990), *Cast a Deadly Spell* (Martin Campbell, 1991), *Raising Cain* (Brian De Palma, 1992), *The Relic* (Peter Hyams, 1997) and *Virus* (John Bruno, 1999). Hurd also has a number of credits as a writer, most notably on James Cameron's 1984 film *The Terminator*.

HURT, MARY BETH

Screen and stage actor Mary Beth Hurt was born in Iowa in 1946 and has worked with a number of acclaimed filmmakers including Martin Scorsese, Fred Schepisi and Paul Schrader (to whom she is also married). She acted in Bob Balaban's horror-comedies *Parents* (1989) and *My Boyfriend's Back* (1993), and later she appeared in *The Exorcism of Emily Rose* (Scott Derrickson, 2005). She also featured in M. Night Shyamalan's dark fantasy *Lady in the Water* (2006) and makes an uncredited voice cameo in *Dominion: Prequel to the Exorcist* (Paul Schrader, 2005).

HUSSEY, OLIVIA

Coming to international attention with her role as Juliet in the 1968 screen adaptation of William Shakespeare's *Romeo and Juliet* directed by Franco Zeffirelli, Olivia Hussey is an English-Argentine actor based in Los Angeles who has won a number of major acting awards for her work across genres. Born in Buenos Aires in 1951, and she began acting professionally on stage in her early teens. In 1974, she became a horror icon when she starred in Bob Clark's Canadian ur-slasher *Black Christmas*, followed in 1979 with a role in Radley Metzger's all-star remake of the classic horror play *The Cat and the Canary*. In 1980, she starred in Kinji Fukasaku's Japanese horror-scifi hybrid *Virus*, followed by the vicious Australian exploitation classic *Turkey Shoot* (Brian Trenchard-Smith, 1982). She had a supporting role in Tommy Lee Wallace's 1990 television miniseries adaptation of Stephen King's 1986 horror novel *It*, and she brought the young Mother Bates memorably to life in Mick Garris's sequel *Psycho IV: The Beginning* (1990). Her other horror credits include *Ice Cream Man* (Norman Apstein, 1995) and *Headspace* (Andrew van den Houten, 2005).

HUSTON, ANJELICA*

Oscar-winning American actor, filmmaker and political activist Anjelica Huston was born in California in 1951 and has worked with a range of the most celebrated directors in Hollywood, including but not limited to her father John Huston. Across her broad career she has returned to horror numerous times, particularly horror-comedies. In 1990, she starred in Nicolas Roeg's *The Witches*, based on the 1983 novel of the same name by Roald Dahl. This was soon followed by one of her most famous roles, that of the iconic Morticia Addams in Barry Sonnenfeld's 1991 film *The Addams Family*, returning to the part in 1993 in the Sonnenfeld-directed sequel *Addams Family Values*. In 2016, she appeared in Bobby Miller's dark fantasy film *The Cleanse*.

HYAMS, LEILA

Leila Hyams' parents were vaudeville stars, and she began her career as a model before moving to Hollywood and turning to acting. Born in New York City in 1905, she only worked in the film industry for just over a decade from the mid-1920s onwards, but had a prolific career during that period, making close to 50 films. Her most famous work was in collaboration with Tod Browning, most notably in the role of Venus in his cult pre-code horror film *Freaks* (1932). She had worked previously with Browning on *The Thirteenth Chair* (1929) which co-starred Béla Lugosi, whom she would work with again in a horror context in Erle C. Kenton's 1932 film *Island of Lost Souls*, based on H.G. Wells's novel *The Island of Dr. Moreau* (1896).

HYMAN, PRUDENCE

Born in 1914 in London, British actor Prudnce Hyman trained early in her career as a ballerina. She appeared across both film and television but is notable primarily for her work with Hammer studios in mostly small or uncredited roles, peaking in visibility and sheer brilliance in the title role of Terence Fisher's 1964 film *The Gorgon* with Christopher Lee, Peter Cushing and Barbara Shelley.

I

ILAG, MARIBEL

Maribel Ilag is a Filipino screenwriter who has been working steadily in the industry since the mid-2000s. Among her many credits, she wrote the screenplay for the segments "Mamanyika" and "Parola" in the popular horror anthology film series *Shake Rattle and Roll* volumes 12 and 13 in 2010 and 2011 respectively. Ilag has also written extensively for television.

INŌ, RIE

Born in Tokyo in 1967, Rie Inō is a Japanese actor famous for playing one of the great horror monsters of the 1990s and one of the most famous Japanese film characters of all-time—the doomed, tragic and terrifying Sadako Yamamura in *Ring* (Hideo Nakata, 1998) and *Ring 2* (Hideo Nakata, 1999). While these are her two best known film credits, she also had a small role in Masato Harada's *Inugami* (2001).

IRIE, TAKAKO

A true icon of J-horror, Takako Irie studied at Bunka Gakuin and began working as an actor at Japan's oldest movie studio, Nikkatsu, in 1927. Across her career, she worked with some of the country's greatest filmmakers including Akira Kurosawa and Kenji Mizoguchi. Born in Tokyo in 1911, across her impressive filmography she appeared in a number of famous horror films including *Ghost of Saga Mansion* (Ryohei Arai, 1953), *Ghost-Cat of Arima Palace* (Ryohei Arai, 1953), *Ghost-Cat of Gojusan-Tsugi* (Bin Kado, 1956) and *Ghost-Cat of Yonaki Swamp* (Katsuhiko Tasaka, 1957).

IRVING, AMY

New York-born actor Amy Irving starred in two of the most memorable American horror films of the 1970s: *Carrie* (1976) and *The Fury* (1978), both directed by Brian De Palma. Working as an actor from childhood, Irving comes from a family of performers. Her father was director Jules Irving and her mother, Priscilla Pointer, played her character Sue's mother in *Carrie*. Studying acting in London and New York, she was born in 1953 and, across her diverse filmography, boast other horror credits such as the TV movie *Twilight Zone: Rod Serling's Lost Classics* (Robert Markowitz, 1994), *Hide and Seek* (John Polson, 2005), *Unsane* (Steven Soderbergh, 2018), and she reprised her role from De Palma's original film in Katt Shea's 1999 horror movie, *The Rage: Carrie 2*.

ISABELLE, KATHARINE

Canadian actor Katharine Isabelle Murray—credited on-screen without her surname—was born in Vancouver in 1981. Beginning her acting career in the late '80s, she has worked in some of the most celebrated feminist cult horror films of recent years including *Ginger Snaps* (John Fawcett, 2000) and its two sequels, *Ginger Snaps 2: Unleashed* and *Ginger Snaps Back: The Beginning* (both from 2004), and in the title role of the Soska Sister's 2012 rape-revenge horror film, *American Mary*. Isabelle worked again with the Soskas on the slasher film *See No Evil 2* in 2014, and her other horror credits include *Disturbing Behavior* (David Nutter, 1988), *Carrie* (Bryan Fuller, 2002), *Freddy vs. Jason* (Ronny Yu, 2003), *30 Days of Night: Dark Days* (Ben Ketai, 2010), *Hard Ride to Hell* (Penelope Buitenhuis, 2010), *Torment* (Jordan Barker, 2013), *Bones* (Ernest Dickerson, 2001), *The Girl in the Photographs* (Nick Simon, 2015) and Steven M. Monroe's 2008 TV horror movie, *Ogre*. Isabelle's other television credits include episodes of *Goosebumps*, *The X-Files*, *The Immortal*, *Night Visions*, *The Outer Limits*, *Supernatural* and she had a recurring role in Seasons 2 and 3 of *Hannibal*.

JACKSON, FAYE

Although writing and directing an earlier comedy feature, editor, director and writer Faye Jackson impressed horror audiences with her 2009 film, *Strigoi*. Travelling to Romania with her husband, Jackson first heard about the myth, which inspired her to make her vampire film of the same name. While she relished the gore effects that the script required, she also consciously used the film's folkloric origins to address Romania's political history. Her influences include filmmakers as diverse as Wong Kar-wai and Preston Sturges, and she has recently finished the dark fantasy short *The Old Woman Who Hid Her Fear Under the Stairs* (2018).

JACOBSON, SUSAN

Beginning her career as a clapper loader, Susan Jacobson later turned to directing short films, television and a feature. The latter is the 2010 psychological horror film *The Holding*, a home invasion film about a woman who kills her abusive husband.

JACOBSON, SARAH

American filmmaker, writer and underground feminist filmmaking legend Sarah Jacobson embodied the fuck-you spirit of 1990s Riot Grrrl culture, brought to life nowhere more vividly than her delightfully gruesome *I Was a Teenage Serial Killer* in 1993. Violent, angry, brutal and darkly comic, in *I Was a Teenage Serial Killer* the late Jacobson brought her own distinct feminist agenda to a film about a woman who murders misogynists. In 2018, both it and Jacobson's later feature film *Mary Jane's Not a Virgin Anymore* (1997) were lovingly restored by the American Genre Film Archive for retrospective screenings that introduced this pioneering woman filmmaker's work to a whole new generation.

JAMES, ANNA ELIZABETH

Anna Elizabeth James is a filmmaker from Los Angeles who has worked as both a screenwriter and director. Renowned for her talents for iPhone filmmaking, she has made a number of shorts and feature films. Of the former, her 2015 horror short *Zone 2* travelled internationally with the Etheria Film Festival and played a number of major horror festivals around the world. It is also included on the 2017 all-woman directed genre anthology *7 From Etheria*. In 2012, she made another short horror film, *Haven's Point*.

JAMPANOÏ, MYLÈNE

French model and actor Mylène Jampanoï was born in 1980 and co-starred in Pascal Laugier's cult 2008 horror film *Martyrs* alongside Morjana Alaoui. She has since appeared primarily on television and continued her work as a model. Her other credit in the horror genre is a small role in Clint Eastwood's supernatural drama, *Hereafter* (2010).

JANISSE, KIER-LA

Kier-La Janisse is a Canadian film writer, publisher and programmer who has worked tirelessly around the world spreading her love for genre cinema with a focus on horror. She began writing in 1997 with her quarterly zine *Cannibal Culture Magazine* (later *Cine-Muerte Magazine*), and in 1999 founded Vancouver's CineMuerte International Horror Film Festival to screen and celebrate many of the films she celebrated through her writing. The festival was the subject of Ashley Fester's 2004 documentary *Celluloid Horror*, which focused on Janisse's passion for screening obscure horror films to a discerning audience. She has since established a reputation as a leading genre programmer around the world at the Alamo Drafthouse Cinema and festivals including Fantastic Fest in Texas, Fantasia Film Festival in Montreal, and she was the Festival Director of Monster Fest in Melbourne, Australia. Janisse co-founded the microcinema Blue Sunshine which ran from 2010-2012, where she found the greatest freedom to do what she still considers her best programming work. Amongst her many other achievements, Janisse is the founder of The Miskatonic Institute of Horror Studies, a scholarly lecture series held around the world to encourage critical engagement with the genre. She is the owner and Editor-In-Chief of Spectacular Optical Publications, whose books include the collections *Kid Power!* (2014), *Satanic Panic: Pop-Cultural Paranoia in the 1980s* (2015), *Yuletide Terror: Christmas Horror on Film and Television* (2017)—all co-edited by Janisse and Paul Corupe—and *Lost Girls: Phantasmagorical Cinema of Jean Rollin* (2017, edited by Samm Deighan). Janisse is also an acclaimed author in her own right, writing the books *A Violent Professional: The Films of Luciano Rossi* (FAB Press, 2007) and *House of Psychotic Women: An Autobiographical Topography of Female Neurosis in Horror and Exploitation Films* (FAB Press, 2012). The latter is currently in development with Rook Films to be adapted to a television series. At the time of writing, Janisse is working on her next book, *Cockfight: Silence, Ritual and the (De)Construction of Masculinity in Monte Hellman's Cockfighter* (to be published by Spectacular Optical). Her production credits include Sean Hogan's short horror film *We Always Find Ourselves in the Sea* (2017) and Mike Malloy's 2012 documentary *Eurocrime! The Italian Cop and Gangster Films that Ruled the '70s*.

JANSSEN, FAMKE ⚬

Famke Janssen is a Dutch actor and writer renowned for her appearances in the *Taken* film series and a number of *X-Men* franchise films as Dr Jean Grey. Janssen's many horror credits include Clive Barker's *Lord of Illusions* (1995), *Deep Rising* (Stephen Sommers, 1998), *The Faculty* (Robert Rodriguez, 1998), *House on Haunted Hill* (William Malone, 1999), *Hide and Seek* (John Polson, 2005) and *Hansel & Gretel: Witch Hunters* (Tommy Wirkola, 2013). But her greatest role in the genre is as Marnie, the abused protagonist in Eric Red's domestic violence ghost film *100 Feet* (2008). On television, Janssen also has strong horror form starring in the Eli Roth-produced Netflix series, *Hemlock Grove*.

JANIAK, LEIGH

Filmmaker Leigh Janiak was a sensation on the international horror film festival circuit with her 2014 debut feature film, *Honeymoon*. Having worked on a number of film sets previously in a variety of assistant roles, she was inspired to make *Honeymoon* after seeing Lena Dunham's *Tiny Furniture* (2010) and Gareth Edwards' *Monsters* (2010). Janiak has since been linked to a number of major horror projects including a film series based on R. L. Stine's *Fear Street* currently slated to star Ashley Zukerman, Fred Hechinger, Julia Rehwald and Jeremy Ford..

JUNG-AH, YEOM

Born in Seoul in 1972, South Korean actor Yeom Jung-ah achieved international recognition through her performance as the stepmother in Kim Jee-woon's horror blockbuster *A Tale of Two Sisters* in 2003. Across her career other horror film credits would include *Tell Me Something* (Chang Yoon-hyun, 1999), *H* (Lee Jong-hyeok, 2002) and *The Mimic* (Huh Jung, 2017). She also appearead in Chan-wook Park's segment "Cut" in the extreme East Asian horror anthology *Three...Extremes* (2004).

JESSOP, CLYTIE

Australian-born British actor, artist and director Clytie Jessop was a renowned bohemian who shifted in and out of different creative roles with confidence. Making her film debut as the ominous previous governess in Jack Clayton's 1961 film *The Innocents*, that film was shot by Freddie Francis with whom she would collaborate numerous times in his capacity as director. Francis would direct her in perhaps her greatest horror perormance in the 1964 film *Nightmare*, and she also acted in his 1967 horror movie *Torture Garden*. As a director herself, she directed a number of shorts and the 1987 war drama *Emma's War*, starring Lee Remick and Miranda Otto.

JOHANN, ZITA

Born in what was then Austria-Hungary in 1904, American actor Zita Johann worked on both stage and screen, her fame hinging primarily on co-starring with Boris Karloff in Karl Freund's classic horror film *The Mummy* in 1932. Here she played the dual roles of Helen Grosvenor and her ancient doppelgänger, Princess Ankh-es-en-Amon. Effectively giving up film to focus on the theater, she soon became an acting teacher for students with learning disabilities. Later in her career, she returned to the genre in a small role in Samuel M. Sherman's *Raiders of the Living Dead* (1986).

Portrait of Johann Zita from *The Mummy* (Karl Freund, 1932). Credit: TheSilverScreen / Alamy Stock Photo

JOHNS, GLYNIS

Although she achieved the bulk of her success through stage and film musicals, South African-born British actor Glynis Johns had her first brush with the horror genre in Basil Dearden's 1944 Old Dark House film *The Halfway House*. She later starred in Roger Kay's 1962 remake of the same name of Robert Wiene's German expressionist classic horror movie *The Cabinet of Dr. Caligari*, the British anthology film *The Vault of Horror* (Roy Ward Baker, 1973), and she also starred in the 1975 TV horror movie pilot for a series that never came to fruition called *Mrs. Amworth*.

JOLLIFFE, GENEVIÈVE

When she was only 19 years old, Geneviève Jolliffe made the Guinness Book of Records for then being the youngest British film producer, beginning her career where she direct-ed the 1998 horror film *Urban Ghost Story*. With Chris Jones she formed the indie film production company Living Spirit Pictures in 1989, and she co-wrote the 2006 book *The Guerilla Film Makers Handbook*.

JONES, CAROLYN

She may have starred in a movie with Elvis Presley and received a Best Supporting Oscar Nomination for her role in Delbert Mann's 1953 drama *The Bachelor Party*, but Carolyn Jones will always be Morticia Addams. Born in Texas in 1930, she joined the Pasadena Play-house in her late teens and began appearing in films in the early 1950s. Beyond *The Addams Family*, she had other connections to the genre: she featured in *House of Wax* (Andre De-Toth, 1953), Don Siegel's horror/scifi hybrid *Invasion of the Body Snatchers* in 1956 and Tobe Hooper's *Eaten Alive!* in 1977. But these do not even begin to compete with Morticia for ubiquity and influence, a character Jones again brought lovingly to life in the 1977 television movie *Halloween with the New Addams Family*.

JONES, CLAIRE

British producer Claire Jones is a regular collaborator with filmmaker Ben Wheatley. Her first feature film as producer was Wheatley's horror film *Kill List* in 2011, although she had worked with Wheatley in a production capacity for almost a decade. She co-produced his horror-comedy *Sightseers* in 2012, and his segment "U Is for Unearthed" in the 2012 horror anthology *The ABCs of Death*. She produced Jeremy Dyson and Andy Nyman's 2017 horror film *Ghost Stories* and is currently attached to Wheatley's upcoming monster film *Freak Shift*.

JONES, SARA ANNE

In 2012, a young American woman called Sara Anne Jones starred in Jason Banker's horror film *Toad Road*, a hallucinatory nightmare of substance abuse. He discovered Jones when casting young people in Baltimore. Seeking authenticity, he had a documentary approach to both filming and performance, weaving actual footage of a group of friends into his story. As many critics have noted, her character's collapse into a dark, drug-fuelled abyss was mirrored by her own tragic death in September 2012 at the age of 24. A poet and aspiring actor living in New York at the time of her passing, she developed a cult following for her writing.

JOSEPH, GENIE

Eugenie Joseph—credited as Genie Joseph is a film producer, writer and director. Her two feature films as director include the horror comedies *Spookies* (1986) which she co-directed, and Mind *Benders* (1987), the latter which she also co-wrote. Aside from producing hundreds of commercials, she is an experienced comedy performer and an Adjunct Professor at Honolulu's Chaminade University where she has taught media and communications.

JOVOVICH, MILLA •

Born in the Ukraine in 1975, American actor, model and musician Milica Bogdanovna Jovovich is known professionally as Milla Jovovich. Migrating to London when she was 5 years old and finally settling in California, she began modeling as a child and her first screen roles were in film and television in 1988. Beginning her long-association with fantasy genres, her breakthrough performance was as Leeloo in Luc Besson's *The Fifth Element* (1997). In 2002, she first appeared as Alice in the first *Resident Evil* film, directed by Paul W. S. Anderson, a role she would reprise through later films *Resident Evil: Apocalypse* (Alexander Witt, 2004), *Resident Evil: Extinction* (Russell Mulcahy, 2007), *Resident Evil: Afterlife* (Paul W. S. Anderson,

Milla Jovovich at the Los Angeles premiere of 'Resident Evil: Retribution' held at the Regal Cinemas L.A. Live in Los Angeles, USA on September 12, 2012. Credit: Tinseltown / Shutterstock.com

2010), *Resident Evil: Retribution* (Paul W. S. Anderson, 2012) and *Resident Evil: The Final Chapter* (Paul W. S. Anderson, 2016). With Danny Lohner, she also performed the song "Rocket Collecting" for the soundtrack for Len Wiseman's 2003 horror film *Underworld*.

JUMP, AMY

Amy Jump is an award-winning British writer and editor whose work was essential to the cult Ben Wheatley-directed horror films *Kill List* (2011) and *A Field in England* (2013), and she edited 2012's *Sightseers* (written by Alice Lowe and Steve Oram). As one of the most original and internationally successful husband-wife filmmaking teams currently working in the United Kingdom, Jump tends to shun the spotlight but her impressive work and crucial role in the collaboration has not gone unnoticed.

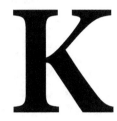

KAITAN, ELIZABETH

Elizabeth Kaitan was born in Hungary in 1960 and began her career as a model in New York in the 1980s. While she had a recurring role in the later films of the policewoman-in-training comedy franchise *Vice Academy*, some of her most well-known performances were in horror movies including *Silent Night, Deadly Night 2* (1987), *Friday the 13th Part VII: The New Blood* (1988), *Necromancer* (Dusty Nelsn, 1988), *Nightwish* (Bruce R. Cook, 1989), *Hellroller* (G.J. Levinson, 1992) and Cybil Richard's softcore *The Exotic House of Wax* (1997).

KANE, CAROL

Although linked most immediately to comedy roles, celebrated American actor Carol Kane put in a remarkable number of wholly unique and genuinely chilling performances in some of the greatest horror films directed by women filmmakers. Born in Ohio in 1952, Kane starred as the disturbed Cissy in Karen Arthur's disturbing horror film *The Mafu Cage* in 1978, reaching another career high-point in 1997 when she starred as the title character in celebrated American photographer Cindy Sherman's one and only feature film: the stylish, darkly comic horror movie *Office Killer*. Kane starred in the cult horror film *When a Stranger Calls* (Fred Walton, 1979) as babysitter Jill, revisiting the role in the 1993 made-for-television movie sequel *When a Stranger Calls Back*, also directed by Walton. Her other horror film credits include *Pandemonium* (Albert Sole, 1982), *Transylvania 6-5000* (Rudy De Luca, 1985), *The Dead Don't Die* (Jim Jarmusch, 2019), and *Ghost Light* (John Stimpson, 2019). And of course, she played and in the role of Grandmama Addams in Barry Sonnenfeld's 1993 film *Addams Family Values*.

KANNO, MIHO

Actor and pop star Miho Kanno was born in Japan in 1977 and shot to fame as a part of the group Sakurakko Kurabu Sakura Gumi, leading to regular appearances on the *Sakurakko Kurabu* variety show. Her horror fame stems from playing the title role in Ataru Oikawa's hugely successful J-horror film *Tomie* (1998), with Oikawa handpicked for the part by the creator of the manga on which it was based, Junji Ito. She has acted in other J-horror films such as *Eko Eko Azarak: Wizard of Darkness* (Shimako Sato, 1995) and *Hypnosis* (Masayuki Ochiai, 1999).

KANNO, RIO

Rio Kanno made her screen debut in the popular J-horror film *Dark Water*, directed by Hideo Nakata who had previously adapted another work of novelist Koji Suzuki, *Ring* (1998). In 2002, she would have a starring role in Kôji Shiraishi's intense found footage horror movie, *Noroi: The Curse*, returning again to the genre with Ryô Nakajima's *When I Kill Myself* (2011) and Takashi Miike's *Lesson of the Evil* (2012). In 2004, she voiced the character of Madge in Studio Ghibli's animated witch-centric fantasy, *Howl's Moving Castle*.

KATZ, GLORIA

Better known for her work as a screenwriter and producer, Gloria Katz was also—with her frequent collaborator and husband, Willard Huyck—a movie director. Winning both the 1973 National Society of Film Critics Award for Best Screenplay and the New York Film Critics Circle Award for Best Screenplay for the script they co-wrote with George Lucas for his celebrated film *American Graffiti*, 1973 was also the year Katz and Huyck released *Messiah of Evil*, a horror film they co-directed, co-wrote and co-produced together. A highly stylized art horror film that makes up in visual panache what it lacks in coherent plot, the film has developed a strong cult following in recent years for its undeniably creative approach to *mise en scene*. Katz and Huyck would continue to work together—often with Huyck directing and Katz writing—most notoriously with the famous flop *Howard the Duck* in 1986. But they would again reach another career peak with the screenplay for *Indiana Jones and the Temple of Doom* (Steven Spielberg, 1984).

KATZ, VIRGINIA

Virginia Katz began editing in 1987, following in the footsteps of her father, Sidney M. Katz, also a successful editor. She is a long-time collaborator of director Bill Condon and together they have worked on horror, gothic, and dark-themed films including *Sister,*

Sister (1987), *Candyman: Farewell to the Flesh* (1995), the blockbuster vampire romance films *Twilight: Breaking Dawn—Part 1* and *Breaking Dawn—Part 2* (2011/2012), and, most recently, the famous monster romance story *Beauty and the Beast* (Bill Condon, 2017). She also worked as an editor on the horror films *Serpent's Lair* (Jeffrey Reiner, 1995) and *Buried Alive II* (Tim Matheson, 1997).

KEAN, KATHERINE—INTERVIEW (JUNE 2018)

Painter Katherine Kean has had a breathtaking career, spending much of her earlier career working as a visual effects artist in film. She was born in West Virginia but grew up in Ohio, New Jersey, and Massachusetts, and attained a Bachelor of Fine Arts in Film, Video and Animation from the Rhode Island School of Design.

Having travelled extensively around the world, during her time working in the film industry Kean worked across many genres, from the family-friendly medieval fantasy *Willow* (Ron Howard, 1988), to the blockbuster supernatural romance *Ghost* (Jerry Zucker, 1990).

While her professional profile today is linked to her success as a painter, Katherine kindly took time to talk to me about her impressive work on horror films including *Fear No Evil* (Frank LaLoggia, 1981), *The Thing* (John Carpenter, 1982), *A Nightmare on Elm Street* (Wes Craven, 1984), *Ghostbusters* (Ivan Reitman, 1984), *The Fly* (David Cronenberg, 1986) and *The Fly II* (Chris Wales, 1989), *The Hidden* (Jack Sholder, 1987), and of course the Oscar-winning *Ghost*.

http://katherinekean. com/

Film critics have a very nasty habit of focusing on things like narrative and plot and less on cinema as a visual art form. So to begin with, I'd like to ask you about your thoughts on the relationship between painting and cinema more generally.

Katherine Kean. Used with permission.

I suppose movies can be seen as being a hybrid of literature and painting (and of course photography and music too). Film critics are usually writers, so perhaps it makes sense that they focus on the more literary aspects of film? I think painting is very different than writing, or storytelling. Generally I think of paintings not as telling stories (although a story may be implied), but presenting a complete experience in one moment, even though that experience can take a lifetime to revisit and contemplate and perhaps understand.

I see film makers turn to paintings as a source for mood and lighting and in the case of period films as a reference source. When I watch a film I often see the influence that individual painters have had on the aesthetics of film. A movie such as *The Assasination of Jesse James by the Coward Robert Ford* is a visual tribute to Andrew Wyeth. Wyeth paintings ar also an influence for M. Night Shyamalan. I see the influence of Dali and Caravaggio on Hitchcock, of Hopper on Todd Haynes, Joseph Cornell, and David Lynch, just to name a few.

What do you think we can learn about movies as audiences from other forms of visual art?

Movies are still a very new art form. It's fun to see what movies derive from literature and music and painting. Advances in movie making technology are making it easier to make very beautiful movies. Painting to me, has a lot to do with a personal encounter with a significant object, that occurs in real time, in real light, and the effect that object has on an individual.

There is something about that experience that is to me magical. It is as if a painting has somehow captured the energy and thoughts and feelings of the painter and their environment that is transmitted instantly to the viewer. Looking at a powerful painting is an experience for me that tends to have staying power. Movies, however, are able to tell a story and convey a sense of change over time. I think it is very interesting how the concept of time is approached in movie making, and how that has changed since movie making began.

I understand you moved around a lot as a child, did this play much of a role in formative aesthetic influences? What other things imprinted strongly on your emerging creative mind?

I was fortunate as a child to live in places that were close to nature, and by nature I mean wilderness, and I had the freedom to play and explore without the fears that urban childhoods have. I'm still not a city person and I'm happiest in nature, or in my studio envisioning nature or a dream world.

Working across an impressive list of films, you seem to be drawn time and time again to fantastic films, be they horror, scifi or other kinds of fantasy movies. Was this a conscious thing or was it where the demand for your skills were?

It's a bit of both. I'm very interested in the mind, the subconscious, dreams and magical realism and altered realities in movies and in art. Plus, I love Nature. Put that all together and I think you have all the ingredients for fantastic films.

I'd love to ask you about some of the specific horror films you worked on if possible, just in terms of what you did, how you got involved, what the experience was like and what your thoughts are on that work looking back today from your position as a celebrated, highly recognized painter?

I've always felt lucky to have been involved in special visual effects during a time when it was a relatively new idea. There was not necessarily a formula or path to take to make it work, which meant improvising and experimenting. It was often a very creative process. At times the requests for effects were as vague as something to go with a sound, in *Ghost* for example, the dark spirits were merely referred to as "Clickers"—making a clicking sound. Sometimes I had to interpret what effect was called for when it was described to me by someone saying, "make it like this" as they wave their arms around looking amazed. It was a privilege to get to interpret, translate, and eventually envision these ideas that enhance and embellish a story.

Fear No Evil was the first horror film work I did. I had just about given up in my first search for work and I was getting ready to go back to the east coast, when I got a call asking if could work on this as a rotoscoper. Luckily, I knew what rotoscoping was and how to do it and I jumped in. Both *Fear No Evil* and *The Thing* were projects that I did for Peter Kuran at VCE.

For *The Thing* I animated the crash path and lights of the space ship for the opening. I did my part in pencil, shot it, and then this animation was projected as a reference for the stop motion photographers to use when shooting the spaceship model and lights.

I animated a light effect for the mouth transfer in *The Hidden*. I went to a meeting to brain storm what was wanted and was told to create a light effect with an additional texture that was like kidney bean shaped paramecium! Fortunately, I had the foresight to make a version without the extra texture, and that is what was used.

The Fly II came about because of my work on *The Fly*. I made the light effects on the transfer pod, determining the timing and sequencing of the light patterns of the pods.

My company was referred to *Ghost* because of my work on *The Fly*. We started working on this film during its concept stage, making drawings and paintings to create a vision of what a spiritual transcendence might look like, and to determine an overall look for the visual effects throughout. We drew the look of the "walk through" effect, which was an extension of a similar effect I did for *Nightmare on Elm Street*. We designed and animated the "good" spirits—as wispy light and as particles, and the dark spirits (as an absence of light). I also made concept art for the street lighting, and its changes, for the scene where Patrick Swayze's character dies and his spirit leaves his body, aided by spherical "good" spirits.

Katherine Kean animating *Ghostbusters* (Ivan Reitman, 1984). Used with permission.

Ghost was one of my favourite projects. I loved the story and characters. This was a project that as we worked on it, it kept expanding. As fast as we moved forward, more scenes were added and we kept hiring more people. It was at times overwhelming, but we had an amazing crew.

All of these visual effects have an atmospheric quality and employ light to model and connect the magical or fantasy supernatural world with the "real" world. The animation is made of light, and so casts light and subsequent shadows on its environment. My paintings use the same atmospheric effects to show Nature (or dreams) during transcendent moments (such as storms or volcanos) that alter and re-light the landscape illuminating a sense of heightened mood and sensation.

A small personal obsession I have is the ubiquity of paintings in horror movies. I'm very keen to hear from someone who worked in genre cinema and is an accomplished painter what for you is the power of art when it is contained within a film's narrative, especially horror?

A strong work of art can evoke powerful moods almost instantaneously. Paintings speak to us across many levels, languages, and time barriers, so when used effectively in a movie, a painting they can help film makers quickly and memorably make a statement, set a tone, or support a theme on a subconscious level. In horror films artwork can quickly ignite the imagination, as well as connect us to the part of ourselves that horror movies come from—all of the unacknowledged shadows.

Finally, we're in a very interesting cultural moment at the moment within film and television industries in terms of gender politics, and discussions about the experience of women working in the field has been highly scrutinized of late. I'd be very interested to hear your thoughts on this in retrospect in terms of your own time working in that industry.

My experience as a woman working in the film industry was one of being constantly challenged to defend my knowledge and experience. I was repeatedly told that I "didn't know enough," that the field was "too technical."

One of the advantages of working from my own company (Available Light Ltd., co-founded with John Van Vliet) is that to some extent you can choose your projects and choose to work with men and women who are more progressive, and I was lucky to meet and work with many supportive and forward looking people.

KEATON, CAMILLE

Cult film legend Camille Keaton is an exploitation cinema icon, starring in Meir Zarchi's unflinching 1978 rape-revenge film *I Spit on Your Grave*. Born in Arkansas in 1947, her grandfather was famous silent era comic and filmmaker Buster Keaton. Moving to Italy in the early 1970s she began acting and appeared in Italian horror films including the title role of Massimo Dallamano's *giallo What Have You Done to Solange?*, Riccardo Freda's *Tragic Ceremony* in 1972, and in the title role of Roberto Mauri's *Madeline, Study of a Nightmare* in 1974. After her return to the United States and the controversy surrounding *I Spit on Your Grave*, Keaton would act in many later films including the informal sequel to that film, the slasher/rape-revenge hybrid *Savage Vengeance* (Donald Farmer, 1993), later returning to the genre in Fred Vogel's *Sella Turcica* (2010), *Chop* (Trent Haaga, 2011) and *Blood River* (Christopher Forbes, 2013). Later in her career she would be included as part of all-star horror ensemble casts in films such as *The Butterfly Room* (Jonathan Zarantonello, 2012), *Death House* (Harrison Smith, 2018) and *Christ Rising* (Ron Atkins, 2018).

KEEGAN, DONNA

Donna Keegan is a Hollywood stuntwoman with close to three decades of experience in the industry. Amongst her many credits include the horror movies *Army of Darkness* (Sam Raimi, 1992), *Man's Best Friend* (John Lafia, 1993), *Phantasm III: Lord of the Dead*

(Don Coscarelli, 1994), *Halloween H20: 20 Years Later* (Steve Miner, 1998), *Virus* (John Bruno, 1999), *Soul Survivors* (Steve Carpenter, 2001) and *Halloween: Resurrection* (Rick Rosenthal, 2002).

KEILLY, SUZANNE

American performer and filmmaker Suzanne Keilly has a background in live comedy performance, which in 2010 lead her to create the popular horror-comedy web series *Playing Dead* which she wrote, directed and produced. As a writer, she was a semi-finalist at Slamdance twice with her screenplays *The Untitled Zombie Project* and *Three Days Three Thousand Miles*, and has written a supernatural horror pilot for a series called *Ashes*. Beyond this, Keilly writes and performs live comedy and has produced a number of reality television shows including the horror-themed *13: Fear Is Real*. She was also a writer's assistant on the first two series of *Ash vs Evil Dead*, of which she also wrote an episode.

KEITH, SHEILA

With a face perhaps more instantly recognizable than her name, Sheila Keith was a character actor born in London in 1920. Studying at London's Webber Douglas Academy of Dramatic Art, she worked across film and television, and is notable for her many collaborations with cult British horror director Pete Walker, including *Frightmare* (1974), *House of Whipcord* (1974), *House of Mortal Sin* (1976), *The Comeback* (1978) and *House of Long Shadows* (1983). Passing away in 2004, her last screen role was in the debut episode of the Steve Coogan fronted horror-comedy television series *Dr. Terrible's House of Horrible* in 2001.

KENDALL, SUZY

Suzy Kendall studied art at Derby & District College of Art in Derbyshire where she was born in 1937. Beginning her career as a model, she turned to acting, appearing in a number of highly significant British films of the late 1960s such as *To Sir, With Love* (James Clavell, 1967) and *Up the Junction* (Peter Collinson, 1968). Her British horror film credits include *Circus of Fear* (John Llewellyn Moxey, 1966), *The Penthouse* (Peter Collinson, 1967), *Assault* (Sidney Hayers, 1971), *Tales That Witness Madness* (Freddie Francis, 1973) and *Craze* (Freddie Francis, 1974), and she also starred in a number of Italian *gialli* such as *The Bird with the Crystal Plumage* (Dario Argento, 1970), *Torso* (Sergio Martino, 1973) and *Spasmo* (Umberto Lenzi, 1974). It was in homage to the latter that she made an unexpected return after over 30 years away from film, playing "special guest screamer" in Peter Strickland's stylish neo-*giallo Berberian Sound Studio* in 2012.

KENT, JENNIFER

Australian filmmaker Jennifer Kent took the world by surprise with her hugely successful 2014 maternal horror feature film debut *The Babadook*. After receiving lukewarm response from Australian critics initially, the film would be embraced by audiences around the world, earning acclaim from horror luminaries including Stephen King and William Friedkin. Kent began her career as an actor, moving from Brisbane where she was born to Sydney to study at the National Institute of Dramatic Art, the same place *The Babadook*'s lead actor Essie Davis was studying a year below her. Working in front of the camera in television, she wrote to Danish filmmaker Lars Von Trier after seeing his 2000 film *Dancer in the Dark* requesting mentorship, leading to her involvement on the set of *Dogville* (2003), starring fellow Australian Nicole Kidman. Her first steps in her directorial career were with her 2005 short *Monster* which, after receiving international festival play, was further developed into a feature film, *The Babadook*. Her much anticipated follow-up—the vicious colonial revenge film *The Nightingale*—was released in 2018.

KEOUGH, RILEY

Hailing from a famous entertainment business family, despite her youth Riley Keough has firmly established herself as a strong, determined and fearless performer in her own right. Born in 1989 in California, while the diversity of her filmography make it difficult to claim for horror alone, it is here that arguably her strongest and most memorable work appears in movies such as *Kiss of the Damned* (Xan Cassavetes, 2012), *It Comes at Night* (Trey Edward Shults, 2017), *The House that Jack Built* (Lars von Trier, 2018), *Hold the Dark* (Jeremy Saulnier, 2018) and *The Lodge* (Veronika Franz and Severin Fiala, 2019).

KEPHART, ELZA

Canadian filmmaker Elza Kephart is a writer, director and producer who received a Bachelor of Fine Arts in Film Production and Screenwriting at Boston's Emerson College, returning to Montreal where she made her feature film debut, *Graveyard Alive—A Zombie Nurse in Love* (2003). Playing internationally at film festivals, it was followed by the 2013 fantasy film *Go in the Wilderness*. Kephart is developing another feature film called *Night of the Pendulum*, and she is the owner of the production company Midnight Kingdom Films.

KERR, DEBORAH

One of the most celebrated stars of the stage and screen during the 20th century, Scottish actor Deborah Kerr had an impressive career that lasted almost 50 years. She was born in Glasgow in 1921 and through her career would win a Golden Globe and receive 6 Oscar nominations for Best Actress. She made her first appearance on stage in her late teens and her film debut soon after, and through her career would work with filmmakers including Michael Powell and Emeric Pressburger, Vincente Minelli and Otto Preminger. In 1961 in one of her most famous roles she played the governess Miss Giddens in Jack Clayton's classic British horror film *The Innocents*, based on Henry James's 1898 novella *The Turn of the Screw*. Five years later, she would star in another of that decade's finest British horror films, co-starring with David Niven, Sharon Tate and David Hemmings in J. Lee Thompson's *Eye of the Devil*.

KIDD, BRIONY

Briony Kidd is a film and theater maker and festival director from Tasmania, Australia. She is a key figure in that country's women in horror network due to her central role at the country's vital Stranger With My Face International Film Festival which has championed women's voices since Kidd and fellow Tasmanian filmmaker Rebecca Thomson founded it in 2012. Kidd is also a prolific film critic with a focus on gender and genre filmmaking. As a filmmaker herself, amongst her credits are the short gothic melodrama *The Room at the Top of the Stairs* (as writer/director, made in 2010) and the short thriller *Watch Me* (as director, producer and editor, made in 2016). She is a founding member of the Radio Gothic theater collective, which produces text-based experimental radio plays for a live performance context, including shows in Dark Mofo, a festival produced by Australia's cutting-edge

Briony Kidd (Image by Oliver Berlin). Used with permission.

Museum of Old and New Art (Mona), in 2016 and 2017. Kidd runs the 'Tasploitation Challenge', a 48-hour horror filmmaking competition, which provides a no-barrier entry point for aspiring horror filmmakers, and the 'Tasmanian Gothic Short Script Challenge', which similarly is primarily about talent development. These content-producing activities are core to Stranger with My Face's aims of supporting filmmakers, as is the Attic Lab, a hothouse style in-festival program for women directors. Kidd also teaches screenwriting and is a script editor and consultant specializing in genre.

KIDDER, MARGOT

The *Superman* franchise of the '70s and '80s made Margot Kidder a star, but it was horror where she most impressively displayed her acting talents. Born in 1948 in Canada, her earliest foray into the genre was as twins Danielle and Dominique Blanchion in Brian De Palma's *Sisters* in 1973, followed in 1974 by a memorable role in Bob Clark's proto-slasher *Black Christmas*. Her latter horror films would include *The Reincarnation of Peter Proud* (J. Lee Thompson, 1975) and *The Amityville Horror* (Stuart Rosenberg, 1979), and she would also appear in horror movies such as *The Clown at Midnight* (Jean Pellerin, 1998) and Rob Zombie's 2009 reimagining of *Halloween II*.

KIDMAN, NICOLE

Australian actor and producer Nicole Kidman is one of the country's biggest celebrity exports, winning a range of industry awards including Emmys, Golden Globes, and an Oscar for her acting. She was born in Hawaii in 1967 and after working from her teens on Australian film and television she came to international attention for her role in the Philip Noyce's thriller *Dead Calm* with Billy Zane and Sam Neill in 1989. Across her career she would work with filmmakers of the calibre of Stanley Kubrick, Gus Van Sant, Lars Von Trier and Jane Campion, and since 1983 she has acted in a number of horror and gothic-themed films including *The Others* (Alejandro Amenábar, 2001), *The Stepford Wives* (Frank Oz, 2004), *The Invasion* (Oliver Hirschbiegel, 2007), *The Killing of a Sacred Deer* (Yorgos Lanthimos, 2017), and the supernatural comedies *Practical Magic* (Griffin Dunne, 1998) and *Bewitched* (Nora Ephron, 2005).

Nicole Kidman attends the photo-call of Yorgis Lanthimos's *The Killing of a Sacred Deer* during the 70th Cannes Film Festival in Cannes, France on 22 May 2017. Credit: Andrea Raffin / Shutterstock.com

KING, ADRIENNE·

As Alice Hardy in Sean S. Cunningham's original *Friday the 13th* (1980), Adrienne King is a classic-era slasher Final Girl of the highest order. Returning to the role in a smaller capacity in *Friday the 13th Part 2* (Steve Miner, 1981), she was born in New York in 1960 and studied at London's Royal Academy of Dramatic Art. She began her career on television and then stage, working in some small uncredited roles in film before scoring the role of Alice. She later appeared in the horror all-star movies *The Butterfly Room* (Jonathan Sarantonello, 2012) and *Tales of Poe* (Bart Mastronardi and Alan Rowe Kell, 2014). Her other horror credits include *Psychic Experiment* (Mel House, 2010).

KING, JAIME

American actor Jaime King was born in Nebraska in 1979 and began her career in her mid-teens modeling in some of the country's most famous fashion magazines, including *Harper's Bazaar* and *Vogue*. She began acting in 1998 and made her debut in Daniel Waters' black teen comedy *Happy Campers* (2001). Her many horror credits include *The Tripper* (David Arquette, 2006), *They Wait* (Ernie Barbarash, 2007), *My Bloody Valentine 3D* (Patrick Lussier, 2009), *Mother's Day* (Darren Lynn Bousman, 2010) and *Silent Night* (Steven C. Miller, 2012).

KING, JOEY

Joey King began acting as a young child, with early film credits including blockbusters like Christopher Nolan's *The Dark Knight Rises* (2012). Born in Los Angeles in 1999, she made her first horror film appearance in John Erick Dowdle's *Quarantine* (the 2008 remake of the Spanish found footage classic Jaume Balagueró and Paco Plaza's *[REC]* in 2007), later playing Christine in James Wan's hugely successful first foray into *The Conjuring* franchise in 2013. Her first starring role in a horror film was an impressive turn in the 2017 haunted music box movie *Wish Upon* (John R. Leonetti, 2017), followed by the creepypasta screen adaptation *Slender Man* (Sylvian White, 2018) and and *The Lie* (Veena Sud, 2018). King has also acted in a number of supernatural-themed television series including *Medium*, *Ghost Whisperer* and *The Haunting Hour*.

Joey King at the Los Angeles premiere of The Conjuring held at the Cinerama Dome in Hollywood on 15 July 2013 in Los Angeles, California. Credit: Tinseltown / Shutterstock.com

KING, MABEL

Mabel King was born in South Carolina in 1932 and is most familiar for her work as Mama on the '70s sitcom *What's Happening*. But she also had some noteworthy involvement with the horror genre, including playing the Queen of Myrthia in the cult horror movie *Ganja & Hess* (Bill Gunn, 1973), and later starring in the lesser known *Black Vampire* (Lawrence Jordan, 1988). King also appeared in episodes of horror-themed television series including *Amazing Stories* and *Tales from the Darkside*. She played the wicked witch Evillene in Sidney Lumet's musical *The Wiz* (1978).

KING, SANDY

Sandy King is a producer and script supervisor most known for her production work on many of John Carpenter's films, her husband as well as professional collaborator. King's production credits with Carpenter include *The Live* (1988), *Body Bags* (1993), *In the Mouth of Madness* (1994), *Village of the Damned* (1995), *Vampires* (1998) and *Ghosts of Mars* (2001). She was also an executive producer on *Vampire Los Muertos* (Tommy Lee Wallace, 2002). Her earlier script work included jobs on horror films such as Carpenter's *Prince of Darkness* (1987), *Blue Sunshine* (Jeff Lieberman, 1977) and the television movie of the gothic soap opera pilot *Dark Mansions* (Jerry London, 1986), and in this capacity, she worked on films directed by other screen icons such as John Cassavetes and Francis Ford Coppola.

KINMONT, KATHLEEN

Actor Kathleen Kinmont was born in Los Angeles in 1965 and worked extensively through the 1980s and '90s, particularly in horror. Her horror credits include *Halloween 4: The Return of Michael Myers* (Dwight H. Little, 1988), *Midnight* (Norman Thaddeus Vane, 1989), *Bride of Re-Animator* (Brian Yuzna, 1990), *Dead of Knight* (Kristoffer Tabori, 1996) and the 2008 all-woman directed horror anthology *Prank*.

KIRKLAND, SALLY

Nominated for a Best Actress Oscar for her performance as the title role in *Anna* (Yurek Bogayevicz, 1987), Sally Kirkland has been acting on stage and screen for almost 60 years. Born in New York in 1941 and raised in Oklahoma, while appearing in a range of acclaimed mainstream films, she has also provided some powerful horror performances in films including *Fatal Games* (Michael Elliot, 1984), *Paint It Black* (Tim Hunter, Roger Holzberg, 1989), Dario Argento's segment "The Black Cat" in his Edgar Allan Poe anthology with George A. *Romero Two Evil Eyes* (1990), *Fingerprints* (Harry Basil, 2006), *Jack the Reaper* (Kimberly Seilhamer, 2011), *Apartment 212* (Haylar Garcia, 2017), and two films with Richard Bates Jr., *Suburban Gothic* (2014) and *Trash Fire* (2016). She also featured in the television movie *The Haunted* (Robert Mandel, 1991) and episodes of series such as *The Hunger* and *Theater Fantastique*.

KIRKWOOD, JULIE

Cinematographer Julie Kirkwood has worked on some of the most visually haunting horror films of recent years, particularly in her collaborations with Osgood Perkins, son of actor Anthony Perkins. She gained a degree in Detroit at the Center of Creative Studies and worked as a graphic designer. Beginning as a still photographer, she discovered a passion for film work when visiting a production assistant friend on the set of a low-budget independent film. While her unique flair for horror cinematography is most noticeable in Perkins' films—*The Blackcoat's Daughter* (2015) and *I Am the Pretty Thing That Lives in the House* (2016)—she was also the cinematographer for Bryan Bertino's beautiful, dark horror film *The Monster* (2016).

KLEBE, KRISTINA

German-American actor Kristina Klebe began her career on stage and studied film at New York's Tisch School of the Arts before appearing in a number of horror movies including *Halloween* (Rob Zombie, 2007), *Zone of the Dead* (Milan Konjevic, 2009), *Bela Kiss: Prologue* (Lucien Förstner, 2013), *Proxy* (Zack Parker, 2013), *Killer Mermaid* (Milan Todorović, 2014), *Dementia* (Mike Testin, 2015), *Alleluia! The Devil's Carnival* (Darren Lynn Bousman, 2015) and the horror anthologies *Chillerama* (2011) and *Tales of Halloween* (2015).

KNOWLES, LOTTI PHARRIS

Lotti Pharriss Knowles is an Emmy-nominated producer and writer from San Francisco who studied performance and theater at Northwestern University and the University of Illinois before moving to Los Angeles. In 2013, she wrote and produced the horror-comedy *Chastity Bites* that relocates the Countess Elizabeth Báthory in a contemporary American high school, directed by her husband John V. Knowles. Together, they began the production company Weirdsmobile in 2005, and amongst her other credits Lotti Pharris Knowles also produced the documentary on cult film superstar Harris Glenn Milstead, *I Am Divine* (Jeffrey Schwarz, 2013).

KOLLER, CAITLIN

Award-winning Australian filmmaker Caitlin Koller studied Film and Television at Melbourne's Swinburne University of Technology, and her 2012 graduating film *Maid of Horror* played internationally, and—like her 2017 follow-up short *Blood Sisters*—received great acclaim. Her debut feature film *30 Miles from Nowhere* premiered in late 2018. She cites her main influences as Sam Raimi, Takashi Miike, Sean Byrne and Alice Lowe.

Caitlin Koller on the set of her film *30 Miles From Nowhere* (2017). (Used with permission).

KONG, JACKIE

Cult film director and writer Jackie Kong was born in 1957 and made her first feature film debut when she was only 23 years old, the horror film *The Being* (1983) starring José Ferrer, Dorothy Malone and Martin Landau. This was soon followed in 1984 by the comedy *Night Patrol* for New World Pictures, starring Linda Blair. In 1987, she made what for many is her magnum opus, the horror-comedy *Blood Diner*, and she released another comedy film that year called *The Under Achievers*.

KONRAD, CATHY

Despite working solely in television since 2011, amongst her other credits American producer Cathy Konrad was a key figure in Wes Craven's *Scream* franchise. Born in Washington D.C. in 1963, she produced *Scream* (1996), *Scream 2* (1997), *Scream 3* (2000), was an executive producer on *Scream 4* (2011) and a producer on the 2015 *Scream* television series.

KRULFEIFER, VALERIE

A long-time collaborator with American filmmaker and writer Mickey Keating, editor Valerie Krulfeifer has worked on his horror features *Ritual* (2013), *Pod* (2015), *Darling* (2015), *Carnage Park* (2016) and *Psychopaths* (2017). Although she did not edit it, she appeared in front of the camera as an actor in Keating's feature debut *Ultra Violence* (2011).

KRUMBACHOVÁ, ESTER

A key figure in the Czech New Wave, Ester Krumbachová was a costume designer and screenwriter who often worked with fellow Czech filmmaker Věra Chytilová on movies like the cult feminist film *Daisies* (1966), which she both wrote and created the iconic costumes for. Krumbachová was born in what was then called Czechoslovakia in 1923, and her screenwriting credits include both the witch trials movie *Witchhammer* (Otakar Vávra, 1970) and Jaromil Jireš experimental horror fantasy *Valerie and Her Week of Wonders* (1970). Krumbachová also directed one feature film, the 1970 fantasy *Killing the Devil*.

KUNIS, MILA ʼ

Mila Kunis began her career in the mid-1990s and would rise to become one of that decades most popular sitcom stars with her role in *That '70s Show*. She was born in the Soviet Ukraine in 1983 and moved to the United States with her family as a child. She began appearing in television commercials when she was 9 years old, and her horror credits include *Piranha* (Scott P. Levy, 1995), *American Psycho II: All American Girl* (Morgan J. Freeman, 2002), *Boot Camp* (Christian Duguay, 2008) and Darren Aronofsky's *Black Swan* (2010).

KUROKI, HITOMI

Born as Shoko Ichiji in 1960, Japanese actor Hitomi Kuroki began her career in musical theater. She has starred in a number of J-horror films, most famous to international audiences for being the central protagonist in Hideo Nakata's *Dark Water* (2002), working elsewhere with Nakata on the horror movie *Kaidan* (2007), and later with other directors on the 1999 television series *Ring: The Final Chapter*. In 1998, she played the title role of *Hausu* (1977) director Nobuhiko Obayashi's *Sada*, a biopic about the notorious Sada Abe who was famous for killing her lover during sex and removing his testicles and penis to keep as mementos.

KURSON, JANE

Editor-turned-painter Jane Kurson worked on Patty Jenkins' Oscar-winning Aileen Wurnos biopic *Monster* in 2003 but was more explicitly linked to horror earlier in her career through her work on editing *Don't Go in the House* (Joseph Ellison, 1979). For cult film fans, however, Kurson's best work arguably remains her editing for Tim Burton's horror-comedy classic *Beetlejuice* (1988).

KUSAMA, KARYN

Raised in Missouri, filmmaker and writer Karyn Kusama is a figurehead in the ever-growing contemporary Women in Horror movement. She studied film at the Tisch School of the Arts in New York where she won a prize for her student film. Working a variety of jobs to support herself in her early career, it was as a nanny for Oscar-nominated indie filmmaker John Sayles that she got her first big break and became his assistant. Her debut film was *Girlfight* in 2000 which won major prizes at both Sundance and Cannes, and after a difficult experience with studio meddling in her sophomore effort *Æon Flux* in 2005, she would turn in 2009 to direct the Diablo Cody-written horror film *Jennifer's Body* with Megan Fox and Amanda Seyfried. At the time misunderstood by critics, *Jennifer's Body* is now championed as a cult feminist horror film well ahead of its time. In 2015, she directed the horror film *The Invitation* that received widespread positive responses from critics and audiences alike. In 2017, Kusama directed the contemporary *Rosemary's Baby* reimagining "Her Only Living Son" as a segment for the highly anticipated all-woman director horror anthology *XX* alongside Jovanka Vuckovic, Annie Clark and Roxanne Benjamin. Her most recent film *Destroyer,* a dark police thriller starring Nicole Kidman, had its world premiere at the 2018 Toronto International Film Festival. Kusama is a vocal advocate for women in the film industry and isn't afraid to call out bullshit when she sees it.

KUZUIC, FRAN RUBEL

While in the 1990s and early 2000s the *Buffy the Vampire Slayer* phenomena was linked primarily to Joss Whedon's television series of the same name, often forgotten in the narrative is the crucial role of Fran Rubel Kuzui. Her debut film *Tokyo Pop* (1988) played at the Cannes Film Festival before she discovered Whedon's script for the *Buffy* film, assisting in developing it further, seeking finance and directing the 1992 feature film version. She would continue to be an executive producer on both the television series of *Buffy* and the later *Angel*, and—continuing her interest in Japanese pop culture demonstrated in her debut feature film as director—she also co-founded Kuzui Enterprises which distributed Japanese cinema in the United States.

KYES, NANCY

Often credited as Nancy Loomis, Virginia-born American actor Nancy Kyes is synonymous with the role of Annie Brackett in John Carpenter's *Halloween* (1978) and *Halloween II* (1981). Her first collaboration was as both an actor and working in the wardrobe department on Carpenter's earlier *Assault on Precinct 13* in 1976. Between the two *Halloween* films she also played Sandy in Carpenter's *The Fog* in 1980, and later appeared in *Halloween III: Season of the Witch* (1982), directed by her then-husband Tommy Lee Wallace. Retiring from acting in the early 1990s, she is now an artist.

LA PLANTE, LAURA

Silent era film star Laura La Plante was born in Missouri in 1904 and began acting in her teens. A prolific and popular actor during the 1920s and into the '30s, her most famous horror film is Paul Leni's 1927 movie *The Cat and the Canary*, in which she starred as the heir to her uncle's fortune in this foundational Old Dark House film. Two years later, she starred again in another Leni-director horror film, 1929's *The Last Warning*.

LAI, ME ME

Stemming from Burmese and British heritage, Me Me Lai worked across both British and Italian horror predominantly throughout the 1970s and 1980s. Her horror credits include *Crucible of Terror* (Ted Hooker, 1971), *Deep River Savages* (Umberto Lenzi, 1972), *Last Cannibal World* (Ruggero Deodato, 1977), and *Eaten Alive!* (Umberto Lenzi, 1980).

LAI, MIU-SUET CAROL

With a background in marketing, Hong Kong filmmaker Carol Lai began her movie career in 1989 in a range of behind-the-scenes roles. She made her debut as both director and writer in 2001 with the teen drama *Glass Tears*, which was included in the Director's Fortnight program at the Cannes Film Festival. This was followed soon after by *The Floating Landscape* (2003), she directed and co-wrote the technological horror film *Naraka 19* in 2007, which starred Hong Kong popstar Gillian Chung Yan-tung from the Cantopop group Twins.

LAM, KAREN—INTERVIEW (JULY 2018)

Working extensively across film, television, and web for almost 20 years, Canadian director, writer, and producer Karen Lam is one of the strongest examples of what women filmmakers can achieve both creatively and ideologically in the horror genre.

Winning an Artistic Innovation Award for Women in Film in Vancouver in 2013, Lam's work has garnered a number of other awards at film festivals around the world for both her features and shorts. Lam's horror shorts include *The Cabinet* (2007), *Doll Parts* (2011), *The Stolen* (2012), and *Chiral* (2015), and she likewise directed, wrote, and produced the features *Stained* (2010) and *Evangeline* (2013). She directed the television series *Very Bad Men* in 2012 that screened on the Investigation Discovery channel, and her web series *Mythos* was awarded the Best Web Series at the 2015 Leo Awards, the major industry accolades for the film and television industry in British Columbia.

Lam has recently been a writer on the SyFy television series *Van Helsing* and *Ghost Wars*, and she at the time of our interview she was in the post-production stage of her next feature film, *The Curse of Willow Song*.

http://karenlamfilms.com/

I'm intrigued in your background as a lawyer: in Australia where I live, one of my favourite filmmakers is a woman called Ana Kokkinos who has a similar background, and I've always wondered what that profession lends of itself in general terms to making films? What inspired the career change?

Law was both the saviour—and aberration—to my career: previously, I had studied music and literature, with a lifelong love for textiles. I was actually enrolled in fashion design at Ryerson University in Toronto when I realized it wasn't for me, dropped out and wrote the LSAT. Law is a fantastic foundation for almost every career but particularly in film. I made the transition from insurance defence to being in-house legal counsel at our provincial funding agency, mainly because I was a terrible lawyer.

But the legal background made producing—which is how I started in film and television—very easy. A lot of producing is contractual and business so coupled with my art background, it seemed like the perfect match. I saw a career working with other artists but providing business cover for them. Of course, things don't always turn out like you plan!

***The Cabinet* is a real little treasure: from Catherine Breillait to Anna Biller, there's something about the *Bluebeard* story that has proven really attractive to women filmmakers. What for your personally is it about that fairy tale that sparked your imagination?**

I have always loved a morality tale and it's why I'm continually drawn to fairy tales and mythology. *Bluebeard* always stuck with me because it was about a greedy girl who married for all the wrong reasons. Would she have met her demise if she had only followed the rules? I'm not saying she deserved her demise—because no one does—but I did see her underlying intentions as being suspect. It's at the heart of horror to me: I don't like "oops" horror, when bad things happen to good people. I like horror where the protagonist is an active participant in their fate. The story couldn't have happened to anyone else, that every choice made leads to the ultimate conclusion. Maybe that's an Asian thing, but I do believe in karma and in being responsible for your own fate.

I first saw *Doll Parts* at Australia's Stranger With My Face film festival, which frankly just blew me away. What for you is the particular power of fantastic genres like horror to tackle very real-world issues like you do here? Could you provide a bit of the back story that inspired you to make this film?

I conceived of the story when I was in Hong Kong. My grandmother was quite ill and having hallucinations every evening: it was clear to me she was already between our world and the next. I was reading *Stories*, edited by Neil Gaiman and Al Sarrantonio, and one stuck out for me "Catch and Release" about a serial killer whose modus operandi was to pick up hitchhikers and decide whether to "release" them.

On the set of *The Curse of Willow Song*. Photo by Tallulah, key crew location scout featuring from left to right: Lindsay Burke (prop master), Darryll Doucette (production designer) Karen Lam (director), Willan Leung (first AD). Used with permission.

The male power over the women's lives irritated me, especially given my already emotional state, and I started really thinking about how that plays out in the rest of our lives. *Doll Parts* came as my anger grew, and I wanted to turn the tables and explore the hitchhiker/killer dynamic in a way that felt satisfying to me.

While *Evangeline* is obviously so much more, I'm really intrigued by how you reimagine—and at times even subvert—the rape-revenge tradition in this film. I'm really fascinated that despite the category so often getting reduced to 'horror', supernatural rape-revenge films are so surprisingly thin on the ground. What made you decide to approach this particular material through a ghost story?

Evangeline is the feature length version of *Doll Parts*, where I wanted to look at my monster's mortal life, seeing what turned her into the thing that she is. The rape-revenge trope is essentially male: we're merely the impetus to the real action, and the rape itself is often a titillating and prolonged rape fantasy: the worse it is, the more justified the male hero's journey. I wanted to reimagine that: to set up Evangeline's life as a real human being with aspirations and a series of choices, not bad choices necessarily, but ones that lead her to where ends up.

Her death is by strangulation and the rape occurs after this death: I wanted to ensure it was as un-sexy as I could. The very nature of the rape scene in male films—with the moaning and screaming and ultimate dominance—sexualizes rape when truly it's merely a function of dominance and power, as we see in prisons. I wanted to reclaim that: the rape is short and ridiculous, all from Evangeline's perspective and from her inner world.

I think the supernatural aspect of the treatment stems from my own belief system: I'm deeply superstitious and believe in the paranormal world, given my own set of personal experiences. It felt like the only way I could tell this particular story.

So much of *Evangeline* obviously relies on the strong connection between you and actor Kat de Lieva. Was the role created with her in mind, or did casting come later? What made her so perfect for the part?

Often when I'm writing, I draw from my own past: people I know, my own experiences and relationships. Apart from specific story structure or themes, I prefer when I can create characters from my real life, rather than referencing other fictional characters. But once the script is done, I like to give it to the universe: I don't try to impose any of my particular ideas onto the actors but to see what they bring and what kind of energy they have that would work for the project.

I met Katerina in the audition project and what I loved about her was the balance of warmth, innocence and yet the core of strength she has. Kat is Eastern European and there's such a femininity about her and yet I wouldn't want to cross her. I knew as soon as I met her that she was the perfect fit for Evangeline. It

On the set of *The Curse of Willow Song*. Photo by Karen Lam. Used with permission.

wasn't until long after we shot and were editing that I realized that Kat is the spitting image of my best friend in elementary school, whose story I roughly used for Evangeline's back story. It wasn't a conscious decision at all, but just a wonderful realization.

Your earlier film *Stained* in many ways deals with different territory than *Evangeline*, but at its heart still lies questions about women, autonomy and trauma. Can you tell me about the origins and development of this project, and how you see it as deviating and overlapping with your other work?

Stained was written as a fever dream: my first feature script and was intended to be a small, strange psychodrama. It was actually inspired by my relationship with my best friend, but I took it to a strange and dark new place. When we made *Stained*, my head was still firmly as a producer: I had a lot of financing contacts and I was still thinking very much like a business person. We raised more money for the project and had a lot of executives and complexity, which led to a lot of creative decisions that were compromises to the creative vision. It was really my own inexperience. At that point, I had only made *The Cabinet*, and I felt very compelled to define my specific style, to the detriment of the film. I learned a lot from the film—in a lot of ways, *Stained* freed me as a filmmaker because it shook me out of the idea that I couldn't fail, couldn't take creative risks.

On the set of *The Curse of Willow Song*. Photo by Karen Lam, featuring left to right, Valerie Tien (lead actress), Monica Correa (key make up), Karen Lam (director). Used with permission.

Now I understand that you will fail if you DON'T take risks, if you try to satisfy everyone, or if you don't protect the creative integrity of the film itself. As a filmmaker, I feel that I'm there merely as a vessel for the ideas. My job is to steer the project, bring on the right people, and prevent it from veering off course. I give guidance to my team, but I also provide a lot of freedom and trust. If I bring you on board, it's because I want to work with you, not undermine you or micromanage.

More broadly, what is it about horror that provides you such a perfect outlet to say what you want to say?

I think I'm drawn to the darkest aspects of human nature. I love human monsters: seeing what makes monsters tick, trying to imagine the thought process in what we consider to be monsters. Horror provides the perfect outlet for me. I can explore gender, politics, pathology and everything that fascinates me in what amounts to adult fairy tales. Also, I can't imagine a world devoid of demons and the supernatural. Horror allows me to combine all of my ideas in the most visual or surreal way that I can dream up—there's no other genre I can work within.

With *Very Bad Men*, what surprised you the most about the shift to a TV documentary series?

Very Bad Men actually came about after my short film, *The Stolen*, and before Evangeline. Speaking of human monsters, I adore true crime and most of my reading veers between mythology and crime fiction/non-fiction. Documentary, unlike fiction, fills my creative tank. As a director and writer on documentary series, you are merely reshaping the stories: you're finding the heart of the material you've gathered and presenting it to the audience in a clear, suspenseful way, that is true to the material and the real-life people involved.

When you're working with real people, their true-life horror stories need to be handled with dignity and with compassion, and it influences how I work in fiction. People are so much more interesting than what we often see in media: they're complicated and their reactions aren't necessarily what appear on movies-of-the-week. Plus, having access to FBI, forensic specialists, journalists and experts in human pathology is invaluable.

Whenever I write fiction, the documentary work is a touchstone for remaining authentic and compassionate. Both horror and true crime (and I see the two as deeply overlapping) require that you keep truth at the heart of your work. It's presented as entertainment but if it's done right, you can be saying so much more.

There's a real move back to your earlier fascination with fairy tale like stories and focus on women and trauma in *Mythos*. Compared to a short or feature film, how did you find the serial nature of a web series as a forum to tease out these ideas both creatively and practically?

I wrote *Mytho*s following the passing of my beloved father, and in a lot of ways, there's a darkness in the web series that was probably reflective of my own emotional state. I partnered with TELUS, our local cable and Internet provider, who literally gave me the money and total creative freedom to make whatever I wanted. I took full advantage of that opportunity.

For me, a web series allows you to explore ideas in a short form, without necessarily needing to think about launching a television series. That's not how everyone looks at it, but I believe that some projects should stand alone by themselves, not just acting as springboards to other, larger projects. *Mythos* is perhaps the purest expression of what I was feeling at the time: it's pure emotion with a visual and musical accompaniment.

There's such a strong international community of women horror filmmakers, other creators and fans under the 'women in horror' umbrella that you are clearly a part of. In Canada alone, I'm always surprised by how many women directors work in the genre. Is this, do you think, a coincidence, or is there something in the cultural imagination that inspires this?

We have long, dark winters…Also when you look at the history of our nation, our literature and our art tends towards the dark. I do wonder whether it has to do with our huge, barren landscapes and living so close to America. It allows for a lot of very dark daydreams.

Having worked in the film and television industry for almost 20 years, I am guessing you have seen and experienced a lot. With the recent very public discussions about gender inequality in this industry, I'd be fascinated to hear your take on this—are things improving?

I don't think there's a woman working in the film or television industry that doesn't have horror stories to share about this inequality, but opening the closet and exposing the monsters is a perfect first step toward rebalance. I don't know that things are improving, but the conversation is. What we need to ensure now is that the conversation is nuanced, and that we're not moving toward a black-and-white interpretation.

That said, whenever power shifts, people with power feel the loss—that they're being stripped of their power and opportunity—and most don't go quietly into the good night. I worry about the backlash, the anger and the hostility toward our efforts, and that it can set us backward. The geopolitical landscape is a perfect example of this: every time we make efforts to move forward, where we think we're going in the right direction, there are people who feel disenfranchised by the shift and fight back with anger. I feel that growing anger now and maybe that's why I like horror so much: I can deal with fictional monsters on-screen, not the ones in my own back yard.

LAMBERT, MARY

Born in Arkansas in 1951, filmmaker Mary Lambert had extensive experience as a music video director, most notably directing some of Madonna's most iconic '80s-era clips such as "Material Girl" and "Like a Prayer". Clearly developing a strong visual style, her feature film debut was the award-winning *Siesta* in 1987. In 1989, she directed the screen adaptation of Stephen King's *Pet Sematary*, followed in 1992 by its sequel *Pet Sematary II*. Later horror directorial work would include *Strange Frequency* (2001), the kids' film *Halloweentown II: Kalabar's Revenge* (2001), *Urban Legends: Bloody Mary* (2005) and *The Attic* in 2007. She would also direct an episode of the television series *Tales from the Crypt*.

LAMPERT, ZOHRA

So synonymous is Zohra Lampert with her eponymous character in John Hancock's 1971 horror masterpiece *Let's Scare Jessica to Death* that it's almost impossible to think of her beyond that role. Born in 1937 in New York, she studied at the University of Chicago and would have a stage and screen career that would span 60 years. Across her impressive career, she would work with filmmakers including John Cassavetes and Elia Kazan, and in 1990 she would return to horror to play George C. Scott's central character's wife in William Peter Blatty's chilling *The Exorcist III*.

LANCHESTER, ELSA

As one of the most famous images of a woman in horror (and privileged on the cover of this very book), as the title character in James Whale's 1935 horror film *Bride of Frankenstein* Elsa Lanchester is one of the most iconic women in the film genre's entire history. Yet she was a performer with a vast range, playing in everything from historical epics to comedies to family films. Born in London in 1902, she began performing early in life, first as a dancer and then acting on stage. She worked steadily from the mid 1920s until her death in the mid '80s. While a third choice for the role of the Bride after Phyllis Brooks and Brigitte Helm, this was the role that would forever associate Lanchester with the horror genre, but her filmography in the category is broad and impressive. While ranging in tone from comic fantasy to eco-horror, Lanchester would appear in *The Ghost Goes West*

Elsa Lanchester in Bride of Frankenstein (James Whale, 1935). Credit: Everett Collection Inc / Alamy Stock Photo

(René Clair, 1935), *The Spiral Staircase* (Robert Siodmak, 1946), *Bell, Book and Candle* (Richard Quine, 1958), *Blackbeard's Ghost* (Robert Stevenson, 1968), *Willard* (Daniel Mann, 1971) and *Terror in the Wax Museum* (Georg Fenady, 1973).

LANDON, LAURENE

Laurene Landon was born in Canada and became a cult figure primarily through her work in the 1980s. Initially training as a police officer, she turned to film extra work in the late 1970s and in 1981 would begin her long professional relationship with filmmaker Larry Cohen with the horror-comedy film *Full Moon High*. Her later horror credits would include *The Stuff* (Larry Cohen, 1985), *Maniac Cop* (William Lustig, 1988), It's *Alive III: Island of the Alive* (Larry Cohen, 1987), *Wicked Stepmother* (Larry Cohen, 1989), *Maniac Cop 2* (William Lustig, 1990) and *The Ambulance* (Larry Cohen, 1990). In 2006, she also acted in Cohen's donation to the Masters of Horror series, "Pick Me Up".

LANGENKAMP, HEATHER ◟

As the Final Girl in Wes Craven's original *A Nightmare on Elm Street* (1984), Heather Langenkamp represented the all-American girl as a tough-as-nails fighter. Actor, producer, director and makeup artist Langenkamp was born in Oklahoma in 1964, and while she had made a few tentative steps into screen acting, it was her casting as Nancy that would make her a horror star. She would return to the franchise with *A Nightmare on Elm Street 3: Dream Warriors* (Chuck Russell, 1987) and *New Nightmare* (Wes Craven, 1994), and would also act in horror films including *Shocker* (Wes Craven, 1989), *The Demolitionist* (Robert Kurtzman, 1995), *Home* (Frank Lin, 2016), *Truth or Dare* (Nick Simon, 2017), *Hellraiser: Judgment* (Gary J. Tunnicliffe, 2018), and would co-star with Barbara Steele in the all-star cast of Jonathan Zarantonello's *The Butterfly Room* (2012). She is the co-owner of AFX Studio who specialize in special effects make up, and in this capacity, she has credits on horror films including *Dawn of the Dead* (Zack Snyder, 2004), *Dead Silence* (James Wan, 2007), *The Cabin in the Woods* (Drew Goddard, 2012), and television series including *American Horror Story* and *Scream Queens*. In 2011, Arlene Marechal's documentary *I Am Nancy* focused on Langenkamp and the role that made her famous, and in 2008 she joined other horror actors-turned-directors Danielle Harris and Ellie Cornell to make the horror anthology *Prank!*

LANGLOIS, LISA

Canadian actor Lisa Langlois made her movie debut in French New Wave director Claude Chabrol's perverse *giallo*-like mystery *Blood Relatives* in 1978, and would later excel in horror. Across a career that saw her work across France, Canada and the United States, born in Ontario in 1959 she worked in both film and television. Langlois's horror credits include John Huston's *Phobia* (1980), J. Lee Thompson's *Happy Birthday to Me* (1981), *Deadly Eyes* (Robert Clouse, 1982), *The Nest* (Terence H. Winkless, 1988) and the made-for-television monster movie *Fire Serpent* (John Terlesky, 2007).

LARK, SHANNON

With her filmography as actor alone in almost 50 films, San Francisco-raised Shannon Lark is the Chief Operating Officer of the Viscera Organization, a non-profit group focused on championing and supporting women horror filmmakers, whose most public facing event is the internationally renowned Viscera Film Festival. Across her wide filmography as an actor include feature films such as *Psychic Experiment* (Mel House, 2010), *The Family* (Joe Hollow and Wolfgang Meyer, 2011), *Towers of Terror* (Matt Gibson, 2013) and *The Girl Who Played with the Dead* (Cory Ulder, 2014). Lark is also a producer, writer and director and has directed and written a number of horror shorts including *It's My Birthday* (2006), *Go Ask Alice* (2008) and *Lip Stick* (2010).

LASSANDER, DAGMAR

German actor Dagmar Lassander was a familiar face in Italian exploitation film, particularly *gialli* and horror movies. Amongst her impressive filmography are Piero Schivazappa's stylish S&M art-*giallo The Laughing Woman* (1969), *A Hatchet for the Honeymoon* (Mario Bava, 1970), *Forbidden Photos of a Lady Above Suspicion* (Luciano Ercoli, 1970), *The Iguana with the Tongue of Fire* (Riccardo Freda, 1971), *Werewolf Woman* (Rino Di Silvestro, 1976), *The Black Cat* (Lucio Fulci, 1981), *The House by the Cemetery* (Lucio Fulci, 1981) and *Devil Fish* (Lamberto Bava, 1984).

LASSEK, LISA

Lisa Lassek is an American editor who has worked regularly with filmmaker Joss Whedon. Originally from Philadelphia and studying at both Boston University and Vassar, Lassek worked on the horror television series *Buffy the Vampire Slayer*, *Angel* and *Tru Calling*, and she edited Drew Goddard's 2012 horror feature *The Cabin in the Woods*.

LAU, LAURA

Born in San Francisco in 1963, American filmmaker Laura Lau often collaborates with Chris Kentis, with whom she co-directed the 2011 horror feature *Silent House* with Elizabeth Olsen, a remake of Gustavo Hernández's 2010 cult Uruguayan film of the same name. Lau also wrote and co-produced their adaptation, and in 2003 they worked on the earlier horror film *Open Water*. While directed by Kentis alone, Lau co-produced and with Kentis was co-cinematographer of *Open Water*. They have been married since 1997, the same year they collaborated on their feature debut *Grind*.

LAURENCE, ASHLEY

As Kirsty Cotton in *Hellraiser* (Clive Barker, 1987), American actor Ashley Laurence began a career that would see her grow a cult reputation in horror, despite appearing in a range of films and television shows. She was cast in the later sequels *Hellbound: Hellraiser II* (Tony Randel, 1988) and *Hellraiser: Hellseeker* (Rick Bota, 2002), as well as the evil child film *Mikey* (Dennis Dimster, 1992), the H. P. Lovecraft adaptation T*he Lurking Fear* (C. Courtney Joyner, 1994), *Warlock III: The End of Innocence* (Eric Freiser, 1999), *Chill* (Serge Rodunsky, 2007) and Lucky McKee's 2008 film *Red*.

LAURIE, PIPER

Rosetta Jacobs has for almost 70 years gone by the stage name Piper Laurie, working earlier in her career alongside some of Classical Hollywood's biggest names. Born in Detroit in 1932 and experiencing a difficult childhood, she was disillusioned with Hollywood both professionally and personally and moved to New York to pursue a career on stage with better roles. She had all but retired from acting and was working as a sculptor when Brian De Palma offered her the role of Margaret White in *Carrie* (1976), launching a spectacular comeback that later saw her receive a Best Supporting Actress nomination for *Children of a Lesser God* (Randa Haines, 1986) and join the ensemble cast of David Lynch and Mark Frost's *Twin Peaks*. Since *Carrie*, Laurie has appeared in a number of horror films such as Curtis Harrington's *Ruby* (1977), Robert Rodriguez's *The Faculty* (1996), Dario Argento's *Trauma* (1993) and the exorcism film *Possessed* (Steven E. de Souza, 2000).

LAZĂR, VERONICA

Born in Romania in 1938, Veronica Lazăr was an Italian actor who was well into her thirties before she began acting in film. Making her debut in the controversial *Last Tango in Paris* (Bernardo Bertolucci, 1972), she worked in many of Bertolucci's later films but is most renowned for her work in horror with Dario Argento. While she had a small role in Argento's rape-revenge film *The Stendhal Syndrome* (1996), she is most readily identifiable for her role as Mater Tenebrarum in *Inferno* (1980), his sequel to 1977's *Suspiria*. Amongst her other roles, she also played Martha in Lucio Fulci's *The Beyond* (1981).

LEANDERSSON, LINA

Iranian/Swedish actor Lina Leandersson stunned horror audiences in 2008 when at only 11 years old she starred as Eli in Tomas Alfredson's groundbreaking vampire film *Let the Right One In*. Born in Dalarna County in central Sweden in 1995, Leandersson began her career in the theater and television before her breakthrough role in *Let the Right One In* and has since appeared in a number of Swedish drama films.

LEASE, MARIA

Under a range of aliases, Maria Lease both directed and acted in a range of adult films, leading to her directing the horror feature, *Dolly Dearest* (1991). Beyond this, Lease has strong form in the low-budget film industry, working a variety of jobs both in front and behind the camera, most famously as an actor in a range of B-grade films from the late 1960s onwards in often small or uncredited roles, including horror movies such as *Dracula vs. Frankenstein* (Al Adasom, 1971) and *Sinthia: The Devil's Doll* (Ray Dennis Steckler, 1970). From the early '70s, Lease also worked in various capacities in script departments, and it is here that she worked on the most mainstream entries in her filmography on films like *Better Off Dead* (Savage Steve Holland, 1985) and TV shows like *Hill Street Blues*, *MacGyver* and *Boston Legal*. This led to Lease's involvement in horror projects such as *Kiss of the Tarantula* (Chris Munger, 1976).

LEE, ANGELICA

Actor Angelica Lee was born in West Malaysia in 1976 and achieved international acclaim for her starring role in Danny and Oxide Pang's Hong Kong/Singapore co-production, the Thai-set horror film *The Eye* (later made in the US in 2008 with Jessica Alba). Lee—who is also married to Oxide—would collaborate on another horror film with the Pang Brothers with 2006's *Re-Cycle*, shown in the *Un Certain Regard* category at the Cannes Film Festival in 2006. In 2008, she also starred in Tsui Hark's horror movie *Missing*.

LEE, TRICIA

British-Canadian Tricia Lee is an award-winning filmmaker who has worked across film, television, web series and short films. As both director and producer, from 2013 to 2016 she had a remarkable 3-for-3 winning streak with the acclaimed horror features *Silent Retreat* (2013), *Clean Break* (2013) and *Blood Hunters* (2017), all of which focus on complex women protagonists.

LEE, IZZY—INTERVIEW (JUNE 2018)

The mother of Nihil Noctem Films, Boston-based writer, director and producer Izzy Lee is a familiar name to anyone who has been to a horror film festival in recent years, her numerous shorts playing internationally to audiences looking for horror films created through the eye of an unabashedly feminist artist.

Her horror shorts include *Legitimate* (2013), *Come Out and Play* (2014), *Picket* (2014), *Invisible Friend* (2015), *A Favor* (2015), *Innsmouth* (2015), *Postpartum* (2015), *For a Good Time, Call...* (2017), *Rites of Vengeance* (2017), *My Monster* (2018), *The Obliteration of the Chickens* (2019) and *Re-Home* (2019), and she has had work included in the portmanteau films *Grindsploitation* (2016) and *60 Seconds to Die* (2017).

Lee has also worked extensively as a film festival programmer, film critic, and is an editor at *ScreenAnarchy*, and writes horror fiction that has appeared in anthologies including *Wicked Witches*, *Now I Lay Me Down to Sleep* and *Lost Films*.

https://www.nihilnoctem.com/

My Monster is so much fun, and that rarest of treasures—a horror-comedy-romcom! Tonally this is different from so much of your other work, what was your inspiration or this project?

The Soska sisters asked me to be part of their 2018 Women in Horror Month Blood Drive PSA. I originally intended to do a much shorter project, but ended up writing a 7-minute script that I needed to make happen. I was able to use a snippet of *My Monster* called "It's in You" to make the PSA while also sending the full film to festivals, where it's gotten great response. I was thrilled to get Brea Grant (*Dexter*, Rob Zombie's *Halloween 2*, *Beyond the Gates*), as well as Adam Egypt Mortimer (director of *Some Kind of Hate*, *Holidays*) to act alongside my hilarious husband Steve, who played the monster.

Every now and then, I need to lighten up and make something a bit funny. I still need some conflict in whatever I make, so I wrote a bit about the female experience of speaking a truth and not being believed, and worse, belittled, even if the intent was good. And why not have an inter-dimensional monster bro-off?

I loved the use of White Zombie in My Monster, too: what's the significance of that film for you?

It's an illustration of a trapped woman, and was perfect for the story. Brea's character is a woman also trapped in a different sense. The other film in there is Horror Express, and that clip shows a frozen monster, who's discovered, packed up in a crate, and locked up; carted off as a curiosity.

Izzy Lee. Photo credit: Jessica Barnthouse. Used with permission.

My Monster, Rites of Vengeance, and For A Good Time, Call… share at their heart a focus on the monstrosity of supposedly 'normal' men, and in each in very different ways the tables are turned. They all deal with women finding a way to settle scores, be it in regards to emotional abuse, revenge porn, or the sexual assault of children by the clergy. Is this a conscious theme that you are interested in, or something you return to almost subconsciously?

That's interesting; I've never really thought of the "normal" guy theme. I suppose that the world is full of those types of normal-seeming people who are secretly awful. I tend to put women front and center in my work because we need more stories where they are the stars of the show. Women are also good at cleaning up messes, and that can include human trash.

There is a special makeup effect in For a Good Time, Call… that reimagines a certain female erogenous zone in a particularly memorable (and hilarious) way. I know you're a makeup whiz, was this your doing?!

I wouldn't say I'm a whiz in the slightest, but having been an artist and having gone to art school has helped. Yes, I made that prosthetic, which was the one major addition I made to the script. It's over the top, but drives home the reflection of the revenge porn theme.

Rites of Vengeance is such a simple but powerful premise, and I have a real weakness for power-nuns in film. What brought you to this kind of religious imagery for this project?

The simple fact that we live in a world where justice is rare, and abuse is rampant within religion. Writing and making films helps take the power back.

***Innsmouth* is such a great film, and I love that you appear in it! Do you like acting—does it present different challenges than directing and writing?**

Thanks. I started out as an actor and writer as a kid; it was something I'd naturally gravitated toward, and every now and then, I'll still do a bit of acting. It's a lot of fun to pretend to be in someone else's shoes, and it's nice to just focus on one thing. If I directed *Innsmouth* over, I wouldn't have acted in it; there was too much to do. However, when you live in the Boston are and film on a holiday weekend, chances are your talent pool is going to be small because everyone is out of town.

Lovecraft is traditionally supposedly such a 'boys club' fandom wise, I love that you reclaimed it here. What's your relationship to Lovecraft, and what inspired *Innsmouth*?

Innsmouth was originally supposed to be part of a mostly European anthology that never happened. The stipulations were nudity, a shocking death, and if possible, something Poe or Lovecraft influenced. I knew I wanted to do something off the wall. I went to sleep one night, wondering, "who is the most fearless person I

Director Izzy Lee with Director of Photography Shaheen Seth. Photo credit: Mary C. Russell.
Used with permission.

know?" Having just worked with Tristan Risk on *For A Good Time, Call...* I knew she had to be involved.

When we were on set and I was applying that homemade prosthetic to her, she'd told me about the very special trick she'd performed to a select audience once upon a time. I'd sort of paused and said, "I'd put that on film!" And then I knew I had to call her up and make that happen with *Innsmouth*.

I adore Poe, but I'd read a few public domain stories from Lovecraft that were bizarre enough to be a bit of what I needed. I took the characters from *The Shadow Over Innsmouth* and made them women, and in some cases, changed their profession and put them in positions of authority. I flipped the script so that the men in the story were window dressing and had no lines, because it's still so unusual to see that. I also know it would have made Lovecraft twitchy, along with that kind of nudity, so too bad.

Postpartum is so joyfully excessive in a way, but also for any mother who's ever gone through a few nights without sleep with a newborn, it actually feeds into a really familiar reality where everything just feels like it falls into chaos. Can you tell me about the roots of this project, and your thoughts on the relationship between horror and motherhood more generally?

I originally started writing it as an absurdist horror-comedy, but it got really dark, really fast. I feel like the stigma of postpartum depression is still out there, and 'how dare you not be joyous after birth no matter what?' It's an ugly truth that some parents, particularly mothers, have a very hard time after bearing children. I wanted to explore that issue within the realm of horror. When you cannot sleep, reality can morph. In those circumstances, we can become monsters. Who can be sure what is real and what's not?

I love A Favor, it was the first film of yours I think I saw. It's a rare one for you in a way because the main character is not only male, but also a relatively nice guy. But then I think: is he?! What was the origin of this project?

He's nice, and yet he's not, he does Liz's dirty work because he's indebted to her, or perhaps she's blackmailing him. This film was originally supposed to be part of another anthology film that never happened, which would have been New England-based.

Your films are marked by some really strong collaborative partnerships even just in front of the camera with actors like Tristan Risk and Diana Porter. What benefits do you find working with the same people across multiple projects?

There's a trust that forms when you work with like-minded collaborators, whether that's in your cast or crew. It's comforting to know that they've got your back while you have theirs, and that you're all working toward the same goals.

A woman of many skills, you've also been writing fiction which I find absolutely fascinating—to move from the visual to the wholly verbal. How have you found this transition, and what can you do in your fiction writing that satisfies you in a way that is different from filmmaking?

Well, I find writing short fiction a lot easier than writing a feature-length screenplay, so far. I write fiction because I've been lucky enough to have a supportive group of author friends who've cheered me on, and being around that positivity has been really encouraging. As a result, I started submitting short fiction horror stories to anthologies and I'm thrilled to say that I've been published in the books: *Lost Films*, *Fright Into Flight*, *Wicked Witches*, *Now I Lay Me Down To Sleep*, and *Hydrophobia*. More to come on that front, I hope.

Another great thing about writing fiction is that unlike making films, you only have to rely on yourself, and it doesn't cost anything but time. It's been a nice relief from filmmaking when I have ideas that there's no way I'd have the budget for. In other words, writing fiction keeps the creativity flowing when I know I can't bring these ideas to film because of money.

LEE, ANNA

Beginning her career in theater at the prestigious Royal Albert Hall in London, Joan Boniface Winnifrith—credited as Anna Lee—was a regular on the popular soap opera *General Hospital*. Born in the UK in 1913 and beginning her career in Britain, she moved to the United States at the onset of World War II and collaborated frequently with director John Ford. She appeared in an impressive range of horror films, including Mark Robson's *Isle of the Dead* (1945) and *Bedlam* (1946), both co-starring Boris Karloff and produced by Val Lewton. Earlier in her career she co-starred with Karloff again in her husband Robert Stevenson's *The Man Who Changed His Mind* (1936), and she played the neighbour of Joan Crawford and Bette Davis's fraught sisters in Robert Aldrich's *What Ever Happened to Baby Jane?* (1962). In 1966, she had a small role in Bert I. Gordon's *Picture Mommy Dead*, and while not a horror movie *per se*, she also acted in Joseph L. Mankiewicz's beloved supernatural romance, *The Ghost and Mrs. Muir* (1947).

LEE, GRACE

Perhaps the only Peabody Award winner to make a zombie film, American director Grace Lee has excelled in both documentary and narrative filmmaking. Attaining a Masters of Fine Arts in Film Directing from UCLA, she describes her 2007 mockumentary *American Zombie* as a "fictional documentary" about a civil rights movement begun by the living dead. Also appearing in the film, while a horror-comedy, Lee's film continues the strong political agenda demonstrated across her broader filmography.

LEE, MARGARET

Born in 1943, British actor Margaret Lee found stardom in Italian cinema during the 1960s and '70s and starred across her career in many horror films. She acted in *Circus of Fear* (John Llewellyn Moxey, 1966), Jess Franco's *Venus in Furs* (1969) and *The Bloody Judge* (1970) and Massimo Dallamano's *Dorian Gray* (1970), as well as the *gialli Double Face* (Riccardo Freda, 1969), The *Killers Are Our Guest* (Vincenzo Rigo, 1974) and *Slaughter Hotel* (Fernando Di Leo, 1971).

LEE, SHERYL

German-born American actor Sheryl Lee was born in 1967. As Laura Palmer in David Lynch and Mark Frost's iconic television series *Twin Peaks* and the 1992 film *Twin Peaks: Fire Walk with Me*, she has offered one of the most powerful and visceral depictions of women and trauma ever put on screen. Lee also starred in John Carpenter's 1998 horror western *Vampires*.

LEERHSEN, ERICA

Beginning her horror career with Joe Berlinger's misunderstood *Book of Shadows: Blair Witch 2* (2000), actor Erica Leerhsen has a long association with the genre that would peak with a key role in *The Texas Chainsaw Massacre* (Marcus Nispel, 2003). Born in New York in 1976, her other horror film credits include *Wrong Turn 2: Dead End* (Joe Lynch, 2007), *Living Hell* (Richard Jefferies, 2008), *Lonely Joe* (Michael Coonce, 2009), *Mischief Night* (Richard Schenkman, 2013) and *Phobia* (Jon Keeyes, 2013).

LEIGH, JANET

One of the women who welcomed the era of the modern horror film as we know it with her legendary performance as doomed petty thief Marion Crane in Alfred Hitchcock's *Psycho* (1960), few have left the imprint on the genre like Janet Leigh. A movie star during

Jamie Lee Curtis and Janet Leigh on Hollywood Boulevard where Curtis was honored with the 2,116th star on the Hollywood Walk of Fame, 3 September 1998. Credit: Featureflash Photo Agency / Shutterstock.com

Hollywood's Golden Age, Leigh was championed by Norma Shearer—a famous star of the silent era—who saw her contracted to MGM studios. Building a strong professional reputation across the 1940s and '50s, it was with *Psycho* that she attained global recognition, nominated for Best Supporting Actress for the role at both the Oscars and the Golden Globes. Born in California in 1927, Leigh was also prolific author, and she appeared in many horror movies including William F. Claxton's eco-horror film *Night of the Lepus* in 1972, co-starring with her daughter and fellow cult horror actor Jamie Lee Curtis in *The Fog* (John Carpenter, 1980) and *Halloween H20: 20 Years Later* (Steve Miner, 1998).

LEIGH, JENNIFER JASON °

While it is difficult to pinpoint the precise moment where Jennifer Jason Leigh became a cult film star, for horror fans at least, it was carved in stone from the outset with her debut film appearance in the 1981 slasher film, *Eyes of a Stranger*. Born in Hollywood in 1962 to parents in the industry, she began working as an actor before she was even 10 years old and, in her teens, studied in New York with Lee Strasberg. As one of the stars of Amy Heckerling's teen comedy *Fast Times at Ridgemont High* (1982), Leigh became a familiar face across the '80s into present day. Returning on many occasions to the genre where her film career began, she notably co-starred in *The Hitcher* (Robert Harmon, 1986), *Sister,*

Jennifer Jason Leigh attends the premiere of Anomalisa during the 72nd Venice Film Festival on 8 September 2015 in Venice, Italy. Credit: Andrea Raffin / Shutterstock.com

Sister (Bill Condon, 1987), *Heart of Midnight* (Matthew Chapman, 1988), and the scifi/ horror hybrids *Existenz* (David Cronenberg, 1999), *Morgan* (Luke Scott, 2016) and *Annihilation* (Alex Garland, 2018). She also acted in the television movie *Buried Alive* (Frank Darabont, 1990), and would return to dark-themed films in movies such as *Single White Female* (Barbet Schroeder, 1992) and the Stephen King adaptation *Dolores Claiborne* (Taylor Hackford, 1995).

LEMMONS, KASI

An important filmmaker in her own right, Kasi Lemmons reputation lies largely as a director of films including *Harriet* (2019) and *Eve's Bayou* (1997), which won numerous awards including Best Director at the 1998 Black Film Awards. For horror fans, Lemmons attained cult status due to her powerful performance in Bernard Rose's *Candyman* (1992). As an actor, Lemmons filmography includes Robert Bierman dark comic fantasy *Vampire's Kiss* in 1989 with Nicolas Cage, and she played Jodie Foster's Clarice Starling's roomate in Jonathan Demme's *The Silence of the Lambs* (1991).

LESTER, KATHY

For close to 40 years, actor Kathy Lester been closely associated with that lavender dress that made her a horror film icon in cult favourite *Phantasm* (Don Coscarelli, 1979). The dress came from her own wardrobe and she selected it herself for her audition, becoming one of the most famous and immediately recognizable motifs from the films.

LETHIN, LORI

Starring in both *Return to Horror High* (Bill Froehlich, 1987) and *Bloody Birthday* (Gerald T. Olson, 1981), American actor Lori Lethin was a familiar face in '80s horror. Working across film and television primarily through the 1980s, she also has a smaller role in Edwin Brown's slasher movie *The Prey* (1980).

LEVENS, OLGA

Very little is known about filmmaker Olga Levens beyond her debut and currently only feature film as director, writer and cinematographer, the 2005 film *Haunted Boat*. What little information there is available about this confirms that, yes, there is a boat, and as its 6 teen protagonists discover, it also just happens to be haunted.

LEVY, JANE

Born in 1989 in California, American actor Jane Levy began her career in community theater and as a dancer, studying at New York's Stella Adler Studio of Acting. Her filmography is marked by a number of impressive forays into horror, including starring in Fede Álvarez's 2013 remake *Evil Dead* and collaborating with the director again in 2016 on the horror movie *Don't Breathe*. Levy also appeared in the 2017 series 3 return of David Lynch and Mark Frost's *Twin Peaks*.

LEWIS, BROOKE.

Brooke Lewis was born in Philadelphia in 1975 and began her career in the theater before moving to film where she would become a horror regular with films including *Kinky Killers* (George Lekovic, 2007), *iMurders* (Robbie Bryan, 2008), *Slime City Massacre* (Greg Lamberson, 2010) and *Dahmer vs. Gacy* (Ford Austin, 2010).

LIBERT, ANNE

Belgian actor Anne Libert was born in 1946 and worked primarily in French exploitation cinema and sex comedies. A frequent collaborator with Jess Franco, her work with him included *Dracula, Prisoner of Frankenstein* (1972), *The Erotic Rites of Frankenstein* (1972), *The Demons* (1973) and—most memorably perhaps—as the Queen of the Night in what arguably remains his horror magnum opus, *A Virgin Among the Living Dead* (1973).

LIGHT, MELANIE

London-based filmmaker Melanie Light has worked for a decade as both a director and art director across film and television. Her experience working on other people's projects inspired her to make her own movies, which includes music videos and short films, the latter including the serial killer film *Switch* (2010), and the shorts *The Herd* (2014) and *The Skin You're In* (2017). Light has also created idents for Britain's FrightFest and the Queen of Horror Festival and was the creative director and producer of the 2014 Women in Horror charity calendar (and also the model for April). She is currently developing her feature film debut called *Covetous* as well as a number of other features built around women protagonists. Most recently, Light has also directed segments for the online short horror platform *Fear Haus*.

LIGGETT, AGNIESZKA

Agnieszka Liggett is an editor based in London who has worked on a range of both fiction and non-fiction projects. Liggett received a MA in drama at the Polish National Film Television and Theater School, and later gained an MA in Editing at Britain's National Film and Television School. A number of projects she has worked on have been nominated for major film awards such as the *Palme d'Or* and the Oscars. Her horror credits include Paul Hyett's 2012 *The Seasoning House* and his 2015 werewolf feature *Howl*, and a number of horror shorts directed by John Dower.

LINAKER, KAY

Kay Linekar was an actor and screenwriter who worked in B-grade genre films during the 1930s and '40s particularly. She was born in Arkansas in 1913, and she is noted primarily for being the person to come up with the name for the cult horror film *The Blob* (Irvin Yeaworth, 1958), also co-writing the screenplay. As an actor, she also had a small uncredited role in A. Edward Sutherland's *The Invisible Woman* (1940).

LINDFORS, VIVECA

Swedish actor Viveca Lindfors was born in 1920 and worked from her early 20s right through to the year of her death in 1995. Finding fame in her homeland after studying at Stockholm's Royal Dramatic Theater School, she worked widely across film and television after relocating to Hollywood. While she appeared in Hammer's *These Are the Damned* (Joseph Losey, 1962), the majority of her horror credits were later in her career in film such as *Cauldron of Blood* (Santos Alcocer, 1971), *The Bell from Hell* (Claudio Guerín, 1973), *The Hand* (Oliver Stone, 1981), *Creepshow* (George A. Romero, 1982), *Silent Madness* (Simon Nuchtern, 1984), *The Exorcist III* (William Peter Blatty, 1990) and Marina Sargenti's *Child of Darkness, Child of Light* (1991). She also starred as Hannah Frankenstein, the title character in the 1986 television miniseries *Frankenstein's Aunt*.

LINDO, SANDRA

Brazilian-born filmmaker Sandra Lindo wrote, directed and produced the 2016 haunted house horror film *Den of Darkness*, having previously taken on the same duties with her horror shorts *Laura* (2009) and *The Attic* (2012). An actor also, Lindo starred as the title character, and worked in front of the camera in a number of thrillers and comedies.

LINÉ, HELGA

German-born actor, model, dancer and acrobat Helga Liné was a Eurohorror superstar, fleeing her homeland during World War II for Portugal, and later settling in Madrid. She would act in a range of horror films and *gialli* from Italy and Spain, including *The Blancheville Monster* (Alberto De Martino, 1963), *Nightmare Castle* (Mario Caiano, 1965) with Barbara Steele, *So Sweet...So Perverse* (Umberto Lenzi, 1969), *Horror Express* (Eugenio Martín, 1972), *My Dear Killer* (Tonino Valerii, 1972), *Horror Rises from the Tomb* (Paul Naschy, 1972), *The Loreley's Grasp* (Amando de Ossorio, 1973) and *Red Rings of Fear* (Alberto Negrin, 1978). She appeared in both León Klimovsky's *The Dracula Saga* (1973) and *The Vampires Night Orgy* (1974), as well as José Ramón Larraz's *Black Candles* (1982) and *Stigma* (1980).

LING, BAI ‹

While her notoriety as a tabloid celebrity may have briefly outshone her work as an actor, it is for her starring role in Fruit Chan's 2004 horror film *Dumplings*—expanded from a shorter segment in the horror anthology *Three...Extremes*—that Bai Ling should be remembered as one of that decade's most spectacular horror performers. Born in China in 1966, Ling began her acting career in the early 1980s first in the theater and moving to the screen. After establishing a career in China, she moved to the United States where she made her film debut in that country in Alex Proyas's cult supernatural revenge film *The Crow* in 1994. Ling's other horror credits include *The Breed* (Michael Oblowitz, 2001), *Chain Letter* (Deon Taylor, 2010), *Go Straight to Hell* (Edward G. Norris, 2011) and *Game of Assassins* (Matt Eskandari, 2013).

LOCKE, SONDRA

Born Sandra Louise Smith on Tennessee in 1944, the late Sondra Locke is perhaps most famous for her many collaborations with Clint Eastwood but has an impressive and broadly underrated career in her own right. She was cast in in Robert Ellis Miller's 1968 *film The Heart is a Lonely Hunter* (based on Carson McCuller's 1940 classic southern gothic novel of the same name) after winning a talent search the previous year, launching her acting career. Amongst her broad filmography include the horror films *Willard* (Daniel Mann, 1971), *A Reflection of Fear* (William A. Fraker, 1972), the horror-western *The Shadow of Chikara* (Earl E. Smith, 1977), the home invasion film *Death Game* (Peter S. Traynor, 1977) and she also appeared in the horror anthology television series *Night Gallery*.

Bai Ling at the Night of Science Fiction, Fantasy & Horror After Party at IATSE Stage 80 on 6 September 2014 in Burbank, California. Credit: Kathy Hutchins / Shutterstock.com

LÓPEZ, ISSA

The first woman to win the Best Horror Film award at Austin's Fantastic Fest, Mexican writer and filmmaker Issa López was—before her film work came to international attention with *Tigers are Not Afraid* (2017)—already a highly acclaimed writer, having won many awards including the National Novel Award from México's Institute of Fine Arts and Literature. She studied directing and screenwriting at México's National University where her award-winning student film *Tan Callando* (1994) brought her instant recognition, and she moved to a hugely successful career in both film and television. Although already having extensive experience as a screenwriter, director and producer, with *Tigers Are Not Afraid*—a magical realist vision of the life of children left behind in the Mexican drug wars—López's substantial talents earned her a high number of film awards at festivals around the world.

LORDS, TRACI ,

There was a time some decades ago when Traci Lords' cult reputation stemmed from her work in adult movies, but since leaving the industry in the late 1980s, she has established herself as a creative force with a range of skills, from music to fashion to writing to acting to directing. Born Nora Louise Kuzma in Ohio in the late 1960s, upon leaving the adult film industry, Lords studied method acting at the prestigious Lee Strasberg Theater Institute in New York. Her mainstream debut was in Jim Wynorski's horror-comedy *Not of This Earth* (1988), and while she would often collaborate with cult filmmakers such as John Waters, she continued a close relationship to the horror genre with later film credits including *Shock 'Em Dead* (Mark Freed, 1990), the television mini-series The *Tommyknockers* (Lawrence D. Cohen, 1993), *Skinner* (Ivan Nagy, 1993), *Blade* (Stephen Norrington, 1998), *Crazy Eights* (Jimi Jones, 2006), *Excision* (Richard Bates, Jr., 2012), *Devil May Call* (Jason Cuadrado, 2013), *Sharkansas Women's Prison Massacre* (Jim Wynorski, 2015) and the made-for-television horror movie *Nightmare Nurse* (Jake Helgren, 2016). Her song "Love Never Dies" also appeared on Mary Lambert's *Pet Sematary 2* (1992).

LORING, LISA

Born in the Marshall Islands in 1958, Lisa Loring's two-year stint as Wednesday Addams on the cult sitcom *The Addams Family* in the mid-1960s made her one of the most instantly recognizable children in the entire horror genre. Despite facing a number of challenges throughout her childhood and adult life, Loring maintained a connection to the show that made her initially so famous with the 1977 television movie *Halloween with the New Addams Family*, and later horror credits include *Blood Frenzy* (Hal Freeman, 1987), *Iced* (Jeff Kwitny, 1988), *Way Down in Chinatown* (Eric Michael Kochmer, 2014) and *Doctor Spine* (John Wesley Norton, 2015).

LORYS, DIANA

Spanish actor Ana María Cazorla Vega was born in Madrid in 1940 and performed under the name Diana Lorys. Working in film and television for almost 50 years, she was cast in a number of cult Eurohorror films including Jess Franco's *The Awful Dr. Orloff* (1962), Amando de Ossorio's *Fangs of the Living Dead* (1969) and Carlos Aured's *Blue Eyes of the Broken Doll* (1973).

LOVE, SUZANNA

Writer and actor Suzanna Love was born in New York in 1950 and studied at Vassar and New York's Neighborhood Playhouse School of the Theater. As an actor and writer, she frequently collaborated with director and then-husband Ulli Lommel on horror films including *The Boogey Man* (1980), *BrainWaves* (1982), *Boogeyman II* (1983) and the perhaps surprisingly explicitly feminist 1983 film *The Devonsville Terror*.

LOWE, ALICE

British actor and writer Alice Lowe was born in 1977 in the Midlands and studied at King's College, Cambridge. Through her early work in theater, she joined the team behind the horror-comedy project *Garth Marenghi* which would begin on stage and later move to television on Channel 4 in 2004. While appearing regularly on UK comedy television, her darkly humorous vision came to life on the cinema screen with her starring in Ben Wheatley's *Sightseers* (2012) which she wrote with her co-star Steve Oram. She also acted in Wheatley's earlier horror movie *Kill List* (2011), the truly unique Oram-written-and-directed *Aaaaaaaah!* (2015), and the bleak psychological horror drama *The Ghoul* (Gareth Tunley, 2016). In 2016 she wrote, directed and starred in the horror-comedy feature *Prevenge* while she was pregnant with her daughter.

LÖWENSOHN, ELINA

Romanian-born actor Elina Löwensohn was linked closely to the film work of American indie auteurs Hal Hartley and Michael Almereyda during the 1990s in particular, the latter of whom directed 1994's *Nadja*, a lo-fi urban New York updating of the *Dracula* story. Amongst her many film credits are also Philippe Grandrieux's 1998 serial killer film *Sombre*, and she also had a small role in Walter Salles 2005 remake of the 2002 J-horror film *Dark Water* as Jennifer Connelly's character's mother. In recent years, her career has been marked by ongoing collaborations with French filmmaker Bertrand Mandico such as the deliciously perverse *The Wild Boys* (2017) and the Cronenbergian burlesque short *Prehistoric Cabaret* (2013).

LOWRY, LYNN

American actor Lynn Lowry has almost a 100 film credits since she began acting in the early 1970s, most famously in horror. Born in Illinois in 1947, she studied theater and moved to New York to pursue acting. It was during this period she met Troma's Lloyd Kaufman which kickstarted her career, and she would appear in a range of impressive horror films including *The Crazies* (George A. Romero, 1973), *Shivers* (David Cronenberg, 1975) and *Cat People* (Paul Schrader, 1982). Disappointed with the roles she was getting in the 1980s, she turned her significant energies elsewhere, but returned to acting and horror movies in the mid 2000s and later horror credits would include a cameo in Breck Eisner's 2010 remake of George A. Romero's *The Crazies*, *Beyond the Dunwich Horror* (Richard Griffin, 2008), *Basement Jack* (Michael Shelton, 2009), *Hack Job* (James Balsamo, 2011), *The Haunting of Whaley House* (Jose Prendes, 2012), *The Legend of Six Fingers* (Sam Qualiana, 2013), *Torture Chamber* (Dante Tomaselli, 2013), *A Grim Becoming* (Adam R. Steigert, 2014), *Ditch Day Massacre* (Joe Hendrick, 2016), Debbie Rochon's feature directorial debut *Model Hunger* (2016) and David Gregory's segment "Sweets" in the 2011 horror anthology *The Theater Bizarre*.

LOY, MYRNA ⚲

Beginning her career in the silent era, Myrna Loy would work well into the 1980s and was a popular actor during Hollywood's Golden Age. Born Myrna Adele Williams in Montana in 1905, early in her career she was often cast in roles as seductive women of color, such as her fascinating pre-code film *Thirteen Women* (George Archainbaud, 1932) which in many tangible ways predates both the rape-revenge film and the body count structure of the slasher movie. As the film's villain Ursula, while her representation of monstrosity is tied closely to her status as a femme fatale woman of color, she is regardless an extraordinarily capable and powerful woman, making the film a difficult yet important horror classic. Decades later, Loy would return to horror in Robert Scheerer's 1977 eco-horror film *Ants*.

LUCAS, ELIZABETH

Filmmaker Elizabeth Lucas is a director of both stage and screen who has experimented broadly with genre. While working extensively as director of musical theater, she has directed stage productions including *Jekyll & Hyde*, and the vampire musical *Zapata, The Cure*. Aside from a number of shorts, from 2009 to 2014 Lucas directed and produced a tryptic of feature films about New York City, each of which was approached through a different genre: her 2009 film *Red Hook* was her horror entry, a slasher film about a scavenger hunt gone wrong.

LUCAS, JESSICA●

Canadian actor Jessica Lucas was born in Vancouver in 1985 and began her career in theater. Starting her screen career on television as an adolescent, she has appeared in a number of horror movies including *The Covenant* (Renny Harlin, 2006), *Cloverfield* (Matt Reeves, 2008), *Amusement* (John Simpson, 2008) and Fede Álvarez's 2013 remake of *Evil Dead*.

Jessica Lucas arrives to the *Super 8* DVD launch on November 22, 2011 in Beverly Hills, California. Credit: DFree / Shutterstock.com

LUCE, ROBIN

Robin Luce—often credited as Robin L. Neal—has an impressive filmography as a makeup artist, with particular talents in horror and other fantasy genres. She has worked for over 20 years in film and television and her credits include *Cujo* (Lewis Teague, 1983), *Friday the 13th: The Final Chapter* (Joseph Zito, 1984), *The Return of the Living Dead* (Dan O'Bannon, 1985), *A Nightmare on Elm Street 2: Freddy's Revenge* (Jack Sholder, 1985), *Flowers in the Attic* (Jeffrey Bloom, 1987), *Priest* (Scott Stewart, 2011) and episodes of *The Elvira Show* and *The X-Files*.

LUND, LUCILLE

Lucille Lund had only one major horror film role, but what a role it was. Born in Washington in 1913, Universal Studios signed her after she won a nation-wide competition to find new talent. While the bulk of the films that she made while working in Hollywood during the 1930s have been forgotten, it was her performance in Edgar G. Ulmer's 1934 perverse horror movie *The Black Cat* that would make Lund a horror icon.

LUPINO, IDA

A groundbreaking figure in the history of cinema, Ida Lupino was an actor-turned-filmmaker notable for being the only woman director (and writer and producer) working within the Hollywood system during the 1950s. Born in London in 1918, she studied at the Royal Academy of Dramatic Art before moving to the United States in the early 1930s and beginning her Hollywood career. Despite her award-winning success as a performer, she had always desired to write and was often unhappy with the poor quality of the characters her contract required her to play. It was while being penalized for refusing to be quiet about precisely these issues that she discovered the action behind the camera was of more interest, leading her and then-husband Collier Young to form their own production company. Making her directorial debut in the late 1940s, she would make a number of films, including the well ahead of its time rape movie *Outrage* in 1950. But it was her 1953 film noir *The Hitch*-Hiker that would remain one of her most famous works as director. While the first woman to direct a film noir, the legacy of Lupino's film would leave a strong imprint on future hitch-hiker horror movies such as *Wolf Creek* (Greg McLean, 2005) and *The Hitcher* (Robert Harmon, 1986). Later in her career, she would also direct horror-themed episodes of series such as *Thriller*, *The Twilight Zone* and the famous domesticated witch sitcom, *Bewitched*. As an actor, her horror credits include *The Devil's Rain* (Robert Fuest, 1975) and *The Food of the Gods* (Bert I. Gordon, 1976).

LUTYENS, ELISABETH

Elisabeth Lutyens was a British composer of such high esteem that she was awarded a Commander of the Most Excellent Order of the British Empire. Born in 1906, while she worked across chamber music, orchestral, opera and musical theater, she also had impressive form as a film score composer, particularly with Hammer Studios. While taking this work out of practical financial necessity, she valued her association with horror with film credits including *Never Take Sweets from a Stranger* (Cyril Frankel, 1960), *Paranoiac* (Freddie Francis, 1963), *The Earth Dies Screaming* (Terence Fisher, 1964), *The Psychopath* (Freddie Francis, 1966), *Dr. Terror's House of Horrors* (Freddie Francis, 1965), *The Skull* (Freddie Francis, 1965) and *Theater of Death* (Samuel Gallu, 1967).

LYNCH, JENNIFER

Jennifer Lynch was born in Philadelphia in 1968 and began her career collaborating on several projects with her father, cult director David Lynch. Working as a production assistant on his 1986 film *Blue Velvet*, Lynch would also write the tie-in book *The Secret Diary of Laura Palmer* in 1990 about the doomed protagonist of the popular television series *Twin Peaks*. Lynch received vicious critical attention for her debut as a feature film director and screenwriter with her dark gothic fairy tale, the 1993 film *Boxing Helena*, which she co-wrote when she was only 19 years old. Returning to filmmaking in 2008 after raising a child and addressing health issues, Lynch perservered as director and writer with later films including *Surveillance* (2008), *Hisss* (2010) and *Chained* (2012), the former winning Lynch the Best Director Award at the New York City Horror Film Festival.

LYON, WENDY

Wendy Lyon is a Canadian actor most instantly recognizable for one of her first film roles as Vicki Carpenter in Bruce Pittman's cult horror film *Hello Mary Lou: Prom Night II* (1987). Lyons other horror credits include *Kaw* (Sheldon Wilson, 2007), *Regression* (Alejandro Amenábar, 2015) and she also appeared in *Friday the 13th: The Series* on television.

LYONNE, NATASHA

Born in New York in 1979, Natasha Lyonne was a familiar face in 1990s teen comedies and, more recently, in the series *Orange is the New Black*. Taking to performing and modeling from a young age, she began her film career in earnest at 16 in the mid-1990s. Lyonne would work in many horror films throughout her career including *Modern Vampires* (Richard Elfman, 1998), *Madhouse* (William Butler, 2004), *Blade: Trinity* (David S. Goyer, 2004), *All About Evil* (Joshua Grannell, 2010) and *Yoga Hosers* (Kevin Smith, 2016). She also featureded in an episode of the horror television series *Night Visions*, played Megan Voorhees in Keenan Ivory Wayans 2001 horror parody *Scary Movie 2*, and recently acted in two horror films alongside fellow actor Chloë Sevigny, Tara Subkoff's *#Horror* in 2015, and Danny Perez's *Antibirth* in 2016.

MACDONALD, SHAUNA

Not to be confused with the Canadian actor of the same name who had a small role in *Saw 3D: The Final Chapter*, Scottish actor Shauna Macdonald was born in 1981 in Malaysia and studied at the Royal Scottish Academy of Music and Drama. Starring in both Neil Marshall's *The Descent* (2005) and *The Descent Part 2* (Jon Harris, 2009) as Sarah Carter, Macdonald's would other horror credits include *Mutant Chronicles* (Simon Hunter, 2008*)*, *The Hike* (Rupert Bryan, 2011), *Howl* (Paul Hyett, 2015) and *Nails* (Dennis Bartok, 2017).

MACCOLL, CATRIONA

Through her early collaborations in the 1980s with director Lucio Fulci and his *Gates of Hell* trilogy, British actor Catriona MacColl is a Eurohorror legend. Born in 1954, she worked in film and television, predominantly in Europe, making her first screen appearances in the late 1970s. With Fulci, she would act in *City of the Living Dead* (1980), *The Beyond* (1981) and *The House by the Cemetery* (1981), and her later horror credits would include *Afraid of the Dark* (Mark Peploe, 1991), *Saint Ange* (Pascal Laugier, 2004), *Chimères* (Olivier Beguin, 2013), *Horsehead* (Romain Basset, 2014) and *Hardware* director Richard Stanley's segment "The Mother of Toads" in the 2011 horror anthology, *The Theatre Bizarre*.

MACLAREN, MICHELLE

Canadian director and producer Michelle MacLaren has worked largely in television, with many of the popular series she has worked on involving horror and dark scifi themes, including *The X-Files* and *The Walking Dead*. Working since the late 1980s, she made her feature film debut in 2006, the rural gothic horror film, *Population 436*.

MADDALENA, MARIANNE

A long-time collaborator of Wes Craven, Marianne Maddalena has worked across many genres but has found success in horror. Born in Michigan in 1963, she was a co-partner of the production company Craven/Maddalena Films whose credits include *Shocker* (1989), *The People Under the Stairs* (1991), *New Nightmare* (1994), *Vampire in Brooklyn* (1995), *Scream* (1996), *Scream 2* (1997), *Scream 3* (2000), *Red Eye* (2005), *Cursed* (2005) and *Scream 4* (2011). She was also a producer of several remakes of Craven's films including *The Hills Have Eyes* (2006) and *The Last House on the Left* (2009), and the television series *Scream*. Her other horror production credits include *Dracula 2000* (Patrick Lussier, 2000) and *The Breed* (Nicholas Mastandrea, 2006).

MADSEN, VIRGINIA •

American actor and producer Virginia Madsen was a familiar face in 1980s genre cinema, but it was her Saturn Award-winning performance for the lead role in Bernard Rose's *Candyman* (1992) that consolidated what would become her lengthy relationship with horror. Born in 1961 in Chicago, her mother Elaine was an author and filmmaker, and her first starring role was in the scifi romcom *Electric Dreams* (Steve Barron, 1984). Although her early career is marked for horror fans by her performance in *Candyman*, she had already appeared in Ron Link's 1987 horror-comedy *Zombie High*, and later horror films including *The Prophecy* (Gregory Widen, 1995), *The Haunting* (Jan de Bont, 1999), *The Haunting in Connecticut* (Peter Cornwell, 2009), *Red Riding Hood* (Catherine Hardwicke, 2011), *Dead Rising: Watchtower* (Zach Lipovsky, 2015) and *Better Watch Out* (Chris Peckover, 2016). She also appeared in the television series *American Gothic* and *Witches of East End*.

Virginia Madsen arrives at the *Red Riding Hood* premiere on 7 March 2011 in Hollywood, California. Credit: DFree / Shutterstock.com

MAINES, NICOLE

Nicole Maines was already a force to be reckoned with long before her spectacular performance as the lead character in Brad Michael Elmore's 2019 queer feminist vampire teen film, Bit. Born in 1997, Maines was the plaintiff in the hugely significant Doe v. Regional School Unit 26 in 2013 where, as a transgender teenager, the court supported her right to use her high school's female bathroom. This led to Maines being the subject of a 2015 book on the case, Amy Ellis Nutt's *Becoming Nicole: The Transformation of an American Family*, and she also appeared in the 2016 documentary *The Trans List*. Following her passion for acting, after her debut on an episode of the television series *Royal Pains* in 2015 Maines would claim the title as the first transgender superhero in 2018 for her role as Nia Nal in The CW series *Supergirl*. But it is as Laurel in Elmore's *BIT* that Maines carved her place in horror history; while not the first transgender woman to appear in a horror film, her performance marks a significant breakthrough not only for the representation of trans women in the genre, but in film in general.

MALFATTI, MARINA

Italian actor Marina Malfatti was born in Florence in 1933 and studied at the *Cours d'Art Dramatique* in Paris. Beginning her career in the theater, she would turn to cinema in the late 1950s. Her horror and *giallo* credits include *The Night Evelyn Came Out of the Grave* (Emilio Miraglia, 1971), *The Red Queen Kills Seven Times* (Emilio Miraglia, 1972), *Seven Blood-Stained Orchids* (Umberto Lenzi, 1972), *All the Colors of the Dark* (Sergio Martino, 1972), *The Bloodstained Lawn* (Riccardo Ghione, 1973) and Marcello Andrei's *A Black Ribbon for Deborah* (1974).

MAGNOLFI, BARBARA—INTERVIEW (JANUARY 2016)

The following interview was published in 2016 at 4:3 Film and is republished with permission. The original article can be found online here https://fourthreefilm.com/2016/01/suspiria-an-interview-with-actress-barbara-magnolfi

In the iconic opening moments of Dario Argento's Italian horror classic *Suspiria*, young American ballet student Suzy Bannion (Jessica Harper) travels from the Munich airport through a technicolor- embossed rainstorm to arrive at her new dance school, the internationally renowned Freiburg Tanzakedemie. Upon her arrival, however, fellow student Pat Hingle (Eva Axén) leaves the building in a clear state of distress. Screaming back inside the building over the sound of the blasting rain, Suzy hears Pat say two words; "iris" and "secret". Structurally, these words offer surface-level a way into the mysteries at the heart of the film, but the joke is of course that the secret of the irises was never a secret at all: there is no surprise revelation that the ballet school is run by a coven of witches, because the word "witch!" is repeated mantra-like throughout Goblin's pounding prog-rock soundtrack that accompanies this famous opening sequence.

But if *Suspiria* mocks our expectations to locate its mysteries within its plot in its first 5 minutes, it stores its more profound enigmas far more deeply. Of these, for me at least, is the figure of Olga, a small but significant character played by Barbara Magnolfi. I spent the bulk of 2014 and 2015 writing a monograph about the film, and while Magnolfi's screen time is less than the film's bigger names—Harper, Alida Valli and Joan Bennett—something about her performance demands our attention, drawing us to her even above the frenzied audio-visual cacophony that so infamously marks the film.

While *Suspiria*'s other characters in large part serve to propel the simple narrative forward—through a series horror vignettes marked by Luciano Tovoli's Gothic Technicolor netherworld to the sound of Goblin's throbbing score—Olga stands apart. Sometimes comic relief, and at other times almost cattily hostile to the protagonist Suzy, Olga feels to be as much a part of the Tanzakedemie's architecture as the Art Nouveau style archways that construct its ribcage-like corridors.

In what is in large part a female ensemble film with only a few minor male characters on the periphery, Magnolfi is a crucial element of *Suspiria*'s parade of strong female characters. Unlike the college-based slasher films that would become popular in North America later in the 1970s and well into the 1980s, *Suspiria* featured women characters of different ages, sizes and personalities, and Olga's vampish little- girl-playing-grown-woman shtick adds in key ways to the film. Snippy and seductive, Olga single- handedly thwarts any suggestion of the female students as solely the victims of the school's teacher- witches: as Magnolfi herself told me recently, "Dario called me 'my wichette', or 'La mia Streghina' in Italian, and that is because Olga is a witch!". There was, says Magnolfi, an intended final scene that that would indicate Olga's survival, but it was never shot "because it was going to take away from the suspense towards the end."

The suggestion that Olga was a part of the coven—one whose task was to recruit other students—is a tantalising one that opens up an already fascinating film to even newer, fresher interpretations. I was introduced to Magnolfi through a mutual contact after the publication of my recent monograph on the film, and this interview has provided me with new insight into the remarkable character of Olga. It was therefore both a delight and a privilege to speak to Barbara not simply about *Suspiria*, but her impressive career more broadly.

http://barbaramagnolfi.com/

I've read that you took to acting very early, appearing in Antonio Pietrangeli's 1969 film *Come, quando, perché* (that also starred the wonderful Horst Buchholz, no less). What do you recall about that experience as a little girl? Was it 'love at first film' for you?

I did it at a very young age, 12 going on 13. I took to ballet dancing much earlier at 4 years old—perhaps to escape a difficult childhood—which I actually consider a blessing in disguise since it led me right to my bliss! On the set of *Come, quando,*

Barbara Magnolfi (right) with Jessica Harper in *Suspiria* (Dario Argento, 1977).
Credit: Photo 12 / Alamy Stock Photo.

perché I felt at home, it was like I had always done this. Pierangeli called me a 'natural', so it's fair to say it was love at first film!

I know that I am not alone in Olga being one of my favourite characters in *Suspiria*. For a film set in an all-girls school, the movie is never exploitative like a lot of other horror films in that setting, yet Olga is the one character that really brings a rare degree of explicitly feminised sexuality to the film. What I love about your performance is that it almost feels like a little girl 'playing' a woman—there's a lot of fun in your Olga. Can you tell me a bit about your thoughts on the character: how you approached her, how you see her now, and her importance to the strong legacy of *Suspiria*?

I approached Olga as a wild cat moving in to catch new prey for Madame Blanc. She was quite a complex character: arrogant but seductive, venomous but sexy, childish but wild, attractive but a bitch—all at the same time. Dario wanted us to play the characters as a child would because the movie was originally meant to be shot with 12 or 13-year-old girls.

I was rereading the original script not so long ago and I looked at Olga on the page again and then thought about how I brought her to life, and I think I really nailed it. It was exactly how Olga was described in the script. Of course, I created those moves and mannerisms, and spiced it up in different ways—even her dresses were my dresses! Olga was a lot of fun to play, and the role was right for me, for sure. I see her now as key to the film's success, because if you take her away it wouldn't be the same at all, would it? In fact, even when the movie came out the media were talking more about Olga then any other character in the movie!

As Olga, you held your own amongst some very big names: Hollywood star Joan Bennett, the legendary Italian actor Alida Valli (who had starred in Hitchcock's *The Paradine Case* and Carol Reed's *The Third Man*), and Jessica Harper (who had recently starred in Brian De Palma's *Phantom of the Paradise*). Were you familiar with your co-stars' earlier works? Was that intimidating at all? One of the things I love about *Suspiria* is that it is for the most part a woman-led ensemble film—there is such great energy between the women in this film!

I was familiar with my co-stars earlier work, absolutely! I had recently watched *Phantom of the Paradise* and loved Jessica's character and her voice. Alida was an amazing actress and person, and she became my mentor on set—we liked each other. Joan Bennett is the one I was most honoured to be in the presence of, a Hollywood legend. Indeed, it was my first day on set when I actually met her and Alida Valli. I could never forget the feeling of that first day, the exhilaration—I was on cloud nine, but at the same time I was terrified. But I held my own—I was prepared as an actress, and all my co-stars were supportive.

I'd love to hear how you got involved in the project, and about the audition process in particular as Dario Argento has quite a reputation for sometimes unusual approaches!

I stared ballet at 4, so by 10 I was the lead ballerina. I believe this had something to do with my getting the role in *Suspiria*, because Olga was supposed to dance in a scene that was never shot—she was meant to be a student in her last year at the academy, and was therefore meant to be a better dancer than the newer students.

I trained for a month or more before we started shooting. The approach the audition—if we could call it that—took was certainly unusual (as is Dario!), but I enjoyed it. I met Dario in his production office and he sat me in a chair. He was sitting on another chair in front of me, and gave me this big thick script that was labelled "Suspiria". He then asked me to take a look at the character Olga, and asked me how I would play her and what I thought about her, so I did. He never asked me to read dialogue, but instead told me to stand in the middle of the half empty room, and move a certain way. He circled around me till he saw what he wanted to see I guess because he became very exited and sent me off shortly after: I was soon given the role! Dario and I became instant friends and throughout the process of production and post production, editing and the creation of the music score of the film, we were often together.

You've often called *Suspiria* a dark fairy tale, which I think is a much better description of it than just as a straightforward horror movie. When you were working on the film, what was the feeling on set? I am guessing that the reputation of Argento's earlier work made it all very exciting, but did you all sense that this was somehow something very different?

I see it as a dark fairy tale, as some children's fairy tales are also really dark if you think about them: even *Little Red Riding Hood* could be made into a horror movie. The feeling on set was quite incredible: the set design—that Art Deco style—was all very grand, and the atmosphere was almost mystic. I guess you could sense that we were in the making of something special: at least I did!

Cinematographer Luciano Tovoli has said similar things, and he had all sorts of amazing stories about how he filmed you poor girls under very hot lights, reflected into mirrors and shone through large frames with velvets and tissue papers to get the intense colors. Did the environment in which you were filming influence performances much?

I remember the sets were quite elaborate and took a long time to build, but Dario wouldn't settle until he got exactly what he wanted. He knew what his vision was, and this went for every little detail, he is a real perfectionist. I believe that enhanced the performance. You had to give it your best.

You have very rightfully been celebrated as a key part of what has made this movie so special, especially in horror fan communities. What are your feelings about the film's legacy more broadly? Did you expect it to be this loved for this long?

It has been quite amazing indeed. This film has been a jewel passed from generation to generation, and it keeps going and will keep going because is like a great song— it is timeless, it doesn't age, and you don't get tired of watching it. It has become a cult classic: I was so overwhelmed when I attended my first convention in the USA! My most memorable tribute from a fan was an amazing poem that brought me right to tears. Someone else told me I was their inspiration to become an actor, and I am honoured to have inspired someone like this, to have made people laugh or to help someone in some way through my performance and work.

Aside from Argento, you worked with two other very big names in Italian genre film: Sergio Martino and Ruggero Deodato. Can you tell me a little about your experiences working with these legendary figures? Did they work in similar ways?

They both marked achievements in my career, but in different ways. Martino's *Suspicious Death of a Minor* (1975) was my first official role in a film and I worked with amazing actors like Mel Ferrer and Claudio Cassinelli. Sergio Martino was such a gentleman and made me feel at ease. I worked with Deodato after [Magnolfi's late husband and actor] Marc Porel's death. Deodato had worked with Marc before, and he reached out to me to give me work at a time when I really needed it to boost my morale. He had me read for a lead role, however my English at the time wasn't perfect so he gave me other one. This gave me the opportunity to work in the USA where we shot my scenes in Miami, and I never forgot how impressed I was and promised myself I would be back to the US one day. And now here I am, residing here!

I am a great admirer of both your work and that of Marc Porel, so am heartbroken that I have yet been able to see Umberto Silva's 1977 film *Difficile Morire*, which you both appear in. I have, of course, seen Enzo Milioni's *giallo Sister of Ursula* that I am assuming is a very different film from Silva's movie! I understand you were unimpressed with the final released version of *Sister of Ursula*?

Difficile Morire is my favourite of my films, along with *Suspiria* and another one I shot with Marc called *Blazing Flowers* (Gianni Martucci, 1978), which also stars Al Cleaver and George Hilton. *Difficile Morire* is a costume historical film, set in 1911. It is also the film where Marc and I met. *Sister of Ursula* a was originally a psychological thriller and quite a good story till in the middle of shooting the producer and director decided to add sex to it to make more money: they did this without my consent and I was the star in the movie! Of course, I was not pleased with the result!

Can you tell me more about your current work, both in front of and behind the camera? In particular, I'm fascinated by your interest in directing: films like *The Babadook* brought much needed attention to women filmmakers in horror, and I believe you are also interested in producing and writing?

I just finished a film with Luigi Cozzi in Rome: Dario Argento, Lamberto Bava, and Antonio Tentori were also involved with it. I did one episode of the My Haunted House TV show for Lifetime last July, and I am currently writing my autobiography and hoping to get that published this year. I continue to audition—I of course would love to book something in a TV show—and I have a couple of film scripts I am reading. More and more I am turning towards production, and even directing: I have a documentary I am looking at producing, in fact. Last but not least, I am looking forward to do more conventions here in US and meet more of my fans. This has been a lot of fun!

MANNING, LESLEY ⸳

If you told most people that the #11 entry on Indiewire's 2017 list of the best-ever British Horror films of all time was directed by a woman, many—even the most dedicated horror fans—might pause to think who this might be. But although writer and filmmaker Lesley Manning may not exactly be a household name, the fruits of her labor as director of the notorious 1991 BBC teleplay *Ghostwatch* has her forever associated with one of Britain's most notorious television events of all-time. Written and created by Stephen Volk, *Ghostwatch* was presented as a live broadcast of a reality-television-style ghost-hunting Halloween special, whose critique of our gullibility was proven to be only too necessary when audiences *en masse* believed it to be real, resulting in complaints, panic, and allegedly, even suicide. A graduate of Beaconsfield's National Film and TV School, Manning worked across both television, later focusing increasingly on feature films—including the psychological thriller *Leila* (2011)—and she is currently developing the feature film *Extrasensory*.

MANOWSKI, BEATRICE

Credited simply as Beatrice M., German actor Beatrice Manowski was born in Berlin in 1968 and for horror fans would be forever linked to the corpse-loving femme fatale in Jörg Buttgereit's notorious *Nekromantik* (1987), later making a small appearance in his sequel, *Nekromantik 2* (1991). She has worked across many genres, particularly on German television, and in 1998 she directed, starred in, and co-wrote the feature film comedy *Drop Out*.

MARGO

Simply credited as Margo, María Marguerita Guadalupe Teresa Estela Bolado Castilla O'Donnell was born in México in 1917 and worked as a dancer and actor from the mid 1930s to the mid '60s when she was a victim of the anti-Communist Hollywood blacklist. One of her most famous films is Jacques Tourneur's horror film *The Leopard Man*—produced by Val Lewton—where she played nightclub performer Clo-Clo.

MARION, FRANCES

Screenwriter Marion Frances was an early film industry power player; a multiple Oscar-winner who was for decades the highest paid screenwriter in Hollywood. Born in 1888 in San Francisco, she began her career as a graphic designer, photographer and newspaper journalist, and in 1914 was hired to write by pioneering filmmaker Lois Weber's production company. Amongst her many credits, Marion wrote the screenplay for the now-lost

George D. Baker 1919 silent film *The Cinema Murder*, and adapted Dorothy Scarborough's 1925 novel *The Wind* to Victor Sjöström's haunting 1928 film of the same name, starring Lillian Gish. Later in her career, she moved to writing novels and stage plays, publishing a memoir in 1972.

MARLINA, LENNY

Born in the mid-1950s, Indonesian actor Lenny Marlina began her career as a beauty queen in her teens and would go on to become an award-winning screen performer. She appeared in a number of Indonesian horror movies, including the title role of M. Shariefudin A.'s *Lisa* (1971)—widely believed to be the first Indonesian horror film—and her other credits in the genre include his latter horror movies *Face of a Killer* (1972) and *Old Building Tenant* (1975), as well as *Snake Queen* (Lilik Sudjio, 1972), *The Ghostly Face* (Yang Sai-King, 1972), *Night Virgin* (Bay Isbahi, 1974) and *Heat of the Night Blanket* (Wahab Abdi, 1982).

MARONEY, KELLI

American actor Kelli Maroney began her acting career in the late 1970s and would act in several cult films during the 1980s, particularly in horror with her frequent collaborator Jim Wynorski. Beginning her career in soap operas, her horror credits include *Slayground* (Terry Bedford, 1983), *Night of the Comet* (Thom Eberhardt, 1984), *Chopping Mall* (Jim Wynorski, 1986) *The Zero Boys* (Nico Mastorakis, 1986), *Not of This Earth* (Jim Wynorski, 1988), *Transylvania Twist* (Jim Wynorski, 1989), *Hard to Die* (Jim Wynorski, 1990), *Servants of Twilight* (Jeffrey Obrow, 1991), *Scream Queen Hot Tub Party* (Fred Olen Ray and Jim Wynorski, 1991) and *Hell's Kitty* (Nicholas Tana, 2018).

MARSH, MARIAN

Violet Ethelred Krauth was credited on-screen as Marian Marsh, an actor born in Trinidad and Tobago in 1913. Contracted to Warner Bros. in the early 1930s, while working across many genres her horror films were important career landmarks, including *Svengali* (Archie Mayo, 1931), *The Mad Genius* (Michael Curtiz, 1931) and *The Black Room* (Roy William Neill, 1935).

MARSHALL, BARBARA

Screenwriter Barbara Marshall hails from Texas and took to reading with a passion early in life, deciding on a career in film at age 7. Writing stories—and later screenplays—through both her school and university years, she was influenced by '80s genre cinema and writers including Stephen King and Toni Morrison. Named one of *Variety*'s "ten screenwriters to watch" in 2013, and she has twice made the highly-regarded Black List of most impressive unproduced scripts. Marshall wrote the screenplays for Henry Joost and Ariel Schulman's 2016 film *Viral*, and John R. Leonetti's *Wish Upon* in 2017.

MARTIN, ANDREA

Andrea Martin is a Canadian-American actor and writer who was born in Portland in 1947. Working across stage and screen since the early 1970s, she studied at Emerson College in Boston and has won several Tony Awards for her work in the theater. In 1973 she appeared in Ivan Reitman's *Cannibal Girls*, followed by Bob Clark's *Black Christmas* (1974), *Believe* (Robert Tinnell, 1999), returning to the genre for Glen Morgan's 2006 remake of *Black Christmas*.

MARTIN, ANNE-MARIE

Anne-Marie Martin is a Canadian actor and writer who was born in Toronto in 1957. Working across film and television, she acted in horror films including *Dr. Strange* (Philip DeGuere, 1978), *Prom Night* (Paul Lynch, 1980), *Savage Harvest* (Robert L. Collins, 1981), *Halloween II* (Rick Rosenthal, 1981) and *The Boogens* (James L. Conway, 1981). She also received a co-writing credit with her husband Michael Crichton the 1996 when-nature-attacks tornado blockbuster *Twister*.

MARTINELLI, ELSA

Despite working across many genres, Italian actor Elsa Martinelli starred in one of the most beloved Eurohorror films of the 1960s, playing Georgia Monteverdi in Roger Vadim's lesbian vampire classic *Blood and Roses* (1960), based on Sheridan Le Fanu's 1872 novella *Carmilla*. Martinelli was born in Tuscany in 1935 and would work in both Europe and the United States with filmmakers including Howard Hawks, Orson Welles and Vittorio De Sica. In 1969, she co-starred with Jean Sorel and Marisa Mell in Lucio Fulci's *giallo Perversion Story*.

MARISSE, ANNE

Anne Marisse was working as an actor on Broadway when she married filmmaker Herb Freed, and she co-wrote screenplays for several of his horror projects including *Haunts* (1976) and *Graduation Day* (1981). She also appeared on screen in Freed's 1980 horror film, *Beyond Evil*.

MASCHERONI, OLIVIA

Olivia Mascheroni is a film executive who has worked with companies including Blumhouse Productions. With a passion for horror and strong women characters, Mascheroni is a graduate of Northwestern University in Illinois, and she previously worked for Maven Pictures and Creative Artists Agency before moving to Blumhouse where she was Chief of Staff. While her influence is broad, her name is credited on many horror films including *Ouija: Origin of Evil* (Mike Flanagan, 2016), *Incarnate* (Brad Peyton, 2016), *The Darkness* (Greg McLean, 2016) and *The Purge: Election Year* (James DeMonaco, 2016).

MASON, MARSHA—INTERVIEW (JUNE 2018)

It feels almost criminal to focus only on horror when Marsha Mason is such an accomplished performer with so many accolades, having worked across a great many genres in film, television and on stage. Receiving Best Actress Oscar nominations for her brilliant performances in *Chapter Two* (Robert Moore, 1979), *Only When I Laugh* (Glenn Jordan, 1981), *Cinderella Liberty* (Mark Rydell, 1973), *The Goodbye Girl* (Herbert Ross, 1977), and winning Golden Globes for Best Actress for the two latter, Mason's formal honours support what anyone has seen her films knows intuitively: she is one of the Hollywood greats.

Born in Missouri, her impressive filmography encompasses films as diverse as *Heartbreak Ridge* (Clint Eastwood, 1986) and *Drop Dead Fred* (Ate De Jong, 1991), and her television credits include *Frasier*, *The Middle*, *Madam Secretary*, *The Good Wife* and *Grace and Frankie*.

Marsha Mason in *Audrey Rose* (Robert Wise, 1977).
Credit: United Artists/Photofest © United Artists.

But it is her important donation to horror that grants her inclusion in this book, and I was fortunate enough to talk to her about her starring role in the great Robert Wise's *Audrey Rose* (1977).

http://restingintheriver.com/

Your role as Janice in *Audrey Rose* is really one of the strongest horror performances of that decade, you bring such depth and urgency to the part. I'm fascinated to hear what lead you to accept this role when you were in such an extraordinary, impressive run in your career—why a horror film, and why then?

I didn't really think of the film as a horror film … perhaps because horror films weren't really as popular then as they are today? I thought of it as a dramatic story about reincarnation … I was studying Hinduism at the time and that was one of the motivating reasons for doing it as well as the fantastic opportunity to work with the director. He was a great going all the way back to Orson Welles where he was his editor…

Robert Wise was wonderful to work with so these two primary reasons were my motivation. The art of filmmaking interested me as well and I wanted to learn from him … I have always been curious…in life and in my work so I was curious to learn his technique!

While horror is notorious for inventing its own—often admittedly quite flimsy!—mythologies, Audrey Rose is based on very real, concrete religious beliefs. What was your own understanding of Hinduism and the concept of reincarnation before the film?

My study of Hinduism was something I had been pursuing since the 60s. In 1964, I began a serious journey to understand religion, life and death, and everything in between. I began to study meditation, Christian Science, Buddhism, Vedanta, Kashmir Shavism, etc.

I started reading a great deal and looking for teachers to learn from and finally, after having been curious about all of the above I met Baba Muktananda, a great teacher of Siddha Yoga and through him learned a great deal about Hinduism and some of the great texts of various forms of Hinduism and my learning continues today.

Despite the fantastic premise of the film, there's a very real-world horror in the first part of the movie especially about a mother's fears for her child. It's such a strong protector role that you play, how did you prepare for the part?

Although I never had children of my own I have two beautiful step daughters … it was easy to relate to the highly dramatic conflict my character went through. When you love and love deeply and totally committed to those you love, the situation my character went through was present for me.

For such a young person, Susan Swift really hit her performance out of the ballpark as your character's daughter, Ivy. How did you find working with her?

Susan was a lovely and natural child and it was easy to relate to her. She was so gifted and seemed to come to it all with understanding and commitment! And Bob Wise was so wonderful with her. He was a soft-spoken man but authoritative in a warm, kind and patient way.

Across your impressive career, you might also be particularly well placed to answer that enduring question: *should* you work with children and animals?!

I seem to have almost always had children in my films … I can think of only two right now that I didn't! *Chapter Two* and *Heartbreak Ridge*…and even in television, I did films with young teenagers—Molly Ringwald, young [Kiefer] Sutherland… and Matthew Broderick! And now I have grandchildren in *The Middle*…ah! but not *Grace and Frankie* although a son was mentioned, and we did do a scene with him the first season I worked on the show. As to animals, I love them and would work with them always no matter what! I did on *Frasier*. He was adorable.

Wikipedia tells me that you were involved in *Dark Shadows* in the late 1960s— I'd love to hear more about this if true!

Yes! I did *Dark Shadows*…I played a prostitute…they were called something else in the script…'Docksie' I think…I was bitten and became a vampire of sorts I think…can hardly remember it. Black-and-white footage!

More recently, I also believe the television series *Nightmares & Dreamscapes* brought you to my neck of the woods in Australia! How was that experience? Were you familiar with Stephen King's work previously?

I came to it through a friend of mine, Bill Haber, who was the producer. I wanted to see Australia and decided "why not!" Spent Thanksgiving there and loved Melbourne. The architecture and the people. I knew of Stephen King's books and some of the material that was dramatized but wasn't really involved in the scary part!

You have such wide-ranging experience as an actor and have seen what I can only imagine are many changes in an industry that receives a high level of public scrutiny. In recent years—the last year especially—there has been an escalation in discussions about gender and Hollywood in particular. I'd love to hear your thoughts on this and how it pertains to your own experience as a hugely successful woman in a notoriously difficult, competitive industry.
I had a rough time like a lot of women … and even when I was married my husband [Neil Simon] didn't think it best to pay me equally with [Richard] Dreyfuss or give me first billing even though I had an Oscar nomination and a Golden

Globe for *Cinderella Liberty*.

It was par for the course then that women were considered difficult to work with if you stood up for yourself or had an opinion. My agent fought for me, but Ray Stark and Neil were of a different opinion and consequently I was never paid what I was worth when working back then.

I did make decent money when I did a series but was treated somewhat meanly for having opinions. I was brought before an entire production staff and told to sit in a chair facing some 20 people of James Brooks' company who all sat in a row facing me and basically, I was called on the carpet for having an opinion and also for standing up for my fellow actors. It was one of the most fearsome moments of my career.

Perhaps if I hadn't fallen in love with my husband, I would have faced even worse experiences after *Cinderella Liberty* … But as for Paul Mazursky and Mark Rydell, as directors and producers they were wonderful to me. They took good care of me as a young actor with no real film experience and treated me well.

Women still aren't paid what they are worth and that is changing now due to the women in film today and I say BRAVA to all of them for standing up, being counted, and fighting back. Brave, brave women all.

MASSEY, ANNA

As Helen Stephens in Michael Powell's *Peeping Tom* (1960), Sussex-born actor Anna Massey starred in one of the most important and controversial British horror films ever made. Becoming a Commander of the Order of the British Empire in 2004 for her remarkable donation to British culture, *Peeping Tom* was one of her earliest screen performances and her career would continue until her death in 2011. She would also appear in Otto Preminger's bleak child abduction thriller *Bunny Lake Is Missing* (1965), Alfred Hitchcock's vicious serial rapist film *Frenzy* (1972), and the horror movies *The Vault of Horror* (Roy Ward Baker, 1973) and *Haunted* (Lewis Gilbert, 1995).

MATONDKAR, URMILA

Indian actor Urmila Matondkar was a child actor who began her screen career in the early 1980s would become an award-winning performer and highly recognized celebrity. Across her impressive career, she starred in three horror movies directed by Ram Gopal Varma: *Kaun* (1999), *Bhoot* (2003) and *Agyaat* (2009), *Bhoot* in particular bringing her widespread acclaim and garnering her a number of major acting awards for her performance as a victim of possession. In 2005, she starred in the main role in Shripal Morakhia's *Naina*—an adaptation of the Pang brother's 2002 film *The Eye*—which would premiere at the Cannes Film Festival.

MATTISON, JENNA

American filmmaker and actor Jenna Mattison began her career on television in popular series in the 1990s such as *Melrose Place* and *Party of Five* before turning her talents towards producing, writing and directing while continuing to work in front of the camera. In 2017, Mattison made her feature film debut when she wrote, directed and produced the horror film *The Sound*, starring Rose McGowan and Christopher Lloyd.

MATTISON, SALLY

Sally Mattison had been working at Concorde-New Horizons for some before Roger Corman gave her an opportunity to make her feature film directorial debut with *Slumber Party Massacre III*. Originally titled *Stab in the Dark*, the title was changed to profit on the women-directed slasher franchise. Mattison also sang on several songs on the film's soundtrack including "Pale Imitation" and "Hold Your Fire". While her only directorial effort, she worked on a number of other horror films in a variety of capacities including producer and casting such as *Masque of the Red Death* (Larry Brand, 1989) and *The Haunting of Morella* (Jim Wynorski, 1990).

MAXA, PAULA

With her surname synonymous with Paris's notorious Grand Guignol theater—without which horror film history would have been very different—French stage and screen actor Paula Maxa is a horror icon. Her story has recently been fictionalized in the feature film *The Most Assassinated Woman in the World* (Franck Ribière, 2018) whose title stems from her claim that she was murdered on stage more than 10,000 times including modes of death such as being shot, disemboweled, hung, drawn and quartered, poisoned and - according to one account—the recipient of a leper's kiss. While the most famous performer at the Grand Guignol and thus a hugely significant (although broadly overlooked) figure in the history of horror, Maxa also appeared on screen in Louis Feuillade's silent crime serial *Les Vampires*.

MCAVOY, MAY

Starring as Olga Redmayne in Roy Del Ruth's proto-slasher film *The Terror* (1928), May McAvoy would not only be an important although often overlooked figure in horror film history, but by appearing in it found herself in the lead role of Warner Bros. studios second sound movie after the widespread introduction of the technology the previous year. McAvoy was born in New York in 1899 and would have close to 100 film credits to her name, including historically significant films such as *Ben-Hur* (Fred Niblo, 1925) and *The Jazz Singer* (Alan Crosland, 1927).

MCCORD, ANNALYNNE

Although most immediately recognizable for her work on mainstream television fare like *Nip/Tuck* and the *90210* reboot, AnnaLynne McCord has shown a flair for horror across a number of unforgettable performances. Born in Atlanta in 1987, she became a model after leaving school and later turned to acting. Her horror credits include *Day of the Dead* (Steve Miner, 2008), *The Haunting of Molly Hartley* (Mickey Liddell, 2008), and two collaborations with filmmaker Richard Bates Jr. in the genre: 2012's *Excision* and *Trash Fire* in 2016.

MCCORMACK, PATTY

Starring as the eponymous evil child in Mervyn LeRoy's 1956 horror film *The Bad Seed* (adapted from William March's 1954 novel of the same name), Patricia McCormack was born in Brooklyn in 1945. She first played the part of the murderous 8-year-old on stage, before earning an Oscar nomination for her performance in the film for Best Supporting Actress (making her the fifth youngest Oscar nominee of all-time). With a star on the Hollywood Walk of Fame, McCormack has worked extensively in film and television for almost 70 years, including horror films such as *Bug* (Jeannot Szwarc, 1975), *Invitation to Hell* (Wes Craven, 1984), *Saturday the 14th Strikes Back* (Howard R. Cohen, 1988), *Mommy* (Max Allan Collins, 1995), *Mommy 2: Mommy's Day* (Max Allan Collins, 1997), *Silent Predators* (Noel Nosseck, 1999), *Inhabited* (Kelly Sandefur, 2003) and *Shallow Ground* (Sheldon Wilson, 2004), as well as episodes of television shows such as *Stan Against Evil*, *Supernatural* and *Freddy's Nightmares*.

MCGEE, VONETTA

In the dual roles of Luva and Tina in William Crain's legendary 1972 film *Blacula*, while Vonetta McGee appeared in many Blaxploitation movies, for horror fans at least this remains the film for which she is best known and most loved. McGee was born in San Francisco in 1945 and turned to acting while studying at San Francisco State University in the 1960s. Across her later work, she would also apper in Dan Curtis's TV horror movie *The Norliss Tapes* in 1973, and had a small role in Alex Cox's 1984 cult classic *Repo Man*.

Vonetta McGee on the set of *Blacula* (William Crain, 1972). Credit: © American International Pictures AIP/ Photofest

MCGOWAN, ROSE·

Today, Rose McGowan is renowned as much as a vocal activist championing women's rights as she is for her film career as an actor, writer and filmmaker. Born in Italy in 1973, she began acting in the early 1990s and came to international attention for her performance in Gregg Araki's *The Doom Generation* in 1995. Her horror film credits include *Scream* (Wes Craven, 1996), *Phantoms* (Joe Chappelle, 1998), *Grindhouse* (Robert Rodriguez and Quentin Tarantino, 2007), *Dead Awake* (Omar Naim, 2010), *Rosewood Lane* (Victor Salva, 2011), *The Tell-Tale Heart* (John La Tier, 2014) and *The Sound* (Jenna Mattison, 2015). From 2001 to 2006, she also played Paige Matthews in the long-running witch series *Charmed*. In 2014, McGowan wrote and directed the dark art-horror-imbued short film *Dawn*.

MCINTOSH, HEATHER

Heather McIntosh began her career as a cellist and bass player, but it is as a composer for film that she has earned her strongest reputation, shortlisted for Oscars for Best Original Score for *Compliance* (2012) and *Z for Zachariah* (2015), both directed by Craig Zobel. Amongst her many other credits are the horror movies *The Rambler* (Calvin Reeder, 2013), *Honeymoon* (Leigh Janiack, 2014) and *Manson Family Vacation* (J. Davis, 2015). In 2014, she was a Sundance Institute Time Warner Foundation Fellow.

MCINTOSH, POLLYANNA

Born in Edinburgh in 1979, Scottish actor and filmmaker Pollyanna McIntosh is familiar to horror fans for her role in Lucky McKee's *The Woman* (2011), which garnered her a nomination for Best Actress at the Fangoria Chainsaw Awards. Regularly working on the television series *The Walking Dead*, her other horror film credits include *White Settlers* (Simeon Halligan, 2014), *Let Us Prey* (Brian O'Malley, 2014), the made-for-television movie *Bats: Human Harvest* (Jamie Dixon, 2007) and Lucky McKee's segment "Ding Dong" in the 2015 horror anthology *Tales of Halloween*. As a director, McIntosh's feature debut is the 2019 sequel to *The Woman* called *Darlin'*, in which she also stars.

MCLEAVY, ROBIN

Australian actor Robin McLeavy was born in Sydney in 1981, graduating from the prestigious National Institute of Dramatic Arts in 2004. Her breakthrough performance was as Lola Stone in Sean Byrne's demented Australian take on the prom night horror movie, *The Loved Ones* in 2009 which McLeavy receive a nomination for the Best Leading Actress award at the 2012 Fangoria Chainsaw Awards. In 2012, she starred as the title character's mother in Timur Bekmambetov's *Abraham Lincoln: Vampire Hunter*, co-produced by Tim Burton. In 2015 she returned to Australia and co-starred with Adrian Brody in Michael Petroni's horror movie *Backtrack*.

MCNAB, MERCEDES

Beginning her career as a child actor, Mercedes McNab was born in Vancouver in 1980 and after making an appearance as a girl scout in Barry Sonnerfield's *The Addams Family* in 1991, she would return again as popular, snooty Amanda Buckman in Sonnenfeld's *Addams Family Values* in 1993. Although retiring in 2011, McNab earlier worked extensively in horror movies such as *Hatchet* (Adam Green, 2006) and a cameo in *Hatchet II* (Adam Green, 2010), *XII* (Michael A. Nickels, 2008), *Vipers* (Brian Katkin, 2008), *Thirst* (Jeffrey Scott Lando, 2010) and *Medium Raw: Night of the Wolf* (Andrew Cymek, 2010).

MCRAE, DONNA—INTERVIEW (JUNE 2018)

In recent years, Australian filmmaker Donna McRae has been determinedly creating some of the most thoughtful and powerful genre films in the country. While opting for clear horror frameworks, McRae uses the genre as a toolbox with which to build her own stories about women haunted—literally and metaphorically—by traumas related to troubled men in the past.

Studying at the Victorian College of the Arts and now a Lecturer in Film & Television at Deakin University in Melbourne, her 2012 feature debut *Johnny Ghost* was a microbudget feature set in Melbourne's vibrant post-punk scene that traces a woman coming to terms with her past through a tattoo removal.

Receiving acclaim internationally and garnering a number of impressive awards, she has just released her follow-up feature, *Lost Gully Road*. Tracing a young woman hiding from a social media-related drama in Melbourne's beautiful Dandenong Ranges, the film uses horror as a metaphoric template with which to think through the ubiquity of violence against women in contemporary Australia.

McRae's first documentary *Cobby: The Dark Side of Cute* also recently played the San Francisco Documentary Film Festival, and she is continuing to develop with producer Tait Brady her feature *Kate Kelly*—a feature-length Western about Ned Kelly's sister—which was selected for Montreal's Frontieres Co-Production Market in 2016.

www.mcraeandvale.com

When was the first moment you remember being fascinated in horror?

As a child watching *Casper the Friendly Ghost*! I loved the imagery of the haunted house, the trio of spooky ghosts (who can forget them lining up with chains laughing as they taught Casper to 'spook'?), and the fact that they could all fly! A few years later *Deadly Earnest* (on TV on Friday nights in Adelaide) introduced me to Val Lewton and the wonderful black-and-white horror films of the 1940s and '50s.

I know you are also a documentary filmmaker also, but your two feature films are fascinating to me because although being quite different in style, tone, and setting, they both use a horror framework to talk about very real issues of women and trauma. What do you think the particular strength of horror is to do this in terms of these two elements in particular?

The particular strength of horror is that you can examine a social issue but wrap it up in a palatable way to audiences using genre. If I presented Lucy's story in social realism it would be very hard to watch. However, using genre tropes I can look at her plight but heighten the experience for the audience. Women have always been a mainstay of horror but have so often been victims of violence through a male gaze.

With *Lost Gully Road* I have told the story very much through a female viewpoint. The violence is there, but it is experiencing it through Lucy, instead of looking *at* her. Her character is clearly flawed, but in the end we are on her side, and we can see what hideous violence can do to a vulnerable woman by herself with no one to help her.

***Johnny Ghost* is not just a great story about a woman struggling with her past, it also feels like a little window back in time to post-punk Melbourne. What's your experience with that scene? There's great live footage in there of some very familiar bands—how did that come about to being incorporated?**

When I moved over to Melbourne in the post punk years I was plunged into the scene of the Seaview Ballroom (my first bar job). I was both fascinated and overwhelmed by this artistic, indulgent and dangerous scene which didn't last very long but produced some very interesting artists, musicians and filmmakers. Those involved moved past that scene but in the last few years it seems to have become iconified by a new generation.

I felt that I needed to include the music of the time in the film for authenticity. Dave Graney and Clare Moore had first hand knowledge and were the obvious choice to score. Mick Harvey and Nick Cave very generously allowed the Birthday Party clip. Even though the story is fictitious it resonates truthfully with those who lived through it—for better or for worse. The film had more interest overseas than here but is available on Ozflix for anyone who would like to see it. I'm very proud of it.

Filmmaker Donna McRae. Used with permission.

Lost Gully Road **reimagines the 'rapist ghost' premise of** *The Entity* **in a specifically Australian context to talk about the widespread, 'faceless' ubiquity of the presence of sexual violence in the lives of Australian women. I'm interested to hear from you if people have been able to draw that subtext easily, or if it's being read as a more straight-forward ghost story. Have any responses to the film surprised you?**

Revelation Film Festival in Perth will be its second screening after Monsterfest, and then we will have the Melbourne Nova screening on July 24th, so it's just beginning to play now. Audiences at Monsterfest were drawn to the comparisons with some of the recent horrific stories of domestic and random violence toward women and quite surprised by the nastiness at the end of the film. They said it was very beautiful too, so it's hard to judge.

It's a slow burn film—so you need to stay with it until the pay-off at the end. It's also quite dark (literally dark—she is in a dark, damp house in the Dandenong Ranges) which adds to the dread. I was sitting next to someone at the Monsterfest screening and they were on the edge of their seat. People were also screaming in parts, which is always good—they then laugh at their own reaction, which is fun.

However, the film is a comment on violence towards women and the enablers that help it to happen. The small twist was very surprising to all, even at script stage, and I wanted to bring home the idea how vulnerable women in these horrific situations can be.

Poster for *Lost Gully Road* (Donna McRae, 2017). Used with permission.

Both *Johnny Ghost* and *Lost Gully Road* rely heavily on the central performances of Anni Finsterer and Adele Perovic respectively, and I'm wondering how you arrived at them for each role. Do you think your own experience as an actor assisted or impeded you working so closely to these women playing very intense, central roles?

I had always admired Anni Finsterer's work—she would turn up in these intense roles on the TV or in film, so when looking for *Johnny Ghost* she was an immediate choice. The role was very demanding—she needed to be able to play music, swim, and of course, carry the film. When we met her, she was perfect—she was a musician (she has her own band), she was a champion swimmer, and had her own experience with the post punk scene!

Laszlo Baranyai (the DOP) suggested Adele Perovic as he had worked with her before. We met, and she also was closely aligned with the character. The role of Lucy in *Lost Gully Road* was even more demanding as she had to build intensity throughout the film and then participate in a series of stunts that only involved her! The film slowly builds to the horrendous crescendo, and Adele's performance is nuanced and deliberate.

I think my time as an actor taught me to trust actors and allow them the space in which to make their own decisions. This process may not result in the performance that you first thought when you wrote the script, but it will be an authentic performance that lives and breathes and feels real. I like to give the character over to the actor and then gently guide them through the machinations of making the film.

I rely heavily on my DOP to make sure they look good within the frame! I am pedantic on lines though—in my films there aren't many so they need to have them down! Obviously you need to cast well to be able to pull off this process. It is very challenging and not all actors like to work this way, but both Annie and Adele excelled—the performances are electric.

You have a number of key collaborators that you return to time and time again: Michael Vale, musicians Dave Graney and Clare Moore, László Baranyai and I am sure there are others. Can you tell me a bit about this team and the benefits of working with people across a number of projects?

It is interesting that I have a team—when I was at film school I thought that it never would happen! I have worked with visual artist Michael Vale on many projects and it seems appropriate that he should be responsible for the 'look' of my films. He is obsessed with tonal and color palettes which adds another visual layer to the work. He is extremely knowledgeable about film and strives to optimise the images contained in my stories.

I met Laszlo Baranyai on the VCA film "LOOP" when I was an actor, and that film was a mini film school of its own. He shot my VCA graduation film and I have been lucky enough to be able to work with him ever since. My greatest fear stepping onto my set is Laszlo saying to me "It will never work"—and there is always at least one occasion when he says this. But that is a good sign of a working partnership. His elegance and fluency with camera and lighting never fails to enhance the emotional impact of my ideas.

I have known Dave Graney and Clare Moore for a number of years, going back to Adelaide days, and they are so versatile. They are legends in their own right and they are incredibly easy to work with. Their scores reveal yet another side of their musical flexibility.

We all have the same taste in music and that binds us together—and they all seem to understand my sensibilities, which is a plus. We have a shorthand now that is effective—along with the chocolate cake that I make!

You've been very actively involved in the Australian women in horror community and have spent time overseas talking to like-minded others. Can you tell me about the benefits of this network for both you as a creator and for the genre in general, and if there's anything you've learned from your peers that you might not have discovered otherwise?

It is crucial to have a network of like-minded filmmakers. This amazing network that we have in place started with Briony Kidd and the Stranger with My Face Film festival. Our tribe—Briony, Rebecca Thomson, Isabel Peppard, Megan Riakos, and Katrina Graham all support each other in a film world which is hard to navigate and run by men.

We met Heidi Honeycutt at the start and wow, is she a supporter of Women in Horror in the US and beyond. With Stacy Pippi she runs Etheria Film Night in Los Angeles which is solely for female horror filmmakers and they take those shorts all around the country. Kier-La Janisse is another Canadian powerhouse who we were lucky enough to have living out here for a couple of years. We try to share information and stand up for visibility—and we need all the help we can get to break through; from film festivals to distribution.

Megan Riakos was instrumental in championing AACTA eligibility for low budget feature films which was such a breakthrough. It's important to belong to a network as it's a really hard industry especially working in horror. There is power in numbers and together we can be a force.

I understand you also teach directing and filmmaking at Deakin University in Melbourne and work in a very hands-on way in mentoring and developing new talent. If you could tell emerging filmmakers what obvious traps to avoid, what would you say? And does working with emerging filmmakers have any benefits for the development of your own practice?

I have been at Deakin for 4½ years now working with Honours Film & Television students. It's very rewarding as they can be ingenious with their decisions—they make short films with no money and some of the ideas they come up with are very inventive. What I try to say to emerging filmmakers is to keep going—no matter what. It won't happen in 5 minutes, you have to keep making films to get better.

Donna McRae with cast on the set of *Johnny Ghost* (2012). Used with permission.

The late Joan Harris, the National Theater Drama school head used to say—"Love the art in yourself, not yourself in the art," and it is so true. Fall in love with the process and it will support you through years of hard work—if you want to be famous, don't become a filmmaker, go on a reality show!

As I mentioned above, you are certainly not limited to just horror film directing, and recently made a documentary. Can you tell us about *Cobby: The Other Side of Cute*, and your work as an artist?

Cobby was a TV show I used to watch in Adelaide when I was a child—the theme song haunted me so I started trawling the internet trying to find information about the show. Finally, I found out that Cobby the chimpanzee was still alive and living in the San Francisco Zoo and the story just took off from there.

I never set out to be a documentary filmmaker, but this story was just too good to pass on. I learnt a lot about animal rights through this project and it is something that I have become passionate about. I am hoping to build awareness with this film.

My work as a visual artist has mainly been in video installation. I find this medium interesting as it is purely visual which helps me with my film practice. I am very invested in 19th century Australian women and have made two multi-channel video works about them.

And I have to ask: when I saw Jane Clifton from *Prisoner* in *Lost Gully Road*'s credits, I almost couldn't believe it! How did you land on her for that role—she's so perfect!

Clare Moore worked her magic on this one! These characters are always written for an actor we would like to work with and Michael had suggested her as Clare was working with Jane on musical projects. She's fantastic, isn't she? Perfect for this role and so much fun on the day.

MCKAY, WANDA

Born Dorothy Quackenbush in Portland in 1915, as a model and actor she would perform professionally as Wanda McKay. Turning to performance after winning a beauty pageant in 1938, although retiring from the screen in the late 1950s, she would appear in several horror films including *Bowery at Midnight* (Wallace Fox, 1942), *Voodoo Man* (William Beaudine, 1944)—both with Béla Lugosi—and Sam Newfield's *The Monster Maker* in 1944.

MEJIAS, ISABELLE

As the title character of Paul Nicholas's 1983 horror film *Julie Darling*, Isabelle Mejias offered the genre one of its most chilling and memorable instances of the killer teenage girl. Although she began her career earlier in the 1980 film *Girls*—directed by *Emmanuelle* and *Story of O* director Just Jaeckin—*Julie Darling* was Mejias's breakthrough role. She would also work in Christian Duguay's *Scanners II: The New Order* in 1991 and episodes of television series including *Alfred Hitchcock Presents*, *Psychic Detectives*, and *Friday the 13th: The Series*.

MENDOZA, NATALIE

Natalie Mendoza was born in Hong Kong in 1978 and grew up in Sydney. Beginning her performance career in Australia, she moved to Britain to study at the Bristol Old Vic Theater School where she received classical training, and it was during this period she was cast as Juno in Neil Marshall's horror film *The Descent* (2005), returning to the part in 2009 for Jon Harris's sequel, *The Descent 2*. That same year she also acted in Terence Daw's horror movie *Surviving Evil*.

MENKE, SALLY

Renowned primarily as a key collaborator of Quentin Tarantino, editor Sally Menke worked on all of his films until her sudden death in 2010, receiving Oscar nominations for her work on both *Pulp Fiction* (1994) and *Inglorious Basterds* (2009). In addition to editing Tarantino's horror film *Death Proof* in 2007 as part of the *Grindhouse* project, Menke also edited Ole Bornedal's 1997 horror movie *Nightwatch* and Michael Lander's dark psychological thriller *Peacock* (2010). After her death, the Sundance Institute established an editing fellowship in her name as a memorial.

MERCER, SHAWNEE

Portland-born filmmaker Shawnee Mercer—often credited as Shawnee McCormack—is a prolific director and writer who has also worked as a producer and actor. Amongst her credits, she wrote and directed the feature-length horror films *Night of a Thousand Screams* (2001), *Revenge of the Unhappy Campers* (2002), *Night of a Thousand Screams 2* (2003), and the neo-giallo *The Killer Knocks Twice* (2017).

MÉRIL, MACHA

Despite working with filmmakers of the calibre of Rainer Werner Fassbinder, Jean-Luc Godard and Luis Buñuel, Macha Méril's face is for cult film audiences linked most readily to her appearance in Italian horror. Stemming from Russian and Ukrainian nobility, Méril was born Princess Maria-Magdalena Vladimirovna Gagarina in 1940 in Morocco. Starring in well over 100 films and television shows since she began acting in the late 1950s, Méril plays as the unfortunate psychic in Dario Argento's *Deep Red* (1975) and stars in Aldo Lado's vicious rape-revenge horror film *Night Train Murders*, a 1975 reimagining of Wes Craven's *The Last House on the Left* (1972) restaged on a moving train.

MERLET, AGNÈS

French filmmaker Agnès Merlet was born in the late 1950s and would through her career work as a director, writer, and producer. Beginning with short films in the mid-1980s, she would later direct four feature films including the 2008 evil child film *Dorothy Mills* with Jenn Murray in the title role and Carice van Houten as her psychiatrist. Merlet also co-wrote the screenplay.

MESQUIDA, ROXANE

Born in Marseille in 1981, French-American actor Roxane Mesquida is of French, Spanish, Italian and American heritage. She was discovered by French director Manuel Pradal who cast her in his film *Marie from the Bay of Angels* (1997), and she would later become a frequent collaborator with another French filmmaker, Catherine Breillat, featuring in the latter's films *Fat Girl* (2001), *Sex is Comedy* (2002) and *The Last Mistress* (2007). Her horror credits include *Sheitan* (Kim Chaprion, 2006), *Rubber* (Quentin Dupieux, 2010), *Sennentuntschi* (Michael Steiner, 2010) and Xan Cassavetes 2012 vampire film *Kiss of the Damned*. Mesquida is also a model, writer and DJ.

MICHAUD, MAUDE

Montreal filmmaker Maude Michaud is a familiar name to anyone with an interest in the contemporary women in horror movement. She published articles from her Masters degree on the subject which she received from Concordia University, and is herself an award-winning screenwriter and director. She made her feature film debut as director in 2014 with the horror movie *Dys-* (released in North America as *At the Door*) which won the Audience Award for Best Canadian Feature at the Fantasia International Film Festival. Additionally, she has made an impressive number of short films such as *Hol-*

Writer and director Maude Michaud www.quirkfilms.ca (used with permission).

lywood Skin (2010), *Snuff* (2010) and *Red* (2011), as well as a documentary web series called *Bloody Breasts: An Exploration of Women, Feminism and Horror Films* (2011). Michaud is also a portrait photographer.

MIERZWA, PATRUSHKHA—INTERVIEW (MAY 2018)

With its screams, screeches and squelches, sound is essential to creating horror's notorious sensory affect, and without the expertise of audio professionals like Patrushkha Mierzwa, the genre more broadly would not make anywhere near the impact on us as audiences that it does. Having worked in the industry for almost 40 years, Mierzwa studied fashion but soon made the switch to sound, establishing a career that has seen her collaborate with filmmakers including Robert Altman, Quentin Tarantino and Robert Rodriguez.

Aside from working on two of the most famous woman-directed cult horror films of all time—Mary Lambert's *Pet Semetary* (1989) and Amy Holden Jones's *The Slumber Party Massacre* (1982)—Mierzwa's impressive horror credits also include *Forbidden World* (aka *Mutant*, Allan Holzman, 1982), *Time Walker* (Tom Kennedy, 1982), *Cujo* (Lewis Teague, 1983*), Friday the 13th: A New Beginning* (Danny Steinmann, 1985), *Once Bitten* (Howard Storm, 1985), *Vamp* (Richard Wenk, 1986), and *Candyman 2: Farewell to the Flesh* (Bill Condon, 1995)

Patrushkha very kindly took the time to speak to me about her move from wardrobe to the sound department, life and learning in the Roger Corman film school, superstar chimpanzees, and covert rubber chickens.

When it comes to sound, you have such a lengthy, impressive filmography, and while we can't claim you for horror alone, it is without doubt a genre you return to time and time and time again. What is it about horror more generally that provides you with the most unique challenges in your craft?

The 1980's were really a time when horror films were in favor, so that's what my work calls were. The collaboration with special effects, stunts and animals are unique factors—there were bloody/noisy/rainy elements and animals are always potentially uncontrollable. There's always an element of danger on a movie set and more so with these, so it's important to have a heightened awareness and be informed about factors such as the intensity of explosions, the payload of guns, the chemical makeup of vapors and smokes.

According to IMDB (which I know we must always take with a pinch of salt!), your first film credit was as a wardrobe supervisor on the great librarian-horror film *The Attic* (George Edwards, 1980), and you worked in the wardrobe departments on a few other films in these early days. Can you tell me a bit about what you remember about working on *The Attic* in particular?

Patrushkha Mierzwa and Miko Hughes on the set of *Pet Sematary* (Mary Lambert, 1989). Used with permission.

My first film credit was actually a feature called *Falling in Love Again*, which happened to be Michelle Pfeiffer's first film as well. I was hired by the same costume designer to do *The Attic*. It starred Carrie Snodgrass, Ray Milland, and a chimpanzee. The story is about a librarian who is stood up at her wedding and then devotes all her energy to her pet. I needed to build a complete wardrobe for the chimp, including a sailor suit. Of course, I asked about meeting him to get measurements; it turned out to be impossible because he was doing a Las Vegas show run, playing duelling banjos with Jerry Van Dyke! I was told to "just make a boy's size but with longer arms and shorter legs". He was incredibly strong and I remember his handler playing poker in the chimpanzee's trailer, betting the chimp's salary—and learned the chimp made more money than I did.

Although I didn't handle men's clothing on *The Attic*, I was asked to help when there was a problem with Ray. He wears a suit and leather shoes in the dramatic climax when Carrie's character walks him in the park. Ray didn't like the black shoes we picked for him and was being difficult. He brought in his handmade Italian leather brown-and-white wingtips and insisted on wearing them. Finally, we said to him, "OK, Ray, that will be fine. Remember you get pushed down the hill and will scuff up those beautiful shoes, so make sure you bring in doubles for your stuntman." He grumbled and snatched the show shoes and walked away… he was quiet after that.

Carrie was sweet and was going through a difficult time: I remember being in her trailer with her during her conversation with Neil Young, informing him that their son Zeke had been diagnosed with a medical problem…and shooting was during a news story about her being assaulted.

The beginning of the shooting schedule took place in Kansas (I wasn't part of that). George, the director, was afraid to fly; he wanted to take a train. Somewhere in Arizona the train broke down; the company was already waiting in Kansas and another train was not available right away, so George took a taxi. Once they were on the road George explained why he wanted to go across state lines, and I heard the taxi driver pitched ideas and scripts the entire trip!

What lead to your shift in career from wardrobe to sound?

I came to film from a career in theater but wanted to stay in Los Angeles after getting my fashion degree. I was relegated to costume workrooms off the set *and* most of the work was shopping for contemporary clothing, which I didn't care for. I asked everyone on the set what they did and, after a short stint as a film loader, I found a good fit in sound—and no one ever asked me to make them sound younger or thinner!

I wanted a job that was where the action was and where I was paid for using my mind. I didn't have to do laundry after work or an actor's personal sewing for free and an additional benefit was that it paid twice as much as costuming. I learned that technology could intimidate people and that made me smile.

Your work on *The Slumber Party Massacre* alone makes you women-in-horror royalty—that film is so important for so many reasons, and even today, almost 40 years since it was first released, it is still so much fun. I'd love to hear how you got involved in the project, what you remember about the shoot, and how—if at all—it contrasted to the other horror films you were working on around the same time, such as *Forbidden World*.

The mixer who introduced me to sound, Mark Ulano, got the call for *Sleepless Night*, the working title of *Slumber Party*. I started booming for Mark after his boom operator decided to move back home. It was a Roger Corman–produced show shot in LA and I have many wonderful memories of my time at the old New World (the lumber yard-turned-movie-"stage"); I was there for the space movie era. I remember our production manager/ co-producer, Aaron Lipstadt, doing a cameo as "the pizza boy". Yes, there were pizza jokes.

The crew got along very well and they enjoyed swimming in the pool at lunchtime. We referred to the show as the "driller killer thriller" and the climax for us was at the end: when the killer is in the pool with his drill and lightning strikes. Unfortunately, the FX people chose a blood product that stained the pool and it had to be drained and re-painted. Our crew photo was taken in the deep end before it was filled up. The Corman experience was like going to film school and I still keep in touch with those friends—and am invited to Aaron's annual birthday bowling party ... of course now he's a well-respected TV director/producer.

Slumber Party contrasted with the other horror films I was doing, such as *Friday the 13th*, in that it was more "terror" than "horror". It was more character and dialogue driven and was more realistic; the other space and horror movies included more special FX, stunts and puppets. *Forbidden World* was known to us as *Mutant*, a title I prefer. We were something of a repertory company at Corman's, many of us went show to show. It was great to have that shorthand about the work so we could focus on the project; there was a true camaraderie. Roger gave many people their start in movies.

The New World building had a hallway and small offices down it, including editing. The hallway had been transformed into a spaceship corridor with the help of McDonald's quarter-pounder Styrofoam containers and paint...if you could think of a script that had these sets, you were given a chance to make your movie. When we shot in the hallway, the editors had to close their door and stop the Movieola.

I remember a lot of silliness: the "scientists" in pink and white jumpsuits and high heels and the tracking shots of the high heels down the corridor. The actress could not maintain a consistent pace so the dolly could follow her. After many takes the dolly grip tied a rope around her so she couldn't change the pace—and she ended up pulling the dolly! The hallway was narrow and I had to ride on the dolly and I thought how strong she was to pull it and the operator, First AC and me. The scene in the animal lab was hard at the time but funny to think back on— the art department got actual dead, frozen animals from the shelter. We broke for

Patrushkha Mierzwa in the foreground with horror author Stephen King making a cameo in the background on the set of *Pet Sematary* (Mary Lambert, 1989). Used with permission.

lunch before finishing the scene and when we came back they had begun thawing. I remember booming across an aisle when drip, drip from a raccoon's nose landed on my arm. Thankfully, we never caught any diseases.

I have Polaroid vacation pictures we took on Zarbia—a few crewmembers jumped into a headless beast and posed. Someone had added a folded napkin over the arm of the mutant in the one-sheet (poster) and added a dialogue bubble: "Do you have a reservation?" I had started a newsletter filled with space/work/interesting articles and gossip about the crew; we were quite close. On Fridays (before crews had to work weekends) the grips made margaritas on the back of their truck. After my 38 years in the movie business I can say the Corman producers were the only ones to ask the crew if they would work late—when a day's shooting wasn't done and the 12-hour mark came, everything stopped and the crew met in the parking lot. A producer would explain why they wanted to work more than 12 hours; then the crew voted. Sometimes we said yes, sometimes no. The decision was honored and when we did stay on, we received a cash bonus.

A bit of history: before Blackwrap was invented, the grips used painted aluminium foil to shield lights. After some usage, the paint would flake off and then a grip was sent to the parking lot to unroll a box of aluminum foil and spray-paint it, then roll it back up.

Like *Slumber Party Massacre*, *Pet Semetary* is a real classic of women-directed horror cinema. Can you talk a little about the experience of working on that movie, too?

Patrushkha Mierzwa and Billy the grip with the rubber chicken on the set of *Pet Sematary* (Mary Lambert, 1989). Used with permission.

It's hard to talk just a little about it, but I'll try. I cherish the time with Fred Gwynne [who played Jud Crandall], a kind, funny, and sweet man. He was a children's book author and illustrator and he gave me several original drawings.

At 2½ years old, Miko [Hughes, who played Gage Creed] was absolutely amazing—he was the youngest Chickasaw to perform a particular long ceremony and dance (something like 25 minutes, I recall). It was during the time I was trying to get pregnant and we became very close. I was his first 3-syllable word.

Denise Crosby [who played Rachel Creed] was fun and funny. While I could write a small book about the making of that film, I'll just say it was quirky.

And I'll finally reveal to the world that for a reason I no longer remember I gave one of the grips a rubber chicken and it became a game to hide it on the different sets. Mary found out about it and angrily demanded that it stop. Sometime after that we shot the night scene when Denise's character is walking at night and sees the closed diner—if you look closely there's a shadow of the chicken hanging in the window. Don't tell Mary.

It might just be a coincidence, but I find it curious that you worked on another animal-based Stephen King horror film adaptation with *Cujo*! It's such an extraordinary movie, and so much of its action spans between the intimate space of the car and the wide-open space of the yard. Did that film in particular present you with any particular challenges, and what are your strongest memories of that film set?

Cujo was shot first and a lot of the crew from the movie we were on went straight to that one. YES! That film had particular challenges, so much so that a book was just written about it, and it is over 500 pages! [Patrushkha and I share a mutual friend, Lee Gambin, whose exhaustive 2017 book *Nope, Nothing Wrong Here: The Making of Cujo* is also published by BearManor Media].

My strongest memory was of Jan de Bont, the DOP. He liked to run a good length of track, operate the camera with one hand and hold a zoom with the other, moving in and out at will, take after take. It was impossible to constantly watch him, move and watch the actors, so I imagined my movie and worked to that. And, dramatically, the main dog, Cubby, died in the middle of filming and we had to use the mean and snarly Moe, as well as a man in a suit (who looks better than some of the real dog shots). We also used a Labrador in a St. Bernard suit.

More recently, you have worked (or are working with) filmmakers like Quentin Tarantino and Robert Rodriguez. Both these directors are really renowned for a kind of 'gonzo', and I wonder if this is the result of painstaking, elaborate dedication to that very aesthetic, or if it is an approach that manifests on set while you're working. Considering how unique their respective films are, I'm curious if there's anything that really stands out to you in terms of the experience of collaborating with these filmmakers in particular?

Both of them like to hold true to the script. Robert is very quiet on the set; it's important to him that you understand what he wants to achieve and then quietly take care of it. I've worked with Quentin as a writer and actor (*Dusk till Dawn*—the movie) and am just starting his *Once Upon a Time in Hollywood*. While I've known him for 20 years, I'm looking forward to working with him as a director.

You've recently produced a few films. Is this something you'd like to do more of, and how different an experience is it from working in sound?

Producing and Sound are not so different, if you're doing it right: working production is a collaborative art form and the true professionals know enough about everyone else's job to be able to anticipate where conflicts may arise between departments and be able to suggest a solution. A better Producer knows everyone's job.

When a project interests me I like to get involved on a deeper level, so I've produced some documentaries and specialty niche videos. I do have an idea for a television series and I'm working on a period feature film script. And I'm writing

3 books about filmmaking and sound. Working production is strenuous and I'll soon be configuring my life to have more time for myself and I hope that's when my writing really takes off.

I have to ask you this as a professional: the story that I've heard is that while some guy actually patented it, Dorothy Arzner basically invented the boom mike when she got a technician to attach a microphone to a fishing rod so she could most effectively record Clara Bow in *The Wild Party* in 1929. Is this just an urban legend? And are there a lot of women working in sound departments today and historically in Hollywood?

I can't shed any more light on the origin; research supports that it was Dorothy Arzner. I trust you know that MOS means minus optical signal; did you know that the word "Nagra" is Polish for record? Polish citizen Stefan Kudelski was the machine's inventor.

When I started in sound there were a few women but most had not stayed in it; I was the only one I knew until the early 1990's (I started in 1980) and now with Facebook we have a group of Hollywood sound women with 123 members. I would like to add that the male Hollywood sound community has been very supportive and inclusive.

MILES, SYLVIA

Two-time Oscar nominee for Best Supporting Actress, Sylvia Miles was born in New York and began her screen career in 1960. Across her lengthy career she collaborated with film-makers including John Schlesinger, Oliver Stone, Abel Ferrara and of course Andy Warhol, the latter of whom she has been closely associated and with whom her cult reputation is closely tied. Her first horror film role was in Richard Hilliard's 1963 exploitation film *Violent Midnight*, and she would later put in a truly unforgettable turn as a lesbian ballet dancer in Michael Winner's 1977 horror movie *The Sentinel*. In 1981, she also played the unlucky fortune teller Madame Zena in Tobe Hooper's slasher movie *The Funhouse*.

MILES, VERA

As plucky investigator Lila Crane who solves the mystery at the heart of Alfred Hitchcock's *Psycho* (1960), Vera Miles is a key figure in the history of women in horror, although her character's sister Marion (played by Janet Leigh) might be more readily remembered. Born in Oklahoma in 1929, Miles turned to acting after a winning streak in a series of beauty pageants in the late 1940s. She was famously championed by Hitchcock who signed her to a long-term contract, the two falling out when she became pregnant and was unable to star in his 1958 film *Vertigo* which he intended to showcase her talents. Although not working with Hitchcock again, Miles would continue to act until the mid-1990s. Her other horror credits include William Castle's horror-comedy *The Spirit Is Willing* (1967), Richard Franklin's *Psycho II* (1983) and Larry Stewart's 1984 slasher, *The Initiation*.

MILLAR, CATHERINE

Australian television directing stalwart Catherine Millar has worked from the early 1980s on some of that country's most popular television series. Across her length filmography are several made-for-television movies, including the stalker films *Every Move She Makes* (1984) and *Without Warning* (1999), the haunted house movie *13 Gantry Row* (1998), and the horror-comedy *Mumbo Jumbo* (1999). From 2007 to 2010, she was the Head of Directing at the Australian Film Television and Radio School, and from 2010 to 2012 she became their Deputy Director of Screen Content.

MILLER, PATSY RUTH

As Esmerelda in Wallace Worsley's 1923 silent screen adaptation of Victor Hugo's 1831 novel *The Hunchback of Notre Dame*, Patsy Ruth Miller was an important woman in the early history of horror cinema. She was discovered by famed Russian-American actor and queer icon Alla Nazimova in her teens and appeared in a number of films from the early 1920s to the early '30s, making a few significant returns to the screen in the 1950s and late '70s. But it was this role with Lon Chaney in *The Hunchback of Notre Dame* which remains her most well-known performance. Bear Manor Media—the publisher of this book—also published Miller's autobiography, *My Hollywood: When Both of Us Were Young*.

MILLER, TERESA ANN

Teresa Ann Miller is an animal trainer who has played a crucial role in bringing some of the most memorable dog-centred horror films to life. The talent runs in the family: her father Karl Lewis Miller established the family tradition in the field as a dog trainer on horror movies including *The Mephisto Waltz* (Paul Wendkos, 1971), *Zoltan, Hound of Dracula* (Albert Band, 1977), *The Pack* (Robert Clouse, 1977), *The Amityville Horror* (Stuart Rosenberg, 1979), *Cujo* (Lewis Teague, 1983), *Dreamscape* (Joseph Ruben, 1984) and *Cat's Eye* (Lewis Teague, 1985). Often taking his work home with him as she was growing up, Teresa Ann and Karl would both work as animal trainers on horror films such as Rob Zombie's *House of 1000 Corpses* (2003) and *The Monster Squad* (Fred Dekker, 1987). Teresa Ann's other horror credits include *Witchboard 2* (Kevin Tenney, 1993) and Kornél Mundruczó's *White God* (2014), which won the impressive *Un Certain Regard* prize at the Cannes Film Festival.

MILLS, JULIET

Along with her sister Hayley, mother Mary, and father Sir John, Juliet Mills is a celebrated actor of stage and screen. Born in London in 1941, while she has worked extensively since the early 1940s in everything from children's films to soap operas to comedies, Mills forever solidified her association with horror for her spectacular performance in Ovidio G. Assonitis's *Beyond the Door* (1974), playing a possessed American housewife called Jessica Barrett. She returned to the genre again in Anthony Hickox's 1992 film *Waxwork II: Lost in Time*.

MINAMIDA, YŌKO

Yōko Minamida was a Japanese actor born in 1933 with almost 140 screen credits to her name. Her international cult film reputation stems from her spectacular performance as Auntie in Nobuhiko Obayashi's unequalled 1977 surreal horror-comedy, *Hausu*. Her other horror credits include the action eco-horror film *Yellow Fangs* (Sonny Chiba, 1990).

MINTER, KELLY JO ▸

Kelly Jo Minter would become a cult favorite in teen movies during the 1980s since her debut in Peter Bogdanovich's *Mask* (1985). Beginning her career working at a video duplication house, she was born in 1966 in New Jersey, and would work across film and television for almost three decades. Her horror credits would include *The Lost Boys* (Joel Schumacher, 1987), *A Nightmare on Elm Street 5: The Dream Child* (Stephen Hopkins, 1989), *Popcorn* (Mark Herrier, 1991), and she played Ruby in Wes Craven's 1991 film *The People Under the Stairs*. In relation to her role as Yvonne in *A Nightmare on Elm Street 5*, she more recently appeared in the documentary *Never Sleep Again: The Elm Street Legacy* (Daniel Farrands and Andrew Kasch, 2010).

MIRANDA, ISA

A *grande dame* of Italian cinema, Ines Isabella Sampietro was born in Milan in 1909 and was known professionally as Isa Miranda. Working with directors including Max Ophüls and Liliana Cavani, her first horror role was Alessandro Blasetti's proto-*giallo The Haller Case* (1933). Later she would work in Massimo Dallamano's horror reimagining of Oscar Wilde's *Dorian Gray* (1970) and Mario Bava's *Twitch of the Death Nerve* (1971).

MIRACLE, IRENE

Born in Oklahoma in 1954, American actor Irene Miracle's breakout performance was *Midnight Express* (Alan Parker, 1978), but for cult film fans she is firmly linked to Italian horror especially for roles in Aldo Lado's *Night Train Murders* (1975) and Dario Argento's sequel to *Suspiria*, 1980's *Inferno*. Her other horror roles would include *In the Shadow of Kilimanjaro* (Raju Patel, 1986), *Puppet Master* (David Schmoeller, 1989), *Nick Knight* (Farhad Mann, 1989) and *Watchers II* (Thierry Notz, 1990).

MIRANDA, SOLEDAD

Only 27 years old when she died in a car accident, Spanish actor Soledad Miranda—born Soledad Rendón Bueno in 1943—attained cult film immortality for her collaborations with fimmaker Jess Franco, particularly the horror movies *Count Dracula* (1970), *She Killed in Ecstasy* (1971) and *Vampyros Lesbos* (1971). She began her performance career as a flamenco dancer as a child, and in her short career worked in more than 30 films. While she worked across different genres, it is horror with which she is most closely associated, and aside from her collaborations with Franco she also featured in the horror movies *Sound of Horror* (Jose Antonio Nieves Conde, 1966) and Pere Portabella's experimental *Cuadecuc, vampir* (1971).

MITCHELL, RADHA

Australian actor Radha Mitchell was born in Melbourne in 1973 and began her career on local film and television before moving to Hollywood. Working across mainstream blockbusters and indie art films, Mitchell also has significant form in horror where her credits include *Pitch Black* (David Twohy, 2000), *Visitor* (Richard Franklin, 2003), *Silent Hill* (Christophe Gans, 2006), *Rogue* (Greg McLean, 2007), *The Crazies* (Breck Eisner, 2010), *Silent Hill: Revelation* (Michael J. Bassett, 2012), *Evidence* (Olatunde Osunsanmi, 2013), *Sacrifice* (Peter A. Dowling, 2016) and *The Darkness* (Greg McLean, 2016).

Radha Mitchell at the world premiere, in Hollywood, of *Silent Hill*, 20 April 2006, Los Angeles, California. Credit: Paul Smith / Featureflash Photo Agency / Shutterstock.com

MITSUYA, UTAKO

Japanese actor Utako Mitsuya was born in Tokyo in 1936 and throughout her acting career she would appear in several cult genre films, most notably Nobuo Nakagawa's classic horror movie *The Sinners of Hell* (1960). Another notable highlight in her filmography is *Evil Brain from Outer Space* (Koreyoshi Akasaka, Teruo Ishii and Akira Mitsuwa, 1965).

MIZUNO, KUMI

A frequent collaborator with filmmakers Toho Kaiju and Ishirō Honda, Japanese actor Kumi Mizuno would work in several horror and scifi films during the 1960s in particular. Born in Niigata in 1937, she studied acting professionally before beginning her film career in the late 1950s. Acting in a number of monster movies featuring national icon Godzilla such as *Invasion of Astro-Monster* (Ishirō Honda, 1965) and *Ebirah, Horror of the Deep* (Jun Fukuda, 1966), her other horror credits include Matango (Ishirō Honda, 1963), *Frankenstein Conquers the World* (Ishirō Honda, 1965) and its sequel, *The War of the Gargantuas* (Ishirō Honda, 1966).

MIZUNO, MIKI

Working across film and television since 1990, Japanese actor Miki Mizuno was born in 1974. As the monstrous title character of Kōji Shiraishi's *Carved: The Slit-Mouthed Woman* (2007)—a poignant horror film about domestic violence told through the urban legend *Kuchisake-onna*—Mizuno proved her flair for the genre, having demonstrated this earlier in Shusuke Kaneko's 1996 monster film *Gamera 2: Attack of Legion*. She would return to dark-themed material again in Sion Sono's *Guilty of Romance* (2011) and Steven Shiel's 2012 Indonesian horror film, *Dead Mine*.

MOFFATT, TRACEY

Unarguably one of Australia's most internationally recognized and celebrated visual artists, Tracey Moffatt has worked primarily as a photographer but also had significant success as a filmmaker. Born in Brisbane in 1960, early shorts like *Nice Colored Girls* (1987) and *Nightcries—A Rural Tragedy* (1989) provide evidence of her skills as both a storyteller and visual stylist, while her 1997 short *Heaven* experiments with cinema authorship and assumptions about the male gaze in a playfully confrontational manner. In 1993, her only feature film as director *beDevil* played at the Cannes Film Festival, to my knowledge the first horror anthology directed by a single woman director.

MONCRIEFF, KAREN

Karen Moncrieff was born in 1963 in California and would go on to become a director and screenwriter after working as an actor in several soap operas. Amongst her directorial credits are 2006's *The Dead Girl* starring Brittany Murphy, Rose Byrne and Toni Collette, a 5-part feature about the impact of a young woman's death on those around her. In 2017, she directed the horror movie *The Keeping Hours*, produced by Blumhouse Productions.

MONREALE, CINZIA

Cinzia Monreale is an Italian actor and producer who was born in Genoa in 1957. Often credited as Sarah Keller, she has appeared in a number of Italian horror films such as *Beyond the Darkness* (Joe D'Amato, 1979), *The Beyond* (Lucio Fulci, 1981), *The Sweet House of Horrors* (Lucio Fulci, 1989), *The Stendhal Syndrome* (Dario Argento, 1996) and the British horror film *Dark Signal* (Edward Evers-Swindell, 2016).

MONROE, MAIKA

Despite acting in a range of films, it was California-born Maika Monroe's 2014 back-to-back releases of the horror films *The Guest* directed by Adam Wingard and David Robert Mitchell's *It Follows* that made her a major player in the indie horror scene. With the latter in particular reaching critical acclaim and making a number of 'best of' lists for the year of its release, less known is Monroe's second career as a professional kiteboarder, which saw her leaving school and studying online to continue her training. In 2018 she starred in Federico D'Alessandro dark scifi thriller *Tau*, followed in 2018 with Neil Jordan's neo-psychobiddy trashfest *Greta* alongside Isabelle Huppert and Chloë Grace Moretz.

MONTEVERDE, ROSELLE Y.

Roselle Y. Monteverde is the Vice President of Filipino production company Regal Entertainment, the daughter of hugely successful producer, hotelier and businesswoman Lily Monteverde. Roselle began working in the industry in 1987 and has produced over 250 feature films and television series, with her many production credits (and a few as writer) on horror films not limited to *The Echo* (Yam Laranas, 2004), *Superstition* (Rahyan Carlos, 2006), *Bahay ni Lola 2* (Joven Tan, 2005), *Txt* (Mike Tuviera, 2006), White Lady (Jeff Tan, 2006), Tiyanaks (Mark A. Reyes, 2007), *Hide and Seek* (Rahyan Carlos, 2007), *Mag-ingat Ka Sa...Kulam* (Jun Lana, 2008), *Da Possessed* (Joyce Bernal, 2014), *Tarot* (Jun Lana, 2009) and *Haunted Forest* (Ian Loreños, 2017). She has also worked on the long-running horror franchise, *Shake, Rattle and Roll*.

MONTEOLIVA, JIMENA

Argentine filmmaker Jimena Monteoliva was born in 1972 and impressed international audiences with her horror features *All Night Long* in 2015 (co-directed with Tamae Garateguy) and *Clementina* (2017). While an impressive writer and director, Monteoliva also has strong form in a production capacity, and in this role was an important figure in Tamae Garateguy's *She Wolf* (2013) amongst others.

MONTFORD, SUSAN

Scottish screenwriter and director Susan Montford studied at the Glasgow School of Art and later moved to the United States to work on a planned feature film debut about the Manson family. Although this project did not eventuate, she was more successful was her 2008 surivval horror film *While She Was Out* starring Kim Bassinger who—along with Guillermo Del Toro—was an executive producer. As a producer herself, her credits also include *Splice* (Vincenzo Natali, 2009) and *Vampire Academy* (Mark Waters, 2014), the latter based on a screenplay by Daniel Waters of *Heathers* fame.

MOORE, EULABELLE

Very little is known of Eulabelle Moore, but according to IMDb.com. she was born in Texas in 1903. Although working mostly on stage, she appeared in Del Tenney's 1964 musical monster film *The Horror of Party Beach*, an important donation to the horror genre because as noted on the *Graveyard Shift Sisters* blog, she was one of the few significant Black characters in any horror movie made in the United States during this period.

MOORE, HEIDI

As founder and director of Wretched Films, Heidi Moore is a director, producer and writer responsible for the feature horror films *Dolly Deadly* (2016) and the forthcoming *Kill Dolly Kill: Dolly Deadly 2*, the latter produced by Troma. Moore has also directed, written, and produced a number of shorts, including the horror films *Boyfriend: Hell Hath No Fury Like a Wo-man Scorned* (2012), *Mommy* (2012) and *Wurms* (2014).

MOORE, JULIANNE °

Although her broader reputation may hinge on more supposedly high-brow material, Oscar-winning actor Julianne Moore has an affection for horror that has permeated her career. Born in North Carolina in 1960, her first feature film was *Tales from the Darkside: The Movie* (John Harrison, 1990), and beyond her work with directors like Todd Haynes, P.T. Anderson and Robert Altman, her horror work has endured. Her other horror credits include the Lovecraftian horror-comedy television movie *Cast a Deadly Spell* (Martin Campbell, 1991), *The Hand That Rocks the Cradle* (Curtis Hanson, 1992), Gus Van Sant's Hitchcock remake *Psycho* (1998), *Hannibal* (Ridley Scott, 2001), *Shelter* (Måns Mårlind and Björn Stein, 2010) and in the role of Margaret White in Kimberly Peirce's 2013 remake of *Carrie*.

Julianne Moore at the *Carrie* Los Angeles Premiere, Arclight, Hollywood, California, 7 October 2013. Credit: s_bukley/Shutterstock.com

MOOREHEAD, AGNES

Forever synonymous with grand witch-matriarch Endora on the long-running television series *Bewitched*, Agnes Moorehead was a hugely successful screen, radio and stage performer who worked from the early 1930s to the mid '70s. She was born in Massachusetts in 1900, a member of the St. Louis Municipal Opera Company, and studied extensively to a postgraduate level at the American Academy of Dramatic Arts. Joining Orson Welles's famous Mercury Theater in the late 1930s, she would be a key member and work with the group on several projects including the Welles-directed films *Citizen Kane* (1941) and *The Magnificent Ambersons* (1942). Her horror film credits include *The Lost Moment* (Martin Gabel, 1947), *The Bat* (Crane Wilbur, 1959), *Hush…Hush, Sweet Charlotte* (Robert Aldrich, 1964), *Dear Dead Delilah* (John Farris, 1972) and *Frankenstein: The True Story* (Jack Smight, 1973).

MORAN, PEGGY

While Hollwyood actor Peggy Moran only had a brief screen career between 1938 until 1943, she starred in a number of fondly remembered B-grade horror films such as *The Mummy's Hand* (Christy Cabanne, 1940) and *Horror Island* (George Waggner, 1941), archival footage from the first film reused later in *The Mummy's Tomb* (Harold Young, 1942).

MORELY, ANGELA

British composer Angela Morley was born Walter Stott in 1924 and is an important figure in film history for being the first openly transgender person to be nominated for an Oscar. Born in Leeds in 1924, Morley's early career was marked by work in British television, but her donation to horror was an impressive and highly memorable one: in 1960, Morely did the drum solo from that famous dance scene in Michael Powell's notorious 1960 British horror film, *Peeping Tom*.

MORETZ, CHLOË GRACE

Actor and model Chloë Grace Moretz was born in Atlanta in 1997, and began her screen career as a child with a key role in Andrew Douglas's 2005 remake of *The Amityville Horror*. Her association with horror would continue throughout her career with key appearances in films such as *Room 6* (Michael Hurst, 2006), *Zombies* (J. S. Cardone, 2006), *Hallowed Ground* (David Benullo, 2007), *The Eye* (David Moreau and Xavier Palud, 2008), *Let Me In* (Matt Reeves, 2010), *Texas Killing Fields* (Ami Canaan Mann, 2011), *Dark Shadows* (Tim Burton, 2012) and *Carrie* (Kimberly Peirce, 2013). In 2018, Moretz starred in Luca Guadagnino's remake of Dario Argento's *Suspiria* and starred alongside Isabelle Huppert in Neil Jordan's grand dame guignol homage, *Greta*.

MORGAN, BONNIE

American contortionist and actor Bonnie Morgan was raised in a family of circus performers, studying classical acting and clowning. These skills have seen her appear in horror films including *The Ring Two* (Hideo Nakata, 2005), *The Burrowers* (J. T. Petty, 2008), *Transylmania* (David and Scott Hillenbrand, 2009), *Piranha 3D* (Alexandre Aja, 2010), *Fright Night* (Craig Gillespie, 2011), *The Devil Inside* (William Brent Bell, 2012), *Fear Clinic* (Robert Green Hall, 2014), *The Last Witch Hunter* (Breck Eisner, 2015), *Bedeviled* (The Vang Brothers, 2016) and *Rings* (F. Javier Gutiérrez, 2017).

MORO, GUISELA

Florida-based Argentine filmmaker Guisela Moro is a director, writer and actor who made her feature film debut in 2016, the horror film *Hollow Creek* set in the Appalachian Mountains. As an actor, she also appeared in the film in a central role, and she had previously directed the comedy short *A World of Pleasure* in 2014.

MULLANEY, KERRY ANNE

Scottish filmmaker Kerry Anne Mullaney made her feature film debut in the 2008 zombie film *The Dead Outside*. Influenced by Japanese horror and movies like *The Dark Crystal* (Jim Henson and Frank Oz, 1982) and *Alien* (Ridley Scott, 1979) when she was growing up, *The Dead Outside* would win her the Best Director award at the Estepona International Horror and Fantasy Film Festival. She was nominated for a number of 2009 Scottish BAFTA awards for the film, including for Best Director and Best Writer.

MULLEN, APRIL

A proud force in strengthening the role of women in the film industry, actor, director and producer April Mullen was, with her 2012 feature film *Dead Before Dawn 3D*, the first woman and youngest person to ever direct a live action feature in stereoscopic 3D, and the first of the latter to be made in Canada. Also acting in and co-producing in this groundbreaking "zemon" film (a hybrid of zombies and demons), Mullen has an extensive filmography as director, producer and actor. Amongst her many credits she directed and co-wrote the revenge film *88* with Katharine Isabelle and has worked on the horror-western television series *Wynonna Earp*.

MULLEAVY, KATE AND LAURA

Sisters Kate and Laura Mulleavy grew up in California and both studied at the University of California in Berkeley. They began their career as fashion designers, with notable credits including working on costumes for *Black Swan* (Darren Aronofsky, 2010). Aside from running their successful fashion label Rodarte, in 2017 they released their feature film debut as co-writers and co-directors, the psychological horror film *Woodshock* starring Kirsten Dunst, who also acted as an executive producer. The film premiered at the Venice International Film Festival.

MUNRO, CAROLINE

One of the great icons of British horror cinema, Caroline Munro is an actor and model who was born in England in 1949. Despite a stint at art school she found her talents lay elsewhere and stumbled across her career as a fashion model almost accidentally, leading to her appearing on the cover of British *Vogue Magazine* while a teenager. Her relationship with horror began with her playing a small but significant role as the deceased wife of Vincent Price's eponymous protagonist in Robert Fuest's *The Abominable Dr. Phibes* (1971) and its sequel, *Dr. Phibes Rises Again* (1972). She was contracted to Hammer Studios, and acted in horror movies including *Dracula A.D. 1972* (Alan Gibson, 1972) and *Captain Kronos—Vampire Hunter* (Brian Clemens, 1974), and her later horror credits would include *I Don't Want to Be Born* (Peter Sasdy, 1975), *Maniac* (William Lustig, 1980), *The Last Horror Film* (David Winters, 1982), *Don't Open till Christmas* (Edmund Purdom, 1984), *Slaughter High* (Mark Ezra, Peter Litten, and George Dugdale, 1986), *Faceless* (Jess Franco, 1988), *Night Owl* (Jeffrey Arsenault, 1993) and *Flesh for the Beast* (Terry M. West, 2003).

MURPHY, BRIANNE

Although not a familiar name even to those with an established interest in women's horror filmmaking, Brianne Murphy is a key figure in cinema history. Born in London in 1933, her work as Director of Photography on the Anne Bancroft directed 20th Century Fox comedy *Fatso* (1980) made Murphy the first woman DOP on a major studio film. Beginning her career as an actor, she worked in rodeos and allegedly crashed a circus performance at Madison Square Garden, pretending to be part of the performance troupe. Beginning her career in indie filmmakng, she won an Academy Award for Scientific and Engineering Achievement in 1982 and received no less than 4 Emmy nominations for her work as cinematographer. While later working on the television series *Acapulco H.E.A.T.* and the teen drama *To Die, to Sleep* (1994) as director, of more immediate interest here is her 1972 directorial effort, the witchcraft movie *Blood Sabbath*. During her lifetime, Murphy also received both a Crystal Award and a Lucy Award for her contributions as a groundbreaking woman in the screen industries.

MURPHY, BRITTANY '

The death of late actor Brittany Murphy caused shockwaves in 2009, causing a widespread revisiting of her impressive filmography that saw her cast in some of the most beloved cult films of the 1990s. Born in Atlanta in 1977, she studied at the Verne Fowler School of Dance and Theater Arts in New Jersey and moved to Los Angeles in her early teens to pursue an acting career. Although perhaps not as well-known as her famous roles in films like *Clueless* (Amy Heckerling, 1995) or *Girl, Interrupted* (James Mangold, 1999), Murphy appeared in a number of horror films. These included *The Prophecy II* (Greg Spence, 1998), Geoffrey Wright's 2000 slasher film *Cherry Falls* and *Deadline* (Sean McConville, 2009).

MUSCHIETTI, BÁRBARA

Argentine producer and writer Bárbara Muschietti is a frequent collaborator with her brother, director Andrés Muschietti. Together they worked on the 2008 short film *Mamá* which would later be developed into the 2013 feature horror film *Mama* (whose script she also co-wrote). Bárbara would also produce the hugely successful 2017 remake of Stephen King's *It*, and its 2019 sequel, *It—Chapter Two* (also directed by her brother).

MUSIDORA

One of the great icons of early cinema, French actor, writer and filmmaker Musidora—borne Jeanne Roques in Paris in 1889—was a pioneer. Her mother was an active feminist and Musidora was nurtured in a creative, politically supportive environment for an ambitious young woman. She had famously written a novel by the time she was in her mid-teens and had appeared in theatrical productions with her friend, the Nobel-prize nominated writer Colette. Musidora was a long-term collaborator of French filmmaker Louis Feuillade, and her relationship to horror is often erroneously linked to her role in his 1915 Gaumont serial *Les Vampires* (which was in fact about a criminal gang rather than vampires as the name suggests). However, both there and in his 1916 serial *Judex*, she established the screen persona of powerful, alluring vamp figures that would impact the representation of strong women in horror cinema (as well as film noir and other genres) for decades to come. With Feuillade as her mentor, she was not satisfied with only acting, however, and would direct ten films, most of which are now lost.

NAGEL, ANNE

Born Anna Marie Dolan in Massachusetts in 1915, Anne Nagel was primarily an actor in genre films across a screen career that extended from the early 1930s to the late '50s. Despite early plans to dedicate her life to religious service as a nun, she quickly changed her mind after working as a model and joining a theater group. Moving to Hollywood, she turned to a career in film, where she starred in several horror films like *Man Made Monster* (George Waggner, 1941), *The Mad Doctor of Market Street* (Joseph H. Lewis, 1942) and *The Mad Monster* (Sam Newfield, 1942).

NAKAMURA, MAMI

Japanese actor Mami Nakamura was born in 1979 and played Tsukiko Izumisawa in the first of the *Tomie* franchise, directed by Ataru Oikawa in 1998. She also appeared in Katsuya Matsumura's horror film *Kirei? The Terror of Beauty* (2004) and Sion Sono's 2008 cult film, *Love Exposure*.

NAVARRO, BERTHA

México City-born film producer Bertha Navarro is a key figure in the nation's film history, working with a range of directors credited with re-energizing the Mexican film industry since the 1960s. Although she has also worked with filmmakers outside of México, in recent years her professional collaborations with filmmakers Alfonso Cuarón and Guillermo del Toro have been worthy of note, the latter of whom she joined in 1998 with sales agent Rosa Borsh to form the production company Tequila Gang. She produced del Toro's debut feature, the horror film *Cronos* (1993), as well as *The Devil's Backbone* (2001) and *Pan's Labyrinth* (2006). In 2008, she was awarded the city of Guadalajara's *Mayahuel de Plata* Lifetime Achievement Award, and she has worked as a coordinator for Latin American scriptwriters at the Sundance Film Institute.

NAVARRO, NIEVES

Often cast as Susan Scott, Nieves Navarro was a familiar face in Italian genre film during the 1960s and '70s. Born in Spain in 1938, she is notable for her lengthy association with *giallo* cinema where her credits include *Death Walks in High Heels* (Luciano Ercoli, 1971), *All the Colors of the Dark* (Sergio Martino, 1972), *So Sweet, So Dead* (Roberto Bianchi Montero, 1972), *Death Walks at Midnight* (Luciano Ercoli, 1972) and *Death Carries a Cane* (Maurizio Pradeaux, 1973). She also acted in Joe D'Amato's *Emanuelle and the Last Cannibals* with Laura Gemser in 1977.

NEGRI, POLA

A major silent era star, Pola Negri was an early movie vamp figure and one of the first European stars to establish a career in Hollywood. Born Barbara Apolonia Chałupec in what was then called the Kingdom of Poland in 1897, it was the 1918 film *The Eyes of the Mummy* directed by Ernst Lubitsch that marked her most important connection to the genre, and would both launch and define Negri, even as she latev worked across a range of genres. After continuing her and Lubitsch's success in Hollywood, Negri would later sign a contract with Paramount Studios, and was one of the most successful Hollywood actors of the silent era.

NEILL, VE

Although identifying her genre work as closer to scifi than horror, makeup artist Ve Neill has had a strong influence on the latter. Of her three Oscars, one was for makeup in Tim Burton's *Beetlejuice* (1988), and she also won an Emmy for her work on Mick Garris' 1997 television miniseries adaptation of Stephen King's novel, *The Shining*. Born Mary Flores in 1951 in California, her other horror credits are in films like *Tourist Trap* (David Schmoeller, 1979), *The Lost Boys* (Joel Schumacher, 1987), *Flatliners* (Joel Schumacher, 1990) and Tim Burton's *Sweeney Todd* (2007).

NERI, ROSALBA

Italian actor Rosalba Neri was born in Italy in 1939 and studied at *il Centro Sperimentale di Cinematografia*. She worked across many genres throughout her career, and her horror credits included includes Mario Bava's *Hercules in the Haunted World* (1961), *Slaughter Hotel* (Fernando Di Leo, 1971), *Smile Before Death* (Silvio Amadio, 1972), *The French Sex Murders* (Ferdinando Merighi, 1972) and *The Devil's Wedding Night* (Luigi Batzella, 1973). Most famously, she starred in Mel Welles's 1971 film *Lady Frankenstein*.

NESSK, MICHELLE

Based in Washington, Michelle Nessk established the production house Gloomy Sunday Productions in 2009 that focuses on film, videogames, photography, music, graphic novels and event planning. As a filmmaker, she works in various capacities, both in front of the camera and behind it. As a director, she has made *The Devil's Fool* (2012), *Shell Shocked* (2017) and the upcoming *Just a Prick* (2018), the latter co-directed with Tonjia Atomic. In 2016, she directed, co-wrote and starred in *O. Unilateralis*, a rare found footage horror film made by a woman.

NEUMANN, LENA

With over 50 film credits to her name, German editor Lena Neumann worked for production companies and studios such as UFA and DEFA across a career that spanned from the mid-1930s to the mid '60s. Among her many credits is the hugely significant German horror film *Fährmann Maria* (Frank Wysbar, 1936), in which Sybille Schmitz's title character battles Death himself.

NEUROTICA, HANNAH—INTERVIEW (SEPTEMBER 2018)

Hailing from Brooklyn and currently based in Vermont, Hannah Neurotica (aka Hannah Forman) is a force to be reckoned with and a central figure in the continually-growing Women in Horror movement. Inspired by discovering feminist film theory when she studied at Washington's Evergreen State College, in 2010 she founded Women in Horror Month and chose February because—with its 28 days—mirror the length of the menstrual cycle that granted her the vernacular name for her now-legendary feminist horror zine Ax Wound.

Along with groups such as the Viscera organization, the mission of Women in Horror Month is clear, described on the official website as "an international, grassroots initiative, which encourages supporters to learn about and showcase the underrepresented work of women in the horror industries."

Neurotica has since developed *Ax Wound* into a film festival to continue providing spaces to nurture women's talents in the field, and Neurotica herself is a prolific writer, filmmaker, animator and mixed media artist.

www.womeninhorrormonth.com

I've always been intrigued by your decision to do *Ax Wound* initially as an old-school printed paper zine at a time when most people had moved online to do websites. Part of the power of *Ax Wound* for me as a reader—aside from its politics and its message and its mission—was just how beautiful it was as an

Hannah "Neurotica" Forman. Used with permission.

object. It felt really special to pick up something physically and read work by women who felt the same way I did about horror. What was the inspiration to *Ax Wound* as an old-school zine and can you tell us a little more about its origins?

The decision to make *Ax Wound* a cut n' paste zine was just a given for me. My life during that period was dominated by riot grrrl and zine culture so DIY publishing was already my main form of art, self-expression, and community.

When I went away to college I became engrossed in Women's Studies for the first time and had this unease start creeping in when I'd watch some of my old favorite films. How could I reconcile big boobie women being chased naked and bloody through the woods by a crazed lunatic? *Ax Wound* was born out of a desire to explore and connect with other women who felt the internal pull between morality and consumption of exploitive films.

It's so easy now to connect with people about the most microscopically niche topics but as you know, that wasn't always the case. When I was going through this identity crisis there wasn't a safe space to explore it. Nobody in my day to day life was interested and when I'd sign on to message boards (social media wasn't part of everyday life yet) it was clear that if the trolls could reach through the screen and collectively beat and rape me they probably would.

One of the less vulgar and most persistent responses was "why do you feminists always have to bring politics into everything?" This notion is actually nuts because no genre (outside of documentary) has historically tackled politics better than horror films. So, I figured out pretty damn quick that not only were women unwelcome in this space but also the average horror fanboy had absolutely zero intention of even *considering* engaging in an intelligent conversation.

It was because of these reasons I sat on my floor cut n' pasting my thoughts/observations/struggles with glue sticks and sharpies to anyone who might listen. I saw that first issue as a fish on a line—putting it out into the world and hoping to catch one or two like-minded punk rock feminist ladies like myself who needed to explore the genre in a deeper way than had ever been done outside of academia.

The term "Final Girl" wasn't part of the culture yet in the slightest. Now it's a commonplace term that the average horror fan can identify without knowing its origin.

Speaking of final girls—Carol Clover's book is often cited as the first substantial work dealing with "feminism and horror" but if one re-visits the book it actually focuses on gender and Freudian psychology: *in fact, in the introduction, she clearly states the book is written with a male audience in mind.* This took me a little while to wrap my brain around but it was that realization which took down that wall of guilt when it came to enjoying and studying horror films.

It wasn't that horror films were feminist in nature but rather had the inherent capability of exploring the themes of gender, history, cultural expectations, social anxieties, and personal demons through the lens of horror.

Even in its earliest days, the impact of *Ax Wound* was extraordinary not just for women fans of horror films, but for horror filmmakers. Can you tell us about some of the zine's earliest supporters—I believe there's some impressive names!

It will never cease to blow my mind that *Ax Wound* became part of the larger horror culture. Not only was it made with glue sticks and sharpies but the spelling and grammar were atrocious and the overall look was just totally messy.

After getting the first 20 copies made I sent out consideration copies to DIY zine distros and indie bookstore. One afternoon I got an email from Gluestick Distro saying she wanted to buy 5 copies of the zine to sell! She wrote, "this isn't aesthetically what I usually carry but the content is really great." The moment is very vivid—it was the first time in my life that I created something I was genuinely proud of and wanted to get out as much as possible. Keep in mind, this zine distro wasn't horror based—none of them were—but the people seeking self-published work were already open to alternative views and new ways to look at the world and pop culture. This allowed *Ax Wound* to stand out because there was nothing else in the catalogs like it.

Wanting to reach more horror fans I begun running my fingers down horror magazine mastheads and jotting down women sounding names from all the movie credits. It was through this action that I was able to start building the Women in Horror community.

The "impressive names" came years later. Not sure if people realize it wasn't like I created *Ax Wound* and was an instant "viral" success. I'd been making it for a microscopic audience (mainly for myself) for *5+ years* before it was noticed.

One day I got an email from a reporter at *Newsweek* asking if he could call me for a phone interview about feminism and horror. During this time period, I was the only person (that I know of!) who was openly talking about the topic. I mean, I was the closest thing to an expert *Newsweek* could find to comment! To this day I wonder how he found me.

When that came out, a few more women contacted me and the community grew a little more. It also opened the door for me to think a bit bigger about what I could do with a possible emerging platform. I began interviewing people from those mastheads and movie credits- women who were the only member of a crew, the only female editors of a genre magazine, university professors. I'd ask them to share their stories for the zine and the results were truly magical.

Later I decided to reach out to filmmakers for the first time and was continually blown away when responses came back. Connecting with filmmakers and actors today is so simple because of social media but before that, I was doing some pretty detailed investigative work. I think people responded because *Ax Wound* was so niche, so necessary, and unlike blogs, it was a physical object I could mail to them.

Herschell Gordon Lewis gave me one of my most favorite press quotes, saying he was my biggest fan. Then Eli Roth asked for a copy and shared it with Quentin Tarantino on the set of *Inglorious Bastards*. It was through my interview with Eli that I met Jen and Sylvia Soska. One of the questions I'd asked him was to share the names of women making horror films that the average fan wouldn't have heard of. He directed me to the Myspace (!) page of Jen and Sylvia who had just finished *Dead Hooker in a Trunk* and were struggling to get people to screen it. We instantly connected, and I featured them in *Ax Wound* for their first print interview! Later, Women in Horrror Month would provide the first screening.

Can you talk us through your thinking to behind the manifesto that led to you creating Women in Horror Recognition Month? Did you expect it to go as big as it did—and as international in scope as it has?

In the years following *Ax Wound* being mentioned in *Newsweek* I would get interview requests every October for seasonal pieces on women and horror films. Unlike today, where 'women and horror' is written about frequently in certain subsections of the horror community/media, this was not the case then.

I wrote for *Bitch Magazine*, was quoted in *The Guardian*, and given shout outs in *Fangoria* and *Rue Morgue*. It was surreal to be supported by artists who I never in a million years thought would know my name!

This was all awesome and well and great but it was still so niche and I'd quickly forget that I was in a bubble when people outside would remark (frequently) how odd it was for women to enjoy such an offensive genre. Or they say things like "there is already so much horror in the world. Why do we need it in our films?"

It was precisely these sorts of questions that, in 2009, a producer at CBC radio asked me on the phone while doing prep research for an upcoming panel I was going to be taking part in.

It was a live segment and I was so deeply nervous. The panel included myself alongside Jovanka Vuckovic (filmmaker, writer) and Aviva Briefel (writer/film studies professor). Jovanka was the only one in the actual studio, so the women interviewing us began spending the time we had on the air commenting on how Jovanka looked—was it hard to get a date with all those tattoos? We were a novelty and this great opportunity that meant so much to all of us was degraded and lost. When you are in a bubble it's hard to remember how much work is left to be done.

Around this time my Dad was very ill with a mysterious illness and was progressively getting worse. We were hanging out and talking about the interview experience. I yelled, "this is all getting so ridiculous! We need, like, a Women in Horror Month or something!" As I've mentioned before, ideas flow out of me constantly, so he just acknowledged it but gave me a look and jokingly said something like, "okay good luck with that!"

In a passionate fit, I pounded out the Women in Horror Recognition Month Manifesto on my now-defunct website. The sentiment was basically "you can come with me or I will celebrate alone every February". Within minutes, the response was huge! Almost everyone I'd come to know through *Ax Wound* was commenting on what a great idea it was and why it was important to them personally.

It was in September that I wrote the call-to-action and it was January when my Dad died. He was going downhill fast and so the months leading up to the inaugural WiHM was during the worst point in my life. In fact, I'd been pasting together what would be the last print issue of *Ax Wound* during that time as well. This was the reason, in my mind, that I'd never been able to make another one. I also wish my Dad could have seen WiHM but those sorts of thoughts are more about ourselves than those who are gone.

Every now and then when people—let's be honest, it's almost always guys—say that they don't get the need for "Women in Horror Recognition Month" because there's always been lots of women in horror movies. Once I've picked my jaw off the ground, I patiently say that firstly, it's about representing women as more than big-breasted disposable victims, but—more importantly—that WiHM is as much (if not more) about making horror movies as it is watching them, about creating both virtual and very real spaces for women filmmakers and creatives to come together not just to work together, but to build a supportive community. Do you get people saying similar things, and what's your response?

The Soska Sisters in Hannah Neurotica's *Ax Wound Zine*. Used with permission.

Yes—it is absolutely *mostly* guys, but it breaks my heart how frequently it is women too. That one hurts the most. One of the most frustrating aspects of WiHM (and my lack of control over it now that its global) is not being able to correct (nor know of!) every person who misunderstands any aspect of it. Behind the scenes I have worked for the past 10 years to re-word/get feedback/re-write that mission and not once has it made a difference. The truth of the matter is most people don't read mission statements—it's all so reactionary. Which means if someone wants to understand what WiHM is all about, they need to take the time to educate themselves. This is a microcosm of a larger ignorance cycle. Plus, as I learned when I was virtually harassed on message boards in the old zine days—most of these folks have zero interest in engaging on an intellectual level regardless of the WiHM intentions.

Honestly, the whole thing drives me nuts and the energy that was eaten up those first few years by my anger and sadness didn't help move our agenda any further. So I needed to put my feelings aside and return focus to the mission. The heart. The good news is I don't get as many death threats now. The first few years had a few truly scary moments but those handful of trolls who banded together couldn't bring me down! (*to the tune of "Hedwig").

It felt very logical—almost natural—to me when you expanded your work with *Ax Wound* and WiHM to create your own film festival. Can you tell us the background of that project and some of its many accomplishments?

I wanted to have a feminist horror film festival for years but I was dealing with mental health struggles (amongst other things) and the time wasn't right. One day I was sitting in a cafe reading the local paper and there was an interview with the director of a community theater right in town. The writer described the space as cavernous, dark; an art gallery encircling a theater used for stage productions and film screenings. I'm not saying that I've got psychic abilities but throughout my life, I've consistently been able to predict the success of an idea the moment it pops in my head. It happened with *Ax Wound* zine, Women in Horror Month, and other creative undertakings and reading this article that familiar pang was in full effect.

The tone of the piece led me to believe the director was hoping the article/interview would attract people who wanted to use the space just as much as enticing people to buy tickets. Everything about it just clicked and I knew right then that the Hooker-Dunham Theater & Gallery in Brattleboro, VT was the future home of the soon-to-exist Ax Wound Film Festival.

I wrote down the contact information and quickly sent an email inquiring about the cost of renting the space and the rest is history.

I'd like to interject a point here though that relates to one of the previous questions about advice for other women. During this moment in my life, I'd just come out of the psychiatric hospital for bipolar depression (again) and was in no way thinking about starting up a film festival. It was hard enough to get my teeth brushed. Money was not coming in, so a fest was truly the last thing on my reality meter. But if you are in tune with your local community it's amazing what connections and opportunities one can carve out for little to no money and in a way that is beneficial to all involved.

It's not that everyone is going to find this, but when you tap into the local community—read the paper—you can get a sense of who is looking for folks to help grow an artistic space.

I'd never ever held a film festival before (let alone screened a film in a theater) so the first year was a complete experiment. You know when your little and have a birthday party but fear nobody is going to show up? That was exactly how it felt, but somehow we sold out and people were standing in the aisles.

I'm so proud that this event has morphed into a truly family-like atmosphere that has fostered some wonderful networking relationships and provided a space for so many great films to reach an audience excited to see them.

The vision I have for this festival is a living zine. Each year I'm able to add more elements to the mix. For example, we have films screenings, filmmaker Q+A panels, presentations on crowdfunding, live podcast recordings, DIY gore demonstrations, and last year an unreal academic presentation on horror in the Trumpian era by Alison Lang. Following that the whole audience started engaging in real social horror discourse!

Unlike other festivals, Ax Wound doesn't and will never give out awards. Women are criminally underrepresented in this field and in order for things to change we need to support each other. We haven't come anywhere near far enough to start dividing ourselves at our own events. I've observed great ladies become less supportive of one another when up for the same awards and it's really disturbing and insidious. For us to advance we need to hire each other and when there are no safe spaces to connect without defences up, this is just not possible. Ax Wound is where you meet the ladies you're going to work on your next film— not compete against.

This leads me to another mission which is to provide our filmmakers with as many tools possible that will support the advancement of their career. I'm deeply grateful to Final Draft (the industry standard screenwriting software) for becoming a sponsor and allowing us to provide filmmakers with a free copy.

I'm blown away by the support we get from larger media companies like AMC's *Shudder*, horror media like *Fangoria* and *Rue Morgue*, to smaller women-owned and operated shops like Ghoulish Delights (who made us Ax Wound bath gel), My Pretty Zombie Cosmetics, and this year Horror Decor is making Ax Wound pillows!

Another aspect that blows my mind is how many insanely talented filmmakers from around the world have been in attendance despite our current inability to provide monetary assistance. Every year we have between 15 to 20! I guess you could say Ax Wound Film Festival is like Women in Horror Month in the sense that it only exists because the community as a whole make it happen.

In terms of the films: my criteria for judges is to abandon the standard rating system provided by FilmFreeway. I mean, rating acting/directing/sound from 1 to 10 doesn't tell me anything. As long as the sound is good and the picture is clear, all films have an equal chance of acceptance. So if you made a $20,000 film and have a recognizable name, your film has no more or less of a chance then a first time filmmaker who used a cell phone and $50. Good work is good work is good work and I wish other festivals would be more thoughtful in how they viewed the artform.

Another thing I work really hard at is extending the call for submissions to spaces outside the usual horror hangouts. I've learned a lot from Women in Horror Month and one of those is just because you use the word "woman" doesn't mean you are being inclusive. Throughout history, the word "woman" has implied white and we all need to make sure we do everything in our power to share the stories of women regardless of age, race, sexuality, or who they are friends with.

When you yourself made the shift to behind the camera yourself, it almost felt inevitable that the woman who had brought so many gifted women together in the joined spirit of horror and its potential for women filmmakers and fans should herself have something really powerful to say in her own film work. Can you tell us a bit about the creation of your short film *Letting* and your other film work?

Letting is a short film I've got a rather complicated relationship with. I will say that the experiences I've had with filmmaking took a real toll on my mental health for many reasons—like being utterly disrespected to the point of panic attacks and made to feel badly about my ideas. All the self-esteem I have worked hard to believe never spilled over to that sector.

At the core, I am a writer—an artist who needs solitude boarding, for better or worse, on isolation. It was always this deep conflict—wanting to turn my scripts into films but not accepting that my mental health was such that it just wasn't in the cards for me that created constant stress and self-hate crap.

It wasn't until last year that I made one of those life altering discoveries. Claymation! Someone on YouTube made this killer horror claymation and it was like, woah. This. This is what I am meant to do.

Here was an artform that involved zine-like creation (sets by hand, etc) and it was all completely solitary. This doesn't mean I won't ever make a film with actual humans in it but right now it's all about expressing my horrors with clay and chicken bones. The first one I made is called "Surprise Egg!" and can be found on Vimeo.

My first official claymation short film will be out by end of the year. It is a re-imaging of a short story from *Scary Stories to Tell in The Dark* and I've named it *Raspberries*.

I'm also interested in exploring horror filmmaking in VR—a truly experimental media that has the potential to be a women-helmed sector of the entertainment industry.

Long story short—this part of my life is only just starting, and I can't wait to express myself more and more as I learn the technical ins and outs of stop-motion.

Is there anything about the explosive global success of the WiHM movement that has surprised you in particular?

Literally everything! The thing that surprised me most and continues to blow me away is that WiHM now exists completely separate from me. After the first year, I was convinced it was all a fluke and attention spans would move elsewhere. It really hit home that WiHM was here to stay when I'd started reading write-ups with people talking about the history of WiHM in ways that were totally not accurate or attributing its origins to the wrong places. While annoying as that was, it was no longer about me. It was finally its own thing. That is how cultural movements and art exist—you can't control them.

In the beginning, I would get so worked up when someone said negative things about WiHM because it felt like a personal attack. I would cry and get angry and then say stupidly impulsive things on Facebook. But just like WiHM has grown, so have I and the biggest lesson for me is that I don't have to (because I physically can't) defend WiHM across the globe.

For those with anxiety disorders you know to focus on what is within your control and I work so hard to apply that to all aspects of my life. I can't control what magazines write or people say on message boards, but I can control how I conduct myself and what actions I take to try and make the world a better place.

It surprises me every year how many different ways people celebrate and recognize the month in their own horror communities. There are events in Second Life, stage performances, live streaming of artists, loads of film festivals around the world, etc. And even chapters started forming on their own like WiHM-Dublin. Honestly, the whole thing still hasn't sunk in and it's about to be a decade!

What's the one piece of advice you give budding women filmmakers and/or feminist activists wanting to shake things up the way you have? What's the one piece of advice you give budding women filmmakers and/or feminist activists wanting to shake things up the way you have?

Don't wait until you have 'enough resources' because that day will never come. You legitimately have everything needed right now to start doing whatever it is you want to explore/create. However, it is a proactive, creative, and bumpy journey that requires an open heart and surrendered ego. If the ultimate goal is to create something one can feel proud, passionate, and connected to then having the slickest new gear or loads of cash will not get you any closer to the heart. Working with what you have is a test in the ultimate creative problem solving. That alone is super impressive! Once others see what you can do with the means available it will inspire them to support your vision.

Hannah Neurotica's *Ax Wound Zine*. Used with permission.

There is a second part to this advice that is critical: *don't stop*. Don't get overwhelmed by the vastness of the world and all the possible outcomes that cause you doubt yourself.

If I gave up all the times I failed when I started *Ax Wound*—I never would have made WiHM, If I gave up all the times I fucked up during WiHM then I never would have the AWFF. And if I never had such unpleasant filmmaking experiences I'd never discover i'm actually meant to be a lone animator.

Like the advice from granny—stay on the path and when the wolves come, let them howl, cry with fear at the sound, and then breathe and move further down the road.

In 50 years from now, what would you like people to remember as your legacy?

In 50 years from now, if I've truly made an impact on the world for the better- it doesn't matter if people remember me. But who am I kidding? I'm human and it would feel good to be remembered as someone with a never-ending wealth of crazy ideas who worked selflessly for most of her life in the hopes of empowering women to claim spaces for themselves and extend that sentiment to support others.

I don't know if I'll ever have kids, so in some way maybe Women in Horror Month is the offspring I will be able to leave behind.

NICOLODI, DARIA

Born in Florence in 1950, actor, producer and screenwriter is far too often a footnote in the careers of her one-time collaborator and partner Dario Argento's and their daughter, Asia. But Nicolodi is a highly accomplished figure in horror history in her own right. Beginning her career in television in the early 1970s, she was mentored early in her career by esteemed director Elio Petri and was thus already an established figure in the Italian industry by the time she began working with Argento in 1975. Collaborating with Argento, she would act in *Deep Red* (1975), *Inferno* (1980), *Tenebrae* (1982), *Phenomena* (1985), *Opera* (1987) and *The Mother of Tears* (2007), as well as being a major researching partner and writer on *Suspiria* in 1977 (in which she has a small cameo during the opening airport scene). Amongst her other horror credits, she would star in Mario Bava's underrated final film *Shock* (1977), as well as being cast in his son Lamberto's 1987 neo-*gialli Delirium* and Michele Soavi's *The Sect* (1991). As a writer, she also wrote the screenplay for Luigi Cozzi's 1989 horror film *Paganini Horror*—in which she also starred—and was an uncredited co-writer on his *Demons 6: De Profundis* that same year. In 2009, she acted in Antonello Grimaldi's Italian television miniseries *Il mostro di Firenze* about the real-life serial killer, the so-called Monster of Florence.

NINAGAWA, MIHO

Japanese actor, painter and musician Miho Ninagawa began her screen career in the late 1980s. Her horror credits include *Marebito* (Takashi Shimizu, 2004), *Deadball* (Yudai Yamaguchi, 2011), *Arcana* (Yoshitaka Yamaguchi, 2013), *Vampire Night* (Shinpei Yamazaki, 2017) and two episodes of the *Masters of Horror* television series, Takashi Miike's "Imprint" and Norio Tsuruta's "Dream Cruise".

NINAGAWA, MIKA

Although her international reputation is based in her success as a commercial photographer (particularly in fashion), Japanese artist Mika Ninagawa is also a hugely talented filmmaker. Transferring her signature visual style from photography to feature film with her geisha drama *Sakuran* (2007), in 2012 she adapted Kyoko Okazaki's horror manga *Helter Skelter* to the screen in a movie of the same name starring Erika Sawajiri. Born in 1972 in Tokyo, Ninagawa has received numerous awards for her work since 1996, and in 2012 Japanese publisher Parco released a glossy photobook of stills from *Helter Skelter*.

NOTO, CLAIR

Clair Noto is something of a mysterious figure and—considering she is renowned for a horror/scifi screenplay that was never produced—her inclusion here at first may seem unusual. But what a screenplay it is: *The Tourist* is frequently described as one of the greatest unproduced screenplays of all-time and a "masterpiece". The inability of *The Tourist* to achieve fruition is widely hailed as one of the great failures of the Hollywood system, its destruction at the hands of overzealous rewriters, personal vendettas, and broader financial blunders saw the collapse of what is broadly documented as Noto's remarkable original vision of the film. Noto had envisaged actors including Hanna Schygulla, Kim Bassinger, Sharon Stone, Teresa Russell and Michelle Pfeiffer for the lead role, but the lack of support meant the film never happened. Despite trying her luck elsewhere with Dino DeLaurentiis and Francis Ford Coppola's Zoetrope, the screenplay ultimately ended up in permanent limbo. Regardless, the influence and legacy of that much-passed-around original is considered to have had a strong impact on later genre cinema.

NORTON, ROSANNA

Recieving an Oscar nomination for her work on the 1982 scifi film *Tron*, American costume designer Rosanna Norton worked across many genres from the early 1970s for almost 40 years. One of her earliest credits was for *Lemora: A Child's Tale of the Super-*

natural (Richard Blackburn, 1973), which was followed by other horror films including both *Phantom of the Paradise* (1974) and *Carrie* (1976) with director Brian De Palma, Joe Dante's *Gremlins 2: The New Batch* (1990), *Casper* (Brad Silberling, 1995), and the television series *Bone Chillers*.

NOXON, MARTI

Marti Noxon was a key figure driving the success of the television series *Buffy the Vampire Slayer* and *Angel* as both co-writer and co-executive producer. In 2011, she wrote the screenplay for Craig Gillespie's remake of *Fright Night* and made a small appearance in the television mini-series *Dr. Horrible's Sing-Along Blog*. She also wrote and directed the feature drama *To the Bone* in 2017 and is a showrunner, creator and producer of the series *Sharp Objects*, based on Gillian Flynn's thriller novel of the same name.

NURMI, MAILA

Known simply by the moniker Vampira, Maila Nurmi is a cult horror icon. Of Finnish and American heritage, she was born in 1922 and moved from Oregon where she grew up to Hollywood to pursue an acting career. Instead, she found fame in fame as a television horror movie host on *The Vampira Show* in the mid 1950s. She would later work in several films, often credited as Vampira. Of these, most famous is Ed Wood's *Plan 9 From Outer Space* (1959), the inspiration for a biopic about the director by Tim Burton in 1994 where Lisa Marie played the Maila Nurmi role.

NYONG'O, LUPITA⸙

Kenyan-Mexican actor Lupita Nyong'o was born in Mexico in 1983 but raised in Kenya from an early age before moving to the United States to study. Beginning her film career behind the camera, she made her acting debut in a short film in 2008, winning a Best Supporting Actress Oscar for her feature film debut in *12 Years a Slave* (Steve McQueen, 2013). Working on both stage and screen, her flexibility as a performer would also become visible through the increasingly high-profile roles she would accept, appearing in everything from the *Star Wars* sequel trilogy (2015–2019) to Ryan Coogler's blockbuster superhero film *Black Panther* (2018). Yet horror fans were still stunned by her mainstream shift into the genre in Jordon Peele's celebrated doppelganger nightmare *Us* in 2019, the same year that she consolidated her place as an unexpected but welcome horror icon through her starring role in Abe Forsythe's charming zom-com, *Little Monsters*.

O'CONNOR, UNA

Character actor Una O'Connor was born in Belfast in 1880 and spent much of her career on the stage before turning to film in her late 40s. One of her first screen performances was in Alfred Hitchcock's *Murder!* in 1930, and she appeared in many other mystery films including Billy Wilder's *Witness for the Prosecution* in 1957 with Charles Laughton, Marlene Dietrich and Elsa Lanchester. The latter would take the title role in the film that would include O'Connor's most famous screen performance, as the housekeeper Minnie in *Bride of Frankenstein* (James Whale, 1935). She also featured in Whale's scifi-horror hybrid *The Invisible Man* (1933), and the horror-comedy *The Canterville Ghost* (Jules Dassin, 1944). Although often cast for comic relief, O'Connor's memorable, expressive face made her work in *Bride of Frankenstein* particularly iconic.

O'DEA, JUDITH

One of the most famous lines ever uttered in a horror movie is surely "They're coming to get you, Barbara!" from George A. Romero's *Night of the Living Dead* (1968). Barbara was, of course, played by Judith O'Dea, a woman who finds herself in the midst of an undead apocalypse upon visiting her mother's grave. Born in Pittsburgh in 1945 where Romero's famous film was made, beyond the role with which her name is now synonymous, O'Dea would not commit fully to acting as a career, making her next appearance ten years later in a made-for-television movie called *The Pirate*. But she would return to horror with a number of performances from the early 2000s onwards, including *Claustrophobia* (Mark Tapio Kines, 2003), *October Moon* (Jason Paul Collum, 2005), *October Moon 2: November Son* (Jason Paul Collum, 2008), *Beast* (Timo Rose, 2009), *Women's Studies* (Lonnie Martin, 2010), *Safe Inside* (Jason Paul Collum, 2017) and in the segment "Gein" in the anthology film *Hole in the Wall* (2014).

O'ROURKE, HEATHER °

One of the most famous faces of 1980s horror, Heather O'Rourke's early death at the age of 12 linked her legacy with ugly conspiracy theories surrounding her association with the supposedly 'haunted' production of Tobe Hooper's *Poltergeist* (1982), in which she starred as Carol Anne Freeling. O'Rourke was born in San Diego in 1975 and played Carol Anne again in both *Poltergeist II* (Brian Gibson, 1986) and *Poltergeist III* (Gary Sherman, 1988), the latter released four months after her premature death and consequently dedicated to her. Beyond some television work, these remained O'Rourke's only feature film roles but the cultural impact of her performance (and her famous "They're here!" line) has been significant both in the horror genre itself and pop culture history more broadly.

OBERLI, BETTINA

Swiss filmmaker Bettina Oberli was born in 1972 in the country's central mountains. She studied directing at the Zürcher Hochschule der Künste and has worked extensively as a director and scriptwriter in feature film, television and theater, as well as making short films and music videos. She has won numerous awards for her work. Her 2009 feature-length horror film, *The Murder Farm*—co-written with Petra Lüschow—was nominated for Best Picture at the Swiss Film Awards and won a Zurich Film Award the following year. *The Murder Farm* was based on Andrea Maria Schenkel's 2006 novel, *Tannöd*, inspired by the Hinterkaifeck murders in 1922.

OHMART, CAROL

Carol Omhart was an American actor born in Utah in 1927 who would work for almost 25 years across film and television. She began her career as a child singing on radio, later performing with live bands, and in 1946, she won the title Miss Utah and was a competitor in the Miss America pageant. Beginning her screen career in commercials, her horror film work includes *House on Haunted Hill* (William Castle, 1959), *Spider Baby* (Jack Hill, 1967) and *The Spectre of Edgar Allan Poe* (Mohy Quandor, 1974).

OKINA, MEGUMI

One-time J-pop singer and actor Megumi Okina was born in 1979 in Hiroshima. She is best known for her starring role as Rika Nishina in Takashi Shimizu's *Ju-On: The Grudge*, released in 2002, which became an international sensation and was remade in the United States in 2004 with Sarah Michelle Geller in the lead role. In 2004 she played the avenging ghost in Masayuki Ochiai's supernatural rape-revenge film, *Shutter*.

OLIVO, AMERICA

American actor, model and musician America Olivio was born in California in 1978 and studied at New York's Juilliard School. Her screen career began with a pilot sitcom based around her band Soluna in 2004, which brought her industry attention. Working across theater, film and television, Olivo has acted in several horror movies such as *The Last Resort* (Brandon Nutt, 2008), *Neighbor* (Robert A. Masciantonio, 2009), *Friday the 13th* (Marcus Nispel, 2009), *Circle* (Michael W. Watkins, 2010), *No One Lives* (Ryuhei Kitamura, 2012) and *Maniac* (Franck Khalfoun, 2012).

America Olivo arriving at the *Friday the 13th* premiere at Mann's Village Theater in Los Angeles, CA. on 9 February 2009. Credit: carrie-nelson / Shutterstock.com

OLSEN, ELIZABETH

At one point, Elizabeth Olsen may have been assumed to be cast in the shadow of her famous sisters, Mary-Kate and Ashley, twin fashionistas who found early fame in the '80s sitcom *Full House*. Although appearing alongside her sisters in some of their early screen work, however, Olsen has gone on to establish a strong reputation and is very much a name in her own right. Born in California in 1989, Olsen would study at Tisch School of the Arts in New York, and in 2011 she launched her career with spectacular back-to-back turns in the dark thriller *Martha Marcy May Marlene* (Sean Durkin, 2011) and the horror film *Silent House*, Laura Lau and Chris Kentis's remake of the 2010 Uruguayan film of the same name. Both films would find Olsen receiving several awards and nominations, including a Fangoria Chainsaw Award for Best Leading Actress for *Si-*

lent House. Her career would only continue to develop, and later roles include a starring role in Gareth Edwards's 2014 American remake of the famous Japanese monster movie, *Godzilla.*

Elizabeth Olsen at the *Godzilla* premiere at Dolby Theater on 8 May 2014 in Los Angeles, California. Credit: Kathy Hutchins / Shutterstock.com

ORR, MELANIE

Despite today being more well known for her work as a script supervisor and director on the popular television series such as *Orphan Black*, Melanie Orr's began her career making feature horror films. Without the access to the equipment necessary to make films as a child, she instead put her creative energies into staging plays and later directed three horror movies; *Grindstone Road* (2008), *The Devil's Mercy* (2008) and *Harm's Way* (2010). Orr has since also directed and been a script supervisor on many other television series episodes and short films.

ORLANDI, NORA

Italian horror of the 1960s and '70s has a reputation—behind the camera at least—of being a notably male-dominated affair. This is one of the many reasons composer Nora Orlandi is such a curious figure. Born in Pavia province in 1933, she was a musician from an early age, demonstrating talent with both the violin and piano. She studied at *Conservatorio di Musica Niccolò Paganini in* Genoa, and from there played with a number of orchestras. Aside from several Spaghetti Westerns, Orlandi was notable for composing the soundracks for many *gialli*; Romolo Guerrieri's *The Sweet Body of Deborah* (1968), Riccardo Freda's *Double Face* (1969), and—most famously—for Sergio Martino's *The Strange Vice of Mrs. Wardh* (1971), starring Edwige Fenech. Orlandi's track "Dies Ires" from the latter has since been reused in films including Quentin Tarantino's *Kill Bill: Vol. 2* (2004) and Bertrand Mandico's *The Wild Boys* (2017).

OTOWA, NOBUKO

Born in 1924, Japanese actor Nobuko Otowa was an extraordinarily prolific screen actor and appeared in well over 100 films in her 44-year career. She was a frequent collaborator of director Kaneto Shindo (whom she married in the late 1970s), and together they would collaborate on two of Japan's most famous horror films: *Onibaba* in 1964, and *Kuroneko* in 1968. Otowa won a Best Actress award at the the Mainichi Film Concours for the latter, and both films are considered important landmarks in Japanese film history.

OUIMET, DANIELE

As the emotionally and physically abused newlywed who turns to the dark side in Harry Kümel's 1971 lesbian vampire film *Daughters of Darkness*, French-Canadian actor Danielle Ouimet earned her place in cult film history for that role alone. She was born in Montreal in 1947 and would work in film and television until the mid 1980s, returning briefly since then in a few shorts, features and television episodes. While she has been less than complimentary about her experience working on *Daughters of Darkness*, she returned to the genre in 1972 in Jean Beaudin's *The Sensual Sorceress*.

OUSPENSKAYA, MARIA

Based on her roles in films *like The Wolf Man* (Curt Siodmak, 1941) and *Frankenstein Meets the Wolf Man* (Roy William Neill, 1943) alone, it would be far too easy to dismiss Maria Ouspenskaya as merely a character actor. But she was much, much more: born in Russia in 1876, she was a celebrated theatrical actor in Moscow, where she co-founded the

Moscow Art Theater which saw her in the same professional network as important figures like Konstantin Stanislavsky. It was when travelling internationally that she found herself in the United States and decided to remain in New York. Here she established the School of Dramatic Art, and as a teacher she taught everyone from comic, actor, screenwriter and director Elaine May to Oscar-winning actor Anne Baxter. As a screen actor she received several Oscar nominations for her film work, but it is her role in *The Wolf Man* for whom Ouspenskaya remains most widely remembered.

P

PALMER, BETSY ✓

Betsy Palmer had already established a long career on stage and screen by the time she tackled the role of Pamela Vorhees—mother of the trouble-making Jason—in Sean S. Cunningham's *Friday the 13th* (1980). Turning to a career in the arts when secretarial work proved less than fulfilling, she studied acting at Chicago's DePaul University and began working on stage, moving to New York and expanding her repertoire to film and television. Immersed in that city's performane lifestyle, she joined The Actors Studio and work extensively on Broadway. But her cult legacy is linked closely to the *Friday the 13th* series, and she would later return to the genre in mostly smaller roles in movies like *The Fear: Resurrection* (Chris Angel, 1999), *Penny Dreadful* (Bryan Norton, 2005) and *Bell Witch: The Movie* (Shane Marr, 2007). *Bell Witch* director Shane Marr would also direct the documentary *Betsy Palmer: A Scream Queen Legend* (2006).

PALMER, KEKE

R&B singer Keke Palmer also has impressive form as an actor with a close association to horror through her role as Kym on the Fox television series, *Scream Queens*. A child actor born Lauren Keyana Palmer in Illinois in 1993, she worked extensively on television and in many feature films, and aside from acting in musicals and family films and voicing animated features, she starred in Brett Simmons's monster movie *Animal* (2014). Palmer's favourite horror film is Mark Jones's *Leprechaun* (1993).

PAQUIN, ANNA ⁰

Born in Canada but raised in New Zealand, Anna Paquin stunned audiences with her breakthrough role in Jane Campion's 1993 film *The Piano*, winning an Oscar for Best Supporting Actress when she was only 11 years old. Born in 1982, she was a passionate musician and dancer before Campion selected her from the 5000 children auditioning for the role. With her starring role as Sookie Stackhouse in the vampire television series *True Blood*, Paquin would be closely linked to the genre, continually returning to it throughout her career. Paquin's most notable horror credits beyond *True Blood* are Jaume Balagueró's *Darkness* in 2002 and in Michael Dougherty's 2007 horror anthology *Trick 'r Treat* where she appears in the segment "Surprise Party".

PARKER, CHRISTINE

Micro-budget independent filmmaker Christine Parker is based in North Carolina and has a clear passion for horror, returning to it with impressive frequency across her many features and shorts. While focusing on more wholesome media production as a career, horror filmmaking remains a passion, and she has made four feature films with her production company Adrenalin, including *Forever Dead* (2007), *Fistful of Brains* (2008), *A Few Brains More* (2012), *Fix it in Post* (2014) and *Blood of the Mummy* (2018). Parker is also the force behind North Carolina's Sick Chick Flicks Festival that champions women-made horror, fantasy and scifi short films.

PARKER, ELEANOR

Three-time Oscar nominee for Best Actress, Eleanor Parker was born in Ohio in 1922, and her credits range from *The Sound of Music* (Robert Wise, 1965) to a number of horror movies. She worked for almost half a century for many of the big studios—Warner Bros., Paramount and MGM—and while she worked primarily in film, she would also turn to television, especially later in her career. Parker's horror credits include *The Mysterious Doctor* (Benjamin Stoloff, 1943), the killer ant eco-horror film *The Naked Jungle* (Byron Haskin, 1954), *Eye of the Cat* (David Lowell Rich, 1969) and John Llewellyn Moxey's 1972 made-for-television horror film, *Home for the Holidays* with Sally Field. She also appeared in an episode of the supernatural anthology television series *Circle of Fear*.

PARKER, JEAN

Jean Parker was born in Montana in 1915 and had intended a career as a visual artist before becoming an actor in Hollywood. Beginning in the early 1930s, she worked extensively for 30 years and worked in over 60 films after being discovered by the secretary of MGM Studios' Louis B. Mayer. Although working earlier in her career in René Clair's supernatural comedy *The Ghost Goes West* with Robert Donat in 1935, 1944 would be the year of her most prolific output with consecutive jobs in Edgar G. Ulmer's famous retelling of *Bluebeard* with John Carradine, Frank McDonald's *One Body Too Many* with Béla Lugosi, and Reginald Le Borg's *Dead Man's Eyes* with Lon Chaney Jr. and Acquanetta.

PARKINS, BARBARA

Finding fame on the popular soap opera *Peyton Place*, Barbara Parkins' cult reputation stems from the trash masterpiece *Valley of the Dolls*, Mark Robson's 1967 film adaptation based on Jacqueline Susan's bestselling novel of the same name. Born in Canada in 1942, she studied dance at high school when she moved to Hollywood in her mid-teens and began making small appearances in film and television in her early 20s. Moving to England soon after the critically (although not commercially) unsuccessful release of *Valley of the Dolls*, it was here that she would be cast in a number of horror films like *The Mephisto Waltz* with an evil, skivvy-wearing pre-*M*A*S*H* Alan Alda (Paul Wendkos, 1971), and in the segment "Frozen Fear" in Roy Ward Baker's Amicus anthology film *Asylum* (1972). In 1971, she would also co-star with Barbara Stanwyck in the made-for-TV horror film *A Taste of Evil*, directed by John Llewellyn Moxey.

PARSONS, NANCY

Born in Minnesota in 1942, Nancy Parsons has the rare privilege of claiming memorable and truly unique roles in two of the most beloved cult films of the 1980s: Bob Clark's *Porkys* (1982), and Kevin Connor's *Motel Hell* (1980). While later also appearing in *Porky's II: The Next Day* (Bob Clark, 1983) and *Porky's Revenge!* (James Komack, 1985), Parsons began her career with small roles in films like the dark schizo-fantasy *I Never Promised You a Rose Garden* (Anthony Page, 1977), and her later credits would include Clint Eastwood's rape-revenge film *Sudden Impact* (1983) and *Steel Magnolias* (Herbert Ross, 1989). But it is as Ida in *Motel Hell* that renders Parsons such an important woman in horror: wild, demented and vicious, she's precisely the kind of actor that keeps the genre alive.

PASCAL, FRANÇOISE

French-Mauritian actor Françoise Pascal was born in 1949 and would in the late 1970s find her greatest fame on the ghastly British sitcom *Mind Your Language*. Her early career would be marked in several sex films made by British directors later more commonly linked to horror—Norman J. Warren and Pete Walker—also having a small uncredited role in Robert Hartford-Davis's 1970 horror film *Incense for the Damned*. In 1973, she starred in Jean Rollin's horror film *The Iron Rose*, followed in 1978 in Rollin's zombie film *The Grapes of Death*, both films establishing her cult reputation and linking her closely to the famous French director.

PATRICK, MILICENT

Until Mallory O'Meara's much-anticipated biography *The Lady from the Black Lagoon: Hollywood Monsters and the Lost Legacy of Milicent Patrick,* little was currently known about enigmatic, prolific and highly influential make-up and special effects artist. Patrick is synonymous with her design work on the 'Gill-man' costume in the Jack Arnold's legendary 1954 monster film *Creature from the Black Lagoon,* and her work has also been an important part of the key designs so important to horror and scifi films including *It Came from Outer Space* (Jack Arnold, 1053), *Abbott and Costello Meet Dr. Jekyll and Mr. Hyde* (Charles Lamont, 1953), *This Island Earth* (Jack Arnold and Joseph M. Newman, 1955), and *The Mole People* (Virgil W. Vogel, 1956). Patrick was also an actor although has largely gone uncredited for many of her roles.

PAUL, ALEXANDRA—INTERVIEW (JUNE 2018) ⸱

Activist, actress, *Baywatch* alumna, and producer Alexandra Paul has worked across a range of genres, but for those interested in horror she is a familiar and always-welcome presence. A performer whose horror work spans desperate innocence and unabashed ferocity, her many credits in the genre include *American Nightmare* (Don McBrearty, 1983), *The Paperboy* (Douglas Jackson, 1994), *Piranha* (Scott P. Levy, 1995), *Spectre* (Scott P. Levy, 1996), and of course John Carpenter's 1983 screen adaptation of Stephen King's novel *Christine,* in which she co-starred with Keith Gordon and John Stockwell.

Alexandra has worked across film, television, and web series, and has co-written and co-produced a number of documentaries and television shows. She also works as a health coach, and in 2005 was named Activist of the Year by the American Civil Liberties Union of Southern California for her dedication to environmental issues, voter rights, and the peace movement.

http://alexandrapaul.com/

I believe one of your first feature film roles was a small but crucial part in the horror film *American Nightmare* – it's quite an unflinching film, what was the experience on set?

American Nightmare was actually my first paid acting gig, although I prefer to forget about it! My boyfriend, Lawrence Day, was starring in the film, so that is how I got the part—I cannot even recall if I auditioned, but I do remember when I got on set they wanted me to take a toke from a marijuana cigarette which I didn't know how to do. I had never smoked or done any drugs in real life, so needless to say I didn't look very expert onscreen.

Alexandra Paul in *Christine* (John Carpenter, 1983). Credit: Columbia/Photofest © Columbia Pictures.

My character, a prostitute, just has one line and then gets killed by the murderer. That line was later dubbed by someone else—I cannot recall if it was because the sound was bad and I was out of town when post production was being done, or because I was so bad the producers wanted to improve my performance! In any case, I was also left off the credits when it played in theaters, which was unfortunately corrected for the video release because I had more of a name by then! After that first acting role, I have played several prostitutes and I have done a much better job, because I have interviewed call girls in person. Luckily, I have never had to smoke for a role since.

Then of course was *Christine*, a film whose impact relies so heavily on the key performances of yourself and Keith Gordon to make the fantastic premise so human and believable. How did you approach your character for that film, and how much did you work with John Carpenter on developing the nuances of Leigh that make her so sympathetic?

John told me later he cast me because I had an innocence he was looking for, so that role was not a stretch. I was still a teenager myself, anyway. I read the Stephen King book upon which the screenplay was based, broke down the script in terms of Leigh's background, motivations, and her shifting feelings about John Stockwell's character Dennis, Keith's Arnie and Christine, the car herself.

The Paperboy is a very traditional horror film in a lot of respects, but also one that has really important things to say about trauma and abuse. I'd love to hear what you took from the experience of making that film, and also your thoughts on your character's role.

Even though I am not a mother in real life, I really enjoy having kids onscreen! My first role as a mom was when I was 23, and because it was a period piece I had 3 children. I am still in touch with Chad Tucker, who was 6 when he played my middle child in that movie (and who is married with kids of his own now), but I was terrified of holding the baby, in case I dropped her! Anyway, in *The Paperboy,* I loved having scenes where I was a loving, fun mom and the scenes where I was the ferocious protective tigress.

Spectre is such a classic haunted house films in so many ways, and such a beautiful location. What was working in Ireland like, and I'm curious how much of that film was sets and real locations?

That film was so fun to shoot. All my projects have been fun to shoot, but I really enjoyed the two Roger Corman films I have done, because I like the ingenuity of figuring out how to make a good movie on a small budget.

This film was shot in Spiddal, Ireland in 1995. The arts minister was from the area, so money had been allocated for a studio to be built there to encourage filmmaking. We were one of the first movies to be shot in Spiddal, and I recall my makeup artist was a housewife who had assisted on the previous movie but who otherwise had no makeup experience and never wore makeup herself! That was all fine with me, as I loved how little time my make-up took and how little we applied.

We filmed entirely on location—the mansion in which my character lived was spectacularly spooky, and the landscape was gorgeous.

I only saw Piranha for the first time recently, and it made me think about your passion for animals. It's an interesting film in terms of the nature-fights-back trope.

The *Piranha* I filmed was an almost word for word remake of the original Corman produced/ John Sayles written/ Joe Dante directed movie done 17 years before. As I said, Corman liked to save money and redoing a project is a great way to do that, especially because we used some of the same piranha footage.

The lesson here is that human beings' hubris, especially when it comes to technology, will come back to bite us in the ass (pun intended!). And that you cannot beat Mother Nature. Which I am all about, as an environmentalist and a vegan.

Having worked across so many genres so successfully in both film and television, as a performer what is unique about horror that no other kind of project allows you to do?

Horror allows women to be fierce! Women get to fight on par with a man, unlike westerns or thrillers where generally she is saved by some guy who takes care of the problem.

Also, I love horror fans. They are so passionate, loyal, and knowledgeable about horror films. I love meeting them at autograph signings and finding out about what they love to watch and to read. *It* seems to be a favorite Stephen King book, which I haven't read or seen because I am too much of a scaredy cat. But I love *making* horror movies as an actress!

PAXSON, MADELLAINE

Madellaine Paxson's filmography is a thing of beauty: there, hidden underneath a seemingly endless stream of screenwriting credits for kids shows including the *Power Rangers*, *Kim Possible*, *Peter Rabbit* and *Kuu Kuu Harajuku*, is one lone, single feature film directing credit. 2014's *Blood Punch* is as far from child-friendly entertainment as you can get. Uniting crystal meth, rehab and interdimensional time-twisting, *Blood Punch* remains Paxson's only feature directorial credit, but for sheer imagination and ambition it is hoped it won't remain so for long.

PAXTON, SARA

Sara Paxton's first real association with horror was as Mari Collingwood in Dennis Iliadis's 2009 remake of *The Last House on the Left*. Paxton was born in California in 1988 and although appearing in a range of genres across her career, her relationship to horror would continue with other credits in movies such as *Shark Night* (David R. Ellis, 2011), *The Innkeepers* (Ti West, 2011), *Enter Nowhere* (Jack Heller, 2011), *Cheap Thrills* (E.L. Katz, 2013) and *The Briar Lakes Murders* (David R. Ellis, 2013). She also starred in the 2006 made-for-television family movie *Return to Halloweentown*, and in 2017 played Vegas-dwelling Candy Shaker in the third series of David Lynch and Mark Frost's *Twin Peaks*.

PEABODY, SANDRA

Sara Paxton may have updated the character of Mari Collingwood for a new generation, but it was Sandra Peabody who played her in Wes Craven's original 1972 version of *The Last House on the Left*. Born in 1948 in Oregon, she had some minor roles on stage before *Last House on the Left*, after which Peabody's career would be affiliated primarily with exploitation movie roles after this, and she worked in a few other horror films including *Voices of Desire* (Mark Ubell, 1972), *Massage Parlor Murders!* (Chester Fox and Alex Stevens, 1973), and *Legacy of Satan* (Gerard Damiano, 1974). She worked for some time behind the scenes on films after becoming disillusioned with the kinds of movies she was appearing in and moved finally to working on children's television as a writer and producer.

PEARL, DOROTHY J.

Known to friends and colleagues as Dottie, Dorothy J. Pearl worked was an award-winning make-up artist who has worked with directors including Tim Burton, Steven Spielberg, Julie Taymor and Martin Scorsese. She made her film debut as the make-up artist on one of the most notorious and beloved horror films of all-time—Tobe Hooper's *The Texas Chain Saw Massacre* in 1974—and would later work with Hooper on *Poltergeist* (1982). Pearl's other horror credits include *Race with the Devil* (Jack Starrett, 1975), *Love at First Bite* (Stan Dragoti, 1979), *11:14* (Greg Marcks, 2003), and Lauren Petzke's 2013 short *Zombiewood*.

PEETERS, BARBARA

Along with Stephanie Rothman, Barbara Peeters was one of two women directors working for Roger Corman's New World Pictures during the 1970s, although she worked in a variety of other roles including writer, actor and production assistant. Peeters began her career doing make-up and script supervision, and across her career would make a variety of films including sex comedies and exploitation film. But it was her 1980 monster film *Humanoids from the Deep* that has made her a cult figure: despite her fame being so closely connected to that film, she was unhappy that Corman made so many changes to it without her permission. Despite her request that her name be removed from the credits, it was not, and her name remains closely tied to the final product. Peeters would go on to work extensively on television and establish her own production company.

PEIRONE, MITZI

With a background in modeling and acting, much of the media excitement about Mitzi Peirone's 2018 feature film debut—the horror film *Braid*—stems from its status as the first film fully funded by cryptocurrency. This aside, the film is groundbreaking in other ways. An intense, at times even psychedelic tale about womens' friendship and identity gone terribly wrong, *Braid* was expanded from Peirone's previous short film *Chaosmos* (2016) in which she also starred, made the same year as her filmmaking debut, the short film *Vesperlings*. Very much Peirone's creation, on *Braid* she was producer, writer and director, premiering at the Tribeca Film Festival.

PEIRCE, KIMBERLY

In 1999, filmmaker Kimberly Peirce stunned audiences with her chilling feature film debut *Boys Don't Cry* about the real-life murder of Brandon Teena, a transgender man raped and murdered in Nebraska in 1993. Later in her career, she would move to horrors of a more traditional nature in her 2013 remake of *Carrie*, originally made by Brian De Palma in 1976. Perice was born in Pennyslvania in 1967 and began her career as a photographer in Japan and New York. After studying literature at the University of Chicago, she gained a Masters of Fine Arts at Columbia University in film where her student film saw her screened at Switzerland's Locarno Film Festival. An early short she made as a student on Brandon Teena's death caught the attention of famed indie producer Christine Vachon, who collaborated with her on developing the project into a feature. The film would go on to critical acclaim, garnering an Oscar for Hilary Swank in the lead role and a nomination for Chloë Sevigny for Best Supporting Actress.

PETERSON, KRISTINE

Kristine Peterson worked in a range of capacities across films both famous, notorious, and unknown. Working in the Zoetrope office during the production of Francis Ford Coppola's *Apocalypse Now* (1979), she would later go on to take a more central role in several horror films as either director of second assistant director. Her work as an assistant director early in her career garnered her credits on horror films including *The Supernaturals* (Armand Mastroianni, 1986), *Chopping Mall* (Jim Wynorski, 1986), Janet Greek's girl-gang rape-revenge film *The Ladies Club* (1986), *Nightflyers* (T.C. Blake, 1987), *Tremors* (Ron Underwood, 1990) and *A Nightmare on Elm Street: The Dream Child* (Stephen Hopkins, 1990). Peterson later turned to directing with a number of features including the horror movies *Deadly Dreams* (1988) and *Critters 3* (1991).

PELUPESSY, RUTH

Indonesian actor Ruth Pelupessy was born in 1940 in what was then the European colony known as the Dutch East Indies. She studied teaching at *Sekolah Guru Kepandaian Putri*, and amongst her many film credits she starred in Sisworo Gautama Putra's 1980 horror film *Satan's Slave* which received widespread international release. Although superficially evoking many key aspects of *Phantasm* (Don Coscarelli, 1979), *Satan's Slave* is noteworthy for its Islamic themes. The following year she worked with Putra again on the sequel to the 1984 Indonesian horror film *Telaga Angker* called *Sundelbolong*, in which she co-starred with horror icon Suzzanna.

PEPPARD, ISABEL—INTERVIEW (JUNE 2018)

Isabel Peppard is the exact opposite of the hackneyed cliché of the blonde haired, tan, bikini-wearing Australian woman and prides herself on it, and her art has as the same powerful, energetic presence as Peppard herself does in person. Based in the Australian city of Melbourne, Peppard's 2012 short dark fantasy animation *Butterflies*—voiced by Rachel Griffiths—played internationally at over 50 film festivals including high profile events such as Sitges International Fantastic Film Festival and the Annecy International Animated Film Festival, and would garner the artist and filmmaker a number of awards.

She was also a recipient of Screen Australia's The Directors Acclaim fund which supported a mentorship in Los Angeles with filmmaker Jennifer Lynch (*Boxing Helena*, *Surveillance*, *Chained*, *Hisss*). In 2015, her feature horror film script *Silk* won a project award at South Korea's prestigious Bucheon International Fantastic Film Festival.

Peppard recently co-directed *Morgana* with Josie Hess, a pro-sex, body-positive documentary about an Australian woman who began a career as a porn star later in life.

www.butterfliesanimation.com

To call you merely a 'filmmaker' does quite the disservice to your remarkable range of skills as both a visual artist and a storyteller—I tend to think of you more as a 'maker', I guess, which sounds simplistic perhaps but feels to more generously encompass the diversity of your talents. How do you identify yourself professionally, if there is indeed even a need to?

I'd probably identify myself as an artist I think. I started in creature effects and used the skills that I learnt in that field to attack a wide variety of art forms, from costume, to murals and even performance. That being said I am more drawn to film than any other medium and a lot of the sculptural and 'making' work I do is designed to create unique visual worlds for my film projects.

What is your first memory of being exposed to and finding pleasure in dark stories or imagery?

I've often wondered why I'm so obsessed with horror and to be honest it is hard to pinpoint but I think I can trace it back to an early age. As a child, I lived in Japan and there was a temple near our home that had two frightening statues of monstrous 'Nio' or temple guardians out the front. As a young girl, I was terrified of them and didn't want to walk past. For some reason that fear became obsession and I fell in love with them. I would pose and pull monstrous faces in an attempt to embody the statues that once scared me so much. After that I was all in!

I was a compulsive reader of fairy tales and mythology, particularly loving stories of Faustian pacts. From that I progressed to wilderness survival stories, the black plague, and medieval torture. Just the average reading list for a young lady!

Artist and filmmaker Isabel Peppard. Used with permission.

You made quite the splash with your beautiful animated dark fantasy film *Butterflies*, which screened internationally and met with such strong acclaim. Can you tell me about the development of that project, whether you expected the response to it that it received, and how Rachel Griffiths got involved?

I first had the seeds of what *Butterflies* became while I was in a deep depression, during a particularly difficult time in my life. I think I personally felt like I was losing my soul or becoming invisible in a way. It was really about using creativity to claw my way back to the land of the living and find my identity again. The seeds of imagery started to come to me and I wrote the first draft with my producer but I was constantly rewriting all the way through the shoot. Even though it was financed through Screen Australia the build and shoot was incredibly gruelling given that I had to function in multiple roles from set building and puppet making to directing and animating.

I wasn't necessarily expecting the response it got but given the personal nature of the material I was glad that people had an emotional response and could relate to my story.

We got Rachel Griffiths involved through a visual pitch combined with the script. She was actually the first human (non-puppet) actor I have ever worked with so it was a real baptism of fire! It ended up being a wonderful experience though. She was very a bright and collaborative woman who actually had a lot to contribute to the role.

You've worked and collaborated with some of Australia's most celebrated artists and filmmakers like Adam Elliot and Patricia Piccinini, and on your latest project, the documentary *Morgana*, you are co-directing with Josie Hess. I'd love to ask you about the benefits of collaboration, and how it stands in contrast to your creative practice as an artist that is clearly more an individual experience? Do you prefer working in a team or by yourself, or do both have benefits?

Artist and filmmaker Isabel Peppard sculpting a maggot. Used with permission.

I've definitely learned a lot from everyone I have worked with and a lot of the skills I have picked up along the way have helped to refine my personal work. When it comes to filmmaking, I love the collaborative aspect. When you have a great team it's really exciting to see something grow from each person putting their individual stamp on it. As a director, you get to watch the seed of your idea germinate and take form with the contribution of the other creatives on the crew, it's exciting! Seeing those images in my head become a reality on film is one of my favourite things about directing.

The only work I really do alone is sculpting and while I enjoy the control it gives me I definitely prefer a collaborative process. In my experience working with the right team and having someone to bounce off can keep the energy in a project and help push ideas forward.

I understand you did a scriptwriting mentorship with Jennifer Lynch in Los Angeles that resulted from funding from Screen Australia. How did that come about, and what was that experience like?

After *Butterflies,* I was awarded The Directors Acclaim fund which allowed me to travel to Los Angeles to work with Jen on my feature script. Working with Jen was an amazing experience and left me with a deep love and respect for her as an artist and a human being. We mainly wrote together and drank a lot of coffee! It was also a great insight into the into the business of making films in LA and how to navigate that world.

While *Morgana* is clearly your primary focus at the moment, I'd love to hear about your horror film script *Silk* that won you a project award at the Bucheon International Fantastic Film Festival in 2015. So many Australian artists seem to be in denial about the reality that we are in closer proximity to Asia than Europe and the United States, it's interesting to me that you have sought inspiration from cultural traditions much closer to home.

I think with *Silk* I was inspired by my childhood in Japan and particularly the Japanese fairy tales that my parents introduced me to around shape shifting weavers and spider women. *Silk* tells the story of two sisters forced to immigrate to the Australian outback after losing their mother. It explores themes of cultural alienation and dehumanization through the lens of a feminist fairy tale/creature feature. I like to think of it as *Pan's Labyrinth* meets *Wake in Fright*!

I've always been fascinated by how you have embraced a gothic aesthetic and sensibility in both your work and your own identity, but have been so defiantly disinterested in restricting that solely to a 'scene'. What is it about this aesthetic that appeals to you?

From *Butterflies* (Isabel Peppard, 2012). Used with permission.

Ha ha, I honestly don't know! I think it just is a product of my lifelong love of horror and dark imagery. I also think that I felt much more at home in my skin when I started art directing my appearance in my early teens. Given that I spend a lot of my time in workshops these days I am usually dressed in grubby overalls and steel capped boots so I am basically 90 percent slob and 10 percent glamour ghoul!

You are a very familiar face in the Australian women in horror community, and have often been involved in Hobart's Stranger With My Face film festival. How did you first discover this community of like-minded others, and what are the benefits of networks like this in a country as small as Australia?

I think I first became part of that community when the wonderful Briony Kidd approached me to screen Butterflies at the festival. Discovering a group of supportive and likeminded women who also made horror was pretty profound for me actually! It felt like I had found my tribe! Everyone comes from different backgrounds and walks of life but there is a real kinship there in our shared experiences of filmmaking and life as women in the world. Stranger With My Face has effectively established an international network of women making horror and really opened up the genre world for us Aussie gals toiling away in the southern hemisphere.

PERELLO, HOPE

Although appearing to cease working in film in the late 1990s, Hope Perello has a fascinating filmography not only in a range of production contexts but also as a director. As a production coordinator, she worked on horror films including *Troll* (John Carl Buechler, 1986), and with Stuart Gordon on both *From Beyond* (1986) and *Dolls* (1987). She also collaborated with director David Schmoeller on films such as *Crawlspace* (1986), *Catacombs* (1988) and *Puppetmaster* (1989), the latter on which she was also second unit director. As a feature film director in her own right, her most notable horror credit is *Howling VI: The Freaks* (1991).

PERFILI, VIRGINIA

Virginia Perfili is closely affiliated with the *Mirror, Mirror* franchise. She studied at Wayne State University and is currently the director of the board of the Lifton Institute for Media Arts and Sciences in Burbank, the media training school of Jimmy Lifton who produced Marina Sargenti's *Mirror, Mirror* in 1990, and directed its sequel, *Mirror, Mirror 2: Raven Dance* (1994). Perfili was an executive director on both *Mirror, Mirror, Mirror, Mirror 2* (which she co-wrote), and *Mirror, Mirror III: The Voyeur* (1995), the latter of which was also her feature film directorial debut. Perfili made a small cameo in the first film in the series, and recently returned to feature filmmaking, writing and co-directing *Cheerleader Chainsaw Chicks*.

PERKINS, EMILY*

Canadian actor Emily Perkins was born in 1977 in Vancouver, and became a horror icon for her dual roles as Brigitte in the *Ginger Snaps* films and Beverly in Tommy Lee Wallace's 1990 made-for-television miniseries adaptation of Stephen King's *It*. Across her filmography, she returned to horror again later in her career in *Blood: A Butcher's Tale* (Mark Tuit, 2010) and Colin Minihan's scifi-horror hybrid *Extraterrestrial* (2014), and she appeared in horror-themed television shows such as *The X-Files*, *Dead Like Me*, *The Twilight Zone* and *Supernatural*.

PETERSEN, CASSANDRA (ELVIRA)—INTERVIEW (2002) ⌐

This interview was originally published in FIEND Magazine in 2002. Many thanks to Jarod Collard and Ground Under Productions (and Lolita).

It's virtually impossible not to read the Elvira phenomenon as a kind of gothic postmodern victory. While Elvira herself obviously carries strong nostalgic references to the hot-rod and horror movie imbued fifties, the life of her alter-ego Cassandra Peterson reads like a who's who of 20th century pop culture; "At the age of 14, I was a go-go dancer and at 17, I became the youngest showgirl in Vegas," starts Peterson. "Somehow it led to me getting career advice from the King himself, Elvis Presley. I left Vegas after that, and cruised around Europe for a year and a half. While in Rome, a chance encounter with an old friend got me an introduction to Fredrico Fellini and I got a small part in his film Roma… After returning to the States and dancing in a show at the Miami Beach Playboy Club, I moved to Los Angeles to pursue acting and after just 12 short years of starving and auditioning, I heard a local TV station was looking for a horror host. I responded."

More correctly, Elvira responded. Motivated by a passion for old horror films and the practical necessity of paid work, Cassandra donned the black wig that has iconised a genre and a star was born. It was through this role, as the televisual hostess for an endless list of B-grade horror and scifi classics that Elvira clawed her way out of the grave of anonymity and into our hearts. Over the course of a long and varied career, her resumé is remarkable: The first nationally syndicated horror show host; the first person to be broadcast in 3D; the first celebrity to market her own beer; and perhaps most astonishing of all, the first female to twirl tassels from her breasts on American network television

"What can I say about my boobs?" she asks. "People question if they're real and I have to admit they're not. I keep the real ones in a safe place and rarely take them out because I don't want to risk getting them lost or stolen."

But her achievements don't stop there: She has been in over 500 television shows; has had pinball machines and comics dedicated to her; and has made many films including her last, *Elvira's Haunted Hills*, a project that has been one of her most difficult to date.

After a series of false starts, Elvira's Haunted Hills was eventually financed by Peterson herself. "Making a film on your own with your own money is a very daunting experience," she says. "It ultimately proved to be a vanity project. I don't know that I'd recommend making a film on your own to anyone unless you just want to do it for the sheer creative experience and not the money". Despite the fiscal pitfalls, responses to the film have thus far been very positive. Shot on location in Romania, *Elvira's Haunted Hills*—as the title implies—carries all the traits of the British styled sexual double entendre that has so endeared the character to audiences for over two decades.

Cassandra Peterson at the "Elvira: Mistress Of The Dark" coffin table book launch at Roosevelt Hotel on 17 October 2016 in Los Angeles, California. Credit: Kathy Hutchins / Shutterstock.com

It's pulp, but Elvira has never pretended to be anything else. Peterson's heart lies in the horror classics, and it is these films that inspire so much of Elvira's camp humour. "They're so naïve, and that quality is gone and lost forever," she bemoans. "I don't call 'slasher' movies horror anymore. I call them the 5:00 news". Elvira's world is not one of victims and perpetrators, and this is perhaps where much of her appeal lies. "I've made a very concerted effort in my career to make sure that Elvira stands up for herself", says Peterson. "No matter what perils befall her, no 'knight in shining armour' shows up to save her.

She does it herself." Peterson continues, "Elvira may not be the smartest woman alive, but she has tremendous courage, self-esteem, and confidence".

However, Peterson is still not sure about how she feels about Elvira as a role model. "She treats men like many men treat women, as sex objects, and isn't afraid of using her physical 'assets' to get what she wants," she says. "I get lots and lots of mail from girls and young women telling me what a strong role model Elvira was for them growing up. In one way that scares me, but in another, it's the best part about playing Elvira". She is clear, however, on her opinion of one subculture that so passionately embraced her: "I love the whole goth culture! I don't mean to sound conceited, but I feel that in some way I actually contributed to it. I was certainly doing that drag long before I saw it on the streets", she says. "When I was a teenager, we didn't have a word for it. I was just a weird looking geek".

PFIEFFER, MICHELLE ₵

Celebrated American actor Michelle Pfeiffer may not be immediately linked to horror, but she has done some impressive and important work in the genre. Born in California in 1958, her relationship to cult film began early in her career with her starring role in *Grease 2* (Patricia Birch, 1982). She began her career in beauty pageants and soon moved to acting, appearing on television from the late 1970s. Amongst her many impressive film credits are her starring roles in George Miller's supernatural comedy *The Witches of Eastwick* (1987), Mike Nichols' *Wolf* (1994), Robert Zemeckis's *What Lies Beneath* (2000), Tim Burton's *Dark Shadows* (2012) and Darren Aronofsky's psychological horror film *Mother!* (2017).

PHILBIN, MARY

A horror superstar of the silent era, Mary Philbin was linked closely to the genre most famously for her iconic performance as Christine in Rupert Julian's 1925 version of *The Phantom of the Opera*, the woman who famously removed Lon Chaney's title character's mask. Philbin was born in 1902 in Chicago, signing to Universal Studios when Erich von Stroheim discovered her after she moved to California after winning a beauty pageant. Although later going on to star in films such as D.W. Griffith's *Drums of Love* (1928), *The Phantom of the Opera* remains her most famous role, and she also starred that same year

Elvira (aka Cassandra Peterson) at the 2016 Knott's Scary Farm at Knott's Berry Farm on 30 September 2016 in Buena Park, California. Credit: Kathy Hutchins / Shutterstock.com

with Conrad Veidt in Paul Leni's horror-romance *The Man Who Laughs*. She largely retired from the film industry in the late 1920s with the onset of sound technology.

PHILLIPS, BIJOU

Born into a celebrity family, model and actor Bijou Phillips has a perhaps surprisingly long relationship with the horror genre. In 2003, she appeared in Marcus Adams's *Octane*, later cast in *Venom* (Jim Gillespe, 2005), Jeremy Kasten's 2007 remake of Herschell Gordon Lewis's 1970 film *The Wizard of Gore* with Crispin Glover, and—most famously—in Eli Roth's *Hostel: Part II* (2007) with Lauren German and Heather Matarazzo. She also starred in Josef Rusnak's 2009 film *It's Alive*, itself a remake of Larry Cohen's 1974 film of the same name. As a singer, Phillips's song "Polite" was included on the soundtrack of Danny Cannon's teen horror blockbuster *I Still Know What You Did Last Summer* (1998).

PICASSO, PALOMA

French born designer Anne Paloma Ruiz-Picasso y Gilot—known simply as Paloma Picasso—may be more instantly renowned for professionally following her famous artist father's interest in the visual arts, and yet her single film credit tantalizingly suggests an alternate career that, had it continued, been just as spectacular. In 1973, she famously played notorious Hungarian serial killer Countess Elizabeth Báthory in Polish auteur Walerian Borowczyk's art-horror masterpiece, *Immoral Tales*. One of the film's most famous images—indeed, one of the most immediately recognizable images from across Borowzyck's entire ouvere—is of Picasso bathing in blood in one of the film's most memorable scenes. To her credit, she bathed in actual pig's blood, granting the scene a strong degree of authenticity. But this fact alone perhaps might indicate why she never acted in another film—horror or otherwise—again.

PIERONI, ANIA

Italian actor Ania Pieroni might be most readily recognizable to horror fans for two small but highly memorable roles in two of Dario Argento's most beloved films. In 1980, she played a music student holding a cat in *Inferno*, a character later revealed to be Mater Lachrymarum (a character she was rumored to have been offered again in Argento's 2007 finale of the *Three Mothers* trilogy, *The Mother of Tears*). As a brunette, she later was cast in Argento's *giallo Tenebrae* as an unfortunate shoplifter early in the film, one of that movie's first victims. In 1981, she played a babysitter in Lucio Fulci's *The House by the Cemetery*, and her final film role was as Countess Oniria in the horror-comedy *Who's Afraid of Dracula?* (Neri Parenti, 1985).

PITT, INGRID

Born Ingoushka Petrov in Warsaw in 1937, horror legend Ingrid Pitt experienced very real horrors early in her life during her imprisonment with her Jewish family by the Nazis in the Stutthof concentration camp. Briefly married to an American soldier after her release, she moved from Berlin to California and then back to Europe where she established herself as a hugely successful screen actor, linked primarily to Hammer studio's horror output of the 1960s and '70s. Although appearing in spy films, historical romances and scifi films, it was with Hammer films including *The Vampire Lovers* (Roy 1970) and *Countess Dracula* (Peter Sasdy, 1971) that her fame largely rests. Her other horror credits include the anthology *The House that Dripped Blood* (Peter Duffell, 1971), *The Wicker Man* (Robin Hardy, 1973), *Underworld* (Clive Barker, 1985), *Minotaur* (Jonathan English, 2006), *Beyond the Rave* (Matthias Hoene, 2008), and *Sea of Dust* (Scott Bunt, 2008). Pitt was also a prolific writer, and her books include *The Ingrid Pitt Bedside Companion for Vampire Lovers* (1998), *The Ingrid Pitt Bedside Companion for Ghost-hunters* (1999) and *The Ingrid Pitt Book of Murder, Torture and Depravity* (2000). In 1998, she provided narration in character as Countess Elizabeth Báthory on Cradle of Filth's album, *Cruelty and the Beast*.

Ingrid Pitt in *The Vampire Lovers* (Roy Ward Baker, 1970). Credit: American International Pictures/Photofest © American International Pictures

PLATT, POLLY

Born in 1939 in Illinois, Polly Platt was a screenwriter, production designer and producer. She met Peter Bogdonavich—with whom she would collaborate with extensively (as well as marry)—when she was working as a costume designer in the New York theater. She was a production co-ordinator on Bogdanovich's *Voyage to the Planet of the Prehistoric Women* (1968), and with Bogdonovich, she co-wrote his remarkable serial killer film *Tar-*

gets (1968), which features Boris Karloff's final film performance. She was a production designer on a number of films including *Targets* and George Miller's *The Witches of East-wick* in 1987 starring Cher, Susan Sarandon and Michelle Pfieffer. Platt was also a long-term collaborator with James L. Brooks and plays a significant part of *The Simpsons* story, and in 1994 she received the Women in Film Crystal Award for her significant services to the screen industry. Just before her death in 2011, she was an executive producer on the documentary *Corman's World: Exploits of a Hollywood Rebel*.

PLATT, RUTH

British actor, filmmaker and screenwriter Ruth Platt studied at University College Oxford and the esteemed Royal Academy of Dramatic Arts (RADA) in London. As an actor, her most highly acclaimed performance was in Roman Polanski's *The Pianist* (2002), but as a writer and director she began her career with the shorts *Stealing Up* (2005) and *The Heart Fails Without Warning* (2013). In 2015, she wrote and directed the horror film *The Lesson*, inspired by the films of Michael Haneke about a teacher who abducts two students (Platt at one stage was a teacher herself).

PLEASENCE, ANGELA

Born Daphne Anne Angela Pleasence in 1941 in Sheffield, while her father Donald may be a horror film icon, although having only a fraction of his genre credits, Angela Pleasence is no less a memorable presence in the few horror films in which she appeared. Studying at London's Royal Academy of Dramatic Art and beginning her career on the stage, she is renowned for her work in historical dramas and literary adaptations on British television. But her work in horror is remarkable: the beautiful and oppressive mood of José Ramón Larraz's magnum opus *Symptoms* (1974) relies heavily on Pleasence's performance, and while a smaller role, her monstrous maternal stranger in Gabrielle Beaumont's *The Godsend* (1980) is one of the most disturbing and ominous performances in a British horror film of the period. Pleasence would appear alongside her father in the segment "An Act of Kindness" in Kevin Connor's 1974 Amicus horror anthology *From Beyond the Grave*, and she was one of many stars from that era to make a cameo in the 2001 horror spoof television series *Dr. Terrible's House of Horrible*.

POINTER, PRISCILLA

Born in New York in 1924, Priscilla Pointer's career was tied closely to her many successes on the stage, but she also had a notable film career. Most famously from a horror perspective is her role in Brian De Palma's *Carrie* (1976) as Mrs Snell, mother of Sue Snell played by Pointer's real-life daughter, Amy Irving. Pointer and Irving would work together again as mother and daughter in both *Honeysuckle Rose* (Jerry Schatzberg, 1980) and *Carried Away* (Bruno Barreto, 1996). Pointer's other horror roles include the anthology *Twilight Zone: The Movie* (1983), *Nightmare on Elm Street 3: Dream Warriors* (Chuck Russell, 1987), *C.H.U.D. II: Bud the C.H.U.D.* (David K. Irving, 1989) and *Disturbed* (Charles Winkler, 1990), as well as working in a number of dark-themed cult films including *Mommie Dearest* (Frank Perry, 1981), *Looking for Mr. Goodbar* (Richard Brooks, 1977) and David Lynch's *Blue Velvet* (1986) as Mrs. Beaumont.

POLLACCHI, PAULA

One of Argentina's first and most prolific women horror film directors, Paula Pollacchi studied at Buenos Aires's Escuela Nacional de Experimentación y Realización Cinematográfica (National School of Film Experimentation and Production) and began her career making commercials and music videos. With influences including Dario Argento and Edgar Allan Poe, she was attracted by the subversive potential of the horror genre from a young age. Beginning directing in 1997, she found horror to be an ideal space for women to express anger at what she feels is their widespread mistreatment in her culture. Pollacchi's extremely low-budget films find her working across a range of roles beyond director, including cinematographer, writer, producer and editor. Aside from several shorts that attracted attention on the international festival circuit, Pollacchi's feature horror films include *Inzomnia* (1997) and *Baño de sangre* (2003).

PONDER, STACIE

Stacie Ponder is a writer, artist and filmmaker from New England in the United States. Renowned for her famous horror blog *Final Girl*, Ponder also shifted her remarkable talents behind the camera as director of the shorts *Itch* (2010) and *Buyer Beware: Soulmates* (2016), as well as directing, writing, producing and acting as cinematographer on her 2010 feature film *Ludlow*, starring cult actor Shannon Lark. Aside from being an active writer on videogames, Ponder also write the book *Death Count: All of the Deaths in the Friday the 13th Film Series, Illustrated* and is currently writing a monograph on *Martyrs* (Pascal Laugier, 2008).

PONS, BEATRICE

Beatrice Pons was a character actor whose career spanned almost four decades. Born in 1906, she worked on both screen and stage extensively, although for horror fans she is best known for her role as the vicious matriarch in Troma's *Mother's Day* (directed by Lloyd Kaufman's brother, Charles Kaufman), where she appeared under the pseudonym Rose Ross.

POWLEY, BEL

Isobel Powley—commonly credited as Bel—is a British actor who was born in London in 1992. She began her acting career in 2007 largely on television, later moving to both film and the theater. In 2017, she played Claire Clairmont in Haifaa al-Mansour's biopic *Mary Shelley* as the stepsister of the famous 19th century horror writer and author of *Frankenstein* (1818), followed in 2018 by a powerful starring role in Fritz Böhm's horror film *Wilding*.

PRESTON, GAYLENE

One of New Zealand's most important and celebrated filmmakers, Gaylene Preston is broadly renowned for her documentary filmmaking with a strong feminist edge, however she has also made numerous fictional feature films. Born on the west coast of New Zealand's South Island in 1947, although making several shorts and documentaries beforehand, her feature film debut was the 1984 horror film *Mr. Wrong* (released in the United States as *Dark of the Night*) about a young woman tormented by a haunted car. In 2003, she returned to dark fictional material with a supernatural edge in *Perfect Strangers* with Rachael Blake and Sam Neill, again in the capacity of writer, producer and director. She has received a number of accolades, including the New Zealand Order of Merit.

PURDY-GORDON, CAROLYN

Born in Michigan in 1947, Carolyn Purdy-Gordon is often associated with her collaborations with cult horror filmmaker Stuart Gordon, who since 1968 has also been her husband. She has appeared in many of his films including *Re-Animator* (1985), *From Beyond* (1986), *Dolls* (1987) and *The Pit and the Pendulum* (1991), and she also later worked behind the scenes on a number of films directed by David DeCoteau, including *Ring of Darkness* (2004) and *Hansel & Gretel: Warriors of Witchcraft* (2013).

QUIGLEY, LINNEA*

Actor Linnea Quigley is synonymous with B-grade horror films of the 1980s and '90s. Born in Iowa in 1958, it was in 1978 that Quigley made her first film appearance in Harry Hurwitz's *Fairy Tales* (1978). From this point onwards, her career would develop rapidly and in 1981 had her first major role in a horror film in Herb Freed's slasher *Graduation Day* (1981). Highlights amongst Quigley's lengthy filmography include *Silent Night, Deadly Night* (Charles E. Sellier Jr., 1984), *The Return of the Living Dead* (Dan O'Bannon, 1985), *Creepozoids* (David DeCoteau, 1987), *Sorority Babes in the Slimeball Bowl-O-Rama* (David DeCoteau, 1988), *Hollywood Chainsaw Hookers* (Fred Olen Ray, 1988), *Night of the Demons* (Kevin S. Tenney, 1988), *A Nightmare on Elm Street 4: The Dream Master* (Renny Harlin, 1988), *Zombiegeddon* (Chris Watson, 2003), *Disciples* (Joe Hollow, 2014), *The Barn* (Justin M. Seaman, 2016) and she has cameos in Doris Wishman's final film, *Each Time I Kill* (2007) and Adam Gierasch's 2009 remake of *Night of the Demons*. Quigley is also a vocal animal rights activist and vegan and has written a number of books including *The Linnea Quigley Bio & Chainsaw Book* (1991), *Skin* (1993) and *I'm Screaming as Fast as I Can: My Life in B-Movies* (1995). In 1990, she released *Linnea Quigley's Horror Workout*, an aerobics video for the darkly inclined.

RAIA, CHRISTINA

Studying at Hunter College where she made her first short film—the psychological thriller *Do Over* (2010)—New York-based filmmaker Christina Raia directed, wrote and produced the 2014 feature film *Summit*. A slasher-inspired film based around a skiing trip in Vermont, Raia's film won Best Horror Film at the Manhattan Film Festival, Best Director at the Rhode Island International Film Festival as well as playing at several other festivals. Amongst her many credits, she also directed, produced and wrote the horror-comedy

Filmmaker Christina Raia. Photo credit: Chris Carroll. Used with permission. www.christinaraia.com

shorts *House Near the End of the Street* (2012), *Hello* (2015) and *Night In* (2016). Her 2016 short thriller *Enough* is currently playing the festival circuit, and she is currently developing her third feature, a horror-comedy called *Silent Night*. A quarter-finalist at the 2016 Slamdance Screenplay Contest, it follows a couple's holiday that goes terribly wrong and Raia plans to begin shooting in 2019.

RAINES, CRISTINA

Born in the Philippines as Tina Herazo in 1952, Cristina Raines worked for almost 20 years across film and television, with early credits including Robert Altman's *Nashville* (1975) and Ridley Scott's *The Duellists* (1977). In 1973, she appeared in Leo Garen's horror film *Hex*, alongside her long-time partner and co-actor Keith Carradine, and in 1977 in Michael Winner's demented *The Sentinel* with Sylvia Miles and Beverly D'Angelo as ballet dancing lesbians and a birthday-hat-wearing cat. Her last horror film was in Joseph Sargent's 1983 anthology *Nightmares* in the segment "Terror in Toganga" with William Sanderson.

RAMKE, YOLANDA

Australian actor and filmmaker Yolanda Ramke wrote and co-directed the 2017 zombie film *Cargo* with Ben Howling, developed from their 2013 award-winning short of the same name that became a viral hit on YouTube. As an actor, Ramke's credits also include the role of a survivor in the short film version of *Cargo*.

RAMPLING, CHARLOTTE

Celebrated British actor Charlotte Rampling has impressive form in the horror genre. Born Tessa Charlotte Rampling in 1946, she began her career in cabaret and modeling before establishing a strong reputation in the late 1960s and '70s as an actor adaptable to a wide range of roles, from chimpanzee-romance *Max, Mon Amour* (Nagisa Oshima, 1986) to the arthouse

Charlotte Rampling attends the *I, Anna* press conference mduring of the 62nd Berlin Film Festival at the Grand Hyatt on 12 February 2012 in Berlin, Germany. Credit: Denis Makarenko / Shutterstock.com

Nazisploitation film *The Night Porter* (Liliana Cavani, 1974) to Consuella the Eternal in John Boorman's cult scifi film *Zardoz* (1974). In 1972, she played Barbara in the segment "Lucy Comes to Stay" in Roy Ward Baker's Amicus horror anthology *Asylum*. In 1977, she starred in Michael Anderson's eco-horror film *Orca*, later appearing in Alan Parker's 1987 voodoo horror film, *Angel Heart*. In 2018, she appeared in Lenny Abrahamson's gothic horror film *The Little Stranger*.

RAMSAY, LYNNE

The films of celebrated Scottish filmmaker Lynne Ramsay have often circled intensely dark themes, stemming back to her early short films. But it was in her 2011 film adaptation of Lionel Shriver's novel *We Need to Talk About Kevin*, that most explicitly linked Ramsay to horror for many critics in its powerful reimagining of the story of a woman disconnected from her troubled, violent son. Born in Glasgow in 1969, Ramsay studied at the National Film and Television School in England after having previously studied Photography. One of the great 'what ifs' of contemporary cinema remains the Ramsay version of Alice Sebold's 2002 supernatural novel, *The Lovely Bones*, which Ramsay originally planned to bring to the screen before Peter Jackson took over. After the wide acclaim that greeted her powerful 2017 thriller *You Were Never Really Here*, Ramsay announced that she was currently writing the screenplay for an eco-horror film.

Lynne Ramsay arriving for the London Critics Circle Film Awards 2012 at the BFI, South Bank, London, 19 January 2012. Credit: Steve Vas / Featureflash Photo Agency / Shutterstock.com

RAMSEY, ANNE*

American actor Anne Ramsey was born Angelina Mobley in Nebraska in 1929. Most famous for her role in Richard Donner's *The Goonies* (1985) and her Oscar-nominated performance in the title role of Danny DeVito's comedy *Throw Momma from the Train* (1987), her career spanned over 30 years on stage and screen. Ramsey played Elvira Parker in Wes Craven's *Deadly Friend* (1986), and appeared in the horror-comedies *Love at Stake* (John C. Moffitt, 1987), *Dr. Hackenstein* (Richard Clark, 1988) and *Meet the Hollowheads* (Thomas R. Burman, 1989).

RANDOLPH, JANE

Born in Ohio in 1915, American actor Jane Roemer took the name Jane Randolph for her professional career, which lasted from the early 1940s to the mid-1950s. Studying acting at a school run by influential director and producer Max Reinhardt, Randolph's career was marked by roles in horror and film noir, the former including roles in the classic Val Lewton-produced RKO horror films *Cat People* (Jacques Tourneur, 1942) and *The Curse of the Cat People* (Robert Wise, 1944). Randolph would return to the genre in a more lighthearted context in 1948 when she starred in Charles Barton's *Abbott and Costello Meet Frankenstein*, alongside not only Bud Abbott and Lou Costello but also Lon Chaney Jr, Béla Lugosi and Lenore Aubert.

RASHIDI, NARGES

Narges Rashidi was born in Iran in 1980 and immigrated to Turkey and then Germany with her family during the Iran-Iraq War. Establishing her acting career primarily in German movies and television series, she has many international credits to her name, most famously her starring role in Babak Anvari's 2016 horror film, *Under the Shadow*. Premiering at the Sundance Film Festival, Rashidi's performance was widely praised.

RATTRAY, CELINE

Celine Rattray is a film producer who co-founded Maven Pictures in 2011 with Trudie Styler which focuses on development, finance and production. Of her 30 production credits, 13 of those films have played at the presitgious Sundance Film Festival. Amongst her horror credits include *After.Life* (Agnieszka Wojtowicz-Vosloo, 2009), *Vanishing on 7th Street* (Brad Anderson, 2010) and *Wilding* (Friedrich Böhm, 2018).

RAVER, LORNA

Born in Pennsylvania in 1943 with an extensive 30-year career across stage and screen, Lorna Raver may have played diverse roles, but it is surely for her stunning performance as Sylvia Ganush in Sam Raimi's 2009 film *Drag Me to Hell* that she is the most remembered. As the terrifying woman who places the narrative-propelling curse on the film's young protagonist, Raver's performance is fun and terrifying in equal measure, a combination she revives to equal effect as the monstrous Rose in Matthew Parkhill's grossly underrated 2011 Puerto Rican horror film, *The Caller*.

READ, MELANIE

While women like Jane Campion and Gayleen Preston might be more readily identifiable names as far as pioneers of New Zealand women's filmmaking, Melanie Read's 1985 horror film *Trial Run* was in fact the first feature film directed by a woman in the country. Known also as Melanie Rodriga, she was born in Malaysia, studied film in the United Kingdom and began her career in Australia as a writer and director predominantly of television dramas and documentaries. *Trial Run* was consciously conceived as a feminist horror film, and the revelation of the true perpetrator at the film's conclusion is as profound and significant today as it was when the film was first released. Although considered a classic of New Zealand gothic, the film is long overdue international reappraisal and solid reclamation by horror fans with an interest in gender politics.

REMICK, LEE

Oscar-nominee for Best Actress in 1962 and a star as much for her work on Broadway as for her work in film and television, American actor Lee Remick trained as a dancer and actor. Performing in musicals and comedies, it is however for her darker material that she is most well-known, including her powerful performance as a rape survivor in Otto Preminger's *Anatomy of a Murder* in 1959 and a self-destructive alcoholic in Blake Edwards's *Days of Wine and Roses* in 1962. Remick appeared in thriller/horror hybrids such as Blake Edwards 1962 serial killer film *Experiment in Terror* and the stage play of *Wait Until Dark* (adapted to the classic home invasion film of the same name in 1967 by Terence Young, starring Audrey Hepburn in the role). But it was two films in the mid-late 1970s that would firmly establish Remick as a horror icon: in Richard Donner's blockbuster *The Omen* (1976) and Jack Gold's supernatural conspiracy horror film *The Medusa Touch* in 1978, co-starring Richard Burton. One of her final roles was William Nicholson's British TV horror movie *The Vision* in 1988 with Dirk Bogarde.

REVILLE, ALMA

Although broadly remembered as 'Alfred Hitchcock's wife', Alma Reville was an extraordinarily gifted editor and screenwriter in her own right, and the acknowledgement of her influence on her husband's work in recent years has been long overdue. Born in Nottingham in 1899, her father worked at a film studio where she got her first job making tea. In her mid-teens she became a negative cutter and worked her way up the ranks, itself an impressive accomplishment for a woman in the British film industry at the time. Both she and Hitchcock—who married in 1926—were establishing their careers when they met, and her practical influence on his filmography is now widely recognized as a writer, director and editor in her own right. Her input from *The Ring* (1927) onwards would prove essential to Hitchcock's work, and her important role both personally and professionally in the creation of his classic horror films *Psycho* (1960) and *The Birds* (1963) was dramatized in *Hitchcock* (Sacha Gervasi, 2012) and *The Girl* (Julian Jarrold, 2012) respectively.

REYRE, MARIE-LAURE

Marie-Laure Reyre has been working as a producer in France since the late 1970s. Amongst her many credits, her role as the sole producer of Andrzej Żuławski›s cult 1981 horror film *Possession* is a stand-out. Her centrality to the production of that film is explicitly discussed on Daniel Bird's 2011 documentary *The Other Side of the Wall: The Making of Possession* where Reyre speaks about her close involvement in the casting process, the bringing into the project special effects heavyweight Carlo Rambaldi, as well as the film's debut in Cannes and its broader cult longevity.

RICCI, CHRISTINA ‹

One of the most successful child stars of the 1980s, Christina Ricci was born in California in 1980 and was discovered in a school play when she was 8 years old. Making her feature film debut in Richard Benjamin's *Mermaids* as Cher's daughter in 1990, her dark, quirky star persona rapidly grew with her casting as Wednesday Addams in *The Addams Family* (Barry Sonnenfeld, 1991) and *Addams Family Values* (Barry Sonnenfeld, 1993), followed soon after by the hybrid live action/animation reboot of *Casper* (Brad Silberling, 1995). As she grew older, Ricci became an important figure in the US indie cinema scene, peaking with Patty Jenkins's Aileen Wuornos serial killer biopic *Monster* (2003) alongside Charlize Theron. Ricci would co-star in Tim Burton's gothic ghost story *Sleepy Hollow* (1999) and have a smaller role in Chuck Russell's 2000 horror film *Bless the Child*. Her later horror credits include *The Gathering* (Brian Gilbert, 2003), *Cursed* (Wes Craven, 2004) and *After.Life* (Agnieszka Wójtowicz-Vosloo, 2009).

Christina Ricci at the world premiere, in Los Angeles, of *Halloween H20*, 27 July 1998.
Credit: Featureflash Photo Agency / Shutterstock.com

RICHARD, CYBIL

Cybil Richards is an American filmmaker whose area of specialization is adult scifi films. A notable exception is her 1997 feature, the softcore horror film *The Exotic House of Wax* (1997).

RICHARDSON, NANCY

Nancy Richardson is an American film editor who gained a Masters of Fine Arts at Berkeley, and is a Professor at UCLA's School of Theater, Film, and Television. Richardson's first job as editor on a feature film was Ramón Menéndez's *Stand and Deliver* (1988) and she would work across many different genres, collaborating often with the same filmmakers across several projects. Of these, her work with Catherine Hardwicke is of particular note—beginning with *Thirteen* in 2003, her collaborations with Hardwicke would also include the vampire romance blockbuster *Twilight* (2008) and Hardwicke's gothic horror reimagining of the fairy tale *Red Riding Hood* (2011). She would return to the *Twilight* franchise in 2010 when she edited David Slade's *The Twilight Saga: Eclipse*, and her other horror credits as editor include Kimberly Peirce's *Carrie* (2013) and Jonathan Levine's *Warm Bodies* (2013).

RICHARDSON, SALLYE •

Studying film at the University of Texas, as editor and assistant director of Tobe Hooper's *The Texas Chain Saw Massacre* (1974), Sallye Richardson is an important but often overlooked figure in 1970s US horror. Meeting Hooper through an early role at Richard Kidd's company Motion Pictures Productions, she was living at Hooper's home during production of the film and was thus intimately familiar with what was needed to be done on set each day, describing her role as doing the work Hooper did not have the time himself for. As the script for the film was also very rough, she has noted that much of the coherency and flow of dialogue was the result of editing, for which she and J. Larry Carroll were both credited.

RIFFEL, RENA

Rena Riffel is a multitalented artist with experience with everything from acting, dancing, singing, modeling, and writing, producing and directing feature films. Familiar perhaps due to onscreen performances in cult films including *Showgirls* (Paul Verhoeven, 1995) and *Mulholland Drive* (David Lynch, 2001), she would later go on to direct, write, edit and produce the sequel to the former, *Showgirls 2: Penny's from Heaven* (2012). Riffel also worked in similar capacities in her two feature-length horror-comedies, *Trasharella* (2009) and *Trasharella Ultra Vixen* (2011) in which she also stars in the title role. Riffel has continued her work in filmmaking, expanding to experimenting with other genres.

RISHER, SARA⁊

Producer Sara Risher is a name perhaps not immediately familiar to horror fans, but she played a key role in the genre, particularly due to her involvement with the *A Nightmare on Elm Street* franchise. Risher was both Head of Production and then Chairman of New Line Cinema for 27 years, and alongside Robert Shaye, she was a central figure not only in the *Elm Street* films, but also played a major part in bringing many of the films of John Waters to a wide audience. Under her guidance, New Line became one of the world's most successful indie film studios, and later in her career she was the president of Nova Filmhouse. Beyond *Elm Street*, Risher's many credits in a production capacity include the horror films *Alone in the Dark* (Jack Sholder, 1982), *Critters* (Stephen Herek, 1986), *My Demon Lover* (Charlie Loventhal, 1987), *Lucky Stiff* (Anthony Perkins, 1988) and *The Demented* (Christopher Roosevelt, 2013).

RISK, TRISTAN

Tristan Risk is a Canadian actor and burlesque performer who has become a familiar face on the indie horror film festival circuit and is closely aligned with the Women in Horror movement. Amongst her many feature film credits, Risk has appeared in *American Mary* (Jen and Sylvia Soska, 2012), *The Editor* (Adam Brooks and Matthew Kennedy, 2014), *Mania* (Jessica Cameron, 2015), *Save Yourself* (Ryan M. Andrews, 2015), *Frankenstein Created Bikers* (James Anthony Bickert, 2016), *Ayla* (Elias, 2017), *Cabaret of the Dead* (Staci Layne Wilson, 2017) and *Odissea della Morte* (Vince D'Amato, 2018). She has also worked in many horror short films, including *Call Girl* (Jill Gevargizian, 2014), *Innsmouth* (Izzy Lee, 2015), *For a Good Time, Call...* (Izzy Lee, 2017), *Haxx Deadroom: A Cyberpunkzz Story* (Dionne Copland, 2017), *Just a Prick* (Tonjia Atomic and Michelle Nessk, 2018) and *Nepenthes* (Ariel Hansen, 2018). Risk also starred in and co-wrote Kate Kroll's short film *Happily Ever Evil* (2014) and both acted in and was an executive producer on Paddy Murphy's 2015 short *Ground Floor*.

ROBBINS, KATE

Producer, writer and director Kate Robbins studied acting at New York University and embarked on additional studies to focus on fiction and playwriting. In the late 1990s, she co-founded Snowfall Films with Suzanne Lyons (author of the 2012 book *Independent Film Producing: The Craft of Low Budget Filmmaking*), later developing a genre division called WindChill Films, whose production credits include Robbins' sole directorial cred-it, the 2006 horror film *Candy Stripers* (which she co-wrote with Jill Garson). Although focusing on her theatrical writing later in her career, as producer Robbins' credits include the horror films *Séance* (Mark L. Smith, 2006), *Desert of Blood* (Don Henry, 2008) and *Portal* (Geoffrey Schaaf, 2009).

ROBERTS, EMMA

Born in New York in 1991, Emma Roberts began acting as a child, making an early ap-pearance in Ted Demme's 2001 crime film *Blow*. While focusing on kid and teen friendly roles such as Nickelodeon's series *Unfabulous* for many years, she broke free from child star typecasting by working in several well received indie films, and aw also cast in many horror films including *Scream 4* (Wes Craven, 2011) alongside Neve Campbell and Court-ney Cox. More recently, she starred in Oz Perkins' stylish *The Blackcoat's Daughter* (2015) and Henry Joost and Ariel Schulman's *Nerve* (2016). Continuing her association with horror, on the small screen she has appeared in series including *American Horror Story* and *Scream Queens*.

Emma Roberts at the Los Angeles Premiere *of The Twilight Saga: New Moon* held at the Mann Village Theater in Westwood, California., on 16 November 2009. Credit: Tinseltown / Shutterstock.com

ROBERTS, JUDITH

While American actor Judith Roberts is most familiar to horror fans for her performance as Mary Shaw in *Dead Silence* (James Wan, 2007), she made an early role in David Lynch's 1977 cult horror film *Eraserhead* credited as the "Beautiful Girl Across the Hall". She also appeared in an uncredited role as Mother Superior in Charles E. Sellier Jr.'s *Silent Night, Deadly Night* (1984), and recently put in a spectacular performance as Joaquin Phoenix's character's *Psycho*-loving mother in Lynne Ramsay's brutal thriller *You Were Never Really Here* (2017).

ROBERTSON, ELISE

Elise Robertson is a filmmaker, actor and teacher who was born in Pittsburgh and studied directing and acting at Northwestern University. She has worked extensively in theater, particularly in Los Angeles and the San Francisco Bay Area. An early film credit was as a character painter on *Tim Burton's The Nightmare Before Christmas* (Henry Selick, 1993), and she has worked as a model maker. In 2011 she made her feature film directorial debut with the horror movie *Donner Pass* (which she also co-wrote), resulting with her being named a "notable woman in Horror" by the Horror Society in 2015.

ROBIE, WENDY

Although most immediately recognizable as the eye-patch-wearing Nadine Hurley from David Lynch and Mark Frost's *Twin Peaks*, Cincinnati-born actor Wendy Robie has a long association with the horror genre. Born in 1953, it was not until 1990 that Robie would first work as an actor, launching her career with her high-profile role in *Twin Peaks*, re-vamping Nadine in 2017 when Lynch returned to the much-anticipated third series. In 1991, she rejoined her *Twin Peaks* co-star Everett McGill in a chilling performance in Wes Craven's *The People Under the Stairs*, later making a small cameo in Craven's *Vampire in Brooklyn* (1995). Robie's other horror credits include *Devil in the Flesh* (Steve Cohen, 1998), *The Dentist 2* (Brian Yuzna, 1998), *The Attic Expeditions* (Jeremy Kasten, 2001) and the made-for-television horror film *Lost Voyage* (Christian McIntire, 2001).

ROBINS, EVA

One of the most iconic scenes across Dario Argento's *giallo* output is that featuring a woman on a beach in the primal scene that lies at the heart of *Tenebrae* (1982), despite her not speaking nor her character being credited with a name. With her red high heels and white dress, Eva Robins played one of the most memorable characters across Argento's entire ouvere. The transgender model was born in Bologna in 1958 and began transitioning in her teens. She would appear in various capacities across film and television primarily in Italy, although another notable role would be Patrick Conrad's *Mascara* (1987) alongside Charlotte Rampling. Robins is still working today and is a vocal transgender activist.

ROCHA DA SILVEIRA, ANITA

Filmmaker Anita Rocha da Silveira was born in Brazil in 1985 and studied film at the Pontifical Catholic University of Rio de Janeiro. A director, writer, editor and producer, she began her career with the short films O *vampiro do meio-dia* (2008), *Handebol* (2010) and *Os Mortos-Vivos* (2012). She made her feature debut in 2015 with the Argentine-Brazilian teen horror film *Kill Me Please,* which played at the Venice Film Festival and won Best Director at the 2015 Rio Festival.

ROCHON, DEBBIE—INTERVIEW (JUNE 2018)

If there was one person who single-handedly embodied the warrior spirit of women in horror at its best, it's unquestioningly cult icon Debbie Rochon. Born in Vancouver, she was a street kid who accidentally found her way to the film industry in the early 1980s, with an early role in Lou Adler's punk masterpiece *Ladies and Gentlemen, The Fabulous Stains!* in 1982.

Moving to New York to pursue acting further, she first worked on stage before moving to film, and across her career would appear in over 200 independent features such as *Santa Claws* (John A. Russo, 1996), *Tromeo and Juliet* (Lloyd Kaufman, 1996), *Final Examination* (Fred Olen Ray, 2003), *Dr. Horror's Erotic House of Idiots* (Paul Scrabo, 2004), *Slime City Massacre* (Greg Lamberson, 2010) and *Disciples* (Joe Hollow, 2014).

Rochon made her feature film directorial debut in 2016 with the horror movie *Model Hunger,* starring fellow horror legend Lynn Lowry.

www.debbierochon.com

> **From the very outset, I must thank you: you have been so open and frank about your early life, it is so important as a template for other young people—perhaps young women especially—who feel they are trapped in inescapable circumstances. You are living proof that life is not merely surviving, but exceling. You've won so many awards and are really such a major horror icon and beloved by so many, how would you frame your remarkable journey for a young person in circumstances not unlike those you found yourself in growing up?**

Cult film legend Debbie Rochon. Used with permission.

I have always looked at my journey as one would look at different movies or books or characters. In chapters—simply put. I think when you take on the idea and then reality of changing something, or your circumstances, you have to be willing to completely let go of all previous concepts of what is possible or logical. For me, I could attribute it to will. If you told me a square peg couldn't fit in a round hole I would understand what you're saying but I would then push, shove, hammer, do whatever I could, to make it fit. I never listened to anyone's advice for the most part as I *knew* what I didn't want as much as I knew what I did want. That tunnel vision is what helped me. I knew where I was, for example living on the streets, but I never accepted it as my reality. So going from the foster care system to street life to moving to NYC to study and join theater companies then to film making seems like a lot of steps but it's not. Why would I say that? Because I never had anything to lose or anything holding me back so taking each step was challenging and sometimes difficult but the alternate reality of staying where I was didn't seem possible.

So, letting go of the past, having no fear of a better future and willing to make big steps, take chances and leap into the unknown was, in a strange way, what I was doing already. I never knew if I was going to eat or where I was going to sleep any given night when I was a pre-teen then teen, taking big leaps didn't feel like it was a big deal. I know it can feel like it's a big deal if you're stuck in something. But turn it around. What do you have to lose? Comfort in the abuse and despair? Many people are more comfortable in what they know no matter how horrible it is. But I wasn't comfortable in it, so I just kept moving.

You have written so beautifully about how your path lead you to cinema and joining the cast of *All Washed Up*. This sounds like such an important moment in your life personally, as of course must have been your involvement in *Ladies and Gentlemen, the Fabulous Stains*. Can you tell me a bit about your life at the time you got involved in that project?

When I walked into the extras audition room for *Ladies and Gentlemen, The Fabulous Stains!* I was literally shoeless! When Lynne Carrow, the casting director, asked if I would be willing to bleach out my hair I said "Of course!". Next I had a full make over by London's (then) top hair dresser Schumi and punk rock journo Caroline Coon headed up my punkification. Once the filming started it gave me a sense of routine, creative outlet, a sense of belonging and a new set of people who came from the US and UK so my mind expanded in many ways—to look at possibilities and experience a new way of approaching life all together. I was on the shoot for three months. That was enough time to really get a sense of the hard work that goes into film making and how creative it is. When it was over I decided my 'other' existence was even less palpable and it gave me a crystal-clear direction.

I sincerely wish more women with public profiles spoke as honestly about their experience of unplanned pregnancy and the decision to terminate. The story

about you watching *Texas Chain Saw Massacre* as you recovered which lead you to decide to study acting to me is one of the great stories about women and horror. You've mentioned Marilyn **Burns's performance in particular as revolutionary for you—what was it about that film, that character, at that moment that you think propelled such a major life decision?**

I watched Marilyn Burns just slam that role out of the ballpark and it blew me away. What resonated for me was the possibility of taking my pain and channelling it via art and that was such a revelation for me. I also knew I needed some damn good training to do this. That's when I knew I had to study acting in NYC where all the serious teachers were. I had to previously cut myself off from my emotions to survive the streets so my next journey would be about reclaiming my emotions and access to them. That was really difficult.

When you are coming from a place of such real-life terror the only way you can survive it is by numbing out. So I had to set a course for un-numbing myself! I remember in one of my first voice classes in NYC just simply doing the breathing exercises brought on such overwhelming emotion I was frightened. I then became agoraphobic. I would have extremely intense panic attacks whenever I left my apartment. This was due to all the emotions that had been so safely tucked away for my survival now being encouraged to come out. Well they came out alright, but I was not ready for the intensity of that. So I went into therapy for quite a while. It helped me but only to a certain degree. It wasn't until I figured out how to channel all my 'stuff' into my art that I was able to fix a huge part of myself.

It took many years. To this day I am not magically fixed, but I know if I can channel the darkness into a role or something creative I can keep using it to my 'advantage'. If I don't do this, it easily comes back and tries to overtake me again. It's a lifelong work.

What does the descriptor "scream queen" mean to you?

I didn't think much of it either way when I first heard the term in the early 90s. Then after about a decade of being called one I could see how terribly limiting it was and at that point the term had taken on a more negative connotation. I then rejected the term. But people love 'handles' and as hard as I fought not to be called one, people would keep doing it regardless. Then I decided I really didn't care either way. I called myself an actress and if others wanted to label me for their convenience or comfort then so be it.

Now, I think it's again become more fashionable. So the term seems like it's here to stay. It's OK with me. I don't mind being called one. Although you'll not find any site or social media app that I run using the term 'Scream Queen' when I describe myself.

I know ImdB is not to be completely trusted, but it tells me that you had an uncredited role in Roberta Findlay's *Lurkers* very early on in your career. Findlay

Debbie Rochon in *Wrath of the Crows* (Ivan Zuccon, 2013). Used with permission.

is quite a notorious figure, so I'm fascinated to hear about that experience!

Yes, I worked with her as an extra on the film *Lurkers*, which was originally titled *Home Sweet Home*. Then I had a featured role in her next movie called *BANNED* which was her last movie and to this day has never released. It's a real shame. I thought it was clever. It's about the leader of a hip young jazz band that becomes possessed by Teddy Homicide a punk rocker who died in the same recording studio the jazz group rented for their first album. It was very funny and a real slice of the 80s. But sadly, never released! I still hope Media Blasters, who owns the rights, releases it.

Roberta is a really funny, unique person. One minute she's having a laugh and the next minute she's screaming at everyone calling them names. I have to give her a ton of credit. When we made *BANNED* in 1989 she had been in the business for a couple of decades at that point and female directors were just not working in the capacity that she was. She is a true NY character! Eccentric and brash and to the point. It made me a little nervous at the time, but I look back now and love it! Makes me laugh—in a good way.

Looking at your filmography, I am constantly reminded how much *fun* your movies are: I think a lot of big budget more mainstream films—both horror and more generally—could learn a lot from this almost punk-rock DIY spirit of delight. What do you like the most about working on indie productions?

My favorite thing about it is the ability to improvise. I usually have my character down pretty good and sometimes the improvised lines or scenes are just as good if not better than what's written. I've come across a number of directors who allow for this in the indie world.

I love many things about it and most importantly the heart these films have. While we always have to be hopeful that a distribution company picks up the film, the content is not shot with that in mind. So you really have far more creative license in the DIY films. They are much closer to art films than the Hollywood movies are. Of course, we have some stunning directors in Hollywood who do make art films but they are not the norm, they are the exception.

Also, the roles for women are a million times better in indie films. A woman can be the driving force in a movie with or without sex appeal, a woman can be the killer, mad scientist—pretty much anything. So roles are superior in indie films for women. There's always the chance the movie doesn't come together very well but…I would rather be in a very rough gem then a polished turd.

You've appeared in quite a few 'horror women all-star' films such as *Psychic Experiment* and the narrator on *Tales of Poe*. There seems to be more broadly such a strong sense of community amongst women in horror that I sense even amongst fan groups. Has this always been the case?

There is a good sense of comradery. There are great women like Brinke Stevens, Lisa Wilcox and Jaime King—the list goes on. Too many to name. But there's always women who will hate on other women. Men have the same problem. But envy or hatred or trolling to make people feel better about themselves is just ugly and stupid. We all face this in one form or another.

I do find there is a terrific amount of women both working in many departments of the business, or who are the fans of the genre, that are supportive, helpful and inspirational. There will always be the 'others' but for me it's not a big thing. I have always referred roles or interviews or merchandise possibilities to other women in the industry to not just help them out but to help the creator who's looking for introductions. I don't expect it in return. I enjoy it. When and if it happens, I am thrilled and deeply appreciative. I love bringing talent together, that's the satisfaction in and of itself.

Model Hunger feels like so much more than just a feature directorial debut— it's a funny yet quite poignant war-cry about the politics of age and femininity in an industry that is notoriously inflexible when it comes to diversity. How did this project come to fruition, was Lynn Lowry always who you imagined as the star, and does this suggest more to come from you in a directorial capacity?

The writer and executive producer James Morgart approached me with the script to direct. He felt I could bring a lot of experience to the project and what it had to say. He was simply a dream to have there supporting me on my first feature. He allowed a lot of changes and left the final cut completely to me and my vision. I tried to achieve a lot of layers, some successful some not, and I am deeply proud of the movie—warts and all.

The cast is just stunning in the film. Lynn Lowry was not the first person I approached to be the lead role of Ginny but I can't tell you how lucky I was that it worked out that way. She gave 110% and created an award-winning performance! I was nothing but blessed to have the talent I had on the film. It was an intense experience and one I will never forget.

As far as directing again…James and I are beginning a new collaboration now. I can't wait to share what it will be and I am excited to be on another directorial journey with my sophomore film!

I'm intrigued that you have worked behind the camera in producer roles on numerous occasions as well. Is this an aspect of filmmaking you get different professional satisfaction from?

I enjoy creating very much. I love making connections and seeing projects come together. I get great satisfaction from assisting other people's visions. My favorite areas of creativity are acting, directing and camera work to be honest. I can do a lot with helping out in producer type jobs but not all of them. For instance, raising money is not something I enjoy. It's painful for me. So I don't usually do it. I do have a shy side so being behind a character or a camera or coaching actors to be their best fits my personality.

Debbie Rochon in *Sick Boy* (Tim T. Cunningham, 2012). Used with permission.

The sheer amount that you work is genuinely gobsmacking—the turnover is just remarkable. Are there any projects in recent years that you would flag as essentials for people new to your work?

That's tough because it depends on their taste and sometimes my favorite characters I've worked on are not always in the 'better' movies. I would say some recent (meaning last 10 years) essentials would be *Exhumed, Slime City Massacre, Tales of Poe, Axe to Grind, Serial Kaller.* And there are the movies that I have not seen yet but should be out later this year—*Fantasma, Death House* and *My Uncle John is a Zombie.* All were super fun to make.

Talking about your career more broadly, if there is one performance across your entire filmography that you feel has gone unrecognized?

I still think the movie *Nowhere Man* never found its audience. It was a very raw looking film, had a Noir style story and we just tore it up emotionally. It was brutal to make—in a good way. Felt absolutely spent inside and out afterward. But because it wasn't horror and it wasn't any specific genre it never seemed to get momentum. That was one of my best performances, I think, because I had a superior director and script, but it's been pretty much buried.

ROCKOW, JILL

A make-up and special effects artist with multiple Emmy awards to her name, Jill Rockow has a long association with genre film and television in particular. Hailing from New Jersey, while later in her career she would work on blockbuster franchises like *Thor* and *Pirates of the Carribean* and television series like *Star Trek: Deep Space Nine*, her early career was marked by a close association with horror. Inspired to become a make-up artist after visiting the circus as a child, she studied cosmetology in her teens, and in 1979 studied at the Joe Blasco Makeup Academy. It was through Blasco she got her first film job, the horror film *Beyond Evil* (Herb Freed, 1980), returning to work with Freed again on the slasher movie *Graduation Day* in 1981 where she worked with Oscar-winning special-effects artist Dick Smith. Rockow's other horror film credits include *Deadly Eyes* (Robert Clouse, 1982), *Frightmare* (Norman Thaddeus Vane, 1983), *Friday the 13th: The Final Chapter* (Joseph Zito, 1984), *Silver Bullet* (Daniel Attias, 1985), *They're Playing with Fire* (Howard Avedis, 1984), *Grim Prairie Tales* (Wayne Coe, 1990), *Ghosts of Mars* (John Carpenter, 2001) and the 1997 television mini-series adaptation of Stephen King's *The Shining*.

ROEL, MARTA

While little information remains in English at least about actor Marta Roel, she was a key figure in Mexican horror cinema of the 1930s. Her credits include her debut as the vamp character Cristina in Fernando de Fuentes's 1934 horror movie *El fantasma del convent*. Filmed in an actual monastery in the Mexican city of Tepotzotlán, the film was made to profit from the success of the 1933 horror film *La Llorona*, which du Fuentes co-wrote.

ROJAS, JULIANA

Born in São Paulo in 1981, Juliana Rojas is a Brazilian director and editor renowned for her collaborations with her filmmaking partner Marco Dutra. Deciding to work together when they discovered a mutal passion for horror films, their first short film together *The White Sheet* was made while they were studying at the University of São Paulo and was selected to play at the 2004 Cannes Film Festival. Although Rojas has directed a number of films independently, it is her work with Dutra that has garnered the most international attention—aside from horror shorts including *A Stem* (2007), and *The Shadows* (2009), they also together made the feature films *Hard Labor* (2011) and the brilliant queer werewolf movie *Good Manners* (2017), the latter winning the Silver Leopard at the Locarno Film Festival.

ROMÁN, MARÍA DEL CARMEN MARTÍNEZ

Despite having worked on a range of horror films and westerns in particular, little is known about Spanish writer María del Carmen Martínez Román. She began her career working in make-up and wardrobe and was the costume supervisor on Jess Franco's *The Awful Dr. Orlof* (1962). Working also across sword-and-sandal films and adventure movies (she wrote the screenplay for a number of *Zorro* films), as a writer Román's horror credits include *House of 1,000 Dolls* (Jeremy Summers and Hans Billian, 1967), *Os cinco Avisos de Satanás* (José Luis Merino, 1970), *Scream of the Demon Lover* (José Luis Merino, 1970), and she is said to have worked in an uncredited capacity on Camillo Mastrocinque's *Crypt of the Vampire* (1964) with co-writers including *giallo* great Ernesto Gastaldi.

ROMERO, TINA

Not to be confused with the daughter of George A. Romero who has at the time of writing recently announced her directorial debut with the upcoming zombie featue *Queens of the Dead*, actor Tina Romero was born in New York City in 1949 and moved to her parent's homeland of México a decade later where she studied acting. Romero has worked extensively across film and television since the mid-1970s, primarily in México but also appearing in several US movies and television programs. In the title role of Juan López Moctezuma's cult horror classic *Alucarda* (1977), Romero established her place in the genre. Her other horror credits include *Silencio de muerte* (Ramiro Meléndez, 1991), *Las lloronas* (Lorena Villarreal, 2004) and the television movie *Violencia a sangre fría* (1989).

ROMAY, LINA

For almost four decades, Spanish actor Lina Romay and her frequent collaborator and long-time partner, filmmaker Jess Franco, together created some of the wildest horror films ever made. Born Rosa María Almirall Martínez in Barcelona in 1954, Romay and Franco's work together frequently straddled his signature affection for horror/erotica hybrids, and while she did not work exclusively with Franco, it is with him that the bulk of her most well-known movies were made. While listing all her horror movies would be an exhaustive task, highlights include *Lorna the Exorcist* (1974), *Female Vampire* (1974), *Jack the Ripper* (1976), *Mondo Cannibale* (1980), *Devil Hunter* (1980), *Revenge in the House of Usher* (1982), *Mansion of the Living Dead* (1982) and *Faceless* (1988).

ROSE, FELISSA

Born in New York City in 1969, Felissa Rose Esposito—credited as Felissa Rose—earned her strong cult reputation based on her dazzling performance as Angela Baker in Robert Kiltzik's 1983 slasher film *Sleepaway Camp* (1983), later revisiting the role in 2008 in Kiltzik's *Return to Sleepaway Camp*. After her famous role as the cult film's protagonist, Rose gave up acting to study and attended New York's Tisch School of the Arts. In the late 1990s, she revived her film career after fan interest inspired her to return to acting, and has since appeared in a number of horror films including *Horror* (Dante Tomaselli, 2002), *Zombiegeddon* (Chris Watson, 2003), *Corpses are Forever* (Jose Prendes, 2003), *Nikos the Impaler* (Andreas Schnaas, 2003), *Satan's Playground* (Dante Tomaselli, 2006), *Zombie Killers: Elephant's Graveyard* (B. Harrison Smith, 2015), *Silent Night, Zombie Night* (Sean Cain, 2009), *2 Jennifer* (Hunter Johnson, 2016), *Death House* (Gunnar Hansen, 2017), *Victor Crowley* (Adam Green, 2017) and she has recently again reprised the role of Angela Baker in Andy Palmer's forthcoming *Camp Cold Brook*.

ROSE, JANE

Jane Rose is a Brooklyn-based horror filmmaker and special effects make-up artist. As a writer and director, her credits include the shorts *Heading Home* (2006) and *The Curse of Coney Island* (2006), and she also directed segments in the horror anthologies *The Horror of H.P. Lovecraft* (2006) and *The Moose Head Over the Mantel* (2017). In her capacity as a makeup and special effects artist, she has worked on horror movies including the shorts *Even* (Ben Jurin, 2008), *Late Night Local* (Jessi Gotta and Patrick Shearer, 2014), *Demons Eat the Mind* (Jeffrey Velaquez, 2008), *Rising Up: The Story of the Zombie Rights Movement* (Laura Moss, 2009), *Insatiable* (Scott W. Perry, 2009), *Anniversary Dinner* (Jessi Gotta, 2012) and *Late Night Local* (Jessi Gotta and Patrick Shearer, 2014), as well as the features *Plague Town* (David Gregory, 2008), *The Sickness* (Carl Paolino, 2008), *The Big Bad* (Bryan Enk, 2011) and *They Will Outlive Us All* (Patrick Shearer, 2013).

ROSE, RUTH

Born in Massachusetts in 1896, although she began her career as an actor on stage and screen in her teens, filmmaker Merian C. Cooper famously hired Ruth Rose to repair the until-then troubled script of his classic monster movie *King Kong* (1933). Rose's work on the screenplay has been recognized as saving the film, her creating some of its most famous lines and her script editing widely credited as streamlining the pacing. While she did not have an extensive career as a screenwriter, amongst her other credits are the similarly ape-focused Ernest B. Schoedsack 1949 film *Mighty Joe Young*, and the influence of her work on *King Kong* was acknowledged by her being credited in both the 1976 and 2005 remakes of the film by John Guillermin and Peter Jackson respectively.

ROSS, GAYLEN

Buried deep within the filmography of the impressive documentary filmmaker and producer Gaylen Ross lies a distant but important past career as an actor, where she played one of the most memorable American horror films of the 1970s. Long before she made documentaries about Nazi gold and Adolf Eichmann, Ross spent four years working as an actor, and her credits include Francine in George A. Romero's zombie classic *Dawn of the Dead* (1978). In 1982, she would collaborate again with Romero on *Creepshow* in the segment "Something to Tide You Over".

ROSS, KATHERINE

Oscar-nominee actor Katharine Ross was born in Hollywood in 1940, and with films such as Mike Nichols' *The Graduate* (1967) and George Roy Hill's *Butch Cassidy and the Sundance Kid* (1969), she was one of the most recognizable stars of the era. Dropping out of university to pursue acting, she began her career on stage and then moved to film and television. Her most famous role for cult film audiences is undeniably her starring performance in Bryan Forbes' feminist nightmare *The Stepford Wives* (1975), but she had previously co-starred with Simone Signoret in the comically macabre *Games* in 1967. In 1978 she appeared in Irwin Allen's killer bee eco-horror film *The Swarm*, co-starring with her real-life husband Sam Elliott that same year in Richard Marquand's horror movie *The Legacy*. In 2001, she was introduced to a new audience with her role as Dr. Lilian Thurman in Richard Kelly's *Donnie Darko*.

ROTHMAN, MARION

American editor Marion Rothman studied Theater Arts at UCLA in California before moving to study French at the prestigious Sorbonne. Beginning her film career as a writer, in the late 1950s she was drawn to the role of editor. Her first credit as editor was on Richard Fleischer's vicious yet hyper-stylized serial killer film *The Boston Strangler* in 1968, and she would later cut cult films including both *Beneath the Planet of the Apes* (Ted Post, 1970) and *Escape from the Planet of the Apes* (Don Taylor, 1971). Her horror credits include *The Island of Dr. Moreau* (Don Taylor, 1977) and *Orca* (Michael Anderson, 1977), and she is renowned as a frequent collaborator with John Carpenter, notably cutting *Starman* (1984) and the horror films *Christine* (1983) and his horror-comedy *Memoirs of an Invisible Man* (1992). Amongst Rothman's other cult film credits are Lamont Johnson's 1976 rape-revenge film *Lipstick*.

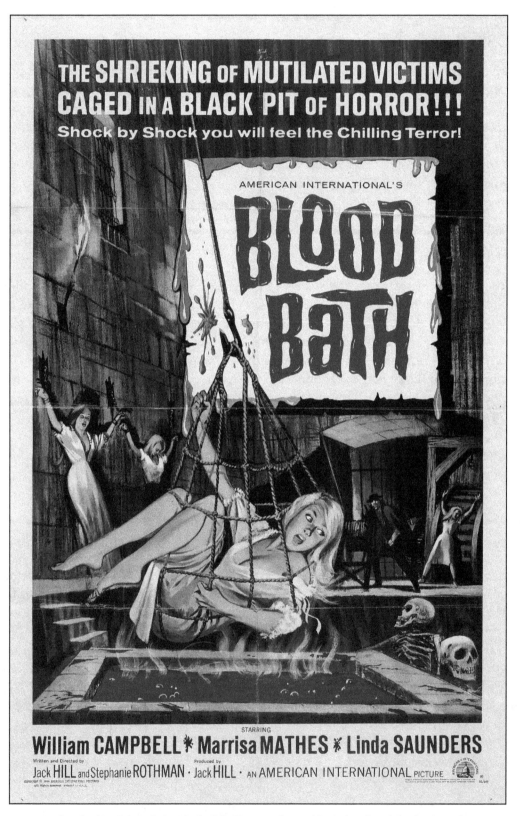

Poster for *Blood Bath* (1966) aka *Track of the Vampire*, directed by Jack Hill and Stephanie Rothman.
Credit: AIP/Photofest © AIP.

ROTHMAN, STEPHANIE

One of the most famous women exploitation filmmakers of the 1960s and '70s, Stephanie Rothman was born in New Jersey in 1936 and would become renowned for her horror movies, action films and sex comedies for producer Roger Corman. Inspired by the work of Ingmar Bergman, Georges Franju and Jean Cocteau, she studied in the Cinema Department of the University of Southern California and was soon the first woman to receive the Directors Guild of America fellowship for student filmmakers. This led to her working with Corman from 1964 in an assistant capacity which required her doing several jobs across screenwriting, casting, editing and directing. Amongst her most famous work as director during this period was her co-credit with Jack Hill on *Blood Bath* (1966) and as writer and director on 1971's *The Velvet Vampire*. Widely recognized as a significant feminist filmmaker, she left Corman in the early 1970s and with her husband Charles S. Swartz played a central role in establishing Dimension Pictures where she worked until the mid-1970s. After finding it increasingly difficult to find work, she left filmmaking altogether, turning first to political activism and then real estate development.

RUBIN, JENNIFER

As angry doomed punk girl Taryn in *A Nightmare on Elm Street 3: Dream Warriors* (Chuck Russell, 1987), Jennifer Rubin would become a much-loved cult horror figure. She began her career notably modeling for Calvin Klein's "Obsession" campaign, and in 1984 was voted Ford International Model of the Year. Focusing in the late '80s on her acting career, later horror credits include *Bad Dreams* (Andrew Fleming, 1988), *Full Eclipse* (Anthony Hickox, 1993), *The Wasp Woman* (Jim Wynorski, 1995), *Little Witches* (Jane Simpson, 1996), *Twists of Terror* (Douglas Jackson, 1997), *Sanctimony* (Uwe Boll, 2000) and *Heebie Jeebies* (Thomas L. Callaway, 2013). She also appeared in episodes of horror and scifi television series including *The Twilight Zone*, *Tales from the Crypt* and *The Outer Limits*.

RUBINSTEIN, ZELDA[a]

One of the most vibrant actors to ever grace the horror screen, Zelda Rubinstein was an intriguing performer and a passionate and vocal AIDS activist. Born in Pennsylvania in 1933, in the late 1970s, she shifted the focus to acting and the film for which she is the most renowned—Tobe Hooper's *Poltergeist* (1982)—was one of her first roles. Although she would act in sopa operas, sitcoms and dramas across her career, it was this role that would largely inform her star persona, and she would return to horror throughout her career in films including the brilliant Spanish horror film *Anguish* (Bigas Luna, 1987*), Little Witches* (Jane Simpson, 1996), *Wishcraft* (Danny Graves and

Richard Wenk, 2002) and *Behind the Mask: The Rise of Leslie Vernon* (Scott Glosserman, 2006), as well as the *Poltergeist* sequels *Poltergeist II: The Other Side* and (Brian Gibson, 1986) and *Poltergeist III* (Gary Sherman, 1988). She was also cast in an episode of the television spin-off *Poltergeist: The Legacy*, as well as epsides of *Tales from the Crypt*, *Jennifer Slept Here*, and she narrated the long-running series *Scariest Places on Earth*.

RUEDA, BELÉN

Spanish actor Belén Rueda was born in Madrid in 1965 and in her homeland is renowned for her work in film and television. Internationally, however, it is her starring role in two horror films that have associated her strongly with the genre: as the protagonist Laura in J. A. Bayona's debut film *The Orphanage* (2007), and in the title role of Guillem Morales 2010 horror film *Julia's Eyes*, produced by Guillermo Del Toro. Rueda was nominated for a Goya Award for Best Actress for her performance in *The Orphanage*.

RUSSELL, ELIZABETH

A familiar face in some of the most loved American horror films of the 1940s, actor Elizabeth Russell was born in 1916 in Pennsylvania. She would collaborate extensively with producer Val Lewton and appeared in several his famous RKO horror films, including *Cat People* (Jacques Tourneur, 1942), *The Seventh Victim* (Mark Robson, 1943), *The Curse of the Cat People* (Gunther von Fritsch and Robert Wise, 1944) and *Bedlam* (Mark Robson, 1946). Her other horror film credits include *The Corpse Vanishes* (Wallace Fox, 1942) and *Weird Woman* (Reginald Le Borg, 1944).

RUSSELL, GAIL

American actor Gail Russell was born in Chicago in 1924 and moved to Los Angeles with her family where she pursued a career as an actor. Her breakout performance was as Stella Meredith in Lewis Allen's classic 1944 horror film *The Uninvited*, one of the most famous American horror films of that decade. Despite it being the role for which she is primarily remembered, Russell's career was dramatically cut short when she tragically passed away in her mid-30s.

RUSSELL, MIA'KATE—INTERVIEW (JULY 2018)

If Mia'Kate Russell's impressive career as a make-up and special effects artist in Australian film and television over a decade and a half isn't enough to convince you of her dedication and talent, then the fact that she has extended her remarkable skills to other roles behind the camera—including directing and writing—should destroy any possible doubts.

An artist with an original voice and a distinct flair for horror storytelling, Russell's directorial work is marked as much by darkness as it is at times a sly, even camp, humor. Her 2016 short *Death by Muff* was a finalist of the *ABCs of Death 2* competition and consequently included on the *ABCs of Death 2.5*, Russell's other work includes the comedy short *Auditioning Fanny* (2012) and 2 very distinct yet equally memorable horror shorts, the horror-comedy *Swallow* (2013) and the more dramatic horror short *Liz Drives* (2017).

As a make-up and special effects artist, Russell's vast credits also include horror films such as *Cannibal Suburbia* (D.A. Jackson and Jean-Luc Syndikas, 2008), *Don't Be Afraid of the Dark* (Troy Nixey, 2010), *Crawlspace* (Justin Dix, 2012), *I, Frankenstein* (Stuart Beattie, 2014), and *Scare Campaign* (Cameron and Colin Cairnes, 2015).

www.maketroublefilms.com

> **To say that you are multiskilled when it comes to horror is an understatement, Mia'Kate! I guess a logical place to start is how you went from makeup and SFX to directing and writing?**

I spent my school years writing and making short films on 8mm then handycams. Followed by 4 years acting training, with 10 years doing some dubious theater performances. I'm one of those people who is grateful their youth happened before social media.

I loved writing, painting, film, and I had a fascination with death. The thought of a normal job horrified me, but I needed a skill for cash, so I made the decision to study film makeup and SFX in 2005. I was lucky to get work right after training and fell in love with being on set. This is when I first met SFX crew and horror nerds who had an equal fascination with death and the macabre. The following years as a makeup artist were wonderful, but also confirmed I wanted to write and direct my own work.

I didn't plan it, but those makeup years are where I met many of the actors and crew that ended up being in my films, and who I'm planning future projects with.

> **What inspired the formation of your company, Make Trouble Films?**

In 2011, I made *Auditioning Fanny* and needed a name for the company. The name 'Make Trouble' I saw in a *Get Smart* TV episode as a teenager. Max entered a beatnik bar and 'Make Trouble' was lit up in a neon sign on the wall. I was desperate for a 'Make Trouble' sign of my own for years after seeing it.

Mia'Kate Russell. Photo credit: Julia Madotti. Used with permission.

Make Trouble Films has actually never been more than me and and my computer in my room. I never had plans of it being a larger production company. Producing was out of necessity to get my films made.

The end goal is to write and direct horror films that have an underbelly of feminism and a social message, so wrapped up in the story that audiences don't notice.

The first film I saw of yours as a director was *Swallow* and I honestly couldn't believe what I was watching: I think I heard it described as John Waters does *Wolf Creek* with werewolves, but even then, I don't think that comes close to doing it justice! There's such joy in this film and it's tonally so different from something like *Liz Drives*—I'd love to hear about where this project originated and the details of the shoot.

Swallow was written with a lot of love and confidence. I knew the actors I was writing for and I wasn't out to impress anyone. I was making it for me.

I bought a Bedazzler and went nuts on the costumes, bought a van and built the interior, even painted pictures for the location walls, and Larry Van Duynhoven from Scarecrow Studios designed, made, and applied the werewolf make-up. Creatively I was very hands-on everywhere and the shoot was a success.

Unfortunately, I'd really over spent, and after I finished the edit, it sat untouched for months. It was also sitting as a 14-minute film, which wasn't great for festivals.

A post producer came on board with some great contacts and he got it to its completion. He also took it to an editor and they edited it down to 9 minutes and added some ADR dialogue.

I was in two minds to be honest about the new cut, but I felt like I had to listen to the producers, they were giving me their time for free and I was deeply grateful. It got into Sitges and did really well. My 14-minute version may not have been as successful? Me-now probably would have fought harder for the story. But me-then wasn't as secure.

Lulu McClatchy has such a strong screen presence, and you have collaborated with her to really great affect across so many of your films, including the upcoming *Maggie-May*. How did you both meet, and what keeps bringing you back to this remarkable performer?

I met Lulu on Nick Ball's short film *The Pistachio Effect* in 2010. She's one of those people that light up a room with old Hollywood glamour, laughter, dry humor, and 100% sarcasm. After only knowing her only a few hours I said, "If I write a short film will you be my lead?" And she said "Yeah". Now she's a close friend and she's acted in 4 of my 5 films.

It's only a matter of time before she's a household feature film name. Can you imagine if Ryan Murphy saw her? She plays Maggie in the short we're currently in post for *Maggie-May*, he'd love her in it. Maybe I should try and send him a copy? I told her when she's famous I'll release her shorts as a box set called *Lulu's Box* and add a scratch n' sniff card. Then I'll just live off the royalties.

I understand your short *Death By Muff* was made for the *ABCs of Death 2* competition, can you tell me how you got involved in that and what it was like being a finalist?

I loved the anthology film *The ABC's of Death* so much and showed as many people the *F—Death by Fart* segment as I could. It was almost a friendship test up there with "do you like my dogs".

When the competition for the M segment the following year was announced, I was overly excited. I recall constantly interrupting conversations with another awesome M way to die. It was probably really annoying for people.

I threw around: "Dying by Monopoly" (that game never ends well) or "*M.A.S.H* re-runs" (but the suicide line would have been too dark) and in the end, decided on "MUFF" (what's not to love!).

I wrote the script really quickly and we built the set inside a studio with discarded materials. It's the only film I've done where the storyboard matched the end result, frame to frame.

When the films were online and the public were voting, I was surprised at what was popular. *Death by MUFF* did better than a couple of the other films that I thought were superior, and the one I thought would win didn't get to top 12. It was a lesson for me that a good budget, production design, and even story, can be pushed aside in favor of an audience-loved gag. Some incredible films missed out. After weeks of watching all the online discussion and debate, it was also an insight for me into who this horror audience was.

The 12 finalists formed a private Facebook group and we're still all in touch. Everyone's very supportive of each other's following work.

It's genuinely staggering to look at the list of awards and nominations *Liz Drives* has received, and as I mentioned above, it's a really notable diversion tonally from some of your other work. What was the inspiration for this project, and did you expect it to be as well received as it has—what is it about the film that you think audiences have connected with so strongly?

I was in my lounge room drinking wine and having a whinge with actress Sophia Davey. I had feature scripts I wanted to direct, no money, and felt my writing was too gory for the funding bodies so I didn't even bother applying (I know, good attitude). So we came up with a plan to make a short where film people might take me more seriously, give her a meaty acting role, and get us both producer credits.

We sent our mate Cassandra Magrath the script, besides being a great actor, she was producing her first feature film. We wanted her for both. It worked, she came on to play Ellie and became the third producer.

My father had just died, and I was in a really dark place. *Liz Drives* was written over a weekend, with a second draft in response to notes from my DOP Tim Egan. He's one of the few opinions I instinctively trust.

I didn't know actor Christopher Kirby, but he had the imposing height and presence for the character I needed, had a beautiful face, and he was Black. I got his email and introduced myself with the script attached.

Liz Drives is predominantly about race. I wanted to know from Chris, as a Black man, how he felt about a white woman telling this story. These are such sensitive times, and I can be heavy footed. Looking back, I think I was subconsciously asking his permission. He wrote back that *Liz Drives* was one of two of the best scripts he'd ever read! He loved a white woman telling this story, and he came on board as our actor. The man is divine.

From storyboarding to the shoot on *Liz Drives* I had this in my thoughts: "try and do it more like others do"—which wasn't meant negatively, just more of a creative challenge for myself to pull back on my more usual camp aesthetic.

The shoot was as great as it could be with a couple of lights, in the middle of the bush, in freezing temperatures. Sophia playing Liz would shoot a dramatic scene, and when I called "CUT" would run to heat up the soup for the crew.

Christopher shot the film over the two free days he had before starting a feature, and at 4am when our shoot wrapped, we drove him 3 hours to the airport so he could start his next film hours later.

The overall main feedback I received from this film's audience is "I didn't see it coming". I think more than the story's theme, that is what has been repeatedly relayed back to me. The ability to surprise them, when they felt they'd seen it all, they really appreciated.

Amy Bradney-George in *Liz Drives* (2017). Stills by Rah Dakota. Used with permission.

Cassandra Magrath, Mia'kate Russell, and Sophia Davey on the set of *Liz Drives* (2017).
Photo credit: Daniel Klaas. Used with permission.

Interestingly, the racial tone of the film has only ever been mentioned in interviews, and generally with appreciation to the point I was trying to make.

You're also an impressively accomplished makeup/SFX artist and I think your work is really central to horror movies like Cameron and Colin Cairnes's 2015 movie *Scare Campaign*. You also work in this capacity beyond horror (I saw you worked on Romi Trower's romcom *What If It Works?*, for example)—what is about these kinds of jobs that you like the most when collaborating with other filmmakers?

Colin and Cameron Cairns were great to work for as a makeup artist, and inspirational to watch as a director. They never lose their cool on set, ever, I've seen people get more worked up over a coffee order going wrong, but they're unflappable.

Sometimes they would shoot a scene on their iPhones to see if it would work. We'd turn up on set and they'd play it for us, with them acting out all the roles, the running girl, madman with axe etc…Always hysterical.

And Romi Tower had a spine operation in the middle of shooting *What if it Works*. The first half of the shoot she was in pain, and the second half, she was in a wheelchair! So she's the poster girl of 'success against all odds'. Again she always kept her cool.

My IMBD profile apparently lists 62 film and TV makeup jobs. I think the female directors in there are only a handful if those. I've definitely seen some incredible directors and absolutely seen some appalling ones too.

I feel that when it is my turn to direct a feature there, can be no room for error. There's a responsibility when you've been asking for your turn to prove yourself; as RuPaul would say… "Don't fuck it up!".

As both a filmmaker and makeup/SFX artist, I'd be fascinated to hear who your most important professional influences were—these are both fields really dominated by men, especially in horror.

All films that have influenced me, and that I have fallen in love with, were directed by men. Two of my favorite films are Pedro Almodovar's *All About My Mother* and Todd Haynes' *Velvet Goldmine*. My favorite TV shows are Ryan Murphy's *American Horror Story*, and *Feud*. And growing up I was, and still am, obsessed with anything by John Waters. Even though they're all men—they're all gay men, which may be a coincidence? But my inner fag hag, says it's not.

Recently Jordan Peele's *Get Out* was a game-changer for me. The idea of intelligent horror with a political message, starring a Black man, winning an Oscar? Awesome.

The women characters seen in the shows mentioned above are what I aspire to create. The characters written for Jessica Lange in *AHS* are nothing short of brilliant. I would love to say there was a woman in my top influencers, but the fact there isn't, is a sign of the lack of opportunities woman have had, not a sign of their work. The next 10 years in horror is going to be sensational for all the right reasons.

You have such a strong presence in the Australian women in horror community, I'd love to hear your thoughts on the value of networks such as these and film festivals like Hobart's Stranger With My Face?

Oh, I adore the horror community! They really are a different breed of film folk. There's no pretension, everyone's genuinely glad to have a chat.

In other film festivals there's a foul hierarchy you often see, or a "I'll only talk to who is important" vibe going on. You never get that in the horror film celebrations.

I went to the Women in Horror Film Festival in Atlanta last year and stayed on site (school camp for horror nerds). For over a week the restaurant/bar area was filled with new horror writers, established producers, celebrated actors, all sitting together talking horror. I've never seen so much cool, and friendliness in one place, and I've only felt that warmth at horror festivals.

It's impossible to leave these festivals without a handful of new friends. And with social media, and years going by, you end up with a large family of women and a really supportive network.

Over the last few years I've seen these women get their first features up, complete scripts, and we celebrate them. Others have tough times, and we give them care. The amount of support for the ups and the downs is equal for both.

I've seen your name linked to a couple of new projects that I'd love to ask you about—*Penny Lane Is Dead, Tommy,* and *Eating Candy* especially?

I met producer Andre Lima on a short film his husband (John Sheedy) was directing and I just adored him. He's passionate about social change, film, and his favorite films are *Thelma and Louise* and *Monster*. Heaven.

I wrote *Maggie-May* a short horror commenting on apathy. He produced, I directed, and we're currently in post. Andre has read both *Penny-Lane is Dead* and *Tommy*, two of my feature scripts and is interested in both. It feels like I've spent a lifetime waiting to meet a producer who both liked my writing, and someone I trusted. We're in very early stages now, talking about getting one of my feature scripts up, and I'm tapping away at something new.

RYDER, WINONA⋆

One of the most recognizable child stars of the 1980s, Winona Ryder would establish herself as an enduring presence in contemporary American film and television across more than three decades. Born in Minnesota in 1971, her popularity as a teen idol was launched by her performance as Lydia in Tim Burton's horror-comedy *Beeltejuice* (1988) and as an accidental serial killer that same year in Michael Lehmann's cult black comedy *Heathers*. Studying acting in San Francisco while growing up in a commune, she was an avid reader as a child and throughout her career she would work with directors including Francis Ford Coppola, Martin Scorsese, James Mangold and Gillian Armstrong. She would collaborate again with Burton on the gothic films *Edward Scissorhands* (1990) and *Frankenweenie* (2012), and her later horror roles include Coppola's *Bram Stoker's Dracula* (1992) where she played Mina Harker, Jean-Pierre Jeunet's *Alien: Resurrection* (1997), *Lost Souls* (Janusz Kamiński, 2000) and *Black Swan* (Darren Aronofsly, 2010). More recently, Ryder has endeared herself to a new generation of horror fans with her role in the horror series *Stranger Things*.

Winona Ryder at the Academy Awards, 24 March 1997. Credit: Paul Smith /
Featureflash Photo Agency / Shutterstock.com

S

SAKULJAROENSUK, APINYA

Born in Thailand in 1990 and often known mononymously as Saiparn, Apinya Sakuljaroensuk is a regional celebrity who works across film, television, music videos and advertising. Sakuljaroensuk made her film debut as the title character in Pen-Ek Ratanaruang's *Ploy*, which premiered at the 2007 Cannes Film Festival. In 2008, she appeared in the first instalment of the popular Thai horror anthology film *4bia* in Paween Purikitpanya's segment "Deadly Charm". Although starring in well over 20 feature films, Sakuljaroensuk would continue to return to horror again in Thanadol Nualsuth and Thammanoon Sakulboonthanom's 2010 movie *The Intruder* as a journalist documenting a cobra invasion. In 2012, Sakuljaroensuk featured in *3AM*—another horror anthology film—starring in Patchanon Thammajira's segment "The Wig". In 2013, she was cast in prolific Thai horror director Piyapan Choopetch's haunted island film *Hashima Project*. Sakuljaroensuk has not since returned to horror, but in 2016 starred in Anocha Suwichakornpong's *By the Time It Gets Dark*, which was chosen as the country's submission to the 90th Academy Awards for the Best Foreign Language Film category.

SALMONOVA, LYDA

Born in Prague in 1889, Lyda Salmonova studied dance as a child and moved to Berlin where she pursued a stage career. Twice marrying a key figure in the German Expressionist movement, Paul Wegener (she was his third and sixth wife), she worked in many horror films that he often co-directed and co-wrote including her debut film *The Student of Prague* (1913), *The Golem* (1915), *The Golem: How He Came into the World* (1920), as well as *Nosferatu* director F.W. Murnau's *The Hunchback and the Dancer* (1920) and Richard Oswald's *Lucrezia Borgia* (1922). Her last film appearance was in Lothar Mendes's *The Island of Tears* in 1923.

SANDWEISS, ELLEN

As a key figure in *The Evil Dead* franchise, Ellen Sandweiss was involved from the outset. Born in 1978 in Detroit, she made her screen debut in Sam Raimi's 1978 short film *Within the Woods*, from which the series was spawned. As Cheryl Williams in Raimi's first feature film of the series from 1981, Sandweiss played protagonist Ash's (Bruce Campbell) sister. In 2006, Sandweiss was cast in Dante Tomaselli's horror film *Satan's Playground*, later playing a character again called Cheryl in Bruce Campbell's *My Name Is Bruce* (2007). That same year, she appeared alongside horror luminaries such as Gunnar Hansen and Mick Garris in Stevan Mena's horror-comedy mockumentary *Brutal Massacre*, as well as Michael Spence's *The Dread*. In 2009, she had a small role in Douglas Schulze's Dee Wallace/David Carradine-fronted horror movie *Dark Fields* and returned to the *Evil Dead* franchise with a voiceover in Fede Alvarez's 2013 remake of Raimi's original film. She also appeared in two episodes of the television series *Ash vs Evil Dead*.

SARANDON, SUSAN˙

With a screen career spanning close to 50 years, political activist and Oscar-winning American actor Susan Sarandon is one of the great screen performers of her generation. Beginning her career on television and moving later to film, she was born in New York in 1946 and studied at The Catholic University of America in Washington D.C. Within her lengthy filmography are several horror film performances, including the horror-musical *The Rocky Horror Picture Show* (Jim Sharman, 1975), *The Hunger* (Tony Scott, 1983) and the supernatural comedy *The Witches of Eastwick* (George Miller, 1987). Sarandon also starred in Peter Jackson's supernatural mystery film *The Lovely Bones* (2009), adapted from Alice Sebold's 2002 novel of the same name.

SARGENTI, MARINA

Marina Sargenti was born in Los Angeles in 1947, and her screen career was brief but significant in the history of women in horror. Her debut film was the cult classic *Mirror, Mirror* (1990)—one of the most fascinating horror films ever directed by a woman—that she also co-wrote with Yuri Zeltser and sisters Annette and Gina Cascone. Sargenti left the *Mirror, Mirror* franchise after her first film and turned her attention to her second and only other horror film, the made-for-television movie *Child of Darkness, Child of Light* in 1991. Punching well above its low-budget weight, this theological horror film tracks the birth of a saviour and the antichrist, and stars Sela Ward (with a brief appearance by Brendan Fraser in his on-screen debut).

SARO-WIWA, ZINA

Zina Saro-Wiwa has worked across journalism, filmmaking and contemporary art. Born in 1976 in Nigeria into a family of writers and activists, she was raised in Britain and studied at the University of Bristol. Often cited as the originator of the term "alt-Nollywood", her short film *Phyllis* was one of two consciously created alt-Nollywood shorts that she made for her 2010 New York exhibition *Sharon Stone in Abuja*, marking Saro-Wiwa's first video installation work as an artist. *Phyllis* played Berlin's 2017 Final Girls Film Festival whose programmers clearly recognised the generic appeal of Saro-Wiwa's experimental video piece. While Saro-Wiwa's work is too diverse to offer *Phyllis* as any definitive indicator of her broader repertoire, on its own merits it is a striking experiment with horror iconography in a national context not typically aligned with the genre in the western imagination at least beyond devil-panic films.

SATŌ, SHIMAKO

Closely associated with the popular *Eko Eko Azarak* J-horror films inspired by Shinichi Koga's manga of the same name, director and screenwriter Shimako Satō was born in Iwate Prefecture in 1964. While she has often worked outside of horror, her beginnings in the industry were grounded in the genre. She made her debut as a screenwriter and director in the Julian Sands-fronted 1992 Edgar Allan Poe adaptation *Tale of a Vampire*, then directed the original 1995 film *Eko Eko Azarak: Wizard of Darkness*, and writing and directing its sequel, *Eko Eko Azarak II: Birth of the Wizard* in 1996. A further four *Eko Eko Azarak* films would follow based on her first two films, but Satō would begin to work both as a screenwriter and director more broadly across thrillers, action films, dramas and comedies. She did not leave horror altogether, however, and directed elements of the horror videogames *Resident Evil Code: Veronica X* (2000) and *Resident Evil* (2002). Satō also wrote screenplay for Tarô Ohtani's *Ghost* (2010), and in 2015, she directed an episode of the *Tales of Terror* series.

SATRAPI, MARJANE

Iranian artist and writer Marjane Satrapi is most immediately associated with the hugely successful adaptation of her *Persepolis* graphic novels to film, but as a director she has more recently experimented with horror and black comedy in *The Voices* (2014) which premiered at the Sundance Film Festival in 2014 to broad critical acclaim. Born in 1969 and raised in Tehran, she went to school during her teen years in Vienna, periods of her life documented in her celebrated graphic novels *Persepolis* (2003) and *Persepolis 2* (2004) which she adapted into a feature length animated film. Co-directed in 2007 Vincent Paronnaud, *Perespolis* won the pair the Jury Prize at the Cannes Film Festival that year and was nominated for an Oscar. Paronnaud and Satrapi would in 2011 again adapt one of Satrapi's graphic novels to the screen in *Chicken with Plums*. In 2012, she wrote the screenplay for the comedy *The Gang of Jotas* which she directed and starred in.

SAUL GUERRERO, GIGI - INTERVIEW (AUGUST 2018)

Born in Mexico City in the 1990 and moving to Canada in her early teens, Gigi Saul Guerrero is a filmmaker and actor whose work has been championed internationally at film festivals, by fans, and across industry.

As co-founder of the production company Luchagore that she formed with fellow filmmakers who she met while studying at Vancouver's Capilano University in 2013, the horror genre has been core to her work that has spanned film, videogames and web series.

Amongst her impressive filmography are the short films *Dia los Muertos* (2013), *Slam* (2014), *Testement* (2014), *El Gigante* (2014), *Bestia* (2017), and the segment "M is for Matador" in the *ABCs of Death 2.5* (2016), as well as 7-part web series *La Quinceañera*. In 2019, the international premiere of her feature debut *Culture Shock* was held at Montreal's Fantasia International Film Festival, produced by Blumhouse as part of their Into the Dark series for Hulu.

www.luchagoreproductions.com

Your web series *La Quinceañera* just played at the 2018 Fantasia Fest in Montreal; I'm absolutely intrigued by this project and would love to ask some questions about it - first of all, the Quinceañera is such a fascinating cultural ritual of feminine transformation, can you tell me a little about it and why you chose that as such a central focus of the series?

Fantasia is seriously one of the most badass and incredible festivals I have had the pleasure to attend. Genre filmmakers MUST go to Fantasia. The wildest crowd I have ever witness haha!

Well for those who don't know what a "Quinceañera" is, it's a Mexican tradition for celebrating the night of a girl's 15th birthday. Which is the night she is supposed to become a woman.

However, in our *Quinceañera* things go terribly wrong and bloody! I personally never had a Quinceañera growing up. Moving from Mexico to Canada right at that age it was hard fitting in, making friends, and I loved the idea to apply my personal experiences into the lead character of the show—who also didn't want a Quinceañera, and didn't know who she really is or wants to become. This really interested me!!! And of course, I am very proud of my roots, so making a project with Latin content is my most favourite. Although…. I end up giving it a horror twist.

Gigi Saul Guerrero (Luchagore Productions). Used with permission. www.luchagoreproductions.com

Gigi Saul Guerrero (Luchagore Productions). Used with permission. www.luchagoreproductions.com

I very recently had the good fortune to see Issa López's *Tigers are Not Afraid*, another Mexican woman-directed horror film that in a very different style from yours also really focuses on the effect of violence linked to cartels on young people. I'd love to hear your thoughts on the relationship between genre film and real-world politics and social issues, and what creative and ideological voice horror especially gives you as an artist to talk about things like this?

Movies are a means to have a voice to shed light on the human condition, be it past or present. Movies like that of Issa López are important and even sometimes hard to see because of the realness of it all. What I love about genre film is that I take that reality and augment it to a point where the audience can experience an extreme version of the issues I am exposing, but at the same time be entertained by it and—not only that—become aware of the social issues. I try and bring realness to my projects and thereby create a consciousness in my audience through a bloody horrific time.

I'm interested to hear your thoughts about making a longer-form narrative in the shape of a web series like *La Quinceañera*: what can you do here that single shorts or feature films might not allow? I understand it was made with Warner Bros.—was that a different experience from the more indie frameworks you'd previously worked in?

Anything with money and having studio behind your back makes it instantly NOT indie haha! Working with such a large studio for *La Quinceañera* was such an amazing experience.

Having the show be a SHORT FORM series worked amazing because that's basically what the world is getting used to now. The attention span of people is shorter and shorter. We all want to see funny cat videos and move on!

So binge-watching a show is totally what people do now, anywhere they can—the bus, their office break, etc. I think this format is fantastic for the busy person.

Having short film experience made this project easier. However, feature length films will always be my favourite format. It's what movies were meant to be like.

So much discussion about "women's filmmaking" I think really unhelpfully pits women and men against each other, but I know you co-founded Luchagore Productions with Luke Bramley and Raynor Shima. Can you tell me about how this all came together—where you all met and what inspired the formation of Luchagore—and how your working relationship has developed?

We met in film school, Luke and I, and joined forces with Raynor later on. Funnily enough, he was from a rival school and don't quote me on this, but we might have been the first film team to join forces despite the rivalry between the schools.

As far as me being a woman in a male dominated industry—and in my case even in my team—it's never an issue because at Luchagore it's not about that, it's about making movies; great movies! We came together to form Luchagore because our love of creating films and wanting to be the best we can as individual filmmakers. Combining our talents to create awesome films, that's what we are about and the respect we have for each other is as important as our passion for film.

Our team has now expanded and brought such talented artists in the other departments, and we never consider gender. A collaborative process is what makes a successful project.

I first discovered your work when your short *El Gigante* played at Monster Fest in Melbourne, Australia, in 2015 where I was co-programming the shorts, and it was honestly one of the wildest things that came across our path that year! What was the inspiration for that project, and were you surprised by its international appeal?

El Gigante is my favourite project thus far. It has so much Latino bad-assery: luchas and tacos! *El Gigante* is based on the first chapter of Shane Mackenzie's novel Muerte con Carne: if you like gore it's a must-read. Just be warned—be prepared to squirm through the last three chapters. I cannot wait to make the feature film adaptation of the book!

"Dia de los Muertos" from the *México Bárbaro* anthology was clearly a really important career milestone for you that brought your work to a lot of people's attention. That must have been a remarkable experience—did it make you realise anything about your direction professionally and as an artist?

Wow "Dia los Muertos" was so long ago ... I was still in school! Man, I feel old hahaha! I never imagined it would travel so far. This project is special to me because it not only was it my graduation film, bit it made it to Netflix and I got to meet a ton of talented people both here in Canada and in Mexico thanks to it. It was my first big project and I loved all the lessons and connections it brought me along the way.

This is also a BIG THANKS TO MEXICAN GORE MASTER Lex Ortega for inviting me to be part of this anthology and allowing the short to be worked on by post-production people I never knew I was going to meet!

Your films have played at so many impressive festivals and won a number of awards, I'd love to ask you a little more about *Bestia*, *Slam* and *Testament* for example. Can you tell me a bit about the creation and reception of each of these?

I am so thankful for all of the festivals we have participated in. Festivals are a great place to network and see what's out there. As for *Bestia*, *Slam* and *Testament*, they all came about the way many of our projects happen: the need to create and film!

Gigi Saul Guerrero (Luchagore Productions). Used with permission. www.luchagoreproductions.com

Budget for us is not a hindrance and we love creating shorts like *Bestia*, *Slam* and *Testament* because it makes us be resourceful and pushes us to create with what we have available, from actors to free locations.

You only get better when you practice and when you do it… that why at Luchagore we are always filming, even if there is no specific reason but to create. Budget should never stop you from making films happen!

I was fascinated to see that you've been working on a videogame, again a very distinct form of visual media. What has that experience been like, and what is different about videogames than film?

CAPCOM has really been a memorable a new learning experience. I was hired to write, and this industry is a lot more competitive and has a lot more departments to think about while writing. Not only that, but your audience are players who have the power to manipulate your story to go in different directions! So as a writer you must think of what those alternative journeys may be.

I loved working on this and I feel even more lucky that I am one of the lead characters on the project. Too bad it takes a year or two to announce it!

What's the most important and the most useless thing you learned at film school?

Most important was to not be afraid of failure! When you fail you learn from your mistakes and that is how you become better. Film school is a safe place to fail.

As far as useless … that's hard because I loved everything they showed me. Well, maybe having to take Physics class because it's a university requirement—filmmakers are not meant to do physics or any kind of math, at least not me. Haha!

So I have to ask: Wikipedia says that you stole a copy of *Child's Play* from a video store when you were a kid but were too freaked out to watch it. Did you ever finish the film, and what did you think of it? I saw recently it's being re-made—would you take the gig if you were offered it?!

Yes I *did* finish it years later… and OMG YES!! I would for sure take a remake gig. But I would love to do a reimagining of the whole franchise … I wouldn't want to continue from where it was left off. Chucky deserves it as much as Pennywise did.

SAWAJIRI, ERIKA

Japanese-Algerian actor, model and musician Erika Sawajira's name is often associated in Japan with words like "controversial" and "outspoken", aspects of her star persona that filmmaker Mika Ninagawa brought to the fore of her 2012 horror film *Helter Skelter* in which Sawajira starred. Making her screen debut in Naoki Hashimoto's *Furenzu* (2003), Sawijara has worked across film and television, particularly in the horror films *The Eyes of Ashura's Castle* (Yôjirô Takita, 2005) and *Ghost Train* (Takeshi Furusawa, 2006) as well as *Helter Skelter*.

SAYERS, BECKY

Growing up in Washington and experimenting as a teen with VHS filmmaking, Becky Sayers studied filmmaking at Chapman University in California. With her husband Nick, they have made a number of horror features - continuing an interest in her earlier film-making experiments -*Break* (2010) and *The Last Buck Hunt* (2013), as well as th earlier short *Among Wolves* (2009), all of which she also wrote.

SCARWID, DIANA

Psycho III is one of the great forgotten sequels, the Anthony Perkins-directed 1986 follow-up to Hitchcock's original film in 1960 and Richard Franklin's *Psycho 2* (1983). The movie is carried in large part by the performance of Diana Scarwid who—born in Savannah, Georgia in 1955 –garnered an Oscar nomination in 1980 for her performance as Louise in Richard Donner's drama *Inside Moves*. Across her career, she collaborated with directors and writers of the calibre of Mike Nichols, Nora Ephron, Terence Davies, Robert Zemeckis and Claudia Weill. Making her screen debut in an episode of *Police Woman* in 1976, her first horror role was in Jerry Thorpe's *The Possessed* in 1977 alongside PJ Soles, with later genre work including the film *Strange Invaders* (Michael Laughlin, 1983), David Greene's 1991 TV movie adaptation of *Night of the Hunter*, and dark-themed fare such as the mini-series *Guyana Tragedy: The Story of Jim Jones* (William A. Graham, 1980), *Mommie Dearest* (Frank Perry, 1981), and two rape-revenge related films in 1986, Janet Greek's *The Ladies Club* and Robert M. Young's *Extremities*. Scarwid also appeared in horror television shows such as *The Outer Limits* and *The X-Files*.

SCHRAGE, LISA

Canadian actor Lisa Schrage was born in Vancouver in 1956 and attained cult status for her performance in the title role of Bruce Pittman's *Hello Mary Lou: Prom Night II* (1987). She also worked in Bert I. Gordon's 1989 horror film *Food of the Gods II* and was cast on television series including *Alfred Hitchcock Presents* and The *Twilight Zone*.

SCHLEIF, DANIELLE

Primarily a producer of documentaries, Barcelona-based Danielle Schleif co-wrote Roberto Busó-García 2012 Spanish haunted house film *The Condemned* (2012) and collaborated on writing duties for the zombie film *Summer Camp* with Alberto Marini. Schleif also worked as an editor on the Marini co-written horror film *Extinction* (Miguel Ángel Vivas, 2015).

SCHMITZ, SYBILLE

One of the most tragic figures in German cinema history, Sybille Schmitz was born in 1909 and died by suicide at only 45 years old. Her first screen role was in Ernö Metzner's crime short *Accident* in 1928, followed in 1929 as Elisabeth in G.W. Pabst's Louise Brooks-fronted *Diary of a Lost Girl*. Her third film is arguably her most famous, as vampire-victim Léone in Carl Theodor Dreyer's classic horror film *Vampyr* (1932), based on Sheridan Le Fanu's short story collection *In a Glass Darkly* (published in 1872). She later starred in Frank Wysbar's horror film *Death and the Maiden* in 1936, as well as earlier appearances in the scifi movies *F.P.1 Doesn't Answer* (Karl Hartl, 1932) and *Master of the World* (Harry Piel, 1934). Starring in Herbert Selpin bizarre Nazi propaganda film *Titanic* in 1943, Schmitz worked steadily until the early-mid 1940s. The final years of her life were the inspiration for Rainer Werner Fassbinder's *Veronika Voss* (1982).

SCHOEMANN, GLORIA

Born in México City in 1910 and with a filmography of over 100 movies, editor Gloria Schoemann had a career that saw her make an important donation to the Golden Age of Mexican cinema, working alongside filmmakers including Julio Bracho, Luis Buñuel, Roberto Gavaldón and Matilde Landeta. Across more than 30 years in the industry, Schoemann worked on horror films including *The Headless Woman* (René Cardona, 1944), *The Headless Horseman* (Chano Urueta, 1957), *The Head of Pancho Villa* (Chano Urueta, 1957), *Cry of the Bewitched* (Alfredo B. Crevenna, 1957), *Macario* (Roberto Gavaldón, 1960), *The Bloody Vampire* (Miguel Morayta, 1962), *The Invasion of the Vampires* (Miguel Morayta, 1963), *Panic* (Julián Soler, 1966), *Pedro Páramo* (Carlos Velo, 1967), *The Specters' Road* (Gilberto Martínez Solares, 1967), *A Stranger in the House* (Alfredo Zacarías, 1968), and a number of horror-themed entries in popular film series including *Blue Demon vs. The Diabolical Women* (Gilberto Martinez Solares, 1969), *Capulina vs. The Vampires* (René Cardona, 1971) and *Chanoc vs. The Tiger and the Vampire* (Gilberto Martínez Solares, 1972).

SCHREIBER, NANCY

The first winner of the American Society of Cinematographers' President Award in 2017 (and the fourth woman to join the prestigious group), Nancy Schreiber has often brought her critically-acclaimed gaze towards horror. Garnering her first on-screen credit with Milton Moses Ginsberg's *The Werewolf of Washington* (1973), she would work on Leszek Burzynski's cannibal film *Trapped Alive* (1988). She dabbled in the supernatural for television on shows like *Monsters* and *Ghost Whisperer* and was the director of photography on *The Baby-Sitters Club* episode "Dawn and the Haunted House". More famously, she worked on Joe Berlinger's *Book of Shadows: Blair Witch 2* in 2000, the much-maligned sequel to the blockbuster original. With well over 100 film and television credits to her name, amongst Schreiber's many other accolades she was awarded the Susan B. Anthony "Failure is Impossible" Award at New York's High Falls Women's Film Festival in 2017.

SCHRÖDER, GRETA

As Ellen Hutter in F. W. Murnau's 1922 silent horror film *Nosferatu: A Symphony of Horror*, Greta Schröder played a Mina Harker-like figure who falls prey to the vampyric Count Orlock (Max Schreck). As Murnau's breakthrough film, *Nosferatu* is still considered one of the highlights of gothic cinema, and its influence on future fim—not just horror, but the art form more generally—has been widely acknowledged. Despite this, little remains known of Schröder herself. Making her debut in Max Reinhardt's *Die Insel der Seligen* (1913), she had a small role in the horror film *The Golem* (1920) from director/actor Paul Wegener, whom she would later marry. While known primarily as an actor, she also wrote the screenplay of Ernst Matray's 1916 German adaptation of Gaston Leroux's beloved *Phantom of the Opera.* Working well into the sound era (her last film credit is for Veit Harlan's *Circus Girl* in 1954), information about her later life remain hazy, but her memory was brought vividly (although largely fictionally) to life in E. Elias Merhige's 2000 meta-horror *Shadow of the Vampire*, where she was played by Catherine McCormack.

SCHUCH, ELIZABETH E.

Elizabeth E. Schuch is a London and Bruges-based creative who works in film and theater as a director, producer, concept artist, production designer and storyboard artist. Amongst her impressive credits is *The Book of Birdie*, her 2016 feature film directorial debut which she co-wrote with Anami Tara Shucart. Filmed in Wisconsin with an all-woman cast, the film marks the screen debut of Ilirida Memedovski in the title role of an adolescent girl pushed to the edge of fantasy and sanity in a strange convent. In the film, a magical realist approach is employed to address issues like miscarriage. *The Book of Birdie* played at film festivals around the world, including Sweden's Göteborg International Film Festival, Brazil's Fantaspoa International Fantastic Film Festival, Spain's Sitges International Festival of Fantastic Cinema, Final Girls Berlin Film Festival, Australia's Stranger With My Face International Film Festival and the Brooklyn Horror Film Festival in New York City, winning awards at the last two.

SCOB, ÉDITH

French actor Édith Scob beame a horror film legend with her performance as the disfigured daughter of a mad scientist in Georges Franju's *Eyes Without a Face* (1960), one of the most famous European horror films ever made. Born in Paris in 1937, she made her screen debut in Franju's earlier film *Head Against the Wall* in 1959, and she would collaborate with the director numerous times in films including *Judex* (1963) and *Thomas the Imposter* (1965). Across her career, she would work with directors such as Luis Buñuel,

Poster from the Edith Scob film *Eyes Without a Face* (aka Les Yeux Sans Visage, Georges Franju, 1959). Credit: Everett Collection, Inc. / Alamy Stock Photo

Leos Carax, Jacques Rivette, Andrzej Żuławski, Olivier Assayas and—most recently—Mia Hansen-Løve. In 1962, she appeared in Julien Duvivier's *The Burning Court*, and Scob later played as the Countess Geneviève de Morangias in Christophe Gans horror film *Brotherhood of the Wolf* in 2001.

SCOTT, JANETTE

Daughter of British comic Dame Thora Bird, Janette Scott was born in 1938 in Lancashire. Working across film and television, Scott made three horror movies in 1963; Steve Sekely's *The Day of the Triffids*, Freddie Francis's *Paranoiac*, and William Castle's *The Old Dark House*. Playing the wife of a scientist who attempts to battle the infamous killer plants in *The Day of the Triffids*, in *The Old Dark House*—a remake of James Whale's 1932 film—she plays deceptively sweet Cecily who, it is revealed, is central to the film's mystery. But it is in the lesser known Hammer film *Paranoiac* that Scott offers her strongest horror performance as the gaslit Eleanor, sister of Oliver Reed's cruel Simon. Scott's film career ended soon after, her final feature film role in Gregg G. Tallas's daft *Bikini Paradise* in 1967.

SCOTT, JORDAN

Jordan Scott comes from a filmmaking family; her father Ridley and uncle Tony are both famous directors, and she is the half-sister of Luke and Jake, filmmakers also. She has spent close to 20 years directing commercials. Her sole feature film directing credit is for the 2009 film *Cracks*, an adaptation of Shelia Kohler's celebrated 1999 novel of the same name. Co-produced by the legendary Christine Vachon, the film is a taut psychological thriller that frequently bleeds into horror territory in its tale of institutionalized abuse at an exclusive British girls' school.

SEBASTIAN, BEVERLY

Dog lover, director, producer and writer Beverly Sebastian received her first film credit in a small role in her husband Ferd Sebastian's 1967 film *I Need a Man*. Often receiving directorial credits alongside Ferd in the many low-budget, drive-in friendly genre films they made together and individually, she received her first director credit alongside his name in the 1971 Richard Nixon-era censorship documentary *Red, White and Blue*. While they made 'Gator Bait in 1974 and its 1988 sequel, *Gatorbait II: Cajun Justice*, *Rocktober Blood* in 1984 is Sebastian's strongest horror film and one for which she receives a sole director credit (although she co-wrote it with Ferd). Following a returned-from-the-dead demonic rock star hellbent on revenge, its soft metal aesthetics and determination to cash in on then-contemporary anxieties about the so-called 'satanic panic' scare at the time, the film is effectively a time capsule, perfectly capturing the look, feel, and frequent silliness of the era.

SEBERG, JEAN

Recognized primarily for her starring role in Jean Luc Godard's French New Wave classic *Breathless* (1960), American actor Jean Seberg made her film debut after famously being picked from thousands of young hopefuls by director Otto Preminger to star in the title role of his epic 1957 biopic *Saint Joan*. Seberg lived much of her later life in France, and on the back of *Breathless* she worked steadily for a few years in primarily European films made by directors including Claude Chabrol and Jean Becker. In 1969, her vocal support of the Black Panthers found her the victim of cruel public attacks on her personal life planted falsely by the FBI, resulting in the premature birth and subsequent death of her baby daughter in 1970. Never fully recovering, Seberg's final years were extremely difficult professionally and personally—widely believed to have been blacklisted, she experienced severe depression that ended only with what is commonly assumed to be her suicide in 1979 at the age of 40. In retrospect, this only adds to her devastating performance in the title role of Robert Rossen's 1964 dark psychological gothic drama film *Lilith* alongside Warren Beatty. In 1973, Seberg appeared in in Juan Antonio Bardem's Spanish *giallo The Corruption of Chris Miller* as the evil stepmother of the title character.

SEIMETZ, AMY

Amy Seimetz is a key figure in contemporary American independent cinema and although perhaps most immediately recognizable as an actor, she is also a director, producer, editor and screenwriter. She was born in Florida in 1981, later moving to Los Angeles to develop her career. Amongst her many acting credits are several horror films including *Bitter Feast* (Joe Maggio, 2010), *A Horrible Way to Die* (Adam WIngard, 2010), *Silver Bullets* (Joe Swanberg, 2011), *You're Next* (Adam Wingard, 2011), *The Sacrament* (Ti West, 2013) and Ridley Scott's horror-scifi hybrid *Alien: Covenant* in 2017. In 2012, she wrote and directed the horror-tinged feature *Sun Don't Shine* starring Kate Lyn Sheil. In 2019, Seimetz starred in Kevin Kolsch and Dennis Widmyer's adaptation of Stephen King's 1983 novel *Pet Sematary*, previously brought to the screen by Mary Lambert in 1989.

SERBEST, DILEK

Model and actor Dilek Serbest was born in Turkey in 1981. She appearead in several music videos and during the 2000s starred in a number of horror movies including *Dark Spells* (Orhan Oğuz, 2004) and *Tramvay* (Olgun Arun, 2006).

SEVIGNY, CHLOË ⁹

Indie darling Chloë Sevigny has long demonstrated an affinity for horror. Born in Massachusetts in 1974, Sevigny's film career began with her performance in Harmony Korine's controversial film *Kids* in 1995, and in 2000, she played Patrick Bateman's unfortunate secretary in Mary Harron's *American Psycho*, adapted from Bret Easton Ellis's 1991 novel of the same name. Her work in horror continued in 2006 in Douglas Buck's remake of Brian De Palma's 1973 film *Sisters*, followed in 2009 with Werner Herzog's horror movie *My Son, My Son, What Have Ye Done?* (based on real-life killer Mark Yarvorsky). In 2015, she appeared alongnside Natasha Lyonne in Tara Subkoff's *#Horror*, joining Lyonne again in Danny Perez's over-the-top gorefest *Antibirth* the following year. Sevigny was also a regular on the television series *American Horror Story*,

Chloë Sevigny at the Antibirth Los Angeles premiere at the Cinefamily Theater on 21 August 2016 in Los Angeles, California. Credit: Kathy Hutchins / Shutterstock.com

featuring in both *Hotel* and *Asylum* series. In 2018, she played legendary real-life acquitted axe-murderer Lizzie Borden in Craig William Macneill's *Lizzie*, followed in 2019 by an appearance in Jim Jarmusch's zombie film *The Dead Don't Die*.

SEYFRIED, AMANDA ⁸

Amanda Seyfried made her film debut in the cult teen comedy *Mean Girls* in 2004, although she already had years of experience in front of the camera as a model and soap opera actor. Although building her reputation on more mainstream fare like *Mamma Mia!* (Phyllida Lloyd, 2008) and *Dear John* (Lasse Hallström, 2010), Seyfried's first horror film was in Daniel Myrick's 2008 film *Solstice*, a remake of Carsten Myllerup's 2003 Swedish-Danish co-production, *Midsommer*. In 2009, she starred alongside Megan Fox in Karyn Kusama and Diablo Cody's *Jennifer's Body*, returning to the genre in 2011 as Valerie, the protagonist in Catherine Hardwicke's gothic reimagining of *Red Riding Hood*. Seyfried also worked in Brian Crano's short horror film *Dog Food* in 2014, returning to the darkside for her incandescent performance as Becky in series 3 of David Lynch and Mark Frost's *Twin Peaks* in 2017. In 2019, Seyfried will co-star with Kevin Bacon in David Koepp's horror film *You Should Have Left*.

SEYRIG, DELPHINE

One of the key figures of European art cinema with star turns in films such as Alain Resnais's *Last Year at Marienbad* (1961), Luis Buñuel's *The Discreet Charm of the Bourgeoisie* (1972) and Chantal Akerman's *Jeanne Dielman, 23 quai du Commerce, 1080 Bruxelles* (1975), Delphine Seyrig is also horror royalty. Born in Beirut to French and Swiss parents, she studied in both France and the United States. After some preliminary appearances in the American series *Sherlock Holmes* in the mid-1950s, Seyrig turned to film after meeting Resnais in New York, moving to Europe soon after. In 1971, she starred as Countess Elizabeth Báthory in Harry Kümel's dreamlike lesbian vampire film, *Daughters of Darkness*. A vocal feminist, Seyrig was also a filmmaker whose efforts on that front included starring and directing a 1976 short adaptation of Valerie Solanas's iconic 1967 feminist masterwork *SCUM Manifesto* (the "Society for Cutting Up Men").

SHADBURNE, SUSAN

Susan Shadburne worked as a filmmaker for 30 years. Working across documentaries, children's films, and feature films, in 1986 she wrote, directed and produced the feature horror film *Shadow Play* which starred Cloris Leachman and Dee Wallace.

SHAPIRO, MILLY

Shocking audiences around the world with her sole film role as Charlie Graham in Ari Aster's 2018 horror film *Hereditary*, few were prepared for how much power adolescent Milly Shapiro could pour into a single horror performance. Born in Florida in 2002, she had previous success on the stage in several Broadway appearances.

SHAYE, LIN

Although a familiar face in horror movies across many decades, Lin Shaye has a much broader filmography that covers both film and television. While working in a number of Farrelly brothers' comedies including *Dumb and Dumber* (1994) and *There's Something About Mary* (1998), as well as no less than four movies directed by Walter Hill, it is in horror that she built her primary reputation. Beginning with small roles in films like *Alone in the Dark* (Jack Sholder, 1982) and Wes Craven's *A Nightmare on Elm Street* (1984), she gained increasing prominence with *Critters* (Stephen Herek, 1986), *Critters 2: The Main Course* (Mick Garris, 1988), *Amityville: A New Generation* (John Murlowski, 1993) and *Wes Craven's New Nightmare* (Wes Craven, 1994). After her breakthrough in mainstream comedy, she returned to horror with *Dead End* (Jean-Baptiste Andrea Fabrice Canepa, 2003), *The Hillside Strangler* (Chuck Parello, 2004), Tim Sullivan's *2001 Maniacs* (2005) and *2001 Maniacs: Field of Screams* (2010), *Hood of Horror* (Stacy Title, 2006), and of course James Wan's 2010 horror blockbuster *Insidious*, where she played demonologist Elise Reiner in a role that saw her receive a number of acting award nominations. Shaye would return to play Elise in *Insidious: Chapter 2* (James Wan, 2013), *Insidious: Chapter 3* (Leigh Whannell, 2015), and *Insidious: The Last Key* (Adam Robitel, 2018). She was also cast in both films of the *Ouija* series—*Ouija* (Stiles White, 2014) and *Ouija: Origin of Evil* (Mike Flanagan, 2016). Shaye's association with the genre also extends to *Rosewood Lane* (Victor Salva, 2011), *Big Ass Spider!* (Mike Mendez, 2013), the 2015 anthology *Tales of Halloween*, *Helen Keller vs. Nightwolves* (Ross Patterson, 2015), *Abattoir* (Darren Lynn Bousman, 2016) and *The Black Room* (Rolfe Kanefsky, 2017).

SHEA, KATT

Katt Shea began her career as an actor and then moved to writing and directing when she collaborated on the script that would become the Roger Corman-produced *The Patriot* (Frank Harris, 1986). Shea made her acting debut in Cliff Bole's television movie *The Asphalt Cowboy* in 1980, also appearing in a small part in Brian De Palma's *Scarface* in 1983. Her first overt connection to horror was playing one of "Mother" Bates' unfortunate victims in the Anthony Perkins-directed *Psycho III* in 1986, and the following year she made her directorial debut with *Stripped to Kill*. As director and co-writer, Shea followed this with the 1989 sequel, *Stripped to Kill 2: Live Girls*, and the vampire film *Dance of the Damned* that same year. Her mainstream breakthrough as director was the psychological thriller *Poison Ivy* in 1992 that famously saw Drew Barrymore shed her good girl image once and for good. In 1999, Shea returned to horror with full force, directing *The Rage: Carrie 2*, the sequel to Brian De Palma's genre classic *Carrie* (1976).

Lin Shaye and The Black Bride at the world premiere of her movie Insidious Chapter 3 at the TCL Chinese Theatre, Hollywood, 5 June 2015, Los Angeles, California. Credit: Jaguar PS / Shutterstock.com

SHEIL, KATE LYN

Born and raised in New Jersey in the mid 1980s, Kate Lyn Sheil studied acting at New York's prestigious Tisch School of the Arts. Despite being most familiar to a wide audience for her appearances in the Netflix series *House of Cards*, Sheil is closely associated with American independent filmmaking, and has worked in a range of horror films. Making her debut in Maxim Dashkin's short film *Aliens* in 2007, her second movie was Carlo Mirabella-Davis's 2009 horror short *Knife Point*. In 2011, she starred in the meta-werewolf film *Silver Bullets*, directed by mumblecore sweetheart Joe Swanberg. She had a small part in Adam Wingard's slasher *You're Next* in 2011, and appeared in both the 2012 anthology *V/H/S* in Ti West's segment "Second Honeymoon" and the West-directed found footage horror film *The Sacrament* in 2013. Sheil has appeared frequently in the films of Alex Ross Perry, including a small role in his

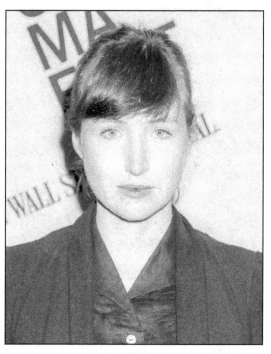

Actress Kate Lyn Sheil attends BAMcinemaFest 2015 *Queen of Earth* premiere at BAM Peter Jay Sharp Building, BAM Rose Cinema in Brooklym June 22, 2015. Credit: Sam Aronov / Shutterstock.com

2015 psychological thriller *Queen of Earth*, clearly influenced by John D. Hancock's cult 1971 horror film *Let's Scare Jessica to Death*. Of all her horror performances, however, her starring role in Robert Hillyer Barnett's brilliant 2015 film *Tears of God* is a standout. Other career highlights include her work in Sarah Adina Smith's haunting *Buster's Mal Heart* in 2016, and her negotiation with the real-life horror story of American newsreader Christine Chubbuck who famously shot herself on live television in Robert Greene's experimental docu-drama *Kate Plays Christine* (2016). In 2012, she also starred in actor Amy Seimetz's dark feature debut, *Sun Don't Shine*.

SHELLEY, BARBARA

Immediately linked with the heyday of Britain's Hammer Horror studios, Barbara Shelley was one of their biggest women stars. While most biographies emphasize her undeniably striking appearance, less attention is paid to how hard she worked across the five decades her acting career spanned. Shelley was born in London in 1932 and was initially a model, later turning to film and television. Although she made a very small appearance in Terence Fisher's crime film *Man in Hiding* in 1953—an early Hammer production—the first phase of her film career was largely in Italian films in small parts across crime movies, dramas and comedies. Her first major horror credit was in the title role of *Cat Girl* (1957), the AIP remake of Jacques Tourneur's *Cat People* (1942), and in 1958 she had a leading part in Henry Cass's *Blood of the Vampire*. In 1960, she played the wife of George Sander's Professor Gordon Zellaby in Wolf Rilla's *Village of the Damned*, and in 1961 she returned to feline horror territory in John Gilling's *The Shadow of the Cat*. In 1964, she collaborated again with Terence Fisher, this time in the Hammer film *The Gorgon* alongside Christopher Lee, Peter Cushing and Prudence Hyman. Although Shelley had established herself as a strong horror actor in years previously, Hammer's *Dracula: Prince of Darkness*—again with Fisher and Lee—granted Shelley her most famous role as the vampire Helen. She worked again with Lee on another Hammer film (Don Sharp's 1966 film *Rasputin: The Mad Monk*) and continued her strong association to the studio with Roy Ward Baker's *Quatermass and the Pit* in 1967 (written by celebrated genre writer Nigel Kneale). While the heyday of her horror career was arguably at an end, she maintained a connection to the genre in *Ghost Story* (Stephen Weeks, 1974), which starred Marianne Faithfull. In recent years, she has been interviewed in several documentaries about her involvement in the genre, including *British Film Forever* (2007) and *A History of Horror with Mark Gatiss* (2010).

SHENTON, KATE

British filmmaker Kate Shenton was born in Staffordshire and studied at the University of York where she discovered a passion for directing, soon pursuing further studies in the field at the University of Essex. Gaining traction with her 2010 horror-comedy short *Bon Appetit*, Shenton became a regular on the UK film festival circuit. She moved to London and made her 2013 documentary *On Tender Hooks* about the human suspension subculture, bringing her international attention. Continuing with short films, her initial attempt at making a zombie romcom as her first feature film collapsed but inspired her to make for what would become 2015's low-budget hit *Egomaniac*, a meta-horror-comedy about a young filmmaker trying to make a zombie romcom whose vision goes askew. Shenton has just released her first web series, *Netfl!x and Kill*.

SHEPARD, JEWEL

Hailing from New York City, Jewel Shepard has worked as a writer and photographer but her association with horror stems largely from acting. It was during her time as a stripper in Los Angeles that Shepard met director Dan O'Bannon which gave her an entry point into acting, and her horror credits include O'Bannon's *The Return of the Living Dead* (1985), *Scanner Cop II* (Steve Barnett, 1995), and *Slasher.com* (Chip Gubera, 2017). In 1992, she published the book *Invasion of the B-Girls* which featured interviews with cult film actors including Kitten Natividad, Linnea Quigley and Mary Woronov, and in 1996 she released her autobiography *If I'm So Famous, How Come Nobody's Ever Heard of Me?*

SHEPARD, PATTY

Although born in the United States in 1945, Patty Shepard moved to Spain when her father relocated for work and it is there where she built her screen career. With a filmography spanning two decades, she made over 50 films including many horror movies. Making films in Italy and France as well as Spain, she worked in several movies with the great Paul Naschy including *The Monsters of Terror* (Tulio Demicheli, 1970) and *Walpurgis Night* (León Klimovsky, 1971). Across her many other horror roles, she also appeared in the *giallo My Dear Killer* (Tonino Valerii, 1972), the psychological thriller *Glass Ceiling* (Eloy de la Iglesia, 1971), *Diabolical Shudder* (George Martin, 1972), *Hannah, Queen of the Vampires* (Julio Salvador and Ray Danton, 1973), *The Witches Mountain* (Raúl Artigot, 1975), *Rest in Pieces* (José Ramón Larraz, 1987), *Slugs* (Juan Piquer Simón, 1988) and *Edge of the Axe* (José Ramón Larraz, 1988).

SHEPHERD, ELIZABETH—INTERVIEW (JULY 2018)

While legendary actor Elizabeth Shepherd can by no means be claimed for horror alone, her work in the genre has earned her a reputation as a key figure for her iconic performances in films like *The Tomb of Ligeia* (Roger Corman, 1967) with Vincent Price, and *Damien: Omen II* (Don Taylor, 1978).

Born in London and spending her early childhood in Burma, Shepherd began acting professionally in the late 1950s and would soon establish an impressive career on stage and British television. She made her debut film appearance in Michael Powell's *The Queen's Guards* (1961) before later appearing alongside Price in *The Tomb of Ligeia* and would continue to work in the theater and in film and television after emigrating to the United States in 1965.

With over 500 television credits alone, Shepherd's celebrated career would unfold across England, Canada, and the United States on both stage and screen, playing characters as diverse as Margaret Thatcher, Simone de Beauvoir and Miss Havisham. She has particular expertise concerning the plays of William Shakespeare especially, playing many of his most famous characters including Juliet, Ophelia, Portia, and Lady Macbeth.

Shepherd's extraordinary knowledge of and experience in performing the great English classics have also garnered her a strong reputation as a teacher at highly-regarded institutions including Columbia University, London Academy of Music and Dramatic Art, and New York's Stella Adler Studio of Acting. Elizabeth very kindly took the time to speak to me about her remarkable career.

www.elizabethshepherdactor.com

Tomb of Ligeia **was without doubt the first horror film I really fell in love with as a child, and it was only as I got older—on one of my many, many revisits in**

my teens—that I clicked that Lady Ligeia and Rowena were played by the same person (I was not known as a particularly bright child, my apologies!). This revelation was absolutely radical for me, and I suspect it was the first time in my life I ever really understood that vital binary of light and dark, of yin and yang. I'm curious to hear about how you approached the process of playing two such striking, unique characters—while you clearly had some impressive collaborators (not just Mr Price and Mr Corman, but Mr Poe himself!), but so much of this dual performance seems to be spawned from somewhere very deep inside of you as an actor.

First, I am glad to read that the film grew on you in such revealing ways.

Here is my history with these two women, Ligeia herself and Rowena. Once I knew I was to do the movie, long before I was sent the script, the first thing I did was read the Poe story of "Ligeia", several times. I fell in love with this amazing woman so admiringly and passionately described by her adoring and un-named husband. The Lady Rowena wife was a mere cipher, no love lost between them, and only a vehicle for the return of the wondrous Lady Ligeia.

So, when I read the script of the movie I was *outraged* on Ligeia›s behalf!

I expressed to Roger my dismay that she was now this evil spirit lurking in mystery and the main story was now with Rowena…Roger heard me, but explained that a drug addicted opium fantasy was not exactly the best cinematic material! Therefore, he and Robert Towne (the screen-writer) searched to find a contemporary equivalence which could serve the story—and came up with Mesmerism. The Lady Rowena of our movie was created by Towne, and is a compelling and sparky wilful character in her own right, whom I did grow to love as much as Ligeia. As portrayed in our story I did see it as a double love story—Ligeia loved him so much she could not bear to let him go, so put the spell on him to keep him close. Rowena loved him because he was by far the most interesting man she had even met, and when she finally realizes the hold Ligeia has on him she has the courage and understanding to impersonate Ligeia in order to free him. Two remarkable women.

In the story, they are not at all alike. In our movie, the kindred spirit I surmised makes sense of the fact that they looked somehow alike—one as dark as the other is fair. In creating the character of Rowena, I had plenty in the script itself, and the daring of her actions, to guide me.

One striking characteristic is how brilliant a horsewoman—so I had to learn to ride side-saddle! Actually, I do not ride at all, but in the end I did all my riding except for the hunt and the jump. Rowena inspired me!

For my image of Ligeia, I went to Poe, and particularly the resonant descriptions of her Voice.

In the script of the hypnotism scene, when Rowena turns into Ligeia, it just said that "it happens during the singing of the song". I was so happy when I found my *link* which precipitated it…

> I have a bonnet trimmed with blue
> Do you wear it, yes I do.
> I will wear it when I can
> Going to the ball with my young man.

Second time through, third line:

> I will *will WILL*…and now I am Ligeia.

Roger Corman went to the Actors' Studio himself so that he could understand an actor's process, and works in detail beforehand on discussing the role, the character we are creating, the relationships, the look and the tone, etc.—and then he entrusts the role to the actor. That saves time on the set, and leaves him free to a create the shots which will tell the story in the most vivid way visually. He is the master of composition.

Vincent Price was a joy to work with, a brilliant (and underestimated) classical actor, and such an attractive man in all ways—accomplished in many arts, amusing raconteur, generous and loved by everyone in the profession. Neither he nor Roger thought of these Poe stories as "horror films"—but rather as Gothic tales, as Poe says "Tales of mystery and imagination". Vincent regarded this work like Shakespeare, heightened language and big emotional stakes. I was experienced in Shakespeare, so we were on the same wavelength.

Vincent was 53 when we made the film, and apparently, Roger Towne thought Verden should be played by a younger man…as if one could imagine *anyone else* in the role! I learned later I was cast because, although I was only 27, I had the maturity of my theater experience and so would pair with Vincent better than an ingénue actress. It was a good match, and I can say that Rowena had no difficulty in falling in love with Verden Fell!

With this emotionally rich material to fill my heart, and these fellow artists to work with, I was able to be at my best—I am proud of the movie, and am amazed it is still so much a part of my life even today. When I go to the Conventions and see how people love the film and me in it, I feel very touched and gratified.

I have great respect for both Vincent and Roger. They call Roger Corman the "King of the Bs"—but, for all that he has contributed to cinema, with his own films and the start in film he has given so many, many others, and his distribution of foreign films to the American cinema public, he is the "King of the Whole Alphabet" as far as I am concerned.

I have a fondness for the entirety of Roger Corman's Poe cycle, but for me *Tomb of Ligeia* is the one with the strongest women: so many women characters in this series seem to interpret 'elegance' as a kind of 'primness' that at times verges on uptight, but in the case of Rowena especially, this is never the case—certainly elegant, but also headstrong and fearless in a way quite unlike her counterparts. I'm curious to hear what your thoughts on women in gothic and

Elizabeth Shepherd in *The Tomb of Ligeia* (Roger Corman, 1964). Credit: American Internaitonal Pictures (AIP)/Photofest © American International Pictures (AIP).

horror films were at the time that you tackled this iconic dual role—I believe this was made only a few years after Alfred Hitchcock's *Psycho*, were you familiar with what was happening in gothic and horror themed cinema at the time or was your performance untethered from them?

I may not have as much to say here as you might like or expect! I really did not have much knowledge of what was happening in Gothic films at the time, though I knew Hitchcock's Psycho. I had not seen any of the other Corman/Price/Poe movies. I only knew Vincent from *Laura*, so I would indeed say I was "untethered"!

From what I have seen since, I would say that both Ligeia and Rowena are remarkably independent women. Not victims—headstrong and fearless both. Hitchcock would have perhaps found them too assertive!

The Hammer Horror films were current in England, and I never was approached by them. *Ligeia* was a one-off for me—and Joan Hart of course, another woman to be reckoned with!

While I realise it's not a horror film, I was fascinated to note that your film acting debut was Michael Powell's tremendous *The Queen's Guards*. From what I've read, Powell made this film with you in between shooting *Peeping Tom* and that film›s notorious release that so unfairly ended his filmmaking career in Britain. I›m very curious to hear from you if you had any sense yourself while working on *The Queen's Guards* that Powell had any idea that the*Peeping Tom* powder-keg was about to explode. And did you find the negativity surrounding *Peeping Tom* at the time of its release affected the way that people spoke about *The Queen's Guards*?

I had no idea about *Peeping Tom* while we were doing *The Queen's Guards*. I did know he had a "reputation"—when I went for my screen test, I was warned "He will try to make you cry"...I did not cry and I got the part, but I saw him make another girl cry with his remarks while we were filming.

The reason *The Queen's Guards* did not have the acclaim of his other films is because it was cut by half. In those days, it was fashionable to make films three or more hours long, with an Intermission. Our story, of soldiers in the Grenadier guards, who are all dressed up with tall black fur helmets for state occasions, but who are also on active combat service, was supposed to span 10 years. I was one of two girlfriends who cycle around the three hero-soldiers over these 10 years.

There was action in the fighting in Kenya and elsewhere—and all the social life in London between engagements. The Producers decided that the 3-hour formula was no longer practical, and ordered Powell to chop the film to pieces. It was released, but Powell never did really own it, though it is being included into his collected works.

When *Peeping Tom* was released to the outcry, that also doused Powell's public standing. I am proud to have worked with him—I wish the whole film could have been restored.

Your role as Joan Hart in *Damien: Omen II* is one of my favourite women-in-horror tropes—the plucky woman journalist—although things don't work out for Joan quite as well as some of her predecessors! The first *Omen* film of course was a cultural phenomenon—did you feel much pressure in making the sequel to live up to the hype of the original? And what was this unforgettable scene like to film with that very naughty bird?!

I was cast in *Damien* by the original director, Mike Hodges, who also co-wrote the script. He certainly intended to take the classy elements from the first "Omen" and make them classier still—visually and in depth. He wanted to explore Damien's dilemma when he discovered the role he had been born to.

At the original reading of the script, the scene between him and his cousin when Damien begs him to support him in his terrible path was absolutely heart-breaking, it was so human...Mike did all the original scenes with Sylvia [Sidney], and the visuals were as lovely as Visconti.

I was supposed to wear a fiber-glass mask of my face over my face for the heavy pecking. I did—and it was scary, as fibre-glass is very thin and the bird of prey's beak was fierce. My eyes were screwed tightly tightly closed. Mike then approached me and said we could not use any close-ups with the mask—would I work with the other bird (trained to land on black hair and peck blue eyes only once!) without the mask?

The bird wrangler was the same man as did the birds for the Hitchcock film—so I knew I would be in good hands. The bird "Big Boy" was tied onto my black wig with black threads and I was given hamburger in my fingers—I look as if I am trying to waft the bird away but I am in fact wafting hamburger to prevent any pecking! Mike wanted the scene to be longer with the tension wrenched up and up before the attack, like in Hitchcock—there seems danger from the birds but then they seem gone and Joan Hart sees rescue ahead—and when she (and we) relax and believe she *is safe THEN THE ATTACK HAPPENS BY SURPRISE—* huge JUMP SHOCK really *SCARY!*

Well—the 20th Century producers decided they wanted to speed things up, blood and gore up front, and then on to the next grisly death. They cheapened the concept, which could have explored the mythical workings of the devil more creatively. So Mike was fired and I had to reshoot my death scene all over again, faster—it is still quite an experience, but not what it could have been.

My stunt double who was hit by the truck in the end of my death scene was really hit by the truck on the first take—she very gamely did it again on the swing to fly up the land on TOP of the truck as intended, but they liked the accident better so that is what is in the film—someone REALLY nearly getting killed...

I loved Joan Hart, and loved working with William Holden (another real gentleman, like Vincent), but I would love to have seen the film Mike Hodges would have made.

The television series *Poltergeist: The Legacy* I recall airing around the same time that *The X-Files* was a big hit, but it was much more explicitly aligned with horror in the spirit of the films that it was based on. This series sadly has not had the same cult impact as *The X-Files*, so I'd love to hear from you some thoughts on your work on the show because I think it's long overdue a comeback.

Poltergeist was fun while it lasted—filmed in Vancouver. Jane Witherspoon was another feisty woman, and I was sorry when she met her demise. Crucifixion—that was another unusual experience! The only thing I was sorry about was that things ended before I had a chance to come back from the dead as others had done. Because I was in and out of the shooting I did not have a chance to bond with the other regulars on the show.

Do agitate for it to be re-released—residuals always come in handy! Incidentally, for those early films like *Ligeia*, residual arrangements were not written into the contract. So I consider the Conventions my Residual now.

I was fascinated to read on your website some of the legendary figures you have played on the stage, including some of the most complex women characters ever conceived: Miss Havisham in *Great Expectations*, Blanche Dubois in *A Streetcar Named Desire*, and Lady Macbeth. While each of these characters are marked by a certain strength, they are also representative each in their own way by a kind of feminine monstrosity—as an actor, what kind of unique creative possibilities do these 'darker' women characters (who are common to horror and the gothic but not unique to them) offer you creatively?

Miss Havisham, Blanche Dubois, Lady Macbeth—all formidably *strong* women, but I would not call them monstrosities—although Lady M's false reputation as a "ball-breaking bitch" has unfortunately become current, even among my Shakespeare students before they actually study the play!

It is mandatory for an actor never to judge the character they are playing but to inhabit them as a human being who for their own reasons (which must be understood) act in a certain way. Bruno Ganz, playing Hitler, said he had to explore the man's whole life to get under his skin, know what it was to *be* the man himself, know how his mind worked thinking his thoughts. To act "monster" is a caricature—the man did do monstrous things, but never himself believing them to be so.

Even playing the most extreme Gothic character, an actor must go there personally, from the inside, and dare to travel to those dark and dangerous places where the character's life force is leading them. If Lady Macbeth had been a ruthless cold-blooded killer, she would not have had to invoke "the spirits that tend on mortal thoughts" to "unsex her" in order to help Macbeth accomplish the murder; she would not have fallen apart as things unravel; she would not have been driven to madness in the end.

As written, she is a woman who is in partnership with her husband to make sure he becomes King. She stiffens his resolve when he wavers about killing King Duncan in their home, because she believes that he needs her to "pour my spirits in thine ears" in order for him to fulfill his dearest ambition. They are in it together—and the tragedy is that it destroys the relationship the further into the dark side he is forced to go. Shakespeare's characters are always very *human*, he sees them as human beings—even the most wicked like Richard the Third, and Iago (tho' he is the *most* irredeemable).

Blanche is one of my most treasured roles. To play her, I did have to go into her extremely vulnerable and frightening emotions—but what guided me was what Tennessee Williams had said about his sister Rose, whose fragile mental state was Blanche's landscape. He spoke of how *gallant* Rose was in dealing with all her difficulties.

I admired how Blanche is fighting always for her own sanity, fighting to make things come out right in the end, and if only that salesman had not been passing through with tales of her past, maybe she *could* have found solace with Mitch "Sometimes there's God so quickly". You cannot play Blanche from the outside, she has to be experienced for real so that her story can touch an audience and give them some visceral idea of what she goes through. Holding onto sanity is an epic task...

Miss Havisham is a wonderfully Gothic figure! In reading the book, I noticed that in the description of her room it told of one shoe gathering cobwebs on her dressing table... so I re-lived how that must have happened. She is in her wedding dress getting ready for the ceremony. She has one shoe on, and the other in her hand ready to put it on, when the letter arrived. She puts the shoe on the dressing table, opens the letter, learns she is being jilted—and everything STOPS DEAD right there for 25 years! Therefore, I chose to play with one shoe on and one shoe off for the whole run of the play! Since it was a co-production between the Derby Playhouse in England and the Walnut St Theater in Philadelphia that was for over two months! In fact, I developed "Miss Havisham's hip" as a result of the in-balance...but more unbalancing was to enter into her own personal nightmare world.

So, as you can see, these unusually complex, dark, and emotionally challenging roles are exciting to play because they demand my most creative energies—they stretch my imagination—they take me into unknown territory. Imagining what it feels like to be somebody else is my job—imagining what it feels like to be a Lady Macbeth, or a Blanche, or a Miss Havisham makes me a better actor for sincerely undertaking to live their difficult lives.

As someone who has been so active on both stage and screen for many decades, I'm curious as to what kinds of films in particular you yourself like to watch—are there any recent films that struck a chord with you? Do you watch horror movies, and if so, have any in particular struck you as particularly noteworthy in recent years? What advice would you give to young women wanting to act in horror or gothic-themed films?

I have to admit that Gothic and horror films are not my special favorites—though I do appreciate and prefer the older "classic" ones, like *Ligeia* certainly, even *Damien*, which are character-driven and not montages of special effects and weird happenings.

Casablanca is one of my all-time favorites, and tears always come to my eyes when she starts singing the "Marseillaise"! Last year I loved a movie called *Maudie* [directed by Aisling Walsh] about a painter—wonderful performances by Sally Hawkins and Ethan Hawke. I just saw the Mr Rogers movie, *Won't You Be My Neighbor?*—most touching and important, especially in today's atmosphere. I remember being powerfully impressed by a New Zealand film *Once Were Warriors* dealing with domestic violence in a creative Maori way. Just a taste—as you see they are all very human stories.

My advice to any young woman wanting to act in horror or Gothic-themed stories is to *expand* your heart and mind wide open to enter into this new unfamiliar world as if you belonged there. Enter into the culture of it.

Understand your character's place in it—it is as everyday real to HER as your everyday is to YOU. Study her inner life as intently as you would a role in a "realism" play or film. Find out how *different* she is from you—and also what you may have in common. *Dare* to go into unknown territory—unleash your imagination—fantasize—surprise yourself—make *discoveries*.

If it is Poe, pay attention to the beauty of the language and relish it.

Above all, make her REAL in her own way and in her own right. Playing "weird" and "horrible" is just grotesque—both Ligeia and Rowena are in extreme Gothic circumstances but yet are true to themselves, have their own truth.

Believe in the character—and believe in yourself as an actor able to find her.

SHEPIS, TIFFANY

Tiffany Shepis is an American actor who was born in New York in 1979. She began acting in her early teens and made her film debut in *Tromeo and Juliet* (James Gunn, 1996). She has worked largely in low-budget indie genre films since the mid 1990s, and her horror credits include *Citizen Toxie: The Toxic Avenger IV* (Lloyd Kaufman, 2000), *Scarecrow* (Emmanuel Itier, 2002), *Bloody Murder 2: Closing Camp* (Rob Spera, 2003), *The Hazing* (Rolfe Kanefsky, 2004), *Nightmare Man* (Rolfe Kanefsky, 2006), *Abominable* (Ryan Schifrin, 2006), *Hoodoo for Voodoo* (Steven Shea, 2007), *Home Sick* (Adam Wingard, 2007), *Dark Reel* (Josh Eisenstadt, 2008), *Bryan Loves You* (Seth Landau, 2008), *Zombies! Zombies! Zombies!* (Jason M. Murphy, 2008), *The Violent Kind* (The Butcher Brothers, 2010) and *Caesar and Otto's Paranormal Halloween* (Dave Campfield, 2015). In 2015 she also starred in Adam Gierasch's segment "Trick" in the horror anthology film *Tales of Halloween*.

SHERMAN, CINDY

One of the most celebrated American visual artists of the 20th century, Cindy Sherman made only one feature film across her lengthy career, the horror movie *Office Killer* in 1997. Born in New Jersey in 1954, Sherman has won awards and fellowships around the world for her photographic work, including the prestigious MacArthur Fellowship in 1995 and the American Academy of Arts and Sciences Award in 2003. Sherman had elsewhere demonstrated an interest in horror in early short films and her "Untitled Horrors" photography series, and although her sole feature film did not generally impress critics at the time of its release, *Office Killer*—starring Carol Kane and Molly Ringwald and co-written by Todd Haynes—is dark, funny and consciously taps into horror's perverse pleasures.

SHERWOOD, ROBIN

American actor Robin Sherwood began her career as an actor and model in the early 1970s. She was born in Miami in 1952, and her horror credits include *The Love Butcher* (Mikel Angel and Don Jones, 1975), *Tourist Trap* (David Schmoeller, 1979), and Brian De Palma's *Blow Out* (1981). She further strengthened her cult film credentials playing Charles Bronson's daughter in *Death Wish II* (Michael Winner, 1982).

SHI, NAN-SUN

Joining the screen industry during the prolific era of the Hong Kong New Wave, Nan-sun Shi began her career in television in the mid-1970s and soon established a career in film production. A hugely successful film executive, she has been highly recognized in the industry and was on the jury for the 2011 Cannes Film Festival and received the Best Independent Producer Award at Switzerland's Locarno Film Festival in 2014. Her many film credits include the horror movies *A Chinese Ghost Story* (Andrew Chan, 1997), *The Era of Vampires* (Wellson Chin, 2003), *Missing* (Tsui Hark, 2008) and *Journey to the West: The Demons Strike Back* (Tsui Hark, 2017).

SHIINA, EIHI

While already having established a successful career as a model, Eihi Shiina is most immediately recognizable for her iconic performance as the sadistic Asami Yamazaki in Takashi Miike's *Audition* (1999). Born on the Japanese island of Kyushu in 1976, her screen debut was in Isao Yukisada's understated drama *Open House* in 1998, but following the international success of *Audition* she would turn increasingly towards horror, appearing in many films directed by Yoshihiro Nishimura such as *Tokyo Gore Police* (2008), *Vampire Girl vs. Frankenstein Girl* (2009), *Helldriver* (2010) and *Meatball Machine Kodoku* (2017), as well as his segment "The Hell Chef" in the 2013 horror anthology *The Profane Exhibit*.

Eihi Shiina as Asami Yamakazi in *Audition* (Takashi Miike, 1999). Credit: Vitagraph/Photofest
© Vitagraph Films LLC

SHIRE, TALIA'

As Adrian Pennino in the *Rocky* movies and Connie Corleone in *The Godfather* films, Talia Shire won several awards for her acting (including two Oscar nominations), but she also appeared in an impressive number of horror films. Shire comes from a family who have attained great success in the field, including her brother Francis Ford Coppola, niece Sofia Coppola, nephews Roman Coppola and Nicolas Cage, and her sons, Robert and Jason Schwartzman. Shire made her film debut in Daniel Haller and Roger Corman's *The Wild Racers* in 1968, appearing in Haller's Sandra Dee-fronted Lovecraft adaptation *The Dunwich Horror* in 1970 that marked her horror debut. Across her career, she would return to the genre in Paulmichel Mielche's *The Butchers* (1973), John Frankenheimer's *Prophecy* (1979) and Robert Malenfant's *The Landlady* (1998).

SHORTLAND, CATE

Born in 1968, Cate Shortland is one of Australia's most celebrated contemporary film directors. She grew up in the country's capital city Canberra, and studied at Sydney's Australian Film, Television and Radio School where the high standard of her work was recognized early. After several shorts and working on television, Shortland's much anticipated debut *Somersault* was nominated for Cannes' prestigious *Un Certain Regard* Award. Shortland's police drama *The Silence* (2006) was followed by the war movie *Lore* (2012), demonstrating a flair for working across different genres that came to the fore in her 2017 psychological horror film, *Berlin Syndrome*, adapted from Melanie Joosten's novel of the same name.

SIDNEY, SYLVIA

As a social worker for the recently deceased in Tim Burton's *Beetlejuice* (1988), New York-born actor Sylvia Sidney topped off a long career that saw frequent career highlights in horror. Born in 1910 as Sophia Kosow, her first small movie role was in Joseph Boyle's *Broadway Nights* in 1927, followed by increasingly larger roles and headlining films by directors including Dorothy Arzner, Fritz Lang, William Wyler and Alfred Hitchcock. Working until 1998, she also appeared on stage and television, and her horror credits include *Damien: Omen II* (Don Taylor, 1978), *God Told Me To* (Larry Cohen, 1976), and the made-for-TV horror movies *Snowbeast* (Herb Wallerstein, 1977) and *Death at Love House* (E.W. Swackhamer, 1976). But it is as *Beetlejuice*'s chain-smoking June that Sidney is most remembered, the actor passing away at the age of 88 from oesophageal cancer, somewhat ironically a result of her own life-long cigarette addiction.

SIEGEL, KATE

As the mute protagonist of Mike Flanagan's *Hush* (2016), Kate Siegel earned a place as one of the strongest horror performers currently working in the genre. Making her debut in Dan Goldman's 2007 horror film *The Curse of the Black Dahlia*, Siegel was born in Maryland in 1982 and would work steadily in film and television until she played the sadistic ghost Marisol in Flanagan's 2013 haunted mirror movie *Oculus*. Siegel and Flanagan would marry in 2016 and continue to collaborate professionally, with Siegel appearing in *Ouija: Origin of Evil* (2016) and *Gerald's Game* (2017), and both starring in and writing *Hush*. Her other horror work as an actor includes appearances in *Demon Legacy* (Rand Vossler, 2014) and the horror shorts *The Program* (Dylan Mulick, 2015) and *Let's Go Down* (Phil Davism 2017). In 2018 she played Theo in Flanagan's widely acclaimed adaptation of Shirley Jackson's 1959 novel *The Haunting of Hill House*.

Kate Siegel arrives at the 42nd Annual Saturn Awards on 22 June 2016 at the Castaway Restaurant in Burbank, California. Credit: CarlaVanWagoner / Shutterstock.com

SIEGER, JACQUELINE

Little is known of Jacqueline Sieger, whose only screen credit is as the "Queen of the Vampires" in Jean Rollin's 1968 film, the French horror classic *The Rape of the Vampire*. As the leader of the undead, Sieger plays her lesbian vampire queen with gusto, albeit admittedly avoiding the pesky trappings of realistic performance. As one of the few Black women cast as a horror film protagonist from this era in European cinema, Sieger's often-ignored importance to genre history should be remedied.

SIGNORET, SIMONE

The career of French actor Simone Signoret was already well-established by the time she starred in Henri-Georges Clouzot's classic *Diabolique* in 1955. Three years later, Signoret would become the first person from France to win an Oscar, and across her career she worked with high calibre directors including Luis Buñuel, René Clément, Costa-Gavras, Stanley Kramer and Sidney Lumet. Born in Germany in 1921, she struggled in her early years in the French film industry as she was an illegal immigrant, a result of her Jewish family's dislocation from Germany during the Nazi regime. In *Diabolique*, Signoret made a significant donation to the history of horror's strong yet monstrous women as the duplicitous and seductive Nicole Horner. She continued this legacy in Curtis Harrington's underrated 1967 film *Games*, where Signoret again plays a master manipulator, this time in the pop-art drenched nightmare world of upper-class New York City alongside Katharine Ross and James Caan. Signoret would also write and perform for the stage, penning her memoirs in 1978 and a novel in 1985.

SIKAMANA, ACHITA

Born in Thailand in 1982, model-turned-actor Achita Sikamana made her first screen appearance in the internationally successful 2004 Thai horror film *Shutter* by Banjong Pisanthanakun and Parkpoom Wongpoom (remade in the United States in 2008). A supernatural rape-revenge film, Sikamana plays Natre, a ghost who returns through camera technology to torment photographer Tun (Ananda Everingham) and his girlfriend Jane (Natthaweeranuch Thongmee). She has continued to act, with further films including a role in the horror-comedy *Ghost Station* (Yuthlert Sippapak, 2007).

SIMON, SIMONE

With a career that crossed the Atlantic, Simone Simon is remembered for her famous role as Irena Dubrovna in Jacques Tournear's *Cat People* (1942). Born in 1910 to a French father and Italian mother in the northern French city of Béthune, the young Simon had a flair for performance and the arts and was discovered by Russian director Victor Tourjansky. She quickly rose to fame in France, moving to Hollywood to continue her successes which at first failed to fully materialize due to conflicts with colleagues and poor health. Frustrated with America, she briefly returned to France but attempted Hollywood again in the early 1940s with the onset of World War II, which lead her to producer Val Lewton and RKO, resulting in both *Cat People* (1942) and *The Curse of the Cat People* (1944). As Irene, Simon granted depth to what could have easily become a comic, exploitative character; the tragic, trapped half-woman, half-feline.

Simone Simon from *Cat People* (Jacques Tourneur, 1942). Credit: Photo 12 / Alamy Stock Photo

SISSEL, SANDI

Beginning her career on television shows like *Saturday Night Live* and *60 Minutes*, Emmy-award winning cinematographer Sandi Sissel initially pursued a career in journalism before turning towards working behind the camera on films including Mira Nair's 1988 film *Salaam Bombay!*. While she has worked extensively in the field of documentary, Sissel was the cinematographer on Anthony Hickox's 1993 werewolf cop television movie *Full Eclipse*, and an episode of the 2005 television reboot of the Kolchak series, *Night Stalker*. Most significantly, she was responsible for the beautiful photography that brought the ominous and often surreal energy of Wes Craven's *The People Under the Stairs* (1991) to life. Sissel is an Associate Professor at New York University's Tisch School of the Arts.

SKLOSS, KAREN

Early in her career, American filmmaker, artist and musician Karen Skloss starred as one of the two lead characters in the surreal teen fantasy *Odile and Yvette at the Edge of the World* (André Burke, 1993), turning her talents as an adult primarily towards editing and, later, directing. Her first feature-length narrative film as director was 2017's *The Honor Farm*, a prom night horror movie with a twist. Filmed in Texas, *The Honor Farm* was shot by Richard Linklater regular, cinematographer Lee Daniel, whose skill behind the camera amplifies Skloss's unique vision.

SKOGLAND, KARI

Award-winning Canadian director Kari Skogland is a champion for women's filmmaking and has achieved success in both film and television. She made her directorial debut on the TV series *Dead at 21* in 1994 and learned the ropes on several other shows and made-for-television movies during the 1990s. Her first work in the genre was on the short-lived series *The Crow: Stairway to Heaven* in 1998, followed by her the straight-to-video sequel, *Children of the Corn 666: Isaac's Return in 1999* with Nancy Allen. Later in her career, she would also direct episodes of popular television series including *The Borgias, Penny Dreadful* and *The Walking Dead*.

SLATER, JEANNE

Canadian editor Jeanne Slater studied with celebrated indie filmmaker and editor Shirley Clarke at UCLA and pursued her passion for editing. She began her editing career as an assistant, working on Nietzchka Keene's Björk-fronted *The Juniper Tree* in 1990. Her first full editorial credit was for Annie O'Donoghue's 1996 short *Love Taps*, and she would work across film and television including a number of notable collaborations with horror director Karen Lam, including the short films *The Cabinet* (2007), *Doll Parts* (2011), *The Stolen* (2012), *Stalled* (2013), *Chiral* (2015) and the feature film *Evangeline* (2013). In 2014, Slater also edited numerous episodes of the children's horror television series *R.L. Stine's The Haunting Hour*.

SMITH, MADELINE

British model and actor Madeline Smith was born in Sussex in 1949, and across her film, television and stage career she appeared in a number of horror movies, including three from Hammer studios. She made her debut in Robert Amram's *The Mini-Mob* (1967), gaining small roles in film and television until she gained a part in *Taste the Blood of*

Dracula (Peter Sasdy, 1970), her first horror movie. That same year she got a much bigger role in Hammer's *The Vampire Lovers* (Roy Ward Baker, 1970) playing Emma Morton, the would-be victim of Ingrid Pitt's lesbian vampire Marcilla. Her final Hammer film was Terence Fisher's *Frankenstein and the Monster from Hell* in 1974, where she was cast alongside Peter Cushing and David Prowse as the title characters. Beyond Hammer, her other donations to the genre include *The Devil's Widow* (Roddy McDowall, 1970) and the Vincent Price film *Theater of Blood* (Douglas Hickox, 1973).

SMITH, SARAH ADINA

Studying in New York City, Sarah Adina Smith acted in a couple of shorts in the early 2000s. Her directorial debut was *Madura* in 2006 which—alongside much of her indie work—she wrote and edited also. Her feature debut was the found footage horror film *The Midnight Swim* (2014) which garnered her several accolades, such as the breakthrough audience award at AFI FEST. Smith followed this up with the segment "Mother's Day", a maternal horror film in the anthology film *Holidays* in 2016 which also included directors like Kevin Smith and Nicholas McCarthy. While also working in television, Smith's dark, sad, and strange follow-up to *The Midnight Swin* was 2016's *Buster's Mal Heart*.

SMITH, SHAWNEE

While also a musician and appearing in several popular sitcoms, American actor Shawnee Smith is linked most immediately to the *Saw* franchise and her continuing role as Amanda Young. Appearing regularly throughout the franchise from James Wan's first film in 2004, Smith's Amanda also appeared in videogames and comic books stemming from the popular series. Smith was born in South Carolina in 1969, and began acting in the theater as a child, soon moving to television commercials. She made her debut in a small role as a dancer in John Huston's adaptation of the popular play *Annie* in 1982. She increasingly worked in television, moving to film including a lead role in Chuck Russell's 1988 remake of *The Blob* with Kevin Dillon, and Adam Grossman and Ian Kessner's 1998 remake of Herk Harvey's 1962 cult horror movie *Carnival of Souls*. During the period, she would also make appearances in the mini-series adaptations of Stephen King's *The Stand* (Mick Garris, 1984) and *The Shining* (Mick Garris, 1997) as well as an episode of *The X-Files*. After her first appearance in the *Saw* films, Smith would maintain her connection to horror beyond the franchise by appearing in Darren Lynn Bousman's 2006 short *Repo! The Genetic Opera* (which he would later develop into a feature film in 2008) and *The Grudge 3* (Toby Wilkins, 2009), as well as the horror mini-series *30 Days of Night: Dust to Dust*, a sequel to David Slade's 2007 film. In 2008, she was a regular guest on the reality TV programme *Scream Queens*, and while Kevin Greutert's *Saw VI* in 2009 was the last time Amanda was seen in the series, she was mentioned in the Spierig Brothers' *Jigsaw* in 2017.

Shawnee Smith at the *Saw 3D* special screening, Chinese 6, Hollywood, California.
27 October 2010. Credit: s_bukley / Shutterstock.com

SMOCZYŃSKA, AGNIESZKA

Polish director Agnieszka Smoczyńska was born in 1978 and took the international film festival circuit by storm with her musical mermaid horror extravaganza *The Lure* in 2015. Consciously intended as an antidote to the Disneyfication of Hans Christian Anderson's *The Little Mermaid*, Smoczyńska brings a burlesque sensibility to her tale of killer fish-women Golden (Michalina Olszańska) and Silver (Marta Mazurek). Having worked on television and short films previously, *The Lure* was her debut feature film, and she has since gone on to work on the horror anthology *The Field Guide to Evil* (2018) with directors including Veronika Franz, Katrin Gebbe and Peter Strickland. In 2016, *The Lure* won the Special Jury Award for Unique Vision and Design, and in 2018, she released her much-anticipated follow up *Fugue*.

SNIVELY, DEVI

Self-identifying "writer/directrix" Devi Snively began her career in the arts as a dedicated ballerina until she was 20, lured to the dark side by influences including *The Wizard of Oz* and *The Nutcracker Suite* and a formative crush on Darth Vader from *Star Wars*. She began as an amateur filmmaker with her first short *A Soap Opera* in 2001, and would follow with a string of alluringly titled comedy-horror shorts including *Teenage Bikini Vampire* (2004), *Confederate Zombie Massacre!* (2005), *Raven Gets a Life* (2006), and the fabulous *I Spit on Eli Roth* (2009), the latter co-starring horror directors Jane Rose and Amy Lynn Best. Since then, as her work has developed to a more polished, professional level, she has made a strong impression on the festival circuit with several shorts includ-

Devi Snively http://brideoffrankie.com (Used with permission).

ing *Last Seen on Dolores Street* (2010) and *Bride of Frankie* (2017). Her feature film debut was *Trippin'* (2011), followed by the web series *Martini Mom and Devil Spawn* (2012). Snively is an alumnus of the AFI Conservatory Directing Workshop for Women (DWW), later selected as one of their 2017 Fox Filmmaker Lab participants where she made her celebrated short *Death in Charge*. Snively is also an adjunct professor of anthropology at the University of Notre Dame in Indiana.

SNODGRESS, CARRIE

Growing up in Chicago, Carrie (short for Caroline) Snodgress was born in 1945 and would famously turn down the role of Adrian in *Rocky* (1976), leading to another horror regular Talia Shire being cast in the role. Regardless, she had a long career, beginning on stage and moving in later years to film and television. Early in her career she had a brief uncredited role in Dennis Hopper's *Easy Rider* (1969) befor her breakout performance in Jack Smight's *Rabbit, Run* with James Caan in 1970. She was nominated for a Best Supporting Actress Oscar that same year for her role as Tina in Frank Perry's comedy *Diary of a Mad Housewife*. Her first horror film saw her as Kirk Douglas's substantially younger lover in Brian De Palma's *The Fury* (1978), and she starred in George Edward's *The Attic* in 1980. Her other horror film performances include *Trick or Treats* (Gary Graver, 1982), *Ed Gein* (Chuck Parello, 2000) and *The Forsaken* (J.S. Cardone, 2001), and she also appeared in *The X-Files*.

SNOWDEN, JULIET

Juliet Snowden wrote the screenplays for several horror films including *Boogeyman* (Stephen Kay, 2005), *The Possession* (Ole Bornedal, 2012) and) and the short film *The Need* (Chris Young, 2006). These were co-written with her husband Stiles White, who directed 2014's *Ouija* which he and Snowden also wrote together. With Stiles, she co-wrote the screenplay Alex Proyas's scifi film *Knowing* (2009).

SOLES, PJ

PJ (Pamela Jayne) Soles is a horror film icon, appearing in two of the most famous horror films of the 1970s; Brian De Palma's *Carrie* (1976) and John Carpenter's *Halloween* (1978). Born in Germany and travelling around the world with her father's work as a child, she moved to Los Angeles in 1975 to dedicate herself to her acting career. Although appearing in a range of films including The Ramones' *Rock 'n' Roll High School* (Allan Arkush, 1979), *Private Benjamin* (Howard Zieff, 1980), *Stripes* (Ivan Reitman, 1981) and *Jawbreaker* (Darren Stein, 1999), Soles is known primarily for horror movies including *Blood Bath* (Joel M. Reed, 1976), *The Possessed* (Jerry Thorpe, 1977), *Innocent Prey* (Colin Eggleston, 1984), *Uncle Sam* (William Lustig, 1996), *Mirror, Mirror IV: Reflection* (Paulette Victor-Lifton, 2000), *Death by Engagement* (Philip Creager, 2005), *The Devil's Rejects* (Rob Zombie, 2005), *The Tooth Fairy* (Stephen J. Cannell, 2006), *Mil Mascaras vs. the Aztec Mummy* (Chip Gubera and Jeff Burr, 2007) and *Alone in the Dark II* (Michael Roesch and Peter Scheerer, 2008).

SOMMER, ELKE

German actor and model Elke Sommer was born in 1940 and her career flourished internationally during the 1960s. Discovered by Italian auteur Vittorio De Sica when she was 18 years old, in the 1970s she appeared in two Mario Bava films: *Baron Blood* with Joseph Cotten in 1972 and *Lisa and the Devil* in 1973, the latter recut and re-released in 1975 *as House of Exorcism* to profit on the success of William Friedkin's *The Exorcist* (1973). In 1992, she would star with Oliver Reed in Damon Santostefano's horror-*comedy Severed Ties*, making a smaller appearance in 2000 in Michael Karen's *Flashback*.

SONDERGAARD, GALE

Born in Minnesotta in 1899, Gale Sondergaard received a Best Supporting Actress Award for her first film role in Mervyn LeRoy's *Anthony Adverse* (1936). While appearing in a range of films during the late 1930s and '40s in particular, her horror work is of note: Sondergard was cast in in *The Cat and the Canary* (Elliott Nugent, 1939), *The Black Cat* (Albert S. Rogell, 1941), *The Invisible Man's Revenge* (Ford Beebe, 1944) and *The Spider Woman Strikes Back* (Arthur Lubin, 1947). A victim of the injustices of the communist witch-hunts of the House Un-American Activities Committee, Sondergaard's career was virtually destroyed by accusations that made her husband Herbert Biberman one of the infamous "Hollywood Ten". After an almost 20-year hiatus, she returned to acting in 1969 and in the later part of her career she appeared in the horror films *Savage Intruder* (Donald Wolfe, 1970) and *Living Nightmare* (Arthur Allan Seidelman, 1982), as well as appearing in the horror television series *Night Gallery*.

SOO-JUNG, IM

South Korean actor Im Soo-jung began her career modeling, moving to the screen for her debut in Kim Jee-woon's internationally acclaimed *A Tale of Two Sisters* (2003). Born in Seoul, while having some experience on television with series such as *The Haunted School*, few anticipated her nuanced performance in what remains one of the most famous and celebrated K-horror films of the 21st century. Since then, she has worked in a range of primarily romantic comedies and dramas, including Chan-wook Park's *I'm a Cyborg, But That's OK* (2006).

SORINA, ALEXANDRA

Belarusian actor Alexandra Sorina was born in 1899 in Minsk in the Russian Empire (now part of Poland). Her screen career lasted only a decade—from 1922 to 1932—but within that time she packed in several significant horror performances. Most prominent of these is her role as Yvonne Orlac in Robert Wiene's expressionist classic *The Hands of Orlac* (1924)—for which she was credited simply as 'Sorina'. Although not technically horror films, there is also certainly generic overlap in two of her later films; *Rasputin, the Holy Sinner* (Martin Berger, 1928) and *Rasputin, Demon with Women* (Adolf Trotz, 1932).

SOSKA, JEN AND SYLVIA—INTERVIEW (JANUARY 2019)

Canadian filmmaking twins Jen and Sylvia Soska (aka The Twisted Twins or The Soska Sisters) are virtually synonymous with the contemporary Women in Horror movement. Born in Vancouver in 1983, they famously directed, wrote and starred in their debut feature *Dead Hooker in a Trunk* (2009), which they made for only $2500. After several short films (including promos for Women in Horror Month), in 2012 they released their breakout feminist deconstruction of the rape-revenge trope *American Mary*, starring Katherine Isabelle of *Ginger Snaps* fame in the title role. A series of further shorts and the segment "T is for Torture Porn" for the horror anthology *ABCs of Death 2* (2014) followed, with their third feature *See No Evil 2* released the same year. Aside from the action film *Vendetta* released in 2015, they have rarely strayed from their beloved horror terrain: they hosted the horror game show *Hellevator* in 2015 and 2016, and when they kindly took time out of their busy schedule to chat to me about their careers, their much-anticipated remake of fellow Canadian David Cronenberg's 1977 film *Rabid* was about to be released on the international horror film festival circuit.

http://twistedtwinsproductions.net/

I'd like to start right back with *Dead Hooker in a Trunk*—there's so few debut films I can think of that have anywhere near the energy of that film, and it really feels like one of the last great punk rock feminist films. The title feels like such a provocation—where in the process did that name come into play, and did people's responses to the film based on its title alone ever surprise you? Do you think the provocative title caught people's attention?

Sylvia: The title came from Jen as a response to the multi-segmented Grindhouse that was in theatres at the time. In particular, *Hobo With A Shotgun*. This was also during the times of the Pickton farm serial killer outcry. Women were going missing and the police did little to help these women as the majority of them worked on the street. We took that and made it the heart of our film. We've had people—with the proper outrage of disrespect of sex workers—come at us, we've had the film banned on title alone, but the film is about a group of fuck-ups trying to make a peaceful end to a murdered woman they find the body of. The violence and tone of the film is very tongue-in-cheek until it comes to the violence against the title character. We wanted that to be real and for the reality of it to be upsetting. We wanted to humanize people who society looks down on.

Jen: You need a good title especially when you're starting out. I needed something that would get stuck in people's heads, get a strong emotional reaction, and say, "I've gotta see that movie". The title definitely turned heads and opened doors as well as closed them. I did not create the phrase, "Dead Hooker In A Trunk", but I did want to make a very self-aware film about respect for life. The whole film is out-of-this-world ridiculousness until you see how the title character died. You feel for her. Everything else is intentionally slap stick. No character has a name in that film. Just a type or role. Hooker, Junkie, Badass, Goody Two Shoes and Geek. Even Cowboy Pimp. We put all our passion into that one and it shows.

I understand *Dead Hooker* was a film school project, and I'd love to hear what you found the most beneficial—and the biggest waste of time—of that kind of formal training?

S: The film industry is one of the most slimiest, underhanded, thieving businesses there is and that starts at film school. We had a terrible agent at the time who had a deal with the school to send people to it. We wanted to stop playing these stereotypical twin roles and wanted to do work we could be proud of. At the time, we were heavily involved with marital arts and wanted to be stunt women. Our agent said only the school upstairs can do that and five figures later, we were even more pissed off and disenchanted than when we started. *Dead Hooker* was a fuck you. It was never planned to be a film. We shot a fake trailer with everything the school had on its list for inappropriate material and added beastiality and necrophilia for good measure. We paid for it ourselves, we acted, wrote, directed, crew'ed, did stunts, you name it and it was the first time we were in control of what we were in—and we loved it. I don't recommend film school.

J: Every film school is a giant waste of time. Put that money into buying equipment and watch YouTube videos to learn for free. Or volunteer on set. Get PAID for an education. Film school is good if you're not really sure what you want to do in film and want to make contacts, but if that's your mindset it will be a difficult profession for you. You need to roll with the punches and think fast on your feet. I'd never recommend any and certainly not the one we attended.

I think it's an understatement, but if *Dead Hooker* had a punk feminist spirit, *American Mary* proved that was more than just luck. I have a few questions

Jen Soska and Sylvia Soska at Superstars for Hope honoring Make-A-Wish, Beverly Hills Hotel, Beverly Hills, California, 15 August 2013. Credit: s_bukley / Shutterstock.com

about this film because it really solidified your reputation in so many ways—I have written two books on rape-revenge film and I'm always surprised by how few women filmmakers tackle it (even though there's a lot more who make films including depictions of sexual violence). What made that a particular area of fascination for you at that particular moment? It feels so ahead of its time, especially with the major focus on sexual assault and harassment we've seen on such a mass scale over the last year or so ...

S: A film comes from your own experiences. *American Mary* was an analogy for our ventures in the film industry. We are identical twins and, in this world, that means being hyper sexualized constantly even at a presexual age. There was no one to save you, you were constantly at the mercy of wolves if you could even get in the door. The film started with differentiating between a male and female killer. How are they different? What is something truly terrifying a woman with that kind of medical training could do to her assailant? Many survivors of assault do not get their justice, but they can watch *American Mary* and that bastard gets it every time.

I think the film scared a lot of people. What Mary does to Dr. Grant is extremely relatable and a lot of women have that level of anger in them for the atrocities of this world. I hope people rediscover it and it have a cathartic experience with it now.

J: The film was certainly ahead of its time and I'm frankly surprised given its content and the reason we wrote it that it would be getting more attention given the TIME'S UP movement. I guess people don't like how Mary dealt with her attacker but as someone who has now heard hundreds if not over a thousand stories from sexual assault survivors about how their assaulter never faced justice, I'm not too happy with how the justice system functions. It's a business. There's only justice for the most wealthy. Most rape kits aren't even *tested*.

I also hate how rape is always sexualized in film. Male gaze, like watching porn, rather than female gaze, watching an assault. We wanted to make a clear distinction despite pressure from our producers to get our lead to be topless for the scene. That film was made under very trying circumstances. It seems every time there is a female celebrating film, there are growing pains of the #MeToo era. *American Mary* was made well before anyone cared what women had to say and it was difficult to tell that story without any support. I'm glad we made it so that those who never got their own closure can receive some through Mary's vengeance.

One of the most important and radical things about *American Mary* for me is that in most rape-revenge films (in fact, almost all of them), when it's a woman seeking vengeance for herself it's almost like rape is some kind of alchemy that 'turns' women into feminists. You guys totally avoided this by making it very, very clear that Mary was *already* a strong feminist character—I think this is just so ground-breaking. Was this a conscious decision? How did you research the role, and what were you wanting to do with this film that you felt was really necessary in the telling of stories about this kind of trauma?

S: I never intended to make a rape revenge, although it can definitely be described as that. Mary has her world ripped apart three times before she changes into someone darker for good. First is when she does the backroom surgery on the Rat in the club, second when she does the elective amputations and surgery on the doll woman, and then last when Grant proves that he only ever saw her as a sexual object. Everything Mary ever held sacred is torn out from under her and she goes numb. She becomes the one who protects her. She goes to sociopathic lengths to try to heal what was done to her by making other people happy with her surgeries while she's secretly chopping up Grant in a storage locker. He's like a little black dress she tries on to feel great about herself. Any bad nights? Time for some more surgery.

J: This touches on what you mentioned before, women tackling this material. No man will ever know what it's like to be a woman and raped by a man. They can know their own abuse, but they cannot get into that mindset. They project feelings rather than understand them. That's why this odd insta-feminist archetype comes into play. Women can't fit into one box. We're too complex. We can't just be victim girl, then badass. And in being a badass there isn't always strength. I'm exhausted by the over correction where women perform incredible feats flawlessly with no training or challenge. That doesn't reflect reality and seeing that doesn't erase all the inequality issues we face. It was important that Mary had a lot going on inside her before. We don't write weak women because I don't believe in representing women that way. Now more than ever we need to be outspoken and we need role models like that.

A simple question, but one I've always really wanted to ask: why did you decide that Mary had to die at the end? (I'm not criticising, it's a fascinating decision and I'd love to hear your thinking!)

S: There were creative challenges with people who did not understand the film who wanted to turn Mary into a magical ghost in the sequels that killed horny teenagers. It was a mercy killing. It was also the way we wanted to end the film because it›s unrealistic that there would be a happy ending in her story that was a tragedy. She was dead in so many ways that after she lost her grandmother, she was beyond lost. She went out on her own terms, as a brilliant surgeon. She could have grabbed her phone, called 911, but she had so little control over her life, her death was her final masterpiece.

J: It was also to have this discussion. Many complain that they wish Mary left with Billy at the end. That just wasn't her. She never wanted him and he only wanted her because of his complex feelings of guilt and desire because he couldn't ever

Jen and Sylvia Soska in *American Mary*. Credit: TCD/Prod.DB/Alamy Stock Photo.

have her. He never knew her beyond his fantasy. Mary was already dead on the inside by then. You can hear it in her voice. I wonder if people would have loved Mary as much if she had lived? There's nothing like a beautiful tragedy.

See No Evil 2 really felt like so much fun, and so well deserved after the really dark terrain of American Mary. It was also so great to see you collaborating again with Katherine Isabelle and working with Danielle Harris. What was that experience like compared to what you'd done previously?

S: We have been huge WWE fans since we were teens—it was such an honour to get to work with Glenn 'Kane' Jacobs (I guess that's actually Mayor Glenn Jacobs) on the revival of the *See No Evil* franchise. There's a lot of history when you do a sequel plus a huge fan expectation. Getting to have Katie back in a comedic role with Scream Queen royalty, Danielle Harris, was a match made in horror heaven. We shot it all in the same partially closed mental hospital so it has a lot of charm!

J: It was nice to work for two huge studios, WWE Studios and Lionsgate. They know what they want. Creativity is limited because you are working to satisfy a client and WWE has very particular standards and desires, or at least they did at the time. Censorship was a huge issue. So it was fun to learn all about what restrictions there are globally. Making a film is so much bigger than most people suspect. There are a lot of people and regions to satisfy. Being big WWE fans, it was a dream come true to work for the company.

We have an extremely wonderful mutual friend, the extraordinary superstar Hannah Neurotica (it was in fact she who first brought you to my attention!). I know you are closely involved in the Women in Horror Movement, can you tell me a little bit from your perspective what the value of that kind of network-building community is for filmmakers, either established like yourself or those who are emerging?

S: I sometimes wonder if Hannah realizes how much Women in Horror Recognition Month has changed the world? She's just so phenomenal. I watched her though all these years and the way she fights for artists and art and even creates great art of her own—she's the real deal! When we made *Dead Hooker*, we were rejected around the globe on title alone. Then the first WiH month has female-centred film fests that got us our first two screenings and the film went from there. It was a life changing experience to get the work out to an audience and that's what WiH month does for past, present, and future artists. It just builds your database of great female artists every year!

J: I didn't receive a lot of support when I started out. I know what a big difference it would have made for me to get someone to ask questions to or ask for feedback from. It's a tough business and it can be really cruel. I've always felt it's important to include everyone. Kindness will get you far. It's the road less travelled but when you look back at your actions you can be proud. I know how much any words of encouragement meant to me. It still means a lot. I want anyone starting out that they can make it. It's scary at first but you can do it. We've heard one group voices telling all the stories for too long. It's time to have new voices, new perspectives.

***Hellevator* was so much fun seeing you guys really take centre stage—how different was it working on a project like that to what you had previously been more used to doing?**

S: We loved doing *Hellevator*! It was like a brain vacation except for memorizing lines and making sure the contestants didn't kill themselves. The hours of stand up with Jen was a blast. It was nice to see our senses of humour used for torture to win money. I'd love to do more reality television like that.

J: It was so much fun. I can't believe they paid us to make fun of scared people. It was nice to not have to worry about the production side of things though I was always concerned, ha ha! And we got to have our lair right next to the critters. I loved playing with tarantulas and rats every day. It was like a petting zoo. But for me. Ha!

It's an understatement to say that the remake of *Rabid* is one of the most anticipated upcoming woman-directed horror films in the world right now. When did you guys first come across the film, how did you find yourselves attached to such a wild project, and what to you is the most sacred part of the original that you'd like to see maintained in your reimagining of the work?

S: Thank you for saying so! It came as a random email one December and we got a meeting the next day. It was a real gig—the producers explained how they came upon the project and then our names came up as directors as we are known to be keen on the great work of the genius filmmaker that is Mr David Cronenberg. We're not fans of remakes but were scared to think of what someone who wasn't such a fun would do. They might even make a film about rabies!

To us, every aspect of the original is sacred, so you are going to see a heavy love fest. As a matter of fact, if you've seen the original, there is so much there for you. Our *Rabid* only exists through David's original brilliant premise, but it is modernized and told through the female gaze. When we spoke with Mr Cronenberg, after we wrapped, he said that the film ended up where it should. That meant a lot to hear. Everyone on the team—including cast and crew from his films - wanted to make something special to celebrate David's amazing body of work.

J: Everything David does is sacred to us. I can't give anything away, but we went to great lengths to honor him and his work. Many of our crew had worked with him before. We got a few of his actors in the film. Everything is a lover letter to him. He's one of our biggest influences. We tried to get every important aspect of the original in our version, in one way or another. You'll see homages to his other works as well. If you're a Cronenberg fan you are certainly in for a treat with this.

Aside from filmmaking, you guys have both also continued acting. I'd love to hear your thoughts on what you find most fulfilling about working in front of the camera in comparison to working behind it—what particular buzz do you get in each role that the other can't quite satisfy?

S: There is something very freeing about being in front of the camera, being able to get lost in a character, express something that you never can quite reach in reality. It's a beautiful artistic experience. I prefer the control of being behind the camera and controlling the world, but that's just me.

J: I love the freedom of acting. Its so important but in a way you've really just got you to manage. I love the ability to direct so many different people and energies to bring a film to life. Directing is like leading an orchestra. It's a lot of work but when it's just right it's magic.

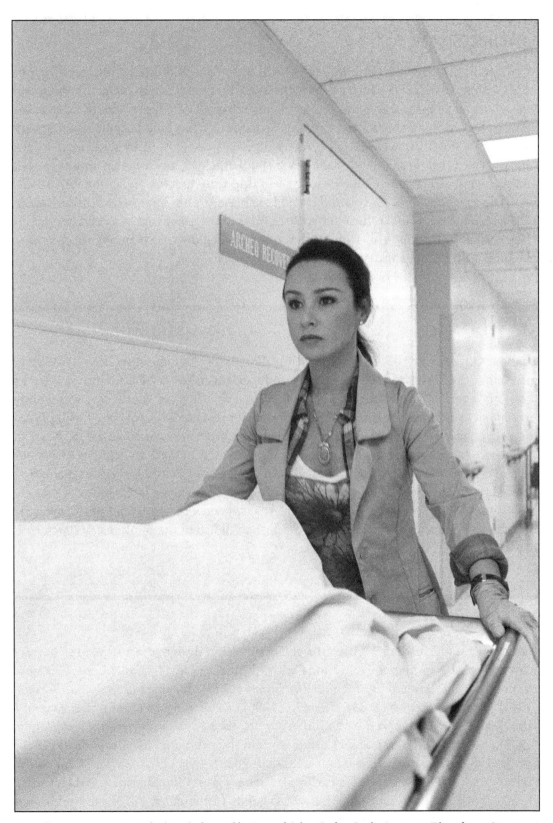

Danielle Harris in *See No Evil 2* (2014), directed by Jen and Sylvia Soska. Credit: Lionsgate/Photofest, © Lionsgate.

SPACEK, SISSY*

With barely any screen experience at the time, Sissy Spacek showed a distinct synchronicity with the dark side in Terrence Malick's 1973 directorial debut, *Badlands*. But it was her performance as the title character in Brian De Palma's 1976 film *Carrie* that made her a horror legend: sympathetic yet terrifying, Spacek's Carrie would become a benchmark for horror acting that has even today rarely been surpassed. Born in Texas in 1949, the film was her breakthrough and made her a star, launching a career that would see her win Academy Awards and Golden Globes, working with directors including Robert Altman, Oliver Stone, Costa-Gavras and David Lynch. Across her impressive film and television career, Spacek would return in two 2015 films to the genre that launched her career; Hideo Nakata's *The Ring Two* with Naomi Watts, and Courtney Solomon's *An American Haunting* with Rachel Hurd-Wood.

SPEED, CAROL

William Girdler's 1974 Blaxploitation film *Abby* is not shy about its debt to William Friedkin's *The Exorcist* (1973), whose producers even took legal action against its distributor for copyright infringement. Yet while the film may not have been wholly original, it brought to the screen the unparalleled presence of Carol Speed who played the title character, a young woman possessed by West African spirit Eshu. Born in 1945 as Carolyn Stewart in California, her Blaxploitation credits include *Disco Godfather* (J. Robert Wagoner, 1979) and *The Big Bird Cage* (Jack Hill, 1972) but she first entered the industry on television in the early 1970s, appearing in episodes of *Sanford and Son* and *Julia*. Aside from starring in *Abby*, Speed also wrote and performed the film's song, "My Soul is a Witness". In 1980, she published the book *Inside Black Hollywood*.

SPIER, CAROL

Carol Spier is a Canadian art director and production designer renowned for her extensive, award-winning collaborations with filmmaker David Cronenberg. Her horror credits with Cronenberg include *The Brood* (1979), *Scanners* (1981), *Videodrome* (1983), *The Dead Zone* (1983), *The Fly* (1986), *Dead Ringers* (1988) and *eXistenZ* (1999), and she also worked with Guillermo del Toro twice on horror movies; *Mimic* (1997) and *Blade II* (2002). Spier's other work in the genre includes *Humongous* (Paul Lynch, 1982), *Bless the Child* (Chuck Russell, 2000), *Dracula 2000* (Patrick Lussier, 2000), *Silent Hill* (Christophe Gans, 2006), *Dream House* (Jim Sheridan, 2011), *Carrie* (Kimberly Peirce, 2013) and *Regression* (Alejandro Amenábar, 2015), and television series such as *Friday the 13th: The Series* and *Black Mirror*.

ST. CROIX, SILVIA

Virtually nothing is known about writer/director 'Silvia St. Croix', the mastermind behind Full Moon Entertainment's *Gingerdead Man 2: Passion of the Crust* (2008) to an almost suspicious degree. While most probably indicating an alias (for a man or woman, who knows), it is more tempting to believe that St. Croix is herself a real-life gingerbread lady who makes horror movies. Or, alternatively for the conspiracy theorists amongst you, she may be a demented baker-turned-filmmaker. What matters most, perhaps, is that the enigmas of the *Gingerdead Man* franchise remain intact.

ST JOHN, BETTA

Dancer, singer and actor Betta St John was born Betty Jean Striegler in 1929. During her screen career, she was cast in *Dream Wife* (Sidney Sheldon, 1953) with Cary Grant and Deborah Kerr and the British film *Hide Tide at Noon* (Philip Leacock, 1957) that was entered in competition at the Cannes Film Festival. Guy Green's 1958 Hammer film *The Snorkel* marked her first major horror appearance, appearing in Robert Day's *Corridors of Blood* with Boris Karloff and Christopher Lee that same year. In 1960, she appeared again with Lee in John Moxey's *Horror Hotel*, having acted in the television series version of *The Invisible Man* the year before.

STANSBURY, HOPE

Born in New York City in 1946, Hope Stansbury is closely linked to the work of cult horror auteur Andy Milligan. Milligan's 1965 short *Vapors* was written by Stansbury (adapted from her stage play), beginning her numerous collaborations with Milligan as she moved to acting in film including *The Degenerates* (1967), *Depraved!* (1967), and the horror films *The Rats Are Coming! The Werewolves Are Here!* (1972) and *Legacy of Satan* (1973). Stansbury also worked in theater, co-starring in the Divine-fronted *The Neon Woman* in New York in 1978 (footage from the play appears in Jeffrey Schwarz's 2013 documentary *I Am Divine*).

STARDUST, CHELSEA

Raised on a farm in Ohio, filmmaker Chelsea Stardust was a horror fan from a young age. She began studying filmmaking while still at high school, moving to university to continue developing her skills. Relocating to Los Angeles, she worked at Blumhouse Productions as Jason Blum's executive assistant which lead to her involvement in some of their biggest horror hits, including series such as *Paranormal Activity*, *Sinister*, *The Purge* and

Insidious. She made her first short *Where Are You?* in 2015, and after a number of other shorts her feature film debut *Satanic Panic* premiered in early 2019, followed soon after by her donation to the Blumhouse-produced "Into the Dark" series with the feature-length, stand-alone episode *All That We Destroy*.

STEEL, AMY⁕

As Ginny in *Friday the 13ᵗʰ Part 2* (Steve Miner, 1981), Amy Steel is one the most cherished Final Girls from slasher's classic era. Born in 1960 in Pennsylvania, she began her screen career in television soap operas. After gaining the role of Ginny through an audition process, Steel consciously sought to distinguish the character from her shallower peers, granting Ginny a sense of maturity that comes to the fore in how she negotiates her experiences. After her role as Ginny, she returned to the genre again in 1986 in Fred Walton's *April Fool's Day*. She later appeared in the horror series *American Gothic*, and would appear alongside fellow women horror icons including Debbie Rochon, Adrienne King, Lesleh Donaldson and Caroline Williams in the 2014 horror anthology *Tales of Poe*.

STEEL, J. A.

J. A. Steel was born Jacquelyn Ruffner in Pennsylvania in 1969 and began acting as a child. In 1991, she was an uncredited story intern on 6 episodes of the *Tales from the Crypt*. Steel wrote and directed her first short film *Vertex* in 2000 and is mostly recognized for her powerful feminist cop film *The Third Society* from 2002. While also making documentaries, comedies, scifi and action films, in 2007 she wrote, directed and acted in the horror film *Salvation* and in 2010 she made the monster movie *Denizen* (later adapted to television in the 2014 series *Denizen: Descent*). In 2010, she wrote and directed the horror short *S.C.A.A.R*, followed in 2012 by the feature-length movie *Blood Fare*. Steel edited and produced much of her own work, and as an actor appeared in Ford Austin's *Aliens vs. A-holes* (2012) and *Cerebral Print: The Secret Files* (2005).

STEEL, PIPPA

Pippa Steel was born in Germany in 1948 and is remembered as one of the essential women of Hammer horror for her performances in *The Vampire Lovers* (Roy Ward Baker, 1970) and *Lust for a Vampire* (Jimmy Sangster, 1971). Along with John Hough's *Twins of Evil* (1971), the three films make up Hammer's Karnstein Trilogy, inspired by Sheridan Le Fanu's famous novella *Carmilla* (1872) and likewise shares its fascination with the figure of the lesbian vampire.

STEELE, BARBARA

As one of the most famous faces of Italian horror cinema, British actor Barbara Steele is inextricably linked to the pierced visage of the witch Asa in Mario Bava's gothic horror classic *Black Sunday* (1960). Born near Liverpool in the United Kingdom in 1937, she made her screen debut on television in 1958 and worked in small and often uncredited movie roles until her breakthrough in the Bava classic. The following year she continued her horror work in Riccardo Freda's *The Horrible Dr. Hichcock*, and while Steele appeared in other genres (including memorable roles in Federico Fellini's celebrated *8½* in 1963 and Volker Schlöndorff's *Young Torless* in 1966), her horror movies include *The Ghost* (Riccardo Freda, 1963), *Castle of Blood* (Sergio Corbucci and Antonio Margheriti, 1964), *The Long Hair of Death* (Antonio Margheriti, 1964), *Terror-Creatures from the Grave* (Massimo Pupillo, 1965), *Nightmare Castle* (Mario Caiano, 1965), *The Doctor and the Devil* (Nicholas Ray, 1965), *She Beast* (Michael Reeves, 1966), *An Angel for Satan* (Camillo Mastrocinque, 1966), *Curse of the Crimson Altar* (Vernon Sewell, 1968), *Shivers* (David Cronenberg, 1975), *Piranha* (Joe Dante, 1978) and *The Silent Scream* (Denny Harris, 1979). More recently, she starred in Jonathan Zarantonello's *The Butterfly Room* (2012) alongside fellow horror icons Heather Langenkamp, Camille Keaton, Adrienne King and P. J. Soles, and made a brief but memorable appearance in Ryan Gosling's directorial debut, the hugely underrated *Lost River* (2014). Steele has also been cast in several television series, including *Alfred Hitchcock Presents*, *Night Galler* and the *Dark Shadows* reboot in 1991.

Barbara Steele in *La Maschera del Demonio* aka *Black Sunday* aka *The Mask of the Demon* aka *The Mask of Satan* aka *The Revenge of the Vampire* (Mario Bava, 1960) Credit: RGR Collection / Alamy Stock Photo

STEGERS, BERNICE

Born in Liverpool in 1949, British actor Bernice Stegers has appeared in work as diverse as voicing characters for the videogame *Final Fantasy XII* in 2006 to a small role in Mike Newell's beloved romcom *Four Weddings and a Funeral* (1994). Her mark on horror is linked to two roles in particular: as Rachael in Harry Bromley Davenport's vicious horror/scifi film *Xtro* (1982), and as the tortured protagonist Jane in Lamberto Bava's *Macabre* (1980). Stegers on-screen career has spanned almost 50 years, and aside from these two key films in her horror repertoire, she also worked in the television series *Tales of the Unexpected*.

STENSGAARD, YUTTE

Danish model-turned-actor Yutte Stensgaard (her first name an anglicized version of Jytte) was born in Jutland in 1946. While only acting for five years, within that period she worked on over 20 films and television shows, including *Scream and Scream Again* (Gordon Hessler, 1970) which starred Vincent Price, Christopher Lee and Peter Cushing. The following year she starred in the dual roles of the vampiric Mircalla and Carmilla Karnstein in Jimmy Sangster's *Lust for a Vampire* (1971). Her final on-screen credit was in the horror anthology television series *Dead of Night* in the early 1970s.

STEPANSKY, BARBARA

Polish-born writer, director and editor Barbara Stepansky was awarded the 2013 Nicholl Fellowship from the Academy of Motion Picture Arts and Science, awarded to develop promising emerging screenwriters, and her other accolades include winning a Mary Pickford Foundation Scholarship and receiving the Franklin J. Schaffner AFI Fellow Award. While having worked across several genres, she directed and co-wrote the 2009 horror feature *Hurt*, followed in 2011 with another horror film, *Fugue*. She also made the short horror film *Road Rage* in 2010, and wrote and directed the segment "Downtown" on the 2011 all-woman directed anthology *I Hate L.A.*

STEVENS, BRINKE—INTERVIEW (AUGUST 2018)

Charlene Elizabeth Brinkman began her horror career as a fan, leading her towards modeling, acting, and screenwriting, and later producing and directing. With well over 150 acting credits alone, Stevens's first major role was in Amy Holden Jones's *The Slumber Party Massacre* in 1982, and her film credits include *Sorority Babes in the Slimeball Bowl-O-Rama* (David DeCoteau, 1988) and *Nightmare Sisters* (David DeCoteau, 1988), with more recent films including *The Small Woman in Grey* (Andrew Sean Eltham-Byers, 2017) and Abby Borden in *Lizzie Borden's Revenge* (Dennis Devine, 2013).

She starred and co-wrote *Teenage Exorcist* (Grant Austin Waldman, 1991) with Fred Olen Ray and Ted Newsom, and her other writing credits include *Dr. Horror's Erotic House of Idiots* (Paul Scrabo, 2004) and *Wild Spirit* (C.B. Tilden, 2003).

Stevens has also appeared on television, including in episodes of *Tales from the Darkside* in 1988, and the web series *Dawn and the Dead*. Brinke generously spoke to me about her hugely impressive and influential career.

www.brinke.com

There's a really offensive cliché about women in horror movies that they're kind of airheaded screaming murder-fodder with big boobs waiting to be butchered. I think I actually reached out to high five you when I read that you studied to a postgraduate level at university, thus pretty much single-handedly putting an end to that stereotype and really challenging it.

I earned a Bachelor's degree in biology and psychology (double major), and then a Masters degree in marine biology. My goal was to specialize in animal behavior, and specifically to study how dolphins communicate with one another. The popular theory in the 1970s was that dolphins talked to each other by making audible noises. I had my own theory that they instead communicate soundlessly with their natural sonar. (Turns out I was 13 years ahead of my time, because it took that long for someone else to test the same theory.) However, my research was frowned upon because thousands of dolphins were being killed in tuna nets, and thus nobody really wanted to talk to them except me. Well, that unpopular research got me kicked out of grad school and I was unable to complete my Ph.D. I immediately landed a job as an environmental consultant for a nuclear power plant near San Diego, California.

A few years later, I accidentally became a Scream Queen. Go figure! To quote a line from *Nightmare Sisters*: "Advanced trigonometry never prepared me for this!"

I understand your career really started from your status as a horror fan. How did this unfold?

I was one of the early founders of San Diego Comic-Con, and I ran the masquerade contest for many years in the 1970s. This came about after I won first place for portraying Vampirella in 1973. Later, I staged elaborate costumed dance routines during the intermission to popular songs such as "Funeral for a Friend", "Killer Queen", "Ballroom Blitz", and so on. I'd say it was Comic-Con and fandom that really prepared me for an acting career by helping me to overcome my innate shyness.

In 1980, I moved from San Diego to Los Angeles CA to marry my college sweetheart, artist Dave Stevens. One fateful day, while looking for a science job, I wandered past the open door of a casting office. I was invited in and immediately got hired as a background extra in *All the Marbles* (Robert Aldrich, 1981). I started to pursue casting calls, and soon landed my first big role in Roger Cor-

Brinke Stevens. Photo credit: JT Seaton. Used with permission.

man's *Slumber Party Massacre* (Amy Holden Jones, 1981).

The Slumber Party Massacre is of course a really beloved cult film for both men and women alike, but especially for those of us interested in feminism and the genre. Can you tell me a little about how you became involved in that project, what it was like to work on, and if any of you had any idea at the time that it would endure and resonate so strongly with future audiences?

I saw a casting notice in *Dramalog* magazine, looking for girls who were willing to get naked and die horribly. I was cast as one of the main leads, but I'd already booked a modeling job at Lake Tahoe that coincided with the film shoot in Los Angeles. So, they had to switch me to a lesser role and kill me off quickly.

Because the script (originally titled "Sleepless Nights") was written by Rita Mae Brown and directed by Amy Jones — and the fact that plucky gals end up besting the male killer —it was considered a "feminist" slasher movie at the time. I don't think they ever set out to make a feminist statement. I thought it was just as bloody as any other slasher movie, though perhaps with more humor.

Another favorite of mine is Sorority Babes in the Slimeball Bowl-O-Rama: Could you tell me a bit about what that film was like to work on?

Sorority Babes was shot on-location at a bowling alley near San Diego. Since it remained open for business during the day, we had to begin shooting at 9pm (when they closed) and work all night till 9am. As such, we felt like real-life vampires, sleeping all day and eating breakfast at 4 pm! For that reason, it was rather difficult. But it was truly an adventure, too.

I shared a hotel room with Michelle Bauer, and I really enjoyed working with the late Robin Stille. I have a fondness for *Sorority Babes* because I'm still in touch with many of that cast and crew. I often work with director Dave DeCoteau, Linnea Quigley and Michelle Bauer, and I occasionally hang out with Andras Jones, Hal Havens and John Wildman. It's a magical little movie for that reason: such a great group of people who made it.

Like Sorority Babes in the Slimeball Bowl-O-Rama, you've been involved in a number of films that are sort of 'horror all-star' movies alongside other women in your field who have similarly strong cult reputations. Can you tell me what that network is like both in terms of filmmaking but also on the convention circuit and socially, things like that?

I'd say there were only three original Scream Queens in the 1980's: me, Linnea Quigley, and Michelle Bauer. In the early days, we constantly ran into each other on auditions and movie jobs. Linnea and I became close friends and hung out together. For a brief time, I was involved in Linnea's all-girl rock band The Skirts.

I included her in some *Playboy* modeling shoots ("Girls of Rock & Roll" and "Flashdancers"). She introduced me to filmmaker David DeCoteau, who cast me in several horror films such as *Nightmare Sisters*. We're all still working together. Recently, our trio appeared in *Cougar Cult, Three Scream Queens, The Trouble with Barry*, and *Trophy Heads*. Women in this business tend to stick together and support one another.

I have to confess I haven't seen it yet, but I've just seen that you were Abby Borden in *Lizzie Borden's Revenge*. What was it like playing someone like that who has such widespread fame in the popular imagination?

I was already booked to shoot *Jonah Lives* in Fall River MA — Lizzie's home town. When I found out I'd gotten cast in the Lizzie Borden movie, I asked the *Jonah Lives* director if I'd have time to visit the Borden Museum while I was soon in town. He immediately cancelled my hotel reservation at a major chain and got me a room at the exact same house where the Borden murders occurred, now a Bed & Breakfast inn and official museum. I stayed on the third floor in what used to be the maid's bedroom. It was fascinating and so incredibly timely to see the museum displays, photographs, actual furniture, and so on. It gave me a clear idea how to look the part of Abby Borden — how to do my hair, make-up, and wardrobe — when I shot that film a month later in Hollywood.

I'd love to ask you about your behind-the-camera work, too. I'm really interested in how you came to scriptwriting after acting for so long: *Teenage Exorcist* looks like it was a real turning point for you professionally?

I've been able to sustain a living for so long in the B-movie business because I expanded laterally and diversified — by doing conventions and mail-order, and creating my own merchandise (photos, comic books, T-shirts, trading cards). I've also continually reinvented myself by becoming a writer, producer, and director.

Teenage Exorcist came about when I was cast in the lead role... and then learned that there wasn't a script yet, just a synopsis. So I offered to write it myself. I'd already written and sold several screenplays before that, and I'd served as the Executive Editor of *Weird Tales* magazine in the mid-1980s.

As actor, writer, producer and director, *Personal Demons* is clearly another hugely important milestone in your already impressive career. Can you tell me about how that project came together, what inspired you, and how Linnea Quigley and Debbie Rochon got involved?

Six years ago, filmmaker Joe Castro invited me to pitch an idea for his new *Terror Toons* anthology. I gave him a brief synopsis for *Personal Demons*, which he really liked. He told me to go ahead and write the screenplay. Then, he liked the finished

Linnea Quigley and Brinke Stevens in their band, The Skirts. Used with permission.

script so much that he asked me to direct it myself to 'stay true to my vision'. For years, I'd been slated to direct one project or another, but they all fell through… so I was thrilled by his offer.

When we shot *Personal Demons*, I hired my pals Linnea Quigley and Debbie Rochon to co-star with me. It was fun and reassuring to work with my good friends on my very first director job. We shot the whole film against a green screen, which made it easier at times yet more confusing at others. [Like asking yourself, 'Does the (invisible) door swing open this way… or that way?']

On the first day of shooting, I loved my cameraman's awed comment, "You're so calm and quiet!" I think male directors are often too loud, fast, frenetic. After working as an actress on almost 200 films, I've learned quite a lot about dealing with actors in a calm patient manner. No one likes to be rushed or hurried up, especially when they're trying to conjure real emotions like grief or fear. You need to give them the time and space to really get into it.

I also believe you are involved both in front of and behind the camera on the web series *Dawn and the Dead*. How did you find that experience, and is it different working on a web series like that than a feature film?

Producer Rick Danford is soon giving me my second directing opportunity on his *Dawn and the Dead* series, and I also play a major recurring character. We'll shoot my episode next month, then put together a package to pitch at the AFM film market in Los Angeles later this year. I worked with Rick several years ago on the film *Web of Darkness* in Florida, and I'm delighted that he kept me in mind for this new project.

Finally, one last question: we're at a very interesting moment in the history not just of film but culturally in general where we have a lot of people asking long-overdue questions about discrimination, harassment and abuse based on gender difference. I'm conscious of not prying here, but if you could give advice to a young woman just starting out in the business, what would your key tip be for surviving the darker side of the business?

Early in my career, nudity was simply the rule… what was expected of us. We just went along with it because we wanted to work. I've never been shy about nudity. Good thing, too—my willingness to undress landed me a lot of good roles and helped to get me better noticed by fans. However, I was never comfortable doing explicit "love scenes" with a guy, so I tended to turn down those kinds of parts. In almost every case, the directors have been very good about asking non-essential personnel to leave the set and we were treated respectfully. I'm actually quite relieved that I've reached such an age where I'm no longer asked to do this.

Though I mostly work in the Horror genre, these films are technically Action flicks. Sometimes actors have to run full-tilt and chase people, or else blindly flee for our lives. We often have vicious fight scenes and use a variety of deadly

Brinke Stevens. Photo credit: Ken Marcus. Used with permission.

Brinke Stevens. Photo credit: Ken Marcus (for the comic book *series Brinke of Destruction*).
Used with permission.

weapons. Safety must come first, and it's astounding to me when young filmmakers forget about that. My peer Debbie Rochon suffered a horrible on-set accident, where she was unknowingly handed a real machete to slay someone—and she consequently sliced open her own palm on the sharp blade. Her medical bills were astronomical, and the production had no insurance nor workman's comp to help her out. I've been rushed to the Emergency Room twice during movie shoots.

When I first started out in the early 1980's, it was much easier then to become a horror film star. Only a few independent Hollywood studios were churning out product. Since then, horror movie production has spread across the nation, with thousands of individuals now shooting films everywhere. My advice to young actresses would be to attend genre conventions, hand out your photo and resume to all the young filmmakers who've set up booths. and just network like crazy.

Normally, a mainstream actress is considered "washed up" by age 40. At that point, they rush to a plastic surgeon and try to keep their career alive a tiny bit longer. Fortunately, I've found it to be very different in the horror community. I've had the same army of loyal fans for 25 years—and now their children are becoming my new fans, as well. I've never encountered the same sort of "age prejudice" in this genre, thank goodness. I get hired just as much as I ever did—but of course, the roles have changed. I'm no longer the nubile co-ed who strips, showers, and dies horribly. These days, I play far more meaty roles, like cops, detectives, professors, doctors and so on. Over the years, I've built up a good reputation as a "reliable" actress, and it still serves me well.

STEWART, CHARLOTTE

Born in California in 1941, American actor Charlotte Stewart began her collaborations with David Lynch when she played Mary X in his cult 1977 horror film *Eraserhead*, later appearing as Betty Briggs in *Twin Peaks*. Working across film and television since the mid-1950s, Stewart's other horror credits include *Tremors* (Ron Underwood, 1990), *Dark Angel: The Ascent* (Linda Hassani, 1994) and *Tremors 3: Back to Perfection* (Brent Maddock, 2001).

STEWART, KRISTEN▸

Born in Los Angeles to an American father and Australian mother in 1990, with both parents working in screen industry Stewart's future career path seemed destined. Beginning in several small and uncredited roles in 1999, her breakthrough performance was alongside Jodie Foster in the David Fincher's 2002 home invasion film *Panic Room*. Gaining increasingly more high-profile roles with directors including Sean Penn and Mike Figgis, in 2007 she starred in the Pang Brothers' horror film *The Messengers*. With Catherine

Hardwicke's first *Twilight* movie released in 2008, Stewart would for many years become synonymous with the popular vampire romance franchise, surprising many when she transcended the teen star label to become a serious player in more highbrow art cinema circles as both an actor and director. In 2016, she starred in Olivier Assayas haunting ghost story *Personal Shopper* which was in contention for the *Palme d'Or* at the Cannes Film Festival. In 2018, she played Lizzie Borden's maid in Craig William Macneill's *Lizzie* alongside Chloë Sevigny in the title role.

STOLER, SHIRLEY

Born in Brooklyn in 1929, Shirley Stoler's was in her mid-twenties before she took to the stage in New York's flourishing experimental theater scene in the 1950s. She came to cinema much later in her career: she was in her early 40s when she co-starred in Leonard Kastle's classic killer couple film *The Honeymoon Killers* (1970) as Martha Beck. While appearing in several other movies (including Lina Wertmüller's Oscar-*nominated Seven Beauties* in 1975), she also appeared in Frank Henenlotter's *Frankenhooker* (1990).

Kristen Stewart attends the *Personal Shopper* photo-call during the 69th Cannes Film Festival on 17 May 2016 in Cannes, France Credit: Andrea Raffin / Shutterstock.com

STONE, IVORY

Blackenstein was the 1973 follow-up to AIP's *Blacula* released the year before. While it does not have a particularly strong reputation as either a horror film or a Blaxploitation film, as Dr Winifred Walker the film boasts the only film performance by Ivory Stone. Seeking a way to help her quadruple amputee fiancé Eddie (Joe De Sue), she is drawn to the research of John Hart's Dr Stein that results in Eddie becoming a Black version of Frankenstein's monster (hence the film's title). While little about Stone is known, her performance as one of Blaxploitation's pluckier horror protagonists makes her worthy of inclusion in this book.

STOPPI, FRANCA

Born in 1946 in Italy, Franca Stoppi was a model and actor who worked closely on stage with her husband, actor and director Simone Mattioli. Her horror roles include George Eastman and Peter Skerl's *Bestialita* (1976), *Beyond the Darkness* (Joe D'Amato, 1979) and *The Other Hell* (Bruno Mattei, 1981), appearing in several Mattei's other exploitation films including the nunsploitation movie *The True Story of the Nun of Monza* (1980), and the women in prison films *Caged Women* (1982) and *Women's Prison Massacre* (1983).

STRIBLING, MELISSA

Most famous for her performance as Mina in Terence Fisher's Hammer horror film *Dracula* (1958), Melissa Stribling was born in Scotland in 1926 and made her first film appeareance in the British crime film *Wide Boy* (Ken Hughes, 1952). Across her film and television career she worked in a number of genres, including horror movies such as *Ghost Ship* (Vernon Sewell, 1952) and *Crucible of Terror* (Ted Hooker, 1971). Horror was a family affair for Stribling: she was married to director Basil Dearden with whom she worked numerous times (his credits include Ealing's 1945 horror anthology *Dead of Night* amongst others), and their son James Dearden directed the horror shorts *The Contraption* (1977) and *Panic* (1978) and wrote the screenplay for Adrian Lyne's *Fatal Attraction* in 1987, based on his 1980 short film *Diversion*.

STRINDBERG, ANITA

Swedish model turned *giallo* star Anita Strindberg brought a defining sense of glamor to the Italian subgenre through a number of iconic performances, although she appeared in a number of other kinds of Italian exploitation films during the 1970s in particular. Born in 1937, she made two Swedish films in the late 1950s, *Blonde in Bondage* (Robert Brandt, 1957) and *Sköna Susanna och gubbarna* (1959). Eleven years later she had a small uncredited role in Massimo Franciosa's *That Clear October Night* (1970), before her breakthrough performance as the unfortunate lover of Florinda Bolkan's protagonist Carol in Lucio Fulci's psychedelic *giallo A Lizard in a Woman's Skin* (1971). This was followed by more central roles in *gialli* including Sergio Martino's *The Case of the Scorpion's Tail* (1971) and Aldo Lado's *Who Saw Her Die?* (1972), and possibly her most famous role in the category, Sergio Martino's *Your Vice Is a Locked Room and Only I Have the Key* (1972) where she starred alongside fellow Italian horror icon Edwige Fenech. Strindberg's other horror roles include *Tropic of Cancer* (Giampaolo Lomi and Edoardo Mulargia, 1972), *Almost Human* (Umberto Lenzi, 1974), *The Antichrist* (Alberto De Martino, 1974) and her last film role, Riccardo Freda's *Murder Syndrome* (1981).

STRÖMBERG, EWA

Co-starring with Soledad Miranda in Jess Franco's *Vampyros Lesbos* (1971), Ewa Strömberg was arguably half of one of the most famous vampire lesbian couples ever put to film. Born in Sweden in 1940, her numerous collaborations with Franco garnered her the most attention, but she had a lengthy filmography and worked with directors including Robert Siodmak and Arne Mattsson. After several comedies and dramas she appeared in three Alfred Vohrer German *krimi* films, *The College Girl Murders* in 1967, *The Zombie Walks* in 1968 and *Terror on Half Moon Street* in 1969. Her first film with Franco was *The Devil Came from Akasava* (1971) which also co-starred Soledad Miranda, the team re-joining that same year for *Vampyros Lesbos* and *She Killed in Ecstasy*. Her other work with Franco included *X312—Flight to Hell* (1971) and Franco's reimagining of the Dr Mabuse mythology in *Dr. M Proposes* (1972).

STUART, GLORIA

As Old Rose in James Cameron's *Titanic*, Gloria Stuart is renowned as the oldest person ever to receive an Oscar nomination for acting, but her screen career began early in life. Born in California in 1910, she started performing at a young age and signed to Universal Studios in the early 1930s, making her screen debut in John Francis Dillon's comedy *The Cohens and Kellys in Hollywood* (1932). A vocal activist with strong left-leaning beliefs, she made her first appearance in a horror film that same year in James Whale's *The Old Dark House* alongside Boris Karloff and Charles Laughton, followed the next year with both Kurt Neumann's *Secret of the Blue Room* and collaborating again with Whale on *The Invisible Man* (1933). Making up to six films a year during the 1930s, she quit acting to become an artist in 1946. After three decades, she made an initially tentative return, with a small role in the Elizabeth Montgomery-fronted television biopic *The Legend of Lizzie Borden* (Paul Wendkos, 1975), sticking predominantly to the small screen until her memorable appearance in *Titanic*. In 2001, she played a small role in the television series *The Invisible Man* as a hat-tip to her performance in the classic 1930s film of the same name, and her final screen role was Wim Wenders' 2004 film *Land of Plenty*.

SUBKOFF, TARA

A woman who excels in several fields, Connecticut-born Tara Subkoff is most immediately recognizable for her work as an actor in movies such as *The Last Days of Disco* (Whit Stillman, 1998), *The Cell* (Tarsem Singh, 2000) and *The Notorious Bettie Page* (Mary Harron, 2005). But Subkoff is also an artist, designer, and—most recently—horror film director. Her acting career began in the mid-1990s with what were television roles predominantly, including an episode of the vampire series *Kindred: The Embraced*. Yet due to her effective blacklisting after an alleged sexual harrassment experience by maligned producer Harvey Weinstein, Subkoff turned to art and design with her fashion collection Imitation of Christ and later to installation and performance art. Joining with her *The Last Days of Disco* co-star and Imitation of Christ collaborator Chloë Sevigny, in 2015 Subkoff directed, wrote and co-produced the social media horror film *#Horror* which played at the Cannes Film Festival.

SUTTON, TAMMI

Tammi Sutton was born in Florida in 1971 and turned to genre filmmaking after a background in music videos. Sutton creates low-budget, fun horror movies including her debut feature *Killjoy 2: Deliverance from Evil* (2002), *Sutures* (2009) and *Whispers* (2015), amongst others. She had previously appeared in front of the camera in Danny Draven's *Horrorvision* (2001) and *Hell Asylum* (2002) as well as *Dead & Rotting* (David P. Barton, 2002), and was both producer and production designer on the latter two. In her capacity as production designer, Sutton also worked on *Witchouse 3: Demon Fire* (2001)—for which she received an additional producer credit—and was production designer on horror films including *The Dead Hate the Living!* (Dave Parker, 2000), *The Vault* (James Black, 2000), *Gorom Lake* (William Shatner, 2002) and *Speck* (Keith Walley, 2002).

SUZZANNA

The undisputed queen of Indonesian horror, Suzzanna Martha Frederika van Osch—credited in her numerous films simply as Suzzanna—was born in 1942 in West Java (then the colony of the Dutch East Indies). She found success early in her life, winning several awards in her teens. While she worked across a range of genres throughout her career, it is horror with which she is most closely aligned due to her roles in films including *Birth in the Tomb* (Awaludin and Ali Shahab, 1972), *Ghost with Hole* (Sisworo Gautama Putra, 1982), *The Snake Queen* (Sisworo Gautama Putra, 1982), *Perkawinan nyi blorong*, Sisworo Gautama Putra, 1983), *The Queen of Black Magic* (Liliek Sudjio, 1983), *Telaga Angker* (Sisworo Gautama Putra, 1984), Ratu sakti calon arang (Sisworo Gautama Putra, 1985), *The White Alligator* (H. Tjut Djalil, 1988), *Santet* (Sisworo Gautama Putra, 1988), *Wanita harimau* (Sisworo Gautama Putra, 1989) and *Titisan Dewi Ular* (Sisworo Gautama Putra,

1990). Outside of her impressive filmography, Suzzanna was closely linked to horror not only due to her on-screen performances but for how they intersected with her alternative lifestyle that emphasised the role of mysticism. Her last film was Koya Pagayo's horror movie *Hantu Ambulance* in 2008, released the year she died.

SWAN, REBECCA

Rebecca Swan is a transgender screenwriter and director most familiar for co-writing John Carpenter's *Masters of Horror* series episode "Cigarette Burns", and writing and co-directing *Maskhead* in 2009 with Fred Vogel. Swan also has written for theater and in 2018 starred in, wrote and was second unit director on Anthony DiBlasi's horror film *Extremity*. Swan also directed and wrote the horror-comedy *Big Junior* (2010), and amongst other credits also wrote Fred Vogel's *The Final Interview* (2017) and co-wrote "Skin and Bones", Larry Fessenden's episode of the series *Fear Itself*.

SWANSON, GLORIA

Gloria Swanson's devastating performance as Norma Desmond in Billy Wilder's 1950 film noir *Sunset Boulevard* is a hugely significant performance upon which the representation of later-in-life monstrous femininity would be modeled upon. The character of Desmond consciously riffed on Swanston's own lengthy screen career that saw her as one of the few stars of her generation to successfully cross from silent movies to talkies. Born in Chicago in 1899, she grew up in Puerto Rico and began her film career working as an extra. One of her first appearances was an uncredited role in Charles Chaplin's short *His New Job* (1915), but it was her work with Cecil B. DeMille when she joined Paramount Studios in 1919 that led to her becoming a star. With films like *Sadie Thompson* (Raoul Walsh, 1928) and *Queen Kelly* (Erich von Stroheim, 1929), Swanson became one of the biggest superstars of the 1920s. With the rise of sound, Swanson saw herself overtaken by a new breed of film star, an intertextual element that plays a concrete role in the plot of *Sunset Boulevard*. Although not Wilder's first choice for the role, it is unimaginable without her and the debt of horror film performances by women that followed it is great. In her later years, Swanson turned to television and appeared in an episode of *The Alfred Hitchcock Hour* in the mid-1960s and Curtis Harrington's television horror movie *Killer Bees* (1974).

SWANSTON, KRISTY *

Long before Sarah Michelle Gellar became synonymous with the role, Kristy Swanson starred as the eponymous *Buffy the Vampire Slayer* in Fran Rubel Kuzui's 1992 cult horror-comedy film of the same name. Born in California in 1969, she was a familiar face in a number of '80s teen films such as John Hughes's 1986 one-two punch of *Pretty in Pink* and *Ferris Bueller's Day Off*. Beginning acting as a child in commercials and moving to television, her first leading role was in Wes Craven's *Deadly Friend* in 1986. The following year, she earned further genre kudos starring as one of the tortured siblings in Jeffrey Bloom's screen adaptation of V.C. Andrews perverse, sadistic blockbuster novel *Flowers in the Attic*. Moving steadily between film and television, the year before *Buffy* she starred in another horror-comedy, *Highway to Hell* (Ate de Jong, 1991), returning to the genre in later years in Erin Berry's *Living Death* (2006).

SWEENEY, MARY

One of the most significant collaborators of cult auteur David Lynch is his long-time producer and editor (and, briefly, wife) Mary Sweeney. Her first film credit is as one of the unnamed titular insect women in Denis Sanders's sexy, demented *Invasion of the Bee Girls* (1973). Born in Wisconsin, Sweeney worked with Lynch for two decades, on films including *Blue Velvet* (1986), *Wild at Heart* (1990), *Twin Peaks: Fire Walk with Me* (1992), *Lost Highway* (1997), *Mulholland Drive* (2001) and *Inland Empire* (2006). She also produced Michael Almereyda's 1994 hipster vampire film *Nadja*. Sweeney is the Dino and Martha De Laurentiis Endowed Professor at the University of Southern California, and the Chair of the Board of Trustees of Film Independent.

SWENSON, ELIZA

Musician and actor Eliza Swenson was born in California in 1982, and has worked both in front of the camera and on the soundtrack to a number of horror movies. As an actor, she appeared in *Satanic* (Dan Golden, 2006), *Candy Stripers* (Kate Robbins, 2006), *Pocahauntus* (Veronica Craven, 2006), *The Haunting of Alice D* (Jessica Sonneborn, 2014) and several films by Leigh Scott, including *Frankenstein Reborn* (2005), *The Beast of Bray Road* (2005) and *Dracula's Curse* (2006). As a composer, her credits include *Exorcism: The Possession of Gail Bowers* (Leigh Scott, 2006), *Dracula's Curse* (Leigh Scott, 2006), *Supercroc* (Scott Harper, 2007), *The Dunwich Horror* (Leigh Scott, 2009), *Sharknado 2: The Second One* (Anthony C. Ferrante, 2014), *Lavalantula* (Mike Mendez, 2015), *Night of the Wild* (Eric Red, 2015), *Evil Nanny* (Jared Coh, 2016), *Alien Convergence* (Rob Pallatina, 2017), *5 Headed Shark Attack* (Nico De Leon, 2017) and *Dream House Nightmare* (Jose Montesinos, 2017).

SWINTON, TILDA

One of the most celebrated actors of our time, British icon Tilda Swinton was born Katherine Matilda Swinton in London in 1960 and studied at Cambridge. Across her impressive filmography, Swinton has frequently explored the potential to further develop her performance range in the context of horror and gothic cinema in films including *We Need to Talk About Kevin* (Lynne Ramsay, 2011), Bong Joon-ho's 2017 monster movie *Okja*, and twice with cult auteur Jim Jarmusch on the art-horror films *Only Lovers Left Alive* (2013) and *The Dead Don't Die* (2019). In 2018, Swinton starred in Luca Guadagino's remake of Dario Argento's Eurohorror classic, *Suspiria* (1977); a not wholly surprising revelation confirmed after the films release is that she played two characters in the film—a man and a woman—recalling the gender-fluidity of her earlier performance in Sally Potter's iconic queer film *Orlando* (1992). In 2019 she made an unforgettable cameo as part of the vampire council in the television series of *What We Do in the Shadows*, adapted from Jemaine Clement and Taika Waititi's 2014 horror-comedy mockumentary of the same name.

Tilda Swinton attends the *Only Lovers Left Alive* photo-call during The 66th Annual Cannes Film Festival at Palais des Festival on 25 May 2013 in Cannes, France. Credit: Denis Makarenko / Shutterstock.com

T

TAKAL, SOPHIA

Sophia Takal is an American actor and filmmaker hailing from New Jersey. In her capacity in the former, she has often worked closely with mumblecore movement, particularly with director Joe Swanberg appearing in his films *The Zone* (2011), *All the Light in the Sky* (2012), and *24 Exposures* (2013). In 2012, she had a role in "Second Honeymoon", Ti West's segment of the first *V/H/S* horror anthology that also co-starred Swanberg and Kate Lyn Shiel. In 2016, Takal directed and co-produced the powerful psychological horror film, *Always Shine*, about two women friends who have competed professionally in their work as actors and the explosive outcomes of the rising tensions between them. In 2018, she directed an episode of Blumhouse's anthology series *Into the Dark* called "New Year, New You," and is set to release a remake of Bob Clarke's *Black Christmas* in December 2019.

TALALAY, RACHEL*

Born to British parents in Chicago in 1958, Rachel Talalay is a director and producer who has worked across film and television, and a Professor in Film at the University of British Columbia. Talalay studied at Yale University and made her feature film debut as director in 1991's *Freddy's Dead: The Final Nightmare*, after acting as a producer on *A Nightmare on Elm Street 4: The Dream Master* (Renny Harlin, 1988), as well as John Waters' *Hairspray* (1988) and *Cry-Baby* (1990). As director, her credits would include the cult film adaptation of Alan Martin and Jamie Hewlett's iconic comic *Tank Girl* (1995), but she remained a key figure in horror, directing feature films including *Ghost in the Machine* (1993) and *The Dorm* (2014). Talalay also has extensive experience as a television director, working on *The Dead Zone, Touching Evil, Supernatural, South of Hell* and cult series including *Sherlock* and *Riverdale*.

TATE, SHARON

Adding insult to quite literal horrific injury, that Sharon Tate has gone down in history only in terms of who murdered her and who she was married to is overwhelmingly offensive in how aggressively it overshadows her status as a remarkable figure in her own right. Born in Dallas, her early career was make primarily by her work as a model, although she did make appearances on television. She made her film debut in a small part in 1961 but it was J. Lee Thompson's 1966 film *Eye of the Devil* that granted Tate her first major film role, an astonishing horror movie where she plays a witch with a suspiciously close relationship with her brother, played by David Hemmings. While the cult film *Valley of the Dolls* in 1967 would be the movie that granted Tate cult film longevity, she returned to horror again with an incandescent performance in Roman Polanski's horror-comedy film, *The Fearless Vampire Killers*, released that same year. Had she not died in such cruel circumstances, Tate would arguably have continued her impressive career trajectory, and we can only imagine that it might have included equally dazzling horror performances.

TAYLOR, ELIZABETH

Across her impressive list of Oscars, BAFTA awards and Golden Globes; her AIDS activism; her perfume brands; and her status as one of the greatest movie stars of the 20th century, it is impossible to claim Elizabeth Taylor only for horror. But make no mistake, Taylor's powerful and totally unique reclamation of the strong yet volatile women characters had an enormous impact on the genre, both directly or indirectly. Born in London in 1932, she was a hugely successful child actor and continued her career well into her later years, working for over six decades in the industry where she worked so hard to become a star. Moving to the United States in the late 1930s, Taylor was in high demand. Her signature depiction of desperate yet highly individual women characters can be seen most clearly in Richard Brooks' screen adaptation of Tennessee Williams' play *Cat on a Hot Tin Roof* (1958), Mike Nichols' adaptation of Edward Albee's play *Who's Afraid of Virginia Woolf?* (1966), *Reflections in a Golden Eye* (John Huston, 1941), *Secret Ceremony* (Joseph Losey, 1968), and *The Driver's Seat* (Giuseppe Patroni Griffi, 1974), all films where Taylor as a performer presents a perfect balance of total control and total surrender, an acting strategy that would also be shared by many of the greatest women horror performers in the genre. While all of these films arguably have a gothic or at least a dark, twisted sensibility to them, in 1973 Taylor also made her most explicit horror film, Brian G. Hutton's *Night Watch*, whose poster—complete with night-time thunderstorms and a spooky, shadowy house—clearly indicates a conscious association with the genre.

TAYLOR, LILI

American actor Lili Taylor was born in Illinois in 1967 and during the 1980s and '90s in particular became a darling of indie cinema. Her numerous horror films include *The Addiction* (Abel Ferrara, 1995), *The Haunting* (Jan de Bont, 1999), *The Secret* (Vincent Perez, 200 7), *The Conjuring* (James Wan, 2013) and *Leatherface* (Julien Maury and Alexandre Bustillo, 2017). In 2019, she is set to star in Ciarán Foy's horror film *Eli*.

TAYLOR-COMPTON, SCOUT ∂

Scout Taylor Compton was born in California in 1989 and began her career as a child actor in television. Her first horror film appearance was in J. S. Cardone's *Wicked Little Things* in 2006, followed by her starring role in the much-hyped 2007 Rob Zombie remake of John Carpenter's 1978 film *Halloween*, where Taylor-Compton revived Jamie Lee Curtis's character Laurie Strode. She followed this in 2008 with the remake of the 1986 slasher *April Fool's Day* and, in 2009, starred in Ron Carlson's *Life Blood*. Despite a desire to move away from horror to establish a more mainstream reputation, Taylor-Compton returned for Zombie's *Halloween II* (2009) and while appearing steadily across a range of genres in both film and television, her later horror credits simultaneously included *247°F* (Levan Bakhia and Beka Jguburia, 2011), *Flight 7500* (Takashi Shimizu, 2014), *Ghost House* (Rich Ragsdale, 2017), *Feral* (Mark H. Young, 2017) and *Edge of Insanity* (Barry Andersson and Joseph Forsberg, 2017).

Scout Taylor-Compton at the Los Angeles premiere of *Lights Out* held at the TCL Chinese Theater in Hollywood, USA on 20 July 2016. Credit: Tinseltown / Shutterstock.com

TAYLOR-JOY, ANYA

Born in Miami in 1996 but primarily raised in Britain, Anya Taylor-Joy became a familiar face to horror fans with her breakout role as Thomasin in Robert Eggars' 2015 film,

The VVitch. Taylor-Joy initially studied as a dancer and began her career as a model, soon turning to acting and breaking through to mainstream attention in *The VVitch* after a small, uncredited role in Mark Waters' 2014 horror-comedy, *Vampire Academy*. She starred in the title role of Luke Scott's horror-scifi hybrid *Morgan* in 2016, and later roles continued her association with horror, including *Split* (M. Night Shyamalan, 2016), *Marrowbone* (Sergio G. Sánchez, 2017), and the psychokiller rich girl black comedy *Thoroughbreds* (Cory Finley, 2017).

TEMPLE, JUNO

One of the most adaptable character actors currently working today, London-born Juno Temple has a long and impressive association with horror although her credits certainly transcend its boundaries. Born in 1989, she began acting in film at the age of 8 and has worked steadily since. While many of her roles straddle gothic-toned thrillers and more traditionally recognizable horror, Temple clearly has a flair for darker characters: beginning with *Cracks* (Jordan Scott, 2009), her later relevant credits would include *Killer Joe* (William Friedkin, 2011), *Magic Magic* (Sebastián Silva, 2013), *Horns* (Alexandre Aja, 2013), *Maleficent* (Robert Stromberg, 2014) and *Unsane* (Steven Soderbergh, 2018).

Juno Temple at the world premiere of *Maleficent* at the El Capitan Theatre, Hollywood, Los Angeles, California, 29 May 2014. Credit: Featureflash Photo Agency / Shutterstock.com

THOMAS, ANNA

Recognized more broadly as a writer, Anna Thomas also directed a feature length horror film called *The Haunting of M* in 1979 as her thesis submission when she was studying at UCLA. Born in Germany but raised in the US, despite its low budget *The Haunting of M* is a beautiful, brooding ghost story filmed in Scotland. Thomas would continue to work in a screenwriting capacity in the industry—her most notable other credit a co-writing acknowledgement on Julie Taymor's 2002 Frida Kahlo biopic *Frida*, starring Salma Hayek. Thomas is the Head of Screenwriting at the American Film Institute Conservatory, and also writes vegetarian cookbooks.

THOMAS, MRS. ROBERT L.

One of the first—if not the first—women credit in what we today might identify as a horror film was the enigmatic "Mrs Robert L. Thomas", who played the title role in Alfred Clark's 1895 film *The Execution of Mary, Queen of Scots* (also known as *The Execution of Mary Stuart*), produced by the Edison Company. In retrospect, this can be identified as one of the first horror movies ever made and one of the first to incorporate what can clearly be understood as a horror special effect with its still-gruesome beheading spectacle. As a number of books focusing on this era of filmmaking have noted, "Mrs" Thompson was in fact played by a man; Robert Thomae, who was the treasurer and secratary of the Edison Comppany during this period. But that the character was both gendered female and credited as such make her a curious but important addition to any history of women in film.

THOMSON, REBECCA

Rebecca Thomson is an award-winning Australian filmmaker from Tasmania. A co-founder of The Stranger With My Face International Film Festival with Briony Kidd in 2012, Thomson's many credits as writer, producer and director include short films such as *Cupcake: A Zombie Lesbian Musical* (2010), *The Jelly Wrestler* (2013) and *I Am Undone* (2015), which have been a staple on the international genre film festival circuit, playing around the world. *I Am Undone* was included on the 2015 horror anthology *A Night of Horror Volume 1*, and *The Jelly Wrestler* featured on the 2017 woman-directed genre anthology *7 From Etheria*.

THORNE, BELLA

Bella Thorne was a popular child star, model and singer who has recently moved into more adult, horror-oriented roles in recent years. Born in Florida in 1997, Thorne was 5 years old when she began working and has worked steadily across film and television in many popular television series and teen films. Her first horror film appearance was as the young Angela Smith in Tyler Oliver's 2009 film *Forget Me Not*, and more recently she has appeared in the horror movies *Amityville: The Awakening* (Franck Khalfoun, 2017), *The Babysitter* (McG, 2017) and *Keep Watching* (Sean Carter, 2017). In 2018, she also starred in Scott Speer's horror movie *I Still See You* and had a small but memorable role in Sam Levison's cult-film-in-the-making, *Assassination Nation*.

THULIN, INGRID

One of the shining lights of European art cinema, Ingrid Thulin was born in Sweden in 1926 and would become renowned for her collaborations with filmmaker Ingmar Bergman. Co-starring with Max Von Sydow and Liv Ullmann, Thulin would play an unforgettable and haunting role in Bergman's iconic 1968 horror film *Hour of the Wolf*, returning to horror again in 1971 with Italian filmmaker Aldo Lado's debut feature, the stylish *giallo Short Night of Glass Dolls*. Despite working with filmmakers ranging from Bergman to Vincente Minnelli to Alain Resnais to Luchino Visconti, Thulin's cult film reputation stems primarily from her extraordinary performance in Tinto Brass's Nazisploitation film *Salon Kitty* (1976).

TICHENOR, EDNA

Edna Tichenor is in the unusual position of being a horror icon despite the fact that the film for which she is most widely known—Tod Browning's *London After Midnight* (1927)—is now considered lost. Born in Minnesota in 1901, Tichenor would elsewhere collaborate with Browning, making her first credited appearance in his 1923 film *Drifting*. Linked closely with the vamp figure, Tichenor would become effectively typecast for this kind of character, but of her surviving films she is most recognizable as the spider woman Luna in Browning's *The Show* (1927).

TILLY, JENNIFER ⬩

Queen of the *Child's Play* franchise, Jennifer Tilly was born Jennifer Ellen Chan in California in 1958. An Oscar nominee who built a strong cult reputation for her co-starring role in The Wachowskis' *Bound* (1996), across her broad career that began in television in the early 1980s Tilly has established a decades-long association with horror. This began

Jennifer Tilly at the world premiere of her movie *The Haunted Mansion*, 23 November 2003.
Credit: Paul Smith / Featureflash Photo Agency / Shutterstock.com

with Neil Jordan's horror-comedy High *Spirits* (1988), followed by *Embrace of the Vampire* (Anne Gousaud, 1995), *The Haunted Mansion* (Rob Minkoff, 2003), *The Caretaker* (Bryce Olsen, 2008) and Stuart Gillard's 2006 made-for-television movie *The Initiation of Sarah*. But it is of course in Ronny Yu's 1998 *Bride of Chucky* that Tilly launched herself as a horror-comedy legend, appearing in the later *Child's Play* sequels *Seed of Chucky* (Don Mancini, 2004) and *Cult of Chucky* (Don Mancini, 2017).

TILLY, MEG ♂

Like her sister Jennifer, Meg Tilly is an American actor who despite the broadness of her career has also made a signficant donation to the horror genre. She was born in California in 1960 and rose to notoriety for her starring role in the controversial Norman Jewison film *Agnes of God* (1985) about a pregnant nun which won her a Golden Globe for Best Actress and garnered her an Oscar nomination. In 1983, she appeared alongside Anthony Perkins and Vera Miles in Richard Franklins' *Psycho II*, continuing her horror work that same year with Tom McLoughlin's *One Dark Night*. In arguably one of her most powerful roles, Tilly put in an unforgettable and broadly underrated performance in Abel Ferrara's often overlooked *Invasion of the Body Snatchers* reimagining, his 1994 film *Body Snatchers*. Returning to horror in 2016, Tilly played a paranoid conspiracy theorist in Danny Perez's glorious psychedelic nightmare *Antibirth*, co-starring Natasha Lyonne and Chloë Sevigny.

TITLE, STACY

American filmmaker, producer and screenwriter Stacy Title made her feature debut in 1995 with the vicious black comedy *The Last Supper* which made an impressive impact on the international arthouse circuit. After her 1999 contemporary updating of *Hamlet* called *Let the Devil Wear Black*, Title would work on two feature-length horror films: directing the horror anthology *Snoop Dogg's Hood of Horror* in 2007 and the urban legend bogeyman film *The Bye Bye Man* in 2017. Title also directed an episode of the horror television series *Freakish*.

TORRENT, ANA

Born in Madrid in 1966, Spanish actor Ana Torrent made her feature film debut starring role before she was even 10 in the haunted gothic tale *The Spirit of the Beehive* (Víctor Erice, 1973). Across her career, she has returned to horror and dark-themed material, most notably starring in Alejandro Amenábar's snuff-centred *Tesis* in 1996, *The Haunting* (Elio Quiroga, 2009), and in Paco Plaza's horror film *Verónica* (2017).

TOWNSEND, NAJARRA

Beginning her career modeling as a small child, Najarra Townsend would appear in short films and television before establishing a career with a notable emphasis on horror. Born in California in 1989, she came to international attention for her performance in Miranda July's *Me and You and Everyone We Know* (2005), but for cult film fans she is most immediately recognizable for her starring role in Eric England's *Contracted* (2013), returning to the role in Josh Forbes's *Contracted: Phase II* (2015). Townsend's other horror roles include *Haunted Echoes* (Harry Bromley Davenport, 2008), *The Telling* (Nick Carpenter and Jeff Burr, 2009), Matt Mercer's 2016 short *Feeding Time*, and two shorts directed by Jill Gevargizian; 2016's *The Stylist*, and *42 Counts* in 2018.

TOYE, WENDY

Despite her extraordinary success, Wendy Toye is barely known to horror fans despite her hugely important role in the genre's film history. An accomplished ballet dancer, she had already played on London's prestigious Royal Albert Hall before she was 5 and choreographed a ballet performance for the London Palladium before she was ten. Born in London in 1917, her career would span well beyond dancing and acting, and she would become a noted theatrical and opera director in London from the mid 1940s through to the mid-1990s when she retired. But it is of course her relation to film that is of particular interest here: her first film as director was the short *The Stranger Left No Card* (1952) which would play at the Cannes Film Festival the following year and whose vocal supporters included the renowned writer, artist, and filmmaker Jean Cocteau. She would make seven feature films as director, mostly dramas and comedies, but in 1955 was one of three directors (four including an uncredited Orson Welles) of the horror anthology *Three Cases of Murder*. Her segment "The Picture" is a classic of the haunted painting trope, and a masterclass in the creation of tone and mood in a dark fantasy-based horror context.

TRACHETENBERG, MICHELLE⸎

Perhaps most famous for her role as Dawn, the sister of the eponymous *Buffy the Vampire Slayer* in the cult television series, American actor Michelle Trachtenberg was born in New York in 1985. She was a child actor who made her first screen appearance at the age of 3, and throughout her career would work across genres. Her association with *Buffy*, however, granetd her a strong relationship to horror, and in 2006 she starred in Glen Morgan's slasher film *Black Christmas*, and John Suits gothic *The Scribbler* alongside fellow *Buffy* alumni Eliza Dushku. Trachtenberg would also appear in the recent television series version of *Sleepy Hollow* and hosted the Discovery Kids horror mytholoy series *Truth or Scare*.

TRUE, RACHEL ⸎

Born in New York in 1966, Rachel True is one quarter of the famous quartet of teen witches from Andrew Fleming's 1996 blockbuster *The Craft*, appearing as Rochelle Zimmerman alongside Fairuza Balk, Robin Tunney and Neve Campbell. True began her career with a recurring role on the sitcom *The Cosby Show* in the early 1990s and would appear on television in a range of popular series. In 1995, she appeared in Anne Goursaud's *Embrace of the Vampire*, and her other horror credits include *Social Nightmare* (Mark Quod, 2013), *Blood Lake: Attack of the Killer Lampreys* (James Cullen Bressack, 2014), *Sharknado 2: The Second One* (Thunder Levin, 2014) and *The Manor* (Jonathon Schermerhorn, 2018).

Rachel True at Hollywood Life Magazine's 9th Annual Young Hollywood Awards. Music Box, Hollywood, California, 22 June, 2007. Credit: s_bukley / Shutterstock.com

TUCKER, PLUMMY

American film editor Plummy Tucker has an extensive filmography but is renowned for her many collaborations with director Karyn Kusama. Landing her first job in the industry as an assistant on Peter Weir's *Dead Poet's Society* (1989), at first Tucker was interested in writing and directing but turned to editing because she felt it would give her the greatest experience to tackle filmmaking more generally. Having edited all of Kusama's feature films since 2000's *Girlfight*, Tucker notably edited Kusama's two full-length horror movies; *Jennifer's Body* (2009) and *The Invitation* (2015).

TÜLLMANN, TINI

German filmmaker Tini Tüllmann was born in Munich in 1977 and studied at the Athanor Academy for Performing Arts in Burghausen, the London Film School, and Cologne's Academy of Media Arts. Graduating in 2003, she worked as a director and in sound and casting, winning the Heinz Badewitz Prize for Best New Director at the Hof International Film Festival for her 2016 feature horror film *Freddy/Eddy* that she both wrote and directed.

TUNNEY, ROBIN ●

Born in Chicago in 1972, American actor Robin Tunney is a familar face on television shows such as *Prison Break* and *The Mentalist*, but her cult horror film fame is linked to her role as Sarah in *The Craft* (Andrew Fleming, 1996), one of that films four teen witch protagonists. Studying at the Chicago Academy for the Arts, she moved to Los Angeles just before she turned 20 and began her career on

Co-stars from *The Craft* Fairuza Balk and Robin Tunney (right) at the MTV Movie Awards in Los Angeles, California. 7 June 1997. Credit: Featureflash Photo Agency / Shutterstock.com

television, impressing audiences the year before *The Craft* with her breakout performance as depressed teenager Debra in Allan Moyle's cult coming-of-age film *Empire Records* (1995). While it was *The Craft* that made Tunney a horror legend, she worked in later films aligned with the genre including Peter Hyams' demonic action film *End of Days* (1999) and Walter Hill's horror-scifi movie *Supernova* in 2000. She also co-starred in Alexander Bulkeley's 2005 film *The Zodiac* about the notorious Zodiac killer.

TURNER, ANN

Australian director Ann Turner directed five feature films in Australia, beginning her career with the Australian gothic classic *Celia*, a dark horror-imbued historical drama about childhood trauma and the escape into fantasy. Born in Adelaide in 1960, Turner studied at Melbourne's Swinburne film school where she made the impressive queer short film *Flesh on Glass* in 1981. Although the genre hybridity of *Celia* at the time of its release saw its initial distribution marred by confused executives, over time it has been celebrated internationally as one of Australia's best horror films of the period. Today, Turner is a successful novelist.

TURNER, GUINEVERE

Actor and screenwriter Guinevere Turner has never been afraid of playing with the transgressive, making her debut as actor and screenwriter in the classic lesbian film *Go Fish* (1994). Born in Boston in 1968, she starred in Stuart Urban's 1997 S+M masterpiece *Preaching to the Perverted* and wrote the screenplay for Mary Harron's 2005 biopic *The Notorious Bettie Page*. In 2000, she and Harron collaborated for the first time when Turner wrote the script for the horror film *American Psycho*, adapted from Bret Easton Ellis's 1991 novel. Amongst Turner's other credits include the screenplay for Uwe Boll's 2005 horror film *BloodRayne*, and co-writing Jamie Babbit's *Breaking the Girls* (2012). Turner also starred in Jane Clark's 2014 horror-comedy *Crazy Bitches*.

TYLER, LIV ✦

Liv Tyler is an American actor and film producer who was born in New York in 1977. She began her acting career in the mid-'90s and would work with directors ranging from Bernardo Bertolucci, Robert Altman and of course with Peter Jackson in the Oscar-winning *Lord of the Rings* films. In 2008, she stunned horror audiences with her unforgettable performance in Bryan Bertino's slasher film *The Strangers*—a role a thousand miles away from the lighter fare which her work with Jackson in particular had cast her. Returning to the genre again in Carter Smith's *Jamie Marks is Dead* (2014) and *Wilding* (Friedrich Böhm, 2018), Tyler also produced the latter.

UDY, HELEN

Born in New Mexico in 1962, Canadian actor and filmmaker Helen Udy began her career appearing in a range of horror films including *My Bloody Valentine* (George Mihalka, 1981), *The Incubus* (John Hough, 1982) and *The Dead Zone* (David Cronenberg, 1983). Although later more renowned for her work on television series like *Dr Quinn: Medicine Woman*, Udy would continue to work extensively in horror in films including *Nightflyers* (T.C. Blake, 1987), *The Last Revenants* (Jim DeVault, 2017), *First House on the Hill* (Matteo Saradini, 2017), *Amityville: Evil Never Dies* (Dustin Ferguson, 2017), *House of Demons* (Patrick Meaney, 2018) and *Stirring* (Troy Escamilla, 2018). Udy has also collaborated on numerous occasions with director David DeCoteau such as *Witches of the Caribbean* (2005), *1313: Frankenqueen* (2012), *3 Wicked Witches* (2014), and *Swamp Freak* (2017). As well as acting, she also directed several shorts and the Daphne Zuniga-fronted romance *Naked in the Cold Sun* (1997).

ULLMANN, LIV

Associated both professionally and personally with filmmaker Ingmar Bergman, Norwegian actor and filmmaker Liv Ullmann was born in Tokyo in 1938. With Bergman, they collaborated on some of the most celebrated European art films of the 20th century, among which Bergman's horror film *Hour of the Wolf* (1968) is a significant entry, as is his infamous psychological horror film *Persona* (1966). Starring in both of these films and in large part granting them their inescapable intensity, Ullmann also starred in the title role of Juan Luis Buñuel's vampire film *Leonor* in 1975. A *Palme d'Or* nominated director herself, as a filmmaker, Ullmann is renowned for her high-quality drama films.

UNGER, DEBORAH KARA

Canadian actor Deborah Kara Unger was born in Vancouver in 1966 and began her career in Australia after studying at Sydney's National Institute of Dramatic Arts. Returning to North America, she came to international attention when she starred in David Cronenberg's *Crash* (1996), and she has worked extensively in horror. While her work is not limited to the genre, her horror credits include *Paranoia 1.0* (Jeff Renfroe and Marteinn Thorsson, 2004), *Messages Deleted* (Rob Cowan, 2009), *Walled In* (Gilles Paquet-Brenner, 2009), *The Hollow* (Sheldon Wilson, 2015) and *Jackals* (Kevin Greutert, 2017). However, her most well-known association with the genre stems from her repeated appearance in the *Silent Hill* franchise, beginning with Christophe Gans' original entry in 2006 and returning in 2012 for Michael J. Bassett's *Silent Hill: Revelation*.

Deborah Kara Unger attends the world premiere of *Silent Hill* held at the Egyptian Theatre in Hollywood, California, 20 April 2006. Credit: Tinseltown / Shutterstock.com

VADHANAPANICH, MARSHA

Thai actor and musician Marsha Vadhanapanich was born in Germany in 1970, and would become famous on-screen for her horror work including the features *Dark Flight* (Issara Nadee, 2012), the segment "In the End" directed by Banjong Pisanthanakun in the 2009 horror anthology *Phobia 2*, and playing identical twins Pim and Ploy in the horror film *Alone* (Banjong Pisanthanakun and Parkpoom Wongpoom, 2007).

VALLI, ALIDA

Sometimes credited simply as Alida, Italian cinema superstar Baroness Alida Maria Laura Altenburger von Marckenstein-Frauenberg—most commonly known as Alida Valli—was one of the most successful and prolific figures of 20th century European cinema. With over 100 credits to her name since she first began acting in 1936. Valli worked with many of cinema's greats, appearing in classic films such as *The Paradine Case* (Alfred Hitchcock, 1947), *The Third Man* (Carol Reed, 1949), *Senso* (Luchino Visconti, 1954) and several films with Bernardo Bertolucci. And, of course, she played the unforgettable Miss Tanner in Dario Argento's Eurohorror classic, *Suspiria* (1977). Born in Italy in 1921 to an aristocratic family, she studied at Rome's Centro Sperimentale di Cinematografia, and throughout her career would win a range of impressive awards. Although focusing primarily on her stage work in the 1950s, she appeared in Georges Franju's famous French horror film *Eyes Without a Face* (1959) later that decade, and would continue her work in the genre in later years in movies such as *Eye in the Labyrinth* (Mario Caiano, 1972), *Lisa and the Devil* (Mario Bava, 1974), *Tender Dracula* (Pierre Grunstein, 1974), *The Antichrist* (Alberto De Martino, 1974), *Killer Nun* (Giulio Berruti, 1979), *Inferno* (Dario Argento, 1980) and *Fatal Frames* (Al Festa, 1996).

VAN ROUVEROY, DORNA

Little is known of Dutch filmmaker Dorna van Rouveroy and, outside of 1999's *An Amsterdam Tale* with Sylvia Kristel, her work has centred primarily on documentary filmmaking. However, under the name Dorna X. De Rouvero, van Rouveroy directed and wrote the Dutch horror movie *Intensive Care* in 1991, starring prolific American actor George Kennedy who won an Oscar for his performance in Stuart Rosenberg's *Cool Hand Luke* (1967).

VAND, SHEILA

Now synonymous with her performance as the eponymous young woman in Ana Lily Amirpour's breakthrough 2014 vampire film *A Girl Walks Home Alone at Night*, California-born Sheila Vand is of Iranian heritage and studied at UCLA. While she has worked in several other genres and is also renowned as a performance artist, Vand's close association with horror has continued with an appearance in Sarah Adina Smith's segment "Mother's Day" in the 2016 horror anthology *Holidays*, and St. Vincent's (aka Annie Clark's) "The Birthday Party" segment in the 2017 horror anthology *XX*.

VELASCO, MANUELA

While for those outside of Spain her name may not be immediately recognizable, for horror fans, the face of Manuela Velasco is synonymous with the internationally successful found footage horror film *[REC]* (Jaume Balagueró Paco Plaza, 2007), also appearing in both *[REC 2]* (Jaume Balagueró Paco Plaza, 2009) and *[REC] 4: Apocalypse* (Jaume Balagueró, 2014). Born in Madrid in 1975, Velasco is famous in Spain both for her acting and as a presenter on television. In 2001, she also appeared in Carlos Gil's slasher film, *School Killer*. For her work in the first *[REC]* film, Velasco received a Goya Award for Best New Actress.

VERDUGO, ELENA

Working across radio, film and television for over 50 years, American actor Elena Verdugo was born in California in 1925, and is best known for her film work in the 1940s. Beginning her career as a child, among her many credits she starred in Erle C. Kenton's *The House of Frankenstein* (1944) with Boris Karloff, Lon Chaney Jr. and John Carradine, and in Harold Young's *The Frozen Ghost* the following year.

VICTOR LIFTON, PAULETTE

Born in Hollywood, Paulette Victor Lifton has a range of skills in post-production, sound editing, casting and direction. Beginning her career as an editor working on country and western music videos, she turned to television and has won several Emmy awards for her work as a sound editor on kids' cartoons. In 2000, Victor Lifton both directed, wrote, edited and produced *Mirror, Mirror IV: Reflection*, the sequel to Marina Sargenti's original in the series. Victor Lifton is the CEO of Oracle Post, a post-production outfit based in New York City and Santa Monica.

VINCENT, CERINA

Las Vegas native Cerina Vincent was born in 1979 and, across her career, has appeared in several teen movies, especially horror films. She began performing as a child and joined a local youth theater group, winning Miss Nevada Teen USA in 1996. Her feature film debut was in Serge Rodnunsky's horror film *Fear Runs Silent* (2000), and her connection to the genre was established with a starring role in Eli Roth's *Cabin Fever* (2002). This was followed by appearances in later horror movies such as *Murder-Set-Pieces* (Nick Palumbo, 2004), *It Waits* (Steven R. Monroe, 2005), *Intermedio* (Andrew Lauer, 2005), *Seven Mummies* (Nick Quested, 2006), *Sasquatch* Mountain (Steven R. Monroe, 2007), *Return to House on Haunted Hill* (Víctor García, 2007), *Freaks of Nature* (Robbie Pickering, 2015), and the short films *Skypemare* (John Fitzpatrick, 2013) and *Brentwood Strangler* (John Fitzpatrick, 2015). In 2015, she starred in Neil Marshall's segment "Bad Seed" on the horror anthology film *Tales of Halloween*.

Cerina Vincent at Weekend of Hell horror-themed fan convention in Dortmund, Germany, April 7-8 2018. Credit: Markus Wissmann / Shutterstock.com

VOGEL, SHELBY

Shelby Vogel is a key part of the dark underbelly of independent US gore studio Toetag Pictures, based in Pittsburgh. The wife of Toetag's founder Fred Vogel, Shelby's credits are extensive and her skills are diverse. Aside from receiving a directorial credit on Toetag's *Murder Collection V.1* (2009), her credits as writer also include *The Redsin Tower* (Fred Vogel, 2006) and *Sella Turcica* (Fred Vogel, 2010). In front of the camera, she has received acting credits for *Murder-Set-Pieces* (Nick Palumbo, 2004), *The Redsin Tower* (Fred Vogel, 2006), *August Underground's Penance* (Fred Vogel, 2007), *Maskhead* (Rebecca Swan and Fred Vogel, 2009), and *The Final Interview* (Fred Vogel, 2017), and she has also worked in a production capacity on many of these films.

VOGELSANG, JUDITH

Judith Vogelsang is a filmmaker with expertise in writing, producing and directing who is based in Los Angeles. While turning later in her career towards documentary filmmaking and television, in 1997 she directed the transplant-based made-for-television horror film *Heartless* with Mädchen Amick. Amongst her many credits as an assistant director includes work on supernatural television series including *Kindred: The Embr*aced and *Charmed*.

VOLTURNO, JEANETTE

Originally running her own production company CatchLight Films, Jeanette Volturno is the Head of Physical Production for Blumhouse Productions and has been a driving force behind some of the biggest horror films of the past decade. Her gobsmackingly impressive credits across a variety of production roles include *Paranormal Activity* (Oren Peli, 2007), *Paranormal Activity 2* (Tod Williams, 2010), and a co-producer of *Paranormal Activity 3* (Henry Joost, Ariel Schulman, 2011), as well as *Sinister* (Scott Derrickson, 2012), *The Lords of Salem* (Rob Zombie, 2012), *Dark Skies* (Scott Stewart, 2013), *The Purge* (James DeMonaco, 2013), *Insidious: Chapter 2* (James Wan, 2013), *Ritual* (Mickey Keating, 2013), *The Purge: Anarchy* (James DeMonaco, 2014), *The Town That Dreaded Sundown* (Alfonso Gomez-Rejon, 2014), *Mercy* (Peter Cornwell, 2014), *Ouija* (Stiles White, 2014), *The Lazarus Effect* (David Gelb, 2015), *The Gift* (Joel Edgerton, 2015), *Visions* (Kevin Greutert, 2015), *Curve* (Iain Softley, 2015), *Insidious: Chapter 3* (Leigh Whannell, 2015), *Sinister 2* (Ciarán Foy, 2015), *The Veil* (Phil Joanou, 2016), *Hush* (Mike Flanagan, 2016), The Darkness (Greg McLean, 2016), *Viral* (Henry Joost and Ariel Schulman, 2016), *Ouija: Origin of Evil* (Mike Flanagan, 2016), *Incarnate* (Brad Peyton, 2016), *Get Out* (Jordan Peele, 2017), *Amityville: The Awakening* (Franck Khalfoun, 2017), *Happy Death Day* (Christopher Landon2017), *Insidious: The Last Key* (Adam Robitel, 2018), *Delirium* (Dennis Iliadis, 2018) and *The First Purge* (Gerard McMurray, 2018).

VON BLANC, CHRISTINA

Although little is known about actor Christina von Blanc, she appeared in some of the most memorable Italian horror films of the 1970s. These include *The Dead Are Alive* (Armando Crispino, 1972), *Bell from Hell* (Claudio Guerin Hill, 1973), and the horror mockumentary *The Evolution of Snuff* (Andrzej Kostenko and Karl Martine, 1978). Most memorable is her performance as Christine in what arguably remains Jess Franco's magnum opus, his 1973 horror film *A Virgin Among the Living Dead*.

VON GARNIER, KATJA

Born in Germany in 1966, filmmaker Katja von Garnier studied at Munich's University of Television and Film, and her student film *Making Up!* (1993) received cinema release and won a German Film Award for Best New Direction. In 1998, she was listed alongside Nick Casavettes, Kevin Smith, Atom Agoyan, and fellow women filmmakers Julie Davis and Mary Harron as upcoming directors to watch in *Vanity Fair*'s Hollywood issue. She has directed many films across a range of genres, most notably the 2007 werewolf film *Blood and Chocolate* starring Agnes Bruckner.

VUCKOVIC, JOVANKA

Canadian director, producer and writer Jovanka Vuckovic's first film was *The Captured Bird* (2012), sweeping awards at films festivals across the globe and with Guillermo del Toro as its executive producer. The following year, the Toronto International Film Festival chose her from a selection of global artists to be a part of their Emerging Filmmakers Competition which was the context within Vuckovic made her two following shorts, *Self Portrait* (2012) and *The Guest* (2013). In 2017 she was an associate producer and driving force behind the all-woman directed horror anthology *XX*, which included her segment "The Box" that she both wrote and directed. Her feature debut is the 2019 scifi/action hybrid *Riot Girls* and she is collaborating on adapting Clive Barker's character Jacqueline Ess from the *Books of Blood* series into a film.

WADDINGTON, ALICE

Alice Waddington is a Spanish filmmaker and artist who was born in Bilbao in 1990. She began her career in advertising, taking a sabbatical to make her extraordinary short film debut, the 2015 baroque horror masterpiece *Disco Inferno*. The film received international acclaim, playing at over 60 film festivals around the world and winning awards at Sitges and Fantastic Fest. Waddington's feature debut—the feminist scifi film *Paradise Hills*—premiered at the 2019 Sundance Film Festival.

WALDY, SOFIA

Born in what was then known as the Dutch East Indies, Indonesian actor and filmmaker Sofia Waldy—often credited as Sofia Waldi or Sofia W.D.—had a long career spanning close to 3 and a half decades, during which time she was in more than 40 films. Of particular note as an actor is her performance in H. Tjut Djalil's 1981 horror film *Mystics in Bali*, a black magic film where she played the memorable Queen of the Leyak. That same year, she also co-starred in Liliek Sudjio's Suzzanna fronted horror *film The Queen of Black Magic*. However, it is the 1962 movie *Badai-Selatan* that Waldy directed that is even more intriguing, which played at the Berlin International Film Festival that year. Yet while listed commonly online as a horror film, little is in fact known about the subject of this film—for many specialists in the field, the first true Indonesian horror film is broadly assumed to be M. Sharieffudin A.'s *Lisa* (1971), starring Lenny Marlina.

WALKER, SHIRLEY

Born in California in 1945, American composer Shirley Walker best known for her film scores to many Hollywood movies. She was among the very first women composers to receive a lone credit score on a large-budget Hollywood film, John Carpenter's horror-comedy *Memoirs of an Invisible Man* (1992). Working from the late 1970s until the mid-

2000s, she began her career as a pianist and studied at San Francisco State University. She initially wrote jingles for commercials and music for industrial films, and her major film work began by her playing synthesizers on the soundtrack for Francis Ford Coppola's *Apocalypse Now* (1979). Across her career, she would have a long association with horror, especially through her work co-composing scores for *Ghoulie*s (Luca Bercovici, 1984), *Nightbreed* (Clive Barker, 1990), *Ritual* (Avi Nesher, 2002), *Willard* (Glen Morgan, 2003) and the first three *Final Destination* films. Her last film credit was for Glen Morgan's 2006 remake of Bob Clark's 1974 slasher film, *Black Christmas*.

WALLACE, DEE

Attaining global fame for her role as Mary in the 1982 blockbuster, *E.T the Extra-Terrestrial* (Steven Spielberg, 1982), Dee Wallace—born Deanna Bowers—has had a lengthy and highly productive relationship with the horror genre since she began acting professionally in the mid-1970s. Born in Kansas in 1948, her horror credits include *The Stepford Wives* (Bryan Forbes, 1975), *The Hills Have Eyes* (Wes Craven, 1977), *The Howling* (Joe Dante, 1981), *Cujo* (Lewis Teague, 1983), *Critters* (Stephen Herek, 1986), *Shadow Play* (Susan Shadburne, 1986), *Popcorn* (Mark Herrier, 1991), *Alligator II: The Mutation* (Jon Hess, 1991), *The Frighteners* (Peter Jackson, 1996), *Headspace* (Andrew van den Houten, 2005), *Boo* (Anthony C. Ferrante, 2005), *Halloween* (Rob Zombie, 2007), *The House of the Devil* (Ti West, 2009), *Dark Fields* (Douglas Schulze, 2009), *The Lords of Salem* (Rob Zombie, 2012), *Hansel & Gretel* (Anthony C. Ferrante, 2013),

Dee Wallace in *Red Christmas* (Craig Anderson, 2016). Photo credit: Douglas Burdorff.
Used with permission (thanks to Craig Anderson).

Apparitional (Andrew P. Jones, 2013), *Ejecta* (Chad Archibald and Matt Wiele, 2014), *Red Christmas* (Craig Anderson, 2016) and *Death House* (Gunnar Hansen, 2017). Wallace is also an author, public speaker and producer, and she has worked extensively on television, and in 2019 is set to appear in Rob Zombie's *3 from Hell* and Cuyle Carvin's *Dolls*.

WALLACE, LOLA

Raised in the Midwest, the thought of becoming a director did not occur to American filmmaker Lola Wallace until her late teens. She studied Film Production at the University of Southern California in 2003, and later was strongly influenced by Lloyd Kaufman's 'Make Your Own Damn Movie' manifesto. With influences including Peter Jackson, Sam Raimi, Robert Rodriguez and Tim Burton, Wallace has worked in a variety of capacities on low-budget indie horror films including *Legend of the Sandsquatch* (2006), *Creek* (2007), and *The Trek* (2008), all of which she also wrote. Her other credits include working extensively in the sound department of films such as *Night of the Dead* (Eric Forsberg, 2006), *The Lonely Ones* (David Michael Quiroz Jr., 2006), *Butcher House* (Christopher Hutson, 2006), *Grim Reaper* (Michael Feifer, 2007), *The Gay Bed and Breakfast of Terror* (Jaymes Thompson, 2007), *Jake's Closet* (Shelli Ryan, 2007) and *Creature of Darkness* (Mark Stouffer, 2009).

WALSH, AISLING

Irish filmmaker and writer Aisling Walsh already had established a strong professional reputation, but it was her 2016 film *Maudie* with Sally Hawkins—a biopic about the Canadian folk artist Maud Lewis—that saw her receive a vast number of awards and nominations around the world. While the bulk of Walsh's work has remained steadfastly loyal to drama territory, her previous feature film directorial effort *The Daisy Chain* (2008) was firmly within the evil child horror film category. Walsh was born in Dublin in 1958 and studied at Dublin's Dún Laoghaire Institute of Art, Design and Technology and the The National Film School in England, working prolifically in television including on popular series such as *The Bill* and the 2005 adapation of Sarah Waters' 2002 novel *Fingersmith* in 2005 (itself which would later be reimagined in Park Chan-wook's 2016 erotic thriller, *The Handmaiden*). While *The Daisy Chain* did not make the same impact as some of her more famous works, her reimagining of the evil child trope certainly indicated a fearless filmmaker with the courage to push the subgenre into new terrain in a thoughtful, sensitive manner.

WALSH, FRAN

New Zealand producer and screenwriter Fran Walsh may not be as well-known as her long-term collaborator (and partner) Peter Jackson, but her importance on their collaborations—which have garnered her three Oscars and sevn nominations—is widely recognized. Born in Wellington in 1959, Walsh had an initial interest in music and fashion, studying literature at Wellington's Victoria University. She had already begun her career as a screenwriter before meeting Jackson when he was making his cult horror film *Bad Taste* (1987), and they would collaborate from that point onwards on many films, including horror, monster and supernatural-themed movies such as *Braindead* (1992), *The Frighteners* (1996), *King Kong* (2005) and *The Lovely Bones* (2009).

WALTERS, JESSICA

While today most immediately known for her work on the popular sitcom *Arrested Development* and voicing the cartoon *Archer*, Walter has impressive form in horror also. In 1971, she put in an incredible performance in Clint Eastwood's stalker film *Play Misty For Me* as the obsessive Evelyn Draper, which saw her nominated for a Golden Globe award for Best Actress. The following year she would appear with an all-star cast in the John Llewellyn Moxey-directed made-for-television horror film *Home for the Holidays* alongside Sally Field, Eleanor Parker and Julie Harris. In 1978 she starred in Philip DeGuere's adaptation of Marvel's supernatural fantasy *Dr. Strange*, again returning to a made-for-TV film in 1979 in E. W. Swackhamer's *Vampire*. In 1993, she also had a smaller role in Rachel Talalay's scifi horror hybrid *Ghost in the Machine*.

WALTON, KAREN

Hailing from Nova Scotia, Karen Walton is a significant horror screenwriter for her award-winning screenplay of John Fawcett's cult 2002 Canadian feminist werewolf film, *Ginger Snaps*. Studying Drama at the University of Alberta, she later joined The Film and Video Arts Society of Alberta co-op after becoming interested in film after doing stunt work on a locally produced horror film. Initially trying her hand at directing, it was not until she was in her 30s that she found script writing was more satisfying and began writing films and radio plays. Influenced by Mary Shelley's *Frankenstein* at a young age, Walton has said it took five years to develop *Ginger Snaps* from the initial script to the final film, but it is a project upon which she established an internationally recognized reputation. She has since worked extensively as a writer and producer aross film and television, including on popular shows such *as Orphan Black* and *Queer as Folk*.

WARD, RACHEL

British-born Australian filmmaker, actor and writer Rachel Ward has in recent years established herself as one of Australia's most interesting directors, but her career as an actor began with a close affiliation with the horror genre. Born in England in 1957, Ward was a successful model who moved from the United Kingdom to the United States to pursue an acting career after studying at London's Byam Shaw School of Art. Her debut role in a feature film was in Ken Hughes's 1981 slasher *Night School* where she plays morally ambiguous exchange student Eleanor Adjai. Although her acting career would expand to incorporate more mainstream and highbrow fare, in these early years her association with horror continued when she co-starred with Daryl Hannah in Andrew Davis's camping slasher film *The Final Terror* (1983), and later—after Ward had moved to Australia—she starred in the Australian abduction nightmare *Fortress* (1985), written by celebrated Australian genre screenwriter Everett De Roche.

WARREN, DERYN

Today an acting coach and script doctor, Deryn Warren has an impressive past history as a horror movie director. Her filmmaking debut was the horror comedy movie *Dead of Night* (1988), followed by *The Boy from Hell* (1988) and *Black Magic Woman* (1991) which she also co-wrote, the latter starring Apollonia Kotero, most famous for her co-starring role in Albert Magnoli's 1984 blockbuster Prince vehicle *Purple Rain*.

WASIKOWSKA, MIA

Born in 1989 in Canberra, Australian actor Mia Wasikowska had ambitions as a child of becoming a professional dancer. Despite intensive training, she later turned to acting and began her career on Australian television. Her first significant film role was in *Wolf Creek* director Greg McLean's *Rogue* (2007), beginning Wasikowska's long professional association with horror and gothic cinema. In 2008, she starred in Spencer Susser's zombie short *I Love Sarah Jane*, making her international breakthrough in the title role of Tim Burton's 2010 adaptation *Alice in Wonderland*. In 2013, Wasikowska worked back-to-back in two of the year's most original and critically celebrated art-horror films, Jim Jarmusch's vampire film *Only Lovers Left Alive* with Tilda Swinton, and Park Chan-wook's *Stoker* alongside fellow Australian actor, Nicole Kidman. In 2015, she starred in Guillermo del Toro's gothic love letter to the films of Mario Bava *Crimson Peak*, and in 2018 she starred in Nicolas Pesce's *Piercing*.

Mia Wasikowska attends the *Damsel* premiere during the 68th Film Festival Berlin at Berlinale Palast on 16 February 2018 in Berlin, Germany. Credit: Denis Makarenko / Shutterstock.com

WATTS, NAOMI ❦

Naomi Watts was born in England in 1968, moving to Australia in 1982 where she began to build her significant career as one of that country's most successful and well-known screen professionals. Her mother Myfanwy worked in Australian film and television as a costume designer and stylist, sparking Naomi's interest in the industry and she would famously become friends with fellow rising star Nicole Kidman during her time working on TV commercials. After many years of struggling to break through in Hollywood, she gained a key role in Rachel Talalay's cult film *Tank Girl* (1995), and during this fledgling period of her career also gained a starring role in Greg Spence's *Children of the Corn IV: The Gathering* (1996). In 2001, she starred in the evil elevator film *The Shaft*, but Watts's career would take a dramatic turn when she was hand-picked by David Lynch to star in his dark surrealist nightmare-noir *Mulholland Drive* in 2001, and stardom soon followed. Watts would famously star in the US remakes of the popular Japanese series *Ringu* in both *The Ring* (Gore Verbinski, 2002) and *The Ring Two* (Hideo Nakata, 2005). In 2007 she starred in Michael Haneke's American remake of his twisted home invasion film *Funny Games*. Later roles in the genre also include Jim Sheridan's *Dream House* (2011) and Farren Blackburn's 2016 film *Shut In*.

WEAVER, SIGOURNEY &

As Ellen Ripley in *Alien* (Ridley Scott, 1979), *Aliens* (James Cameron, 1986), *Alien 3* (David Fincher, 1992) and *Alien Resurrection* (Jean-Pierre Jeunet, 1997), Sigourney Weaver became one of the most prominent and important women in horror due to her groundbreaking role in the famous horror-scifi franchise. Born in New York in 1949, across her career she has been nominated for Tony Awards, Oscars and Emmys and winning Golden Globe, BAFTA and Saturn Awards. Weaver came from a showbusiness family and studied at both Stanford and Yale, gaining her Masters in Drama from the latter in the mid-1970s. Beginning her career on stage, she had small roles in film until she gained the part of Ripley. Across her career, Weaver has appeared in horror films including *The Cabin in the Woods* (Drew Goddard, 2012), *Red Lights* (Rodrigo Cor-

Sigourney Weaver at the premiere of *Alien Resurrection* in Los Angeles, California, 20 November 1997. Credit: Featureflash Photo Agency / Shutterstock.com

tés, 2012), *Vamps* (Amy Heckerling, 2012) and *A Monster Calls* (J. A. Bayona, 2016), as well as famous supernatural comedies *Ghostbusters* (Ivan Reitman, 1984), *Ghostbusters II* (Ivan Reitman, 1989), and a cameo in Paul Feig's 2016 dude-bro trolling reboot, *Ghostbusters*. Weaver was also cast in the television movie *Snow White: A Tale of Terror* (Michael Cohn, 1997).

WEBER, PEGGY

Born in Texas in 1925, Peggy Webber was famously only 2-years-old when she began working as a stage performer, moving to radio at age 11 and writing, directing and producing her own television shows before she was even 20. With a list of radio credits well into the thousands, Webber she is best known to horror fans for her starring performance in Alex Nicol's low-budget horror classic *The Screaming Skull* (1958) where she played the tormented young wife Jenni Whitlock, and she also appeared in the horror television series *Panic!* and *Night Gallery*.

WEBER, LOIS

Pioneering American filmmaker, writer and actor Lois Weber is one of the most important women in the history of American cinema, her notable achievements amongst many including directing films with the first full-frontal nudity scene with a woman in her 1915 movie *Hypocrites*. Weber was the first woman in the United States to run her own studio, and one of the first—if not the first—filmmakers to use split-screen in her 1913 film, *Suspense*. Weber was born in Pennsylvania in 1879 and took to performing from an early age, first exceling at the piano, and later moving to the theater as an actor and singer. With the assistance of earlier pioneering woman filmmaker Alice Guy, Weber moved to film as a writer and director, also acting in some of her own films. With a career output and importance the scale of which should make her reputation equal to D.W. Griffith, *Suspense* in particular is a key film in Weber's filmography from a horror perspective as it is a proto-home invasion story that relies heavily on excessive film style to communicate extremely dark vibes.

WEIXLER, JESS

Jess Weixler is an American actor who was born in the early 1980s in Kentucky. She studied at Juilliard and began her screen career in her early 20s, her performance in Mitchell Lichtenstein's cult horror film *Teeth* in 2007 remaining her most famous role. In 2019, she appeared in Andy Muschietti's *It Chapter Two*.

WENDEL, LARA

Born in Munich in 1965, Lara Wendel would make her first film appearance at the age of 7 in the *giallo My Dear Killer* (Tonio Valerii, 1972), beginning her 20-year long association with Italian film and television. Despite acting in movies made by Michelangelo Antonioni and Federico Felini, it was in horror that Wendel made her most famous film appearances, including Francesco Barilli's *The Perfume of the Lady in Black* 1974, *Ring of Darkness* (Pier Carpi, 1979), Dario Argento's *Tenebrae* (1982), *Zombie 5: Killing Birds* (Claudio Lattanzi, 1988) and *Ghosthouse* (Umberto Lenzi, 1988).

WEST, GABBY

Gabby West is an American actor who was born in Los Angeles in 1985. After winning the 2010 horror-themed reality television competition *Scream Queens*, she was cast as Kara in Kevin Greutert's *Saw 3D* (2010). In 2011, she appeared in Tim Sullivan's segment "I Was a Teenage Werebear" in the horror anthology *Chillerama*.

WEST, VERA

Born in New York in 1900, while the mysterious circumstances surrounding the death of American costume designer Vera West have been an ongoing subject of fascination for film fans across many decades, her role as the chief designer of Universal Pictures from 1928 to 1947 saw her work on several the studio's most famous horror films of the era. Her first solo credit as designer was on Paul Leni's classic horror film *The Man Who Laughs* (1928), and her later work includes many notable horror movies such as *The Mummy* (Karl Freund, 1932), *Son of Frankenstein* (Rowland V. Lee, 1939), *The Invisible Man Returns* (Joe May, 1940), *Tower of London* (Rowland V. Lee), *Black Friday* (Arthur Lubin, 1940), *The Invisible Woman* (A. Edward Sutherland, 1940), *Hold That Ghost* (Arthur Lubin, 1941), *The Wolf Man* (George Waggner, 1941), *The Ghost of Frankenstein* (Erle C. Kenton, 1942), *Frankenstein Meets the Wolf Man* (Roy William Neill, 1943), *Phantom of the Opera* (Arthur Lubin, 1943), *Son of Dracula* (Robert Siodmak, 1943), *House of Frankenstein* (Alder C. Kenton, 1944) and *She-Wolf of London* (Jean Yarbrough, 1946).

WEXLER, JENN

A key figure at Larry Fessenden's US production company Glass Eye Pix, Jenn Wexler has not only significant form as a producer but is just as impressive a director and writer on her own merits. Her production credits include the Fessenden-directed 2013 film *Beneath*, Mickey Keating's *Darling* (2015) and Ana Asensio's brilliant *Most Beautiful Island* (2017). Wexler is the force behind the shorts *Slumber Party* (2012) and *Halloween Bash* (2013), and her 2018 feature directorial debut *The Ranger* received international festival play, introducing global audiences to her work.

WEYHER, RUTH

Born in what was then West Prussia (now Poland) in 1901, German silent actor Ruth Weyher appeared in almost 50 films during her 10-year film career that began in 1920. Of her many roles, most iconic is her performance as the unnamed wife of the count at the heart of the dramas of Arthur Robison's German Expressionist horror classic, the hallucinatory 1923 film *Warning Shadows*.

WHITE, JENNIFER B.

Jennifer B. White is a novelist, screenwriter, producer and director whose talents range from writing taglines for Universal Pictures to making her own feature film, the 2014 horror movie *Mary Loss of Soul*. Aside from the short mystery *Nora's Return* (2016) and a 2014 music video, *Mary Loss of Soul* remains White's only feature credit as both director, writer and producer. Her supernatural novels include *The Witch and the Devil's Son* (2002), *Otherwise* (2011) *and Dead Asleep* (2011), and she is a principal figure at the production company OakIvy Productions.

WHITELAW, BILLIE

Widely noted for her ongoing work with renowned playwright Samuel Beckett, for cult film fans Billie Whitelaw is most immediately recognizable as Mrs. Blaylock in Richard Donner's *The Omen* (1976). Born in England in 1932, she began acting as a child and later moved to radio. She studied acting at the Royal Academy of Dramatic Arts in London and launched a successful stage and screen career, appearing in movies including John Gilling's mad doctor film *The Flesh and the Fiends* (1960), Roy Boulting's psychological horror film *Twisted Nerve* (1969) and Alfred Hitchcock's vicious *Frenzy* (1972).

WILBUR, EMILY LOU

Emily Lou Wilbur is an American filmmaker who was born in California and studied at San Francisco State University where she was awarded the Julie Irving Award for Excellence in Direction. Her feature film debut was the 2011 horror-comedy *The Selling*, on which she was also a producer.

WILCOX, LISA

As Alice Johnson in *A Nightmare on Elm Street 4: The Dream Master* (Renny Harlin, 1989) and *A Nightmare on Elm Street 5: The Dream Child* (Stephen Hopkins, 1989), American actor Lisa Wilcox is a much-loved part of the franchise. Born in Missouri in 1964, she began working on television in her early 20s, with the *Elm Street* films marking her first major film appearances. She was also cast in John Carl Buechler's 1998 horror film *Watchers Reborn*, *Savage* (Jordan Blum, 2011), *Sebastian* (Gregori J. Martin, 2011), *Imago*

(Chris Warren, 2013), *Clinger* (Michael Steves, 2015), *Red Hollow* (Pressly Parrish, 2017) and the 2009 FEARnet web series *Fear Clinic* with other horror alumni Robert Englund, Kane Hodder and Danielle Harris. In 2010, she appeared in Daniel Farrands and Andrew Kasch's documentary *Never Sleep Again: The Elm Street Legacy*.

WILDE, BARBIE—INTERVIEW (AUGUST 2018)

All-round renaissance woman Barbie Wilde might be most readily recognized as the woman Cenobite in Tony Randel's horror classic *Hellbound: Hellraiser II* (1988), but her accomplishments and talents are broad.

While born in Canada in 1960 and growing up in the United States, it was in Britain that Wilde's many talents would ultimately lead her to cult stardom. Wilde studied mime in the late 1970s and from this she spawned the punk burlesque troupe SHOCK who would tour with some of the biggest British New Wave bands of the 1980s.

As well as appearing in a number of cult films beyond *Hellbound: Hellraiser II*, Wilde worked as both host and writer of a number of film and music review television programs in the UK during the 80s and 90s, and in recent years has established a strong body of work as an author with highlights including the short story "Sister Cilice" in Paul Kane and Marie O'Regan's *Hellbound Hearts* anthology in 2009.

She published many more short stories and in 2012 she released her debut novel *The Venus Complex* with Comet Press, today continuing her career as a prolific author: *Fangoria Magazine* has called Wilde "one of the finest purveyors of erotically charged horror fiction around".

www.barbiewilde.com

Many of us first got to know you as a Cenobite, your performance in *Hellbound: Hellraiser II*. How did you find yourself playing a character almost all women horror fans (and many male ones) I know want to be?!

Before I returned to acting in the mid-1980s, I'd explored classical mime in London, England. Then bizarrely, I moved into the realms of the New Romantic music movement with the group SHOCK, which incorporated mime, dance, music and wild theatrics. SHOCK supported such artists as Gary Numan, Adam and the Ants, Depeche Mode and Ultravox. We were signed to RCA Records for a couple of years and released two singles. After SHOCK broke up, I began to write my own material and tried to break into the music biz, but I didn't have any luck. After appearing as a thug in *Death Wish 3* and a drummer for an electronica band in *Grizzly II: The Concert* AKA *Grizzly 2: The Predator*. I moved into hosting movie review and pop music shows. I must say, I felt more comfortable as a TV presenter, as I was more in control and wrote my own scripts.

Then my agent called one day and asked if I wanted to go to an audition to play a Cenobite in the second *Hellraiser* film. "And to think, I hesitated" (as

Doug Bradley and Barbie Wilde in *Hellraiser II: Hellbound* (Tony Randel, 1988).
Credit: AF archive / Alamy Stock Photo.

Dr Channard says in *Hellbound*). But I did, simply because I thought that they wanted me to play the Chatterer and that character really disturbed me.

In the end, of course, I did go to the audition and had a nice chat with director Tony Randel. Rule One of any audition: don't be argumentative with the director! However, when Tony said that he though that Clive had made up the word, Cenobite, I corrected him (twice) and said: "No, it means a person who is a member of an order, normally a religious one." I guess that Tony was impressed by my vast knowledge of everything Cenobitical and he cast me in the role.◻ Also, I know that Clive is very interested in mime and perhaps the fact that I was a classically trained mime artist was a factor. I felt that my training helped me get that all important feeling of "being centered" that was so necessary for playing a Cenobite. It's the heavy ominous stillness of the Cenobites that has always intrigued me. They are so much more mysterious than the usual run-of-the mill monsters that shriek and run crazily through the woods with chain saws, chasing girls wearing boob tubes and hot pants.

I've always been really touched by how strong the bond is between the *Hellraiser* alumni—so many of you seem to support each other and continue working together. Was this something you felt would happen at the time you were making *Hellbound: Hellraiser II*?

Absolutely. I think that when you get a group of actors who are all under pressure during the makeup and costume process with very early starts and long hours in the makeup chair, then you do achieve a certain camaraderie. Also, as with any movie, there was a lot of waiting around, so we had to entertain ourselves.

There was a time when we lost touch with each other, but soon found ourselves at horror conventions, which are a huge amount of fun and a great way to connect with fans. (As well as getting the news out about what we're all doing now.)

I didn't know until I saw it on your website that you were a drummer in *Grizzly II*! That project sounded incredible, how did you come to be involved?

My boyfriend at the time, Richard James Burgess, was producing the music for Predator, the electronica band that was going to appear in the movie. He was going to play the drummer, then he got the call to produce Adam Ant in Sweden, so he took that job instead. He suggested me for the role, even though I've never held a pair of drum sticks in my life. However, he taught me the basics and I rehearsed like mad. Luckily, I was using an extraordinary set of his electronic Simmons Drums. When the sound of the drums was turned off, you couldn't hear if I was out of sync or not (thank goodness), so all I had to do was look like I was in time and "mime drum" like the devil, which I did.

Grizzly II was a strange project, starring Louise Fletcher, John Rhys-Davies, Steve Inwood, Deborah Raffin, and including "red shirt" extras such as Charlie

Sheen, Laura Dern and George Clooney, who were all eaten by the bear in the first half hour. Sadly, I never met them, as all my time was taken up performing with the band on the massive concert stage that had been built in the middle of a national park in Hungary.

In the end, the film never saw the light of day (except for excerpts up on You-Tube). Financial woes were the main reason, I believe. I wish that someone would buy the rights and finish it off, as it would be fun to see it in all its crazy glory.

Speaking of music, it is so clearly a large part of your personal and professional life, how did that relationship begin and how has it evolved over time?

I was always very musical. Over the years, I've taken piano, guitar, recorder and harpsichord lessons. I even learned how to play the bagpipe at University! And I loved singing in school musicals and at drama school. Funnily enough, when I started out in the biz, I always imagined that I'd end up in musical theater, however, it just didn't work out. (The closest I came was singing "Mein Herr" from *Cabaret* to a bemused LittleJohn, the makeup artist in *Hellbound*.)

The fact that SHOCK were signed by RCA Records was facilitated by our producers, Richard James Burgess and Rusty Egan. It seemed like a natural for us to combine all the music and movement skills we had with writing our own material, which Tim Dry, one of the other members of SHOCK, and I did with Richard. However, sadly, success eluded SHOCK and we all ended up going our own ways.

So many women I have spoken to involved in horror are often multiskilled, multitalented, and refuse to lock themselves down to one single professional identity. You might just be the reigning queen of this, a veritable polymath! Can you tell me a little about all the different things you've done as a creator, and how they intersect and deviate? Did you arrive at any one creative field initially and branch out from there, or did it all emerge from your creative spirit more organically?

Well, I think that when folks view one's career, they imagine that I must have planned this amazing creative narrative arc, but it was really more of an organic (and perhaps frantic) "what do I do now?" kind of thing. I suppose that I've never been afraid of trying new disciplines like mime, or music, or even roller skating (for a Andrew Lloyd Webber musical that I didn't get in), with varying degrees of success.

I think that the things that I was most successful at: acting, TV presenting and writing, are the ones that I cared the most about. I'm a big believer in following your passions (or to "follow your bliss" as author Joseph Campbell says). Writing is number one now. I'm the one creating the worlds, the mythologies and the characters and it's very rewarding. When you're on a roll, writing something that you love, there is no better feeling of satisfaction and creativity.

Barbie Wilde on the set of *Grizzy 2*. Used with permission.

And finally, in a practical sense, the more skills you possess, the easier it is to be employed, especially in show biz.

I'm really intrigued in your fiction writing that the erotic and horror sit so organically together in a way that feels so far beyond exploitation, verging really into the realm of almost abstracted poetry. "Sex and death" is one of the great clichés of horror perhaps; what is it do you think from your own perspective that has granted you insight into creating something so fresh and original in terms of these themes in particular?

Thank you! When I first approached the idea of writing a book about a serial killer (which eventually became *The Venus Complex*), it was from the viewpoint of the plucky forensic psychiatrist on the trail of a vicious murderer. Then I got bored. It was like so many other books that I'd read before. I wanted to create something different. So I did my research and wrote the book from the male perspective — from the viewpoint of the killer himself. And boy, was it liberating. To me, sex is such an important aspect of human behavior and yet no one wants to talk about it. (I often feel like I'm back in the late 1960s trying to persuade my parents to spill the beans on sex education.)

To write a novel exploring the sexual fantasies and mindscape of a serial killer was my goal, and I'm very proud of *The Venus Complex*, because according to a policeman friend of mine, I not only cracked the police procedural part of the book, but I also revealed the secrets of what men really think of women sexually.

I also have to give credit to a friend of mine who was a professional dominatrix. (She had a Masters Degree in Human Sexuality as well.) She taught me a lot about human desire and how far people are willing to go to fulfill their fantasies.

I do have to point something out: with many of my short horror stories (which you can find in my illustrated collection, *Voices of the Damned*, published by SST Publications), I don't start out with the overriding idea of writing erotica. It just happens to come along and insert itself into the story. I suppose it's because I like writing about humans and as I say above, sex is a very important part of being human.

As a writer, does reading for you feel a little bit like research or is it a space where you can let go of your more intellectual and professional interests? I'd love to hear about some of your favourite books and authors.

I read for both pleasure and research and since I always choose subjects that fascinate me, then research ends up being a joy for me. One of my favorite non-fiction authors is Colin Wilson. My top picks of his work are *Criminal History of Mankind*, *Order of Assassins* (the book that first got me interested in serial killers) and *Written in Blood*, which is about the history of forensic science. Another standout book about psychopaths is *Without Conscience* by Dr Robert Hare.

As far as fiction and film are concerned, my favorite writers are: Patricia Highsmith, Shirley Jackson, Margaret Atwood, Raymond Chandler, Dashiell Hammett, Hemingway, Rod Serling, Guillermo del Toro and last, but certainly not least, Clive Barker—especially for *The Hellbound Heart*, the novella that was the basis for the Hellraiser films.

I'd also like to give a special mention to *Dracula* by Bram Stoker. It was one of the first gothic horror novels that I'd ever read. Stoker and Mary Shelley were both influences on me when I was growing up.

One of the books that made a major impression on me in the last few years was a brilliant novella called *Whitstable* by Stephen Volk. Set in 1971 after the death of horror icon Peter Cushing's beloved wife Helen, Volk channels Cushing in the most moving and compelling way: we feel Cushing's grief, his fear, his anger, his love for Helen, and how even in death, she gives him the strength to go on. There are no supernatural monsters in this beautifully written tale, just human ones. A reprint of *Whitstable* will be available in October 2018 in a collection called *The Dark Masters Trilogy*, along with Volk's other novellas *Leytonstone* and *Netherwood*.

Do you watch a lot of horror films? Is there a particular trend that you would like to see more—or less—of?

I'm very selective about what I watch, simply because I write horror (not only books and stories, but scripts as well) and when you have that kind of stuff in your head all day long, sometimes you just want to kick back and watch a film with palm trees in it and drink a margarita.

However, there are some horror films that have made a big impression on me: *American Mary* and *Dead Hooker in a Trunk* by the Soska Sisters. (And I can't wait for their imaginative and unique reimagining of *Rabid*, which they're in the midst of doing now.) I also loved *The Autopsy of Jane Doe* by André Øvredal, *The Love Witch* by Anne Biller, *Only Lovers Left Alive* by Jim Jarmusch, *Audition* by Takeshi Miike and *Sinister* by Scott Derrickson. And anything by Guillermo del Toro.

However, I'm a bit old school too: most of my all-time favs are either Hammer Horror or old black-and-white horror like *The Innocents* (1961), *The Haunting* (1963), *The Thing from Another World* (1951) and *Invasion of the Body Snatchers* (1956). And I do love '80s horror like Carpenter's *The Thing*, *Alien*, *Halloween* and of course, *Hellraiser*.

Although it's not a horror film, you are amazing in *Death Wish 3* (I love that makeup so much!). How did you come to that role, and what was the experience like of filming it?

Again, my agent put me up for the part. It was a fun experience and Michael Winner was a real character. He had the reputation for always bringing in his movies under time and under budget, so there was no lingering on scenes.

One thing did happen though, which was a bit of a shock. We were nearly at the end of the shoot and were about to start with a rare (for me anyway) indoor scene. Mr. Winner asked me if I had anything else to wear instead of the usual jeans, motorcycle boots, leather jacket that I had been wearing every day. I came back dressed in what I'd worn to work: a pink leopard skin mini skirt, black fish net tights, pink leather stilettos and a pink *Earth VS The Flying Saucers* T-shirt. (Hey, it was the 80s!)

Anyway, I'm afraid that this outfit gave Mr Winner some ideas and he told me that he'd like me to do the scene topless, which was really unexpected. It wasn't in the script and I had no warning. I kept thinking about my Mom, who was a lapsed Catholic, and I thought to myself: I can't do this, she'd never forgive me.

Also, I was a bit miffed about being placed in such an uncomfortable position at such late notice. In my opinion, it's really unprofessional for a director to spring something like that on an actress just before you go on set.

Barbie Wilde "Female Cenobite" artwork by Andrew Tong. Used with permission.

I pushed back the only way I knew how: I asked for more money! He refused to pay me extra, saying that "no one was making any money on this movie, darling." I said, "Hey, I just read in the newspaper that you've just pre-sold the video rights for 600,000 pounds alone." I insisted that I wouldn't do it and he ordered me off the set. Whew! Maternal disappointment averted! The funny thing was, he got another actress in to do the same scene after I left and he didn't ask her to take her top off. So there ya go!

Both personally and professionally you've really set a very high bar for what women can achieve in the broader realm of horror. What do you think stops more women from staking a claim as artists in the field, and do you think that's changing?

I think we know what stops women in the field. It's just really hard to be taken seriously in an entitled white man's world. However, as director Kathryn Bigelow (*Zero Dark Thirty*) said: "If there's specific resistance to women making movies, I just choose to ignore that as an obstacle for two reasons: I can't change my gender, and I refuse to stop making movies. I can't change my sex and I don't want to do anything else, so you just have to keep on persevering."

So my motto is: "Never give up; never surrender" as Commander Peter Quincy Taggart says in *GalaxyQuest*.

Do I think it's changing? Yes, as there are a lot more women in the horror realm, showing their love for the genre, either as writers, directors, producers, etc. We just have to keep on working and getting our stuff out there. And we shouldn't be afraid of speaking up and demanding to be noticed. Sometimes I think that women are a bit too polite. We've got to use our elbows and force our way to the top.

WILLIAMS, ALLISON

As Rose Armitage in Jordan Peele's Oscar-winning horror film *Get Out* (2017), American Allison Williams brought to life in an undeniably memorable way the cloying hypocrisy of white liberalism in one of the most important and effective horror films made in the last decade. Born in Connecticut in 1988, Williams has also appeared on the HBO series *Girls* and Netflix's *A Series of Unfortunate Events*. In 2018 she co-starred with Logan Browning in Richard Shepard's neo-grindhouee horror film *The Perfection*, a film that takes the concept of complex women characters to audacious, excessive lengths.

Allison Williams arrives for the *Get Out* Los Angeles premiere on 10 February 2017 in Los Angeles, California. Credit: DFree / Shutterstock.com

WILLIAMS, ASHLEY C.

Born in Boston in 1984, despite an impressive career as a theatrical actor, Ashley C. Williams for most horror fans at least will always maintain a strong place in their collective hearts for her role as the central 'segment' of Tom Six's notorious 2009 film *The Human Centipede*. Williams began acting as a child, and apart from her stage work she has also appeared across a range of film and television genres. Her other horror credits include *Empty* (C.S. Drury, 2011), *Paranormal Movie* (Kevin Farley, 2013), *Hallows' Eve* (Sean McGarry, 2013), *Julia* (Matthew A. Brown, 2014) and *Selene Hollow* (Mathew Provost, 2015).

WILLIAMS, CAROLINE

Caroline Williams is best known as Stretch from *The Texas Chainsaw Massare* films, but her impressive work across the genre as both actor and producer has spanned more than four decades. Born in Texas in 1957, Williams's horror credits include *The Texas Chainsaw Massacre 2* (Tobe Hooper, 1986), *Stepfather II* (Jeff Burr, 1989), *Halloween II* (Rob Zombie, 2009), *The Unleashed* (Manuel H. Da Silva, 2011), *Hatchett III* (BJ McDonnell and Robert Green Hall, 2013), *Contracted* (Eric England, 2013), *Blood Valley: Seed's Revenge* (Marcel Walz, 2014), *Contracted: Phase II* (Josh Forbes, 2015) and *Fantasma* (Brett Mullen, 2017). She has also appeared in the anthology films *Tales of Poe* (2014) and *Tales of Halloween* (2015) and made a cameo as Stretch in *Sharknado: The 4th Awakens* (Anthony C. Ferrante, 2016). She is currently working on a feature film directed by Kansas Bowling of *B.C. Butcher* (2016) fame.

WILLIAMS, GIGI

Gigi Williams began her career as a makeup artist in 1975, initially collaborating with Diane von Fustenberg for publications including *Vogue* and *Interview*, moving to film and television at the end of that decade. With credits ranging from *Pearl Harbor* (Michael Bay, 2001) to *Gone Girl* (David Fincher, 2014) to *Inherent Vice* (Paul Thomas Anderson, 2014), Williams also has an impressive CV when it comes to horror, having worked on movies like *Nocturna* (Harry Tampa, 1979), *The Howling* (Joe Dante, 1981), *My Demon Lover* (Charlie Loventhal, 1987), *A Return to Salem's Lot* (Larry Cohen, 1987), *Lord of Illusions* (Clive Barker, 1995), *Nightwatch* (Ole Bornedal, 1997) and *When a Stranger Calls* (Simon West, 2006), as well as television series such as *Tales from the Darkside*.

WILSON, BELINDA M.

Actor, cinematographer and filmmaker Belinda M. Wilson has worked on stage and screen, beginning her directorial career with a number of shorts before her feature debut, the action film *X-Scape* (2011). Her career is notable for directing two feature-length horror movies; the women-in-prison film Women's Playground (2013) and the occult fantasy *Black Mamba* (2016). Wilson also appeared on-screen in both of these films and receives an acting credit in Dom Franklin's 2018 horror film *The Church*, co-starring Bill Moseley and Lisa Wilcox.

WILSON, LULU

One of the youngest women in this book, Lulu Wilson's flair for horror is as strong as many of her much older colleagues. Born in 2005 in New York, Wilson's work in horror has elevated the quality of the films she has appeared in due to her sensitivity to the nuance and intelligence she brings to the roles she plays. Career highlights include *Deliver Us from Evil* (Scott Derrickson, 2014), *Ouija: Origin of Evil* (Mike Flanagan, 2016), and *Annabelle: Creation* (David F. Sandberg, 2017). In 2018, she appeared in Flanagan's Netflix series *The Haunting of Hill House*, adapted from Shirley Jackson's famous 1959 novel of the same name.

Lulu Wilson at the *It* premiere at the TCL Chinese Theater IMAX on 5 September 2017 in Los Angeles, California. Credit: Kathy Hutchins / Shutterstock.com

WILSON, STACI LAYNE

Staci Layne Wilson is a director, writer and producer with an extensive list of feature film and shorts. She began her career as a film critic for magazines including *Rue Morgue* and *Fangoria*, using her knowledge of horror to make her own films. As director, her feature films include *Fetish Factory* (2017, also known as *Cabaret of the Dead*), and the forthcoming *Good Family Times* and *Dead Slate,* the former two of which she also wrote. Wilson also made the shorts *The Night Plays Tricks* (2011) and *Psycho Therapy* (2016) and has worked on the web series such as *Ms. Vampy's Love Bites*. Wilson is also a prolific author, who has written many fiction and non-fiction books.

WINSTEAD, MARY ELIZABETH

Mary Elizabeth Winstead began acting in 1997 at only 13 years old. Born in North Carolina, while she has broad experience across film and television, she is renowned for her work in horror that began in earnest with her appearance in the 2004 made-for-television movie *Monster Island*, starring Carmen Electra. Later credits in the genre include *The Ring Two* (Hideo Nakata, 2005), *Final Destination Three* (James Wong, 2006), *Black Christmas* (Glen Morgan, 2006), Quentin Tarantino's *Death Proof* (2007), *The Thing*

Mary Elizabeth Winstead at *The Thing* world premiere, AMC Citywalk Stadium 19, Universal City, California, 11 October 2011. Credit: s_bukley / Shutterstock.com

(Matthijs van Heijningen Jr., 2011), and *10 Cloverfield Lane* (Dan Trachtenberg, 2016). Winstead also starred in the supernatural television drama series *Wolf Lake*. In 2006, she won a Scream Award for Best Scream Queen for her performance in *Black Christmas* and won a Saturn Award for Best Actress for her role in *10 Cloverfield Lane* at the 2017 Saturn Awards.

WINTERS, SHELLEY

Working for well over half a century on stage and screen, Shelley Winters is a Hollywood icon with a long, illustrious relationship to horror. Born in St. Louis in 1920 and studying at New York's The New School, she began her career as a model, initially cast in stereotypical 'blonde bombshell' roles. Determined to move beyond such shallow assumptions of her skills, she proved them memorably wrong in an impressive career that saw her co-star in everything from George Stevens' *A Place in the Sun* (1951) to Stanley Kubrick's *Lolita* (1955). But it was films like Charles Laughton's *The Night of the Hunter* (1955) that would firmly establish Winters' flair for dark-themed and gothic material, flourishing in horror during the 1970s in particular. During this era, her horror credits include *The Mad Room* (Bernard Girard, 1969), *Revenge* (Jud Taylor, 1971), *Whoever Slew Auntie Roo?* (Curtis Harrington, 1971), *The Devil's Daughter* (Jeannot Szwarc, 1973), *Poor Pretty Eddie* (Richard Robinson, 1975), *The Tenant* (Roman Polanski, 1976), *Tentacles* (Ovidio G. Assonitis, 1977), *Black Journal* (Mauro Bolognini, 1977), *The Initiation of Sarah* (Robert Day, 1978) and Giulio Paradisi's impressively weird *The Visitor* (1979). In 1995, she returned to the genre with a small role in *Raging Angels*, credited to the illustrious pseudonym Alan Smithee.

WISHMAN, DORIS

Exploitation queen Doris Wishman is not just an important woman in the history of trash cinema, but a vital figure in the history of women's filmmaking for her determination, longevity and refusal to play by any traditional rulebook regarding the types of movies women should or shouldn't make. Born in New York in 1912, Wishman was linked primarily to sexploitation films, beginning with nudist films like *Hideout in the Sun* (1958) and then going on to make some of her most famous films including *Bad Girls Go to Hell* (1965), and her collaborations with Chesty Morgan, *Deadly Weapons* and *Double Agent 73* (both in 1974). Although many of Wishman's sexploitation films dabbled in violence, she made two explicit horror films in her career; *A Night to Dismember* (1983) was such a negative experience that she gave up filmmaking for almost 20 years. She returned in her later years, the highlight being the posthumously released horror film *Each Time I Kill*—shot in 2002 but released in 2008—made just before Wishman passed away from lymphoma at the age of 90. The film includes cameos by John Waters and Linnea Quigley.

WLOSINSKI, STEPHANIE

Often credited as Stephanie Andrews, Stephanie Wlosinski is filmmaker who has worked both behind and in front of the camera with a focus on the horror genre. With Adam R. Steigert she co-directed three horror feature films; *Bitez* (2008), *Gore* (2009) and *The Final Night and Day* (2011). She co-wrote, shot and acted in all three films, and recieved a producer credit for both *Gore* and *The Final Night and Day.*

WOJTOWICZ-VOSLOO, AGNIESZKA

Polish-American filmmaker Agnieszka Wojtowicz-Vosloo was born in 1975 in Warsaw. Living in Paris before moving to the United States, she collborated with a range of artists and musicians (including avant garde icon Laurie Anderson) after launching her career with the impressive short post-apocalyptic film *Pâté* (2001). In 2008, *Filmmaker Magazine* named her one of the "25 New Faces of Independent Film" which preceded the release of her impressive 2009 feature film debut, the horror movie *After.Life* that she both directed and co-wrote, starring Christina Ricci and Liam Neeson.

WOLTER, HILDE

Actor Hildegard Elise Alwine Wollschläger was credited in her many silent films made in Germany simply as Hilde Wolter. She was born in Berlin in 1898, and between 1919 and 1923 she experienced the peak of her career, making her debut in the title role of the famous German silent horror film *Alurane,* directed by Eugen Illés and Joseph Klein. Beginning her career on the stage in Germany and Austria in her late teens, she was only 20 when she appeared in her famous first film, and while she would go on to appear in several other movies, that would remain the role for which she was most renowned. *Alurane* would be remade numerous times: in 1928 and 1930, both starring Brigitte Helm, and in 1952 with Hildegard Knef.

WONG, JULIA

Award-winning American editor Julia Wong has been working in the film industry for over 20 years and her credits include blockbusters such as *X-Men: The Last Stand* (Brett Ratner, 2003). She has collaborated with filmmaker Catherine Hardwicke on several occasions—notably her her gothic fairy tale *Red Riding Hood* (2011) and the stalker film *Plush* (2013)—and in 2016 she edited Greg McLean's horror film *The Belko Experiment.*

WORONOV, MARY

The cult fame of artist, writer and underground superstar Mary Woronov is linked to her collaborations with Roger Corman and Andy Warhol, and her creative output since the mid-1960s is prolific and influential. Born in Florida in 1943, aside from her work with Warhol in his experimental films, Woronov has appeared in a number of cult and horror films including *Silent Night, Bloody Night* (Theodore Gershuny, 1972), *Seizure* (Oliver Stone, 1974), *Blood Theater* (Rick Sloane, 1984), *Nomads* (John McTiernan, 1986), *Night of the Comet* (Thom Eberhardt, 1984), *TerrorVision* (Ted Nicolaou, 1986), *Chopping Mall* (Jim Wynorski, 1986), *Warlock* (Steve Miner, 1989), *Watchers II* (Thierry Notz, 1990), *Frog-g-g!* (Cody Jarrett, 2004), *The Halfway House* (Kenneth J. Hall, 2004), *The Devil's Rejects* (Rob Zombie, 2005) and *The House of the Devil* (Ti West, 2009).

WRAY, ARDEL

Screenwriter Ardel Wray is a key figure in the success of the wealth of Val Lewton-produced low-budget horror films made at RKO studios during the 1940s. Born in Washington in 1907, her parents were both actors and her step-father was a film director. She began her career as a model before working for almost four decades as both a screenwriter and story editor, beginning her work in film as a reader for Warner Bros. studios before moving to RKO as part of their Young Writers' Project in the early 1940s. While at RKO, her work with Lewton would include writing credits on *I Walked with a Zombie* (Jacques Tourneur, 1943), *The Leopard Man* (Jacques Tourneur, 1943) and Mark Robson's *Isle of the Dead* (1945). After writing a script for Lewton inspired by the life of the notorious Lucrezia Borgia called A *Mask for Lucrezia*, Wray's career suffered when she refused to provide names of suspected communists in the ugly context of the McCarthy-era witch hunts. Finally made as *Bride of Vengeance* (Mitchell Leisen, 1949), Wray was not named in the film's credits. A similar fate is alleged to have fallen her Blackbeard adaptation, *Blackbeard the Pirate* (Raoul Walsh, 1952). Unable to work in this political climate for a decade and a half, when she returned to the industry she worked primarily in television and did not return to horror.

WRAY, FAY ‡

One of the most famous images of 20th century cinema is surely that of Fay Wray as Ann Darrow in the clutches of the skyscraper-climbing giant ape King Kong in Merian C. Cooper and Ernest B. Schoedsack's 1933 blockbuster of the same name. One of the most beloved monster movies of all-time, Wray's performance is essential not only to the narrative but to the humanity of the film, granting it its heart and compassion. Born in Canada in 1907, Wray would work for almost 60 years, and often returned to horror, although

Fay Wray from *King Kong* (Directed by Ernest B. Schoedsack and Merian C. Cooper, RKO, 1933).
Credit: cineclassico / Alamy Stock Photo.

no other roles could challenge *King Kong* for popularity. She was in her mid-teens when she made her film debut, and in the years surrounding *King Kong* her credits included *Doctor X* (Michael Curtiz, 1932), *The Most Dangerous Game* (Ernest B. Schoedsack and Irving Pichel, 1932), *Mystery of the Wax Museum* (Michael Curtiz, 1933), *The Vampire Bat* (Frank R. Strayer, 1933) and *Black Moon* (Roy William Neill, 1934).

WRIGHT, JENNY

Born in New York in 1962, Jennifer G. Wright—often credited as Jenny Wright—was a familiar face in the 1980s and '90s. Across her many cult film appearances were several memorable horror movies: of these, the most instantly recognizable is surely Kathryn Bigelow's southern gothic vampire film *Near Dark* (1987). Lesser known but equally deserving of a cult reputation is Tibor Takács's underrated *I, Madman* (1989), and she also played the love interest of Jeff Fahey's Jobe in Brett Leonard's *The Lawnmower Man* (1992).

WYSS, AMANDA

As Tina in Wes Craven's *A Nightmare on Elm Street* (1984), Amanda Wyss was assured a permanent place in horror history. Born in California in 1960, she worked throughout the '80s primarily in teen movies and would later work extensively across both film and television. Before *Elm Street*, Wyss appeared in the made-for-television horror movie *This House Possessed* (William Wiard, 1991), and her later horror credits include *To Die For* (Deran Sarafian, 1988), *Shakma* (Tom Logan and Hugh Parks, 1990), *The Graves* (Brian Pulido, 2009) and *The Sandman* (Peter Sullivan, 2017).

XUXA

Maria da Graça Meneghel is a star of Brazilian children's film and television, known simply as Xuxa. Hosting her own children's television series on Brazilian television from the mid-1980s, despite the comparative lack of international recognition, she was the first Brazilian person to make *Forbes Magazine*'s rich list. Of her many films to include supernatural themes and monsters are *Super Xuxa Versus Satan* (Anna Penido and David Sonnenschein, 1988), *Xuxa Abracadabra* (Moacyr Góes, 2003) and *Xuxinha and Guto against the Space Monsters* (Moacyr Góes and Clewerson Saremba, 2005).

Y

YARU, MARINA

Of all the representations of the devil in 20th century cinema, few actors have remained more fascinating—and more elusive—than Marina Yaru. Starring as the ball-throwing, white-dress clad devil-child in Federico Fellini's segment "Toby Dammit" in the breathtaking 1968 horror anthology *Spirits of the Dead*, as the demonic yet innocent-looking antagonist to Terence Stamp's title character, child actor Yaru—in her single film credit—provides one of the most memorable horror performances of the decade.

YIP YUEN-TING, SHIRLEY

Hong Kong film editor Shirley Yip Yuen-Ting—also credited as Ye Wan-Ting—has been working steadily in the film industry since 2007, including on a number of horror movies such as *Naraka 19* (Carol Lai Miu-Suet, 2007), *Blood Stained Shoes* (Raymond Yip Wai-Man, 2012), *Twilight Online* (Maggie To Yuk-Ching, 2014), *Phantom of the Theatre* (Wai Man Yip, 2016) and *Witch Doctor* (Wu Zongqiang, 2016).

YORK, SUSANNAH

Born in London in 1939, BAFTA Award-winning British actor Susannah York worked across both stage and screen throughout a career that lasted almost half a century. Drawn to the stage after a positive experience in a school play as a child, she excelled at London's Royal Academy of Dramatic Arts where she graduated in 1958. In a film career that saw her work across the Atlantic, many of York's most famous roles are dark, gothic or outright horror movies including Robert Altman's *Images* (1972), Jerzy Skolimowski's *The Shout* (1978), Mike Newell's *The Awakening* (1980), Richard Franklins' *Visitors* (2003) and Colin Finbow's 1985 made-for-television movie, *Daemon*.

YOUNG, REYNA

San Francisco's Reyna Young—aka Miss Misery—has worked in horror in a range of capacities including as a director, producer, actor and film festival director. Young was a model and worked as a film extra as a child. Continuing her passion for film as she grew older, she turned her attention to directing in university. The founder of Last Doorway Productions, it is in this context that she has made an impressive number of films. Aside from the many horror shorts for which she has directorial credits, Young also wrote and directed features including *Monster of Golden Gate* (2013), *Forgotten Tales* (2016) and *Doll Murder Spree* (2017) as well as directing the documentary *Welcome to My Darkside!* in 2009 about women in the horror genre. With her husband, John Gillette, she also founded and ran San Francisco's horror shorts festival A Nightmare To Remember, and she has turned her talents towards the small screen with the series *Miss Misery's Movie Massacre* and *The Last Doorway Show with Miss Misery*.

YOUNG, SEAN •

American actor Sean Young was born in Kentucky in 1959. Closely associated to scifi for her roles in Ridley Scott's *Blade Runner* (1982) and David Lynch's *Dune* (1984), Young also has impressive form in horror with her appearances including *Dr. Jekyll and Ms. Hyde* (David Price, 1995), *The Garden* (Don Michael Paul, 2006), *Parasomnia* (William Malone, 2008), *Attack of the 50 Foot Cheerleader* (Kevin O'Neill, 2012), *Gingerclown* (Balázs Hatvani, 2013), *Bone Tomahawk* (S. Craig Zahler, 2015), *Jug Face* (Chad Crawford Kinkle, 2013) and Mickey Keating's *Darling* (2015).

YOUNG-HEE, SEO

Despite working across film and television, South Korean actor Seo Young-hee is famous for her connection to horror and tonally related genres. In 2009, she played Kim Mi-jin in Na Hong-jin's brutal serial killer film, *The Chaser*, and she won a Best Actress Award at the Korean Film Awards, Puchon International Fantastic Film Festival, Fantasporto Oporto International Film Festival and Austin's Fantastic Fest for her devastating starring role in Jang Cheol-soo's horror film, *Bedevilled* (2010). Her other horror credits include *Bloody Reunion* (Dae-wung Lim, 2006) and the gothic *Shadows in the Palace* (Mi-jung Kim, 2007).

YUN, JAE-YEON

South Korean filmmaker Jae-yeon Yun made her feature film debut *Whispering Corridors 3: Wishing Stairs* in 2003 after her earlier short *Psycho Drama* garnered her a prize at the Seoul Women's Film Festival. In 2009, she followed the success of her entry to the popular *Whispering Corridors* franchise with the stand-alone horror film *Yoga*, another cult K-horror film.

YURKA, BLANCHE

American actor Blanche Yurka began her career as an opera singer and would later turn to film and stage, the latter where she also worked as a director. Born Blanch Jurka in Minnesota in 1887, and although her performance career stretched over five decades, she was almost 50 before she worked on film. Amongst her many screen credits are the horror-comedy *One Body Too Many* (Frank McDonald, 1944), and she had a key role in Henry Levin's *Cry of the Werewolf* (1944) alongside Nina Foch.

Z

ZABRISKIE, GRACE

Forever to be remembered as Laura Palmer's tormented mother Sarah in David Lynch and Mark Frost's *Twin Peaks*, American actor Grace Zabriskie was born in New Orleans in 1941. She began acting in the late 1970s and, while she returned to work with Lynch in both *Wild at Heart* (1990) and *Inland Empire* (2006), she appeared in many horror films across her career, beginning with the Roger Corman production *Galaxy of Terror* (Bruce D. Clark, 1982), *Child's Play 2* (John Lafia, 1990), *Servants of Twilight* (Jeffrey Obrow, 1991), *The Devil's Child* (Bobby Roth, 1997), *R.S.V.P.* (Mark Anthony Galluzzo, 2002) and *They Crawl* (John Allardice, 2001). In 2017 she returned with terrifying aplomb as Sarah in the much-anticipated series 3 of *Twin Peaks*.

ZANCOLÒ, SILVANA—INTERVIEW (JULY 2018)

Italian filmmaker Silvana Zancolò has a passion for genre, be it horror, scifi, or thrillers. Working across feature films, shorts and documentaries in a variety of capacities—director, writer, cinematographer, editor, and producer—Zancolò encapsulates the DIY spirit of women's independent filmmaking.

Her 2007 horror film *The Shadow Within* came after she had made a number of shorts and a straight-to-video thriller called *The Root of Evil* (2006) that was adapted from Pascal Françaix's 1998 book *Les meres noires*. Starring Hayley J Williams, Laurence Belcher, and Beth Winslet, it is a dark and moving horror film about motherhood, grief and the duty of care set in the 1940s.

Silvana spoke to me about the film, her thoughts on the horror genre and the state of Italian horror today.

www.silvanazancolo.com

The Shadow Within is such a fascinating and powerful film, but before we begin I'd like to ask you about your background—did you study filmmaking,

Director Silvana Zancolò on the set of *The Shadow Within* (2007). Used with permission.

and I believe you have also made commercials, documentaries and short films?

I started with doing shorts at age of 17, and when I was 20 I went to a film and television school situated in a small town of Northern Italy. But it was when I moved to Milan that I started to work as director for an animation Company and I did some commercials, educational films, and pilots.

The Shadow Within **was such a discovery for me, and really reminded me of the power of the horror genre to talk about women's experiences in a way quite unlike any other kind of movie, especially in regard to the relationship between motherhood and horror.**

Life is magic, but the act of birth itself is—even today—brutal and bloody, as Nature can be sometimes. The relationship between mother and child is something unique, but at the same time can be pathological in many ways, and for this reason it has fascinated a lot of famous psychologists. Horror addresses fear and the unconscious, and women's fears and obsessions have always fascinated me particularly.

This act of childbirth and the experience of motherhood is so powerfully depicted in the film's opening scene—it's a very beautiful image that appears again later in the film's climax. Was it difficult to shoot?

The underwater scene was for me one of the scenes in the movie that addresses the unconsciousness. When you are shooting an indie film, every scene can be difficult because you are faced with many problems. But scenes like this are really difficult if you don't have an actress that supports you: it can be a nightmare. I was super lucky because the actress that played Marie [Hayley J. Williams]—this was her first movie—was very good and supportive, and she played her role with relaxed enthusiasm.

How did you discover the Pascal Françaix story that the film is based on and what inspired you to make a movie out of it?

The book was suggested to me by a friend of mine: it's a French book that I liked from the title, *Les meres noires*. I read it in one breath and immediately wanted to visualize it. The story was written in the form of a child's diary, and it wasn't easy to find the key that would allow me to adapt it into a movie.

There are major questions in *The Shadow Within* about children and morality and issues of child abuse. Do you think horror has a particular ability to address such important subjects?

In the past, horror and genre films in general have addressed many social matters. Traditionally, horror is a genre with a strong social character, channeling the fears of particular historical periods. To wit: *Invasion of the Body Snatchers* and *Night of the Living Dead* can be seen as metaphors for The Cold War and Vietnam War, but also the fear of technology is apparent in movies like *Videodrome* and *The Ring*, while the fear of globalization lies at the heart of *They Live*. I love this kind of horror.

I was very impressed simply by how beautiful *The Shadow Within* looks—there are films made for a hundred times more money that are not as stylish! What was your budget, and how did you stretch it so well to such great effect?

I don't know exactly what the budget was, but I just know that every time I asked for something the answer was: "We haven't got the money for that!"
The idea was to use the beauty of Italy's artistic heritage and landscape: there is still so much of the past in Italy that we could reproduce the 1940s without buying or hiring almost anything. We did a lot of research, and finally we were able to find old houses, an old cemetery, and even old furnishings just by asking around. Naturally, the people that worked on the movie were very motivated: for most of them, it was their first experience of filmmaking!

From *The Shadow Within* (Silvana Zancolò, 2007). Used with permission.

The main house in the film is extraordinary, how did you discover this incredible location?

The set designer and I had been looking for the right house for weeks in many places (including other countries), and then… the house that you see in the movie was just 15 kilometres from where I was born! Funny, isn't it?

The Shadow Within is a film that relies on very strong performances, and I'd not seen any of these actors' before. In particular, how did you find Laurence Belcher, Hayley J. Williams, and Beth Winslet?

I had a great casting director [Carol Crane], I must say. We together auditioned a lot of children and women, both famous actresses and those for whom it was their first experience. Both Hayley and Beth were being considered for the mother Marie at beginning: I choose Hayley because I loved her sexy, cold face, and I felt she was perfect for the role.

At the same time, I felt bad for not choosing Beth. When the woman I chose for the role of the doctor changed her mind and left, I remembered Beth's wonderful face and re-cast her for this new role. She had a child in the meantime and became even sweeter, so she was perfect for the new part.

Laurence was the last child I auditioned, he came to us by chance because he was at another casting call the same day at the same time. I had already chosen another child at that time and auditioned him with the idea of just seeing him for a couple of minutes. But when I saw him reading a couple of lines through the camera, I was hit by lightning strike. He changed my mind about who would play Maurice!

At times, *The Shadow Within* feels like a Classical Hollywood movie or even suggests the influence of 1970s and '80s British and North American horror films like Peter Medak's *The Changeling*. What were your cinematic influences on this film and on you more broadly?

It's hard to say. I am a huge film watcher and I love horror and scifi. Influences are from everywhere, but maybe you're right about the Anglo-Saxon influences, they are strong. I love horror movies from the past, especially B-movies: not big budget ones, but with the freedom to tell their stories. The list is too long! Just before shooting The Shadow Within, I watched Wolf Rillas's *Village of the Damned* (1960) many times.

Are there any recent horror films you have liked?

Of course, there are some horror films mostly from the US that I liked, including *The Conjuring, Insidious, The VVitch, It Follows, Get Out...*

Beth Winslet in make-up on the set of *The Shadow Within* (2007). Used with permission.

There is obviously a very long, celebrated tradition of Italian horror cinema that you are now a part of: can you tell me what it is like being an Italian woman horror film director? There are lots of famous men directing horror from your country, but not as many women?

True! This is a big subject for me that I face every day in one way or another. First of all, most of the Italian directors that you are referring to are not making movies anymore: they are from the past. Horror is a tradition that we have lost. There are still some very low budget indie horror films—sort of arthouse—but none of them are able to find proper distribution and overcome the obstacles.

There are no longer producers that believe in horror nowadays in this country, and this is a pity, because as you said, Italy was famous for those big horror directors.

In general, doing horror in Italy is very difficult, and it's worse if you are a woman. Usually women do documentaries or little drama films, and that's all. I am still trying to make my third horror film, and it's as if I were making my debut.

I understand *The Shadow Within* was your second feature film: can you tell me about the first—*The Root of Evil*—and what you are working on now?

The first movie was a direct-to-video thriller that Giovanni Eccher (the screenplay writer) and I shot with 5 friends in a friend's house. Sounds like a million of first time directors' stories, doesn't it?

Next, I would love to do an Italian *giallo*, like those that made Mario Bava, Dario Argento, and Lucio Fulci in the past.

ZELLWEGER, RENÉE

Born in Texas in 1969, actor Renée Zellweger has widespread mainstream appeal, but made her breakthrough with a starring role in Kim Henkel's *Texas Chainsaw Massacre: The Next Generation* (1994). She began her career with small roles on television commercials and a very early appearance was a small part in Bob Balaban's 1993 horror-comedy *My Boyfriend's Back* that was eventually cut. Later in her career—once established as a star—she returned to the genre with a lead role in Christian Alvart's psychological horror film, *Case 39* (2009).

ZIYI, ZHANG

Chinese actor Zhang Ziyi was born in Beijing in 1979 and studied at that city's Central Academy of Drama. She attained widespread recognition for her role in Ang Lee's Oscar-nominated *wuxia Crouching Tiger, Hidden Dragon* (2000), and would later in her career star in both Jonas Åkerlund›s horror film *Horsemen* (2009) and the horror-scifi reboot *The Cloverfireld Paradox* (Julius Onah, 2018).

ZOMBIE, SHERI MOON

Born Sheri Lyn Skurkis in California in 1970, although also a model, designer and dancer in her own right, Sheri Moon Zombie is primarily recognized for her collaborations with her filmmaker/musician husband, Rob Zombie. Initially appearing in music videos for his now-defunct band White Zombie, she would soon star in his feature films *House of 1000 Corpses* (2003), *The Devil's Rejects* (2005), *Halloween* (2007), *Halloween II* (2009), *The Lords of Salem* (2012), *31* (2016) and his forthcoming *3 from Hell*. She also voiced Suzi-X in Zombie's 2009 animated horror feature *The Haunted World of El Superbeasto* and appeared in his fake trailer "Werewolf Women of the SS" that was included in Robert Rodriguez and Quentin Tarantino's 2007 *Grindhouse* project. While working primarily with her husband, she has also been cast in films and television series helmed by other directors, most notably Tobe Hooper's 2004 film *Toolbox Murders*.

ZUBARRY, OLGA

One of the great stars of Argentine cinema, Olga Zubiarriaín—credited broadly as Olga Zubarry—was born in Buenos Aires in 1929. Across her career that lasted well over five decades, she worked in more than 80 movies, first coming to the public's attention with a semi-nude scene in Carlos Hugo Christensen's *The Naked Angel* (1946). She won a Silver Condor Award for Best Actress in 1954 for her extraordinary lead performance of Román Viñoly Barreto's *The Black Vampire*, which reworks Fritz Lang's famous German horror film *M* (1931) from a notably female perspective. In 1975, Zubarry would return to less highbrow horror territory in Bernardo Arias's exploitation film, *The Inquisitor*. She died in 2012, working in film and television right up to her death at 83 years old.

ZURBORG, JILL RAE

Jill Rae Zurborg is an American director, writer, and actor whose feature film debut was the 1991 horror-comedy *Beauty Queen Butcher*. As an actor, she has also appeared in *A Compulsion to Murder* (Jeff Carney, 1990) and *The Creeper* (Jeff Carney, 1995).

APPENDIX:
SELECTED FILMOGRAPHY

THE FOLLOWING IS AN INCOMPLETE LIST of feature-length horror films directed by women. The definition of 'horror' here, as outlined at length in the Introduction to this book, is loosely applied and thus incorporates everything from kids' movie to porn, animation to made-for-television movies. However, what unites them is that all the films included here are in some way deemed to fall under a horror umbrella in some way and clock in at over the 50 minute mark as a minimum benchmark for my practical definition of feature film. As also discussed in the Introduction, the archive can be a tricky beast when it comes to remembering women horror filmmakers, so I am in large part at the mercy of websites like IMDb; films have been checked and double checked where possible, so fingers crossed the information here is reliable as not all films (sadly, not even half) are readily accessible for viewing.

#Horror (Tara Subkoff, 2015)

3 (Lou Simon, 2018)

3 Day Weekend (Renee S. Warren Peoples and Tarjatta Rose, 2009)

3 mukhi (Aishwarya Addala, 2018)

5-tsu kazoereba kimi no yume (Yûki Yamato, 2014)

6 Days Dark (Miona Bogovic, 2014)

The 6th Friend (Letia Miller, 2016)

7 Deadly Sins: Inside the Ecomm Cult (Michelle Bolvox and Kay Kayos, 2009)

10 Days to Die (Casie Coddington, Elaine Niessner and Michael Sergi, 2010)

12:06 Rumah Kucing (Chiska Doppert, 2017)

13 Dolls in Darkness (Zeda Müller, 2017)

13 Gantry Row (Catherine Millar, 1998)

21 Days (Kathleen Behun, 2014)

30 Miles from Nowhere (Caitlin Koller, 2018)

666 (Honey Blanca and Celso Ad. Castillo, 2010)

869 (Brittany Miles, 2014)

1993 (Elle Millie, 2017)

4426 (Fathimath Nahula and Ahmed Shinan, 2016)

The Abduction of Jennifer Grayson (Corynn Egreczky, 2017)

Abortifacient (Fatima Hye, 2018)

An Accidental Zombie (Named Ted) (Anne Welles, 2017)

Action Figures (Danielle Sage, 2011)

Actual Images: The Valley Murder Tapes (Blaze Lovejoy, 2008)

After.Life (Agnieszka Wojtowicz-Vosloo, 2009)

The Afterglow (Yolanda Torres and Joan Álvarez, 2014)

Agoraphobia (Lou Simon, 2015)

Alice: Boy from Wonderland (Eunhee Huh, 2015)

Alice D (Jessica Sonneborn, 2014)

Alice in the Underworld: The Dark Märchen Show!! (Mari Terashima, 2009)

All That We Destroy (Chelsea Stardust, 2019)

All the Creatures Were Stirring (Rebekah McKendry and David Ian McKendry, 2018)

All Girls Weekend (Lou Simon, 2016)

All Night Long (Tamae Garateguy and Jimena Monteoliva, 2015)

Allure (Jillian Martin, 2018)

El almohadon (Alicia Violante, 1990)

Alpatraum (Ana Pieterbarg, 2017)

Always Shine (Sophia Takal, 2016)

Amer (Hélène Cattet and Bruno Forzani, 2009)

American Burger (Johan Bromander and Bonita Drake, 2014)

American Mary (Jen and Sylvia Soska, 2012)

American Psycho (Mary Harron, 2000)

American Zombie (Grace Lee, 2007)

Among Friends (Danielle Harris, 2013)

Die Ahnfrau (Luise and Jacob Fleck, 1919)

Angry (Yohanna Idha and Christopher Stone, 2010)

Ánimas (Jose F. Ortuño and Laura Alvea, 2018)

Anita (Luise and Jacob Fleck, 1920)

Aphra and Aradia (Celia Hay, 2018)

The Apparition of Roxanne (Debbie McAlister, 2010)

Are You Here (Jill Wong, 2015)

As They Fall (Janelle Morrissey, 2008)

Assignment: Witches Talisman (Kelly Helen Thompson, 2013)

At the Door (Maude Michaud, 2014)

At the End of the Tunnel (Claire Wasmund, 2018)

Aune, or On Effective Demise (Maija Timonen, 2013)

The Attic (Mary Lambert, 2007)

The Awakened (Lou Simon, 2012)

B.C. Butcher (Kansas Bowling, 2016)

The Babadook (Jennifer Kent, 2014)

The Bad Batch (Ana Lily Amirpour, 2017)

Bad Fruit (Kimberley Crossman, 2015)

Ballet Blanc (Anne-Sophie Dutoit, 2018)

Banned (Roberta Findlay, 1989)

Baño de sangre (Paula Pollacchi, 2003)

Beast Lover (Amy McCullough and Jimmie Buchanan Jr., 2013)

The Beast of Beauty (Hilde Heier, 2003)

Beauty Queen Butcher (Jill Rae Zurborg, 1991)

Bedevil (Tracey Moffatt, 1993)

The Being (Jackie Kong, 1983)

Benavidez's Case (Laura Casabé, 2016)

Between Worlds (Maria Pulera, 2018)

Berlin Syndrome (Cate Shortland, 2017)

Best Friends Forever (Brea Grant, 2013)

Beyond Bizarro (Maggie Hardy, 2013)

Bikini Vampire Babes (Ted West and Margaret Root, 2010)

Bilocation (Mari Asato, 2013)

Bird Box (Susanne Bier, 2018)

Bitch (Marianna Palka, 2017)

Bite Me (Meredith Edwards, 2019)

Bitez (Adam R. Steigert and Stephanie Andrews, 2008)

Black Christmas (Sofia Takal, 2019)

Black Friday (Crescentia Volz, 2017)

Black Magic Woman (Deryn Warren, 1991)

Black Mamba (Belinda M. Wilson, 2016)

Black Rock (Katie Aselton, 2012)

Black Tower Temptation (Catherien Taylor, 2009)

Blind Sun (Joyce A. Nashawati, 2015)

Blood (Bernadette Manton, 2010

Blood Bath (Jack Hill and Stephanie Rothman, 1966)

Blood Child (Jennifer Phillips, 2017)

Blood and Chocolate (Katja von Garnier, 2007)

Blood Diner (Jackie Kong, 1987)

Blood and Donuts (Holly Dale, 1995)

Blood Drive: The Movie (Sophia Robbins, 2013)

Blood Fare (J. A. Steel, 2012)

Blood Games (Tanya Rosenberg, 1990)

Blood Hunters (Tricia Lee, 2017)

Blood of the Mummy (Christine Parker, 2018)

Blood Punch (Madellaine Paxson, 2013)

Blood Rites (Dorothy Booraem, 2010)

Blood Rogues (Jeremy Childs and Karen Garcia, 2009)

Blood Sabbath (Brianne Murphy, 1972)

Blood Sisters (Roberta Findlay, 1987)

Blood of the Tribades (Michael J. Epstein and Sophia Cacciola, 2016)

Blood Vow (Victoria Sutton, 2017)

Bloodbath Test (Carla Forte and Vincente Forte, 2018)

Bloodshed and Emeralds (Ann Cochran, 1999)

Bloody Tarot (Aurora Martinez, 1990)

The Blue Eyes (Eva S. Aridjis, 2012)

Blue My Mind (Lisa Brühlmann, 2017)

Bluebeard (Amy Hesketh, 2012)

Body Parts (Michael Paul Girard and Jan Marlyn Reesman, 1992)

Bohemian Moon (MarieAnna Dvorak, 1999)

Bongo: Killer Clown (Geraldine Winters, 2014)

The Book of Birdie (Elizabeth E. Schuch, 2017)

Born to Love You (Shelly Lyons, 1999)

Boxing Helena (Jennifer Lynch, 1993)

The Boy from Hell (Deryn Warren, 1988)

Braid (Mitzi Peirone, 2018)

Break (Becky Sayers and Nicholas Sayers, 2010)

Bride of Beyond Bizarro (Maggie Hardy, 2014)

Bride of Scarecrow (Louisa Warren, 2018)

Branded (Darla Enlow, 2006)

Brothel (Amy Waddell, 2008)

Brutal (Darla Rae and Michael Patrick Stevens, 2012)

Buffy the Vampire Slayer (Fran Rubel Kuzui, 1992)

The Bug in the Bathroom (Catherine Dawson, 2009)

Bugs: A Trilogy (Simone Kisiel, 2018)

Butter on the Latch (Josephine Decker, 2013)

The Bye Bye Man (Stacy Title, 2017)

Cabaret of the Dead (Staci Layne Wilson, 2017)

Cabin of Horror (Sean Michael Williams and Emily Kuheli Rahma, 2015)

The Camera's Eye (Wendy Shear, 2010)

Candy Stripers (Kate Robbins, 2006)

Cannibal Hookers (Donald Farmer and Caroline Kopko, 2018)

Cannibalism (Lizzy Borden, 2002)

Capture (Georgia Lee, 2017)

The Caretaker (Shannon Casto and Michelle Henderson, 2008)

Cargo (Yolanda Ramke and Ben Howling, 2017)

Carrie (Kimberly Peirce, 2013)

Carver (Emily DiPrimio, 2015)

The Catcher (Guy Crawford and Yvette Hoffman, 1999)

Celia (Ann Turner, 1989)

Cellular Girlfriend (Mari Asato, 2011)

Central Park Dark (Cybil Lake, 2018)

Chained (Jennifer Lynch, 2012)

The Changeover (Miranda Harcourt and Stuart McKenzie, 2018)

Chanthaly (Mattie Do, 2012)

Charm (Sarah Reed and Sadie Shaw, 2002)

The Chasing World 3 (Mari Asato, 2012)

The Chasing World 4 (Mari Asato, 2012)
The Chasing World 5 (Mari Asato, 2012)
Chastity Bites (Lotti Pharriss Knowles, 2013)
Cherry Creek Freaks (Molly Kruger, 2015)
Child of Darkness, Child of Light (Marina Sargenti, 1991)
Children of the Corn 666 (Kari Skogland, 1999)
Chill: The Killing Games (Noelle Bye and Meredith Holland, 2013)
Cilla (Yurie Collins and Nora Reilly, 2014)
The Citadel (Snow Marie Reese, 2015)
Circuito Interno (Leticia De Bortoli and Larissa Vaiano, 2015)
Clara's Ghost (Bridey Elliott, 2018)
Claudia Qui (Tonjia Atomic, 2012)
Clean Break (Tricia Lee, 2013)
Clementina (Jimena Monteoliva, 2017)
Cleveland Abduction (Alex Kalymnios, 2015)
A Closer Walk with Thee (John C. Clark and Brie Williams, 2017)
Clownstrophobia (Geraldine Winters, 2009)
Cocki—The Running Doctor (Svetlana Baskova, 1998)
Cold Light of Day (Fhiona-Louise, 1989)
The Commune (Elisabeth Fies, 2009)
Corruptor (Dorothy Booraem, 2016)
The Countess (Julie Delpy, 2009)
Cousin Sarah (Jenni Gold, 2011)
Cracks (Jordan Scott, 2009)
Cravenous (Carolyn Cavallero and James Oliver Bullock, 2012)
The Craving (Valerie R. Castro, 2011)
Crazy Bitches (Jane Clark, 2014)
Credo (Susanne Bier, 1997)
Credo (Toni Harman, 2008)
Creepshow 3 (Ana Clavell and James Dudelson, 2006)
Creek (Lola Wallace, 2007)
Critters 3 (Kristine Peterson, 1991)
Crushed (Megan Riakos, 2015)
The Cry (Bernadine Santistevan, 2007)
A Cry from Within (Zach Miller and Deborah Twiss, 2014)
Crystal Force (Laura Keats, 1990)
Crystal Nights (Tonia Marketaki, 1992)
The Curse (Jacqueline Garry, 2001)
Curse of Scarecrow (Louisa Warren, 2018)
Cut Her Out (Tiffany Heath, 2014)
D'Anothers (Joyce E. Bernal, 2005)
Da Possessed (Joyce E. Bernal, 2014)
Daily Chicken (Lilly Grote, 1997)
The Daisy Chain (Aisling Walsh, 2008)

Dance of the Damned (Katt Shea, 1989)

Dark Angel: The Ascent (Linda Hassani, 1994)

Dark Circus (Julia Ostertag, 2016)

Dark House: The Legend of Dark House (Sheila Evans, 2018)

Dark Mountain (Tara Anaïse, 2013)

Dark Spaces (Shannon Casto and Michelle Henderson, 2009)

Dark Sunrise (Hilary Philips, 2018)

Dark Touch (Marina de Van, 2013)

Darken (Audrey Cummings, 2017)

Darlin' (Pollyanna McIntosh, 2018)

Day 665 (Erykah del Mundo, 2013)

Day of the Dead 2: Contagium (Ana Clavell and James Dudelson, 2005)

Days of the Iguanas (Christine Whitlock, 2013)

Dead Before Dawn 3D (April Mullen, 2012)

Dead Dicks (Chris Bavota and Lee Paula Springer, 2019)

Dead Hooker in a Trunk (Jen and Sylvia Soska, 2009)

Dead Innocent (Sara Botsford, 1997)

Dead of Night (Deryn Warren, 1988)

The Dead Outside (Kerry Anne Mullaney, 2008)

Dead Woman's Hollow (Libby McDermott, 2013)

Deadly Dreams (Kristine Peterson, 1988)

Deadly Waters (Tyler-James and Catherine Carpenter, 2015)

Dear John (Catherine Ord, 1987)

Dearest Sister (Mattie Do, 2016)

Deathly Love (Sandra Tuerk, 2013)

The Decayed (Delia Ruffin and Nicolas Wood, 2017)

The Deeper You Dig (Toby Poser, John Adams and Zelda Adams, 2019)

Dementia: Alone (Carla Saunders, 2010)

Demon Hunter (Zoe Kavanagh, 2016)

Demon Hunters: Fear the Silence (Chris Eilenstine and Debra Higgins, 2013)

A Demon in My View (Petra Haffter, 1991)

Demonica's Reign (Daniela Garcia, 2011)

Den of Darkness (Sandra Lindo, 2016)

Denizen (J. A. Steel, 2010)

Detrás de la Muerte (Leticia Melo, 2009)

The Devil's Doorway (Aislinn Clarke, 2018)

Devil's Grove (Michael J. Hein and R. Zoe Judd, 2008)

The Devil's Mercy (Melanie Orr, 2008)

Die Kinder Der Toten (Kelly Copper and Pavol Liška, 2019)

Djinns (Hugues Martin and Sandra Martin, 2010)

Dokumushi (Kayoko Asakura, 2016)

The Doll (Susannah O'Brien, 2017)

Doll Murder Spree (Reyna Young, 2017)

Dolly Deadly (Heidi Moore, 2016)

Dolly Dearest (Maria Lease, 1991)

Don't Look (Luciana Faulhaber, 2018)

Don't Look Back (Marina de Van, 2009)

Donner Pass (Elise Robertson, 2011)

Dorothy Mills (Agnès Merlet, 2008)

The Dorm (Rachel Talalay, 2014)

Down by the Riverside (Brad Davison and Marama Killen, 2007)

Dracu (Desire Dubonet, 2003)

Dracula de Denise Castro (Denise Castro, 2018)

Draug (Klas Persson and Karin Engman, 2018)

Drifting Into Chaos (Sachi Hamano, 1989)

Drink Slay Love (Vanessa Parise, 2017)

Dyke Hard (Bitte Anderson, 2014)

Each Time I Kill (Doris Wishman, 2008)

The Earl Sessions (Ginnetta Correli, 2011)

Eat Me! (Katie Carman, 2010)

Egest (Angela Williams and Zebulun Dinkins, 2013)

Egomaniac (Kate Shenton, 2016)

Eko Eko Azarak: Wizard of Darkness (Shimako Satō, 1995)

Eko Eko Azarak II: Birth of the Wizard (Shimako Satō, 1996)

Embrace of the Vampire (Anne Goursaud, 1995)

Encounter (Susannah O'Brien, 2016)

End (Megan Welch, 2009)

An Ending (Jessica Cameron, 2018)

The Endless Day (Alessia Chiesa, 2018)

Endzeit - Ever After (Carolina Hellsgård, 2018)

Episode 50 (Joe Smalley and Tess Smalley, 2011)

El Escondite (Sandra Becerril, 2011)

Están Aquí (Sandra Becerril, 2014)

Ever After (Carolina Hellsgård, 2018)

Evangeline (Karen Lam, 2013)

Every Move She Makes (Catherine Millar, 1984)

The Evil Gene (Kathryn F. Taylor, 2015)

Evil Has Come to Prey (Dianne Dennis, 2016)

Evolution (Lucile Hadžihalilović, 2015)

The Exotic House of Wax: Legacy of Lust (Cybil Richards, 1997)

F5 Teraphobia (Kimberly Taylor Fagan, 2018)

The Faith Community (Faith R. Johnson, 2017)

Family (Veronica Kedar, 2017)

Family Demons (Ursula Dabrowsky, 2009)

Fatal Frame (Mari Asato, 2014)

The Father's Shadow (Gabriela Amaral Almeida, 2019)

Feed Me (Claudia Demasceno, 2013)

A Few Brains More (Christine Parker, 2012)

A Filha (Solveig Nordlund, 2003)

The Final Haunting (Flamina Graziadei, 2014)

The Final Night and Day (Adam R. Steigert and Stephanie Andrews, 2011)

Fistful of Brains (Christine Parker, 2008)

Five Bottles of Vodka (Svetlana Baskova, 2001)

Fix it in Post (Christine Parker, 2014)

Following the Wicca Man (Jacqueline Kirkham, 2013)

For One Night Only (Belinda Green-Smith, 2010)

Forced Entry (Lizzy Borden, 2002)

The Forbidden House (Hélène Angel, 2011)

Forever Dead (Christine Parker, 2007)

Forgotten Tales (Reyna Young, 2016)

The Forsaken (Yolanda Torres, 2015)

Frankenpimp (Vivita, Tony Watt and John A. Kelly, 2009)

Freddy/Eddy (Tini Tüllmann, 2016)

Freddy's Dead: The Final Nightmare (Rachel Talalay, 1991)

Friday Night Horror (Barbara Graftner, 2012)

Friendly Beast (Gabriela Amaral Almeida, 2017)

Frostbite (Bridget Machete, 2013)

Fugue (Barbara Stepansky, 2011)

Gary and the Underworld (Amy McCullough and Jimmie Buchanan Jr., 2018)

Geisterstunde (Tanja Brzakovic, 2006)

Get Dead (Markus Baldwin and Julie Mitchell, 2014)

Ghost in the Machine (Rachel Talalay, 1993)

Ghostwatch (Lesley Manning, 1992)

Gingerdead Man 2: Passion of the Crust (Silvia St. Croix, 2008)

A Girl Walks Home Alone at Night (Ana Lily Amirpour, 2014)

The Girl Who Married a Ghost (Sandra Sawatzky, 2004)

Girls, Dance with the Dead (Kayoko Asakura, 2015)

Gless (Rick Gawel and Melissa Malan, 2010)

Go Home (Luna Gualano, 2018)

The Godsend (Gabrielle Beaumont, 1980)

Gomennasai (Mari Asato, 2011)

Good Evening to Everyone (Lupita A. Concio, 1976)

Good Manners (Juliana Rojas and Marco Dutra, 2017)

Goodnight Mommy (Veronika Franz and Severin Fiala, 2014)

Gore (Adam R. Steigert and Stephanie Andrews, 2009)

Gory Gory Hallelujah (Sue Corcoran, 2003)

Grandma's House (Bonnie Kathleen Ryan, 2018)

Graveyard Alive (Elza Kephart, 2003)

The Green Elephant (Svetlana Baskova, 1999)

The Grid: Zombie Outlet Maul (Linda Andersson and MJ Lallo, 2015)

Grindstone Road (Melanie Orr, 2008)

El guardavías (Daniel Celeya and Andrea Trigo, 2004)

Guardian of the Frontier (Maja Weiss, 2002)
Gut Instincts (Michelle Henderon, 2012)
Haint (Alyssa Taylor Wendt, 2018)
Halloweentown II: Kalabar's Revenge (Mary Lambert, 2001)
The Halloween Store Zombie Wedding Movie (Victoria Sutton, 2016)
Hard Ride to Hell (Penelope Buitenhuis, 2010)
Harm's Way (Melanie Orr, 2010)
Haruko's Paranormal Laboratory (Lisa Takeba, 2015)
Haunted Boat (Olga Levens, 2005)
The Haunting of Sarcnoia Buttercup (Amanda Dyar, 2012)
The Haunting of M (Anna Thomas, 1979)
HazMat (Lou Simon, 2013)
He Belongs to Us (Gigi Hozimah, 2018)
Head Count (Elle Callahan, 2018)
Heart of Death (Alicia Norman, 2011)
Heartless (Judith Vogelsang, 1997)
Hell at Heathridge (Caroline Abbey and Tyler Pina, 2013)
Helter Skelter (Mika Ninagawa, 2012)
The Hidden (Jessie Kirby, 2007)
The Hitch-Hiker (Ida Lupino, 1953)
His Will Be Done (Shannon Casto and Michelle Henderson, 2009)
Hisss (Jennifer Lynch, 2010)
The Holding (Susan Jacobson, 2010)
Hollow Creek (Guisela Moro, 2016)
Home Sweet Home (Netie Pena, 1981)
Honeymoon (Leigh Janiak, 2014)
The Honor Farm (Karen Skloss, 2017)
Hotel (Jessica Hausner, 2004)
House of Sweat and Tears (Sonia Escolano, 2018)
HOUSED: The Feature (Simone Kisiel, 2017)
Housekeeping (Jennifer Harrington, 2015)
How to Kill a Zombie (Tiffany McLean, 2014)
Howling VI: The Freaks (Hope Perello, 1991)
Humanoids from the Deep (Barbara Peeters, 1980)
Hurt (Barbara Stepansky, 2009)
Hypnagogic (Janet Llavina, 2015)
I Dare You to Open Your Eyes (Hope Muehlbauer, 2018)
The Ice Cream Truck (Megan Freels Johnston, 2017)
Id (Kei Fujiwara, 2005)
In Memorium (Amanda Gusack, 2005)
In My Skin (Marina de Van, 2002)
In the Blood (Victoria Cocks, 2018)
In Their Sleep (Caroline and Eric du Potet, 2010)
Incubus (Anya Camilleri, 2006)

The Incubus (Marcie Gorman and Shayne Leighton, 2010)

Inner Demon (Ursula Dabrowsky, 2014)

Innocence (Hilary Brougher, 2013)

Innocence (Lucile Hadžihalilović, 2004)

Inside: A Chinese Horror Story (Lili Bai, 2017)

Intensive Care (Dorna van Rouveroy, 1991)

The Invitation (Karyn Kusama, 2015)

Inzomnia (Paula Pollacchi, 1997)

Isis Rising: Curse of the Lady Mummy (Lisa Palencia, 2013)

It's a Beautiful Day (Kayoko Asakura, 2013)

It's a Wonderful Afterlife (Gurinder Chadha, 2010)

Jack of Hearts (Cynthia Roberts, 1993)

Jack 'O' Slasher (Jennifer Valdes, 2012)

Jack the Reaper (Kimberly Seilhamer, 2011)

Jacob's Hammer (Angie Bojtler, 2012)

Jake's Closet (Shelli Ryan, 2007)

Jelly Dolly (Susannah Gent, 2004)

Jennifer's Body (Karyn Kusama, 2009)

Jesus and Her Gospel of Yes (Alfred Eaker and Cheryl Townsend, 2004)

The Jinn (Iris Green, 2007)

Jogo de Copo (Amanda Maya, 2014)

John the Violent (Tonia Marketaki, 1973)

Johnny Ghost (Donna McRae, 2011)

Ju-On: Black Ghost (Mari Asato, 2009)

Kapital (Greg Hall and Rebecca Finlay-Hall, 2007)

Karma (Adriana Ledesma, 2013)

The Keeping Hours (Karen Moncrieff, 2017)

Kill By Inches (Diane Doniol-Valcroze and Arthur K. Flam, 1999)

Kill Me Please (Anita Rocha da Silveira, 2015)

Killer Ants (Carolyn Banks, 2009)

Killer Bees (Penelope Buitenhuis, 2002)

The Killer in the Forest (Dianne Dennis, 2012)

The Killer Knocks Twice (Shawnee Mercer, 2017)

The Killing Secret (Sheena Herod and Wardell Richardson, 2013)

Killjoy 2: Deliverance from Evil (Tammi Sutton, 2002)

Kimmy Dora and the Temple of Kiyeme (Joyce E. Bernal, 2012)

Kiss of the Damned (Xan Cassavetes, 2012)

Kissed (Lynne Stopkewich, 1996)

The Last Buck Hunt (Becky Sayers and Nicholas Sayers, 2013)

The Last Nightmare (Leilani Amour Arenzana, 2011)

The League of Legend Keepers: Shadows (Elizabeth Blake-Thomas, 2017)

Left for Dead (Gwen Riffo, 2004)

Legacy (Rachel Wilson, 2015)

The Legend of Granny Brown (Jennifer Goodman and William Mullins, 2008)

Legend of the Red Reaper (Tara Cardinal, 2013)
Legend of the Sandsquatch (Lola Wallace, 2006)
The Legend of Wasco (Shane Beasley and Leya Taylor, 2015)
The Lesson (Ruth Platt, 2015)
Level 16 (Danishka Esterhazy, 2018)
Libertaria (Sabrina Pena Young, 2013)
The Lie (Veena Sud, 2018)
A Light in the Woods (Elizabeth Hansen, 2014)
Lilith's Awakening (Monica Demes, 2016)
Limbo (Tina Krause, 1999)
Lineage (Alyssa Clark, 1997)
Little Joe (Jessica Hausner, 2019)
Little Witches (Jane Simpson, 1996)
Livescream (Michelle Iannantuono, 2018)
Las Llorona (Lorena Villarreal, 2004)
The Lodge (Veronika Franz and Severin Fiala, 2019)
Lonely Hearts (Jessica Hunt and Sam Mason-Bell, 2018)
The Long Walk (Mattie Do, 2019)
Loon (Andrew Bassett and Lillian Langston, 2017)
Lost Gully Road (Donna McRae, 2017)
Louis Lake (Ingrid Clay, 2012)
The Love Witch (Anna Biller, 2016)
Loverboy (Erica Summers, 2012)
Lucifer's Bride (Zoi Florosz, 2015)
Ludlow (Stacie Ponder, 2010)
Ludo (Katrin Ottarsdottir, 2014)
The Lure (Agnieszka Smoczyńska, 2015)
Lurkers (Roberta Findlay, 1988)
The Lurking Man (Jenn Page 2017)
Lyle (Stewart Thorndike, 2014)
M.F.A (Natalia Leite, 2017)
The Mafu Cage (Karen Arthur, 1978)
Make a Wish (Sharon Ferranti, 2002)
Makua Charley (Albert J. Cloutier and Jayne Coutier, 2013)
Mania (Jessica Cameron, 2015)
Manos Returns (Tonjia Atomic, 2018)
Marina Monster (Christine Whitlock, 2008)
Marla Mae (Lisa van Dam-Bates, 2018)
Le Marquis de la Croix (Amy Hesketh, 2012)
Mary Loss of Soul (Jennifer B. White, 2014)
Maskhead (Fred Vogel and Rebecca Swan, 2009)
Massacre at Bluff's Ridge (Tiffany Nettles, 2018)
Mega Python vs. Gatoroid (Mary Lambert, 2011)
Menagerie (Sarah Martin, 2018)

Messiah of Evil (Walter Huyck and Gloria Katz, 1973)
Metal Maniac (Susana Kapostasy, 2012)
Midnight Show (Ginanti Rona Tembang Sari, 2016)
The Midnight Swim (Sarah Adina Smith, 2014)
The Mime (Maria Gilbert, 2015)
Mind Benders (Genie Joseph, 1987)
Mirror (Zarina Abdullah, 2007)
Mirror, Mirror (Marina Sargenti, 1990)
Mirror, Mirror III: The Voyeur (Virginia Perfili, 1995)
Mirror, Mirror IV: Reflection (Paulette Victor Lifton, 2000)
Mister White (Erica Summers, 2013)
Il Misterio di Villa De Mahl (Elena D'Atri, 2007)
Mistress of Seduction (Ellyn Michaels, 1998)
Model Hunger (Debbie Rochon, 2016)
Moonlight (Wong Pak Kei, 2011)
Monster of Golden Gate (Reyna Young, 2013)
Monster: The Prehistoric Project (Lisa Palencia, 2015)
The Monument (Kristine Hipps, 2005)
Moscow Zero (María Lidón, 2006)
The Moth Diaries (Mary Harron, 2011)
Most Beautiful Island (Ana Asensio, 2017)
Mr Wrong (Gaylene Preston, 1986)
Mumbo Jumbo (Catherine Millar, 1999)
Munchies (Tina Hersch, 1987)
The Murder Farm (Bettina Oberli, 2009)
The Museum (Jeanette Murray and Michael Bemma, 2013)
Mutant Man (Suzanne deLaurentiis, 1996)
My Boo (Erica D. Hayes, 2013)
My Dead Selfie (Joy Shannon, 2018)
My Sucky Teen Romance (Emily Hagins, 2011)
Naraka 19 (Carol Lai, 2007)
Near Dark (Kathryn Bigelow, 1987)
Nefarious (Sarah Martin, 2017)
The Next Big Thing (Michelle Henderson, 2010)
Night of a Thousand Screams (Shawnee McCormack, 2001)
Night of a Thousand Screams 2 (Shawnee McCormack, 2003)
A Night to Dismember (Doris Wishman, 1983)
The Night Visitor (Jennifer Blanc-Biehn, 2013)
No Exit (Sarah Wilson, 2018)
Non Compos Mentis (Geraldine Winters, 2010)
Nothing Bad Can Happen (Katrin Gebbe, 2013)
O. Unilateralis (Michelle Nessk, 2016)
Off Season (Katie Carman, 2012)
Office Killer (Cindy Sherman, 1997)

Olalla (Amy Hesketh, 2015)
On the Edge (Danielle Sunley, 2012)
One (Tristan Baumeister, Kayli Ross and Olivia Watry, 2014)
The Open House (Matt Angel and Suzanne Coote 2018)
Or So the Story Goes: Happy Thoughts (Theresa Labreglio, 2015)
The Oracle (Roberta Findlay, 1985)
Orgia de terror (Martha Rodriguez, 1990)
Orazio's Clan (Riccardo Bernasconi and Francesca Reverdito, 2017)
Organ (Kei Fujiwara, 1996)
The Other Lamb (Małgorzata Szumowska, 2019)
Out of the Shadows (Dee McLachlan, 2017)
Outside of Nowhere (Gwendolyn, 2004)
Pathogen (Emily Hagins, 2006)
Patient 001 (Katie Fleischer, 2018)
Pelican Blood (Katrin Gebbe, 2019)
Penaggal: The Curse of the Malayan Vampire (Ellie Suriati Omar, 2013)
Perfect Strangers (Gaylene Preston, 2003)
Pet Sematary (Mary Lambert, 1989)
Pet Sematary II (Mary Lambert, 1992)
Phaedra (Scarlet Moreno, 2018)
The Phobic (Margo Romero, 2006)
Pinup Dolls on Ice (Geoff Klein and Melissa Mira, 2013)
Plaster Rock (Jacqueline Giroux, 2010)
Plot 7 (Farnaz Samiinia, 2007)
Plush (Catherine Hardwicke, 2013)
Pocahauntus (Veronica Craven, 2006)
Pocong keliling (Viva Westi, 2010)
Population 436 (Michelle MacLaren, 2006)
Powerplegic (Natalie Degennaro, 2013)
Pox (Lisa Hammer, 2011)
Predatory Moon (Shiva Rodriguez, 2017)
Prepper's Grove (Lisa Enos, 2018)
Prevenge (Alice Lowe, 2016)
Prime Evil (Roberta Findlay, 1988)
Protégé (Shannon Casto and Michelle Henderson, 2010)
Psycho-Path (Geraldine Winters, 2011)
Psychopath (Jennifer Blanc-Biehn, 2016)
Psychomentary (Luna Gualano, 2014)
Psychos (Sandy Chukhadarian, 2017)
Pumpkins (Maria Lee Metheringham, 2018)
Puppy (Jennifer Emsley and Sony Green, 2007)
Pure (Susan Aronovitz and Scott MacLaughlin, 2002)
The Purgation (Elaine Chu, 2015)
Puss Bucket (Lisa Hammer, 1991)

Pyromaniac (Greg Finton and Catherine Lane, 1995)

The Quacks (Elaine Watts, 2011)

The Quarantine Hauntings (Arnold Perez and Bianca Biasi, 2015)

The Queen of Screams (Margot Romero, 2009)

The Quiet (Jamie Babbit, 2005)

Rabid (Jen and Sylvia Soska, 2019)

Rabidus (Rosalind Woods, 2015)

Radius (Caroline Labrèche and Steve Léonard, 2017)

The Rage: Carrie 2 (Katt Shea, 1999)

Rage: Midsummer's Eve (Tii Ricks, 2015)

Raggedy DemAnn (Amanda Dyar, 2012)

The Ranger (Jenn Wexler, 2018)

Ravenous (Antonia Bird, 1990)

Raw (Julia Ducournau, 2016)

Raw: The Curse of Grete Müller (Natascha R. and Marcel Walz, 2013)

Razortooth (Patricia Harrington, 2007)

Reanimator Academy (Judith Priest, 1992)

Rebound (Megan Freels, 2014)

Red Hook (Elizabeth Lucas, 2009)

Red Riding Hood (Catherine Hardwicke, 2011)

The Retelling (Emily Hagins, 2009)

Revenge (Coralie Fargeat, 2017)

Revenge of Beyond Bizarro (Maggie Hardy, 2015)

Revenge of the Unhappy Campers (Shawnee McCormack, 2002)

Revisited (Kimberley Saylor, 2011)

Rio Grande (Samantha Candice, 2015)

Rivershine (Elena Altman, 2016)

Rock, Paper and Scissors (Macarena García Lenzi and Martín Blousson, 2019)

Rocktober Blood (Beverly Sebastian, 1984)

Roman (Angela Bettis, 2006)

Roommates (Eun-kyung Kim, 2006)

Rosemary's Baby (Agnieszka Holland, 2014)

Run for Your Life (Patricia Riggen, 2018)

The Sacrificial Temptation of the Void (as Night Slowly Falls, We Make Love)
      (Cassandra Troyan, 2012)

Saint Maud (Rose Glass, 2019)

Salvación (Denise Castro, 2016)

Salvation (J. A. Steel, 2007)

Santa Jaws (Misty Talley, 2018)

Sarah Landon and the Paranormal Hour (Lisa Comrie, 2007)

Satanic Panic (Chelsea Stardust, 2019)

Savage Lagoon (MarieAnna Dvorak, 2007)

Sawbones (Catherine Cyran, 1995)

Scareycrows (Lucy Townsend, 2017)

Scarlet Samurai: Incarnation (Tara Cardinal, 2013)
School Spirit (Allison Eckert, 2017)
Sea Fever (Neasa Hardiman, 2019)
The Seashell and the Clergyman (Germaine Dulac, 1928)
The Secret of Pine Cove (Penelope Buitenhuis, 2008)
See No Evil 2 (Jen and Sylvia Soska, 2014)
Segunda Mano (Joyce E. Bernal, 2011)
Seligo (Allison Albano Knight, 2017)
Seligo Il Venari (Allison Albano Knight, 2018)
The Selling (Emily Lou Wilbur, 2011)
Serpent (Amanda Evans, 2017)
Severe Injuries (Amy Lynn Best, 2003)
Sexual Labyrinth (Morgana Mayer, 2017)
Shadow Play (Susan Shadburne, 1986)
The Shadow Within (Silvana Zancolò, 2007)
The Shadows (Sabrina Mansfield, 2011)
Shewolf (Tamae Garateguy, 2013)
Shadowhunters: Devilspeak (Monique Dupree, 2015)
Sharp Teeth (Christine Whitlock, 2006)
Shock Attack (Jaclyn Chessen, 2015)
Shriek of the Mutilated (Robert Findlay and Roberta Findlay, 1974)
Sibling Rivalry (Margot Romero, 2009)
Sickhouse (Hannah Macpherson, 2016)
Sick-o-pathics (Brigida Costa and Massimo Lavagnini, 1995)
Silent House (Chris Kentis and Laura Lau, 2012)
Silent Retreat (Tricia Lee, 2013)
Silent Screamplay (Denise Riley, 2003)
Silver Clutch (Kay Bouma, 2012)
Sinner (Shannon Casto and Michelle Henderson, 2008)
Sinners and Saints and Sinners (Melantha Blackthorne, 2004)
The Sisterhood of Night (Caryn Waechter, 2014)
Six Degrees of Separation from Lilia Cuntapay (Antoinette H. Jadaone, 2011)
Slaughtered (Kate Glover, 2010)
Slaughterhouse Bride (Luke McEwan and Zoe Rae, 2013)
Sleep When You're Dead (Alyssa Clark, 1997)
Slender (Aliha Thalien, 2018)
The Slumber Party Massacre (Amy Holden Jones, 1982)
Slumber Party Massacre II (Deborah Brock, 1987)
Slumber Party Massacre III (Sally Mattison 1990)
Snoop Dogg's Hood of Horror (Stacy Title, 2007)
Snow Doesn't Melt Forever (Victoria Markina, 2009)
Snow Woman (Kiki Sugino, 2016)
Snuff (Michael and Roberta Findlay, 1976)
Song of the Vampire (Denise Duff, 2001)

Sorority House Massacre (Carol Frank, 1986)

Sorority Sister Slaughter (Susan Hippen, 2007)

Soulmate (Axelle Carolyn, 2011)

The Sound (Jenna Mattison, 2017)

South African Spook Hunter (Kathryn MacCorgarry Gray and Daniel Rands, 2018)

Spellbinder (Janet Greek, 1988)

Spicy Sister Slumber Party (Amy Lynn Best, 2004)

Spin the Bottle: The Kiss of Death (ShaRhonda 'Roni' Brown, 2011)

Splatter Movie: The Director's Cut (Amy Lynn Best, 2008)

A Split Personality (June Daguiso and Connie Lamothe, 2013)

Spookies (Genie Joseph, 1986)

Spooky Bunch (Ann Hui, 1980)

Starved (Guy Crawford and Yvette Hoffman, 1999)

Stepford Wife: The Barbie Serial Killer (Amanda Dyar, 2012)

Steve: Death Collector (Missy Dawn, 2015)

The Strange Color of Your Body's Tears (Hélène Cattet and Bruno Forzani, 2013)

Strange Frequency (Mary Lambert and Bryan Spicer, 2001)

Strigoi (Faye Jackson, 2009)

Stripped to Kill (Katt Shea, 1987)

Stripped to Kill 2: Live Girls (Katt Shea, 1989)

The Stitcher (Darla Enlow, 2007)

The Stockholm Bloodbath (Stephanie Ohlsson, 2015)

Suicide Girls Must Die! (Sawa Suicide, 2010)

Summer in the Shade (Alice Millar, 2018)

Summer of 84 (Anouk Whissell, François Simard and Yoann-Karl Whissell, 2018)

Summit (Christina Raia, 2014)

Sun Don't Shine (Amy Seimetz, 2012)

Sunset Society (Phoebe Dollar, 2018)

Surveillance (Jennifer Lynch, 2008)

Surviving Evidence (Mara Katria, 2013)

Suster N (Viva Westi, 2007)

Sutures (Tammi Sutton, 2009)

Tale of a Vampire (Shimako Satō, 1992)

Tales from the Lodge (Abigail Blackmore, 2019)

Tarot (Elisaveta Abrahall, 2016)

Teeth and Blood (Al Franklin and Pamela J. Richardson, 2015)

Temple of Fear (Jennifer Abbott, 2004)

Temporary Madness: Trash and Insidious Tales (Izabel Grondin, 2004)

Ten (Michael J. Epstein and Sophia Cacciola, 2014)

Tenement (Roberta Findlay, 1985)

Thinking Speed (Lisa Menzel, 2014)

The Third Eye (Leah Walker, 2007)

Thou Wast Mild And Lovely (Josephine Decker, 2014)
Tick Tock Trick (Bronwyn Edwards, 2013)
Tigers are Not Afraid (Issa Lopez, 2017)
Time and Again (Penelope Buitenhuis, 2007)
Toe Tags (Darla Enlow, 2003)
Tormented (Audrey Cummings, 2014)
Touch of the Devil (Virginia Mariposa Dale, 2013)
Tower: A Bright Day (Jagoda Szelc, 2017)
Trail of the Blood on the Trail (Kate Lavin, 2015)
Trapped (Wendy Whitbeck, 2008)
Trasherella (Rena Riffel, 2009)
Trasherella Ultra Vixen (Rena Riffel, 2011)
The Trek (Lola Wallace, 2008)
Trial Run (Melanie Read, 1984)
Trippin' (Devi Snively, 2011)
Trouble Every Day (Claire Denis, 2000)
Truth or Dare (Jessica Cameron, 2013)
Truth or Double Dare (Shaquita Smith, 2018)
The Turning (Floria Sigismondi, 2019)
Twilight (Catherine Hardwicke, 2008)
Twilight Online (Maggie To Yuk-Ching, 2014)
Twilight Syndrome: Dead Go Round (Mari Asato, 2008)
TYFTB (Thank You from the Bottom) (Sylvia Toy St Louis, 2014)
U Get What U Kiss (Camelia Popa, 2018)
The Underlords (Elizabeth Tomic, 2018)
Underworld: Blood Wars (Anna Foerster, 2016)
Urban Ghost Story (Geneviève Jolliffe, 1998)
Urban Legends: Bloody Mary (Mary Lambert, 2005)
Vampie (Melissa Tracy, 2014)
Vampire Carmilla (Tom Le Pine and Denise Templeton, 1999)
Vampire Dentist (Christine Whitlock, 2006)
Vampires in Venice (Deborah Goodwin, 2013)
Vampires of Sorority Row (Dennis Devine and Kathryn Glass, 1999)
Vamps (Amy Hecklering, 2012)
The Velvet Vampire (Stephanie Rothman, 1971)
The Viper's Hex (Addison Heath and Jasmine Jakupi, 2018)
Visible Secret (Ann Hui, 2001)
Vixen Highway 2006: It Came from Uranus! (Tony Watt and Vivita, 2010)
The Voices (Marjane Satrapi, 2014)
Walking the Dead (Melanie Ansley, 2010)
Wake the Witch (Dorothy Booraem, 2008)
War Z Day One (Lana Titova, 2013)
Watch Me (Melanie Ansley, 2006)
Watcher in the Woods (Melissa Joan Hart, 2017)

We Have Always Lived in the Castle (Stacie Passon, 2018)
We Need to Talk About Kevin (Lynne Ramsay, 2011)
The Well (Samantha Lang, 1997)
While She Was Out (Susan Montford, 2008)
Whispering Corridors 3: Wishing Stairs (Jae-yeon Yun, 2003)
Whispers (Tammi Sutton, 2015)
White Devil (Elena Altman, 2017)
Wild Blue Moon (Francesca Fisher and Taggart Siegel, 1992)
The Wind (Emma Tammi, 2018)
The Witch Hunt (Anja Breien, 1981)
Witchcraft III: The Kiss of Death (Rachel Feldman, 1991)
Witchcraft VI: The Devil's Mistress (Julie Davis, 1994)
Within (Hanelle M. Culpepper, 2009)
Without Warning (Catherine Millar, 1999)
Wolf's Hole (Věra Chytilová, 1987)
Wolf Devil Woman (Pearl Chang, 1982)
Das Werwolfspiel (Johanna Rieger, 2013)
Women's Playground (Belinda M. Wilson, 2013)
Woodshock (Kate and Laura Mulleavy, 2017)
Yoga (Jae-yeon Yun, 2009)
You're Not Getting Out Alive (Kristine Hipps, 2011)

CPSIA information can be obtained
at www.ICGtesting.com
Printed in the USA
LVHW061528130521
687357LV00006B/282